The works of that learned and judicious divine Mr. Richard Hooker, containing eight books of the laws of ecclesiastical polity, and several other treatises : To which is prefixed the life of the author, by Isaac Walton. To this edition is subjoined a new

Richard Hooker, Izaak Walton, John Exon

THE WORKS
OF
THAT LEARNED AND JUDICIOUS DIVINE
MR. RICHARD HOOKER,
CONTAINING
EIGHT BOOKS
OF THE
LAWS
OF
ECCLESIASTICAL POLITY,
AND
SEVERAL OTHER TREATISES.

TO WHICH IS PREFIXED

THE LIFE OF THE AUTHOR,

BY

ISAAC WALTON.

TO THIS EDITION IS SUBJOINED

A NEW INDEX TO THE WHOLE.

VOLUME THE SECOND.

OXFORD:
PRINTED AT THE CLARENDON PRESS.
MDCCXCIII.

LAWS

OF

ECCLESIASTICAL POLITY.

BOOK V.

Concerning their fourth Assertion, That touching several publick Duties of Christian Religion, there is amongst us much Superstition retained in them; and concerning Persons, which for performance of those Duties are endued with the Power of Ecclesiastical Order, our Laws and Proceedings according thereunto, are many ways herein also corrupted.

The Matter contained in this Fifth Book.

24. *Of*

62. *Whether*

BOOK V. *regard of due Information what their quality is that enter into holy Orders.*

81. *Of the Learning that should be in Ministers, their Residence, and the number of their Livings.*

True Religion is the root of all true Virtues and the stay of all well ordered Commonweals.

FEW there are of so weak capacity but publick evils they easily espy; fewer so patient, as not to complain when the grievous inconveniencies thereof work sensible smart. Howbeit, to see wherein the harm which they feel consisteth, the seeds from which it sprang, and the method of curing it, belongeth to a skill, the study whereof is so full of toil and the practice so beset with difficulties, that wary and respective Men had rather seek quietly their own, and wish that the World may go well, so it be not long of them, than with pain and hazard make themselves advisers for the common good. We which thought it at the very first a sign of cold affection towards the Church of God, to prefer private ease before the labour of appeasing publick disturbance, must now of necessity refer events to the gracious Providence of Almighty God, and in discharge of our duty towards him, proceed with the plain and unpartial defence of a common Cause. Wherein our endeavour is not so much to overthrow them with whom we contend, as to yield them just and reasonable causes of those things, which for want of due consideration heretofore they misconceived, accusing Laws for Men's over-sights, imputing evils grown through personal defects unto that which is not evil, framed unto some sores unwholsome plaisters, and applying othersome where no sore is. To make therefore our beginning that which to both parts is most acceptable, we agree, that pure and unstained Religion ought to be the highest

highest of all cares appertaining to publick Regiment, as well in regard of that aid and protection which they who faithfully serve God confess they receive at his merciful hands, as also for the force which Religion hath to qualify all sorts of Men, and to make them in publick affairs the more serviceable; * Governors the apter to rule with conscience; Inferiors for conscience-sake the willinger to obey. It is no peculiar conceit, but a matter of sound consequence, that all duties are by so much the better performed, by how much the Men are more religious from whose abilities the same proceed. For if † the course of politick affairs cannot in any good sort go forward without fit Instruments, and that which fitteth them be their Virtues, let Polity acknowledge itself indebted to Religion; Godliness being the ‡ chiefest top and well-spring of all true Virtues, even as God is of all good things. So natural is the union of Religion with Justice, that we may boldly deem there is neither, where both are not. For how should they be unfeignedly just, whom Religion doth not cause to be such; or they religious, which are not found such by the proof of their just actions? If they which employ their labour and travail about the publick administration of Justice, follow it only as a trade, with unquenchable and unconscionable thirst of gain, being not in heart persuaded that || Justice is God's own work, and themselves his Agents in this business, the Sentence of Right God's own Verdict, and themselves his

BOOK V.

Psal. cxliv. 2.

* C. Th. lib xvi. tit. 2. Gaudere et gloriari ex fide semper volumus, scientes magis religionibus quam officiis et labore corporis vel sudore nostram republicam contineri.

† Ἔστι δ' οὐδὲν ἐν τοῖς πολιτικοῖς δυνατὸν πρᾶξαι ἄνευ τοῦ ποιόν τινα εἶναι, λέγω δὲ οἷον σπουδαῖον. Τὸ δὲ σπουδαῖον εἶναί ἐστι τὸ τὰς ἀρετὰς ἔχειν. Arist. Magn. Moral lib. i. cap. i.

‡ Ἀρχὴ δ' ἀρίστη πάντων τῶν ὄντων Θεὸς, ἀρετῶν δ' εὐσέβεια. Philo. de Dec Præcept.

|| 2 Chron. xix. 6. Ἀγαπητὸν μὲν γὰρ κἂν ἑνὶ μόνῳ, κάλλιον δὲ καὶ θειότερον ἔθνει καὶ πόλεσιν. Arist Ethic. lib. i. cap. 2. Eccles. xii. 10. Wisd. xvii. 13.

BOOK V. Priests to deliver it, Formalities of Justice do but serve to smother Right, and that which was necessarily ordained for the common Good is through shameful abuse made the cause of common Misery. The same Piety, which maketh them that are in authority desirous to please and resemble God by Justice, inflameth, every way, Men of action with zeal to do good (as far as their place will permit) unto all. For that, they know, is most noble and divine. Whereby, if no natural or casual inability cross their desires, they always delighting to inure themselves with actions more beneficial to others, cannot but gather great experience, and through experience the more wisdom; because conscience, and the fear of swerving from that which is right, maketh them diligent observers of circumstances, the loose regard whereof is the nurse of vulgar folly, no less than Solomon's attention thereunto, was of natural furtherances the most effectual to make him eminent above others. For he gave good heed, and pierced every thing to the very ground, and by that means became the Author of many Parables. Concerning Fortitude, sith evils great and unexpected (the true touchstone of constant Minds) do cause oftentimes even them to think of divine Power with fearfullest suspicions, which have been otherwise the most secure despisers thereof; how should we look for any constant resolution of Mind in such cases, saving only where unfeigned affection to God-ward hath bred the most assured confidence to be assisted by his hand? For proof whereof, let but the Acts of the ancient Jews be indifferently weighed, from whose magnanimity, in causes of most extreme hazard, those strange and unwonted resolutions have grown; which for all circumstances, no People under the roof of Heaven did ever hitherto match. And that which did always animate them was their meer Religion. Without which, if so be it were possible, that all other ornaments of Mind might be had in

their

their full perfection, neverthelefs the Mind that fhould poffefs them, divorced from Piety, could be but a fpectacle of commiferation; even as that Body is, which adorned with fundry other admirable beauties, wanted Eye-fight, the chiefeft grace that Nature hath in that kind to beftow. They which commend fo much the felicity of that innocent World, wherein it is faid that Men of their own accord did embrace fidelity and honefty, not for fear of the Magiftrate or becaufe revenge was before their eyes, if at any time they fhould do otherwife, but that which held the People in awe was the fhame of ill-doing, the love of equity, and right itfelf, a bar againft all oppreffions which greatnefs of power caufeth: they which defcribe unto us any fuch eftate of happinefs amongft Men, though they fpeak not of Religion, do notwithftanding declare that which is in truth her only working. For if Religion did poffefs fincerely and fufficiently the hearts of all Men, there would need no other reftraint from evil. This doth not only give life and perfection to all endeavours wherewith it concurreth; but what event foever enfues, it breedeth, if not joy and gladnefs always, yet always patience, fatisfaction, and reafonable contentment of Mind. Whereupon it hath been Pfal. i. 3.
fet down as an axiom of good experience, that all things religioufly taken in hand are profperoufly ended; becaufe, whether Men in the end have that which Religion did allow them to defire, or that which it teacheth them contentedly to fuffer, they are in neither event unfortunate.* But left any Man fhould here conceive, that it greatly fkilleth not of what fort our Religion be, inafmuch as Heathens, Turks, and Infidels, impute to Religion a great part of the fame effects which ourfelves afcribe

* Τὸν γὰρ ὡς ἀληθῶς ἀγαθὸν καὶ ἔμφρονα πάσας οἰόμεθα τὰς τύχας εὐσχημόνως φέρειν, καὶ ἐκ τῶν ὑπαρχόντων ἀεὶ τὰ κάλλιστα πράττειν. Arift. Ethic. lib. i. cap. 10.

hereunto,

BOOK V hereunto, they having ours in the ſame deteſtation that we theirs, it ſhall be requiſite to obſerve well, how far forth there may be agreement in the effects of different Religions. Firſt, by the bitter ſtrife which riſeth oftentimes from ſmall differences in this behalf, and is by ſo much always greater as the matter is of more importance; we ſee a general agreement in the ſecret opinion of Men, that every Man ought to embrace the Religion which is true; and to ſhun, as hurtful, whatſoever diſſenteth from it, but that moſt, which doth fartheſt diſſent. The generality of which perſuaſion argueth, that God hath imprinted it by Nature, to the end it might be a ſpur to our induſtry in ſearching and maintaining that Religion, from which as to ſwerve in the leaſt points is error, ſo the capital Enemies thereof God hateth as his deadly Foes, Aliens, and without Repentance, Children of endleſs Perdition. Such, therefore, touching Man's immortal ſtate after this life, are not likely to reap benefit by their Religion, but to look for the clean contrary, in regard to ſo important contrariety between it and the true Religion. Nevertheleſs, in as much as the errors of the moſt ſeduced this way have been mixed with ſome truths, we are not to marvel, that although the one did turn to their endleſs woe and confuſion, yet the other had many notable effects, as touching the affairs of this preſent life. There were in theſe quarters of the World, ſixteen hundred years ago, certain ſpeculative Men whoſe authority diſpoſed the whole Religion of thoſe times. By their means it became a received opinion that the Souls of Men departing this life do flit out of one Body into ſome other. Which opinion, though falſe, yet entwined with a true, that the Souls of Men do never periſh, abated the fear of death in them which were ſo reſolved, and gave them courage unto all adventures. The Romans had a vain ſuperſtitious cuſtom, in moſt of their enterpriſes, to conjecture before-hand of the event by certain tokens which they noted in Birds, or in

Cæſ de Bell. Gall. lib. vi.

in the intrails of Beaſts, or by other the like frivolous Divinations. From whence notwithſtanding as oft as they could receive any ſign which they took to be favourable, it gave them ſuch hope, as if their Gods had made them more than half a promiſe of proſperous ſucceſs. Which many times was the greateſt cauſe that they did prevail, eſpecially being Men, of their own natural inclination, hopeful and ſtrongly conceited, whatſoever they took in hand. But could their fond Superſtition have furthered ſo great attempts without the mixture of a true perſuaſion concerning the unreſiſtable force of divine Power? Upon the wilful violation of Oaths, execrable Blaſphemy, and like contempts, offered by deriders of Religion, even unto falſe Gods, fearful tokens of divine Revenge have been known to follow. Which occurrents the devouter ſort did take for manifeſt arguments, that the Gods whom they worſhipped were of power to reward ſuch as ſought unto them, and would plague thoſe that feared them not. In this they erred. For (as the Wiſe Man rightly noteth concerning ſuch) it was not the power of them by whom they ſware, but the vengeance of them that ſinned, which puniſhed the offences of the ungodly. It was their hurt untruly to attribute ſo great power unto falſe Gods. Yet the right conceit which they had, that to perjury vengeance is due, was not without good effect as touching the courſe of their lives, who feared the wilful violation of Oaths in that reſpect. And whereas we read ſo many of them ſo much commended, ſome for their mild and merciful diſpoſition, ſome for their virtuous ſeverity, ſome for integrity of life, all theſe were the fruits of true and infallible principles delivered unto us in the Word of God, as the Axioms of our Religion, which being imprinted by the God of Nature in their hearts alſo, and taking better root in ſome than in moſt others, grew, though not from, yet with and amidſt the heaps of manifold repugnant errors; which errors of

Wiſd. xiv. 31.

 of corrupt Religion had alſo their ſuitable effects in the lives of the ſelf-ſame Parties. Without all controverſy, the purer and perfecter our Religion is, the worthier effects it hath in them who ſtedfaſtly and ſincerely embrace it, in others not. They that love the Religion which they profeſs, may have failed in choice, but yet they are ſure to reap what benefit the ſame is able to afford; whereas the beſt and ſoundeſt profeſſed by them that bear it not the like affection yieldeth them, retaining it in that ſort, no benefit. David was a *Man after God's own heart*, ſo termed becauſe his affection was hearty towards God. Beholding the like diſpoſition in them which lived under
1 Chr xxix. 17. him, it was his prayer to Almighty God, *O keep this for ever in the purpoſe, and thoughts of the heart of this People.* But when, after that David had ended his days in peace, they who ſucceeded him in place, for the moſt part followed him not in quality; when their Kings (ſome few excepted) to better their worldly eſtate (as they thought) left their own and their People's ghoſtly condition uncared for, by woeful experience they both did learn, that to forſake the true God of Heaven, is to fall into all ſuch evils upon the face of the Earth, as Men either deſtitute of Grace divine may commit, or unprotected from above, endure. Seeing therefore it doth thus appear that the ſafety of all Eſtates dependeth upon Religion; that Religion unfeignedly loved perfecteth Men's abilities unto all kinds of virtuous ſervices in the Commonwealth; that Men's deſire in general is to hold no Religion but the true; and that whatſoever good effects do grow out of their Religion, who embrace inſtead of the true a falſe, the roots thereof are certain ſparks of the light of Truth intermingled with the darkneſs of error; becauſe no Religion can wholly and only conſiſt of untruths, we have reaſon to think, that all true virtues are to honour true Religion as their Parent, and all well ordered Commonweals to love her as their chiefeſt ſtay.

2. They

The most extreme opposite to true Religion, is affected Atheism.

2. They of whom God is altogether unapprehended are but few in number, and for grossness of wit such, that they hardly and scarcely seem to hold the place of human being. These we should judge to be of all others most miserable, but that a wretcheder sort there are on whom, whereas Nature has bestowed riper capacity, their evil disposition seriously goeth about therewith to apprehend God as being not God. Whereby it cometh to pass, that of these two sorts of Men, both godless, the one having utterly no knowledge of God, the other study how to persuade themselves that there is no such thing to be known. The *fountain and well-spring of which impiety, is a resolved purpose of mind to reap in this World what sensual profit or pleasure soever the World yieldeth, and not to be barred from any whatsoever means available thereunto. And that this is the very radical cause of their Atheism no Man (I think) will doubt, which considereth what pains they take to destroy their principal spurs and motives unto all Virtue, the Creation of the World, the Providence of God, the Resurrection of the Dead, the Joys of the Kingdom of Heaven, and the endless Pains of the Wicked, yea, above all things, the Authority of the Scripture, because on these points it evermore beateth, and the Soul's Immortality, which granted, draweth easily after it the rest as a voluntary train. Is it not wonderful, that base desires should so extinguish in Men the sense of their own excellency, as to make them willing that their Souls should be like to the Souls of Beasts, mortal and corruptible with their Bodies? Till some admirable or unusual accident happen (as it hath in some) to work the beginning of a better alteration in their Minds, disputation about the knowledge of God with such kind of persons

* Wisd. ii. 21. Such things they imagine and go astray because their own wickedness hath blinded them. Ἐστι γὰρ ἡ κακία φθαρτικὴ ἀρχῆς. Arist. Eth. lib. vi. cap. 5.

commonly

BOOK V. commonly prevaileth little. For how ſhould the brightneſs of Wiſdom ſhine, where the windows of the Soul are of very ſet purpoſe cloſed?* True Religion hath many things in it, the only mention whereof galleth and troubleth their minds. Being therefore loth that enquiry into ſuch matters ſhould breed a perſuaſion in the end contrary unto that they embrace, it is their endeavour to baniſh, as much as in them lieth, quite and clean from their cogitation whatſoever may ſound that way. But it cometh many times to paſs (which is their torment) that the thing they ſhun doth follow them; Truth, as it were, even obtruding itſelf into their knowledge, and not permitting them to be ſo ignorant as they would be. Whereupon, in as much as the nature of Man is unwilling to continue doing that wherein it ſhall always condemn itſelf, they continuing ſtill obſtinate to follow the courſe which they have begun, are driven to deviſe all the ſhifts that wit can invent for the ſmothering of this light, all that may but with any the leaſt ſhew of poſſibility ſtay their Minds from thinking that true, which they heartily wiſh were falſe, but cannot think it ſo without ſome ſcruple and fear of the contrary.† Now becauſe that judicious learning, for which we commend moſt worthily the ancient Sages of the World, doth not in this caſe ſerve the turn, theſe trenchermates (for ſuch the moſt of them be) frame to themſelves a way more pleaſant, a new method they have of turning things that are ſerious into mockery, an art of contradiction by way of ſcorn, a learning wherewith we were long ſithence forwarned that the miſerable time whereunto we are fallen ſhould abound. This they ſtudy, this they practiſe, this they grace with a wanton ſuperfluity of wit, too much

2 Pet. iii. 3. Jude, Verſ. 18.

* Suſan. ver. 9. They turned away their mind, and caſt down their eyes that they might not ſee Heaven, nor remember juſt judgments

† Hæc eſt ſumma delicti, nolle agnoſcere quem ignorare non poſſis. Cypr. de Idol. Vanit.

insulting

insulting over the patience of more virtuously disposed minds. For towards these so forlorn Creatures we are (it must be confest) too patient. In zeal to the glory of God, Babylon hath exceeded Sion. We want that decree of Nebuchodonosor; the fury of this wicked brood hath the reins too much at liberty; their tongues walk at large; the spit-venom of their poisoned hearts breaketh out to the annoyance of others; what their untamed lust suggesteth, the same their licentious mouths do every where set abroach. With our contentions their irreligious humour is also much strengthened. Nothing pleaseth them better than these manifold oppositions upon the matter of Religion, as well for that they have hereby the more opportunity to learn on one side how another may be oppugned, and so to weaken the credit of all unto themselves, as also because by this hot pursuit of lower controversies among Men professing Religion, and agreeing in the principal foundations thereof, they conceive hope that about the higher principles themselves time will cause altercation to grow For which purpose, when they see occasion, they stick not sometime in other Men's Persons, yea, sometime without any vizard at all, directly to try what the most religious are able to say in defence of the highest points whereupon all Religion dependeth. Now for the most part it so falleth out, touching things which generally are received, that although in themselves they be most certain; yet because Men presume them granted of all, we are hardliest able to bring such proof of their certainty as may satisfy gainsayers, when suddenly and besides expectation they require the same at our hands. Which impreparation and unreadiness when they find in us, they turn it to soothing up of themselves in that cursed fancy, whereby they would fain believe that the hearty devotion of such as indeed fear God, is nothing else but a kind of harmless error, bred and confirmed in them by the sleights of wiser Men. For a politick

Dan. iii. 29.

BOOK V. uſe of Religion they ſee there is, and by it they would alſo gather that Religion itſelf is a meer politick device, forged purpoſely to ſerve for that uſe. Men fearing God are thereby a great deal more effectually, than by poſitive Laws, reſtrained from doing evil; in as much as thoſe Laws have no farther power than over our outward actions only, whereas unto Men's *inward cogitations, unto the privy intents and motions of their hearts, Religion ſerveth for a bridle. What more ſavage, wild and cruel than Man, if he ſee himſelf able either by fraud to over-reach, or by power to over bear the Laws whereunto he ſhould be ſubject? Wherefore in ſo great boldneſs to offend, it behoveth that the World ſhould be held in awe, not by a vain ſurmiſe, but a true apprehenſion of ſomewhat, which no Man may think himſelf able to withſtand. This is the politick uſe of Religion. In which reſpect there are, of theſe wiſe malignants, ſome who have vouchſafed it their marvellous favourable countenance and ſpeech; very gravely affirming, That Religion honoured, addeth greatneſs; and contemned, bringeth ruin unto Commonweals: that Princes and States which will continue, are above all things to uphold the reverend regard of Religion, and to provide for the ſame by all means in the making of their Laws. But when they ſhould define what means are beſt for that purpoſe, behold, they extol the wiſdom of Paganiſm; they give it out as a myſtical Precept of great importance, that Princes and ſuch as are under them in moſt authority and credit with the People, ſhould take all occaſions of rare events, and from what cauſe ſoever the ſame do proceed, yet wreſt them to the ſtrengthning of their Religion, and not make it nice for ſo good a purpoſe to

Mach. Diſc. l. i. c. 11, 12, 13, 14

* Vos ſcelera admiſſa punitis, apud nos et cogitare peccare eſt; vos conſcios timetis, nos etiam conſcientiam ſolam, ſine quâ eſſe non poſſumus. Minu. Fel. in Octav. Summum præſidium regni eſt juſtitia ob apertos tumultus, et religio ob occultos. Carda. de Sapien. lib. iii.

uſe

ufe, if need be, plain forgeries. Thus while they ftudy to bring to pafs that Religion may feem but a matter made, they lofe themfelves in the very maze of their own difcourfes, as if Reafon did even purpofely forfake them, who of purpofe forfake God the Author thereof. For furely, a ftrange kind of madnefs it is, that thofe Men, who though they be void of Piety, yet becaufe they have wit cannot chufe but know that Treachery, Guile, and Deceit, are things which may for a while, but do not ufe long to go unefpied, fhould teach, that the greateft honour to a State, is perpetuity; and grant that alterations in the Service of God, for that they impair the credit of Religion, are therefore perilous in Commonweals, which have no continuance longer than Religion hath all reverence done unto it; and withal acknowledge (for fo they do) that when People began to efpy the falfhood of Oracles, whereupon all Gentilifm was built, their hearts were utterly averted from it; and notwithftanding counfel Princes in fober earneft, for the ftrengthening of their States, to maintain Religion, and for the maintenance of Religion, not to make choice of that which is true, but to authorife that they make choice of by thofe falfe and fraudulent means which in the end muft needs overthrow it. Such are the counfels of Men godlefs, when they would fhew themfelves politick devifers, able to create God in Man by art.

Of Superftition, and the root thereof, either mifguided Zeal, or ignorant Fear of divine Glory.

3. Wherefore to let go this execrable crew, and to come to extremities on the contrary hand, two affections there are, the forces whereof, as they bear the greater or leffer fway in Man's heart, frame accordingly the ftamp and character of his Religion, the one Zeal, the other Fear. Zeal, unlefs it be rightly guided, when it endeavoureth moft bufily to pleafe God, forceth upon him thofe unfeafonable offices which pleafe him not. For which caufe, if they who this way fwerve be compared with fuch fincere, found and difcreet, as Abraham was in matter

BOOK V. of Religion; the ſervice of the one, is like unto flattery; the other, like the faithful ſedulity of friendſhip. Zeal, except it be ordered aright when it bendeth itſelf unto conflict with all things either in deed, or but imagined to be oppoſite unto Religion, uſeth the razor many times with ſuch eagerneſs, that the very life of Religion itſelf is thereby hazarded; through hatred of tares the corn in the field of God is plucked up. So that Zeal needeth both ways a ſober Guide. Fear, on the other ſide, if it have not the light of true underſtanding concerning God, wherewith to be moderated, breedeth likewiſe Superſtition. It is therefore dangerous, that in things divine we ſhould work too much upon the ſpur either of Zeal or Fear. Fear is a good Solicitor to Devotion. Howbeit, ſith Fear in this kind doth grow from an apprehenſion of Deity endued with irreſiſtable power to hurt, and is of affections (anger excepted) the unapteſt to admit any conference with Reaſon; for which cauſe the wiſe Man doth ſay of Fear, that it is a betrayer of the forces of reaſonable underſtanding; therefore, except Men know before-hand what manner of ſervice pleaſeth God, while they are fearful they try all things which fancy offereth. Many there are who never think on God but when they are in extremity of Fear, and then becauſe, what to think, or what to do they are uncertain, perplexity not ſuffering them to be idle, they think and do, as it were, in a phrenſy, they know not what. Superſtition neither knoweth the right kind, nor obſerveth the due meaſure of actions belonging to the Service of God, but is always joined with a wrong opinion touching things divine. Superſtition is, when things are either abhorred or obſerved with a zealous or fearful, but erroneous relation to God. By means whereof, the ſuperſtitious do ſometimes ſerve, though the true God, yet with needleſs offices, and defraud him of duties neceſſary, ſometime load others than him with ſuch honours as properly are his. The one, their overſight

2 Chron xx. 7. Abraham thy friend

Wiſd. xvii. 11.

fight who miss in the choice of that wherewith they are affected; the other, theirs who fail in the election of him towards whom they shew their devotion: this, the crime of Idolatry; that, the fault of voluntary either niceness or superfluity in Religion. The Christian World itself being divided into two grand parts, it appeareth by the general view of both, that with matter of Heresy the West hath been often and much troubled; but the East part never quiet till the deluge of misery, wherein now they are, overwhelmed them. The chiefest cause whereof doth seem to have lien in the restless wits of the Grecians, evermore proud of their own curious and subtile inventions; which when at any time they had contrived, the great facility of their language served them readily to make all things fair and plausible to Men's understanding. Those grand Heretical Impieties therefore, which most highly and immediately touched God and the glorious Trinity, were all in a manner the monsters of the East. The West bred fewer a great deal, and those commonly of a lower nature, such as more nearly and directly concerned rather Men than God; the Latins being always to capital Heresies less inclined, yet unto gross Superstition more: Superstition, such as that of the Pharisees was, by whom divine things indeed were less, because other things were more divinely esteemed of than Reason would. The Superstition that riseth voluntarily, and by degrees which are hardly discerned, mingling itself with the Rites even of very divine Service done to the only true God, must be considered of as a creeping and incroaching evil; an evil, the first beginnings whereof are commonly harmless, so that it proveth only then to be an evil, when some farther accident doth grow unto it, or itself come unto farther growth. For in the Church of God, sometimes it cometh to pass, as in over-battle grounds, the fertile disposition whereof is good; yet because it exceedeth due proportion, it bringeth forth abundantly,

Mark vii. 9.

through too much ranknefs, things lefs profitable; whereby, that which principally it fhould yield being either prevented in place, or defrauded of nourifhment, faileth. This (if fo large a difcourfe were neceffary) might be exemplified even by heaps of Rites and Cuftoms, now fuperftitious in the greateft part of the Chriftian World, which in their firft original beginnings, when the ftrength of virtuous, devout, or charitable affection bloomed them, no Man could juftly have condemned as evil.

Of the Redrefs of Superftition in God's Church, and concerning the Queftion of this Book.

4. But howfoever Superftition doth grow; that wherein unfounder times have done amifs, the better ages enfuing muft rectify as they may. I now come therefore to thofe accufations brought againft us by Pretenders of Reformation. The firft in the rank whereof is fuch, that if fo be the Church of England did at this day therewith as juftly deferve to be touched, as they in this caufe have imagined it doth, rather would I exhort all forts to feek pardon even with tears at the hands of God, than meditate words of defence for our doings, to the end that Men might think favourably of them. For as the cafe of this World, efpecially now, doth ftand, what other ftay or fuccour have we to lean unto, faving the teftimony of our Confcience and the comfort we take in this, that we ferve the living God (as near as our wits can reach unto the knowledge thereof) even according to his own Will, and do therefore truft that his Mercy fhall be our fafeguard againft thofe enraged Powers abroad, which principally in that refpect are become our Enemies? But fith no Man can do ill with a good Confcience, the confolation which we herein feem to find is but a meer deceitful pleafing of ourfelves in error, which at the length muft needs turn to our greater grief, if that which we do to pleafe God moft, be for the manifold defects thereof offenfive unto him. For fo it is judged, our Prayers, our Sacraments, our Fafts, our Times and Places of publick meeting together for the Worfhip and Service

vice of God; our Marriages, our Burials, our Functions, Elections and Ordinations Ecclesiastical, almost whatsoever we do in the exercise of our Religion according to Laws for that purpose established, all things are some way or other thought faulty, all things are stained with Superstition. Now, although it may be the wiser sort of Men are not greatly moved hereat, considering how subject the very best things have been always unto cavil, when Wits possessed either with disdain or dislike thereof have set them up as their mark to shoot at: safe notwithstanding it were not therefore to neglect the danger which from hence may grow, and that especially in regard of them, who desiring to serve God as they ought, but being not so skilful as in every point to unwind themselves where the snares of glosing speech do lie to intangle them, are in mind not a little troubled, when they hear so bitter invectives against that which this Church hath taught them to reverence as holy, to approve as lawful, and to observe as behoveful for the exercise of Christian Duty. It seemeth therefore, at least for their sakes, very meet, that such as blame us in this behalf be directly answered, and they which follow us, informed plainly in the reasons of that we do. On both sides, the end intended between us is to have Laws and Ordinances, such as may rightly serve to abolish Superstition and to establish the Service of God with all things thereunto appertaining in some perfect form. There is an inward reasonable, and there is a solemn outward serviceable Worship belonging unto God. Of the former kind are all manner of virtuous Duties, that each Man in reason and conscience to God-ward oweth. Solemn and serviceable Worship we name for distinction sake, whatsoever belongeth to the Church or publick Society of God by way of external Adoration. It is the latter of these two, whereupon our present question groweth. Again, this latter being ordered partly, and as touching principal matters, by none but Precepts divine only; partly, and as con-

 concerning things of inferior regard, by Ordinances as well human as divine, about the ſubſtance of Religion, wherein God's only Law muſt be kept, there is here no controverſy. The crime now intended againſt us is, that our Laws have not ordered thoſe inferior things as behoveth, and that our Cuſtoms are either ſuperſtitious or otherwiſe amiſs, whether we reſpect the exerciſe of publick Duties in Religion, or the Functions of Perſons authoriſed thereunto.

Four general Propoſitions demanding that which may reaſonably be granted concerning matters of outward form in the exerciſe of true Religion. And fifthly, of a Rule not ſafe nor reaſonable in theſe caſes.

5. It is with Teachers of Mathematical Sciences uſual, for us in this preſent queſtion neceſſary, to lay down firſt certain reaſonable demands, which in moſt particulars following are to ſerve as Principles whereby to work, and therefore muſt be before-hand conſidered. The Men whom we labour to inform in the Truth, perceive that ſo to proceed is requiſite. For to this end they alſo propoſe, touching Cuſtoms and Rites indifferent, their general Axioms, ſome of them ſubject unto juſt exceptions, and, as we think, more meet by them to be farther conſidered than aſſented unto by us. As that, *In outward things belonging to the Service of God, reformed Churches ought by all means to ſhun Conformity with the Church of Rome*; that, *The firſt reformed ſhould be a pattern whereunto all that come after, ought to conform themſelves*; that, *Sound Religion may not uſe the things, which being not commanded of God, have been either deviſed or abuſed unto Superſtition.* Theſe and the reſt of the ſame conſort we have in the Book going before examined. Other Canons they alledge, and Rules not unworthy of approbation, as, *That in all ſuch things the glory of God, and the edification or ghoſtly good of his People muſt be ſought, that nothing ſhould be undecently or unorderly done.* But foraſmuch as all the difficulty is, in diſcerning what things do glorify God and edify his Church, what not; when we ſhould think them decent and fit, when otherwiſe: becauſe theſe Rules being too general, come not near enough unto the matter which we have in hand, and the former Principles being nearer the purpoſe, are too far

far from Truth; we must propose unto all Men certain Petitions incident, and very material in causes of this nature, such as no Man of moderate judgment hath cause to think unjust or unreasonable. BOOK V.

6. The first thing therefore which is of force to cause approbation with good conscience towards such Customs or Rites as publickly are established, is, when there ariseth from the due consideration of those Customs and Rites in themselves apparent reason, although not always to prove them better than any other that might possibly be devised, (for who did ever require this in Man's Ordinances?) yet competent to shew their conveniency and fitness, in regard of the use for which they should serve. Now touching the nature of religious Services, and the manner of their due performance, thus much generally we know to be most clear; that whereas the greatness and dignity of all manner of Actions is measured by the worthiness of the Subject from which they proceed, and of the Object whereabout they are conversant, we must of necessity in both respects acknowledge that this present World affordeth not any thing comparable unto the publick Duties of Religion. For if the best things have the perfectest and best operations, it will follow, that seeing Man is the worthiest Creature upon Earth; and every Society of Men more worthy than any Man; and of Societies that most excellent which we call the Church; there can be in this World no work performed equal to the exercise of true Religion, the proper operation of the Church of God. Again, forasmuch as Religion worketh upon him who in Majesty and Power is infinite, as we ought we account not of it, unless we esteem it even according to that very height of excellency which our hearts conceive, when divine sublimity itself is rightly considered. In the powers and faculties of our Souls God requireth the uttermost which our unfeigned affection towards him is able to yield: so that if we affect

The first Proposition touching judgment, what things are convenient in the outward publick ordering of Church affairs.

John iv. 24.

BOOK V.

Wisd. vi 10
1 Chron. xxix. 17.

affect him not far above and before all things, our Religion hath not that inward perfection which it should have, neither do we indeed worship him as our God. That which inwardly each Man should be, the Church outwardly ought to testify. And therefore the Duties of our Religion which are seen, must be such as that affection which is unseen ought to be. Signs must resemble the things they signify. If Religion bear the greatest sway in our Hearts, our outward religious Duties must shew it as far as the Church hath outward ability. Duties of Religion performed by whole Societies of Men, ought to have in them, according to our power, a sensible excellency, correspondent to the Majesty of him whom we worship. Yea, then are the publick Duties of Religion best ordered, when the militant Church doth resemble by sensible means *, as it may in such cases, that hidden Dignity and Glory wherewith the Church triumphant in Heaven is beautified. Howbeit, even as the very heat of the Sun itself, which is the life of the whole World, was to the People of God in the desart a grievous annoyance, for ease whereof his extraordinary Providence ordained a cloudy Pillar to over-shadow them; so things of general use and benefit (for in this World, what is so perfect that no inconvenience doth ever follow it?) may by some accident be incommodious to a few. In which case, for such private evils, remedies there are of like condition, though publick Ordinances, wherein the common good is respected, be not stirred. Let our first demand be therefore, that in the external Form of Religion such things as are apparently, or can be sufficiently proved effectual and generally fit to set forward Godliness, either as betokening the

2 Chron. ii. 5.

* Ἐκκλησία ἐστὶν ἐπίγειος οὐρανός. Germa. περὶ τῶν ἱερουργουμένων. Delectatio Domini in Ecclesia est; Ecclesia vero est imago Cœlestium. Ambros. de interpel. Dav. Facit in terris opera cœlorum. Sidon. Apol. Epist. lib. vi.

Greatness

Greatneſs of God, or as beſeeming the Dignity of Religion, or as concurring with celeſtial impreſſions in the minds of Men, may be reverently thought of; ſome few, rare, caſual, and tolerable, or otherwiſe curable inconveniencies notwithſtanding. BOOK V.

7. Neither may we in this caſe lightly eſteem what hath been allowed as fit in the judgment of Antiquity, and by the long continued practice of the whole Church; from which unneceſſarily to ſwerve, experience never as yet have found it ſafe. For Wiſdom's ſake we reverence them no leſs that are young, or not much leſs than if they were ſtricken in years. And therefore of ſuch it is rightly ſaid, that their ripeneſs of Underſtanding is *grey Hairs*, and their Virtues *old Age*. But becauſe Wiſdom and Youth are ſeldom joined in one, and the ordinary courſe of the World is more according to Job's obſervation, who giveth Men advice to ſeek *Wiſdom amongſt the Ancient, and in the length of Days, Underſtanding*; therefore if the compariſon do ſtand between Man and Man which ſhall hearken unto other, ſith the Aged for the moſt part are beſt experienced, leaſt ſubject to raſh and unadviſed paſſions; it hath been ever judged reaſonable, that their ſentence in matter of counſel ſhould be better truſted, and more relied upon than other Mens. The goodneſs of God having furniſhed Men with two chief inſtruments, both neceſſary for this life, Hands to execute, and a Mind to deviſe great things, the one is not profitable longer than the vigour of Youth doth ſtrengthen it; nor the other greatly, till Age and Experience have brought it to perfection. In whom therefore Time hath not perfected Knowledge, ſuch muſt be contented to follow them in whom it hath. For this cauſe none is more attentively heard, than they whoſe ſpeeches are, as David's were, *I have been young, and now am old*, much I have ſeen and obſerved in the World. Sharp and ſubtile diſcourſes of wit procure many times very great applauſe; but being laid in the

The ſecond Propoſition.

Wiſd. iv. 9.

Job xii. 12.

BOOK V. the balance with that which the habit of ſound experience plainly delivereth they are over-weighed. God may endue Men extraordinarily with underſtanding as it pleaſeth him: but let no Man preſuming thereupon neglect the inſtructions, or deſpiſe the ordinances of his Elders, ſith he, whoſe gift Wiſdom is, hath ſaid, *Ask thy Father, and he will ſhew thee; thine Ancients, and they ſhall tell thee.* It is therefore the Voice both of God and Nature, not of Learning only, that, eſpecially in matters of Action and Policy, *The ſentences and judgments of Men experienced, aged and wiſe, yea though they ſpeak without any proof or demonſtration, are no leſs to be hearkened unto, than as being demonſtrations in themſelves; becauſe ſuch Men's long obſervation is as an eye, wherewith they preſently and plainly behold thoſe principles which ſway over all actions.* Whereby we are taught both the cauſe wherefore wiſe Men's Judgments ſhould be credited, and the means how to uſe their Judgments to the increaſe of our own Wiſdom. That which ſheweth them to be wiſe, is, the gathering of Principles out of their own particular Experiments. And the framing of our particular Experiments, according to the rule of their Principles, ſhall make us ſuch as they are. If therefore even at the firſt, ſo great account ſhould be made of wiſe Men's Counſels touching things that are publickly done, as time ſhall add thereunto continuance and approbation of ſucceeding ages, their Credit and Authority muſt needs be greater. They which do nothing but that which Men of account did before them, are, although they do amiſs, yet the leſs ‡ faulty, becauſe they are not the Authors of harm, and doing well, their actions are freed from prejudice and novelty. To the beſt and wiſeſt while they live, the World is continually

Deut xxxi. 7.

Arist Eth vi cap. 11.

‡ Πρὸς τοὺς ἐκ ποδῶν, φθόνος οὐδεὶς φύεται Philo.
Πᾶσα δυσμένεια τῷ βίῳ τούτῳ συναποτίθεται. Syneſ
Τὸ ἐκ ποδῶν οὐκ' ἀντίπιπτει καὶ τετίμηται ἀφθόνως. Gregor. Naz. ἐν Στιχ.

a froward

a froward opposite, a curious observer of their defects and imperfections; their virtues, it afterwards as much admireth. And for this cause many times that which most deserveth approbation, would hardly be able to find favour, if they which propose it were not content to profess themselves therein Scholars and Followers of the Ancients. For the World will not endure to hear that we are wiser than they have been which went before. In which consideration there is cause why we should be slow and unwilling to change, without very urgent necessity, the ancient Ordinances, Rites and long approved Customs of our venerable Predecessors. The love of things ancient doth argue * staidness; but levity and want of experience maketh apt unto innovations. That which Wisdom did first begin, and hath been with good Men long continued, challengeth allowance of them that succeed, although it plead for itself nothing. That which is new, if it promise not much, doth fear condemnation before trial; until trial, no Man doth acquit or trust it, what good soever it pretend and promise. So that in this kind, there are few things known to be good, till such time as they grow to be ancient. The vain pretence of those glorious names, where they could not be with any truth, neither in reason ought to have been so much alledged, hath wrought such a prejudice against them in the Minds of the common sort, as if they had utterly no force at all; whereas (especially for these observances which concern our present question) Antiquity, Custom and Consent in the Church of God, making with that which Law doth establish, are themselves most sufficient reasons to uphold the same, unless some notable publick inconvenience

* Ὅσοι δ' εὐστάθειαν τρόπων τὸ τῆς ἀρχαιότητος σεμνὸν τοῦ καινοπρεποῦς προετίμησαν καὶ ἀπαραποίητον τῶν παλαιῶν διεφύλαξαν τὴν παράδοσιν κατά τε χώραν καὶ πόλιν ταύτῃ κέχρηνται τῇ φωνῇ. Basil de Spirit. Sanct. cap. VII.

enforce

BOOK V. enforce the contrary. For * a ſmall thing in the eye of Law is as nothing. We are therefore bold to make our ſecond Petition this; that in things, the fitneſs whereof is not of itſelf apparent, nor eaſy to be made ſufficiently manifeſt unto all, yet the Judgment of Antiquity concurring with that which is received, may induce them to think it not unfit, who are not able to alledge any known weighty inconvenience which it hath, or to take any ſtrong exception againſt it.

The third Propoſition. 8. All things cannot be of ancient continuance which are expedient and needful for the ordering of ſpiritual affairs: but the Church being a Body which dieth not, hath always power, as occaſion requireth, no leſs to ordain that which never was, than to ratify what hath been before. To preſcribe the Order of doing in all things, is a peculiar prerogative which Wiſdom hath, ‡ as a Queen or ſovereign Commandreſs over other Virtues. This in every ſeveral Man's actions of common life appertaineth unto moral; in publick and politick ſecular affairs, unto civil Wiſdom. In like manner, to deviſe any certain Form for the outward Adminiſtration of publick Duties in the Service of God, or things belonging thereunto, and to find out the moſt convenient for that uſe, is a point of Wiſdom Eccleſiaſtical. It is not for a Man, which doth know or ſhould know what Order is and what peaceable Government requireth, to aſk, *Why we ſhould hang our judgment upon our Church's ſleeve*; and, *why in matters of Order, more than in matters of Doctrine.* The Church hath authority to eſtabliſh that for an Order at one time, which at another time it may aboliſh, and in both may do well. But that which in Doctrine

T. C. l. iii p. 171.

* Ὁ μὲν μικρὸν τοῦ εὖ παρεκβαίνων, οὐ ψέγεται. Ariſt. Ethic. 2. c. ix.

Modici nulla fere ratio haberi ſolet. Tiraquel de jud. in reb. exig. Cap. x.

‡ Ἡ μὲν φρόνησις περὶ τὰ ποιητέα ὅρους αὐτοῖς τίθεισα. Philo. pag 35.

the

the Church doth now deliver rightly as a Truth, no Man will ſay that it may hereafter recal, and as rightly avouch the contrary. Laws touching matter of Order are changeable by the power of the Church; Articles concerning Doctrine, not ſo. We read often in the writings of catholick and holy Men touching matters of Doctrine, *This we believe, this we hold, this the Prophets and Evangeliſts have declared, this the Apoſtles have delivered, this Martyrs have ſealed with their blood, and confeſſed in the midſt of torments, to this we cleave, as to the anchor of our Souls, againſt this, though an Angel from Heaven ſhould preach unto us, we would not believe.* But did we ever in any of them read touching matters of meer Comelineſs, Order and Decency, neither* commanded nor prohibited by any Prophet, any Evangeliſt, any Apoſtle, *Although the Church wherein we live do ordain them to be kept, although they be never ſo generally obſerved, though all the Churches in the World ſhould command them, though Angels from Heaven ſhould require our ſubjection thereunto, I would hold him accurſed that doth obey?* Be it in matter of the one kind or of the other, what Scripture doth plainly deliver, to that the firſt place both of Credit and Obedience is due; the next whereunto is, whatſoever any Man can neceſſarily conclude by force of Reaſon; after theſe, the voice of the Church ſucceedeth. That which the Church by her Eccleſiaſtical Authority ſhall probably think and define to be true or good, muſt in congruity of Reaſon over-rule all other inferior judgments whatſoever. To them which aſk, why we thus hang our judgments on the Church's ſleeve, I anſwer with Solomon, becauſe *two are better than one.* *Yea ſimply* (ſaith Baſil) *and univerſally, whether it be in works of Nature, or of voluntary choice and counſel, I ſee not any thing done as it ſhould be, if it be wrought by an agent*

BOOK V.

Eccleſ. iv. 9.

* Baſil. Ep. 68. d. d 8. c. Quæ contra. Turpis eſt omnis pars univerſo ſuo non congruens.

ſingling

BOOK V. *fingling itfelf from conforts.* The Jews had a fentence of good advice, *Take not upon thee to be Judge alone, there is no Judge but one only; fay not to others, Receive my fentence, when their authority is above thine.* The bare confent of the whole Church fhould itfelf in thefe things ftop their mouths, who living under it, dare prefume to bark againft it. *There is* (faith Caffianus) *no place of audience left for them, by whom obedience is not yielded to that which all have agreed upon.* Might we not think it more than wonderful, that Nature fhould in all Communities appoint a predominant judgment to fway and over-rule in fo many things; or that God himfelf fhould allow fo much authority and power unto every poor Family for the ordering of all which are in it; and the City of the Living God, which is his Church, be able neither to command, nor yet to forbid any thing which the meaneft fhall in that refpect, and for her fole authority's fake be bound to obey? We cannot hide or diffemble that evil, the grievous inconvenience whereof we feel. Our diflike of them, by whom too much heretofore have been attributed unto the Church, is grown to an error on the contrary hand; fo that now from the Church of God too much is derogated. By which removal of one extremity with another the World feeking to procure a remedy, hath purchafed a meer exchange of the evil which before was felt. Suppofe we, that the facred Word of God can at their hands receive due honour, by whofe incitement the holy Ordinances of the Church endure every where open contempt? No, it is not poffible they fhould obferve as they ought the one, who from the other withdraw unneceffarily their own or their Brethrens obedience. Surely the Church of God in this bufinefs is neither of capacity, I truft, fo weak, nor fo unftrengthened, I know, with Authority from above; but that her Laws may exact obedience at the hands of her own Children, and enjoin Gainfayers filence, giving them roundly to underftand, that where our duty

R. Ifhmael in Cap. Patr.

Caffian. de Incarn. l. ii. c. 6.

duty is submission, weak oppositions betoken pride. We therefore crave, thirdly, to have it granted, that where neither the evidence of any Law divine, nor the strength of any invincible Argument otherwise found out by the light of Reason, nor any notable publick Inconvenience doth make against that which our own Laws Ecclesiastical have, although but newly, instituted, for the ordering of these affairs, the very Authority of the Church itself, at the least in such cases, may give so much credit to our own Laws, as to make their sentence touching fitness and conveniency, weightier than any bare or naked conceit to the contrary; especially in them, who can owe no less than child-like obedience to her that hath more than motherly power. BOOK V.

9. There are ancient Ordinances, Laws (which on all sides are allowed to be just and good, yea Divine and Apostolick Constitutions) which the Church, it may be, doth not always keep, nor always justly deserve blame in that respect. For in evils that cannot be removed, without the manifest danger of greater to succeed in their rooms; Wisdom (of necessity) must give place to Necessity. All it can do in those cases is, to devise how that which must be endured may be mitigated, and the inconveniences thereof countervailed as near as may be; that when the best things are not possible, the best may be made of those that are. Nature, than which there is nothing more constant, nothing more uniform in all her ways, doth notwithstanding stay her hand, yea, and change her course, when that which God by Creation did command, he doth at any time by Necessity countermand. It hath therefore pleased himself sometime to unloose the very tongues even of dumb Creatures, and to teach them to plead this in their own defence, lest the cruelty of Man should persist to afflict them for not keeping their wonted course, when some invincible impediment hath hindered. If we leave Nature and look into Art, the Work-man hath in his heart

The fourth Proposition.

Numb. xxii. 28.

BOOK V. heart a purpose, he carrieth in mind the whole form which his work should have; there wanteth not in him skill and desire to bring his labour to the best effect, only the matter which he hath to work on is unframeable. This Necessity excuseth him; so that nothing is derogated from his credit, although much of his work's perfection be found wanting. Touching actions of common life, there is not any defence more favourably heard than theirs who alledge sincerely for themselves, that they did as Necessity constrained them. For when the Mind is rightly ordered and affected as it should be, in case some external impediment crossing well advised desires shall potently draw Men to leave what they principally wish, and to take a course which they would not if their choice were free; what Necessity forceth Men unto,* the same in this case it maintaineth, as long as nothing is committed simply in itself evil, nothing absolutely sinful or wicked, nothing repugnant to that immutable Law, whereby whatsoever is condemned as evil, can never any way be made good. The casting away of things profitable for the sustenance of Man's life, is an unthankful abuse of the fruits of God's good Providence towards Mankind. Which consideration, for all that, did not hinder St. Paul from throwing corn into the sea, when care of saving Men's lives made it necessary to lose that which else had been better saved. Neither was this to do evil, to the end that good might come of it; for of two such evils, being not both evitable, the choice of the less is not evil. And evils must be in our construction judged inevitable if there be no apparent ordinary way to avoid them; because, where counsel and advice bear rule, of God's extraordinary Power without extraordinary warrant, we cannot presume. In civil affairs, to declare what sway Necessity hath ever been accustomed to bear, were labour infinite. The Laws of

Acts xxvii. 38.

* Necessitas, quicquid coegit, defendit. Senec. Controv. lib. ix.

all

all States and Kingdoms in the World have ſcarcely of any thing more common uſe. Should then only the Church ſhew itſelf inhuman and ſtern, abſolutely urging a rigorous obſervation of ſpiritual Ordinances without relaxation or exception, what Neceſſity ſoever happen? We know the contrary practice to have been commended by him, upon the warrant of whoſe Judgment the Church, moſt of all delighted with merciful and moderate courſes, doth the oftner condeſcend unto like equity, permitting in caſes of Neceſſity that which otherwiſe it diſalloweth and forbiddeth. Caſes of Neceſſity being ſometime but urgent, ſometime extreme, * the conſideration of publick utility is with very good advice judged at the leaſt equivalent with the eaſier kind of Neceſſity. Now that which cauſeth numbers to ſtorm againſt ſome neceſſary tolerations, which they ſhould rather let paſs with ſilence, conſidering that in Polity as well Eccleſiaſtical as Civil, there are and will be always evils which no art of Man can cure, breaches and leaks more than Man's wit hath hands to ſtop; that which maketh odious unto them many things, wherein notwithſtanding the truth is that very juſt regard hath been had of the publick good; that which in a great part of the weightieſt cauſes belonging to this preſent Controverſy, hath inſnared the judgments both of ſundry good, and of ſome well learned Men, is the manifeſt truth of certain general Principles, whereupon the Ordinances that ſerve for uſual practice in the Church of God are grounded. Which Principles Men knowing to be moſt ſound, and that the ordinary practice accordingly framed is good, whatſoever is over and beſides that ordinary, the ſame they judge repugnant to thoſe true Principles. The cauſe of which error is ignorance, what reſtraints and limitations all ſuch Principles have in regard of

BOOK V.

Luke vi. 4.

* Cauſa neceſſitatis et utilitatis æquiparantur in jure. Ab. Panor. ad c. ut ſuper nu. 15. de Reb. Eccleſ. non alien.

ſo manifold varieties,* as the matter whereunto they are appliable, doth commonly afford. Theſe varieties are not known but by much experience, from whence to draw the true bounds of all Principles, to diſcern how far forth they take effect, to ſee where and why they fail, to apprehend by what degrees and means they lead to the practice of things in ſhow, though not indeed repugnant and contrary one to another, requireth more ſharpneſs of wit, more intricate circuitions of diſcourſe, more induſtry and depth of judgment, than common ability doth yield. So that general Rules, till their limits be fully known, (eſpecially in matter of publick and Eccleſiaſtical affairs) are, by reaſon of the manifold ſecret exceptions which lie hidden in them, no other to the eye of Man's underſtanding than cloudy miſts caſt before the eye of common ſenſe. They that walk in darkneſs know not whither they go: and even as little is their certainty, whoſe opinions Generalities only do guide. With groſs and popular capacities nothing doth more prevail than unlimited Generalities, becauſe of their plainneſs at the firſt ſight: nothing leſs with Men of exact judgment, becauſe ſuch Rules are not ſafe to be truſted over far. General Laws are like general Rules of Phyſick, according whereunto as no wiſe Man will deſire himſelf to be cured, if there be joined with his diſeaſe ſome ſpecial accident, in regard whereof that whereby others in the ſame infirmity, but without the like accident, recover health, would be to him either hurtful, or at the leaſt unprofitable: ſo we muſt not, under a colourable commendation of holy Ordinances in the Church, and of reaſonable cauſes whereupon they have been grounded for the common good, imagine that all Men's caſes ought to have one meaſure. Nor without ſingular wiſdom

* Ἐν τοῖς περὶ τὰς πράξεις λόγοις οἱ μὲν καθόλου κενώτεροί εἰσιν, οἱ δ' ἐπὶ μέρους ἀληθινώτεροι· περὶ γὰρ τὰ καθ' ἕκαστα αἱ πράξεις. Eth. l. i. c. 7.

therefore

therefore it hath been provided, that as the ordinary course of common affairs is difpofed of by general Laws, fo likewife Men's rarer incident neceffities and utilities fhould be with fpecial equity confidered. From hence it is, that fo many Privileges, Immunities, Exceptions and Difpenfations have been always with great equity and reafon granted, not to turn the edge of Juftice, nor to make void at certain times, and in certain Men, through meer voluntary grace or benevolence, that which continually and univerfally fhould be of force (as fome Men underftand it), but in very truth to practife general Laws according to their right meaning. We fee in Contracts, and other dealings which daily pafs between Man and Man, that, to the utter undoing of fome, many things by ftrictnefs of Law may be done, which Equity and honeft meaning forbiddeth. Not that the Law is unjuft, but unperfect; nor Equity againft, but above the Law; binding Mens confciences in things which Law cannot reach unto. Will any Man fay, that the virtue of private Equity is oppofite and repugnant to that Law, the filence whereof it fupplieth in all fuch private dealing? No more is publick Equity againft the Law of publick affairs; albeit the one permit unto fome, in fpecial confiderations, that which the other, agreeably with general Rules of Juftice, doth in general fort forbid. For, fith all good Laws are the voices of right Reafon, which is the Inftrument wherewith God will have the World guided; and impoffible it is that Right fhould withftand Right; it muft follow, that Principles and Rules of Juftice, be they never fo generally uttered, do no lefs effectually intend, than if they did plainly exprefs an exception of all particulars, wherein their literal practice might any way prejudice Equity. And becaufe it is natural unto all Men to wifh their own extraordinary benefit, when they think they have reafonable inducements fo to do; and no Man can be prefumed a competent judge what Equity doth require in his own

BOOK V.

caſe; the likelieſt mean whereby the wit of Man can provide, that he which uſeth the benefit of any ſpecial benignity above the common courſe of others, may enjoy it with good conſcience, and not againſt the true purpoſe of Laws, which in outward ſhew are contrary, muſt needs be to arm with Authority ſome fit both for quality and place to adminiſter that, which in every ſuch particular ſhall appear agreeable with Equity: wherein, as it cannot be denied, but that ſometimes the practice of ſuch Juriſdiction may ſwerve through error even in the very beſt, and for other reſpects where leſs integrity is; ſo the watchfulleſt Obſervers of inconveniences that way growing, and the readieſt to urge them in diſgrace of authoriſed proceedings, do very well know, that the diſpoſition of theſe things reſteth not now in the hands of Popes, who live in no worldly awe or ſubjection, but is committed to them whom Law may at all times bridle, and ſuperior power controul; yea to them alſo in ſuch ſort, that Law itſelf hath ſet down to what Perſons, in what Cauſes, with what Circumſtances, almoſt every faculty or favour ſhall be granted, leaving in a manner nothing unto them more than only to deliver what is already given by Law. Which maketh it by many degrees leſs reaſonable, that under pretence of inconveniences ſo eaſily ſtopped, if any did grow, and ſo well prevented that none may, Men ſhould be altogether barred of the liberty that Law with equity and reaſon granteth. Theſe things therefore conſidered, we laſtly require, that it may not ſeem hard, if in caſes of Neceſſity, or for common utility's ſake, certain profitable Ordinances ſometimes be releaſed, rather than all Men always ſtrictly bound to the general rigor thereof.

The Rule of Men's private ſpirits not ſafe in theſe caſes to be followed.

10. Now where the Word of God leaveth the Church to make choice of her own Ordinances, if againſt thoſe things which have been received with great reaſon, or againſt that which the ancient practice of the Church hath continued time out of mind

or

or againſt ſuch Ordinances as the Power and Authority of that Church under which we live hath in itſelf deviſed for the publick good, or againſt the diſcretion of the Church in mitigating ſometimes with favourable Equity that rigour which otherwiſe the literal generality of Eccleſiaſtical Laws hath judged to be more convenient and meet; if againſt all this it ſhould be free for Men to reprove, to diſgrace, to reject at their own liberty what they ſee done and practiſed according to Order ſet down; if in ſo great variety of ways as the wit of Man is eaſily able to find out towards any purpoſe, and in ſo great liking as all Men eſpecially have unto thoſe inventions, whereby ſome one ſhall ſeem to have been more enlightened from above than many thouſands, the Church did give every Man licence to follow what himſelf imagineth that God's Spirit doth reveal unto him, or what he ſuppoſeth that God is likely to have revealed to ſome ſpecial Perſon whoſe virtues deſerve to be highly eſteemed; what other effect could hereupon enſue, but the utter confuſion of his Church under pretence of being taught, led and guided by his Spirit? the gifts and graces whereof do ſo naturally all tend unto common peace, that where ſuch ſingularity is, they whoſe hearts it poſſeſſeth ought to ſuſpect it the more; in as much as if it did come of God, and ſhould for that cauſe prevail with others, the ſame God which revealeth it to them, would alſo give them power of confirming it to others, either with miraculous operation, or with ſtrong and invincible remonſtrance of ſound Reaſon, ſuch as whereby it might appear that God would indeed have all Men's judgments give place unto it; whereas now the error and unſufficiency of their arguments do make it on the contrary ſide againſt them a ſtrong preſumption, that God hath not moved their hearts to think ſuch things as he hath not enabled them to prove. And ſo from Rules of general direction, it reſteth that now we deſcend

 to

BOOK V. to a more diſtinct explication of Particulars, wherein those Rules have their ſpecial efficacy.

Places for the publick Service of God.

II. Solemn Duties of publick Service to be done unto God, muſt have their places ſet and prepared in ſuch ſort as beſeemeth actions of that regard. Adam, even during the ſpace of his ſmall continuance in Paradiſe, had where to preſent himſelf before the Gen. iii 8. Lord. Adam's Sons had out of Paradiſe in like ſort Gen. iv 3 whither to bring their Sacrifices. The Patriarchs uſed Gen. xiii. 4 xxii. 1. xxi 33. Altars, and Mountains, and Groves, to the ſelf-ſame purpoſe. In the vaſt Wilderneſs, when the People of God had themſelves no ſettled habitation, Exod. xxvi. yet a moveable Tabernacle they were commanded of God to make. The like charge was given them againſt the time they ſhould come to ſettle themſelves in the Land which had been promiſed unto their Fa- *Deut. xii. 5. thers, *Ye ſhall ſeek that Place which the Lord your God ſhall chooſe.* When God had choſen Jeruſalem, and Chron. iii. 1. in Jeruſalem Mount Moriah, there to have his ſtanding habitation made, it was in the chiefeſt of David's 2 Chron. vi. 7. deſires to have performed ſo good a work. His Pſal. cxxxii. 5. grief was no leſs that he could not have the honour to build God a Temple, than their anger is at this day, who bite aſunder their own tongues with very wrath, that they have not as yet the power to pull down the Temples which they never built, and to level them with the ground. It was no mean thing which he purpoſed. To perform a work ſo majeſtical and ſtately was no ſmall charge. Therefore he in- 2 Chron. xxv. 9. cited all Men unto bountiful contribution, and procured towards it with all his power, gold, ſilver, braſs, iron, wood, precious ſtones in great abundance. Yea 2 Chron. xxix 3. moreover, *Becauſe I have* (ſaith David) *a joy in the Houſe of my God, I have of my own gold and ſilver, beſides all that I have prepared for the Houſe of the Sanctuary, given to the Houſe of my God three thouſand talents of gold, even the gold of Ophir, ſeven thouſand talents of* Ezra iii. 12. *fined ſilver.* After the overthrow of this firſt Houſe Agge ii. 4. of God, a ſecond was inſtead thereof erected; but

with

with ſo great odds, that they wept which had ſeen the former, and beheld how much this latter came behind it, the beauty whereof notwithſtanding was ſuch, that even this was alſo the wonder of the whole World. Beſides which Temple, there were both in other parts of the Land, and even in Jeruſalem, by proceſs of time, no ſmall number of Synagogues for Men to reſort unto. Our Saviour himſelf, and after him the Apoſtles frequented both the one and the other. The Church of Chriſt which was in Jeruſalem, and held that profeſſion which had not the publick allowance and countenance of authority, could not ſo long uſe the exerciſe of Chriſtian Religion but in private only. So that as Jews they had acceſs to the Temples and Synagogues, where God was ſerved after the cuſtom of the Law, but for that which they did as Chriſtians, they were of neceſſity forced other where to aſſemble themſelves. And as God gave increaſe to his Church, they ſought out both there and abroad for that purpoſe not the fitteſt (for ſo the times would not ſuffer them to do) but the ſafeſt places they could. In proceſs of time, ſome whiles by ſufferance, ſome whiles by ſpecial leave and favour, they began to erect to themſelves Oratories; not in any ſumptuous or ſtately manner, which neither was poſſible by reaſon of the poor eſtate of the Church, and had been perilous in regard of the World's envy towards them. At the length, when it pleaſed God to raiſe up Kings and Emperors favouring ſincerely the Chriſtian Truth, that which the Church before either could not or durſt not do, was with all alacrity performed. Temples were in all places erected, no coſt was ſpared, nothing judged too dear which that way ſhould be ſpent. The whole World did ſeem to exult, that it had occaſion of pouring out gifts to ſo bleſſed a purpoſe. That chearful devotion which David this way did exceedingly delight to behold, and wiſh that the ſame in the Jewiſh People might be perpetual, was then in Chriſtian People

Ezr. iii. 12. Agge ii. 4.

Act. i 13. & ii. 1. & 46.

1 Chron. xxix. 17, 18.

BOOK V.

every where to be ſeen. Their actions, till this day, always accuſtomed to be ſpoken of with great honour, are called openly into queſtion They, and as many as have been Followers of their example in that thing; we eſpecially that worſhip God, either in Temples which their hands made, or which other Men ſithence have framed by the like pattern, are in that reſpect charged no leſs than with the very Sin of Idolatry. Our Churches in the foam of that good Spirit which directeth ſuch fiery tongues, they term ſpitefully the Temples of Baal, idle Synagogues, abominable Sties.

The Solemnity of erecting Churches condemned by Bar. p. 130 The hallowing and dedicating of them ſcorned, p. 141.

12. Wherein the firſt thing which moveth them thus to caſt up their poiſon, are certain Solemnities uſual at the firſt erection of Churches. Now although the ſame ſhould be blame-worthy, yet this Age (thanks be to God) hath reaſonably well forborn to incur the danger of any ſuch blame. It cannot be laid unto many Men's charge at this day living, either that they have been ſo curious as to trouble the Biſhops with placing the firſt Stone in the Churches they built, or ſo ſcrupulous as after the erection of them to make any great ado for their Dedication. In which kind notwithſtanding as we do neither allow unmeet, nor purpoſe the ſtiff defence of any unneceſſary Cuſtom heretofore received; ſo we know no reaſon wherefore Churches ſhould be the worſe, if at the firſt erecting of them, at the making of them publick, at the time when they are delivered, as it were, into God's own poſſeſſion, and when the uſe whereunto they ſhall ever ſerve is eſtabliſhed, Ceremonies fit to betoken ſuch intents, and to accompany ſuch actions be uſual, as * in the pureſt times they have been. When Conſtantine had finiſhed an Houſe

Durand. rational lib 1. cap 6. & de Conſec d 1. c tabernaculum. Greg. Mag lib. x. epiſt. 12. & lib vii epiſt 71 & lib viii. epiſt 63.

Vide Euſeb. de vita Conſtant. lib. iv c. 41, 43, 44, 45.

* Ἐγκαίνια τιμᾶσθαι παλαιὸς νόμος, καὶ καλῶς ἔχων, μᾶλλον δὲ τὰ νέα τιμᾶσθαι δι' ἐγκαινίων. Καὶ τοῦτο οὐχ ἅπαξ, ἀλλὰ καὶ πολλάκις, ἑκάστης τοῦ ἐνιαυτοῦ περιτροπῆς τὴν αὐτὴν ἡμέραν ἐπαγούσης, ἵνα μὴ ἐξίτηλα τῷ χρόνῳ γένηται τὰ καλά.

for

for the Service of God at Jerufalem, the Dedication he judged a matter not unworthy, about the folemn performance whereof the greateft part of the Bifhops in Chriftendom fhould meet together. Which thing they did at the Emperor's motion, each moft willingly fetting forth that action to their power, fome with Orations, fome with Sermons, fome with the facrifice of Prayers unto God for the peace of the World, for the Church's fafety, for the Emperor's and his Children's good. By Athanafius the like is recorded concerning a Bifhop of Alexandria, in a work of the like devout magnificence. So that whether Emperors or Bifhops in thofe days were Church-founders, the folemn Dedication of Churches they thought not to be a work in itfelf either vain, or fuperftitious. Can we judge it a thing feemly for any Man to go about the building of an Houfe to the God of Heaven with no other appearance, than if his end were to rear up a kitchen, or a parlour, for his own ufe? Or when a work of fuch nature is finifhed, remaineth there nothing but prefently to ufe it, and fo an end? It behoveth that the place where God fhall be ferved by the whole Church, be a publick place, for the avoiding of privy Conventicles, which covered with pretence of Religion may ferve unto dangerous practices. Yea, though fuch Affemblies be had indeed for Religion's fake; hurtful neverthelefs they may eafily prove, as well in regard of their fitnefs to ferve the turn of Hereticks, and fuch as privily will fooneft adventure to inftil their poifon into Men's minds; as alfo for the occafion which thereby is given to malicious Perfons, both of fufpecting, and of traducing with more colourable fhew thofe actions, which in themfelves being holy, fhould be fo ordered that no Man might probably otherwife think of them. Which confiderations have by fo much the greater weight, for that of thefe inconveniencies the Church

Athanafius Apol. ad Conftantium.

BOOK V. Church heretofore had ſo plain experience, when Chriſtian Men were driven to uſe ſecret meetings, becauſe the liberty of publick places was not granted them. There are which hold, that the preſence of a Chriſtian Multitude, and the Duties of Religion performed amongſt them, do make the place of their Aſſembly publick; even as the preſence of the King and his Retinue maketh any Man's Houſe a Court. But this I take to be an error, in as much as the only thing which maketh any place publick, is the publick aſſignment thereof unto ſuch Duties. As for the Multitude there aſſembled, or the Duties which they perform, it doth not appear how either ſhould be of force to infuſe any ſuch prerogative. Nor doth the ſolemn Dedication of Churches ſerve only to make them publick, but farther alſo to ſurrender up that right which otherwiſe their Founders might have in them, and to make God himſelf their Owner. For which cauſe, at the Erection and Conſecration as well of the Tabernacle, as of the Temple, it pleaſed the Almighty to give a manifeſt ſign that he took poſſeſſion of both. Finally, it notifieth in ſolemn manner the holy and religious uſe, whereunto it is intended ſuch Houſes ſhall be put. Theſe things the wiſdom of Solomon did not account ſuperfluous. He knew how eaſily that which was meant ſhould be holy and ſacred, might be drawn from the uſe whereunto it was firſt provided; he knew how bold Men are to take even from God himſelf; how hardly that Houſe would be kept from impious profanation he knew; and right wiſely therefore endeavoured by ſuch Solemnities to leave in the minds of Men that impreſſion which might ſomewhat reſtrain their boldneſs, and nouriſh a reverend affection towards the Houſe of God. For which cauſe when the firſt Houſe was deſtroyed, and a new in the ſtead thereof erected by the Children of Iſrael after their return from captivity, they kept the Dedication even of this Houſe alſo with joy.

Exod. xl. 34. 1 Reg. viii 11. Exod. xl. 9. 1 Reg. viii. Levit. xvi. 2. The place named holy. Ezr. vi. 16.

The

The argument which our Saviour uſeth againſt Prophaners of the Temple he taketh from the uſe whereunto it was with Solemnity conſecrated. And as the Prophet Jeremy forbiddeth the carrying of burdens on the Sabbath, becauſe that was a ſanctified Day, ſo becauſe the Temple was a Place ſanctified, our Lord would not ſuffer no not the carriage of a veſſel through the Temple. Theſe two Commandments therefore are in the Law conjoined, *Ye ſhall keep my Sabbaths, and reverence my Sanctuary.* Out of thoſe the Apoſtle's words, *Have ye not Houſes to eat and drink in?* albeit Temples, ſuch as now, were not then erected for the Chriſtian Religion, it hath been nevertheleſs not abſurdly conceived, that he teacheth what difference ſhould be made between Houſe and Houſe; that what is fit for the Dwelling-place of God, and what for Man's Habitation he ſheweth; he requireth that Chriſtian Men at their own home take common food, and in the Houſe of the Lord none but that food which is heavenly; he inſtructeth them, that as in the one place they uſe to refreſh their Bodies, ſo they may in the other learn to ſeek the nouriſhment of their Souls, and as there they ſuſtain temporal life, ſo here they would learn to make proviſion for eternal. Chriſt could not ſuffer that the Temple ſhould ſerve for a place of mart, nor the Apoſtle of Chriſt that the Church ſhould be made an inn. When therefore we ſanctify or hallow Churches, that which we do is only to teſtify that we make them places of publick reſort, that we inveſt God himſelf with them, that we ſever them from common uſes. In which action, other Solemnities than ſuch as are decent and fit for that purpoſe we approve none. Indeed we condemn not all as unmeet, the like whereunto have either been deviſed or uſed haply amongſt Idolaters. For why ſhould conformity with them in matter of Opinion be lawful when they think that which is true, if in Action when they do that which is meet, it be not lawful

BOOK V.

Matt xxi. 13.

Jer. xvii. 24.

Mark xi. 16.

Levit. xxvi. 2.

1 Cor xi. 22.

Pet. Cluniac.

to

BOOK V. to be like unto them? Are we to forsake any true Opinion because Idolaters have maintained it? or to shun any requisite Action only because we have in the practice thereof been prevented by Idolaters? It is no impossible thing, but that sometimes they may judge as rightly what is decent about such external affairs of God, as in greater things what is true. Not therefore whatsoever Idolaters have either thought or done, but let whatsoever they have either thought or done idolatrously, be so far forth abhorred. For of that which is good, even in evil things, God is Author.

Of the Names whereby we distinguish our Churches.

13. Touching the Names of Angels and Saints whereby the most of our Churches are called, as the custom of so naming them is very ancient, so neither was the cause thereof at the first, nor is the use and continuance with us at this present hurtful. That Churches were consecrated unto none but the Lord only, the very general name itself doth sufficiently shew, in as much as by plain grammatical construction, * Church doth signify no other thing than the Lord's House. And because the multitude as of Persons, so of things particular causeth variety of proper names to be devised for distinction sake, Founders of Churches did herein that which best liked their own conceit at the present time; yet each intending, that as oft as those Buildings came to be mentioned, the name should put Men in mind of some memorable thing or person. Thus therefore it cometh to pass that all Churches have had their names, some as memorials of peace, some of wisdom, some in memory of the Trinity itself, some of Christ under sundry titles, of the blessed Virgin not a few, many of one Apostle, Saint, or Martyr, many of all. In which respect their commendable purpose being not of every one understood, they have been in latter

Vid Socr l. i c. 16. Ev. Lib. iv. c. 30. Hist. Trip. l. iv c. 18.

* From Κυριακή, Kyre, and by adding letters of aspiration, Chyrch.

ages

ages construed as though they had superstitiously meant, either that those places which were denominated of Angels and Saints should serve for the worship of so glorious Creatures, or else those glorified Creatures for defence, protection, and patronage of such places. A thing which the Ancients do utterly disclaim. To them, saith St. Augustin, we appoint no Churches, because they are not to us as Gods. Again, *The Nations to their Gods erected Temples, we not Temples to our Martyrs as unto God, but memorials as unto dead Men, whose Spirits with God are still living.* * Divers considerations there are for which Christian Churches might first take their names of Saints; as either because by the ministry of Saints it pleased God there to shew some rare effect of his power; or else in regard of death, which those Saints having suffered for the testimony of Jesus Christ, did thereby make the places where they died venerable; or thirdly, for that it liked good and virtuous Men to give such occasion of mentioning them often, to the end that the naming of their Persons might cause enquiry to be made, and meditation to be had of their Virtues. Wherefore, seeing that we cannot justly account it Superstition, to give unto Churches those fore-rehearsed names, as memorials either of holy Persons or Things; if it be plain that their Founders did with such meaning name them, shall not we in otherwise taking them offer them injury? Or if it be obscure or uncertain what they meant, yet this construction being more favourable, Charity (I hope) constraineth no Man which standeth doubtful of their minds, to lean to the hardest and worst interpretation that their words can carry. Yea, although it were clear, that they all (for the error of some is manifest in this behalf) had therein a superstitious

V. Aug 8. de civi Dei. c xxvii. l. 22. c. x. Epist. xlix. ad Deo gra.

* The Duty which Christian Men performed in keeping Festival Dedications St. Basil termeth λατρείαν τοῦ Θεοῦ, acknowledging the same to have been withal τιμὴν εἰς τοὺς Μάρτυρας. Basil in Psal. cxiv.

intent,

BOOK V. intent, wherefore ſhould their fault prejudice us, who (as all Men know) do uſe by way of mere Diſtinction the names which they of Superſtion gave? In the uſe of thoſe names whereby we diſtinguiſh both Days and Months, are we culpable of Superſtition, becauſe they were who firſt invented them? The ſign Caſtor and Pollux ſuperſtitiouſly given unto that ſhip wherein the Apoſtle ſailed, polluteth not the Evangeliſt's pen, who thereby doth but diſtinguiſh that ſhip from others. If to Daniel there had been given no other name but only Beltiſhazzar, given him in honour of the Babylonian Idol Belti, ſhould their Idolatry which were the Authors of that name cleave unto every Man which had ſo termed him by way of perſonal difference only? Were it not to ſatisfy the minds of the ſimpler ſort of Men, theſe nice curioſities are not worthy the labour which we beſtow to anſwer them.

Acts xxviii. 11.

Dan iv. 5. Vide Scal. de emendat. temp. l. vi. p. 277.

Of the faſhion of our Churches.

14. The like unto this is a fancy which they have againſt the faſhion of our Churches, as being framed according to the pattern of the Jewiſh Temple. A fault no leſs grievous, if ſo be it were true, than if ſome King ſhould build his Manſion-houſe by the model of Solomon's Palace. So far forth as our Churches and their Temple have one end, what ſhould let, but that they may lawfully have one form? The Temple was for Sacrifice, and therefore had rooms to that purpoſe, ſuch as ours have none. Our Churches are places provided, that the people might there aſſemble themſelves in due and decent manner, according to their ſeveral degrees and order. Which thing being common unto us with Jews, we have in this reſpect our Churches divided by certain partitions, although not ſo many in number as theirs. They had their ſeveral for Heathen Nations, their ſeveral for the People of their own Nation, their ſeveral for Men, their ſeveral for Women, their ſeveral for their Prieſts, and for the High Prieſt alone their ſeveral. Their being in ours for local diſtinction between

tween the Clergy and the reſt (which yet we do not with any great ſtrictneſs or curioſity obſerve neither) but one partition, the cauſe whereof at the firſt (as it ſeemeth) was, that as many as were capable of the holy Myſteries, might there aſſemble themſelves, and no other creep in amongſt them; this is now made a matter ſo heinous, as if our Religion thereby were become even plain Judaiſm; and as though we retained a Moſt Holy Place, whereinto there might not any but the High Prieſt alone enter, according to the cuſtom of the Jews.

The ſumptuouſneſs of Chuches.

15. Some it highly diſpleaſeth, that ſo great expences this way are employed: *The mother of ſuch magnificence* (they think) *is but only a proud ambitious deſire to be ſpoken of far and wide. Suppoſe we that God himſelf delighteth to dwell ſumptuouſly? or taketh pleaſure in chargeable pomp? No; then was the Lord moſt acceptably ſerved, when his Temples were rooms borrowed within the houſes of poor Men. This was ſuitable unto the nakedneſs of Jeſus Chriſt, and the ſimplicity of his Goſpel.* What thoughts or cogitations they had which were Authors of thoſe things, the uſe and benefit whereof hath deſcended unto ourſelves, as we do not know, ſo we need not ſearch. It cometh (we grant) many times to paſs, that the works of Men being the ſame, their drifts and purpoſes therein are divers. The charge of Herod about the Temple of God was ambitious; yet Solomon's virtuous, Conſtantine's holy. But howſoever their hearts are diſpoſed by whom any ſuch thing is done in the world, ſhall we think that it baneth the work which they leave behind them, or taketh away from others the uſe and benefit thereof? Touching God himſelf, hath he any where revealed that it is his delight to dwell beggarly? and that he taketh no pleaſure to be worſhipped, ſaving only in poor cottages? Even then was the Lord as acceptably honoured of his People as ever, when the ſtatelieſt places and things in the whole World were

ſought

BOOK V. sought out to adorn his Temple. This is most suitable,* decent, and fit for the greatness of Jesus Christ, for the sublimity of his Gospel, except we think of Christ and his Gospel as † the Officers of Julian did. As therefore the Son of Syrach giveth verdict concerning those things which God hath wrought,
Eccles. xxxix. 34. *A Man need not say, This is worse than that, this more acceptable to God, that less; for in their season they are all worthy praise:* the like we may also conclude, as touching these two so contrary ways of providing, in meaner or in costlier sort, for the honour of Almighty God, *A Man need not say, This is worse than that, this more acceptable to God, that less; for with him they are in their season both allowable;* the one, when the state of the Church is poor; the other, when God hath enriched it with plenty. When they which had seen the beauty of the first Temple built by Solomon in the days of his great prosperity and peace, beheld how far it excelled the second, which had not builders of like ability, the tears of their
Agg. ii. 5, 10. grieved eyes the Prophets endeavoured with comforts to wipe away. Whereas if the House of God were by so much the more perfect, by how much the glory thereof is less, they should have done better to rejoice than weep, their Prophets better to reprove than comfort. It being objected against the Church in the times of universal persecution, that her Service done to God was not solemnly performed in Temples fit for the honour of Divine Majesty,
Minut. Fœl. in Octav. their most convenient answer was that *The best Temples which we can dedicate to God, are our sanctified Souls and Bodies.* Whereby it plainly appeareth how the Fathers, when they were upbraided with that

* Ἔργον τὸ μέγα καὶ καλὸν τίμιον, τοῦ γὰρ τοιούτου ἡ θεωρία θαυμαστή. Arist. Eth. l. iv. c 2. τὰ αἰσθήσει καλὰ καὶ νοήσει καλῶν εἰκόνες. Philo. Jud.

† Fœlix, thesauri imperialis quæstor, conspicatus sacrorum vasorum pretia; En, inquit, qualibus vasis ministratur Mariæ filio. Theodoret. Hist. Eccles. l. iii. c. 12.

defect,

defect, comforted themselves with the meditation of God's most gracious and merciful nature, who did not therefore the less accept of their hearty affection and zeal, rather than took any great delight, or imagined any high perfection in such their want of external ornaments, which when they wanted, the cause was their only lack of ability: ability serving, they wanted them not. Before the Emperor Constantine's time, under Severus, Gordian, Philip and Galienus, the state of Christian affairs being tolerable, the former buildings which were but of mean and small estate contented them not; spacious and ample Churches they erected throughout every city. No envy was able to be their hinderance, no practice of Satan or fraud of Men available against their proceedings herein, while they continued as yet worthy to feel the aid of the arm of God extended over them for their safety. These Churches Dioclesian caused by solemn edict to be afterwards overthrown. Maximinus with like authority giving them leave to erect them, the hearts of all Men were even rapt with divine joy, to see those places, which tyrannous impiety had laid waste, recovered, as it were, out of mortal calamity, Churches *reared up to an height immeasurable, and adorned with far more beauty in their restauration than their Founders before had given them.* Whereby we see how most Christian minds then stood affected; we see how joyful they were to behold the sumptuous stateliness of Houses built unto God's glory If we should over and besides this, alledge the care which was had that all things about the Tabernacle of Moses might be as beautiful, gorgeous and rich, as art could make them, or what travel and cost was bestowed that the goodliness of the Temple might be a spectacle of admiration to all the World; this, they will say, was figurative, and served by God's appointment but for a time, to shadow out the true everlasting glory of a more divine Sanctuary; whereunto Christ being long sithence entered, it seemeth that

BOOK V.

Euseb. l. viii. c. 1.

Euseb l. viii. c. 2.

Euseb. l. x. c. 2.

BOOK V. that all thoſe curious exornations ſhould rather ceaſe. Which thing we alſo ourſelves would grant, if the uſe thereof had been merely and only myſtical. But, ſith the Prophet David doth mention a natural conveniency which ſuch kind of bounteous expences have, as well for that we do thereby give unto God a teſtimony of our chearful affection, which thinketh nothing too dear to be beſtowed about the furniture of his Service, as alſo becauſe it ſerveth to the World for a witneſs of his Almightineſs, whom we outwardly honour with the chiefeſt of outward things, as being of all things himſelf incomparably the greateſt. Beſides, were it not alſo ſtrange, if God ſhould have made ſuch ſtore of glorious Creatures on Earth, and leave them all to be conſumed in ſecular vanity, allowing none but the baſer ſort to be employed in his own Service? To ſet forth the Majeſty of Kings, his Vicegerents in this World, the moſt gorgeous and rare treaſures which the World hath are procured. We think, belike, that he will accept what the meaneſt of them would diſdain. If there be great care to build and beautify thoſe corruptible Sanctuaries, little or none, that the living Temples of the Holy Ghoſt, the dearly redeemed Souls of the People of God may be edified; huge expences upon timber and ſtone, but towards the relief of the Poor ſmall devotion; coſt this way infinite, and in the mean while Charity cold: we have in ſuch caſe juſt occaſion to make complaint as St. Jerom did, *The walls of the Church there are enough contented to build, and to underſet it with goodly pillars, the marbles are poliſhed, the roofs ſhine with gold, the Altar hath precious ſtones to adorn it, and of Chriſt's Miniſters no choice at all.* The ſame Jerom, both in that place and elſewhere, debaſeth with like intent the glory of ſuch magnificence (a thing whereunto Men's affections in thoſe times needed no ſpur) thereby to extol the neceſſity ſometimes of Charity and Alms, ſometimes of other the moſt principal Duties belonging

1 Chron. xxviii. 14.

2 Chron. ii. 5.

Matth. vi. 29.

Malac. i. 8

Ad Nepotian de vita Cleric.

Ad Demetr. Epiſt. xii ad Gaudentium.

ing

ing unto Chriſtian Men; which Duties were neither ſo highly eſteemed as they ought, and being compared with that in queſtion, the directeſt ſentence we can give of them both, as unto me it ſeemeth, is this; *God who requireth the one as neceſſary, accepteth the other alſo as being an honourable work.*

What Holineſs and Virtue we aſcribe to the Church, more than other places.

16. Our opinion concerning the force and virtue which ſuch Places have, is, I truſt, without any blemiſh or ſtain of Hereſy. Churches receive, as every thing elſe, their chief perfection from the end whereunto they ſerve. Which end being the publick Worſhip of God, they are in this conſideration Houſes of greater Dignity than any provided for meaner purpoſes. For which cauſe they ſeem after a ſort even to mourn, as being injured and defrauded of their right, when places not ſanctified, as they are, prevent them unneceſſarily in that pre-eminence and honour. Whereby alſo it doth come to paſs, that the Service of God hath not then itſelf ſuch perfection of grace and comelineſs, as when the dignity of place which it wiſheth for doth concur. Again, albeit the true worſhip of God be to God in itſelf acceptable, who reſpecteth not ſo much in what place, as with what affection he is ſerved, and therefore Moſes in the midſt of the ſea, Job on the dunghill, Ezekiah in bed, Jeremy in mire, Jonas in the whale, Daniel in the den, the Children in the furnace, the Thief on the croſs, Peter and Paul in priſon, calling unto God were heard, as St. Baſil noteth: manifeſt notwithſtanding it is, that the very majeſty and holineſs of the place where God is worſhiped hath in regard of us great virtue, force and efficacy, for that it ſerveth as a ſenſible help to ſtir up devotion; and in that reſpect, no doubt, bettereth even our holieſt and beſt actions in this kind. As therefore we every where exhort all Men to worſhip God; even ſo, for performance of this Service by the People of God aſſembled, we think not any place ſo good as the Church, neither any ex-

Exhort. ad bapt. et pœnitent.

 hortation

BOOK V. hortation so fit as that of David, *O worship the Lora in the beauty of holiness.*
Psal. xcvi 9.

Their pretence that would have Churches utterly razed. Ps cxxxvii. 7.

17. For of our Churches thus it becometh us to esteem, howsoever others, rapt with the pang of a furious zeal, do pour out against them devout blasphemies, crying, *Down with them, down with them, even to the very ground: For to Idolatry they have been abused. And the places where Idols have been worshiped, are by the Law of God devote to utter destruction. For execution of which Law, the Kings that were godly, as Asa, Jehosophat, Ezechia, Josiah, destroyed all the high Places, Altars and Groves, which had been erected in Juda and Israel. He that said, Thou shalt have no other Gods before my face, hath likewise said, Thou shalt utterly deface and destroy all these Synagogues and places where such Idols have been worshiped. This Law containeth the temporal punishment which God hath set down, and willeth that Men execute for the breach of the other Law. They which spare them therefore, do but reserve, as the Hypocrite Saul did, execrable things to worship God withal.* The truth is, that as no Man serveth God, and loveth him not; so neither can any Man sincerely love God, and not extremely abhor that sin which is the highest degree of Treason against the Supreme Guide and Monarch of the whole World, with whose Divine Authority and Power it investeth others. By means whereof the state of Idolaters is two ways miserable First, in that which they worship they find no succour; and secondly, at his hands whom they ought to serve there is no other thing to be looked for but the effects of most just displeasure, the withdrawing of Grace, dereliction in this World, and in the World to come confusion. Paul and Barnabas, when Infidels admiring their virtues went about to sacrifice unto them, rent their Garments in token of horror, and as frighted persons ran crying through the press of the People, *O Men, wherefore do ye these things?* They knew the force of that dreadful curse whereunto Idolatry maketh subject. Nor is there cause why the guilty

Deut xii. 2
2 Chron. xvii 6.
2 Chron. xxix
2 Chron iii

Isa viii. 21. xlv 20.
Hos. xiv 4.
Isa. xlii. 24
Ps cxv 8. lxxxi. xiii.
Rom i. 24
Judic. vi. 13
Apoc. xxi 8.
Isa. ii 21.
Acts xiv. 14.
Deut. xxvii. 20.

sustaining

ſuſtaining the ſame, ſhould grudge or complain of injuſtice. For, whatſoever evil befalleth in that reſpect, themſelves have made themſelves worthy to ſuffer it. As for thoſe things either whereon, or elſe wherewith Superſtition worketh, polluted they are by ſuch abuſe, and deprived of that dignity which their nature delighteth in. For there is nothing which doth not grieve, and, as it were, even loath itſelf, whenſoever iniquity cauſeth it to ſerve unto vile purpoſes. Idolatry therefore maketh whatſoever it toucheth the worſe. Howbeit ſith creatures which have no underſtanding can ſhew no will; and where no will is, there is no ſin, and only that which ſinneth, is ſubject to puniſhment; which way ſhould any ſuch creature be puniſhable by the Law of God? There may be cauſe ſometime to aboliſh or to extinguiſh them, but ſurely never by way of puniſhment to the things themſelves. Yea farther, howſoever the Law of Moſes did puniſh Idolaters, we find not that God hath appointed for us any definite or certain temporal judgment, which the Chriſtian Magiſtrate is of neceſſity for ever bound to execute upon Offenders in that kind, much leſs upon things that way abuſed as mere inſtruments. For what God did command touching Canaan, the ſame concerneth not us any otherwiſe than only as a fearful pattern of his juſt diſpleaſure and wrath againſt ſinful Nations. It teacheth us, how God thought good to plague and afflict them; it doth not appoint in what form and manner we ought to puniſh the ſin of Idolatry in all others. Unleſs they will ſay, that becauſe the Iſraelites were commanded to make no covenant with the People of that Land, therefore leagues and truces made between ſuperſtitious Perſons, and ſuch as ſerve God aright, are unlawful altogether; or becauſe God commanded the Iſraelites to ſmite the Inhabitants of Canaan, and to root them out, that therefore reformed Churches are bound to put all others to the edge of the ſword. Now whereas commandment was alſo given to deſtroy all places where the Canaanites had

Jer. ii. 17.

Deut. xii. 2.

BOOK V. had ſerved their Gods, and not to convert any one of them to the honour of the true God; this precept had reference unto a ſpecial intent and purpoſe, which was, that there ſhould be but one only place in the whole Land, whereunto the People might bring ſuch Offerings, Gifts and Sacrifices, as their Levitical Law did require. By which Law, ſevere charge was given them in that reſpect, not to convert thoſe places to the Worſhip of the Living God, where Nations
Deut. xii. 4, 5. before them had ſerved Idols, *But to ſeek the place which the Lord their God ſhould chooſe out of all their Tribes*. Beſides, it is reaſon we ſhould likewiſe conſider how great a difference there is between their proceedings, who erect a new Commonwealth, which is to have neither People nor Law, neither Regiment nor Religion the ſame that was, and theirs, who only reform a decayed Eſtate, by reducing it to that perfection from which it hath ſwerved. In this caſe we are to retain as much, in the other as little of former things as we may. Sith therefore Examples have not generally the force of Laws which all Men ought to keep, but of counſels only and perſuaſions not amiſs to be followed by them whoſe caſe is the like, ſurely where caſes are ſo unlike as theirs and ours, I ſee not how that which they did ſhould induce, much leſs any way enforce us to the ſame practice, eſpecially conſidering that Groves and Hill-altars were, while they did remain, both dangerous in regard of the ſecret acceſs, which People ſuperſtitiouſly given, might have always thereunto with eaſe; neither could they remaining, ſerve with any fitneſs unto better purpoſe: whereas our Temples (their former abuſe being by order of Law removed) are not only free from ſuch peril, but withal ſo conveniently framed for the People of God to ſerve and honour him therein, that no Man beholding them, can chooſe but think it exceeding great pity they ſhould be ever any otherwiſe employed. Yea but the cattle of Amalek (you will ſay) were fit for ſacrifice, and this was the very conceit

which

which ſometime deceived Saul. It was ſo. Nor do I any thing doubt, but that Saul upon this conceit might even lawfully have offered to God thoſe reſerved ſpoils, had not the Lord in that particular caſe given ſpecial charge to the contrary. As therefore notwithſtanding the commandment of Iſrael to deſtroy Canaanites, Idolaters may be converted and live: ſo the Temples which have ſerved Idolatry as inſtruments, may be ſanctified again and continue, albeit to Iſrael commandment have been given that they ſhould deſtroy all idolatrous places in their Land; and to the good Kings of Iſrael commendation for fulfilling, to the evil for diſobeying the ſame commandment, ſometimes puniſhment, always ſharp and ſevere reproof hath even from the Lord himſelf befallen. Thus much it may ſuffice to have written in defence of thoſe Chriſtian Oratories, the overthrow and ruin whereof is deſired, not now by Infidels, Pagans or Turks, but by a ſpecial refined Sect of Chriſtian Believers; pretending themſelves exceedingly grieved at our Solemnities in erecting Churches, at the Names which we ſuffer them to hold, at their form and faſhion, at the ſtatelineſs of them and coſtlineſs, at the opinion which we have of them, and at the manifold ſuperſtitious abuſes whereunto they have been put.

Of publick teaching, or preaching, and the firſt kind thereof, Catechiſing.

18. Places of publick reſort being thus provided for, our repair thither is eſpecially for mutual conference, and as it were commerce to be had between God and us. Becauſe therefore want * of the knowledge of God is the cauſe of all iniquity amongſt Men, as contrariwiſe the ground of all our happineſs, and the ſeed of whatſoever perfect virtue groweth

* Contraria fortia in quibus homines ſibi invicem opponantur ſecundum exercitia et deſideria et opiniones, omnia proveniunt ex ignorantia. ſicut cæcus ex privatione ſui viſus vagatur ubique et læditur. Scientia veritatis tollit hominum inimicitiam et odium. Hoc promiſit ſancta Theologia dicens, Habitabit agnus cum lupo Et aſſignat rationem, Repleta eſt terra ſapientia Domini. Moſes Ægypt. in Mor. Hannebuch. lib. iii. cap. 12.

from

BOOK V. from us, is a right opinion touching things divine, this kind of knowledge we may justly set down for the first and chiefest thing which God imparteth unto his People, and our duty of receiving this at his merciful hands, for the first of those religious Offices wherewith we publickly honour him on Earth. For the instruction therefore of all sorts of Men to eternal Life it is necessary, that the sacred and saving Truth of God be openly published upon them. Which open publication of heavenly Mysteries, is by an excellency termed Preaching. For otherwise there is not any thing publickly notified, but we may in that respect, rightly and properly say it is preached. So that when the School of God doth use it as a word of art, we are accordingly to understand it with restraint to such special matter as that School is accustomed to publish. We find not in the World any People that have lived altogether without Religion. And yet this duty of Religion, which provideth that publickly all sorts of Men may be instructed in the fear of God, is to the Church of God, and hath been always so peculiar, that none of the Heathens, how curious soever in searching out all kinds of outward Ceremonies like to ours, could ever once so much as endeavour to resemble herein the Church's care for the endless good of her Children. Ways of teaching there have been sundry always usual in God's Church. For the first introduction of Youth to the knowledge of God, * the Jews even to this day have their Catechisms. With Religion it fareth as with other Sciences; the first delivery of the Elements thereof must, for like consideration, † be

Luc viii. 39. xii. 3.

Vide Tertul. de præscr advers. Hær.

* The Jews Catech. called Lekach Tob.

† Incipientibus brevius ac simplicius tradi præcepta magis convenit. Aut enim difficultate institutionis tam numerosæ atque perplexæ deterreri solent, aut eo tempore quo præcipue alenda ingenia atque indulgentia quadam enutrienda sunt, asperiorum rerum tractatu atteruntur. Fab. procem. l. viii. Incipientibus nobis exponere jura populi Romani, ita videntur posse tradi commodissime, si primo levi ac simplici via, post deinde diligentissima atque

framed according to the weak and ſlender capacity of young Beginners: unto which manner of teaching Principles in Chriſtianity, the Apoſtle in the ſixth to the Hebrews is himſelf underſtood to allude. For this cauſe therefore, as the Decalogue of Moſes declareth ſummarily thoſe things which we ought to do; the Prayer of our Lord, whatſoever we ſhould requeſt or deſire, ſo either by the Apoſtles, or at the leaſtwiſe out of their Writings, we have the ſubſtance of Chriſtian Belief compendiouſly drawn into few and ſhort Articles, to the end that the weakneſs of no Man's wit might either hinder altogether the knowledge, or excuſe the utter ignorance of needful things. Such as were trained up in theſe rudiments, and were ſo made fit to be afterwards by Baptiſm received into the Church, the Fathers uſually in their writings do term * Hearers; as having no further communion or fellowſhip with the Church, than only this, that they were admitted to hear the Principles of Chriſtian Faith made plain unto them. Catechiſing may be in Schools, it may be in private Families; but when we make it a kind of Preaching, we mean always the publick performance thereof in the open hearing of Men; becauſe things are preached not in that they are taught, but in that they are publiſhed.

BOOK V.

Vide Ruff. in Symb.

atque exactiſſima interpretatione ſingula traduntur Alioqui ſi ſtatim ab initio rudem adhuc et infirmum animum ſtudioſi multitudine ac varietate rerum oneraverimus, duorum alterum, aut deſertorem ſtudiorum efficiemus, aut cum magno labore ejus, ſæpe etiam cum diffidentia (quæ plerumque juvenes avertit) ſerius ad id perducemus, ad quod leviore via ductus ſine magno labore et ſine ulla diffidentia maturius perduci potuiſſet. Inſtitut. Imper. l. i, tit. 1.

* Tert. de pœniten. An alius eſt tinctis Chriſtus, alius audientibus? Audientes optare intinctionem non præſumere oportet. Cyprian. Epiſt. xvii. l. 3. Audientibus ſignantia veſtra non deſit Rupert de divin. Offic. lib. iv. cap. 18. Audiens quiſque regulam fidei Catechumenus dicitur. Catechumenus namque Auditor interpretatur.

19. Moſes

BOOK V.

Of Preaching, by reading publickly the Books of holy Scripture, and concerning supposed untruths in those Translations of Scripture, which we allow to be read, as also of the choice which we make in reading.

19. Moſes and the Prophets, Chriſt and his Apoſtles, were in their times all Preachers of God's Truth; ſome by word, ſome by writing, ſome by both. This they did partly as faithful Witneſſes, making mere relation what God himſelf had revealed unto them; and partly as careful Expounders, Teachers, Perſuaders thereof. The Church in like caſe preacheth ſtill, firſt publiſhing by way of Teſtimony or relation the Truth which from them ſhe hath received, even in ſuch ſort as it was received, written in the ſacred volumes of Scripture: ſecondly by way of explication, diſcovering the Myſteries which lie hid therein. The Church as a Witneſs preacheth his meer revealed Truth by reading publickly the ſacred Scripture. So that a ſecond kind of Preaching is the reading of holy Writ. For thus we may the boldlier ſpeak, being ſtrengthened with the example of ſo reverend a Prelate as ſaith, that Moſes from the time of antient generations and ages long ſince paſt, had amongſt the cities of the very Gentiles them that preached him, in that he was read every Sabbath-day. For ſo of neceſſity it muſt be meant, in as much as we know that the Jews have always had their weekly readings of the Law of Moſes; but that they always had in like manner their weekly Sermons upon ſome part of the Law of Moſes, we no where find. Howbeit ſtill we muſt here remember, that the Church by her publick reading of the Book of God preacheth only as a Witneſs. Now the principal thing required in a Witneſs is Fidelity. Wherefore as we cannot excuſe that Church, which either through corrupt Tranſlations of Scripture delivereth inſtead of divine Speeches any thing repugnant unto that which God ſpeaketh; or, through falſified additions propoſeth that to the People of God as Scripture, which is in truth no Scripture, ſo the blame which in both theſe reſpects hath been laid upon the Church of England is ſurely altogether without cauſe. Touching Tranſlations of holy

Acts xv. 21

holy Scripture, albeit we may not disallow of their painful travels herein who strictly have tied themselves to the very original letter; yet the judgment of the Church, as we see by the practice of all Nations, Greeks, Latins, Persians, Syrians, Æthiopians, Arabians, hath been ever, that the fittest for publick audience are such, as following a middle course between the rigour of literal Translators, and the liberty of Paraphrasts, do with greatest shortness and plainness deliver the meaning of the Holy Ghost. Which being a labour of so great difficulty, the exact performance thereof we may rather wish than look for. So that, except between the words of Translation and the mind of the Scripture itself there be contradiction, every little difference should not seem an intolerable blemish necessarily to be spunged out. Whereas therefore the Prophet David in a certain Psalm doth say concerning Moses and Aaron, that they were obedient to the Word of God, and in the self-same place our allowed Translation saith, they were not obedient, we are for this cause challenged as manifest Gainsayers of Scripture, even in that which we read for Scripture unto the People. But for as much as words are resemblances of that which the mind of the Speaker conceiveth, and conceits are images representing that which is spoken of; it followeth that they who will judge of words, should have recourse to the things themselves from whence they rise. In setting down that Miracle, at the sight whereof Peter fell down astonished before the feet of Jesus, and cried, *Depart, Lord, I am a sinner*; the Evangelist St. Luke saith, the store of the fish which they took was such, that the net they took it in brake, and the ships which they loaded therewith sunk; St. John recording the like Miracle saith, that albeit the fishes in number were so many, yet the net with so great a weight was not broken. Suppose they had written both of one Miracle; although there be in their words a manifest shew of jar, yet none, if we look

BOOK V.

Psal. cv. 28.

Luke v. 6, 7

John xxi. 11.

BOOK V look upon the difference of matter, with regard whereunto they might have both ſpoken even of one Miracle, the very ſame which they ſpake of divers, the one intending thereby to ſignify that the greatneſs of the burden exceeded the natural ability of the inſtruments which they had to bear it; the other, that the weakneſs thereof was ſupported by a ſupernatural and miraculous addition of ſtrength. The nets, as touching themſelves, brake, but through the power of God they held. Are not the words of

Mich. v 2. Math ii. 6. the Prophet Micheas touching Bethleem, *Thou Bethleem the leaſt?* And doth not the very Evangeliſt tranſlate theſe words, *Thou Bethleem not the leaſt?* The one regarding the quantity of the place, the other the dignity. Micheas attributeth unto it ſmallneſs in reſpect of circuit; Matthew greatneſs in regard of honour and eſtimation, by being the native ſoil of our Lord and Saviour Chriſt. Sith therefore ſpeeches which gainſay one another, muſt of neceſſity be applied both unto one and the ſelf-ſame ſubject; ſith they muſt alſo the one affirm, the other deny the ſelf-ſame thing; what neceſſity of contradiction can there be between the Letter of the Prophet David and our authoriſed Tranſlation thereof, if he underſtanding Moſes and Aaron do ſay *They were not diſobedient*; we applying our ſpeech to Pharaoh and the Egyptians, do ſay of them *They were not obedient?* Or (which the matter itſelf will eaſily enough likewiſe ſuffer) if the Ægyptians being meant by both, it be ſaid that they, in regard of their

Exod. x. 24 offer to let go the People, when they ſaw the fearful darkneſs, diſobeyed not the Word of the Lord; and yet that they did not obey his Word, in as much as the ſheep and cattle at the ſelf-ſame time they withheld. Of both Tranſlations the better I willingly acknowledge that which cometh nearer to the very letter of the original verity; yet ſo, that the other may likewiſe ſafely enough be read, without any peril at all of gainſaying as much as the leaſt jot or

ſyllable

ſyllable of God's moſt ſacred and precious Truth. Which Truth, as in this we do not violate, ſo neither is the ſame gainſayed or croſt, no not in thoſe very Preambles placed before certain readings, wherein the ſteps of the Latin Service-book have been ſomewhat too nearly followed. As when we ſay, Chriſt ſpake *to his Diſciples*, that which the Goſpel declareth he ſpake *unto the Phariſees*. For doth the Goſpel affirm he ſpake to the Phariſees only? Doth it mean that they, and beſides them no Man elſe, was at that time ſpoken unto by our Saviour Chriſt? If not, then is there in this diverſity no contrariety. I ſuppoſe it ſomewhat probable, that St. John and St. Matthew, which have recorded thoſe Sermons, heard them, and being Hearers did think themſelves as well reſpected as the Phariſees, in that which their Lord and Maſter taught concerning the paſtoral care he had over his own Flock, and his offer of Grace made to the whole World; which things are the matter whereof he treateth in thoſe Sermons. Whereof as yet there is nothing found, wherein we read for the Word of God that which may be condemned as repugnant unto his Word. Furthermore, ſomewhat they are diſpleaſed, in that we follow not the method of reading which * in their judgment is moſt commendable, the method uſed in ſome foreign Churches, where Scriptures are read before the time of divine Service, and without either choice or ſtint appointed by any determinate Order. Nevertheleſs, till ſuch time as they will vouchſafe us ſome juſt and ſufficient reaſon to the contrary, we muſt by their patience, if not allowance, retain the † ancient

BOOK V.

The Goſpel on the ſecond Sunday after Eaſter, and on the twentieth after Trinity. John x. 11. Matt xxii. 1.

* T. C. l. ii. p. 381. Although it be very convenient which is uſed in ſome Churches, where before Preaching-time the Church aſſembled hath the Scriptures read, yet neither is this, nor any other Order of bare publick Reading in the Church neceſſary. h. d.

† Aug. de Civ. Dei, l. xxii. c. 8. Facto ſilentio, Scripturarum ſunt lecta divina ſolennia. That for ſeveral times ſeveral pieces of

BOOK V.

received customs which we now observe. For with us the reading of the Scripture in the Church is a part of our Church-liturgy, a special portion of the Service which we do to God, and not an exercise to spend the time when one doth wait for another's coming, till the assembly of them which shall afterwards worship him be complete. Wherefore, as the form of our publick Service is not voluntary, so neither are the parts thereof left uncertain, but they are all set down in such order, and with such choice as hath in the wisdom of the Church seemed best to concur, as well with the special occasions, as with the general purpose which we have to glorify God.

On Preaching by the publick reading of other profitable instructions; and concerning Books Apocryphal.

20. Other publick Readings there are of Books and Writings not Canonical, whereby the Church doth also preach, or openly make know the doctrine of virtuous conversation, whereupon, besides those things in regard whereof we are thought to read the Scriptures of God amiss, it is thought amiss, that we read in our Churches any thing at all besides the Scriptures. To exclude the reading of any such profitable instruction as the Church hath devised for the better understanding of Scripture, or for the easier training up of the People in holiness and righteousness of life, they ‡ plead, that God in the Law would have nothing brought into the Temple, neither besoms, nor flesh-hooks, nor trumpets, but those only which were sanctified; that for the expounding of

of Scripture were read as parts of the Service of the Greek Church, the Fathers thereof in their sundry Homilies and other writings do all testify. The like Order in the Syrian Churches is clear by the very inscriptions of Chapters throughout their Translation of the New Testament. See the Edition at Vienna, Paris and Antwerp.

‡ T. C. l. 1, p. 196. Neither the Homilies nor the Apocrypha are at all to be read in the Church. Wherein, first, it is good to consider the Order which the Lord kept with his People in times past, when he commanded, Exod. xxx. 29, that no vessel nor no instrument, either besom or flesh-hook or pan should once come into the Temple, but those only which are

sanctified

darker places, we ought to follow the Jews § polity, who under Antiochus, where they had not the commodity of Sermons, appointed always at their meetings somewhat out of the Prophets to be read together with the Law, and so by the one made the other plainer to be understood; that before and after our Saviour's coming they neither read Onkelos nor Jonathan's Paraphrase, though having both; but contented themselves with the reading only of Scripture; that if in the primitive Church there had been any thing read besides the monuments of the Prophets and Apostles, Justin Martyr and Origen, who mention these, would have spoken of the other likewise: that the most ancient and best Councils forbid any thing to be read in Churches, saving canonical Scripture only: that when other things were afterwards permitted, fault was found with it, it succeeded but ill, the Bible itself was thereby in time quite and clean thrust out. Which arguments, if they be only brought in token of the Author's good-will and meaning towards the cause which they would set forward, must accordingly be accepted of by them who already are persuaded the same way. But if their drift and purpose be to persuade others, it would be demanded, by what rule the legal hallowing of besoms and flesh-hooks must needs exclude all other Readings in the Church save Scripture. Things sanctified were thereby in such sort appropriated unto God, as that they might never afterwards again be made common. For which cause, the Lord to sign and mark them as his own, appointed oil of holy ointment, the like whereunto it was not lawful to make for ordinary and daily uses. Thus the anoint-

Acts xiii. 15. Acts xv. 21. Justin Apol. 2. Origen. Hom 1. super Exod. et in Judic. Conc. Laod ca. 59. Concil. Vasens 2. Concil. Coln. par. 2. Exod. xxx. 25, 32. Exod xl. 15.

sanctified and set apart for that use. And in the Book of Numbers he will have no other trumpets blown to call the People together but those only which are set apart for that purpose. Numb x. 2.

§ T. C. l. i. p. 197. Besides this, the Polity of the Church of God in times past is to be followed, &c.

ing

 ing of Aaron and his Sons tied them to the Office of the Priesthood for ever, the anointing, not of those silver trumpets (which Moses as well for secular as sacred uses was commanded to make, not to sanctify) but the Unction of the Tabernacle, the Table, the Laver, the Altar of God, with all the Instruments appertaining thereunto, this made them for ever holy unto him, in whose service they were employed. But what of this? Doth it hereupon follow that all things now in the Church, from the greatest to the least, are unholy, which the Lord hath not himself precisely instituted? for so *those Rudiments, they say, do import. Then is there nothing holy, which the Church by her authority hath appointed; and consequently all positive Ordinances that ever were made by Ecclesiastical Power touching spiritual affairs, are prophane, they are unholy. I would not wish them to undertake a work so desperate as to prove that for the People's instruction no kind of Reading is good, but only that which the Jews devised under Antiochus, although even that also be mistaken. For, according to Elias the Levite (out of whom it doth seem borrowed) the thing which Antiochus forbad, was the publick Reading of the Law, and not Sermons upon the Law. Neither did the Jews read a portion of the Prophets together with the Law to serve for an interpretation thereof, because Sermons were not permitted them; but instead of the Law, which they might not read openly, they read of the Prophets that which in likeness of matter came nearest to each section of their Law. Whereupon, when afterwards the liberty of reading the Law was restored, the self-same custom as touching the Prophets did continue still. If neither

Numb. x. 2.

Exod. xxvii. iii. & xxx. 26, 27, 28.

Elias Thesb. in verbo Patar.

Acts xv. 21.

Acts xiii. 15.

* T. C. l. i. p. 197. The Lord would by these Rudiments and Pædagogies teach, that he would have nothing brought into the Church but that which he hath appointed.

the

the Jews have uſed publickly to read their Paraphraſts, nor *the primitive Church for a long time any other writings than Scripture, except the cauſe of their not doing it were ſome Law of God, or Reaſon forbidding them to do that which we do, why ſhould the latter ages of the Church be deprived of the liberty the former had? Are we bound while the World ſtandeth, to put nothing in practice, but only that which was at the very firſt? Concerning the Council of Laodicea, as it forbiddeth the reading of thoſe things which are not Canonical, ſo it maketh ſome things not Canonical which are. Their judgment in this we may not, and in that we need not follow. We have by thus many years experience found, that exceeding great good, not incumbered with any notable inconvenience, hath grown by the Cuſtom which we now obſerve. As for the harm whereof judicious Men have complained in former times; it came not of this, that other things were read beſides the Scripture, but that ſo evil choice was made. With us there is never any time beſtowed in divine Service without the reading of a great part of the holy Scripture, which we account a thing moſt neceſſary. We dare not admit any ſuch Form of Liturgy, as either appointeth no Scripture at all, or very little to be read in the Church. And therefore the thruſting of the Bible out of the Houſe of God, is rather there to

The Apocalyps.

* T. C. l. i. p. 197. This practice continued ſtill in the Churches of God after the Apoſtles' times, as may appear by the ſecond Apology of Juſtin Martyr. Idem, p. 198 It was decreed in the Council of Laodicea, that nothing ſhould be read in the Church but the Canonical Books of the Old and New Teſtament. Afterwards, as corruptions grew in the Church, the reading of Homilies and of Martyrs' lives was permitted. But, beſides the evil ſucceſs thereof, that uſe and cuſtom was controlled, as may appear by the Council of Colle[illegible], albeit otherwiſe Popiſh. The bringing in of Homilies and Martyrs' lives hath thruſt the Bible clean out of the Church, or into a corner.

be

BOOK V. be feared where Men esteem it a matter *so indifferent, whether the same be by solemn appointment read publickly or not read, the bare Text excepted, which the Preacher happily chooseth out to expound. But let us here consider what the practice of our Fathers before us hath been, and how far forth the same may be followed. We find that in ancient times there was publickly read first the †Scripture, as namely something out of the Books of the ‡ Prophets of God which were of old; something out of § the Apostles' Writings; and lastly out of the holy Evangelists ‖ some things which touched the Person of our Lord Jesus Christ himself. The cause of their reading first the Old Testament, then the New, and always somewhat out of both, is most

Just. quæst. 101. likely to have been that which Justin Martyr and St. Augustin observe in comparing the two Testaments.

Aug. quæst. 33 in Num. *The Apostles* (saith the one) *hath taught us as themselves did learn, first the Precepts of the Law, and then the Gospels. For what else is the Law but the Gospel foreshewed? What other the Gospel, than the Law ful-*

* T. C. l. ii. p. 381. It is untrue, that simple reading is necessary in the Church. A number of Churches which have no such Order of simple reading, cannot be in this point charged with the breach of God's commandment, which they might be, if simple reading were necessary. [By simple reading he meaneth the Custom of bare reading more than the Preacher at the same time expoundeth unto the People.]

† Coimus ad divinarum literarum commemorationem. Tertul. Apol. p. 692.

‡ Judaicarum Historiarum libri traditi sunt ab Apostolis legendi in Ecclesiis. Orig. in Jos. Hom. 15.

§ Πάντων κατὰ πόλεις ἢ ἀγρὲς μενόντων ἐπὶ τὸ αὐτὸ συνέλευσις γίνεται, καὶ τὰ απομνημονεύματα τῶν Ἀποςόλων ἢ τὰ συγγράμματα τῶν Προφητῶν ἀναγινώσκεται. Justin. Apol ii. p. 162. Factum est ut ista die Dominica, Prophetica lectione jam lecta, ante altare adstante qui lectionem St. Pauli proferret beatissimus Antistes Ambrosius, &c. Sulpit. Sever. l 3. de vita St. Mart.

‖ Vide Concil. Val. ii. habitum an. Dom. 444. tom Concil. ii. p. 19. Item. Synod. Laod. c. xvi. Cypr. l. ii epist. 5. and l. iv. epist. 5 Amb. l i. Offic. c. viii. et epist. 75. et lib. de Helia atque jejunio, cap. xx.

filled

filled? In like ſort the other, *What the Old Teſtament hath, the very ſame the new containeth; but that which lieth there as under a ſhadow, is here brought forth into the open ſun. Things there prefigured, are here performed.* Again, *In the Old Teſtament there is a cloſe comprehenſion of the New; in the New, an open diſcovery of the Old.* To be ſhort, the method of their publick readings either purpoſely did tend, or at the leaſtwiſe doth fitly ſerve, *That from ſmaller things the minds of the Hearers may go forward to the knowledge of greater, and by degrees climb up from the loweſt to the higheſt things.* Now beſides the Scripture, the Books which they called Eccleſiaſtical were thought not unworthy ſometime to be brought into publick audience, and with that name they intituled the Books which we term Apocryphal. Under the ſelf-ſame name they alſo compriſed certain, no otherwiſe annexed unto the New than the former unto the Old Teſtament, as a Book of Hermes, Epiſtles of Clement, and the like. According therefore to the phraſe of antiquity, theſe we may term the new, and the other the old Eccleſiaſtical Books or Writings. For we being directed by a ſentence (I ſuppoſe) of Saint Jerom, who ſaith that *All Writings not Canonical are Apocryphal,* uſe not now the title Apocryphal as the reſt of the Fathers ordinarily have done, whoſe cuſtom is ſo to name for the moſt part only ſuch as might not publickly be read or divulged. Ruffinus therefore having rehearſed the ſelf-ſame Books of Canonical Scripture, which with us are held to be only Canonical, addeth immediately, by way of caution, *We muſt know that other Books there are alſo which our Foreſathers have uſed to name not Canonical but Eccleſiaſtical Books, as the Book of Wiſdom, Eccleſiaſticus, Toby, Judith, the Maccabees, in the Old Teſtament; in the New, the Book of Hermes, and ſuch others: All which Books and Writings they willed to be read in Churches, but not to be alledged as if their authority did bind us to build upon them our Faith. Other*

Walaf Stra. de rebus Eccleſiaſt. cap. xxii.

Hieron. in prolog. Galeat.

Ruffinus in Symbol. Apoſt. apud Cypr.

BOOK V. *Writings they named Apocryphal, which they would not have read in Churches. These things delivered unto us from the Fathers we have in this place thought good to set down.* So far Ruffinus. He which considereth notwithstanding what store of false and forged Writings, dangerous unto Christian Belief, and yet bearing glorious inscriptions, began soon upon the Apostles' times to be admitted into the Church, and to be honoured as if they had been indeed Apostolick, shall easily perceive what cause the provincial Synod of Laodicea might have as then to prevent especially the danger of Books made newly Ecclesiastical, and, for fear of the fraud of Hereticks, to provide that such publick readings might be altogether taken out of the Canonical Scripture. Which Ordinance respecting but that abuse which grew through the intermingling of Lessons human with sacred, at such time as the one both affected the credit and usurped the name of the other (as by the Canon* of a later Council providing remedy for the self-same evil, and yet allowing the old Ecclesiastical Books to be read, it doth more plainly and clearly appear), neither can be construed, nor should be urged utterly to prejudice our use of those old Ecclesiastical Writings; much less of Homilies, which were a third kind of readings used in former times, a most commendable institution, as well then to supply the casual, † as now the necessary defect of Sermons. In the heat of general Persecution, whereunto Christian Belief was subject upon the first promulgation thereof throughout the World, it much confirmed the courage and constancy of weaker Minds, when publick relation was made unto them after

Vide Gelas decret. tom. Concil. ii p. 462.

Circa An. Dom. 366.

* Concil. Carthag. iii. c. 47. Præter Scripturas Canonicas nihil in Ecclesiis legatur sub nomine divinarum scripturarum. Circa An Dom. 401.

† Concil. Valen. ii. habitum An. Dom. 444. tom. Concil. ii. p 19. Si Presbyter, aliqua infirmitate prohibente, per seipsum non potuerit prædicare, Sanctorum Patrum Homiliæ a Diaconibus recitentur.

what

what manner God had been glorified through the sufferings of Martyrs, famous amongst them for holiness during life, and at the time of their death admirable in all Men's eyes through miraculous evidence of Grace divine assisting them from above. For which cause the virtues of some being thought expedient to be annually had in remembrance above the rest, this brought in a fourth kind of publick reading, whereby the lives of such Saints and Martyrs had at the time of their yearly memorials solemn recognition in the Church of God. The fond imitation of which laudable Custom being in latter ages resumed, where there was neither the like cause to do as the Fathers before had done, nor any care, conscience, or wit in such as undertook to perform that work, some brainless Men have by great labour and travel brought to pass, that the Church is now ashamed of nothing more than of Saints. If therefore Pope Gelasius did so long sithence see those defects of judgment, even then, for which the reading of the Acts of Martyrs should be, and was at that time forborn in the Church of Rome; we are not to marvel, that afterwards Legends being grown in a manner to be nothing else but heaps of frivolous and scandalous vanities, they have been even with disdain thrown out, the very nests which bred them abhorring them. We are not therefore to except only Scripture, and to make confusedly all the residue of one sute, as if they who abolish Legends could not without incongruity retain in the Church either Homilies or those Ecclesiastical Books. Which Books in case myself did think, as some others do, safer and better to be left publickly unread; nevertheless as in other things of like nature, even so in this, *my private judgment I should be loth to oppose against the force of their reverend authority, who rather considering the divine excellency of some things in

BOOK V.

Concil. Carthag. 11 Can. 13 & Greg. Turon. de gloria mart ca. 86. & Hadrian epist. ad Carol. Magn.

Gelas circa. An Dom. 492. to Concil. 11. p. 161.

Concil Colon celebrat An. Dom 1536 par 11. cap. 6. Melch. Can locor. theol lib. xi Viv de trad. disc. lib v.

* In errorum barathrum faciliter ruant qui conceptus proprios patrum definitionibus anteponunt. c. unde Relig d. in extra.

BOOK V. in all, and of all things in certain of thoſe Apocrypha which we publickly read, have thought it better to let them ſtand as a liſt or marginal border unto the Old Teſtament, and though with divine, yet as human compoſitions, to grant at the leaſt unto certain of them publick audience in the Houſe of God. For in as much as the due eſtimation of heavenly Truth dependeth wholly upon the known and approved authority of thoſe famous Oracles of God, it greatly behoveth the Church to have always moſt ſpecial care, leſt through confuſed mixture at any time, human uſurp the room and title of divine Writings. Wherefore albeit for the People's more plain inſtruction (as the ancient uſe hath been) we read in Churches certain Books beſides the Scripture, yet as the Scripture we read them not. All Men know our profeſſed opinion touching the difference whereby we ſever them from the Scripture. And if any where it be ſuſpected that ſome one or other will happily miſtake a thing ſo manifeſt in every Man's eye, there is no lett, but that as often as thoſe Books are read, and need ſo requireth, the ſtile of their difference may expreſly be mentioned, to bar even all poſſibility of error. It being then known, that we hold not the Apocrypha for ſacred (as we do the holy Scripture) but for human compoſitions, the ſubject whereof are ſundry divine matters; let there be reaſon ſhewed, why to read any part of them publickly it ſhould be unlawful or hurtful unto the Church of God. I hear it ſaid, that many things in them are very frivolous and unworthy of publick audience; yea, many contrary, *plainly contrary to the holy Scripture*. Which hitherto is neither ſufficiently proved by him who ſaith it, and if the proofs thereof were ſtrong, yet the very allegation itſelf is weak. Let us therefore ſuppoſe (for I will not demand to what purpoſe it is, that againſt our Cuſtom of reading Books not Canonical, they bring exceptions of matter in thoſe Books which we never uſed to read), ſuppoſe (I ſay) that what faults ſoever they have obſerved throughout the

Hieron præf. ad libros Salom. Aug de præd. Sanct l. 1 c. 14. Præfat gloſſ. ord. & Lyr. ad prol. Hieron. in Tob

T. C. l. ii. p. 400 401.

BOOK V.

the passages of all those Books, the same in every respect were such as neither could be construed, nor ought to be censured otherwise than even as themselves pretend. Yet as Men, through too much haste oftentimes forget the errand whereabout they should go; so here it appeareth, that an eager desire to rake together whatsoever might prejudice or any way hinder the credit of Apocryphal Books, hath caused the Collector's pen so to run as it were on wheels, that the mind which should guide it had not leisure to think, whether that which might haply serve to with-hold from giving them the authority which belongeth unto sacred Scripture, and to cut them off from the Canon, would as effectually serve to shut them altogether out of the Church, and to withdraw from granting unto them that publick use wherein they are only held as profitable for instruction. Is it not acknowledged, that those Books are holy, that they are ecclesiastical and sacred, that to term them divine, as being for their excellency next unto them which are properly so termed, is no way to honour them above desert; yea, even that the whole Church of Christ, as well as at the first as sithence, hath most worthily approved their fitness for the publick informations of life and manners? Is not thus much, I say, acknowledged, and that by them, who notwithstanding receive not the same for any part of the Canonical Scripture; by them who deny not but that they are faulty; by them who are ready enough to give instances wherein they seem to contain matter scarce agreeable with holy Scripture? So little doth such their supposed faultiness in moderate Men's judgments enforce the removal of them out of the House of God, that still they are judged to retain worthily those very titles of commendation; than which, there cannot greater be given to Writings, the Authors whereof are Men. As in truth, if the Scripture itself, ascribing to the persons of Men righteousness in regard of their manifold virtues, may not rightly be construed as though

Haim. Confes. sect. 1. Bel. con art. 6. Lubert de princip. Christ d gm. l. i. c. 5.

BOOK V.

it did thereby clear them and make them quite free from all faults, no reason we should judge it absurd to commend their Writings as reverend, holy and sound, wherein there are so many singular perfections, only that the exquisite wits of some few peradventure are able dispersedly here and there to find now a word and then a sentence, which may be more probably suspected than easily cleared of error by us which have but conjectural knowledge of their meaning. Against immodest invectives therefore whereby they are charged as being fraught with *outragious Lies*, we doubt not but their more allowable censure will prevail, who without such passionate terms of disgrace do note a difference great enough between Apocryphal and other Writings, a difference such as Josephus and Epiphanius observe: the one declaring, that amongst the Jews, Books written after the days of Artaxerxes were not of equal credit with them which had gone before, in as much as the Jews sithence that time had not the like exact succession of Prophets; the other acknowledging that they are profitable,* although denying them to be divine, in such construction and sense as the Scripture itself is so termed. With what intent they were first published those words of the Nephew of Jesus do plainly enough signify, *After that my Grandfather Jesus had given himself to the reading of the Law and the Prophets, and other Books of our Fathers, and had gotten therein sufficient judgment, he purposed also to write something pertaining to learning and wisdom, to the intent that they which were desirous to learn, and would give themselves to these things, might profit much more in living according to the Law.* Their end in writing, and ours in reading them, is the same. The Books of Judith, Toby, Baruch, Wisdom, and Ecclesiasticus, we read, as serving most unto that end. The rest

The Libel of Metaphys. Schoolp. art. 34

Josceph. cont. App. lib. 1.

Præfat. ad. lib. Eccles.

* Epiph. in Ancyret. Κρήσιμοι μέν εἰσι καὶ ὠφέλιμοι, ἀλλ' εἰς ἀριθμὸν ῥητῶν ὀυκ ἀναφερονται.

we

we leave unto Men in private. Neither can it be reasonably thought, because upon certain solemn occasions, some Lessons are chosen out of those Books, and of Scripture itself some Chapters not appointed to be read at all, that we thereby do offer disgrace to the Word of God, or lift up the Writings of Men above it For in such choice we do not think, but that fitness of speech may be more respected than worthiness. If in that which we use to read there happen by the way any clause, sentence or speech that soundeth towards error; should the mixture of a little dross constrain the Church to deprive her self of so much gold, rather than to learn how by art and judgment to make separation of the one from the other? To this effect very fitly, from the counsel that St. Jerom giveth Læta, of taking heed how she read the Apocrypha, as also by the help of other learned Men's judgments delivered in like case, we may take direction. But surely the arguments that should bind us not to read them, or any part of them publickly at all, must be stronger than as yet we have heard any.

Of preaching by Sermons; and whether Sermons be the only ordinary way of teaching whereby Men are brought to the saving knowledge of God's Truth.

21. We marvel the less that our reading of Books not Canonical is so much impugned, when so little is attributed unto the reading of Canonical Scripture itself; that now it hath grown to be a question, whether the Word of God be any ordinary mean to save the Souls of Men, in that it is either privately studied or publickly read, and so made known; or else only as the same is preached, that is to say, *explained by a lively voice* and applied to the People's use as the *Speaker in his wisdom thinketh meet.* For this alone is it which they use to call Preaching. The public reading of the Apocrypha they condemn altogether as a thing effectual unto evil; the bare reading in like sort of whatsoever, yea even of Scriptures themselves, they mislike as a thing uneffectual to do that good which we are persuaded may grow by it. Our desire is in this present Controversy, as in the rest, not to be carried up and down with the waves of uncertain ar-

guments

BOOK V guments, but rather positively to lead on the minds of the simpler sort by plain and easy degrees, till the very nature of the thing itself do make manifest what is Truth. First therefore, because whatsoever is spoken concerning the efficacy or necessity of God's Word, the same they tie and restrain only unto Sermons, howbeit not Sermons read neither (for such they also abhor in the Church) but Sermons without book, Sermons which spend their life in their birth, and may have publick audience but once; for this cause, to avoid ambiguities wherewith they often entangle themselves, not marking what doth agree to the Word of God itself, and what in regard of outward accidents which may befall it, we are to know that the Word of God is his heavenly Truth touching matters of eternal life revealed and uttered unto Men, unto Prophets and Apostles by immediate divine Inspiration, from them to us by their Books and Writings. We therefore have no Word of God but the Scripture. Apostolick Sermons were unto such as heard them his Word, even as properly as to us their Writings are. Howbeit not so our own Sermons, the exposition which our discourse of wit doth gather and minister out of the Word of God. For which cause, in this present question we are, when we name the Word of God, always to mean the Scripture only. The end of the Word of God is to save, and therefore we term it the Word of Life. The way for all Men to be saved, is by the knowledge of that Truth which the Word hath taught. And sith eternal Life is a thing of itself communicable unto all, it behoveth that the Word of God, the necessary mean thereunto, be so likewise. Wherefore the Word of Life hath been always a Treasure, though precious, yet easy, as well to attain, as to find; lest any Man desirous of Life should perish through the difficulty of the way. To this end the Word of God no otherwise serveth, than only in the nature of a doctrinal instrument. It saveth, because it maketh *wise unto Salvation.*

tion. Wherefore the ignorant it ſaveth not; they which live by the Word, muſt know it. And being itſelf the inſtrument which God hath purpoſely framed, thereby to work the knowledge of Salvation in the hearts of Men, what cauſe is there wherefore it ſhould not of itſelf be acknowledged a moſt apt and a likely mean to leave an apprehenſion of things divine in our underſtanding, and in the mind an aſſent thereunto? For touching the one, ſith God who knoweth and diſcloſeth beſt the rich treaſures of his own Wiſdom, hath by delivering his Word made choice of the Scriptures as the moſt effectual means whereby thoſe treaſures might be imparted unto the World, it followeth, that to Man's underſtanding the Scripture muſt needs be even of itſelf intended as a full and perfect diſcovery, ſufficient to imprint in us the lively character of all things neceſſarily required for the attainment of eternal Life. And concerning our aſſent to the Myſteries of heavenly Truth, ſeeing that the Word of God for the Author's ſake, hath credit with all that confeſs it (as we all do) to be his Word, every propoſition of holy Scripture, every ſentence being to us a principle; if the principles of all kinds of knowledge elſe have that virtue in themſelves, whereby they are able to procure our aſſent unto ſuch concluſions as the induſtry of right diſcourſe doth gather from them; we have no reaſon to think the principles of that Truth which tendeth unto Men's everlaſting happineſs, leſs forcible than any other, when we know that of all other they are for their certainty the moſt infallible. But as every thing of price, ſo this doth require travel. We bring not the knowledge of God with us into the World. And the leſs our own opportunity or ability is that way, the more we need the help of other Men's judgments to be our direction herein. Nor doth any Man ever believe, into whom the doctrine of belief is not inſtilled by inſtruction, ſome way received at the firſt from others. Wherein whatſoever fit means there are

BOOK V. to notify the Myſteries of the Word of God, whether publickly (which we call Preaching) or in private howſoever, the Word by every ſuch mean even ordinarily doth ſave, and not only by being delivered unto Men in Sermons. Sermons are not the only Preaching which doth ſave Souls. For, concerning the uſe and ſenſe of this word Preaching, which they ſhut up in ſo cloſe a priſon, although more than enough have already been ſpoken to redeem the liberty thereof, yet becauſe they inſiſt ſo much, and ſo proudly inſult thereon, we muſt a little inure their ears with hearing how others whom they more regard, are in this caſe accuſtomed to uſe the ſelf-ſame language with us, whoſe manner of ſpeech they deride. Juſtin Martyr doubteth not to tell the Grecians, that even in certain of their Writings the very Judgment to come is preached; nor the Council of Vaus to inſinuate, that Preſbyters, abſent through infirmity from the Churches, might be ſaid to preach by thoſe Deputies who in their ſtead did but read Homilies; nor the Council of Toledo, to call the uſual publick reading of the Goſpels in the Church, Preaching; nor others, long before theſe our days to write, that by him who but readeth a Leſſon in the ſolemn Aſſembly as part of divine Service, the very office of Preaching is ſo far forth executed. Such kind of ſpeeches were then familiar, thoſe phraſes ſeemed not to them abſurd, they would have marvelled to hear the * outcries which we do, becauſe we think that the Apoſtles in writing, and others in reading to the Church thoſe Books which the Apoſtles wrote, are neither untruly nor unfitly ſaid to preach. For although Men's Tongues and their Pens differ, yet to one and the ſelf-ſafe general if not particular effect,

Paraenet. ad Gent. p. 17

Concil Vaſin. II c. 2.

Concil Tol. iv c. 11.

Repert de Divin. Offic l. i c. 12, 13
Iſid de Eccleſ Offic. l. i. c. 10.

* The Libel of Schoolp. art. 11. T. C lib. ii. page 388. St. Paul's writing is no more preaching, than his pen or his hand is his tongue ſeeing they cannot be the ſame, which cannot be made by the ſame inſtruments.

they

they may both ſerve. It is no good argument, St. Paul could not write with his tongue, therefore neither could he preach with his pen. For Preaching is a general end whereunto writing and ſpeaking do both ſerve. Men ſpeak not with the inſtruments of writing, neither write with the inſtruments of ſpeech; and yet things recorded with the one, and uttered with the other, may be * preached well enough with both. By their patience therefore be it ſpoken, the Apoſtles preached as well when they wrote as when they ſpake the Goſpel of Chriſt; and our uſual publick reading of the Word of God for the People's inſtruction is Preaching. Nor about words would we ever contend, were not their purpoſe in ſo reſtraining the ſame, injurious to God's moſt ſacred Word and Spirit. It is on both ſides confeſt, that the Word of God outwardly adminiſtered (his Spirit inwardly concurring therewith) converteth, edifieth and ſaveth Souls. Now whereas the external adminiſtration of his Word is as well by reading barely the Scripture, as by explaining the ſame when Sermons thereon be made; in the one, they deny that the Finger of God hath ordinarily certain principal operations, which we moſt ſteadfaſtly hold and believe that it hath in both.

John vi. 46. Mat. xvi. 17. 2 Cor iv. 6. 1 Cor xii 3. Acts xvi. 14.

What they attribute to Sermons only, and what we to reading alſo.

22. So worthy a part of divine Service we ſhould greatly wrong if we did not eſteem Preaching as the bleſſed ordinance of God, Sermons as keys to the Kingdom of Heaven, as wings to the Soul, as ſpurs to the good affections of Man, unto the ſound and healthy as food, as phyſic unto diſeaſed Minds. Wherefore how highly ſoever it may pleaſe them with words of truth to extol Sermons, they ſhall not herein offend us. We ſeek not to derogate from any thing which they can juſtly eſteem, but our deſire is to uphold the juſt eſtimation of that from which it ſeemeth

* Evangelizo manu et ſcriptione. Raimol. de Rom. Eccleſ. Idol præf. ad Co. Eſſex.

unto

BOOK V. unto us they derogate more than becometh them. That which offendeth us is, firſt, the great diſgrace which they offer unto our Cuſtom of bare reading the Word of God and to his gracious Spirit, the principal virtue whereof thereby manifeſting itſelf for the endleſs good of Men's Souls, even the virtue which it hath to convert, to edify, to ſave Souls; this they mightly ſtrive to obſcure: and, ſecondly, the ſhifts wherewith they maintain their opinion of Sermons, whereunto while they labour to appropriate the ſaving power of the Holy Ghoſt, they ſeparate from all apparent hope of Life and Salvation thouſands whom the goodneſs of Almighty God doth not exclude. Touching therefore the uſe of Scripture, even in that it is openly read, and the ineſtimable good which the Church of God by that very mean hath reaped; there was, we may very well think, ſome cauſe which moved the Apoſtle St. Paul to require that thoſe things which any one Church's affairs gave particular occaſion to write, might, for the inſtruction of all be publiſhed, and that by reading.

1 Theſ. v. 27
Coloſ. iv. 16

1. When the very having of the Books of God, was a matter of no ſmall charge and difficulty, in as much as they could not be had otherwiſe than only in written copies, it was the neceſſity not of preaching things agreeable with the Word, but of reading the Word itſelf at large to the People, which cauſed Churches throughout the World to have publick care that the ſacred Oracles of God, being procured by common charge, might with great ſedulity be kept both entire and ſincere. If then we admire the providence of God in the ſame continuance of Scripture, notwithſtanding the violent endeavours of Infidels to aboliſh, and the fraudulence of Hereticks always to deprave the ſame, ſhall we ſet light by that cuſtom of Reading, from whence ſo precious a benefit hath grown? 2. The voice and teſtimony of the Church, acknowledging Scripture to be the Law of the Living God, is for the truth and certainty thereof no mean evidence.

dence. For if with reaſon we may preſume upon things which a few Men's depoſitions do teſtify, ſuppoſe we that the minds of Men are not both, at their firſt acceſs to the School of Chriſt exceedingly moved, yea and for ever afterwards alſo confirmed much, when they conſider the main conſent of all the Churches in the whole World witneſſing the ſacred Authority of Scriptures, ever ſithence the firſt publication thereof even till this preſent day and hour? And that they all have always ſo teſtified, I ſee not how we ſhould poſſibly wiſh a proof more palpable, than this manifeſt received and every where continued cuſtom of reading them publickly as the Scriptures. The Reading therefore of the Word of God, as the uſe hath ever been, in open Audience, is the plaineſt evidence we have of the Church's aſſent and acknowledgement that it is his Word. 3. A further commodity this cuſtom hath, which is to furniſh the very ſimpleſt and rudeſt ſort with ſuch infallible Axioms and Precepts of ſacred Truth, delivered even in the very letter of the Law of God, as may ſerve them for Rules whereby to judge the better all other Doctrines and Inſtructions which they hear. For which end and purpoſe I ſee not how the Scripture could be poſſibly made familiar unto all, unleſs far more ſhould be read in the People's hearing than by a Sermon can be opened. For whereas in a manner the whole Book of God is by reading every year publiſhed, a ſmall part thereof, in compariſon of the whole, may hold very well the readieſt Interpreter of Scripture occupied many years. 4. Beſides, wherefore ſhould any Man think, but that Reading itſelf is one of the ordinary means, whereby it pleaſeth God of his gracious goodneſs to inſtill that celeſtial Verity which being but ſo received, is nevertheleſs effectual to ſave Souls? Thus much therefore we aſcribe to the Reading of the Word of God as the manner is in our Churches. And becauſe it were odious, if they on their part ſhould altogether deſpiſe the ſame, they

John. v 39.
Iſa. viii. 20.

yield

BOOK V. yield that Reading may ſet forward, but not begin the work of Salvation; that Faith may be nouriſhed therewith, but not bred; that herein Men's attention to the Scriptures, and their ſpeculation of the Creatures of God have like efficacy, both being of power to augment, but neither to effect Belief without Sermons, that if any believe by Reading alone, we are to account it a miracle, an extraordinary work of God. Wherein that which they grant, we gladly accept at their hands, and wiſh that patiently they would examine how little cauſe they have to deny that which as yet they grant not. The Scripture witneſſeth, that when the Book of the Law of God had been ſometime miſſing and was after found; the King, which heard it but only read, tare his cloaths and with tears confeſſed, *Great is the wrath of the Lord upon us, becauſe our Fathers have not kept his Word, to do after all things which are written in this Book.* This doth argue, that by bare Reading (for of Sermons at that time there is no mention) true Repentance may be wrought in the hearts of ſuch as fear God, and yet incur his diſpleaſure, the deſerved effect whereof is eternal death. So that their Repentance (although it be not their firſt entrance) is notwithſtanding the firſt ſtep of their re-entrance into Life, and may be in them wrought by the Word only read unto them. Beſides, it ſeemeth that God would have no Man ſtand in doubt, but that the Reading of Scripture is effectual, as well to lay even the firſt foundation, as toadd degrees of farther perfection in the fear of God; and therefore the Law ſaith, *Thou ſhalt read this Law before all Iſrael, that Men, Women and Children may hear, yea even that their Children, which as yet have not known it, may hear it,* and by hearing it ſo read, *may learn to fear the Lord.* Our Lord and Saviour was himſelf of opinion, that they which would not be drawn to amendment of Life by the Teſtimony which Moſes and the Prophets hath given concerning the miſeries that follow Sinners after death, were not likely to be perſuaded

T. C. l. ii. p. 376, 377, 395. Pag. 378. Pag. 383.

2 Chron. xxxiv. 18.

2 Chron. xxxiv. 3.

Deut. xxxi. 13.

Luke xvi. 20.

perſuaded by other means, although God from the very dead ſhould have raiſed them up Preachers. Many hear the Books of God, and believe them not. Howbeit, their unbelief in that caſe we may not impute unto any weakneſs or inſufficiency in the mean which is uſed toward them, but to the wilful bent of their obſtinate hearts againſt it. With Minds obdurate nothing prevaileth. As well they that preach, as they that read unto ſuch, ſhall ſtill have cauſe to complain with the Prophets which were of old, *Who will give credit unto our teaching?* But with whom ordinary means will prevail, ſurely the power of the Word of God, even without the help of Interpreters in God's Church, worketh mightily, not unto their confirmation alone which are converted, but alſo to their converſion which are not. It ſhall not boot them who derogate from Reading to excuſe it, when they ſee no other remedy, as if their intent were only to deny that Aliens and Strangers from the Family of God are won, or that Belief doth uſe to be wrought at the firſt in them without Sermons. For they know it is our cuſtom of ſimple Reading, not for converſion of Infidels eſtranged from the Houſe of God, but for inſtruction of Men baptized, bred and brought up in the boſom of the Church, which they deſpiſe as a thing uneffectual to ſave ſuch Souls. In ſuch they imagine that God hath no ordinary mean to work Faith without Sermons. The reaſon why no Man can attain Belief by the bare contemplation of Heaven and Earth, is, for that they neither are ſufficient to give us much as the leaſt ſpark of light concerning the very principal Myſteries of our Faith; and whatſoever we may learn by them, the ſame we can only attain to know according to the manner of natural Sciences, which meer diſcourſe of Wit and Reaſon findeth out; whereas the things which we properly believe be only ſuch, as are received upon the credit of divine Teſtimony. Seeing therefore,

G that

BOOK V. that he which confidereth the Creatures of God findeth therein both thefe defects, and neither the one nor the other in Scriptures, becaufe he that readeth unto us the Scriptures, delivereth all the Myfteries of Faith, and not any thing amongft them all more than the mouth of the Lord doth warrant; it followeth in thofe two refpects, that our confideration of Creatures, and attention unto Scriptures are not in themfelves, and without Sermons, things of like difability to breed or beget Faith. Small caufe alfo there is, why any Man fhould greatly wonder as at an extraordinary work, if without Sermons, Reading be found to effect thus much. For I would know by fome fpecial inftance, what one Article of Chriftian Faith, or what Duty required neceffarily unto all Men's Salvation there is, which the very Reading of the Word of God is not apt to notify. Effects are miraculous and ftrange when they grow by unlikely means. But did we ever hear it accounted for a wonder, that he which doth read fhould believe and live according to the will of Almighty God? Reading doth convey to the Mind that Truth without addition or diminution, which Scripture hath derived from the Holy Ghoft. And the end of all Scripture is the fame which St. John propofeth in the writing of that moft divine Gofpel, namely Faith, and through Faith Salvation. Yea, all Scripture is to this effect in itfelf available, as they which wrote it were perfuaded; unlefs we fuppofe, that the Evangelifts, or others, in fpeaking of their own intent to inftruct and to fave by writing, had a fecret conceit which they never opened to any, a conceit that no Man in the World fhould ever be that way the better for any fentence by them written, till fuch time as the fame might chance to be preached upon, or alledged at the leaft in a Sermon. Otherwife, if he which writeth doth that which is forcible in itfelf, how fhould he which readeth be thought

Exod. xxiv. 7.

John xx. 31

Prov. i. 2, 3, 4

Rom. i. 16.

2 Tim. iii. 15.

thought to do that which in itſelf is of no force to work Belief, and to ſave Believers. Now, although we have very juſt cauſe to ſtand in ſome jealouſy and fear, leaſt by thus overvaluing their Sermons, they make the price and eſtimation of Scripture, otherwiſe notified, to fall; nevertheleſs ſo impatient they are, that being but requeſted to let us know what cauſes they leave for Men's encouragement to attend to the Reading of the Scripture, if Sermons only be the power of God to ſave every one which believeth; that which we move for our better learning and inſtruction ſake, turneth unto anger and choler in them, they grow altogether out of quietneſs with it; they anſwer fumingly, that they are *aſhamed to defile their pens by making anſwer to ſuch idle queſtions:* yet in this their mood they caſt forth ſomewhat, wherewith under pain of greater diſpleaſure we muſt reſt contented. They tell us, the profit of Reading is ſingular, in that it ſerveth for a preparative unto Sermons; it helpeth prettily towards the nouriſhment of Faith, which Sermons have once engendered; it is ſome ſtay to his Mind which readeth the Scripture, when he findeth the ſame things there which are taught in Sermons, and thereby perceiveth how God doth concur in opinion with the Preacher; beſides, it keepeth Sermons in memory, and doth in that reſpect, although not feed the Soul of Man, yet help the retentive force of that ſtomach of the Mind which receiveth ghoſtly food at the Preacher's hands. But the principal cauſe of writing the Goſpel was, that it might be preached upon or interpreted by publick Miniſters apt and authorized thereunto. Is it credible that a ſuperſtitious conceit (for it is no better) concerning Sermons, ſhould in ſuch ſort both darken their eyes, and yet ſharpen their wits withal, that the only true and weighty cauſe why Scripture was written, the cauſe which in Scripture is ſo often mentioned, the cauſe which

T. C. l. ii. p. 375.

 all

BOOK V. all Men have ever till this present day acknowledged, this they should clean exclude, as being no cause at all, and load us with so great store of strange concealed causes, which did never see light till now? In which number the rest must needs be of moment, when the very chiefest cause of committing the sacred Word of God unto Books, is surmised to have been, lest the Preacher should want a Text whereupon to scholy. Men of learning hold it for a slip in judgment, when offer is made to demonstrate that as proper to one thing, which Reason findeth common unto more. Whereas therefore they take from all kind of teachings, that which they attribute to Sermons, it had been their part to yield directly some strong reason, why between Sermons alone and Faith, there should be ordinarily that coherence which causes have with their usual effects, why a Christian Man's Belief should so naturally grow from Sermons, and not possibly from any other kind of teaching. In Belief there being but these two operations, Apprehension and Assent, do only Sermons cause Belief, in that no other way is able to explain the Mysteries of God, that the Mind may rightly apprehend or conceive them as behoveth? We all know that many things are believed although they be intricate, obscure and dark, although they exceed the reach and capacity of our wits, yea although in this World they be no way possible to be understood. Many things believed are likewise so plain, that every common Person may therein be unto himself a sufficient Expounder. Finally, to explain even those things which need and admit explication, many other usual ways there are besides Sermons. Therefore Sermons are not the only ordinary means whereby we first come to apprehend the Mysteries of God. Is it in regard then of Sermons only, that apprehending of the Gospel of Christ, we yield thereunto our unfeigned assent, as to a thing infallibly true? They which rightly

rightly consider after what sort the heart of Man hereunto is framed, must of necessity acknowledge, that whoso assenteth to the words of eternal Life, doth it in regard of his Authority whose words they are. This is in Man's conversion unto God, τὸ ὅθεν ἡ ἀρχὴ τῆς κινήσεως, the first step whereat his race towards Heaven beginneth. Unless therefore, clean contrary to our own experience, we shall think it a miracle, if any Man acknowledge the divine Authority of the Scripture till some Sermon have persuaded him thereunto, and that otherwise neither conversation in the bosom of the Church, nor religious education, nor the reading of learned Men's Books, nor information received by conference, nor whatsoever pain and diligence in hearing, studying, meditating day and night on the Law, is so far blest of God as to work this effect in any Man; how would they have us to grant, that Faith doth not come but only by hearing Sermons? Fain they would have us to believe the Apostle Saint Paul himself to be Author of this their Paradox, only because he hath said, that *it pleaseth God by the foolishness of Preaching to save them which believe*; and again, *How shall they call on him in whom they have not believed? How shall they believe in him of whom they have not heard? How shall they hear without a Preacher? How shall Men preach except they be sent?* To answer therefore both allegations at once; the very substance of what they contain is in few but this. Life and Salvation God will have offered unto all; his will is that Gentiles should be saved as well as Jews. Salvation belongeth unto none but such *as call upon the Name of our Lord Jesus Christ*. Which Nations as yet unconverted neither do, nor possibly can do till they believe. What they are to believe, impossible it is they should know till they hear it. Their hearing requireth our preaching unto them. Tertullian, to draw even Paynims themselves unto Christian Belief, willeth the Books of the Old Testament to be searched, which were at that time in Ptolemy's Library. And if Men

BOOK V.

T. C. l. ii. p. 375.

1 Cor. i. 21.

Rom. x. 14.

did

BOOK V. did not lift to travel fo far, though it were for their endlefs good, he addeth that in Rome and other places the Jews had Synagogues, whereunto every one which would might refort; that this kind of liberty they purchafed by payment of a ftanding tribute: that there they did openly read *the Scriptures; and whofoever *will hear* (faith Tertullian) *he fhall find God*, *whofoever will ftudy to know*, *fhall be alfo fain to believe*. But fith there is no likelihood that ever voluntarily they will feek inftruction at our hands, it remaineth that, unlefs we will fuffer them to perifh, Salvation itfelf muft feek them; it behoveth God to fend them Preachers as he did his elect Apoftles throughout the World. There is a Knowledge which God hath always revealed unto them in the works of Nature. This they honour and efteem highly as profound Wifdom; howbeit this Wifdom faveth them not. That which muft fave Believers is *the knowledge of the Crofs of Chrift*, the only fubject of all our Preaching. And in their eyes what feemeth this but Folly? It pleafeth God by *the Foolifhnefs of Preaching* to fave. Thefe words declare how admirable force thefe Myfteries have which the World do deride as Follies; they fhew that the Foolifhnefs of the Crofs of Chrift is the Wifdom of true Believers; they concern the Object of our Faith, the Matter preached of, †and believed in by Chriftian Men. This we know that the Grecians or Gentiles did account Foolifhnefs; but that they did ever think it a fond or unlikely way to feek Men's Converfion by Sermons, we have not heard. Manifeft therefore it is, that the Apoftle ap-

* Apologet. c xi. in fine. This they did in a tongue which to all learned Men amongft the Heathens, and to a great part of the fimpleft was familiarly known; as appeareth by a fupplication offered unto the Emperor Juftinian, wherein the Jews made requeft that it might be lawful for them to read the Greek Tranflations of the LXX Interpreters in their Synagogues, as their cuftom before had been. Authent. cxlvi. Col. 10. incipit, Æquum fane.

† The Apoftle ufeth the word κήρυγμα and not κήρυξις.

plying

plying the name of *Foolishness* in such sort as they did, must needs, by the *Foolishness of Preaching* mean the Doctrine of Christ which we learn that we may be saved; but that Sermons are the only manner of teaching whereby it pleaseth our Lord to save, he could not mean. In like sort, where the same Apostle proveth that as well the sending of the Apostles, as their preaching to the Gentiles was necessary, dare we affirm it was ever his meaning, that unto their Salvation, who even from their tender Infancy never knew any other Faith or Religion than only Christian, no kind of Teaching can be available saving that which was so needful for the first universal Conversion of Gentiles hating Christianity; neither the sending of any sort allowable in the one case, except only of such as had been in the other also most fit and worthy Instruments? Belief in all sorts doth come by hearkening and attending to the Word of Life, which Word sometime proposeth and preacheth itself to the Hearer; sometime they deliver it, whom privately zeal and piety moveth to be Instructors of others by conference; sometime of them it is taught, whom the Church hath called to the publick either Reading thereof, or Interpreting. All these tend unto one effect, neither doth that which St. Paul or other Apostles teach concerning the necessity of such teachings as theirs was, or of sending such as they were for that purpose unto the Gentiles, prejudice the efficacy of any other way of public instruction, or enforce the utter disability of any other Men's vocation thought requisite in this Church for the saving of Souls, where means more effectual are wanting. Their only proper and direct proof of the thing in question had been to shew, in what sort, and how far Man's Salvation doth necessarily depend upon the Word of God; what Conditions, Properties and Qualities there are, whereby Sermons are distinguished from other kinds of administring the Word unto that purpose; and what special Property or Quality that is,

BOOK V. is, which being no where found but in Sermons, maketh them effectual to save Souls, and leaveth all other doctrinal means besides destitute of vital efficacy. These pertinent instructions, whereby they might satisfy us and obtain the cause itself for which they contend; these things which only would serve they leave; and (which needeth not) sometime they trouble themselves with fretting at the ignorance of such as withstand them in their opinion; sometime they *fall upon their poor Brethren which can but read, and against them they are bitterly eloquent. If we alledge what the Scriptures themselves do usually speak for the saving force of the Word of God, not with restraint to any one certain kind of delivery, but howsoever the same shall chance to be made known, yet by one trick or other they always restrain it unto Sermons. Our Lord and Saviour hath said, *Search the Scriptures, for in them ye think to have eternal life.* But they tell us he spake to the Jews, which Jews before had heard his Sermons; and that peradventure it was his mind they should search, not by reading nor by hearing them read, but by attending whensoever the Scriptures should happen to be alledged in Sermons. Furthermore, having received Apostolical Doctrine, the Apostle St. Paul hath taught us to esteem the same as the supreme Rule whereby all other Doctrines must for ever be examined. Yea, but in as much as the Apostle doth here speak of that he had preached, he flatly maketh (as they strangely affirm) his Preachings or Sermons the Rule whereby to examine all. And then, I beseech you, what Rule have we whereby to judge or examine any? For if Sermons must be our Rule, because the Apostles' Sermons were so to their Hearers; then, sith we are not as they were, Hearers of the Apostles' Sermons, it resteth that either the Sermons

T. C. l. ii. p. 37. John v. 39.

Gal. i. 9.

* T. C. l ii p. 373 This tail of Readers. The Bishops more than beggarly presents. Those Rascal Ministers.

which

which we hear ſhould be our Rule, or (that being abſurd) there will (which yet hath greater abſurdity) no Rule at all be remaining for trial what Doctrines now are corrupt, what conſonant with heavenly Truth. Again, let the ſame Apoſtle acknowledge all Scripture profitable to teach, to improve, to correct, to instruct in Righteouſneſs; ſtill notwithſtanding we err, if hereby we preſume to gather, that Scripture read will avail unto any one of all theſe uſes; they teach us the meaning of the words to be, that ſo much the Scripture can do, if the Miniſter that way apply it in his Sermons, otherwiſe not. Finally they never hear ſentence which mentioneth the Word or Scripture, but forthwith their gloſſes upon it are, the Word preached, the Scripture explained or delivered unto us in Sermons. Sermons they evermore underſtand to be that Word of God, which alone hath vital operation; the dangerous ſequel of which conſtruction I wiſh they did more attentively weigh. For, ſith Speech is the very image whereby the Mind and Soul of the Speaker conveyeth itſelf into the boſom of him which heareth, we cannot chooſe but ſee great reaſon wherefore the Word that proceedeth from God, who is himſelf very Truth and Life, ſhould be (as the Apoſtle to the Hebrews noteth) lively and mighty in operation, *ſharper than any two-edged Sword*. Now, if in this and the like places we did conceive that our own Sermons are that ſtrong and forcible Word, ſhould we not hereby impart even the moſt peculiar glory of the Word of God unto that which is not his Word? For, touching our Sermons, that which giveth them their very being is the wit of Man, and therefore they oftentimes accordingly taſte too much of that over-corrupt fountain from which they come. In our ſpeech of moſt holy things, our moſt frail affections many times are bewrayed. Wherefore when we read or recite the Scripture, we then deliver to the People properly the Word of God. As for our Sermons, be they never ſo ſound and perfect, his

1 Tim iii. 16

Heb. iv 12.

BOOK V. his Word they are not as the Sermons of the Prophets were; no, they are but ambiguously termed his Word, because his Word is commonly the Subject whereof they treat, and must be the Rule whereby they are framed. Notwithstanding, by these and the like shifts they derive unto Sermons alone whatsoever is generally spoken concerning the Word. Again, what seemeth to have been uttered concerning Sermons, or their efficacy or necessity in regard of divine matter, and must consequently be verified in sundry other kinds of teaching if the matter be the same in all; their use is to fasten every such Speech unto that one only manner of teaching which is by Sermons, that still Sermons may be all in all. Thus, because Solomon declareth that the *People decay, or perish, for want of Knowledge* where no Prophecying at all is, they gather, that the hope of Life and Salvation is cut off where Preachers are not which prophecy by Sermons, how many soever they be in number that read daily the Word of God, and deliver, though in other sort, the self-same matter which Sermons do. The People which have no way to come to the knowledge of God, no prophecying, no teaching, perish. But that they should of necessity perish, where any one way of knowledge lacketh, is more than the words of Solomon impart. Another usual point of their art in this present question, is to make very large and plentiful Discourses how Christ is by Sermons lifted up higher and more apparent to the eye of Faith, how the savour of the Word is more sweet, being brayed, and more able to nourish, being divided by Preaching, than by only Reading proposed; how Sermons are the Keys of the Kingdom of Heaven and do open the Scriptures, which being but read, remain in comparison still clasped, how God giveth richer increase of grace to the ground that is planted and watered by Preaching, than by bare and simple Reading. Out of which premises declaring how attainment

T. C. l. ii. p. 391. Prov xxix. 18.

T. C. l. ii. p. 379. Joh. iii. 14. 2 Cor. ii. 16. 2 Tim. ii. 15. Matth. xvi. 19

1 Cor iii. 6.

tainment unto life is eaſier where Sermons are, they conclude an * impoſſibility thereof where Sermons are not. Alcidamas the Sophiſter hath many arguments to prove that voluntary and extemporal far excelleth premeditated ſpeech. The like whereunto, and in part the ſame, are brought by them who commend Sermons, as having (which all Men, I think, will acknowledge) ſundry peculiar and proper virtues, T. C. l. ii. p. 394. ſuch as no other way of teaching beſides hath. Aptneſs to follow particular occaſions preſently growing, to put life into words by countenance, voice and geſture, to prevail mightily in the ſudden affections of Men, this Sermons may challenge. Wherein notwithſtanding ſo eminent properties whereof Leſſons are haply deſtitute, yet Leſſons being free from ſome inconveniencies whereunto Sermons are more ſubject, they may in this reſpect no leſs take, than in other they might give the hand which betokeneth preeminence. For there is nothing which is not ſome way excelled, even by that which it doth excel. Sermons therefore and Leſſons may each excel other in ſome reſpects without any prejudice unto either, as touching that vital force which they both have in the work of our Salvation. To which effect, when we have endeavoured as much as in us doth lie to find out the ſtrongeſt cauſes, wherefore they ſhould imagine that Reading is itſelf ſo unavailable, the moſt we can learn at their hands is, that Sermons are the Ordinance of God, the Scriptures dark, and the labour of Reading eaſy. Firſt, therefore, as we T. C. l. ii. p. 396. know that God doth aid with his grace, and by his ſpecial providence evermore bleſs with happy ſucceſs thoſe things which himſelf appointeth; ſo his Church, we perſuade ourſelves, he hath not in ſuch ſort given over to a reprobate ſenſe, that whatſoever it deviſeth for the good of the Souls of Men, the ſame he doth

* T. C. l. ii. No Salvation to be looked for, where no Preaching is.

ſtill

BOOK V. ſtill accurſe and make fruſtrate. Or if he always did defeat the Ordinances of his Church, is not Reading the Ordinance of God? Wherefore then ſhould we think that the force of his ſecret grace is accuſtomed to bleſs the labour of dividing his Word according unto each Man's private diſcretion in publick Sermons, and to withdraw itſelf from concurring with the publick delivery thereof by ſuch ſelected portions of Scriptures, as the whole Church hath ſolemnly appointed to be read for the People's good, either by ordinary courſe, or otherwiſe, according to the exigence of ſpecial occaſions? Reading (ſaith Iſidore) is to the Hearers no ſmall edifying. To them whoſe delight and meditation is in the Law, ſeeing that happineſs and bliſs belongeth, it is not in us to deny them the benefit of heavenly Grace. And I hope we may preſume that a rare thing it is not in the Church of God, even for that very Word which is read to be both preſently their joy, and afterwards their ſtudy that hear it. St. Auguſtine ſpeaking of devout Men noteth how they daily frequented the Church, how attentive ear they gave unto the Leſſons and Chapters read, how careful they were to remember the ſame, and to muſe thereupon by themſelves. St. Cyprian obſerveth, * that Reading was not without effect in the Hearts of Men. Their joy and alacrity was to him an argument that there is in this Ordinance a Bleſſing, ſuch as ordinarily doth accompany the adminiſtration of the Word of Life. It were much if there ſhould be ſuch a difference between the hearing of Sermons preached, and of Leſſons read in the Church, that he which preſenteth himſelf at the one, and maketh his Prayer with the Prophet David, *Teach me, O Lord, the way of thy Statutes, direct me in the way of thy Command-*

Deut xxxi. 13.

De Eccleſ. Offic l li. c 10.

Pſal. i. 2.

Pſal. cxix. 16.

Aug. in Pſal. lxvi.

Pſal. cxix. 33, 35.

* Cyprian. l. ii Epiſt 5. Lector perſonat verba ſublimia. Evangelium Chriſti legis a fratribus conſpicitur, cum gaudio fraternitatis auditur.

ments,

ments, might have the ground of uſual experience whereupon to build his hope of prevailing with God, and obtaining the Grace he ſeeketh; they contrariwiſe not ſo, who crave the like aſſiſtance of his Spirit, when they give ear to the Reading of the other. In this therefore Preaching and Reading are equal, that both are approved as his Ordinances, both aſſiſted with his Grace. And if his Grace do aſſiſt them both to the nouriſhment of Faith already bred, we cannot, without ſome very manifeſt cauſe yielded, imagine that in breeding or begetting Faith, his Grace doth cleave to the one and utterly forſake the other. Touching hardneſs, which is the ſecond pretended impediment, as againſt Homilies being plain and popular inſtructions it is no bar, ſo neither doth it infringe the efficacy, no not of Scriptures, although but read. The force of Reading, how ſmall ſoever they will have it, muſt of neceſſity be granted ſufficient to notify that which is plain or eaſy to be underſtood. And of things neceſſary to all Men's ſalvation we have been hitherto accuſtomed to hold (eſpecially ſithence the publiſhing of the Goſpel of Jeſus Chriſt, whereby the ſimpleſt having now a key unto Knowledge which the Eunuch in the Acts did want, our Children may of themſelves by Reading underſtand that which he without an Interpreter could not) they are in Scripture plain and eaſy to be underſtood. As for thoſe things which at the firſt are obſcure and dark, when memory hath laid them up for a time, judgment afterwards growing, explaineth them. Scripture therefore is not ſo hard, but that the only reading thereof may give life unto willing Hearers. The eaſy performance of which holy labour is in like ſort a very cold objection to prejudice the virtue thereof. For what though an Infidel, yea, though a Child may be able to read; there is no doubt, but the meaneſt and worſt amongſt the People under the Law had been as able as the Prieſts themſelves were to offer Sacrifice; did this

BOOK V.

T. C. l. iii. p. 383. 384. 392.

Acts viii. 31.

BOOK V. this make Sacrifice of no effect unto that purpose for which it was instituted? In Religion some duties are not commended so much by the hardness of their execution, as by the worthiness and dignity of that acceptation wherein they are held with God. We admire the goodness of God in Nature, when we consider how he hath provided that things most needful to preserve this life, should be most prompt and easy for all living Creatures to come by. Is it not as evident a sign of his wonderful Providence over us, when the Food of eternal Life, upon the utter want whereof our endless death and destruction necessarily ensueth, is prepared and always set in such a readiness, that those very means, than which nothing is more easy, may suffice to procure the same? Surely, if we perish, it is not the lack of Scribes and learned Expounders that can be our just excuse. The Word which saveth our Souls is near us; we need for knowledge but to read and live. Apoc. i, 3. The Man which readeth the Word of God, the Word itself doth pronounce blessed, if he also observe the same. Now all these things being well considered, it shall be no intricate matter for any Man to judge with indifferency on which part the good of the Church is most conveniently sought; whether on ours, whose opinion is such as hath been shewed, or else on theirs, who leaving no ordinary way of Salvation for them unto whom the Word of God is but only read, do seldom name them but with great disdain and contempt who execute that service in the Church of Christ. T. C. l. ii. p. 363, 373. By means whereof it hath come to pass, that Churches which cannot enjoy the benefit of usual Preaching, are judged as it were even forsaken of God, forlorn, and without either hope or comfort: contrariwise, those places which every day, for the most part, are at Sermons as the flowing sea, do by their emptiness at times of Reading, and by other apparent tokens shew to the Voice of the Living God, this way sounding in the ears of Men,

Men, a great deal leſs reverence than were meet. But if no other evil were known to grow thereby, who can chooſe but think them cruel which doth hear them ſo boldly teach, that if God (as to him there is nothing impoſſible) do haply ſave any ſuch as continue where they have all other means of inſtruction, but are not taught by continual Preaching, yet this is miraculous, and more than the fitneſs of ſo poor inſtruments can give any Man cauſe to hope for; that Sacraments are not effectual to Salvation, except Men be inſtructed by Preaching before they be made Partakers of them; yea, that both Sacraments and Prayers alſo, where Sermons are not, *do not only not feed, but are ordinarily to further condemnation*; what Man's heart doth not riſe at the mention of theſe things? It is true, that the weakneſs of our wits, and the dulneſs of our affections do make us, for the moſt part, even as our Lord's own Diſciples were for a certain time, hard and ſlow to believe what is written. For help whereof Expoſitions and Exhortations are needful, and that in the moſt effectual manner. The principal Churches throughout the Land, and no ſmall part of the reſt, being in this reſpect by the goodneſs of God ſo abundantly provided for, they which want the like furtherance unto knowledge, wherewith it were greatly to be deſired that they alſo did abound, are yet, we hope, not left in ſo extreme deſtitution, that juſtly any Man ſhould think the ordinary means of eternal Life taken from them, becauſe their teaching is in publick for the moſt part but by Reading. For which cauſe amongſt whom there are not thoſe helps that others have to ſet them forward in the way of Life, ſuch to diſhearten with fearful ſentences, as though their Salvation could hardly be hoped for, is not in our underſtanding ſo conſonant with Chriſtian Charity. We hold it ſafer a great deal, and better to give them encouragement; to put them in mind, that it is not the deepneſs of their Knowledge, but the ſingleneſs of their Belief which God accepteth; that

Pag. 364, 375, 380, 383, 384.

Page 392.

Page 364.

Eccleſ. ii. 26, 27. Matth. xii. 20

1 Tim. i. 5.

Rom. xiv. 1.

1 Theſ. iii. 10.

they

BOOK V. they which *hunger and thirst after Righteousness, shall be satisfied*; that no imbecility of means can prejudice the truth of the Promise of God herein; that the weaker their helps are, the more their need is to sharpen the edge of their own industry; and that painfulness by feeble means shall be able to gain that, which in the plenty of more forcible instruments is through sloth and negligence lost. As for the Men, with whom we have thus far taken pains to confer about the force of the Word of God, either read by itself or opened in Sermons, their speeches concerning both the one and the other are in truth such, as might give us very just cause to think that the reckoning is not great which they make of either. For howsoever they have been driven to devise some odd kind of blind uses whereunto they may answer that Reading doth serve, yet the Reading of the Word of God in publick, more than their Preachers bare Text, who will not judge that they deem needless, when if we chance at any time to term it necessary, as being a thing which God himself did institute amongst the Jews for purposes that touch as well us as them; a thing which the Apostles commend under the Old, and ordain under the New Testament; a thing whereof the Church of God hath ever sithence the first beginning reaped singular commodity; a thing which without exceeding great detriment no Church can omit, they only are the Men, that ever we heard of, by whom this hath been crossed and gain-said; they only the Men which have given their peremptory sentence to the contrary: *It is untrue that simple Reading is necessary in the Church.* And why untrue? *Because, although it be very convenient which is used in some Churches, where before Preaching-time the Church assembled hath the Scriptures read in such order, that the whole Canon thereof is oftentimes in one Year run through; yet a number of Churches which have no such order of simple Reading, cannot be in this point charged with breach of God's commandment, which they might be if simple*

Mat. v 6. Phil i. 6. 1 Pet. v 10 Matth. iii. 9. 1 Thes. iv. 18. Heb x. 24. Jude ver. 20. 1 Pet. iv. 10. Luke xi. 31.

T. C l. ii. p. 381.

ſimple Reading were neceſſary. A poor, a cold and an hungry cavil! Shall we therefore to pleaſe them change the word *neceſſary*, and ſay, that it hath been a commendable Order, a Cuſtom very expedient, or an Ordinance moſt profitable (whereby they know right well that we mean exceedingly behoveful) to read the Word of God at large in the Church, whether it be as our manner is, or as theirs is, whom they prefer before us? It is not this that will content or ſatisfy their minds. They have againſt it a marvellous deep and profound axiom, that *Two things to one and the ſame end cannot but very improperly be ſaid moſt profitable.* And therefore if Preaching be moſt profitable to Man's Salvation, then is not Reading; if Reading be, then Preaching is not. Are they reſolved then at the leaſtwiſe, if Preaching be the only ordinary mean whereby it pleaſeth God to ſave our Souls, what kind of Preaching it is which doth ſave? Underſtand they, how or in what reſpect there is that force or virtue in Preaching? We have reaſon wherefore to make theſe demands; for that, although their pens run all upon Preaching and Sermons, yet when themſelves do practiſe that whereof they write, they change their dialect, and thoſe words they ſhun as if there were in them ſome ſecret ſting. It is not their phraſe to ſay they preach, or to give to their own inſtructions and exhortations the name of Sermons; the pain they take themſelves in this kind is either opening, or lecturing, or reading, or exerciſing, but in no caſe Preaching. And in this preſent Queſtion, they alſo warily proteſt that what they aſcribe to the virtue of Preaching, they ſtill mean it of good Preaching. Now one of them ſaith that a good Sermon muſt expound and apply a large portion of the Text of Scripture at one time. Another giveth us to underſtand, that ſound Preaching *is not to do as one did at London, who ſpent moſt of his time in invectives againſt good Men, and told his Audience how the Magiſtrate ſhould have an eye to ſuch as troubled the peace of the Church.*

T. C. l. ii. p. 372.

T. C. l. ii. p. 385.

Complaint of the Commonalty.

Dr. Somes, Painter. p. 21.

BOOK V. *Church.* The beſt of them hold it for no good Preaching, *when a Man endeavoureth to make a glorious ſhew of eloquence and learning, rather than to apply himſelf to the capacity of the ſimple.* But let them ſhape us out a good Preacher by what pattern ſoever pleaſeth them beſt, let them exclude and incloſe whom they will with their definitions, we are not deſirous to enter into any contention with them about this, or to abate the conceit they have of their own ways, ſo that when once we are agreed what Sermons ſhall currently paſs for good, we may at length underſtand from them, what that is in a good Sermon which doth make it the Word of Life unto ſuch as hear. If ſubſtance of matter, evidence of things, ſtrength and validity of arguments and proofs, or if any other virtue elſe which words and ſentences may contain, of all this, what is there in the beſt Sermons being uttered, which they loſe by being read? But they utterly deny that the Reading either of Scriptures, or Homilies and Sermons can ever by the ordinary grace of God ſave any Soul. So that although we had all the Sermons word for word which James, Paul, Peter, and the reſt of the Apoſtles made, ſome one of which Sermons was of power to convert thouſands of the Hearers unto Chriſtian Faith; yea, although we had all the Inſtructions, Exhortations, Conſolations which came from the gracious lips of our Lord Jeſus Chriſt himſelf, and ſhould read them ten thouſand times over, to Faith and Salvation no Man could hope hereby to attain. Whereupon it muſt of neceſſity follow, that the vigour and vital efficacy of Sermons doth grow from certain accidents, which are not in them, but in their Maker: His virtue, his geſture, his countenance, his zeal, the motion of his body, and the inflection of his voice, who firſt uttereth them as his own, is that which given them the form, the nature, the very eſſence of inſtruments available to eternal Life. If they like neither that nor this, what remaineth but that their final concluſion be, *Sermons we*

T C l ii. p. 385.

know

know are the only ordinary means to Salvation, but why or how we cannot tell? Wherefore to end this tedious Controversy, wherein the too great importunity of our over-eager Adversaries hath constrained us much longer to dwell, than the barrenness of so poor a cause could have seemed at the first likely either to require or to admit, if they which without partialities and passions are accustomed to weigh all things and accordingly to give their sentence, shall here sit down to receive our audit, and to cast up the whole reckoning on both sides; the sum which Truth amounteth unto will appear to be but this, that as Medicines, provided of Nature and applied by Art for the benefit of bodily health, take effect sometime under and sometime above the natural proportion of their virtue, according as the mind and fancy of the Patient doth more or less concur with them; so, whether we barely read unto Men the Scriptures of God; or by Homilies concerning Matter of Belief and Conversation seek to lay before them the Duties which they owe unto God and Man; whether we deliver them Books to read and consider of in private at their own best leisure, or call them to the hearing of Sermons publickly in the House of God; albeit every of these and the like unto these means do truly and daily effect that in the hearts of Men for which they are each and all meant; yet the operation which they have in common being most sensibly and most generally noted in one kind above the rest, that one hath in some Men's opinions drowned altogether the rest, and injuriously brought to pass that they have been thought not less effectual than the other, but without the other uneffectual to save souls. Whereas the cause why Sermons only are observed to prevail so much, while all means else seem to sleep and do nothing, is in truth but that singular affection and attention which the People sheweth every where towards the one, and their cold disposition to the other; the reason hereof being partly the art which our Adversaries

 use

BOOK V. use for the credit of their Sermons, to bring Men out of conceit with all other Teaching besides; partly a custom which Men have to let those things carelesly pass by their ears which they have oftentimes heard before, or know they may hear again whenever it pleaseth themselves; partly the especial advantages which Sermons naturally have to procure attention, both in that they come always new, and because by the Hearer it is still presumed, that if they be let slip for the present, what good soever they contain is lost, and that without all hope of recovery. This is the true cause of odds between Sermons and other kinds of wholesome Instruction. As for the difference which hath been hitherto so much defended on the contrary side, making Sermons the only ordinary means unto Faith and eternal Life, sith this hath neither evidence of Truth, nor proof sufficient to give it warrant, a cause of such quality may with far better grace and conveniency ask that pardon, which common humanity doth easily grant, than claim in challenging manner that assent, which is as unwilling, when reason guideth it, to be yielded where it is not, as withheld where it is apparently due. All which notwithstanding, as we could greatly wish that the rigour of this their opinion were allayed and mitigated; so, because we hold it the part of religious ingenuity to honour virtue in whomsoever, therefore it is our most hearty desire, and shall always be our Prayer unto Almighty God, that in the self-same fervent zeal wherewith they seem to affect the good of the Souls of Men, and to thirst after nothing more than that all Men might by all means be directed in the way of Life, both they and we may constantly persist to the World's end. For in this we are not their Adversaries, though they in the other hitherto have been ours.

Of Prayer. 23. Between the Throne of God in Heaven, and his Church upon Earth here militant, if it be so that Angels have their continual intercourse, where should

we

we find the ſame more verified than in thoſe two ghoſtly exerciſes, the one Doctrine, and the other Prayer? For what is the aſſembling of the Church to learn, but the receiving of Angels deſcended from above? What to pray, but the ſending of Angels upwards? His heavenly Inſpirations, and our holy Deſires are as ſo many Angels of intercourſe and commerce between God and us. As Teaching bringeth us to know that God is our ſupreme Truth; ſo Prayer teſtifieth that we acknowledge him our ſovereign Good. Beſides, ſith on God, as the moſt High, all inferior Cauſes in the World are dependant; and the higher any Cauſe is, the more it coveteth to impart virtue unto things beneath it, how ſhould any kind of ſervice we do or can do, find greater acceptance than Prayer, which ſheweth our concurrence with him in deſiring that wherewith his very Nature doth moſt delight? Is not the name of Prayer uſual to ſignify even all the Service that ever we do unto God? And that for no other cauſe, as I ſuppoſe, but to ſhew that there is in Religion no acceptable Duty which devout Invocation of the Name of God doth not either preſuppoſe or infer. Prayers are thoſe *Calves of Men's lips*; thoſe moſt gracious and ſweet odours; thoſe rich preſents and gifts, which being carried up into Heaven, do beſt teſtify our dutiful affection, and are, for the purchaſing of all favour at the hands of God, the moſt undoubted means we can uſe. On others what more eaſily, and yet what more fruitfully beſtowed than our Prayers? If we give Counſel, they are the ſimpler only that need it; if Alms, the poorer only are relieved, but by Prayer we do good to all. And whereas every other Duty beſides is but to ſhew itſelf as time and opportunity require, for this all times are convenient: when we are not able to do any other things for Men's behoof, when through maliciousneſs or unkindneſs they vouchſafe not to accept any other good at our hands, Prayer is that which we always have in our power to beſtow,

Oſe. xiv 3. Rev v 8. Acts x 4.

Rom i 9. 1 Theſ. v. 17. Luke xviii 1.

 and

BOOK V. and they never in theirs to refuse. Wherefore *God forbid*, saith Samuel, speaking unto a most unthankful People, a People weary of the benefit of his most virtuous Government over them, *God forbid that I should sin against the Lord, and cease to pray for you.* It is the first thing wherewith a righteous life beginneth, and the last wherewith it doth end. The knowledge is small which we have on Earth concerning things that are done in Heaven. Notwithstanding, thus much we know even of Saints in Heaven, that they pray. And therefore Prayer being a work common to the Church as well triumphant as militant, a work common unto Men with Angels, what should we think, but that so much of our Lives is celestial and divine as we spend in the exercise of Prayer? For which cause we see that the most comfortable Visitations which God hath sent Men from above, have taken especially the times of Prayer as their most natural opportunities.

1 Sam xii. 23

Dan ix 20 Acts x 30.

Of publick Prayer.

24. This holy and religious Duty of Service towards God concerneth us one way in that we are Men, and another way in that we are joined as parts to that visible mystical Body, which is his Church. As Men, we are at our own choice both for time and place and form, according to the exigence of our own occasions in private, but the Service, which we do as Members of a publick Body is publick, and for that cause must needs be accounted by so much worthier than the other, as a whole Society of such condition exceedeth the worth of any one. In which consideration unto Christian Assemblies there are most special Promises made. St. Paul, though likely to prevail with God as much as any one, did notwithstanding think it much more, both for God's glory and his own good, if Prayers might be made and Thanks yielded in his behalf by a number of Men. The Prince and People of Nineveh assembling themselves as a main army of Supplicants, it was not in the power of God to withstand them. I speak no otherwise concerning the force of publick Prayer in the Church

Psal lv. 18 Dan. ix 3. Acts x. 9.

Mat. xviii. 20

2 Cor. i 11.

Jonah iv. 11.

Church of God than before me Tertullian hath done, *We come by Troops to the place of Assembly, that being bonded as it were together, we may be Supplicants enough to besiege God with our Prayers: These Forces are unto him acceptable.* * When we publickly make our Prayers, it cannot be but that we do it with much more comfort than in private, for that the things we ask publickly are approved as needful and good in the judgment of all, we hear them sought for and desired with common consent. Again, thus much help and furtherance is more yielded, in that, if so be our zeal and devotion to God-ward be slack, the alacrity and fervour of others serveth as a present spur. † *For even Prayer itself* (saith St. Basil) *when it hath not the consort of many Voices to strengthen it, is not itself.* Finally the good which we do by publick Prayer is more than in private can be done, for that besides the benefit which is here, is no less procured to ourselves, the whole Church is much bettered by our good example; and consequently whereas secret neglect of our duty in this kind is but only our own hurt, one Man's contempt of the common Prayer of the Church of God may be and oftentimes is most hurtful unto many. In which considerations, the Prophet David so often voweth unto God the Sacrifice of Praise and Thanksgiving in the Congregation; so earnestly exhorteth others to sing Praises unto the Lord in his Courts, in his Sanctuary, before the memorial of his Holiness; and so much complaineth of his own uncomfortable exile, wherein although he sustained many most grievous indignities, and endured the want of sundry both pleasures and honours before enjoyed, yet as if this one were his only grief, and the rest not felt, his speeches are all of the heavenly benefit of publick Assemblies, and the happiness of such as had free access thereunto.

BOOK V

Apolog. 39.

Psal cxxii. 1.

Psal xxvi. 12 xxxiv. 18

Psal xxx. 4, & xcvi. 9.

Psal. xxvii. 4. & xlii. 4. & lxxxiv. 1.

* Ambrose l. de Pœn Multi minimi dum congregantur unanimes, sunt magni, & multorum preces impossibile est contemni

† Καὶ αὐτὴ ἡ προσευχὴ μὴ ἔχουσα τοὺς συμφωνοῦντας ἀνανδροτέρα πολλῷ ἑαυτῆς. Basil. Epist. lxviii.

BOOK V.

Of the Form of common Prayer.

25. A great part of the cause wherefore religious Minds are so inflamed with the love of publick Devotion is that virtue, force and efficacy, which by experience they find that the very form and reverend solemnity of common Prayer duly ordered hath to help that imbecility and weakness in us, by means whereof we are otherwise of ourselves the less apt to perform unto God so heavenly a service, with such affection of heart, and disposition in the power of our Souls as is requisite. To this end therefore all things hereunto appertaining, have been ever thought convenient to be done with the most solemnity and majesty that the wisest could devise. It is not with publick as with private Prayer. In this, rather secrecy is commanded than outward shew; whereas that being the publick act of a whole Society, requireth accordingly more care to be had of external appearance. The very assembling of Men therefore unto this service hath been ever solemn. And concerning the place of assembly, although it serve for other uses as well as this, yet seeing that our Lord himself hath to this, as to the chiefest of all other, plainly sanctified his own Temple, by entituling it *the House of Prayer*, what pre-eminence of dignity soever hath been either by the Ordinance, or through the special favour and providence of God annexed unto his Sanctuary, the principal cause thereof must needs be in regard of common Prayer. For the honour and furtherance whereof, if it be as the gravest of the ancient Fathers seriously were persuaded, and do oftentimes plainly teach, affirming that the House of Prayer is a Court, beautified with the presence of celestial Powers; that there we stand, we pray, we sound forth Hymns unto God, having his Angels intermingled as our Associates; and that with reference hereunto, the Apostle doth require so great care to be had of decency for the Angels' sake; how can we come to the House of Prayer, and not be moved

Matth. vi. 5, 6.

Math. xxi. 13.

Chrys Hom. xv ad Hebr. & xxiv. in Act.

1 Cor xi. 10.

moved with the very glory* of the place itself so to frame our affections praying, as doth best beseem them whose suits the Almighty doth there sit to hear, and his Angels attend to further? When this was ingrafted in the minds of Men, there needed no penal Statutes to draw them unto publick Prayer. The warning sound was no sooner heard, but the Churches were presently filled;† the pavements covered with bodies prostrate, and washed with their tears of devout joy. And as the place of publick Prayer is a circumstance in the outward form thereof which hath moment to help devotion; so the Person much more with whom the People of God do join themselves in this action, as with him that standeth and speaketh in the presence of God for them. The authority of his place, the fervour of his zeal, the piety and gravity of his whole behaviour, must needs exceedingly both grace and set forward the service he doth. The authority of his calling is a furtherance, because if God hath so far received him into favour, as to impose upon him by the Hands of Men that Office of blessing the People in his Name and making intercession to him in theirs; which Office he hath sanctified with his own most gracious Promise, and ratified that Promise by manifest actual performance thereof, when others before in like place have done the same, is not his very Ordination a seal, as it were to us, that the self-same divine Love which hath chosen the instrument to work with, will by that instrument effect the thing whereunto he ordained it, in blessing his People, and accepting the Prayers which his Servant offereth up unto God for them? It was in this respect a comfortable Title which the Ancients used to give unto God's Ministers, terming them usually *God's most beloved*, which

BOOK V.

Numb. vi. 23. 2 Chron. xxx. 27.

Cod. l. 1. tit. 3. de Epi & Cler. 43. & 44. sæpe.

* Psal. xcvi 6. Power and Beauty are in his Sanctuary.

† Ad domos statim Dominicas currimus, corpora humi sternimus, mixtis cum fletu gaudiis supplicamus. Salvian. de Prov. l. vii.

were

BOOK V. were ordained to procure by their Prayers his love and favour towards all. Again if there be not zeal and fervency in him which proposeth for the rest those suits and supplications which they by their joyful acclamations must ratify; if he praise not God with all his might; if he pour not out his Soul in Prayer; if he take not their causes to heart, and speak not as Moses, Daniel and Ezra did for their People, how should there be but in them frozen coldness, when his affections seem benummed from whom theirs should take fire? Virtue and Godliness of life are required at the hands of the Minister of God, not only in that he is to teach and instruct the People; who for the most part are rather led away by the ill example, than directed aright by the wholesome instruction of them, whose Life swerveth from the rule of their own Doctrine; but also much more in regard of this other part of his Function; whether we respect the weakness of the People, apt to loath and abhor the Sanctuary when they which perform the service thereof are such as the Sons of Heli were; or else consider the inclination of God himself, who requireth the lifting up of pure hands in Prayers, and hath given the World plainly to understand that the Wicked, although they cry, shall not be heard. They are not fit Supplicants to seek his mercy on the behalf of others, whose own unrepented sins provoke his just indignation. *Let thy Priests* therefore, O Lord, *be* evermore *cloathed with Righteousness, that thy Saints may* thereby with more devotion *rejoice and sing!* But of all helps for due performance of this Service, the greatest is that very set and standing Order itself, which framed with common advice, hath both for matter and form prescribed whatsoever is herein publickly done. No doubt, from God it hath proceeded, and by us it must be acknowledged a work of singular care and providence, that the Church hath evermore held a prescript Form of Common-Prayer, although not in all things every where the same, yet for the most part

1 Tim. ii 8. John ix 31. Jer xi 11 Ezech. viii. 18

Psal. cxxxii 9.

BOOK V.

part retaining ſtill the ſame analogy. So that if the Liturgies of all ancient Churches throughout the World be compared amongſt themſelves, it may be eaſily perceived they had all one original mould, and that the publick Prayer of the People of God in Churches thoroughly ſettled, did never uſe to be voluntary dictates, proceeding from any Men's extemporal wit. To him which conſidereth the grievous and ſcandalous inconveniences whereunto they make themſelves daily ſubject, with whom any blind and ſecret corner is judged a fit Houſe of common Prayer, the manifold confuſions which they fall into, where every Man's private Spirit and Gift (as they term it) is the only Biſhop that ordaineth him to his Miniſtry; the irkſome deformities whereby through endleſs and ſenſeleſs effuſions of indigeſted Prayers, they oftentimes diſgrace in moſt unſufferable manner, the worthieſt part of Chriſtian duty towards God, who herein are ſubject to no certain Order, but pray both what and how they liſt; to him, I ſay, which weigheth duly all theſe things, the reaſons cannot be obſcure why God doth in publick Prayer ſo much reſpect the Solemnity of Places where, the Authority and Calling of Perſons by whom, and the preciſe appointment even with what Words or Sentences, his Name ſhould be called on amongſt his People.

2 Chron vi. 20. Joel ii. 17. 2 Chron. xx v. 30.

26. No Man hath hitherto been ſo impious, as plainly and directly to condemn Prayer. The beſt ſtratagem that Satan hath, who knoweth his Kingdom to be no one way more ſhaken than by the publick devout Prayers of God's Church, is by traducing the form and manner of them to bring them into contempt, and ſo to ſhake the force of all Men's devotion towards them. From this, and from no other forge, hath proceeded a ſtrange conceit, that to ſerve God with any ſet Form of Common-Prayer is ſuperſtitious. As though God himſelf did not frame to his Prieſts the very ſpeech wherewith they were charged to bleſs the People; or as if our Lord, even of purpoſe to

Of them which like not to have any ſet Form of Common-Prayer.

Num. vi. 23

preſcribe

BOOK V. prevent this fancy of extemporal and voluntary Prayers, had not left us of his own framing one which might both remain as a part of the Church Liturgy, and ſerve as a pattern whereby to frame all other Prayers with efficacy, yet without ſuperfluity of words. If Prayers were no otherwiſe accepted of God than being conceived always new, according to the exigence of preſent occaſions; if it be right to judge him by our own bellies, and to imagine that he doth loath to have the ſelf-ſame ſupplications often iterated, even as we do to be every day fed without alteration or change of diet; if Prayers be actions which ought to waſte away themſelves in the making; if being made to remain that they may be reſumed and uſed again as Prayers, they be but inſtruments of Superſtition; ſurely, we cannot excuſe Moſes, who gave ſuch occaſion of ſcandal to the World, by not being contented to praiſe the Name of Almighty God according to the uſual naked ſimplicity of God's Spirit, for that admirable victory given them againſt Pharaoh, unleſs ſo dangerous a precedent were left for the caſting of Prayers into certain poetical moulds, and for the framing of Prayers which might be repeated often, although they never had again the ſame occaſions which brought them forth at the firſt. For that very Hymn of Moſes grew afterwards to be a part of the ordinary Jewiſh Liturgy; not only that, but ſundry other ſithence invented. Their Books of Common-Prayer contained partly Hymns taken out of the holy Scripture, partly Benedictions, Thankſgivings, Supplications, penned by ſuch as have been from time to time, the Governors of that Synagogue. Theſe they ſorted into their ſeveral times and places, ſome to begin the ſervice of God with, and ſome to end, ſome to go before, and ſome to follow, and ſome to be interlaced between the divine Readings of the Law and Prophets. Unto their cuſtom of finiſhing the Paſſover with certain Pſalms, there is not any thing more probable, than that the holy

holy Evangelist doth evidently allude, saying, That after the Cup delivered by our Saviour unto his Apostles; * they sung, and went forth to the Mount of Olives. As the Jews had their Songs of Moses, and David, and the rest; so the Church of Christ from the very beginning hath both used the same, and besides them other of like nature, the Song of the Virgin Mary, the Song of Zachary, the Song of Simeon, such Hymns as the Apostle doth often speak of, saying, *I will pray and sing with the Spirit.* Again, *in Psalms, Hymns, and Songs, making melody unto the Lord, and that heartily.* Hymns and Psalms are such kinds of Prayer as are not wont to be conceived upon a sudden; but are framed by Meditation beforehand, or else by prophetical Illumination are inspired, as at that time it appeareth they were, when God by extraordinary gifts of the Spirit enabled Men to all parts of service necessary for the edifying of his Church.

1 Cor. xiv. 15. Ephes v. 19.

27. Now, albeit the Admonitioners did seem at the first to allow no prescript Form of Prayer at all, but thought it the best that their Minister should always be left at liberty to pray as his own discretion did serve; yet because this opinion upon better advice they afterwards retracted, their Defender and his Associates have sithence proposed to the World a Form such as themselves like, and, to shew their dislike of ours, have taken against it those exceptions which, whosoever doth measure by number must needs be greatly out of love with a thing that hath so many faults; whosoever by weight, cannot choose but esteem very highly of that, wherein the wit of so scrupulous Adversaries hath not hitherto observed any defect which

Of them who allowing a set Form of Prayer, yet allow not ours.

* Matth. xxvi. 30. ὑμνήσαντες, having sung the Psalms which were usual at that Feast, those Psalms which the Jews call the great Hallelujah, beginning at the cxiii and continuing to the end of the cxviii. See Paul Burgens. in Psal. cxiii. addit. 1. and Scal. de emendat. tempor.

themselves

BOOK V. themselves can seriously think to be of moment. Gross Errors and manifest Impiety they grant we have taken away. Yet * many things in it they say are amiss; many instances they give of things in our Common-Prayer, not agreeable as they pretend with the Word of God. It hath in their eye too great affinity with the Form of the Church of Rome; it differeth too much from that which Churches elsewhere reformed allow and observe; our attire disgraceth it; it is not orderly read nor gestured as beseemeth; it requireth nothing to be done, which a Child may not lawfully do; it hath a number of short cuts or shreddings, which may be better called Wishes than Prayers; it intermingleth Prayings and Readings in such manner, as if Supplicants should use in proposing their suits unto mortal Princes all the World would judge them mad; it is too long, and by that mean abridgeth Preaching; it appointeth the People to say after the Minister; it spendeth time in singing and in reading the Psalms by course, from side to side; it useth the Lord's Prayer too oft; the Songs of *Magnificat*, *Benedictus* and *Nunc Dimittis*, it might very well spare; it hath the Litany, the Creed of Athanasius and *Gloria Patri*, which are superfluous; it craveth earthly things too much; for deliverance from those evils against which we pray it giveth no Thanks; some things it asketh unseasonably, when they need not to be prayed for, as deliverance from Thunder and Tempest, when no danger is nigh; some in too abject and diffident manner, as that God would give us that which we for our unworthiness dare not

* T. C. l. i. p 131. afterwards, p. 135. Whereas Mr. Doctor affirmeth that there can be nothing shewed in the whole Book which is not agreeable unto the Word of God; I am very loth, &c Notwithstanding, my duty of defending the Truth, and Love which I have first towards God, and then towards my Country, constraineth me being thus provoked, to speak a few words more particularly of the Form of Prayer, that when the blemishes thereof do appear, it may please the Queen's Majesty, and her honourable Council, with those of the Parliament, &c.

ask;

aſk; ſome which ought not to be deſired, as the deliverance from ſudden Death, riddance from all Adverſity, and the extent of ſaving Mercy towards all Men. Theſe and ſuch like are the Imperfections, whereby our Form of Common-Prayer is thought to ſwerve from the Word of God A great Favourer of that part, but yet (his error that way excepted) a learned, painful, a right virtuous and good Man, did not fear ſometime to undertake, againſt Popiſh Detractors, the general maintenance and defence of our whole Church-Service, as having in it nothing repugnant to the Word of God: and even they which would file away moſt from the largeneſs of that offer, do notwithſtanding in more ſparing terms acknowledge little leſs. For when thoſe oppoſite judgments which never are wont to conſtrue things doubtful to the better, thoſe very tongues which are always prone to aggravate whatſoever hath but the leaſt ſhew whereby it may be ſuſpected to favour of, or to ſound towards any evil, do by their own voluntary ſentence clearly free us from groſs errors, and from manifeſt impiety herein; who would not judge us to be diſcharged of all blame, which are confeſt to have no great fault, even by their very word and teſtimony in whoſe eyes no fault of ours hath ever hitherto been accuſtomed to ſeem ſmall? Neverthelefs, what they ſeem to offer us with one hand, the ſame with the other they pull back again. They grant we err not in palpable manner, we are not openly and notoriouſly impious; yet Errors we have, which the ſharp inſight of theſe wiſeſt Men do eſpy; there is hidden Impiety, which the profounder ſort are able enough to diſcloſe. Their ſkilful ears perceive certain harſh and unpleaſant diſcords in the ſound of our Common-Prayer, ſuch as the Rules of divine Harmony, ſuch as the Laws of God cannot bear.

28. Touching

BOOK V.

The Form of our Liturgy too near the Papists, too far different from that of other reformed Churches, as they pretend.

28. Touching our Conformity with the Church of Rome, as also of the difference between some reformed Churches and ours, that which generally hath been already answered, may serve for answer to that exception which in these two respects they take particularly against the Form of our Common-Prayer. To say, that in nothing they may be followed which are of the Church of Rome, were violent and extreme. Some things they do, in that they are Men, in that they are wise Men, and Christian Men, some things, in that they are Men misled and blinded with error. As far as they follow Reason and Truth, we fear not to tread the self-same steps wherein they have come, and to be their Followers. Where Rome keepeth that which is ancienter and better, others whom we much more affect leaving it for newer and changing it for worse; we had rather follow the perfections of them whom we like not, than in defect resemble them whom we love. For although they profess they agree with us touching a *prescript Form of Prayer to be used in the Church*; yet in that very Form which they say is *agreeable to God's Word and the use of reformed Churches*, they have by special protestation declared, that their meaning is not, it shall be prescribed as a thing whereunto they will tie their Minister. *It shall not* (they say) *be necessary for the Minister daily to repeat all these things before-mentioned, but beginning with some like Confession, to proceed to the Sermon, which ended, he either useth the Prayer for all States before-mentioned, or else prayeth as the Spirit of God shall move his heart.* Herein therefore we hold it much better, with the Church of Rome, to appoint a prescript Form, which every Man shall be bound to observe, than with them to set down a kind of direction, a Form for Men to use if they list, or otherwise to change as pleaseth themselves. Furthermore, the Church of Rome hath rightly also considered, that publick Prayer is a Duty entire in itself, a Duty requisite to be performed

T. C. l. 1. p. 155 A Book of the Form of Common-Prayer tendered to the Parliament. p. 46.

formed much oftner than Sermons can poſſibly be made. For which cauſe, as they, ſo we have likewiſe a publick Form how to ſerve God both Morning and Evening, whether Sermons may be had or no. On the contrary ſide, their Form of reformed Prayer ſheweth only what ſhall be done *upon the days appointed for the preaching of the Word*; with what words the Miniſter ſhall begin, *when the hour appointed for the Sermon is come*; what ſhall be ſaid or ſung before Sermon, and what after. So that according to this Form of their's, it muſt ſtand for a Rule, *No Sermon, no Service*. Which over-ſight occaſioned the French ſpitefully to term Religion, in that ſort exerciſed, a meer Preach. Sundry other more particular defects there are, which I willingly forbear to rehearſe, in conſideration whereof, we cannot be induced to prefer their reformed Form of Prayer before our own, what Church ſoever we reſemble therein.

Page 22.

Page 24.

Attire belonging to the Service of God.

29. The Attire which the Miniſter of God is by Order to uſe at times of divine Service, being but a matter of meer formality, yet ſuch as for comelineſs-ſake hath hitherto been judged by the wiſer ſort of Men, not unneceſſary to concur with other ſenſible notes, betokening the different kind or quality of Perſons and Actions whereto it is tied, as we think not ourſelves the holier becauſe we uſe it, ſo neither ſhould they, with whom no ſuch thing is in uſe, think us therefore unholy,* becauſe we ſubmit ourſelves unto that which in a matter ſo indifferent the wiſdom of Authority and Law hath thought comely. To ſolemn actions of Royalty and Juſtice, their ſuit-

* T. C. l. i. p. 71. We think the Surplice eſpecially unmeet for a Miniſter of the Goſpel to wear p 75. It is eaſily ſeen by Solomon, Eccleſ viii. 9. that to wear a white Garment was highly eſteemed in the eaſt parts, and was ordinary to thoſe that were in any eſteem, as black with us, and therefore was no ſeveral Apparel for the Miniſters to execute their Miniſtry in.

BOOK V. able ornaments are a beauty. Are they only in Religion a ſtain? *Divine Religion,* ſaith St. Jerom (he ſpeaketh of the prieſtly Attire of the Law) *hath one kind of Habit wherein to miniſter before the Lord, another for ordinary uſes belonging unto common life.* Pelagius having carped at the curious neatneſs of Men's Apparel in thoſe days, and through the ſourneſs of his diſpoſition ſpoken ſomewhat too hardly thereof, affirming; that the *glory of Cloaths and Ornaments was a thing contrary to God and Godlineſs*; St. Jerom, whoſe cuſtom is not to pardon over-eaſily his Adverſaries, if any where they chance to trip, preſſeth him as thereby making all ſorts of Men in the World *God's Enemies. Is it enmity with God* (ſaith he) *if I wear my Coat ſomewhat handſome?* If a Biſhop, a Prieſt, Deacon, and the reſt of the Eccleſiaſtical Order *come to adminiſter the uſual Sacrifice in a white Garment,** are they hereby God's Adverſaries? *Clerks, Monks, Widows, Virgins, take heed, it is dangerous for you to be otherwiſe ſeen than in foul and ragged Cloaths. Not to ſpeak any thing of ſecular Men, which have proclaimed to have war with God as oft as ever they put on precious and ſhining Cloaths.* By which words of Jerom, we may take it at the leaſt for a probable collection, that his meaning was to draw Pelagius into hatred, as condemning by ſo general a ſpeech even the neatneſs of that very Garment itſelf, wherein the Clergy did then uſe to adminiſter publickly the holy Sacrament of Chriſt's moſt bleſſed Body and Blood; for that they did then uſe ſome ſuch Ornament, the words of Chryſoſtom give plain teſtimony, who ſpeaking to the Clergy of Antioch, telleth them, that if they did ſuffer notorious Malefactors to come to the Table of the Lord and not put them by, it would be as heavily revenged upon them, as if themſelves had ſhed his Blood; that for

Hieron. in xliv Ezech. Hiero. Adver Pelag. l. 1. c. 9.

Chryſoſt. ad popul. Antioch. tom. v. Serm. 60.

* T. C. l. i. p. 77. By a white Garment is meant a comely Apparel, and not ſlovenly.

this

this purpose God hath called them to the rooms which they held in the Church of Christ; that this, they should reckon was their dignity, this their safety, this their whole crown and glory; and therefore this they should carefully intend, and not when the Sacrament is administered, imagine themselves called only *to walk up and down in a white and shining Garment.* Now, whereas these speeches of Jerom and Chrysostom do seem plainly to allude unto such ministerial Garments as were then in use; to this they answer, that by Jerom nothing can be gathered, but only that the Ministers came to Church in handsome Holy-day Apparel, and that himself did not think them bound by the Law of God to go like slovens, but the Weed which we mean he defendeth not; that Chrysostom meaneth indeed the same which we defend,* but seemeth rather to reprehend than allow it as we do. Which Answer wringeth out of Jerom and Chrysostom that which their words will not gladly yield. They both speak of the same Persons, (namely, the Clergy) and of their Weed at the same time when they administer the blessed Sacrament; and of the self-same kind of Weed, a white Garment, so far as we have wit to conceive; and for any thing we are able to see, their manner of speech is not such as doth argue either the thing itself to be different whereof they speak, or their judgments concerning it different; although the one do only maintain it against Pelagius, as a thing not therefore unlawful because it was fair or handsome, and the other make it a matter of small commendation in itself, if they which wear it do nothing else but wear the Robes which their place requireth. The honesty, dignity and estimation of

* T. C. l. i. p. 75. It is true, Chrysostom maketh mention of a white Garment, but not in commendation of it, but rather to the contrary: for he sheweth that the dignity of the Ministry was in taking heed that none unmeet were admitted to the Lord's Supper, not in going about the Church with a white Garment.

BOOK V. white Apparel in the eaſtern part of the World, is a token of greater fitneſs for this ſacred uſe, wherein it were not convenient that any thing baſely thought of ſhould be ſuffered. Notwithſtanding, I am not bent to ſtand ſtifly upon theſe probabilities, that in Jerom's and Chryſoſtom's time any ſuch Attire was made ſeveral to this purpoſe. Yet ſurely the words of Solomon are very impertinent to prove it an Ornament, therefore not ſeveral for the Miniſters to execute their miniſtry in, becauſe Men of credit and
Ecclef. xlv. 7. eſtimation wore their ordinary Apparel white. For we know that when Solomon wrote thoſe words, the ſeveral Apparel for the Miniſters of the Law to execute their miniſtry in, was ſuch. The wiſe Man which feared God from his heart, and honoured the Service that was done unto him, could not mention ſo much as the Garment of Holineſs, but with effectual ſignification of more ſingular reverence and love. Were it not better that the love which Men bear to God ſhould make the leaſt things which are employed in his Service amiable, than that their over-ſcrupulous diſlike of ſo mean a thing as a Veſtment, ſhould from the very Service of God withdraw their hearts and affections? I term it rather a mean thing, a thing not much to be reſpected, becauſe even they ſo account of it, whoſe firſt Diſputations againſt it were ſuch as if Religion had ſcarcely any thing of
T. C. l. 1. p. 79. greater weight. Their allegations were then, *That if a Man were aſſured to gain a thouſand by doing that which may offend any one Brother, or be unto him a cauſe of falling, he ought not to do it; that*
71. *this Popiſh Apparel, the Surplice eſpecially, hath been by Papiſts abominably abuſed; that it hath been a*
75. *mark and a very Sacrament of Abomination, that remaining, it ſerveth as a monument of Idolatry, and not*
72. T C l. ii. p. 403. *only edifieth not, but as a dangerous and ſcandalous Ceremony doth exceeding much harm to them of whoſe good we*
l. 1. p. 73, 76. l. ii. p. 403. *are commanded to have regard, that it cauſeth Men to periſh, and make ſhipwreck of Conſcience;* for ſo themſelves

ſelves profeſs they mean, when they ſay the Weak are offended herewith; *that it hardeneth Papiſts, hindereth the Weak from profiting in the knowledge of the Goſpel, grieveth godly Minds, and giveth them occaſion to think hardly of their Miniſters; that if the Magiſtrates may command, or the Church appoint Rites and Ceremonies, yet ſeeing our abſtinence from things in their own nature indifferent if the weak Brother ſhould be offended, is a flat Commandment of the Holy Ghoſt which no Authority either of Church or Commonwealth can make void; therefore neither may the one nor the other lawfully ordain this Ceremony, which hath great incommodity and no profit, great offence and no edifying, that by the Law it ſhould have been burnt and conſumed with fire as a thing infected with Leproſy; that the example of Ezekiah beating to powder the Brazen Serpent, and of Paul abrogating thoſe abuſed Feaſts of Charity, enforceth upon us the duty of aboliſhing altogether a thing which hath been, and is ſo offenſive; finally, that God by his Prophet hath given an expreſs Commandment, which in this caſe toucheth us no leſs than of old it did the Jews; Ye ſhall pollute the covering of the Images of Silver, and the rich Ornament of your Images of Gold, and caſt them away as a ſtained rag; thou ſhalt ſay to it, Get thee hence.* Theſe and ſuch like, were their firſt diſcourſes touching that Church-attire which with us for the moſt part is uſual in publick Prayer, our Eccleſiaſtical Laws ſo appointing, as well becauſe it hath been of reaſonable continuance, and by ſpecial choice was taken out of the number of thoſe holy Garments which (over and beſides their myſtical reference) ſerved for comelineſs under the Law; and is in the number of thoſe Ceremonies which may with choice and diſcretion be uſed to that purpoſe in the Church of Chriſt; as alſo for that it ſuiteth ſo fitly with that lightſome affection of joy, wherein God delighteth when his Saints praiſe him; and ſo lively reſembleth the glory of the Saints in Heaven, together with the beauty wherein Angels have appeared unto Men, that they which are to appear for Men in the

Lib. i p. 76. Page 81. Page 78. Iſa. xxx. 22. Exod. xxviii. 2. Exod xxxix. 27. Pſal. cxlix. 2. Apoc xv. 6. Mar. xvi. 5.

BOOK V. presence of God as Angels, if they were left to their own choice, and would choose any, could not easily devise a Garment of more decency for such a Service. As for those fore-rehearsed vehement allegations against it, shall we give them credit, when the very Authors from whom they came confess they believe not their own sayings? For when once they began to perceive how many, both of them in the two Universities, and of others who abroad having Ecclesiastical Charge, do favour mightily their cause, and by all means set it forward, might by persisting in the extremity of that opinion, hazard greatly their own estates, and so weaken that part which their places do now give them much opportunity to strengthen; they asked counsel as it seemed from some abroad, who wisely considered that the Body is of far more worth than the Raiment. Whereupon, for fear of dangerous inconveniences, it hath been thought good to add, that sometimes Authority *must and may with good Conscience be obeyed, even where Commandment is not given upon good ground; that the duty of Preaching is one of the absolute Commandments of God, and therefore ought not to be forsaken for the bare inconveniency of a thing which in its own nature is indifferent; that one of the foulest spots in the Surplice, is the offence which it giveth in occasioning the weak to fall, and the wicked to be confirmed in their wickedness; yet hereby there is no unlawfulness proved, but only an inconveniency, that such things should be established, howbeit no such inconveniency neither as may not be born with; that when God doth flatly command us to abstain from things in their own nature indifferent, if they offend our weak Brethren, his meaning is not we should obey his Commandment herein, unless we may do it, and not leave undone that which the Lord hath absolutely commanded. Always provided, that whosoever will enjoy the benefit of this dispensation, to wear a scandalous badge of Idolatry rather than forsake his Pastoral Charge, do (as occasion serveth) teach nevertheless still the incommodity of the thing itself, admonish the weak*

T. C. l. i. p. 74. & l. ii. p. 250. Index l iii. c 8. l. iii. p. 262, 263.

Lib. iii p. 263.

Page 263.

weak Brethren that they be not, and pray unto God ſo to ſtrengthen them that they may not be offended thereat. So that whereas before, they which had Authority to inſtitute Rites and Ceremonies were denied to have power to inſtitute this, it is now confeſſed, that this they may alſo lawfully, but not ſo conveniently appoint; they did well before, and as they ought, who had it in utter deteſtation and hatred as a thing abominable; they now do well, which think it may be both born and uſed with a very good Conſcience; before, he which by wearing it were ſure to win thouſands unto Chriſt, ought not to do it if there were but one which might be offended; now, though it be with the offence of thouſands, yet it may be done rather than that ſhould be given over whereby notwithſtanding we are not certain we ſhall gain one. The examples of Ezekias and of Paul, the charge which was given to the Jews by Eſay, the ſtrict Apoſtolical prohibition of things indifferent, whenſoever they may be ſcandalous, were before ſo forcible Laws againſt our Eccleſiaſtical Attire, as neither Church nor Commonwealth could poſſibly make void; which now one of far leſs Authority than either, hath found how to fruſtrate, by diſpenſing with the breach of inferior Commandments, to the end that the greater may be kept. But it booteth them not thus to ſolder up a broken cauſe, whereof their firſt and laſt diſcourſes will fall aſunder, do what they can. Let them ingeniouſly confeſs that their invectives were too bitter, their arguments too weak, the matter not ſo dangerous as they did imagine. If thoſe alledged teſtimonies of Scripture did indeed concern the matter to ſuch effect as was pretended, that which they ſhould infer, were unlawfulneſs, becauſe they were cited as prohibitions of that thing which indeed they concern. If they prove not our Attire unlawful, becauſe in truth they concern it not, it followeth that they prove not any thing againſt it, and conſequently not ſo much as uncomelineſs or inconveniency. Unleſs therefore

BOOK V. fore they be able thoroughly to resolve themselves, that there is no one Sentence in all the Scriptures of God which doth controul the wearing of it in such manner, and to such purpose as the Church of England alloweth; unless they can fully rest and settle their minds in this most sound persuasion, that they are not to make themselves the only competent Judges of decency in these cases, and to despise the solemn judgment of the whole Church, preferring before it their own conceit, grounded only upon uncertain suspicions and fears, whereof if there were at the first some probable cause, when things were but raw and tender, yet now very tract of time hath itself worn that also; unless, I say, thus resolved in mind they hold their Pastoral Charge with the comfort of a good Conscience, no way grudging at that which they do, or doing that which they think themselves bound of duty to reprove, how should it possibly help or further them in their course, to take such occasions as they say are requisite to be taken, and in pensive manner to tell their Audience, "*Brethren, our hearts desire is, that* "*we might enjoy the full liberty of the Gospel, as in other* "*reformed Churches they do elsewhere, upon whom the* "*heavy hand of Authority hath imposed no grievous bur-* "*then. But such is the misery of these our days, that so* "*great happiness we cannot look to attain unto. Were it* "*so, that the equity of the Law of Moses could prevail,* "*or the zeal of Ezechias be found in the hearts of those* "*Guides and Governors under whom we live, or the* "*voice of God's own Prophets be duly heard; or the ex-* "*amples of the Prophets of Christ be followed; yea, or* "*their precepts be answered with full and perfect obedi-* "*ence; these abominable Rags, polluted Garments, marks* "*and Sacraments of Idolatry, which Power as you see,* "*constraineth us to wear, and Conscience to abhor, had* "*long ere this day been moved both out of sight and out* "*of memory. But, as now things stand, behold to what* "*narrow streights we are driven; on the one side we* "*fear the words of our Saviour Christ,* Woe be to them

"by

" by whom ſcandal and offence cometh; *on the other* " *ſide, at the Apoſtle's ſpeech we cannot but quake and* " *tremble*; If I preach not the Goſpel, woe be unto " me. *Being thus hardly beſet, we ſee not any other re-* " *medy but to hazard your Souls the one way, that we* " *may the other way endeavour to ſave them. Touching* " *the offence of the Weak, therefore, we muſt adventure it.* " *If they periſh, they periſh. Our Paſtoral Charge is God's* " *moſt abſolute commandment. Rather than that ſhall be* " *taken from us, we are reſolved to take this filth and* " *put it on, although we judge it to be ſo unfit and incon-* " *venient that as oft as ever we pray or preach ſo ar-* " *rayed before you, we do as much as in us lieth to caſt* " *away your Souls that are weak-minded, and to bring* " *you unto endleſs perdition. But we beſeech you, Bre-* " *thren, have a care of your own ſafety, take heed to* " *your ſteps that ye be not taken in thoſe ſnares which* " *we lay before you. And our Prayer in your behalf to* " *Almighty God is, that the poiſon which we offer you,* " *may never have the power to do you harm.* Advice and counſel is beſt ſought for at their hands which either have no part at all in the cauſe whereof they inſtruct; or elſe are ſo far engaged, that themſelves are to bear the greateſt adventure in the ſucceſs of their own counſels. The one of which two conſiderations maketh Men the leſs reſpective, and the other the more circumſpect. Thoſe good and learned Men which gave the firſt direction to this courſe, had reaſon to wiſh that their own proceedings at home might be favoured abroad alſo, and that the good affection of ſuch as inclined towards them might be kept alive. But if themſelves had gone under thoſe ſails which they require to be hoiſed up, if they had been themſelves to execute their own Theory in this Church, I doubt not but eaſily they would have ſeen, being near at hand, that the way was not good which they took of adviſing Men, firſt to wear the Apparel that thereby they might be free to continue their preaching, and then of requiring them ſo to preach,

as

BOOK V. as they might be ſure they could not continue, except they imagine that Laws which permit them not to do as they would, will endure them to ſpeak as they liſt, even againſt that which themſelves do by conſtraint of Laws; they would have eaſily ſeen that our People being accuſtomed to think evermore that thing evil which is publickly under any pretence reproved, and the Men themſelves worſe which reprove it and uſe it too, it ſhould be to little purpoſe for them to ſalve the wound, by making proteſtations in diſgrace of their own actions, with plain acknowledgment that they are ſcandalous, or by uſing fair intreaty with the weak Brethren; they would eaſily have ſeen how with us it cannot be endured to hear a Man openly profeſs that he putteth fire to his Neighbour's houſe, but yet ſo halloweth the ſame with Prayer that he hopeth it ſhall not burn. It had been therefore perhaps ſafer and better for ours to have obſerved St. Baſil's advice, both in this and in all things of like nature: *Let him which approveth not his Governors Ordinances, either plainly (but privately always) ſhew his diſlike if he have* λόγον ἰσχυρὸν, *ſtrong and invincible reaſon againſt them, according to the true will and meaning of Scripture; or elſe let him quietly with ſilence do what is enjoined.* Obedience with profeſſed unwillingneſs to obey, is not better than manifeſt diſobedience.

Baſil Aſcet. reſponſ. ad inter. 47.

Of geſture in Praying, and of different places choſen to that purpoſe.

T. C. l. 1. p 154.

30. Having thus diſputed whether the Surplice be a fit Garment to be uſed in the ſervice of God, the next Queſtion whereinto we are drawn is, whether it be a thing allowable or no that the Miniſter ſhould ſay Service in the Chancel, or turn his Face at any time from the People, or before Service ended remove from the place where it was begun? By them which trouble us with thoſe doubts, we would more willingly be reſolved of a greater doubt; whether it be not a kind of taking God's Name in vain to debaſe Religion with ſuch frivolous diſputes, a ſin to beſtow time and labour about them? Things of ſo mean regard and quality although neceſſary to be ordered,

dered, are notwithſtanding very unſavory when they come to be diſputed of: becauſe diſputation preſuppoſeth ſome difficulty in the matter which is argued, whereas in things of this nature they muſt be either very ſimple, or very froward, who need to be taught by diſputation what is meet. When we make profeſſion of our Faith, we ſtand; when we acknowledge our Sins, or ſeek unto God for favour, we fall down; becauſe the geſture of conſtancy becometh us beſt in the one, in the other the behaviour of humility. Some parts of our Liturgy conſiſt in the reading of the Word of God, and the proclaiming of his Law, that the People may thereby learn what their duties are towards him; ſome conſiſt in words of praiſe and thankſgiving, whereby we acknowledge unto God what his bleſſings are towards us; ſome are ſuch as albeit they ſerve to ſingular good purpoſe, even when there is no Communion adminiſtered, nevertheleſs being deviſed at the firſt for that purpoſe, are at the Table of the Lord for that cauſe alſo commonly read; ſome are uttered as from the People, ſome as with them unto God, ſome as from God unto them, all as before his ſight whom we fear, and whoſe preſence to offend with any the leaſt unſeemlineſs we would be ſurely as loth as they who moſt reprehend or deride that we do. Now, becauſe the Goſpels which are weekly read, T. C. l. i. p. 203. do all hiſtorically declare ſomething which our Lord Jeſus Chriſt himſelf either ſpake, did, or ſuffered in his own Perſon, it hath been the cuſtom of Chriſtian Men then eſpecially in token of the greater reverence to ſtand, to utter certain words of acclamation, and at the Name of Jeſus to bow. Which harmleſs Ceremonies, as there is no Man conſtrained to uſe; ſo we know no reaſon wherefore any Man ſhould yet imagine it an unſufferable evil. It ſheweth a reverend regard to the Son of God above other Meſſengers, Mark xii. 6. although ſpeaking as from God alſo. And againſt Infidels, Jews, Arians, who derogate from the honour of Jeſus Chriſt, ſuch Ceremonies are thus profitable.

As

BOOK V. As for any erroneous eſtimation, advancing the Son above the Father and the Holy Ghoſt, ſeeing that the truth of his Equality with them is a Myſtery ſo hard for the wits of mortal Men to riſe unto, of all Hereſies that which may give him ſuperiority above them is leaſt to be feared. But to let go this as a matter ſcarce worth the ſpeaking of, whereas if fault be in theſe things any where juſtly found, Law hath referred the whole diſpoſition and redreſs thereof to the Ordinary of the place; they which elſewhere complain that diſgrace and injury is offered even to the meaneſt Pariſh Miniſter when the Magiſtrate appointeth him what to wear, and leaveth not ſo ſmall a matter as that to his own diſcretion, being preſumed a Man diſcreet and truſted with the care of the Peoples Souls, do think the graveſt Prelates in the Land no competent Judges to diſcern and appoint where it is fit for the Miniſter to ſtand, or which way convenient to look praying. From their Ordinary therefore they appeal to themſelves, finding great fault that we neither reform the thing againſt the which they have long ſince given ſentence, nor yet make anſwer unto what they bring, which is, that Saint Luke declaring how *Peter ſtood up in the midſt of the Diſciples*, did thereby deliver an unchangeable rule, that whatſoever is done in the Church, ought to be done in the midſt of the Church; and therefore not Baptiſm to be adminiſtered in one place, Marriage ſolemnized in another, the Supper of the Lord received in a third, in a fourth Sermons, in a fifth Prayers to be made; that the cuſtom which we uſe is Levitical, abſurd, and ſuch as hindereth the underſtanding of the People; that if it be meet for the Miniſter, at ſome time to look towards the People, if the Body of the Church be a fit place for ſome part of divine Service, it muſt needs follow, that whenſoever his face is turned any other way, or any thing done any other where, it hath abſurdity. All theſe reaſons, they ſay, have been brought, and were hitherto never anſwered; beſides a number of merriments

T. C. l. iii. p. 215.

T. C. l. i. p. 74.

T. C. l. i. p. 134. l. iii. p. 187.

Acts i. 15. T. C. l. i. p. 134. l. iii. p. 187.

merriments and jests unanswered likewise, wherewith they have presently moved much laughter at our manner of serving God. Such is their evil hap to play upon dull spirited Men. We are still persuaded that a bare denial is answer sufficient to things which meer fancy objecteth; and that the best apology to words of scorn and petulancy, is Isaac's apology to his Brother Ismael, the Apology which patience and silence maketh. Our Answer therefore to their Reasons is, No; to their Scoffs, nothing. BOOK V.

Easiness of praying after our form.

31. When they object that our Book requireth nothing to be done, which a Child may not do as *lawfully and as well as that Man wherewith the Book contenteth itself*,* is it their meaning that the Service of God ought to be a matter of great difficulty, a labour which requireth great learning and deep skill, or else that the Book containing it, should teach what Men are fit to attend upon it, and forbid either Men unlearned, or Children, to be admitted thereunto? In setting down the form of Common Prayer there was no need that the Book should mention either the learning of a fit, or the unfitness of an ignorant Minister, more than that he which describeth the manner how to pitch a field, should speak of moderation and sobriety in diet. And concerning the duty itself, although the hardness thereof be not such as needeth much art, yet surely they seem to be very far carried besides themselves, to whom the dignity of publick Prayer doth not discover somewhat more fitness in Men of gravity and ripe discretion, than in *Children of ten years of age* for the decent discharge and performance of that office. It cannot be that they who speak thus, should thus judge. At the board and in private

* T. C. l. i. p. 133. & l. iii. p. 184. Another fault in the whole Service or Liturgy of England is, for that it maintaineth an unpreaching Ministry in requiring nothing to be done by the Minister which a Child of ten years old cannot do as well, and as lawfully as that Man, wherewith the Book contenteth itself.

it

BOOK V. it very well becometh Children's innocency to pray, and their Elders to ſay *Amen*. Which being a part of their virtuous education, ſerveth greatly both to nouriſh in them the fear of God, and to put us in continual remembrance of that powerful grace which openeth the mouths of Infants to ſound his Praiſe. But publick Prayer, the Service of God in the ſolemn Aſſembly of Saints, is a work, though eaſy, yet withal ſo weighty and of ſuch reſpect, that the great facility thereof, is but a ſlender argument to prove it may be as well and as lawfully committed to Children, as to Men of years, howſoever their ability of learning be but only to do that in decent order, wherewith the Book contenteth itſelf. The Book requireth but orderly reading. As in truth, what ſhould any preſcript Form of Prayer framed to the Miniſter's hand require, but only ſo to be read as behoveth. We know that there be in the World certain voluntary Overſeers of all Books, whoſe cenſure in this reſpect would fall as ſharp on us, as it hath done on many others, if delivering but a Form of Prayer, we ſhould either expreſs or include any thing, more than what doth properly concern Prayer. The Miniſter's greatneſs or meanneſs of knowledge to do other things, his aptneſs or inſufficiency otherwiſe than by reading to inſtruct the Flock, ſtandeth in this place as a ſtranger with whom our Form of Common-Prayer hath nothing to do. Wherein their exception againſt eaſineſs, as if that did nouriſh ignorance, proceedeth altogether out of a needleſs jealouſy. I have often heard it enquired of by many, how it might be brought to paſs, that the Church ſhould every where have Preachers to inſtruct the People; what impediments there are to hinder it; and which were the ſpeedieſt way to remove them. In which conſultation, the multitude of Pariſhes, the paucity of Schools, the manifold diſcouragements which are offered unto Men's inclinations that way, the penury of the Eccleſiaſtical Eſtate, the irrecoverable loſs of ſo many

Livings

Livings of principal value, clean taken away from the Church long ſithence by being appropriated, the daily bruiſes that ſpiritual promotions uſe to take by often falling, the want of ſomewhat in certain Statutes which concern the State of the Church, the too great facility of many Biſhops, the ſtony hardneſs of too many Patron's hearts, not touched with any feeling in this caſe: ſuch things oftentimes are debated, and much thought upon by them that enter into any diſcourſe concerning any defect of knowledge in the Clergy. But whoſoever be found guilty, the Communion-Book hath ſurely deſerved leaſt to be called in queſtion for this fault. If all the Clergy were as learned as themſelves are that moſt complain of ignorance in others, yet our Book of Prayer might remain the ſame; and remaining the ſame it is, I ſee not how it can be a lett unto any Man's ſkill in preaching; which thing we acknowledge to be God's good gift, howbeit no ſuch neceſſary element, that every act of Religion ſhould be thought imperfect and lame, wherein there is not ſomewhat exacted that none can diſcharge but an able Preacher.

32. Two faults there are which our Lord and Saviour himſelf eſpecially reproved in Prayer; the one, when oſtentation did cauſe it to be open; the other, when ſuperſtition made it long. As therefore Prayers the one way are faulty, not whenſoever they be openly made, but when Hypocriſy is the cauſe of open praying; ſo the length of Prayer is likewiſe a fault, howbeit not ſimply, but where error and ſuperſtition cauſeth more than convenient repetition or continuation of ſpeech to be uſed. It is not, as ſome do imagine, (ſaith St. Auguſtin) that long praying is that fault of much ſpeaking in Prayer, which our Saviour did reprove; for then would not he himſelf in Prayer have continued whole nights. *Uſe in Prayer no vain ſuperfluity of words as the Heathens do, for they imagine that their much ſpeaking will cauſe them to be heard:* whereas in truth the thing which God doth regard is

The length of our Service. T. C. l. i. p. 133 & l. iii. p. 184.

Aug. Ep. 121. Luke vi. 12.

how

BOOK V. how virtuous their Minds are, and not how copious their Tongues in Prayer; how well they think, and not how long they talk who come to preſent their Supplications before him. Notwithſtanding for as much as in publick Prayer we are not only to conſider what is needful in reſpect of God, but there is alſo in Men that which we muſt regard; we ſomewhat the rather incline to length, leſt over-quick diſpatch of a duty ſo important, ſhould give the World occaſion to deem that the thing itſelf is but little accounted of, wherein but little time is beſtowed. Length thereof is a thing which the gravity and weight of ſuch actions doth require. Beſide, this benefit alſo it hath, that they whom earneſt letts and impediments do often hinder from being Partakers of the whole, have yet through the length of divine Service, opportunity left them, at the leaſt, for acceſs unto ſome reaſonable part thereof. Again, it ſhould be conſidered, how it doth come to paſs that we are ſo long. For if that very Service of God in the Jewiſh Synagogues, which our Lord did approve and ſanctify with the preſence of his own Perſon, had ſo large portions of the Law and the Prophets, together with ſo many Prayers and Pſalms read day by day, as do equal in a manner the length of ours, and yet in that reſpect was never thought to deſerve blame, is it now an offence that the like meaſure of time is beſtowed in the like manner? Peradventure the Church hath not now the leiſure which it had then, or elſe thoſe things whereupon ſo much time was then well ſpent, have ſithence that loſt their dignity and worth. If the reading of the Law, the Prophets and Pſalms, be a part of the Service of God as needful under Chriſt as before, and the adding of the New Teſtament as profitable as the ordaining of the Old to be read; if therewith, inſtead of Jewiſh Prayers, it be alſo for the good of the Church to annex that variety which the Apoſtle doth commend, ſeeing that the time which we ſpend is no more than the orderly

1 Tim. ii. 1.

orderly performance of these things necessarily required, why are we thought to exceed in length? Words, be they never so few, are too many when they benefit not the Hearer. But he which speaketh no more than edifieth, is undeservedly reprehended for much speaking. That as *the Devil under the colour of long Prayer drave Preaching out of the Church* heretofore, *so we in appointing so long Prayers and Readings, whereby the less can be spent in Preaching, maintain an unpreaching Ministry*, is neither advisedly nor truly spoken. They reprove long Prayer, and yet acknowledge it to be in itself a thing commendable; for so it must needs be, if the Devil have used it as a colour to hide his malicious practices. When malice would work that which is evil, and in working avoid the suspicion of any evil intent, the colour wherewith it overcasteth itself is always a fair and plausible pretence of seeking to further that which is good. So that if we both retain that good which Satan hath pretended to seek, and avoid the evil which his purpose was to effect, have we not better prevented his malice, than if, as he hath under colour of long Prayer driven Preaching out of the Church, so we should take the quarrel of Sermons in hand, and revenge their cause by requital, thrusting Prayer in a manner out of doors under colour of long Preaching? In case our Prayers being made at their full length did necessarily enforce Sermons to be the shorter, yet neither were this to uphold and maintain an unpreaching Ministry, unless we will say that those ancient Fathers, Chrysostom, Augustin, Leo, and the rest whose Homilies in that consideration were shorter for the most part than our Sermons are, did then not preach when the Speeches were not long. The necessity of shortness causeth Men to cut off impertinent discourses, and to comprise much matter in few words. But neither did it maintain inability, nor at all prevent opportunity of Preaching, as long as a competent time is granted for that purpose. *An hour and an half* is, they

BOOK V.

T C l. iii. p. 184.

they ſay, in reformed Churches ordinarily thought reaſonable, for *their whole Liturgy or Service.* Do we then continue, as Ezra did, in reading the Law from morning till mid-day? or, as the Apoſtle St. Paul did, in Prayer and Preaching, till Men through wearineſs be taken up dead at our feet? The huge length whereof they make ſuch complaint is but this, that if our whole Form of Prayer be read, and beſides an hour allowed for a Sermon, we ſpend ordinarily in both more time than they do by half an hour. Which half-hour being ſuch a matter as the *age of ſome, and the infirmity of other ſome, are not able to bear*; if we have any ſenſe of the *common imbecility*, if any care to preſerve Men's wits from being broken with the very *bent of ſo long attention*, if any love or deſire to provide that things moſt holy be not with hazard of Men's Souls abhorred and loathed, this half-hour's tedious-neſs muſt be remedied, and that only by cutting off the greateſt part of our Common-Prayer. For no other remedy will ſerve to help ſo dangerous an inconvenience.

Neh. viii. 3

Acts xx. 9.

Inſtead of ſuch Prayers as the Primitive Churches have uſed, and thoſe that be reformed now uſe, we have (they ſay) divers ſhort cuts or ſhreddings, rather wiſhes than Prayers. T. C. l. i. p. 138. & l. iii. p. 210, 211.

33. The Brethren in Ægypt (ſaith St. Auguſtin, Epiſt. cxxi.) are reported to have many Prayers, but every one of them very ſhort, as if they were darts thrown out with a kind of ſudden quickneſs, leſt that vigilant and erect attention of mind which in Prayer is very neceſſary, ſhould be waſted or dulled through continuance, if their Prayers were few and long. But that which St. Auguſtin doth allow, they condemn. Thoſe Prayers whereunto devout Minds have added a piercing kind of brevity, as well in that reſpect which we have already mentioned, as alſo thereby the better to expreſs that quick and ſpeedy expedition wherewith ardent affections, the very wings of Prayer, are delighted to preſent our ſuits in Heaven, even ſooner than our tongues can deviſe to utter them; they in their mood of contradiction ſpare not openly to deride, and that with ſo baſe terms as do very ill beſeem Men of their gravity. Such ſpeeches are ſcandalous, they

ſavour

ſavour not of God in him that uſeth them, and unto virtuouſly diſpoſed Minds they are grievous corroſives. Our caſe were miſerable, if that wherewith we moſt endeavour to pleaſe God were in his ſight ſo vile and deſpicable, as Men's diſdainful ſpeech would make it.

Leſſons intermingled with our Prayers.

34. Again, for as much as effectual Prayer is joined with a vehement intention of the inferior powers of the Soul, which cannot therein long continue without pain, it hath been therefore thought good ſo by turns to interpoſe ſtill ſomewhat for the higher part of the Mind, the Underſtanding, to work upon, that both being kept in continual exerciſe with variety, neither might feel any great wearineſs, and yet each be a ſpur to other. For Prayer kindleth our deſire to behold God by ſpeculation, and the Mind, delighted with that contemplative ſight of God, taketh every where new inflammations to pray, the riches of the Myſteries of heavenly Wiſdom continually ſtirring up in us correſpondent deſires towards them. So that he which prayeth in due ſort is thereby made the more attentive to hear, and he which heareth, the more earneſt to pray, for the time which we beſtow as well in the one as the other. But for what cauſe ſoever we do it, this intermingling of Leſſons with Prayers is,* in their taſte, a thing as unſavoury, and as unſeemly in their ſight, as if the like ſhould be done in ſuits and ſupplications before ſome mighty

* We have no ſuch forms in Scripture as that we ſhould pray in two or three lines, and then after having read awhile ſome other thing, come and pray as much more, and ſo the twentieth or the thirtieth time, with pauſes between. If a Man ſhould come to a Prince, and having very many things to demand, after he had demanded one thing, would ſtay a long time and then demand another, and ſo the third; the Prince might well think that either he came to aſk before he knew what he had need of, or that he had forgotten ſome piece of his ſuit, or that he were diſtracted in his underſtanding, or ſome other like cauſe of the diſorder of his ſupplication T. C. l. i. p. 138. This kind of reaſon the Prophet in the matter of Sacrifices doth uſe. T. C. l. iii. p. 210.

Prince.

BOOK V. Prince of the World. Our ſpeech to worldly Superiors we frame in ſuch ſort as ſerveth beſt to inform and perſuade the minds of them who otherwiſe neither could nor would greatly regard our neceſſities: whereas, becauſe we know that God is indeed a King, but a great King; who underſtandeth all things before-hand, which no other King beſides doth, a King which needeth not to be informed what we lack; a King readier to grant than we to make our requeſts; therefore in Prayer we do not ſo much reſpect what precepts art delivereth, touching the method of perſuaſive utterance in the preſence of great Men, as what doth moſt avail to our own edification in piety and godly zeal. If they on the contrary ſide do think, that the ſame rules of decency which ſerve for things done unto terrene Powers, ſhould univerſally decide what is fit in the ſervice of God; if it be their meaning to hold it for a maxim, that the Church muſt deliver her publick Supplications unto God, in no other form of ſpeech than ſuch as were decent, if ſuit ſhould be made to the great Turk or ſome other Monarch, let them apply their own rule unto their own form of Common-Prayer. Suppoſe that the People of a whole town, with ſome choſen Men before them, did continually twice or thrice a week reſort to their King, and every time they come, firſt acknowledge themſelves guilty of Rebellions and Treaſons, then ſing a Song, and after that explain ſome Statute of the Land to the Standers by, and therein ſpend at the leaſt an hour; this done, turn themſelves again to the King, and for every ſort of his Subjects crave ſomewhat of him; at the length ſing him another Song, and ſo take their leave: might not the King well think, that either they knew not what they would have, or elſe that they were diſtracted in mind, or ſome other ſuch like cauſe of the diſorder of their Supplication? This form of ſuing unto Kings were abſurd: this form of praying unto God they

they allow. When God was ſerved with legal Sacrifices, ſuch was the miſerable and wretched diſpoſition of ſome Men's minds, that the beſt of every thing they had being culled out for themſelves, if there were in their flocks any poor, ſtarved, or diſeaſed thing, not worth the keeping, they thought it good enough for the Altar of God, pretending (as wiſe Hypocrites do, when they rob God to enrich themſelves) that the fatneſs of Calves doth benefit him nothing: to us the beſt things are moſt profitable; to him all is one, if the mind of the Offerer be good, which is the only thing he reſpecteth. In reproof of which their devout fraud, the Prophet Malachy alledgeth, that Gifts are offered unto God, not as * ſupplies of his want indeed, but yet as teſtimonies of that affection wherewith we acknowledge and honour his greatneſs. For which cauſe, ſith the greater they are whom we honour, the more regard we have to the quality and choice of thoſe Preſents which we bring them for honour's ſake; it muſt needs follow that if we dare not diſgrace our worldly Superiors with offering unto them ſuch refuſe as we bring unto God himſelf, we ſhew plainly that our acknowledgment of his Greatneſs is but feigned; in heart we fear him not ſo much as we dread them. *If ye offer the blind for a Sacrifice, is it not evil? Offer it now unto thy Prince; will he be content or accept thy Perſon? ſaith the Lord of Hoſts. Curſed be the Deceiver which hath in his flock a male, and having made a vow, ſacrificeth unto the Lord a corrupt thing: For I am a great King, ſaith the Lord of Hoſts.* Should we hereupon frame a Rule, that what form of ſpeech or behaviour ſoever is fit for

Mal. i. 8, 14

* Μέρη τιμῆς τὰ δῶρα, τὰ παρ' ἑκάστοις τίμια. Καὶ γὰρ τὸ δῶρόν ἐστι κτήματος δόσις καὶ τιμῆς σημεῖον. Διὸ καὶ οἱ φιλοχρήματοι καὶ οἱ φιλότιμοι ἐφίενται αὐτῶν. Ἀμφότεροι γὰρ ἔχει ὧν δέονται. Καὶ γὰρ κτῆμά ἐστιν οὗ ἐφίενται οἱ φιλοχρήματοι, καὶ τιμὴν ἔχει οὗ οἱ φιλότιμοι. Ariſt. Rhet. lib. i. cap. 5.

BOOK V Suiters in a Prince's Court, the ſame and no other beſeemeth us in our Prayers to Almighty God?

The number of our Prayers for earthly things, and our oft rehearſing of the Lord's Prayer.

35. But in vain we labour to perſuade them that any thing can take away the tedioufneſs of Prayer, except it be brought to the very ſame, both meaſure and form, which themſelves aſſign. Whatſoever therefore our Liturgy hath more than theirs, under one deviſed pretence or other they cut it off. We have of Prayers for earthly things in their opinion too great a number; ſo oft to rehearſe the Lord's Prayer in ſo ſmall a time is, as they think, a loſs of time; * the People's praying after the Miniſter, they ſay, both waſteth time, and alſo maketh an unpleaſant ſound, the Pſalms they would not have to be made (as they are) a part of our Common-Prayer, nor to be ſung or ſaid by turns, nor ſuch Muſick to be uſed with them; thoſe Evangelical Hymns they allow not to ſtand in our Liturgy, the Litany, the Creed of Athanaſius, the Sentence of Glory, wherewith we uſe to conclude Pſalms—theſe things they cancel, as having been inſtituted in regard of occaſions peculiar to the times of old, and as being therefore now ſuperfluous. Touching Prayers for

* I can make no geometrical and exact meaſure, but verily I believe there ſhall be found more than a third part of the Prayers, which are not Pſalms and Texts of Scripture, ſpent in praying for, and praying againſt the commodities and incommodities of this life, which is contrary to all the arguments or contents of the Prayers of the Church ſet down in the Scripture, and eſpecially of our Saviour Chriſt's Prayer, by the which ours ought to be directed. T. C. l. i. p. 136. What a reaſon is this, we muſt repeat the Lord's Prayer oftentimes, thereſore oſtentimes in half an hour, and one in the neck of another? Our Saviour Chriſt doth not there give a preſcript Form of Prayer whereunto he bindeth us but giveth us a Rule and Square to frame all our Prayers by. I know it is neceſſary to pray, and pray often. I know alſo that in a few words it is impoſſible for any Man to frame ſo pithy a Prayer, and I confeſs that the Church doth well in concluding their Prayers with the Lord's Prayer: but I ſtand upon this, that there is no neceſſity laid upon us to uſe theſe very words and no more. T. C. l. i. p. 219.

things

things earthly, we ought not to think that the Church hath ſet down ſo many of them without cauſe. They peradventure, which find this fault, are of the ſame affection with Solomon; ſo that if God ſhould offer to grant them whatſoever they aſk, they would neither crave riches, nor length of days, nor yet victory over their enemies, but only an underſtanding heart; for which cauſe themſelves having eagles wings, are offended to ſee others fly ſo near the ground. But the tender kindneſs of the Church of God it very well beſeemeth to help the weaker ſort, which are by ſo great odds more in number, although ſome few of the perfecter and ſtronger may be therewith for a time diſpleaſed. Ignorant we are not, that of ſuch as reſorted to our Saviour Chriſt being preſent on Earth, there came not any unto him with better ſucceſs for the benefit of their Souls' everlaſting happineſs, than they whoſe bodily neceſſities gave them the firſt occaſion to ſeek relief, where they ſaw willingneſs and ability of doing every way good unto all. The graces of the Spirit are much more precious than worldly benefits; our ghoſtly evils of greater importance than any harm which the body feeleth. Therefore our deſires to Heaven-ward ſhould both in meaſure and number no leſs exceed, than their glorious Object doth every way excel in value. Theſe things are true and plain in the eye of a perfect judgment. But yet it muſt be withal conſidered, that the greateſt part of the World are they which be fartheſt from perfection. Such being better able by ſenſe to diſcern the wants of this preſent life, than by ſpiritual capacity to apprehend things above ſenſe which tend to their happineſs in the World to come, are in that reſpect the more apt to apply their minds even with hearty affection and zeal at the leaſt unto thoſe branches of publick Prayer wherein their own particular is moved. And by this mean there ſtealeth upon them a double benefit; firſt, becauſe that good affection which

BOOK V. things of ſmaller account have once ſet on work is by ſo much the more eaſily raiſed higher; and ſecondly, in that the very cuſtom of ſeeking ſo particular aid and relief at the hands of God, doth by a ſecret contradiction withdraw them from endeavouring to help themſelves by thoſe wicked ſhifts, which they know can never have his allowance whoſe aſſiſtance their Prayer ſeeketh. Theſe multiplied Petitions of worldly things in Prayer have therefore, beſides their direct uſe, a ſervice, whereby the Church under-hand, through a kind of heavenly fraud, taketh therewith the Souls of Men as with certain baits. If then their calculation be true (for ſo they reckon) that a full third of our Prayers be allotted unto earthly benefits, for which our Saviour in his platform hath appointed but one Petition amongſt ſeven, the difference is without any great diſagreement; we reſpecting what Men are, and doing that which is meet in regard of the common imperfection; our Lord contrariwiſe propoſing the moſt abſolute proportion that can be in Men's deſires, the very higheſt mark whereat we are able to aim. For which cauſe alſo our cuſtom is both to place it in the front of our Prayers as a guide, * and to add it in the end of ſome principal limbs or parts, as a complement which fully perfecteth whatſoever may be defective in the reſt. Twice we rehearſe it ordinarily, and oftener as occaſion requireth more ſolemnity or length in the form of divine Service; not miſtruſting, till theſe new curioſities ſprang up, that ever any Man would think our labour herein miſſpent, the time waſtefully conſumed, and the Office itſelf made worſe, by ſo repeating that which otherwiſe would more hardly be made familiar to the ſimpler ſort; for the good of whoſe Souls there is

* Præmiſſa legitima et ordinaria oratione, quaſi fundamento, accidentium jus eſt deſideriorum, jus eſt ſuperſtruendi extrinſecus petitiones. Tertul. de Orat.

not

not in Chriſtian Religion any thing of like continual uſe and force throughout every hour and moment of their whole lives. I mean not only becauſe Prayer, but becauſe this very Prayer is of ſuch efficacy and neceſſity: for that our Saviour did but ſet Men a bare example how to contrive or deviſe Prayers of their own, and no way bind them to uſe this, is no doubt an error. John the Baptiſt's Diſciples, which had been always brought up in the boſom of God's Church from the time of their firſt infancy, till they came to the ſchool of John, were not ſo brutiſh that they could be ignorant how to call upon the Name of God; but of their Maſter they had received a form of Prayer amongſt themſelves, which form none did uſe ſaving his Diſciples, ſo that by it, as by a mark of ſpecial difference, they were known from others. And of this the Apoſtles having taken notice, they requeſt that as John had taught his, ſo Chriſt would likewiſe teach them to pray. Tertullian and St. Auguſtin do for that cauſe term it, *Orationem legitimam*, the Prayer which Chriſt's own Law hath tied his Church to uſe in the ſame preſcript form of words wherewith he himſelf did deliver it; and therefore what part of the World ſoever we fall into, if Chriſtian Religion have been there received, the ordinary uſe of this very Prayer hath with equal continuance accompanied the ſame, as one of the principal and moſt material duties of honour done to Jeſus Chriſt. *Seeing that we have* (ſaith St. Cyprian) *an Advocate with the Father for our ſins, when we that have ſinned come to ſeek for pardon, let us alledge unto God the words which our Advocate hath taught. For ſith his promiſe is our plain warrant, that in his Name what we aſk we ſhall receive, muſt we not needs much the rather obtain that for which we ſue, if not only his Name do countenance, but alſo his Speech preſent our requeſts?* Though Men ſhould ſpeak with the Tongues of Angels, yet words ſo pleaſing to the ears of God as thoſe which the Son of God himſelf hath compoſed, were

Luke xi. 1.

Cypr. in Orat. Dom.

BOOK V. were not poſſible for Men to frame. He therefore which made us to live, hath alſo taught us to pray, to the end that, ſpeaking unto the Father in his Son's own preſcript form, without ſcholy or gloſs of ours, we may be ſure that we utter nothing which God will either diſallow or deny. Other Prayers we uſe many beſides this, and this oftener than any other; although not tied ſo to do by any Commandment of Scripture, yet moved with ſuch conſiderations as have been before ſet down: the cauſeleſs diſlike whereof which others have conceived, is no ſufficient reaſon for us as much as once to forbear, in any place, a thing which, uttered with true devotion and zeal of heart, affordeth to God himſelf that glory, that aid to the weakeſt ſort of Men, to the moſt perfect that ſolid comfort which is unſpeakable.

The People's ſaying after the Miniſter.

36 With our Lord's Prayer they would find no fault, ſo that they might perſuade us to uſe it before or after Sermons only (becauſe ſo their manner is), and not (as all Chriſtian People have been of old accuſtomed) inſert it ſo often in the Liturgy. But the People's cuſtom to repeat any thing after the Miniſter, they utterly miſlike.* Twice we appoint that the words which the Miniſter firſt pronounceth, the whole Congregation ſhall repeat after him: as firſt in the publick Confeſſion of Sins, and again in rehearſal of our Lord's Prayer preſently after the bleſſed Sacrament of his Body and Blood received—a thing no way offenſive, no way unfit or unſeemly to be done, although it had been ſo appointed oftener than with

* Another fault is, that all the People are appointed in divers places to ſay after the Miniſter, whereby not only the time is unprofitably waſted, and a confuſed noiſe of the People (one ſpeaking after another) cauſed, but an opinion bred in their heads, that thoſe only be their Prayers which they pronounce with their own mouths after the Miniſter, otherwiſe than the order which is left to the Church doth bear, 1 Cor xiv. 16. and otherwiſe than Juſtin Martyr ſheweth the cuſtom of the Churches to have been in his time. T. C. l. i. p. 139, & l. iii. p. 211, 212, 213.

us

us it is. But ſurely, with ſo good reaſon it ſtandeth in thoſe two places, that otherwiſe to order it were not in all reſpects ſo well. Could there be any thing deviſed better, than that we all, at our firſt acceſs unto God by Prayer, ſhould acknowledge meekly our ſins, and that not only in heart but with tongue; all which are preſent being made ear-witneſſes even of every Man's diſtinct and deliberate aſſent unto each particular branch of a common indictment drawn againſt ourſelves? How were it poſſible that the Church ſhould any way elſe with ſuch eaſe and certainty provide that none of her Children may, as Adam, diſſemble that wretchedneſs, the penitent confeſſion whereof is ſo neceſſary a preamble, eſpecially to common Prayer? In like manner, if the Church did ever deviſe a thing fit and convenient, what more than this, that when together we have all received thoſe heavenly Myſteries wherein Chriſt imparteth himſelf unto us, and giveth viſible teſtification of our bleſſed Communion with him, we ſhould, in hatred of all Hereſies, Factions and Schiſms, the Paſtor as a Leader, the People as willing Followers of him ſtep by ſtep, declare openly ourſelves united as Brethren in one, by offering up with all our hearts and tongues that moſt effectual Supplication,* wherein he unto whom we offer it hath himſelf not only comprehended all our neceſſities, but in ſuch ſort alſo framed every Petition, as might moſt naturally ſerve for many, and doth, though not always require, yet always import a multitude of Speakers together? For which cauſe Communicants have ever uſed it, and we at that time by the form of our very utterance do ſhew we uſe it, yea, every word and ſyllable of it, as Communicants. In the reſt we obſerve that cuſtom whereunto St. Paul alludeth, and whereof the Fathers of the Church in their writings make often mention, to ſhew indefi- 1 Cor xiv. 16.

* Τὶς γὰρ ἔτι ἐχθρὸν ἡγεῖσθαι δύναται μεθ' οὗ μίαν ἀφῆκε πρὸς Θεὸν τὴν φωνήν. Baſil. Præf. in Pſal.

nitely

BOOK V. nitely what was done, but not universally to bind for ever all Prayers unto one only fashion of utterance. The reasons which we have alledged, induce us to think it still a good work, which they in their pensive care for the well bestowing of time account waste. As for unpleasantness of sound, if it happen, the good of Men's Souls doth either deceive our ears that we note it not, or arm them with patience to endure it. We are not so nice as to cast away a sharp knife, because the edge of it may sometimes grate; and such subtil opinions, as few but Utopians are likely to fall into, we in this climate do not greatly fear.

Our manner of reading the Psalms otherwise than the rest of the Scripture.

37. The complaint which they make about Psalms and Hymns, might as well be overpast without any answer, as it is without any cause brought forth. But our desire is to content them, if it may be, and to yield them a just reason even of the least things, wherein undeservedly they have but as much as dreamed or suspected that we do amiss. They seem sometimes so to speak, as if it greatly offended them that such Hymns and Psalms as are Scripture should in Common-Prayer be otherwise used than the rest of the Scripture is wont;* sometimes displeased they are at the artificial Musick which we add unto Psalms of this kind, or of any other nature else; sometime the plainest and the most intelligible rehearsal of them yet they favour not, because it is done by interlocution, and with a mutual return of sentences from side to side. They are not ignorant what difference there is between other parts of Scripture and Psalms. The choice and flower of † all things profitable in other Books, the

* They have always the same profit to be studied in, to be read, and preached upon, which other Scriptures have, and this above the rest, that they are to be sung But to make daily Prayers of them, hand over head, or otherwise than the present estate wherein we be doth agree with the matter contained in them, is an abusing of them. T. C. l. iii. p. 206.

† Ἡ περιεκτικὴ τῶν πανιέρων ὑμνολογία. Dionys. Hierar. Eccles. cap. iii.

Psalms

Pſalms do both more briefly contain, and more movingly alſo expreſs, by reaſon of that poetical form wherewith they are written. The Ancients, when they ſpeak of the Book of Pſalms, uſe to fall into large diſcourſes, ſhewing how this part above the reſt doth of purpoſe ſet forth and celebrate all the conſiderations and operations which belong to God; it magnifieth the holy meditations and actions of divine Men; it is of things heavenly an univerſal declaration, working in them whoſe hearts God inſpireth with the due conſideration thereof, an habit or diſpoſition of mind whereby they are made fit veſſels, both for receipt and for delivery of whatſoever ſpiritual perfection. What is there neceſſary for Man to know, which the Pſalms are not able to teach? They are to beginners an eaſy and familiar introduction, a mighty augmentation of all virtue and knowledge in ſuch as are entered before, a ſtrong confirmation to the moſt perfect amongſt others. Heroical Magnanimity, exquiſite Juſtice, grave Moderation, exact Wiſdom, Repentance unfeigned, unwearied Patience, the Myſteries of God, the Sufferings of Chriſt, the Terrors of Wrath, the Comforts of Grace, the Works of Providence over this World, and the promiſed Joys of that World which is to come, all good neceſſarily to be either known, or done, or had, this one celeſtial Fountain yieldeth. Let there be any grief or diſeaſe incident unto the Soul of Man, any wound or ſickneſs named, for which there is not in this Treaſure-houſe a preſent comfortable remedy at all times ready to be found. Hereof it is, that we covet to make the Pſalms eſpecially familiar unto all. This is the very cauſe why we iterate the Pſalms oftener than any other part of Scripture beſides; the cauſe wherefore we inure the People together with their Miniſter, and not the Miniſter alone, to read them as other parts of Scripture he doth.

Of Muſick with Pſalms.

38. Touching muſical Harmony whether by inſtrument or by voice, it being but of high and low in

ſounds

BOOK V. ſounds a due proportionable diſpoſition, ſuch notwithſtanding is the force thereof, and ſo pleaſing effects it hath in that very part of Man which is moſt divine, that ſome have been thereby induced to think that the Soul itſelf by nature is, or hath in it Harmony; a thing which delighteth all ages, and beſeemeth all ſtates; a thing as ſeaſonable in grief as in joy; as decent being added unto actions of greateſt weight and ſolemnity, as being uſed when Men moſt ſequeſter themſelves from action. The reaſon hereof is an admirable facility which Muſick hath to expreſs and repreſent to the Mind, more inwardly than any other ſenſible mean, the very ſtanding, riſing and falling, the very ſteps and inflections every way, the turns and varieties of all Paſſions, whereunto the Mind is ſubject; yea, ſo to imitate them, that, whether it reſemble unto us the ſame ſtate wherein our Minds already are, or a clean contrary, we are not more contentedly by the one confirmed, than changed and led away by the other. In Harmony the very image and character even of Virtue and Vice is perceived, the Mind delighted with their reſemblances, and brought by having them often iterated into a love of the things themſelves. For which cauſe there is nothing more contagious and peſtilent than ſome kinds of Harmony, than ſome, nothing more ſtrong and potent unto good. And that there is ſuch a difference of one kind from another we need no proof but our own experience, in as much as we are at the hearing of ſome more inclined unto ſorrow and heavineſs, of ſome more mollified and ſoftened in mind; one kind apter to ſtay and ſettle us, another to move and ſtir our affections; there is that draweth to a marvellous grave and ſober mediocrity; there is alſo that carrieth as it were into ecſtaſies, filling the Mind with an heavenly joy, and for the time in a manner ſevering it from the body: ſo that, although we lay altogether aſide the conſideration of ditty or matter, the very Harmony of ſounds being framed in due ſort, and carried from

the

the ear to the ſpiritual faculties of our Souls, is by a native puiſſance and efficacy greatly available to bring to a perfect temper whatſoever is there troubled, apt as well to quicken the ſpirits as to allay that which is too eager, ſovereign againſt melancholy and deſpair, forcible to draw forth tears of devotion, if the Mind be ſuch as can yield them, able both to move and to moderate all affections. The Prophet David having therefore ſingular knowledge, not in Poetry alone, but in Muſick alſo, judged them both to be things moſt neceſſary for the Houſe of God, left behind him to that purpoſe a number of divinely indited Poems, and was further the Author of adding unto Poetry Melody in publick Prayer, Melody both vocal and inſtrumental for the raiſing up of Men's hearts and the ſweetening of their affections towards God. In which conſiderations the Church of Chriſt doth likewiſe at this preſent day retain it as an ornament to God's ſervice, and an help to our own devotion. They which, under pretence of the Law Ceremonial abrogated, require the abrogation of inſtrumental Muſick, approving nevertheleſs the uſe of vocal Melody to remain, muſt ſhew ſome reaſon wherefore the one ſhould be thought a Legal Ceremony and not the other. In Church Muſick curioſity and oſtentation of art, wanton, or light, or unſuitable harmony, ſuch as only pleaſeth the ear, and doth not naturally ſerve to the very kind and degree of thoſe impreſſions which the matter that goeth with it leaveth, or is apt to leave in Men's Minds, doth rather blemiſh and diſgrace that we do, than add either beauty or furtherance unto it. On the other ſide, the faults prevented, the force and efficacy of the thing itſelf, when it drowneth not utterly, but fitly ſuiteth with matter altogether ſounding to the praiſe of God, is in truth moſt admirable, and doth much edify, if not the underſtanding, becauſe it teacheth not, yet ſurely the affection, becauſe therein it worketh much. They muſt have hearts very dry and tough, from

whom

BOOK V. whom the melody of the Psalms doth not sometime draw that wherein a Mind religiously affected delighteth. Be it as Rabanus Maurus observeth, that at the first the Church in this exercise was more simple and plain than we are; that their singing was little more than only a melodious kind of pronunciation; that the custom which we now use was not instituted so much for their cause which are spiritual, as to the end that into grosser and heavier minds, whom bare words do not easily move, the sweetness of Melody might make some entrance for good things. St. Basil himself acknowledging as much, did not think that from such inventions, the least jot of estimation and credit thereby should be derogated: **For* (saith he) *whereas the holy Spirit saw that Mankind is unto Virtue hardly drawn, and that Righteousness is the least accounted of, by reason of the proneness of our affections to that which delighteth; it pleased the Wisdom of the same Spirit to borrow from Melody that pleasure which, mingled with heavenly Mysteries, causeth the smoothness and softness of that which toucheth the ear, to convey, as it were by stealth, the treasure of good things into Man's Mind. To this purpose were those harmonious tunes of Psalms devised for us, that they which are either in years but young, or touching perfection of Virtue as yet not grown to ripeness, might, when they think they sing, learn. O the wise conceit of that heavenly Teacher which hath by his skill found out a way, that doing those things wherein we delight we may also learn that whereby we profit!*

* Ἐπειδὴ γὰρ εἶδε τὸ Πνεῦμα τὸ ἅγιον δυσάγωγον πρὸς ἀρετὴν τὸ γένος τῶν ἀνθρώπων, καὶ διὰ τὸ πρὸς ἡδονὴν ἐπιῤῥεπὲς τοῦ ὀρθοῦ βίου καταμελοῦντας ἡμᾶς, τί ποιεῖ; τὸ ἐκ τῆς μελωδίας τερπνὸν τοῖς δόγμασιν ἐγκατέμιξεν, ἵνα τῷ προσηνεῖ καὶ λείῳ τῆς ἀκοῆς τὸ ἐκ τῶν λόγων ὠφέλιμον λανθανόντως ὑποδεξώμεθα. Διὰ τοῦτο, τὰ ἐναρμόνια ταῦτα μέλη τῶν ψαλμῶν ἡμῖν ἐπινενόηται, ἵνα οἱ παῖδες τὴν ἡλικίαν ἢ καὶ ὅλως οἱ νεαροὶ τὸ ἦθος τῷ μὲν δοκεῖν μελῳδῶσι, τῇ δὲ ἀληθείᾳ τὰς ψυχὰς ἐκπαιδεύωνται· ὢ τῆς σοφῆς ἐπινοίας τοῦ διδασκάλου ὁμοῦ τε ᾄδειν ἡμᾶς καὶ τὰ λυσιτελῆ μανθάνειν μηχανωμένου. Basil. in Psal.

39. And

Of singing or saying Psalms and other parts of Common-Prayer, wherein the People and Minister answer one another by course.

39. And if the Prophet David did think that the very meeting of Men together, and their accompanying one another to the House of God, should make the Bond of their Love insoluble, and tie them in a league of inviolable amity, Psal. liv. 14;* how much more may we judge it reasonable to hope that the like effects may grow in each of the People towards other, in them all towards their Pastor, and in their Pastor towards every of them; between whom there daily and interchangeably pass in the hearing of God himself, and in the presence of his holy Angels, so many heavenly Acclamations, Exultations, Provocations, Petitions, Songs of Comfort, Psalms of Praise and Thanksgiving? in all which particulars, as when the Pastor maketh their suits, and they with one voice testify a general assent thereunto; or when he joyfully beginneth, and they with like alacrity follow, dividing between them the sentences wherewith they strive which shall most shew his own and stir up others zeal, to the glory of that God whose Name they magnify, or when he proposeth unto God their necessities and they their own requests for relief in every of them; or when he lifteth up his voice like a trumpet to proclaim unto them the Laws of God, they adjoining, though not as Israel did, by way of generality a chearful promise, *All that the Lord hath commanded, we will do*; yet that which God doth no less approve, that which savoureth more of meekness, that which testifieth rather a feeling knowledge of our common imbecility, unto the several branches thereof, several

Exod. xix 8. and xxiv 3. Deut. v 27. and xxvi. 17. Josh. xxiv. 16.

* For the singing of Psalms by course, and side after side, although it be very ancient, yet it is not commendable; and so much the more to be suspected, for that the Devil hath gone about to get it so great Authority, partly by deriving it from Ignatius's time, and partly in making the World believe that this came from Heaven, and that the Angels were heard to sing after this sort: which as it is a mere fable, so it is confuted by Historiographers, whereof some ascribe the beginning of this to Damasus, some other unto Flavianus and Diodorus. T. C. l. i. p. 203.

 lowly

BOOK V. lowly and humble requests for Grace at the merciful hands of God, to perform the thing which is commanded; or when they wish reciprocally each other's ghostly happiness; or when he by exhortation raiseth them up, and they by protestation of their readiness declare he speaketh not in vain unto them. These interlocutory forms of speech what are they else, but most effectual, partly testifications and partly inflammations of all Piety? When, and how this custom of singing by course came up in the Church, it is not certainly known. Socrates maketh Ignatius, the Bishop of Antioch, in Syria, the first beginner thereof, even under the Apostles themselves. But against Socrates they set the authority of Theodoret, who draweth the original of it from Antioch, as Socrates doth; howbeit ascribing the invention to others, Flavian and Diodore, Men which constantly stood in defence of the Apostolick Faith against the Bishop of the Church, Leontius, a favourer of the Arians. Against both Socrates and Theodoret, Platina is brought as a witness to testify that Damasus, Bishop of Rome, began it in his time. Of the Latin Church, it may be true which Platina saith. And therefore, the eldest of that Church which maketh any mention thereof is St. Ambrose,* Bishop of Milan, at the same time when Damasus was of Rome. Amongst the Grecians, St. Basil having brought it into his Church before they of Neocæsarea used it, Sabellius the Heretick, and Marcellus, took occasion thereat to incense the Churches against him, as being the Author of new devices in the Service of God. Whereupon, to avoid the opinion of novelty and singularity, he

Socrat Hist. Eccl. lib. vi. c. 8.

Theod. lib. ii. cap 24.

Plat. in vita Damasi.

Basil Epist. 63.

* Bene mari plerumque comparatur Ecclesia, quæ primo ingredientis populi agmine totis vestibulis undas vomit; deinde in oratione totius plebis tanquam undis refluentibus stridet; tum responsoriis Psalmorum, cantu virorum, mulierum, virginum, parvulorum consonus undarum fragor resultat. Hexam. lib. ii. cap. 5.

alledgeth

alledgeth for that which he himſelf did the example BOOK V.
of the Churches of Egypt, Libya, Thebes, Paleſtina, Tharabians, Phœnicians, Syrians, Meſopotamians, and, in a manner, all that reverenced the cuſtom of ſinging Pſalms, together. If the Syrians had it then before Baſil, Antioch, the Mother Church of thoſe parts, muſt needs have uſed it before Baſil, and conſequently before Damaſus. The queſtion is then, how long before, and whether ſo long, that Ignatius, or as ancient as Ignatius, may be probably thought the firſt Inventors. Ignatius in Trajan's days ſuffered Martyrdom. And of the Churches in Pontus and Bithynia, to Trajan the Emperor, his own Vicegerent there affirmeth, that the only crime he knew of them was, they uſed to meet together at a certain day, and to praiſe Chriſt with Hymns as a God, *ſecum invicem*, one to another amongſt themſelves. Which, for any thing we know to the contrary, might be the ſelf-ſame form which Philo Judæus expreſſeth, declaring how the Eſſenes were accuſtomed with Hymns and Pſalms to honour God, ſometime all exalting their voices together in one, and ſometime one part anſwering another, wherein as he thought they ſwerved not much from the pattern of Moſes and Miriam. Whether Ignatius did at any time hear the Angels praiſing God after that ſort or no, what matter is it? If Ignatius did not, yet one which muſt be with us of great authority did. *I ſaw the Lord* (ſaith the Prophet Iſaiah) *on an high Throne*; *the Seraphim ſtood upon it*; *one cried to another*, *ſaying*, *Holy*, *holy*, *holy*, *Lord God of Hoſts*, *the whole World is full of his glory*. But whoſoever were the Author, whatſoever the time, whenſoever the example of beginning this Cuſtom in the Church of Chriſt; ſith we are wont to ſuſpect things only before trial, and afterwards either to approve them as good, or if we find them evil, accordingly to judge of them; their counſel muſt need ſeem very unſeaſonable, who adviſe Men now to ſuſpect that wherewith the World

Plin Secund. Epiſt. lib. x. p. 97.

Exod. xv. 1, 21.

Iſa. vi. 3.

BOOK V. hath had, by their own account, twelve hundred years acquaintance and upwards, enough to take away ſuſpicion and jealouſy. Men know by this time, if ever they will know, whether it be good or evil which hath been ſo long retained. As for the Devil, which way it ſhould greatly benefit him to have this manner of ſinging Pſalms accounted an invention of Ignatius, or an imitation of the Angels of Heaven, we do not well underſtand. But we very well ſee, in them who thus plead, a wonderful celerity of diſcourſe. For perceiving, at the firſt, but only ſome cauſe of ſuſpicion and fear leſt it ſhould be evil, they are preſently in one and the ſelf-ſame breath reſolved, *that *what beginning ſoever it had, there is no poſſibility it ſhould be good.* The potent arguments which did thus ſuddenly break in upon them, and overcome them, are; firſt, that it is not unlawful for the People all jointly to praiſe God in ſinging of Pſalms. Secondly, that they are not any where forbidden by the Law of God, to ſing every verſe of the whole Pſalm, both with heart and voice, quite and clean throughout. Thirdly, that it cannot be underſtood what is ſung after our manner. Of which three, foraſmuch as lawfulneſs to ſing one way, proveth not another way inconvenient, the former two are true allegations, but they lack ſtrength to accompliſh their deſire; the third ſo ſtrong, that it might

* From whenceſoever it came it cannot be good, conſidering, that when it is granted, that all the People may praiſe God (as it is in ſinging of Pſalms) then this ought not to be reſtrained unto a few; and where it is lawful, both with heart and voice, to ſing the whole Pſalm, there it is not meet that they ſhould ſing but the one half with their heart and voice, and the other with their heart only. For where they may both with heart and voice ſing, there the heart is not enough. Therefore beſides the incommodity which cometh this way, in that being toſſed after this ſort, Men cannot underſtand what is ſung, thoſe other two inconveniencies come of this form of ſinging, and therefore it is baniſhed in all reformed Churches. T. C. l. i. p. 203.

might perſuade, if the truth thereof were not doubtful. And ſhall this enforce us to baniſh a thing which all Chriſtian Churches in the World have received; a thing which ſo many ages have held; a thing which the moſt approved Councils and Laws have ſo oftentimes ratified; a thing which was never found to have any inconvenience in it; a thing which always heretofore the beſt Men and wiſeſt Governors of God's People did think they could never commend enough; a thing which, as Baſil was perſuaded, did both ſtrengthen the meditation of thoſe holy words which were uttered in that ſort, and ſerve alſo to make attentive, and to raiſe up the hearts of Men; a thing whereunto God's People of old did reſort with hope and thirſt, that thereby eſpecially their ſouls might be edified; a thing which filleth the Mind with comfort and heavenly delight, ſtirreth up fragrant deſires and affections correſpondent unto that which the words contain; allayeth all kind of baſe and earthly cogitations, baniſheth and driveth away thoſe evil ſecret ſuggeſtions which our inviſible Enemy is always apt to miniſter, watereth the heart to the end it may fructify, maketh the virtuous in trouble full of magnanimity and courage, ſerveth as a moſt approved remedy againſt all doleful and heavy accidents which befall Men in this preſent life; to conclude, ſo fitly accordeth with the Apoſtle's own exhortation, *Speak to yourſelves in Pſalms and Hymns, and ſpiritual Songs, making melody, and ſinging to the Lord in your hearts*; that ſurely there is more cauſe to fear leſt the want thereof be a maim, than the uſe a blemiſh to the Service of God. It is not our meaning, that what we attribute unto the Pſalms, ſhould be thought to depend altogether on that only form of ſinging or reading them by courſe, as with us the manner is; but the end of our ſpeech is to ſhew, that becauſe the Fathers of the Church, with whom the ſelf-ſame Cuſtom was ſo many ages ago in uſe, have uttered all

BOOK V.

Eph. v. 1.

BOOK V. theſe things concerning the fruit which the Church of God did then reap, obſerving that and no other form, it may be juſtly avouched, that we ourſelves retaining it, and beſides it alſo the other more newly and not unfruitfully deviſed, do neither want that good which the latter invention can afford, nor loſe any thing of that for which the Ancients ſo oft and ſo highly commend the former. Let novelty therefore in this give over endleſs contradictions, and let ancient Cuſtom prevail.

Of Magnificat, Benedictus, and Nunc dimittis.

40. We have already given cauſe ſufficient for the great conveniency and uſe of reading the Pſalms oftner than other Scriptures. Of reading or ſinging likewiſe *Magnificat*, *Benedictus*, and *Nunc dimittis*, oftner than the reſt of the Pſalms, the cauſes are no whit leſs reaſonable; ſo that if the one may very well monthly, the other may as well even daily be iterated. They are Songs which concern us ſo much more than the Songs of David, as the Goſpel toucheth us more than the Law, the New Teſtament than the Old. And if the Pſalms for the excellency of their uſe deſerve to be oftner repeated than they are, but that the multitude of them permitteth not any oftner repetition, what diſorder is it, if theſe few Evangelical Hymns, which are in no reſpect leſs worthy, and may be by reaſon of their paucity imprinted with much more eaſe in all Men's memories, be for that cauſe every day rehearſed? In our own behalf it is convenient and orderly enough, that both they and we make day by day Prayers and Supplications the very ſame; why not as fit and convenient to magnify the Name of God day by day with certain the very ſelf-ſame Pſalms of Praiſe and Thankſgiving? Either let them not allow the one, or elſe ceaſe to reprove the other. For the ancient received uſe of intermingling Hymns and Pſalms with divine readings, enough hath been written. And if any may fitly ſerve unto that purpoſe, how ſhould it better have been deviſed, than that a competent

number

number of the Old being firſt read, theſe of the New ſhould ſucceed in the place where now they are ſet? In which place notwithſtanding, there is joined with *Benedictus* the hundredth Pſalm; with *Magnificat* the ninety-eighth; the ſixty-ſeventh with *Nunc dimittis*; and in every of them the choice left free for the Miniſter to uſe indifferently the one for the other. Seeing therefore they pretend no quarrel at other Pſalms, which are in like manner appointed alſo to be daily read, why do theſe ſo much offend and diſpleaſe their taſte? They are the firſt gratulations wherewith our Lord and Saviour was joyfully received at his entrance into the World, by ſuch as in their hearts, arms, and very bowels embraced him; being prophetical diſcoveries of Chriſt already preſent, whoſe future coming the other Pſalms did but fore-ſignify; they are againſt the obſtinate incredulity of the Jews the moſt luculent teſtimonies that Chriſtian Religion hath; yea, the only ſacred Hymns they are that Chriſtianity hath peculiar unto itſelf, the other being Songs too of Praiſe and Thankſgiving, but Songs wherewith as we ſerve God, ſo the Jew likewiſe. And whereas they tell us, theſe Songs were fit for that purpoſe when Simeon and Zachary and the bleſſed Virgin uttered them, but cannot ſo be to us which have not received like benefit; *ſhould they not remember how expreſsly Hezekiah, amongſt many other good things, is commended for this alſo, that the Praiſes of God were through his appointment daily ſet forth, by uſing in publick divine Service the Songs of David and Aſaph unto that very end? Either there wanted wiſe Men to give Hezekiah advice, and to inform him of that which in his caſe was as true as it is in

BOOK V.

2 Chron. xxix. 30.

* Theſe thankſgivings were made by occaſion of certain particular Benefits, and are no more to be uſed for ordinary Prayers, than the *Ave Maria*. So that both for this cauſe, and the other before alledged of the Pſalms, it is not convenient to make ordinary Prayers of them. T. C. lib. iii. p. 208.

BOOK V. ours; namely, that without ſome inconvenience and diſorder he could not appoint thoſe Pſalms to be uſed as ordinary Prayers, ſeeing that although they were Songs of Thankſgiving, ſuch as David and Aſaph had ſpecial occaſion to uſe, yet not ſo the whole Church and People afterwards whom like occaſions did not befal; or elſe Hezekiah was perſuaded as we are, that the Praiſes of God in the mouths of his Saints are not ſo reſtrained to their own particular, but that others may both conveniently and fruitfully uſe them; firſt, becauſe the myſtical Communion of all faithful Men is ſuch as maketh every one to be intereſted in thoſe precious bleſſings which any one of them receiveth at God's hands: ſecondly, becauſe when any thing is ſpoken to extol the Goodneſs of God, whoſe *Mercy endureth for ever*, albeit the very particular occaſion whereupon it riſeth do come no more; yet, the Fountain continuing the ſame, and yielding other new effects which are but only in ſome ſort proportionable, a ſmall reſemblance between the benefits which we and others have received may ſerve to make the ſame words of Praiſe and Thankſgiving fit, though not equally in all circumſtances fit for both; a clear demonſtration whereof we have in all the ancient Fathers' Commentaries and Meditations upon the Pſalms. Laſt of all, becauſe even when there is not as much as the ſhew of any reſemblance; nevertheleſs by often uſing their words in ſuch manner, our Minds are daily more and more enured with their affections.

Of the Litany.

41. The publick eſtate of the Church of God amongſt the Jews hath had many rare and extraordinary Occurrences; which alſo were occaſions of ſundry * open Solemnities and Offices, whereby the

* We pray for the avoiding of thoſe dangers which are nothing near us; as from lightning and thundering in the midſt of winter; from ſtorms and tempeſt, when the weather is moſt fair, and the ſeas moſt calm. It is true, that upon ſome urgent calamity

People did with general consent make shew of correspondent affection towards God. The like Duties appear usual in the ancient Church of Christ, by that which Tertullian speaketh of Christian Women themselves matching with Infidels. *She cannot content the Lord with performance of his Discipline, that hath at her side a Vassal whom Satan hath made his Vice-agent to cross whatsoever the Faithful should do. If her presence be required at the time of Station, or standing Prayer, he chargeth her at no time but that to be with him in his baths; if a Fasting-day come, he hath on that day a banquet to make; if there be cause for the Church to go forth in solemn Procession, his whole Family have such business come upon them that no one can be spared.* These Processions, as it seemeth, were first begun for the interring of holy Martyrs, and the visiting of those places where they were intombed. Which

Tertul. lib. ii. ad Uxor.

mity a Prayer may, and ought to be framed, which may beg either the commodity for want whereof the Church is in distress, or the turning away of that mischief which either approacheth, or is already upon it. But to make those Prayers, which are for the present time and danger, ordinary and daily Prayers, I cannot hitherto see any, either Scripture, or example of the primitive Church. And here, for the Simple's sake, I will set down after what sort this abuse crept into the Church There was one Mamercus, Bishop of Vienna, which, in the time of great earthquakes which were in France, instituted certain Supplications which the Grecians (and we of them) call the Litany, which concerned that matter: there is no doubt but as other discommodities rose in other Countries, they likewise had Prayers accordingly. Now Pope Gregory either made himself, or gathered the Supplications that were made against the calamities of every Country, and made of them a great Litany or Supplication, as Platina calleth it, and gave it to be used in all Churches: which thing albeit all Churches might do for the time, in respect of the case of the calamity which the Churches suffered; yet there is no cause, why it should be perpetual that was ordained but for a time; and why all lands should pray to be delivered from the incommodities that some land hath been troubled with. T. C. lib. 1. pag. 137. Exod. xv. 20. Wisd. x. 20. 2 Sam. vi. 2. 1 Chron. xiii. 5. 2 Chron. xx. 3. Joel ii. 15.

thing,

thing, the name itſelf applied by Heathens unto the Office of Exequies, and partly the ſpeeches of ſome of the Ancients delivered concerning * Chriſtian Proceſſions, partly alſo the very droſs which Superſtition thereunto added, I mean, the Cuſtom of invocating Saints in Proceſſion, heretofore uſual, do ſtrongly inſinuate. And as things invented to one purpoſe are by uſe eaſily converted to more, it grew, that Supplications, with this Solemnity for the appeaſing of God's wrath and the averting of publick evils, were of the Greek Church termed Litanies, Rogations of the Latin. To the People of Vienna (Mamercus being their Biſhop above four hundred and fifty years after Chriſt) there befel many things, the ſuddenneſs and ſtrangeneſs whereof ſo amazed the hearts of all Men, that the City they began to forſake as a place which Heaven did threaten with imminent Ruin. It beſeemeth not the Perſon of ſo grave a Prelate to be either utterly without counſel, as the reſt were, or in a common perplexity to ſhew himſelf alone ſecure. Wherefore as many as remained he earneſtly exhorteth to prevent portended Calamities, uſing thoſe virtuous and holy means wherewith others in like caſe have prevailed with God. To which purpoſe he perfecteth the Rogations or Litanies before in uſe, and addeth unto them that which the preſent neceſſity required. Their good ſucceſs moved Sidonius, Biſhop of Averna, to uſe the ſame ſo corrected Rogations at ſuch time as he and his People were after afflicted with famine and beſieged with potent Adverſaries. For till the empty name of the Empire came to be ſettled in Charles the Great, the fall of the Romans huge Dominion concurring with other univerſal evils, cauſed thoſe times to be days of much affliction and trouble

Terent. Andr.

Socrat. lib. vi. c. 8. Sozom lib. viii. c 8. Theod lib. xvi. l. xxx. L. iii c. 10. Novel lxviii. 51. Baſil. Epiſt. lxiii. Niceph. lib. xiv. c. 3 Codren. in Theodoſ.

Sidon. lib. vii. Epiſt. 1.

* Hier. Epiſt. xxii ad Euſt. Martyres tibi quærantur in cubiculo tuo. Nunquam cauſa deerit procedendi, ſi ſemper quando neceſſe eſt, progreſſura ſis.

throughout

throughout the World: ſo that Rogations or Litanies were then the very ſtrength, ſtay, and comfort of God's Church. Whereupon in the year five hundred and ſix, it was by the Council of Aurelia decreed, that the whole Church ſhould beſtow yearly at the Feaſt of Pentecoſt three days in that kind of proceſſionary Service. About half an hundred years after, to the end that the Latin Churches which all obſerved this Cuſtom, might not vary in the order and form of thoſe great Litanies which were ſo ſolemnly every where exerciſed, it was thought convenient by Gregory the Firſt, and the beſt of that name, to draw the flower of them all into one. But this iron began at length to gather ruſt; which thing the Synod of Colen ſaw, and in part redreſſed within that Province; neither denying the neceſſary uſe for which ſuch Litanies ſerve, wherein God's clemency and mercy is deſired by publick ſuit, to the end that plagues, deſtructions, calamities, famines, wars, and all other the like adverſities, which for our manifold ſins we have always cauſe to fear, may be turned away from us and prevented through his Grace; nor yet diſſembling the great abuſe whereunto as ſundry other things, ſo this had grown by Men's improbity and malice; to whom, that which was deviſed for the appeaſing of God's diſpleaſure, gave opportunity of committing things which juſtly kindled his wrath. For remedy whereof it was then thought better, that theſe and all other Supplications and Proceſſions ſhould be no where uſed, but only within the walls of the Houſe of God, and Place ſanctified unto Prayer. And by us not only ſuch inconveniencies being remedied, but alſo whatſoever was otherwiſe amiſs in form or matter, it now remaineth a work, the abſolute perfection whereof upbraideth with error or ſomewhat worſe them whom in all parts it doth not ſatisfy. As therefore Litanies have been of longer continuance than that we ſhould make either Gregory or Mamercus the Author of them; ſo they

Concil. tom. ii. p. 513.

Concil. tom. v. Anno 1536.

BOOK V. they are of more permanent uſe than that now the Church ſhould think it needeth them not. What dangers at any time are imminent, what evils hang over our heads, God doth know, and not we. We find by daily experience that thoſe calamities may be neareſt at hand, readieſt to break in ſuddenly upon us, which we in regard of times or circumſtances may imagine to be fartheſt off. Or if they do not indeed approach, yet ſuch miſeries as being preſent, all Men are apt to bewail with tears, the Wiſe by their Prayers ſhould rather prevent. Finally, if we for ourſelves had a privilege of immunity, doth not true Chriſtian Charity require that whatſoever any part of the World, yea any one of all our Brethren elſewhere doth either ſuffer or fear, the ſame we account as our own burthen? What one Petition is there found in the whole Litany, whereof we ſhall ever be able at any time to ſay that no Man living needeth the Grace or Benefit therein craved at God's hands? I am not able to expreſs how much it doth grieve me, that things of principal excellency ſhould be thus bitten at by Men whom God hath endued with graces, both of wit and learning, for better purpoſes.

Of Athanaſius' Creed, and Gloria Patri.

42. We have from the Apoſtles of our Lord Jeſus Chriſt received that brief Confeſſion of Faith which hath been always a badge of the Church, a mark whereby to diſcern Chriſtian Men from Infidels and Jews: *This Faith, received from the Apoſtles, and their Diſciples* (ſaith Irenæus), *the Church, though diſperſed throughout the World, doth notwithſtanding keep as ſafe, as if it dwelt within the walls of ſome one houſe, and as uniformly hold, as if it had but one only heart and ſoul; this as conſonantly it preacheth, teacheth, and delivereth, as if but one tongue did ſpeak for all. As one Sun ſhineth to the whole World; ſo there is no Faith but this one publiſhed, the brightneſs whereof muſt enlighten all that come to the knowledge of the Truth. This Rule* (ſaith Tertullian) *Chriſt did inſtitute; the ſtream and current of this rule hath gone as far, it hath continued as long as the*

Iren. lib. i. cap. 3.

Tertul de Præſcr. adverſ. Hæret. & adverſ. Prax.

the very promulgation of the Gospel. * Under Constantine the Emperor, about three hundred years and upward after Christ, Arius, a Priest in the Church of Alexandria, a subtle-witted and a marvellous fair-spoken Man, but discontented that one should be placed before him in honour, whose superior he thought himself in desert, became through envy and stomach prone unto contradiction and bold to broach at the length that Heresy wherein the Deity of our Lord Jesus Christ, contained but not opened in the former Creed, the Co-equality and Co-eternity of the Son with the Father, was denied. Being for this impiety deprived of his place by the Bishop of the same Church, the punishment which should have reformed him did but increase his obstinacy, and give him occasion of labouring with greater earnestness elsewhere to intangle unwary Minds with the snares of his damnable opinion. Arius in short time had won to himself a number both of Followers and of great Defenders, whereupon much disquietness on all sides ensued. The Emperor, to reduce the Church of Christ unto the unity of sound Belief, when other means whereof trial was first made took no effect, gathered that famous Assembly of three hundred and eighteen Bishops in the Council of Nice; where, besides order taken for many things which seemed to need redress, there was with common consent, for the settling of all Men's minds, that other Confession of Faith set down, which we call the Nicene Creed, whereunto the Arians themselves which were present subscribed also; not that they meant sincerely and indeed to forsake

* The like may be said of the Gloria Patri, and the Athanasius Creed. It was first brought into the Church, to the end that Men thereby should make an open profession in the Church of the Divinity of the Son of God against the detestable opinion of Arius and his Disciples, wherewith at that time marvellously swarmed almost the whole Christendom. Now that it hath pleased the Lord to quench that fire, there is no such cause why these things should be used in the Church, at the least, why that Gloria Patri should be so often repeated. T. C. lib i. p. 137.

their

BOOK V. their error; but only to escape deprivation and exile, which they saw they could not avoid; openly persisting in their former opinions when the greater part had concluded against them, and that with the Emperor's royal assent. Reserving therefore themselves unto future opportunities, and knowing it would not boot them to stir again in a matter so composed, unless they should draw the Emperor first, and by his means the chiefest Bishops unto their part; till Constantine's death and somewhat after, they always professed love and zeal to the Nicene Faith, yet ceased not in the mean while to strengthen that part which in heart they favoured, and to infest by all means, under colour of other quarrels, their greatest Adversaries in this cause. Amongst them Athanasius especially, whom by the space of forty-six years, from the time of his consecration to succeed Alexander, Archbishop in the Church of Alexandria, till the last hour of his life in this World, they never suffered to enjoy the comfort of a peaceable day: the heart of Constantine stolen from him: Constantius, Constantine's Successor, his scourge and torment by all the ways that malice armed with sovereign authority could devise and use: under Julian no rest given him; and in the days of Valentinian, as little: crimes there were laid to his charge many; the least whereof, being just, had bereaved him of estimation and credit with Men, while the World standeth: his judges evermore the self-same Men, by whom his Accusers were suborned; yet the issue always on their part shame, on his triumph. Those Bishops and Prelates, who should have accounted his cause theirs, and could not many of them but with bleeding hearts and with watered cheeks, behold a Person of so great place and worth constrained to endure so foul indignities, were sure, by bewraying their affection towards him, to bring upon themselves those molestations, whereby if they would not be drawn to seem his Adversaries, yet others should be taught how unsafe it was to continue his Friends.

Friends. Whereupon it came to paſs in the end, that (very few excepted) all became ſubject to the ſway of time; other odds there was none amongſt them, ſaving only that ſome fell ſooner away, ſome later from the ſoundneſs of Belief; ſome were Leaders in the hoſt of impiety, and the reſt as common Soldiers, either yielding through fear, or brought under with penury, or by flattery enſnared, or elſe beguiled through ſimplicity, which is the faireſt excuſe that well may be made for them. Yea, (that which all Men did wonder at) Oſius the ancienteſt Biſhop that Chriſtendom then had, the moſt forward in defence of the Catholick cauſe, and of the contrary part moſt feared; that very Oſius, with whoſe hand the Nicene Creed itſelf was ſet down, and framed for the whole Chriſtian World to ſubſcribe unto, ſo far yielded in *the end, as even with the ſame hand to ratify the Arians' Confeſſion, a thing which they neither hoped to ſee, nor the other part ever feared till with amazement they ſaw it done. Both were perſuaded, that although there had been for Oſius no way but either preſently ſubſcribe or die, his anſwer and choice would have been the ſame that Eleazar's was, *It doth not become our age to diſſemble, whereby many young Perſons might think that Oſius an hundred years old and upward were now gone to another Religion; and ſo through mine hypocriſy (for a little time of tranſitory life) they might be deceived by me, and I procure malediction and reproach to my old age. For though I were now delivered from the torments of Men, yet could I not eſcape the hand of the Almighty, neither alive nor dead.* But ſuch was the ſtream of thoſe times that all Men gave place unto it, which we cannot but impute partly to their own overſight: for at the firſt the Emperor was theirs, the determination of the Council of Nice was for them; they had the Arians' hands to that Council. So great advantages are never changed ſo far to the contrary, but by great error. It plainly appeareth, that the firſt thing which weakened them was their

BOOK V.

2 Mac. vi. 24.

Major Centenario. Sulpit. Sever. Hiſt. l. ii.

BOOK V. their ſecurity. Such as they knew were in heart ſtill affected towards Arianiſm, they ſuffered by continual nearneſs to poſſeſs the Minds of the greateſt about the Emperor, which themſelves might have done with very good acceptation, and neglected it. In Conſtantine's life-time to have ſettled Conſtantius the ſame way, had been a duty of good ſervice towards God, a mean of peace, and great quietneſs to the Church of Chriſt; a labour eaſy; and how likely we may conjecture, when after that ſo much pains was taken to inſtruct and ſtrengthen him in the contrary courſe, after that ſo much was done by himſelf to the furtherance of Hereſy, yet being touched in the end voluntarily with remorſe, nothing more grieved him than the memory of former proceedings in the cauſe of Religion; and that which he now foreſaw in Julian, the next phyſician, into whoſe hands the body that was thus diſtempered muſt fall. Howbeit this we may ſomewhat excuſe, in as much as every Man's particular care to his own charge was ſuch, as gave them no leiſure to heed what others practiſed in Princes Courts. But of the two Synods of Arimine and Seleucia, what ſhould we think? Conſtantius, by the Arians' ſuggeſtion, had deviſed to aſſemble all the Biſhops of the whole World about this controverſy; but in two ſeveral places, the Biſhops of the Weſt at Arimine in Italy, the Eaſtern at Seleucia the ſame time. Amongſt them of the Eaſt there was no ſtop, they agreed without any great ado, gave their ſentence againſt Hereſy, excommunicated ſome chief Maintainers thereof, and ſent the Emperor word what was done. They had at Arimine about four hundred which held the truth; ſcarce of the adverſe part, four ſcore; but theſe obſtinate, and the other weary of contending with them: whereupon by both it was reſolved to ſend to the Emperor ſuch as might inform him of the cauſe, and declare what hindered their peaceable agreement. There are choſen for the

the Catholick side, * such Men as had in them nothing to be noted but boldness, neither gravity, nor learning, nor wisdom. The Arians, for the credit of their faction, take the eldest, the best experienced, the most wary, and the longest practised Veterans they had amongst them. The Emperor, conjecturing of the rest on either part, by the quality of them whom he saw, sent them speedily away, and with them a certain Confession of Faith, ‡ ambiguously and subtilly drawn by the Arians, whereunto unless they all subscribed they should in no case be suffered to depart from the place where they were. At length it was perceived, that there had not been in the Catholicks, either at Arimine, or at Seleucia, so much foresight as to provide that true intelligence might pass between them what was done. Upon the advantage of which error, their Adversaries abusing each with persuasion that other had yielded, surprised both. The Emperor the more desirous and glad of such events, for that, besides all other things wherein they hindered themselves, the gall and bitterness of certain Men's writings, who spared him little for honour's sake, made him for their sakes the less inclinable to that Truth which he himself should have honoured and loved. Only in Athanasius there was nothing observed throughout the course of that long tragedy, other than such as very well became a wise Man to do, and a righteous to suffer. So that this was the plain condition of those times; the whole World against Athanasius, and Athanasius against it; half an hundred of years spent in doubtful trial which of the two in the end would prevail,

* Ex parte nostra leguntur homines adolescentes, parum docti, parum cauti. Ab Arianis autem missi senes, callidi et ingenio valentes veterano, perfidia imbuti, qui apud Regem facile superiores extiterunt. Sulpit. lib. ii.

‡ Eisdemque conscripta ab improbis fidem tradit verbis fallentibus involutam, quæ Catholicam disciplinam perfidia latente loqueretur. Ibid.

BOOK V. the ſide which had all, or elſe the part which had no friend but God and Death; the one a Defender of his innocency, the other a Finiſher of all his troubles. Now although theſe contentions were cauſe of much evil, yet ſome good the Church hath reaped by them, in that they occaſioned the learned and ſound in Faith to explain ſuch things as Hereſy went about to deprave. And in this reſpect, the Creed of Athanaſius, firſt exhibited unto Julius, Biſhop of Rome, and afterwards (as we may probably gather) ſent to the Emperor Jovinian for his more full information concerning that Truth which Arianiſm ſo mightily did impugn, was both in the Eaſt and the Weſt Churches accepted as a treaſure of ineſtimable price, * by as many as had not given up even the very ghoſt of belief. Then was the Creed of Athanaſius written, howbeit not then ſo expedient to be publickly uſed as now in the Church of God; becauſe while the heat of diviſion laſteth, Truth itſelf enduring oppoſition doth not ſo quietly and currently paſs throughout all Men's hands, neither can be of that account which afterwards it hath when the World once perceiveth the virtue thereof, not only in itſelf, but alſo by the conqueſt which God hath given it over Hereſy. That which Hereſy did by ſiniſter interpretations go about to pervert in the firſt and moſt ancient Apoſtolical Creed, the ſame being by ſingular dexterity and plainneſs cleared from thoſe Heretical corruptions, partly by this Creed of Athanaſius, written about the year three hundred and forty, and partly by that other ſet down in the Synod of Conſtantinople forty years after, comprehending together with the Nicene Creed an addition of other Articles which the Nicene Creed omitted, becauſe the controverſy then in hand needed no mention to be made of them; theſe

That Creed which in the Book of Common-Prayer, followeth immediately after the reading of the Goſpel.

* Ταύτην μοι δοκοῦσιν αἰδούμενοι τὴν ὁμολογίαν οὔτε τῆς ἑσπερίας καὶ τῆς ἑῴας ὅσαν βιώσιμοι. Greg. Nazian. de Atha.

Catholick

Catholick Declarations of our Belief delivered by them, which were so much nearer than we are unto the first publication thereof, and continuing needful for all Men at all times to know, these Confessions as testimonies of our continuance in the same Faith to this present day, we rather use than any other gloss or paraphrase devised by ourselves, which though it were to the same effect, notwithstanding could not be of the like authority and credit. For that of Hilary unto St. Augustin hath been ever, and is likely to be always true; *Your most religious wisdom knoweth how great their number is in the Church of God, whom the very authority of Men's names doth keep in that opinion which they hold already, or draw unto that which they have not before held.* Touching the Hymn of Glory, our usual conclusion to Psalms, the glory of all things is that wherein their highest perfection doth consist; and the glory of God, that divine excellency, whereby he is eminent above all things, his omnipotent, infinite, and eternal Being, which Angels and glorified Saints do intuitively behold; we on Earth apprehend principally by Faith, in part also by that kind of knowledge which groweth from experience of those effects, the greatness whereof exceedeth the powers and abilities of all Creatures both in Heaven and Earth. God is glorified, when such his excellency above all things is with due admiration acknowledged. Which dutiful acknowledgment of God's excellency by occasion of special effects, being the very proper subject, and almost the only matter purposely treated of in all Psalms, if that joyful Hymn of Glory have any use in the Church of God, whose Name we therewith extol and magnify, can we place it more fitly than where now it serveth as a close or conclusion to Psalms? Neither is the form thereof newly or unnecessarily invented. *We must* (saith St. Basil) *as we have received, even so baptize, and as we baptize, even so believe; and as we believe, even so give Glory.*

BOOK V.

Hilar Arela Epist. ad Aug.

1 Cor xv. 40. Exod. xxxiii. 18. Heb. i. 3 Matt. xviii. 10.

Josh vii. 19 Psal. xxii. 23.

Basil. Epist. lxxviii.

BOOK V. Baptizing, we use the Name of the Father, of the Son, and of the Holy Ghost: confessing the Christian Faith, we declare our Belief in the Father, and in the Son, and in the Holy Ghost: ascribing Glory unto God, we give it to the Father, and to the Son, and to the Holy Ghost. It is ἀπόδειξις τῦ ὀρθῦ φρονήματ☉, *the token of a true and sound understanding* for matter of Doctrine about the Trinity, when in ministring Baptism, and making Confession, and giving Glory, there is a conjunction of all three, and no one of the three severed from the other two. Against the Arians, affirming the Father to be greater than the Son in Honour, Excellency, Dignity, Majesty, this form and manner of glorifying God was not at that time first begun, but received long before, and alledged at that time as an argument for the truth. *If* (saith Fœbadius) *there be that inequality which they affirm, then do we every day blaspheme God, when, in Thanksgivings and Offerings of Sacrifice, we acknowledge those things common to the Father and the Son.* The Arians therefore, for that they perceived how this did prejudice their cause, altered the Hymn of Glory; whereupon ensued in the Church of Antioch, about the year three hundred forty-nine, that jar which Theodoret and Sozomen mention. *In their Quires, while they praised God together, as the manner was, at the end of the Psalms which they sung, it appeared what opinion every Man held; for as much as they glorified some the Father,* and *the Son,* and *the Holy Ghost*; *some the Father* by *the Son,* in *the Spirit*; *the one sort thereby declaring themselves to embrace the Son's Equality with the Father, as the Council of Nice had defined*; *the other sort, against the Council of Nice, his inequality.* Leontius their Bishop, although an Enemy to the better part, yet wary and subtile, as in a manner all the heads of the Arians' Faction are, could at no time be heard to use either form, perhaps lest his open contradiction of them whom he favoured not might make them

Fœbad lib. contra Arian

Theod lib. ii. cap. 24. Sozom. lib iv. cap. 19.

them the more eager, and by that mean the leſs apt to be privately won; or peradventure for that, though he joined in opinion with that ſort of Arians who denied the Son to be equal with the Father; yet from them he diſſented, which thought the Father and Son, not only unequal, but unlike, as Aetius did upon a frivolous and falſe ſurmiſe, that becauſe the Apoſtle hath ſaid, *One God of whom, one Lord by whom, one Spirit in whom*, his different manner of ſpeech doth argue a different Nature and Being in them of whom he ſpeaketh. Out of which blind collection it ſeemeth that this their new deviſed Form did firſt ſpring. But in truth, even that very Form which the Arians did then uſe (ſaving that they choſe it to ſerve as their ſpecial mark of recognizance, and gave it ſecretly within themſelves a ſiniſter conſtruction) hath not otherwiſe as much as the ſhew of any thing which ſoundeth towards impiety. For albeit, if we reſpect God's Glory within itſelf, it be the equal right and poſſeſſion of all three, and that without any odds, any difference; yet, touching his manifeſtation thereof unto us by continual effects, and our perpetual acknowledgment thereof unto him likewiſe by virtuous offices, doth not every tongue both ways confeſs, that the brightneſs of his Glory hath ſpread itſelf throughout the World *by* the Miniſtry of his only begotten Son, and is *in* the manifold Graces of the Spirit every way marvellous? Again, that whatſoever we do to his Glory, it is done *in* the Power of the Holy Ghoſt, and made acceptable *by* the Merit and Mediation of Jeſus Chriſt? So that Glory to the Father, *and* the Son, or Glory to the Father *by* the Son, ſaving only where evil Minds do abuſe and pervert holy things, are not elſe the voices of Error and Schiſm, but of ſound and ſincere Religion. It hath been the Cuſtom of the Church of Chriſt to end ſometimes Prayers, and Sermons always, with words of glory; wherein, as long as the Bleſſed

1 Cor. viii. 6.
1 Cor. xii. 3, 4, 13.

BOOK V. Trinity had due honour, and till Arianifm had made it matter of great fharpnefs and fubtilty of wit to be a found believing Chriftian, Men were not curious what fyllables or particles of fpeech they ufed. Upon which confidence and truft notwithftanding, when St. Bafil began to practife the like indifferency, and to conclude publick Prayers, glorifying fometime the Father, with the Son, and the Holy Ghoft; fometime the Father, by the Son, in the Spirit; whereas long cuftom had enured them unto the former kind alone, by means whereof the latter was new and ftrange in their ears; this needlefs experiment brought afterwards upon him a neceffary labour of excufing himfelf to his Friends, and maintaining his own act againft them; who, becaufe the light of his candle too much drowned theirs, were glad to lay hold on fo colourable matter, and exceeding forward to traduce him as an Author of fufpicious innovation. How hath the World forfaken that courfe which it fometime held? How are the judgments, hearts, and affections of Men altered? May we not wonder, that a Man of St. Bafil's authority and quality, an Arch-prelate in the Houfe of God, fhould have his name far and wide called in queftion, and be driven to his painful apologies to write in his own defence whole volumes, and yet hardly to obtain with all his endeavour a pardon; the crime laid againft him being but only a change of fome one or two fyllables in their ufual Church Liturgy? It was thought in him an unpardonable offence to alter any thing; in us as intolerable that we fuffer any thing to remain unaltered. The very Creed of Athanafius, and that facred Hymn of Glory, than which nothing doth found more heavenly in the ears of faithful Men, are now reckoned as fuperfluities which we muft in any cafe pare away left we cloy God with too much fervice. Is there in that Confeffion of Faith any thing which doth not at all times edify and inftruct the attentive Hearer? Or is our Faith in the Bleffed Trinity

nity a matter needleſs to be ſo oftentimes mentioned BOOK V. and opened in the principal part of that duty which we owe to God, our publick Prayer? Hath the Church of Chriſt from the firſt beginning, by a ſecret univerſal inſtinct of God's good Spirit, always tied itſelf to end neither Sermon, nor almoſt any ſpeech of moment which hath concerned matters of God, without ſome ſpecial words of Honour and Glory to that Trinity which we all adore; and is the like concluſion of Pſalms become now at length an eye-ſore, or a galling to their ears that hear it? Thoſe flames of Arianiſm, they ſay, are quenched, which were the cauſe why the Church deviſed in ſuch ſort to confeſs and praiſe the glorious Deity of the Son of God. Seeing therefore the ſore is whole, why retain we as yet the plaiſter? When the cauſe why any thing was ordained doth once ceaſe, the thing itſelf ſhould ceaſe with it; that the Church being eaſed of unprofitable labours, needful offices may the better be attended. For the doing of things unneceſſary, is many times the cauſe why the moſt neceſſary are not done. But in this caſe ſo to reaſon, will not ſerve their turns. For firſt, the ground whereupon they build is not certainly their own, but with ſpecial limitations. Few things are ſo reſtrained to any one end or purpoſe, that the ſame being extinct, they ſhould forthwith utterly become fruſtrate. Wiſdom may have framed one and the ſame thing to ſerve commodiouſly for divers ends, and of thoſe ends any one be ſufficient cauſe for continuance, though the reſt have ceaſed; even as the tongue, which Nature hath given us for an inſtrument of ſpeech, is not idle in dumb Perſons, becauſe it alſo ſerveth for taſte. Again, if time have worn out, or any other mean altogether taken away, what was firſt intended, uſes not thought upon before may afterwards ſpring up, and be reaſonable cauſes of retaining that which other conſiderations did formerly procure to be inſtituted. And it cometh ſometime to paſs that a thing unne-

BOOK V. ceſſary in itſelf, as touching the whole direct purpoſe whereunto it was meant or can be applied, doth notwithſtanding appear convenient to be ſtill held, even without uſe, leſt, by reaſon of that coherence which it hath with ſomewhat moſt neceſſary, the removal of the one ſhould endamage the other. And therefore Men which have clean loſt the poſſibility of ſight, keep ſtill their eyes nevertheleſs in the place where Nature ſet them. As for theſe two branches whereof our queſtion groweth, Arianiſm was indeed ſome occaſion of the one, but a cauſe of neither, much leſs the only entire cauſe of both. For albeit, conflict with Arians brought forth the occaſion of writing that Creed which long after was made a part of the Church Liturgy, as Hymns and Sentences of Glory were a part thereof before; yet cauſe ſufficient there is why both ſhould remain in uſe, the one as a moſt divine explication of the chiefeſt Articles of our Chriſtian Belief, the other as an heavenly acclamation of joyful applauſe to his praiſes in whom we believe; neither the one nor the other unworthy to be heard ſounding as they are in the Church of Chriſt, whether Arianiſm live or die. Againſt which poiſon likewiſe, if we think, that the Church at this day needeth not thoſe ancient preſervatives, which ages before us were ſo glad to uſe, we deceive ourſelves greatly. The weeds of Hereſy being grown unto ſuch ripeneſs as that was, do even in the very cutting down ſcatter oftentimes thoſe ſeeds which for a while lie unſeen and buried in the Earth, but afterward freſhly ſpring up again no leſs pernicious than at the firſt. Which thing they very well know, and I doubt not will eaſily confeſs, who live to their great both toil and grief, where the blaſphemies of Arians, Samoſatenians, Tritheits, Eutychians and Macedonians, are renewed by them who to hatch their Hereſy have choſen thoſe Churches as fitteſt neſts where Athanaſius's Creed is not heard; by them, I ſay, renewed, who, following the courſe of extreme Reformation, were wont in the pride of

their

their own proceedings to glory that whereas Luther did but blow away the roof, and Zuinglius batter but the walls of Popiſh Superſtition, the laſt and hardeſt work of all remained, which was to raze up the very ground and foundation of Popery, that Doctrine concerning the Deity of Chriſt, which *Satanaſius* (for ſo it pleaſed thoſe impious forſaken Miſcreants to ſpeak) hath in this memorable Creed explained. So manifeſtly true is that which one of the Ancients hath concerning Arianiſm, *Mortuis authoribus hujus veneni, ſcelerata tamen eorum doctrina non moritur.* The Authors of this venom being dead and gone, their wicked Doctrine notwithſtanding continueth.

Fœbad. contra Ar.

Our want of particular Thankſgiving.

43. Amongſt the heaps of theſe exceſſes and ſuperfluities, there is eſpied the want of a principal part of duty, *There are no Thankſgivings for the Benefits for which there are Petitions in our Book of Prayer.** This they have thought a point material to be objected. Neither may we take it in evil part to be admoniſhed, what ſpecial duties of thankfulneſs we owe to that merciful God, for whoſe unſpeakable Graces the only requital which we are able to make, is a true, hearty, and ſincere acknowledgment how precious we eſteem ſuch benefits received, and how infinite in goodneſs the Author from whom they come. But that to every Petition we make for things needful, there ſhould be ſome anſwerable ſentences of thanks provided particularly to follow ſuch requeſts obtained; either it is not a matter ſo requiſite as they pretend; or if it be, wherefore have they not then in ſuch order framed their own Book of Common-Prayer?

* As ſuch Prayers are needful, whereby we beg releaſe from our diſtreſſes, ſo there ought to be as neceſſary Prayers of Thankſgiving, when we have received thoſe things at the Lord's hand which we aſked. T. C. l. i. p. 138. I do not ſimply require a ſolemn and expreſs Thankſgiving for ſuch benefits; but only upon a ſuppoſition, which is, that if it be expedient that there ſhould be expreſs Prayers againſt ſo many of their earthly miſeries, that then alſo it is meet that upon the deliverance there ſhould be an expreſs Thankſgiving. T. C. l. iii p. 209.

Why

BOOK V. Why hath our Lord and Saviour taught us a form of Prayer containing so many Petitions of those things which we want, and not delivered in like sort as many several forms of Thanksgiving to serve when any thing we pray for is granted? What answer soever they can reasonably make unto these demands, the same shall discover unto them how causeless a censure it is, that there are not in our Book Thanksgivings for all the benefits for which there are Petitions.* For concerning the Blessings of God, whether they tend unto this life or the life to come, there is great cause why we should delight more in giving thanks than in making requests for them, in as much as the one hath pensiveness and fear, the other always joy annexed; the one belongeth unto them that seek, the other unto them that have found happiness; they that pray do but yet sow, they that give thanks declare they have reaped. Howbeit, because there are so many Graces, whereof we stand in continual need, Graces for which we may not cease daily and hourly to sue, Graces which are in bestowing always, but never come to be fully had in this present life; and therefore, when all things here have an end, endless Thanks must have their beginning in a state which bringeth the full and final satisfaction of all such perpetual desires: again, because our common necessities, and the lack which we all have as well of ghostly as of earthly favours, is in each kind so easily known; but the gifts of God, according to those degrees and times which he in his secret wisdom seeth meet, are so diversely bestowed, that it seldom appeareth what all receive, what all stand in need of, it seldom lieth hid; we are not to marvel, though the Church do oftner concur in Suits than in Thanks unto God for particular benefits. Nevertheless, lest God should be

* The default of the Book, for that there are no Forms of Thanksgiving for the release from those common calamities from which we have Petitions to be delivered. T. C. l. iii. p. 208.

any

any way unglorified, the greateſt part of our daily Service, they know, conſiſteth, according to the bleſſed Apoſtle's own preciſe rule, in much variety of Pſalms and Hymns, for no other purpoſe but only that out of ſo plentiful a treaſure there might be for every Man's heart to chuſe out his own Sacrifice, and to offer unto God by particular ſecret inſtinct what fitteth beſt the often occaſions which any ſeveral either Party or Congregation may ſeem to have. They that would clean take from us, therefore, the daily uſe of the very beſt means we have to magnify and praiſe the Name of Almighty God for his rich Bleſſings, they that complain of our reading and ſinging ſo many Pſalms for ſo good an end; they, I ſay, that find fault with our ſtore, ſhould of all Men be leaſt willing to reprove our ſcarcity of Thankſgiving. But becauſe peradventure they ſee, it is not either generally fit or poſſible that Churches ſhould frame Thankſgivings anſwerable to each Petition, they ſhorten ſomewhat the reins of their cenſure; there are no forms of Thankſgiving, they ſay, for releaſe of thoſe common calamities from which we have Petitions to be delivered. *There are Prayers ſet forth to be ſaid in the common calamities and univerſal ſcourges of the Realm, as plague, famine, &c. And indeed ſo it ought to be by the Word of God But as ſuch Prayers are needful, whereby we beg releaſe from our diſtreſſes, ſo there ought to be as neceſſary Prayers of Thankſgiving, when we have received thoſe things at the Lord's hands which we aſked in our Prayers.* As oft, therefore, as any publick or univerſal ſcourge is removed, as oft as we are delivered from thoſe, either imminent or preſent calamities, againſt the ſtorm and tempeſt whereof we all inſtantly craved favour from above, let it be a queſtion what we ſhould render unto God for his Bleſſings univerſally, ſenſibly and extraordinarily beſtowed. A Prayer of three or four lines inſerted into ſome part of our Church Liturgy? No, we are not perſuaded that when God doth in trouble enjoin us the

Epheſ. v. 9. Coloſ. iii. 16.

T. C. l. i. p. 138.

BOOK V. the duty of invocation, and promiſe us the benefit of deliverance, and profeſs that the thing he expecteth after at our hands is to glorify him as our mighty and only Saviour, the Church can diſcharge, in manner convenient, a work of ſo great importance, by fore-ordaining ſome ſhort Collect wherein briefly to mention Thanks. Our Cuſtom therefore, whenſoever ſo great occaſions are incident, is by publick Authority to appoint, throughout all Churches, ſet and ſolemn Forms as well of Supplication, as of Thankſgiving, the preparation and intended complements whereof may ſtir up the minds of Men in much more effectual ſort, than if only there ſhould be added to the Book of Prayer that which they require. But we err in thinking that they require any ſuch matter. For albeit their words to our underſtanding be very plain, that in our Book *there are Prayers ſet forth* to be ſaid when *common calamities* are felt, as *plague, famine,* and ſuch like; again, that *indeed ſo it ought to be by the Word of God:* that likewiſe *there ought to be as neceſſary Prayers of Thankſgiving when we have received thoſe things:* finally, that the want of ſuch Forms of Thankſgiving for the releaſe from thoſe common calamities from which we have Petitions to be delivered, is the *default of the Book of Common-Prayer:* yet all this they mean but only by way of *ſuppoſition if expreſs Prayers* againſt ſo many earthly miſeries were convenient, that then indeed as many expreſs and particular Thankſgivings ſhould be likewiſe neceſſary. Seeing therefore we know that they hold the one ſuperfluous, they would not have it ſo underſtood as though their minds were that any ſuch addition to the Book is needful, whatſoever they ſay for argument's ſake concerning this pretended defect. The truth is, they wave in and out, no way ſufficiently grounded, no way reſolved what to think, ſpeak, or write, more than only that becauſe they have taken it upon them, they muſt (no remedy now) be oppoſite.

44. The

In ſome things the matter of our Prayer, as they affirm, unſound.

44. The laſt ſuppoſed fault concerneth ſome few things, the very matter whereof is thought to be much amiſs. In a Song of Praiſe to our Lord Jeſus Chriſt we have theſe words: *When thou hadſt overcome the ſharpneſs of death, thou didſt open the Kingdom of Heaven to all Believers.* Which maketh ſome ſhew of giving countenance to their error, who think that the Faithful which departed this life before the coming of Chriſt, were never till then made partakers of joy, but remained all in that place which they term the Lake of the Fathers. In our Liturgy requeſt is made, that we may be preſerved *from ſudden death.* This ſeemeth frivolous, becauſe the Godly ſhould always be prepared to die. Requeſt is made, that God would give thoſe things which we for our unworthineſs dare not aſk. *This*, they ſay, *carrieth with it the note of Popiſh ſervile fear, and ſavoureth not of that confidence and reverent familiarity that the Children of God have, through Chriſt, with their Heavenly Father.* Requeſt is made, that we may evermore be defended from all adverſity. For this *there is no promiſe in Scripture*; and therefore *it is no Prayer of Faith, or of the which we can aſſure ourſelves that we ſhall obtain it.* Finally, requeſt is made, that God *would have Mercy upon all Men.* This is impoſſible, becauſe ſome are Veſſels of Wrath, to whom God will never extend his Mercy.

When thou hadſt overcome the ſharpneſs of death, thou didſt open the Kingdom of Heaven unto all Believers.

45. As Chriſt hath purchaſed that heavenly Kingdom, the laſt perfection whereof is *Glory in the life to come*, Grace in this life, a preparation thereunto; ſo the ſame he hath opened to the World in ſuch ſort, that whereas none can poſſibly without him attain Salvation, by him all that believe are ſaved. Now whatſoever he did or ſuffered, the end thereof was to open the doors of the Kingdom of Heaven which our iniquities had ſhut up. But becauſe by aſcending after that the ſharpneſs of death was overcome, he took the very local poſſeſſion of Glory, and that to the uſe of all that are his, even as himſelf before had witneſſed, *I go to prepare a place for you*; and again, *whom thou haſt*

BOOK V. *haſt given me, O Father, I will that where I am, they be alſo with me, that my glory which thou haſt given me, they may behold*, it appeareth, that when Chriſt did aſcend, he then moſt liberally opened the Kingdom of Heaven, to the end that with him, and by him, all Believers might reign. In what eſtate the Fathers reſted which were dead before, it is not hereby either one way or other determined. All that we can rightly gather is, that as touching their Souls, what degree of joy or happineſs ſoever it pleaſed God to beſtow upon them, his Aſcenſion which ſucceeded procured theirs, and theirs concerning the Body muſt needs be not only of, but after his. As therefore Helvidius, againſt whom St. Jerom writeth, abuſed greatly thoſe words of Matthew concerning Joſeph and the Mother of our Saviour Chriſt, *He knew her not till ſhe had brought forth her Firſt-born*, thereby gathering, againſt the honour of the Bleſſed Virgin, that a thing denied with ſpecial circumſtance doth import an oppoſite affirmation when once that circumſtance is expired: after the ſelf-ſame manner, it ſhould be a weak collection, if whereas we ſay, that when Chriſt had *overcome the ſharpneſs of death, he* then *opened the Kingdom of Heaven to all Believers*; a thing in ſuch ſort affirmed with circumſtance, were taken as inſinuating an oppoſite denial before that circumſtance be accompliſhed, and conſequently, that, becauſe when the ſharpneſs of death was overcome he then opened Heaven as well to believing Gentiles as Jews, Heaven till then was no receptacle to the Souls of either. Wherefore, be the Spirits of the juſt and righteous before Chriſt truly or falſely thought excluded out of heavenly joy, by that which we in the words alledged before do attribute to Chriſt's Aſcenſion, there is to no ſuch opinion, nor to the Favourers thereof, any countenance at all given. We cannot better interpret the meaning of theſe words than Pope Leo himſelf expoundeth them, whoſe Speech concerning our Lord's Aſcenſion may ſerve inſtead of a marginal gloſs: *Chriſt's Exaltation is our Promotion*;

John xiv. 2. & xvii. 24.

Jerom contra Helvid. Auguſt. Her. lxxxiv.

Lyr ſuper Gen. xxix. Th p. 3, q. 52, or 5.

Promotion; and whither the glory of the Head is already gone before, thither the hope of the Body alſo is to follow. For at this day, we have not only the poſſeſſion of Paradiſe aſſured unto us; but in Chriſt we have entered the higheſt of the Heavens. His *opening the Kingdom of Heaven,* and his entrance thereinto, was not only to his own uſe, but for the benefit of *all Believers.*

Leo. Ser 1. de Aſcenſ.

Touching Prayer for deliverance from ſudden death.

46. Our good or evil eſtate after death dependeth moſt upon the quality of our lives. Yet ſomewhat there is, why a virtuous Mind ſhould rather wiſh to depart this World with a kind of treatable diſſolution, than to be ſuddenly cut off in a moment; rather to be taken than ſnatched away from the face of the Earth. Death is that which all Men ſuffer, but not all Men with one mind, neither all Men in one manner. For being of neceſſity a thing common, it is, through the manifold perſuaſions, diſpoſitions, and occaſions of Men, with equal deſert both of praiſe and diſpraiſe, ſhunned by ſome, by others deſired. So that abſolutely we cannot diſcommend, we cannot abſolutely approve either willingneſs to live, or forwardneſs to die. And concerning the ways of death, albeit the choice thereof be only in his hands who alone hath power over all Fleſh, and unto whoſe appointment we ought with patience meekly to ſubmit ourſelves (for to be agents voluntarily in our own deſtruction is againſt both God and Nature); yet there is no doubt, but in ſo great variety our deſires will and may lawfully prefer one kind before another. Is there any Man of worth and virtue, although not inſtructed in the School of Chriſt, or ever taught what the ſoundneſs of Religion meaneth, that had not rather end the days of this tranſitory life as Cyrus in Xenophon, or in Plato Socrates are deſcribed, than to ſink down with them of whom Elihu hath ſaid *Momento moriuntur,* there is ſcarce an inſtant between their flouriſhing and their not being? But let us which know what it is to die as Abſalon, or Ananias and Saphira died; let us beg of God, that when the hour of our reſt is come, the

Job xx. 20.

BOOK V. the patterns of our dissolution may be Jacob, Moses, Joshua, David; who leisurably ending their lives in peace, prayed for the mercies of God to come upon their Posterity; replenished the hearts of the nearest unto them with words of memorable consolation; strengthened Men in the fear of God, gave them wholesome instructions of life, and confirmed them in true Religion; in sum, taught the World no less virtuously how to die, than they had done before how to live. To such as judge things according to the sense of natural Men and ascend no higher, suddenness, because it shorteneth their grief, should in reason be most acceptable. That which causeth bitterness in death, is the languishing attendance and expectation thereof ere it come. And therefore Tyrants use what art they can to increase the slowness of death. Quick riddance out of life is often both requested and bestowed as a benefit. Commonly therefore it is, for virtuous considerations, that Wisdom so far prevaileth with Men as to make them desirous of slow and deliberate death against the stream of their sensual inclination, content to endure the longer grief and bodily pain, that the Soul may have time to call itself to a just account of all things past, by means whereof Repentance is perfected, there is wherein to exercise patience, the joys of the Kingdom of Heaven have leisure to present themselves, the pleasures of sin and this World's vanities are censured with uncorrupt judgment, Charity is free to make advised choice of the soil wherein her last seed may most fruitfully be bestowed, the Mind is at liberty to have due regard of that disposition of worldly things which it can never afterwards alter; and because the nearer we draw unto God, the more we are oftentimes enlightened with the shining beams of his glorious presence, as being then even almost in sight, a leisurable departure may in that case bring forth, for the good of such as are present, that which shall cause them for ever after from the bottom of their hearts to pray, *O let us die the death of the Righteous,*

Heb. xi. 21. Deut. xxxiii. Josh. xxiv. 1 Kings ii.

Cypr. de Mortal.

Righteous, and let our laſt end be like theirs. All which benefits and opportunities are by ſudden death prevented. And beſides, for as much as death howſoever is a general effect of the wrath of God againſt ſin, and the ſuddenneſs thereof a thing which happeneth but to few; the World in this reſpect feareth it the more as being ſubject to doubtful conſtructions, which as no Man willingly would incur, ſo they whoſe happy eſtate after life is of all Men's the moſt certain, ſhould eſpecially wiſh that no ſuch accident in their death may give uncharitable minds occaſion of raſh, ſiniſter and ſuſpicious verdicts, whereunto they are over prone. So that whether evil Men or good be reſpected, whether we regard ourſelves or others, to be preſerved from ſudden death, is a bleſſing of God. And our Prayer againſt it importeth a twofold deſire, firſt, that death when it cometh may give us ſome convenient reſpite; or, ſecondly, if that be denied us of God, yet we may have wiſdom to provide always beforehand; that thoſe evils overtake us not, which death unexpected doth uſe to bring upon careleſs Men; and that although it be ſudden in itſelf, nevertheleſs, in regard of our prepared minds, it may not be ſudden.

Prayer that thoſe things which we for our unworthineſs dare not aſk, God for the worthineſs of his Son would vouchſafe to grant.

47. But is it credible that the very acknowledgment of our own unworthineſs to obtain, and in that reſpect our profeſſed fearfulneſs to aſk any thing, otherwiſe than only for his ſake to whom God can deny nothing, that this ſhould be noted for a Popiſh error: that this ſhould be termed baſeneſs, abjection of mind, or ſervility, is it credible? That which we for our unworthineſs are afraid to crave, our Prayer is, that God for the worthineſs of his Son would notwithſtanding vouchſafe to grant. May it pleaſe them to ſhew us which of theſe words it is that carrieth the note of Popiſh and ſervile fear? * In

* This requeſt carrieth with it ſtill the note of the Popiſh ſervile fear, and ſavoureth not of that confidence and reverent familiarity that the Children of God have, through Chriſt, with their Heavenly Father. T. C. l. i. p. 136.

BOOK V. reference to other Creatures of this inferior World, Man's worth and excellency is admired. Compared with God, the trueſt inſcription wherewith we can Pſal. xxxix. 5. circle ſo baſe a coin is that of David, *Univerſa vanitas eſt omnis homo*; whoſoever hath the name of a mortal Man, there is in him whatſoever the name of vanity doth comprehend. And therefore what we ſay of our own unworthineſs there is no doubt but Truth will ratify; alledged in Prayer, it both becometh and behoveth Saints. For as humility is in Suiters a decent virtue; ſo the teſtification thereof by ſuch effectual acknowledgments, not only argueth a ſound apprehenſion of his ſuper-eminent Glory and Majeſty before whom we ſtand, * but putteth alſo into his hands a kind of pledge or bond for ſecurity againſt our unthankfulneſs, the very natural root whereof is always either Ignorance, Diſſimulation, or Pride — Ignorance, when we know not the Author from whom our good cometh: Diſſimulation, when our hands are more open than our eyes upon that we receive: Pride, when we think ourſelves worthy of that which mere Grace and undeſerved Mercy beſtoweth. In Prayer, therefore, to abate ſo vain imaginations with the true conceit of unworthineſs, is rather to prevent than commit a fault. It being no error thus to think, no fault thus to ſpeak of ourſelves when we pray; is it a fault, that the conſideration of our unworthineſs maketh us fearful to open our mouths by way of ſuit? While Job had proſperity and lived in honour, Men feared him for his authority's ſake, and in token of their fear, when they ſaw him, they
Job xxix 8 hid themſelves. Between Elihu and the reſt of Job's Familiars, the greateſt diſparity was but in years: and he, though riper than they in judgment, doing
Job xxxii. 6. them reverence in regard of age, ſtood long † doubtful

* Μεμνημένος γὰρ τῆς ἰδίας παρὰ πάντα οὐδενείας, μεμνήσῃ καὶ τῆς τοῦ Θεοῦ παρὰ πάντα ὑπερβολῆς. Phil. de Sacrif. Abel. et Cain.

† Amongſt the parts of honour Ariſtotle reckoneth προσκυνήσεις and ἐκστάσεις. Rhet. l. i. c. 5.

ful and very loth to adventure upon ſpeech in his Elders' hearing. If ſo ſmall inequality between Man and Man make their modeſty a commendable virtue, who reſpecting Superiors, as Superiors, can neither ſpeak nor ſtand before them without fear; that the Publican approacheth not more boldly to God; that when Chriſt in mercy draweth near to Peter, he in humility and fear craveth diſtance, that being to ſtand, to ſpeak, to ſue in the preſence of ſo great Majeſty, we are afraid, let no Man blame us. * In which conſideration notwithſtanding, becauſe to fly altogether from God, to deſpair that Creatures unworthy ſhall be able to obtain any thing at his hands, and under that pretence to ſurceaſe from Prayers as bootleſs or fruitleſs offices, were to him no leſs injurious than pernicious to our own Souls; even that which we tremble to do we do, we aſk thoſe things which we dare not aſk. The knowledge of our own unworthineſs is not without belief in the Merits of Chriſt. With that true fear which the one cauſeth, there is coupled true boldneſs, and encouragement drawn from the other. The very ſilence which our unworthineſs putteth us unto, doth itſelf make requeſt for us, and that in the confidence of his Grace. Looking inward we are ſtricken dumb; looking upward, we ſpeak and prevail. O happy mixture, wherein things contrary do ſo qualify and correct the one the danger of the other's exceſs, that neither boldneſs can make us preſume, as long as we are kept under with the ſenſe of our own wretchedneſs; nor, while we truſt in the Mercy of God through Jeſus Chriſt, fear be able to tyrannize over us! As therefore our fear excludeth not that boldneſs which becometh Saints,

BOOK V.

Rom. v. 2, 8, 15. Heb. x. 19.

* The Publican did indeed not lift up his eyes. So that if by his example we ſhould ſay, we dare aſk nothing, we ought alſo to aſk nothing; otherwiſe, inſtead of teaching true humility, we open a ſchool to Hypocriſy, which the Lord deteſteth. T. C. l. iii. p. 203.

BOOK V. so if our familiarity with God do not savour of this fear, it draweth too near that irreverent confidence wherewith true Humility can never stand.

Prayer to be evermore delivered from all adversity.

48. Touching continual deliverance in the World from all Adversity, their conceit is that we ought not to ask it of God by Prayer, forasmuch as in Scripture there is no promise that we shall be evermore free from vexations, calamities, and troubles. *Minds religiously affected are wont in every thing of weight and moment, which they do or see, to examine, according unto rules of Piety, what dependency it hath on God, what reference to themselves, what coherence with any of those duties whereunto all things in the World should lead, and accordingly they frame the inward disposition of their minds, sometime to admire God, sometime to bless him and give him thanks, sometime to exult in his Love, sometime to implore his Mercy. All which different elevations of Spirit unto God are contained in the name of Prayer. Every good and holy desire, though it lack the form, hath notwithstanding in itself the substance, and with him the force of a Prayer, who regardeth the very moanings, groans and sighs of the heart of Man. Petitionary Prayer belongeth only to such as are in themselves impotent and stand in need of relief from others. We thereby declare unto God what our own desire is, that he by his power should effect. It presupposeth therefore in us, first, the want of that which we pray for: secondly, a feeling of that want: thirdly, an earnest willingness of mind to be eased therein: fourthly, a declaration of this our desire in the sight of God; not as if he should be otherwise ignorant of our necessities, but because we this way shew we honour him as our

* Forasmuch as there is no Promise in the Scripture, that we should be free from all adversity, and that evermore; it seemeth that this Prayer might have been better conceived, being no Prayer of Faith, or of the which we can assure ourselves that we shall obtain it. T. C. l. 1. p 136.

God,

BOOK V.

God, and are verily perſuaded that no good thing can come to paſs which he by his omnipotent Power effecteth not. Now becauſe there is no Man's Prayer acceptable whoſe Perſon is odious, neither any Man's Perſon gracious without Faith, it is of neceſſity required that they which pray, do believe. The Prayers which our Lord and Saviour made were for his own worthineſs accepted; ours God accepteth not but with this condition, * if they be joined with belief in Chriſt. The Prayers of the Juſt are accepted always, but not always thoſe things granted for which they pray. For in Prayer, if Faith and Aſſurance to obtain were both one and the ſame thing, ſeeing that the effect of not obtaining is a plain teſtimony that they which pray were not ſure they ſhould obtain; it would follow, that their Prayer being without certainty of the event, was alſo made unto God without Faith, and conſequently that God abhorred it. Which to think of ſo many Prayers of Saints as we find have failed in particular requeſts, how abſurd were it! His faithful People have this comfort, that whatſoever they rightly aſk, the ſame (no doubt, but) they ſhall receive, ſo far as may ſtand with the glory of God and their own everlaſting good, unto either of which two, it is no virtuous Man's purpoſe to ſeek, or deſire to obtain any thing prejudicial; and therefore that clauſe which our Lord and Saviour in the Prayer of his agony did expreſs, we in Petitions of like nature do always imply; *Pater, ſi poſſibile eſt*, If it may ſtand with thy will and pleaſure. Or if not, but that there be ſecret impediments and cauſes, in regard whereof the thing we pray for is denied us; yet the Prayer itſelf which we make is a pleaſing Sacrifice to God, who both accepteth and rewardeth it ſome other

* Oratio, quæ non fit per Chriſtum, non ſolum non poteſt delere peccatum, ſed etiam ipſa fit peccatum. Aug. Enar. i. in Pſal. cviii.

 way.

BOOK V. way. So that Sinners, in very truth, are denied when they seem to prevail in their Supplications, because it is not for their sakes, or to their good, that their suits take place; the Faithful contrariwise, because it is for their good oftentimes that their Petitions do not take place, prevail even then when they most seem denied. *Our Lord God in anger hath granted some impenitent Men's requests; as on the other side the Apostles suit he hath of Favour and Mercy not granted* (saith St. Augustin). To think we may pray unto God for nothing but what he hath promised in holy Scripture we shall obtain, is perhaps an error. For of Prayer there are two uses. It serveth as a mean to procure those things which God hath promised to grant when we ask; and it serveth as a mean to express our lawful desires also towards that, which whether we shall have or no, we know not, till we see the event. Things in themselves unholy or unseemly, we may not ask; we may whatsoever, being not forbidden, either Nature or Grace shall reasonably move us to wish as importing the good of Men; albeit God himself have no where by promise assured us of that particular which our Prayer craveth. To pray for that which is in itself, and of its own nature, apparently a thing impossible, were not convenient. Wherefore, though Men do without offence wish daily that the affairs which with evil success are past, might have fallen out much better; yet to pray that they may have been any other than they are, this being a manifest impossibility in itself, the Rules of Religion do not permit. Whereas contrariwise, when things of their own nature contingent and mutable, are by the secret determination of God appointed one way, though we the other way make our Prayers, and consequently ask those things of God, which are by this supposition impossible, we notwithstanding do not hereby in Prayer transgress our lawful bounds. That Christ, as the only begotten Son of God, having no Superior,

Numb xi. 33. 1 Sam. viii. 7. Job i 12. & ii. 6 Luke viii. 32. 2 Cor. xii. 7, 8, 9. Aug. Epist. cxxi. Ad probam viduam.

Superior, and therefore owing honour unto none, neither ſtanding in any need, ſhould either give thanks or make petition unto God, were moſt abſurd. As Man, what could beſeem him better, whether we reſpect his affection to God-ward, or his own neceſſity, or his charity and love towards Men? Some things he knew ſhould come to paſs, and notwithſtanding prayed for them, becauſe he alſo knew that the neceſſary means to effect them were his Prayers. As in the Pſalm it is ſaid, *Aſk of me, and I will give thee the Heathen for thine inheritance, and the ends of the Earth for thy poſſeſſion.* (Pſal. ii. 8.) Wherefore, that which here God promiſeth his Son, the ſame in the ſeventeenth of John he prayeth for: *Father, the hour is come, glorify thy Son, that thy Son alſo may glorify thee, according as thou haſt given him power over all fleſh.* (John xvii. 1, 2.) But had Chriſt the like promiſe concerning the effect of every particular for which he prayed? That which was not effected could not be promiſed. And we know in what ſort he prayed for removal of that bitter cup, which he taſted notwithſtanding his Prayer. (Matt. xxvi. 39. Mark xiv. 36 Luke xxii. 42.) To ſhift off this example they anſwer firſt, * *That as other Children of God, ſo Chriſt had a promiſe of deliverance as far as the glory of God in the accompliſhment of his vocation would ſuffer.* And if we ourſelves have not alſo in that ſort the promiſe of God to be evermore delivered from all adverſity, what meaneth the ſacred Scripture to ſpeak in ſo large terms? *Be obedient, and the Lord thy God will make thee plenteous in every work of thy hand, in the fruit of thy body, and in the fruit of thy cattle, and in the fruit of the land for thy wealth.* (Deut. xxx. 9.) Again, *Keep his Laws, and thou ſhalt be bleſt above all people; the Lord ſhall take from thee all infirmities.* (Deut. vii. 15) *The Man whoſe* (Pſal. i. 4.)

* Neither did our Saviour Chriſt pray without promiſe, for as other the Children of God, to whoſe condition he had humbled himſelf, have, ſo had he a promiſe of deliverance ſo far as the glory of God in that accompliſhment of his vocation would ſuffer. T. C. l. iii. p. 200.

BOOK V. *delight is in the Law of God, whatsoever he doth, it shall prosper. For the ungodly there are great plagues remaining; but whosoever putteth his trust in the Lord, Mercy embraceth him on every side.* Not only that Mercy which keepeth from being overlaid or oppressed, but Mercy which saveth from being touched with grievous miseries, Mercy which turneth away the course of *the great water-floods*, and permitteth them not to *come near*. Nevertheless, because the Prayer of Christ did concern but one calamity, they are still bold to deny the lawfulness of our Prayer for deliverance out of all, yea, though we pray with the same exception that he did, *If such deliverance may stand with the pleasure of Almighty God, and not otherwise.* For they have, secondly, found out a Rule, that Prayer ought only to be made for deliverance *from this or that particular adversity, whereof we know not, but upon the event, what the pleasure of God is.* Which quite overthroweth that other principle, wherein they require unto every Prayer which is of Faith, an assurance to obtain the thing we pray for. At the first to pray against all adversity was unlawful, because we cannot assure ourselves that this will be granted. Now we have licence to pray against any particular adversity, and the reason given, because we know not, but upon the event, what God will do. If we know not what God will do, it followeth, that for any assurance we have he may do otherwise than we pray, and we may faithfully pray for that which we cannot assuredly presume that God will grant. Seeing therefore neither of these two answers will serve the turn, they have a third; which is, *that to pray in such sort is but idly mispent labour, because God hath already revealed his will touching this request; and we know that the suit

Psal. xxxii. 11.

Id. v. 7.

T. C. l. iii. p. 201.

* We ought not to desire to be free from all adversity, if it be his will, considering that he hath already declared his will therein. T. C. l. iii. p. 201.

we

we make is denied before we make it. Which neither is true, and if it were, was Chriſt ignorant what God had determined touching thoſe things which himſelf ſhould ſuffer? To ſay, *He knew not what weight of ſufferances his Heavenly Father had meaſured unto him*, is ſomewhat hard; harder, that although *he knew them*, notwithſtanding for the preſent time *they were forgotten through the force of thoſe unſpeakable pangs which he then was in.* The one againſt the plain expreſs words of the holy Evangeliſt, *He knew all things that ſhould come upon him*, the other leſs credible, if any thing may be of leſs credit than what the Scripture itſelf gainſaith. Doth any of them which wrote his ſufferings make report that memory failed him? Is there in his words and ſpeeches any ſign or defect that way? Did not himſelf declare before whatſoever was to happen in the courſe of that whole tragedy? Can we gather by any thing after taken from his own mouth, either in the place of publick judgment, or upon the altar of the Croſs, that through the bruiſing of his Body ſome part of the treaſures of his Soul were ſcattered and ſlipt from him? If that which was perfect both before and after did fail at this only middle inſtant, there muſt appear ſome manifeſt cauſe how it came to paſs. True it is, that the pangs of his heavineſs and grief were unſpeakable; and as true, that becauſe the minds of the afflicted do never think they have fully conceived the weight or meaſure of their own woe, they uſe their affection as a whetſtone both to wit and memory; theſe as nurſes do feed grief, ſo that the weaker his conceit had been touching that which he was to ſuffer, the more it muſt needs in that hour have helped to the mitigation of his anguiſh. But his anguiſh we ſee was then at the very higheſt whereunto it could poſſibly riſe; which argueth his deep apprehenſion, even to the laſt drop of the gall which that cup contained, and of every circumſtance wherein there was any force to augment heavineſs;

BOOK V.

T. C. l. iii. p. 201.

John xviii. 4.

but

 but above all things, the resolute determination of God and his own unchangeable purpose, which he at that time could not forget. To what intent then was his Prayer, which plainly testifieth so great willingness to avoid death? Will, whether it be in God or Man, belongeth to the Essence or Nature of both. The Nature therefore of God being one, there are not in God divers Wills, although the Godhead be in divers Persons, because the power of willing is a natural, not a personal propriety. Contrariwise, the Person of our Saviour Christ being but one, there are in him two Wills; because two Natures, the Nature of God, and the Nature of Man, which both do imply this faculty and power. So that in Christ there is a divine, and there is an human Will, otherwise he were not both God and Man. Hereupon the Church hath of old condemned Monothelites as Hereticks, for holding that Christ had but one Will. The Works and Operations of our Saviour's human Will were all subject to the Will of God, and framed according to his Law: *I desire to do thy Will, O God, and thy Law is within mine heart.* Now as Man's Will, so the Will of Christ hath two several kinds of operation, the one natural or necessary, whereby it desireth simply whatsoever is good in itself, and shunneth as generally all things which hurt; the other deliberate, when we therefore embrace things as good, because the eye of understanding judgeth them good to that end which we simply desire. Thus in itself we desire health, physick only for health's sake. And in this sort special Reason oftentimes causeth the Will by choice to prefer one good thing before another, to leave one for another's sake, to forego meaner for the attainment of higher desires, which our Saviour likewise did. These different inclinations of the Will considered, the reason is easy, how in Christ there might grow desires seeming, but being not indeed opposite; either the one of them unto the other,

Psal. xl. 8.

other, or either of them to the Will of God. For BOOK V. let the manner of his ſpeech be weighed: *My Soul* John xii. 27. *is now troubled, and what ſhall I ſay? Father, ſave me out of this hour. But yet for this very cauſe I am come unto this hour.* His purpoſe herein was moſt effectually to propoſe to the view of the whole World two contrary objects, the like whereunto in force and efficacy were never preſented in that manner to any, but only to the Soul of Chriſt. There was preſented before his eyes in that fearful hour, on the one ſide, God's heavy indignation and wrath towards Mankind, as yet unappeaſed, Death as yet in full ſtrength, Hell as yet never maſtered by any that came within the confines and bounds thereof, ſomewhat alſo peradventure more than is either poſſible or needful for the wit of Man to find out; finally, himſelf fleſh and blood * left alone to enter into Matt. xxvii. 46. conflict with all theſe: on the other ſide, a World to be ſaved by One, a pacification of wrath through the dignity of that Sacrifice which ſhould be offered, a conqueſt over Death through the power of that Deity which would not ſuffer the Tabernacle thereof to ſee corruption, and an utter diſappointment of all the forces of infernal Powers, through the purity of that Soul which they ſhould have in their hands and not be able to touch. Let no Man marvel that in this caſe the Soul of Chriſt was much troubled. For what could ſuch apprehenſions breed, but (as their

* Non potuit divinitas humanitatem et ſecundum aliquid deſeruiſſe, et ſecundum aliquid non deſeruiſſe? Subtraxit protectionem, ſed non ſuperavit unionem. Sic ergo dereliquit ut non adjuvaret, ſed non dereliquit ut recederet. Sic ergo humanitas a divinitate in paſſione derelicta eſt. Quam tamen mortem quia non pro ſua iniquitate, ſed pro noſtra redemptione ſuſtinuit, quare ſit derelicta requiret, non quaſi adverſus Deum de pœna murmurans, ſed nobis innocentiam ſuam in pœna demonſtrans. Hug. de Sacra, lib. ii. part 1. cap. 10. Deus meus, utquid dereliquiſti me? Vox eſt nec ignorantiæ, nec diffidentiæ, nec querelæ, ſed admirationis tantum, quæ aliis inveſtigandæ cauſæ ardorem et diligentiam acuat.

BOOK V. nature is) inexplicable paſſions of mind, deſires abhorring what they embrace, and embracing what they abhor: in which agony, *how ſhould the tongue go about to expreſs what the Soul endureth?* When the griefs of Job were exceeding great, his words accordingly to open them were many; howbeit, ſtill unto his ſeeming they were undiſcovered: *Though my talk* (ſaith Job) *be this day in bitterneſs, yet my plague is greater than my groaning.* But here to what purpoſe ſhould words ſerve, when Nature hath more to declare than groans and ſtrong cries, more than ſtreams of bloody ſweats, more than his doubled and tripled Prayers can expreſs, who thrice putting forth his hand to receive the cup, beſides which there was no other cauſe of his coming into the World, he thrice pulleth it back again, and as often, even with tears of blood, craveth, *If it be poſſible, O Father; or if not, even what thine own good pleaſure is*; for whoſe ſake the Paſſion, that hath in it a bitter and a bloody conflict, even with Wrath, and Death, and Hell, is moſt welcome. Whereas therefore we find in God a will reſolved that Chriſt ſhall ſuffer; and in the human will of Chriſt two actual deſires, the one avoiding, and the other accepting death; is that deſire which firſt declareth itſelf by Prayer, againſt that wherewith he concludeth Prayer, or either of them againſt his mind to whom Prayer in this caſe ſeeketh? We may judge of theſe diverſities in the Will, by the like in the Underſtanding. For as the intellectual part doth not croſs itſelf, by conceiving Man to be juſt and unjuſt when it meaneth not the ſame Man, nor by imagining the ſame Man learned and unlearned; if learned in one ſkill, and in another kind of learning unſkilful, becauſe the parts of every true oppoſition do always both concern the ſame ſubject, and have reference to the ſame thing, ſith otherwiſe they are but in ſhew oppoſite, and not in truth: ſo the Will about one and the ſame thing may in contrary reſpects have contrary inclinations, and

Job xxiii. 2.

and that without contrariety. The Miniſter of Juſtice may, for publick example to others, virtuouſly will the execution of that party whoſe pardon another for conſanguinity's ſake as virtuouſly may deſire. Conſider Death in itſelf, and Nature teacheth Chriſt to ſhun it. Conſider Death as a mean to procure the Salvation of the World, and Mercy worketh in Chriſt all willingneſs of mind towards it. Therefore in theſe two deſires there can be no repugnant oppoſition. Again, compare them with the Will of God, and if any oppoſition be, it muſt be only between his appointment of Chriſt's death and the former deſire which wiſheth deliverance from death. But neither is this deſire oppoſite to the Will of God. The Will of God was, that Chriſt ſhould ſuffer the pains of death. Not ſo his Will, as if the torment of innocency did in itſelf pleaſe and delight God; but ſuch was his Will, in regard of the end whereunto it was neceſſary, that Chriſt ſhould ſuffer. The death of Chriſt in itſelf, therefore, God willeth not, which to the end we might thereby obtain life, he both alloweth and appointeth. In like manner, the Son of Man endureth willingly to that purpoſe thoſe grievous pains, which ſimply not to have ſhunned had been againſt Nature, and by conſequent againſt God. I take it therefore to be an error, that Chriſt either knew not what himſelf was to ſuffer, or elſe had forgotten the things he knew. The root of which error was an overreſtrained conſideration of Prayer, as though it had no other lawful uſe but only to ſerve for a choſen mean, whereby the Will reſolveth to ſeek that which the Underſtanding certainly knoweth it ſhall obtain: whereas Prayers, in truth, both ours are, and his were, as well ſometime a preſentation of mere deſires, as a mean of procuring deſired effects at the hand of God. We are therefore taught by his example, that the preſence of dolorous and dreadful objects, even in minds moſt perfect, may as clouds overcaſt

Iſai. liii. 10.
Job x. 15.

BOOK V. overcaſt all ſenſible joy; that no aſſurance touching future victories can make preſent conflicts ſo ſweet and eaſy, but Nature will ſhun and ſhrink from them; Nature will deſire eaſe and deliverance from oppreſſive burthens; that the contrary determination of God is oftentimes againſt the effect of this deſire, yet not againſt the affection itſelf, becauſe it is naturally in us; that in ſuch caſe our Prayers cannot ſerve us as means to obtain the thing we deſire; that notwithſtanding they are unto God moſt acceptable ſacrifices, becauſe they teſtify we deſire nothing but at his hands, and our deſires we ſubmit with contentment to be over-ruled by his Will; and in general they are not repugnant unto the natural Will of God, which wiſheth to the works of his own hands, in that they are his own handy-work, all happineſs; although perhaps for ſome ſpecial cauſe in our own particular, a contrary determination have ſeemed more convenient; finally, that thus to propoſe our deſires which cannot take ſuch effects as we ſpecify, ſhall notwithſtanding otherwiſe procure us his heavenly grace, even as this very Prayer of Chriſt obtained Angels to be ſent him as comforters in his agony. (Luke xxii. 43.) And, according to this example, we are not afraid to preſent unto God our Prayers for thoſe things, which that he will perform unto us we have no ſure nor certain knowledge. St. Paul's Prayer for the Church of Corinth was, (2 Cor. xiii. 7.) that they might not do any evil, although he knew that no Man liveth which ſinneth not, although he knew that in this life we always muſt pray, * *Forgive us our Sins.* It is our frailty, that in many things we all do amiſs; but a virtue, that we would do amiſs in nothing; and a teſtimony of that virtue, when we pray that what occaſion of ſin ſoever do offer

* We may not pray in this life, to be free from all ſin, becauſe we muſt always pray, Forgive us our Sins. T. C. lib. iii. p. 200.

itſelf,

itſelf, we may be ſtrengthened from above to withſtand it. They pray in vain to have ſin pardoned, which ſeek not alſo to prevent ſin by Prayer, even every particular Sin, by Prayer againſt all Sin; except Men can name ſome tranſgreſſion wherewith we ought to have truce. For in very deed, although we cannot be free from all Sin collectively, in ſuch ſort that no part thereof ſhall be found inherent in us, yet diſtributively, at the leaſt, all great and grievous actual offences, as they offer themſelves one by one, both may and ought to be by all means avoided. So that in this ſenſe, to be preſerved from all Sin, is not impoſſible. Finally, concerning deliverance itſelf from all Adverſity, we uſe not to ſay Men are in adverſity whenſoever they feel any ſmall hindrance of their welfare in this World, but when ſome notable affliction or croſs, ſome great calamity or trouble befalleth them. Tribulation hath in it divers circumſtances, the Mind ſundry faculties to apprehend them: it offereth ſometime itſelf to the lower powers of the Soul, as a moſt unpleaſant ſpectacle; to the higher ſometimes, as drawing after it a train of dangerous inconveniencies; ſometime as bringing with it remedies for the curing of ſundry evils, as God's inſtrument of revenge and fury ſometimes; ſometime as a rod of his juſt, yet moderate ire and diſpleaſure; ſometime as matter for them that ſpitefully hate us to exerciſe their poiſoned malice; ſometime as a furnace of trial for virtue to ſhew itſelf, and through conflict to obtain glory. Which different contemplations of adverſity do work for the moſt part their anſwerable effects. Adverſity either apprehended by Senſe as a thing offenſive and grievous to Nature, or by Reaſon conceived as a ſnare, an occaſion of many Men's falling from God, a ſequel of God's indignation and wrath, a thing which Satan deſireth and would be glad to behold; Tribulation thus conſidered being preſent cauſeth ſorrow, and being imminent breedeth fear.

For

BOOK V. For moderation of which two affections, growing from the very natural bitterness and gall of adversity, the Scripture much alledgeth contrary fruits, which (Psal. cxix. 71.) Affliction likewise hath whensoever it falleth on them that are tractable, the Grace of God's Holy Spirit concurring therewith. But when the Apostle St. Paul teacheth, *That every one which will live godly in Christ Jesus, must suffer persecution*, (2 Tim. iii. 12.) * and, *by many tribulations we must enter into the Kingdom of Heaven*, because in a forest of many wolves, sheep cannot choose but feed in continual danger of life; or when St. James exhorteth to *account it a matter of exceeding joy, when we fall into divers temptations*, (Jam. i. 3.) because *by the trial of Faith, Patience* is brought forth; was it, suppose we, their meaning to frustrate our Lord's admonition, *Pray that ye enter not into temptation?* When himself pronounceth them blessed that should for his Name's sake be subject to all kinds of ignominy and opprobrious malediction, was it his purpose that no Man should ever pray with David, *Lord, remove from me shame and contempt?* (Psal. cxix. 22.) In those tribulations, saith St. Augustin, (Aug. Epist 121. c. 14.) *which may hurt as well as profit, we must say with the Apostle, What we should ask as we ought we know not; yet because they are tough, because they are grievous, because the sense of our weakness flieth them, we pray according to the general desire of the will of Man, that God would turn them away from us: owing in the mean while this devotion to the Lord our God; that if he remove them not, yet we do not therefore imagine ourselves in his sight despised, but rather with godly sufferance of evils expect greater good at his merciful hands. For thus is virtue in weakness perfected.* To the Flesh (as the Apostle himself granteth) all Affliction is naturally grievous. Therefore Nature, which causeth to fear, teacheth to

* To pray against persecution, is contrary to that word which saith, That every one which will live godly in Christ Jesus, must suffer persecution. T. C. lib. iii. p. 200.

pray

BOOK V.

pray against all Adversity. Prosperity in regard of our corrupt inclination to abuse the blessings of Almighty God, doth prove for the most part a thing dangerous to the Souls of Men Very ease itself is death to the Wicked, *and the prosperity of Fools slayeth them:* their table is a snare, and their felicity their utter overthrow. Few Men there are which long prosper and sin not. Howbeit, even as these ill effects, although they be very usual and common, are no bar to the hearty Prayers whereby most virtuous minds wish peace and prosperity always where they love, because they consider that this in itself is a thing naturally desired: so because all Adversity is in itself against Nature, what should hinder to pray against it, although the Providence of God turn it often unto the great good of many Men? Such Prayers of the Church to be delivered from all Adversity are no more repugnant to any reasonable disposition of Men's minds towards death, much less to that blessed patience and meek contentment which Saints by heavenly inspiration have to endure (what cross or calamity soever it pleaseth God to lay upon them) than our Lord and Saviour's own Prayer before his Passion was repugnant unto his most gracious resolution to die for the Sins of the whole World. Prov. i. 32.

Prayer, that all Men may find Mercy, and of the Will of God that all Men might be saved

49. In praying for deliverance from all Adversity, we seek that which Nature doth wish to itself; but by intreating for Mercy towards all, we declare that affection wherewith Christian Charity thirsteth after the good of the whole World, we discharge that duty which the Apostle himself doth impose on the Church of Christ, as a commendable office, a sacrifice acceptable in God's sight, a service according to his heart, whose desire is to have all Men saved: a work most suitable with his purpose, who gave himself to be the price of redemption for all, and a forcible mean to procure the conversion of all such as are not yet acquainted with the Mysteries of that Truth which must save their Souls. Against it, 1 Tim. ii. 3.

BOOK V. there is but the bare shew of this one impediment, that all Men's Salvation, and many Men's eternal condemnation or death, are things, the one repugnant to the other; that both cannot be brought to pass; that we know there are Vessels of Wrath, to whom God will never extend Mercy, and therefore that wittingly we ask an impossible thing to be had. The truth is, that as life and death, mercy and wrath are matters of mere understanding or knowledge, all Men's Salvation, and some Men's endless perdition, are things so opposite, that whosoever doth affirm the one must necessarily deny the other; God himself cannot effect both, or determine that both shall be. There is in the knowledge both of God and Man this certainty, that Life and Death hath divided between them the whole body of Mankind. What portion either of the two hath, God himself knoweth; for us he hath left no sufficient means to comprehend, and for that cause neither given any leave to search in particular who are infallibly the Heirs of the Kingdom of God, who cast-aways. Howbeit, concerning the state of all Men with whom we live (for only of them our Prayers are meant) we may till the World's end, for the present, always presume, that as far as in us there is power to discern what others are; and as far as any duty of ours dependeth upon the notice of their condition in respect of God, the safest axioms for Charity to rest itself upon, are these: *He which believeth already, is*; and *he which believeth not as yet, may be the Child of God.* It becometh not us, *during life, altogether to condemn any Man, seeing that* (for any thing we know) *there is hope of every Man's forgiveness; the possibility of whose repentance is not yet cut off by death.* And therefore Charity, which *hopeth all things*, prayeth also for all Men. Wherefore to let go personal knowledge touching Vessels of Wrath and Mercy, what they are inwardly in the sight of God it skilleth not; for us there is cause sufficient in all Men, whereupon to ground our prayers unto God in their behalf.

Sidon. Apol lib. vi. Epist.

1 Cor. xiv. 7.

behalf. For whatsoever the Mind of Man apprehendeth as good, the will of Charity and Love is to have it enlarged in the very uttermost extent, that all may enjoy it to whom it can any way add perfection. Because, therefore, the farther a good thing doth reach, the nobler and worthier we reckon it; our Prayers for all Men's good, no less than for our own, the Apostle with very fit terms commendeth as being καλὸν, a work commendable for the largeness of the affection from whence it springeth; even as theirs which have requested at God's hands the salvation of many with the loss of their own Souls; drowning, as it were, and overwhelming themselves in the abundance of their love towards others, is proposed as being in regard of the rareness of such affections ὑπερκαλὸν, more than excellent. But this extraordinary height of desire after other Men's salvation, is no common mark. The other is a duty which belongeth unto all, and prevaileth with God daily. For as it is in itself good, so God accepteth and taketh it in very good part at the hands of faithful Men. Our Prayers for all Men do include both them that shall find mercy, and them also that shall find none. For them that shall, no Man will doubt but our Prayers are both accepted and granted. Touching them for whom we crave that mercy which is not to be obtained, let us not think that our Saviour did mis-instruct his Disciples, willing them to pray for the peace even of such as should be uncapable of so great a blessing; or that the Prayers of the Prophet Jeremy offended God, because the answer of God was a resolute denial of favour to them for whom supplication was made. And if any Man doubt how God should accept such Prayers in case they be opposite to his Will, or not grant them if they be according unto that which himself willeth, our answer is, that such suits God accepteth in that they are conformable unto his general inclination, which is that all Men might be saved;

BOOK V.

Rom ix. 3, 8. x. 1.

Matth. x. 11, 12.

Jer xv. 1.

 yet

yet always he granteth them not, for as much as there is in God ſometimes a more private occaſioned Will which determineth the contrary. So that the other being the rule of our actions, and not this; our requeſts for things oppoſite to this Will of God are not therefore the leſs gracious in his ſight. There is no doubt but we ought in all things to frame our wills to the Will of God, and that otherwiſe in whatſoever we do we ſin. For of ourſelves, being ſo apt to err, the only way which we have to ſtrengthen our paths is by following the rule of his Will, whoſe footſteps naturally are right. If the eye, the hand, or the foot, do that which the Will commandeth, though they ſerve as inſtruments to ſin, yet is ſin the commander's fault and not theirs, becauſe Nature hath abſolutely, and without exception, made them ſubjects to the Will of Man, which is Lord over them. As the Body is ſubject to the Will of Man, ſo Man's Will to the Will of God; for ſo it behoveth that the better ſhould guide and command the worſe. But becauſe the ſubjection of the Body to the Will is, by natural neceſſity, the ſubjection of the Will unto God voluntary; we therefore ſtand in need of direction after what ſort our Wills and Deſires may be rightly conformed to his: which is not done, by willing always the ſelf-ſame thing that God intendeth. For it may chance, that his purpoſe is ſometime the ſpeedy death of them whoſe long continuance in life if we ſhould not wiſh we were unnatural. When the object or matter therefore of our deſires is (as in this caſe) a thing both good of itſelf, and not forbidden of God; when the end for which we deſire it is virtuous and apparently moſt holy; when the root from which our affection towards it proceedeth is Charity; Piety that which we do in declaring our deſire by Prayer; yea, over and beſides all this, ſith we know, that to pray for all Men living is but to ſhew the ſame affection which towards every of them our Lord Jeſus Chriſt hath

hath borne, who knowing only as God who are his,* did as Man taste death for the good of all Men; surely, to that Will of God which ought to be, and is the known rule of all our actions, we do not herein oppose ourselves, although his secret determination happily be against us; which if we did understand, as we do not, yet to rest contented with that which God will have done, is as much as he requireth at the hands of Men. And concerning ourselves, what we earnestly crave in this case, the same as all things else that are of like condition, we meekly submit unto his most gracious will and pleasure. Finally, as we have cause sufficient why to think the practice of our Church allowable in this behalf, so neither is ours the first which hath been of that mind. For to end with the words of Prosper, *This Law of Supplication for all Men* (saith he), *the devout zeal of all Priests, and of all faithful Men, doth hold with such full agreement, that there is not any part of all the World, where Christian People do not use to pray in the same manner. The Church every where maketh Prayers unto God, not only for Saints, and such as already in Christ are regenerate; but for all Infidels and Enemies of the Cross of Jesus Christ, for all Idolaters, for all that persecute Christ in his Followers, for Jews to whose blindness the light of the Gospel doth not yet shine, for Hereticks and Schismaticks, who from the unity of Faith and Charity are estranged. And for such, what doth the Church ask of God but this, that, leaving their errors, they may be converted unto him, that Faith and Charity may be given them, and that out of the darkness of ignorance they may come to the knowledge of his Truth? which because they cannot themselves do in*

Prosp. de Vocat. Gen. l i. c 4. inter opera Ambros.

* Propterea nihil contrarietatis erat, si Christus homo secundum affectum pietatis quam in humanitate sua assumpserat aliquid volebat, quod tamen secundum voluntatem divinam, in quâ cum Patre omnia disponebat, futurum non esse præsciebat; quia et hoc ad veram humanitatem pertinebat, ut pietate moveretur, et hoc ad veram divinitatem, ut a sua dispositione non moveretur. Hug. de Quat. Christi Volunt.

their

 their own behalf, as long as the sway of evil custom overbeareth them, and the chains of Satan detain them bound, neither are they able to break through those errors wherein they are so determinately settled, that they pay unto falsity the whole sum of whatsoever love is owing unto God's Truth, our Lord merciful and just requireth to have all Men prayed for; that when we behold innumerable multitudes drawn up from the depth of so bottomless evils, we may not doubt, but (in part) God hath done the thing we requested; nor despair, but that being thankful for them, towards whom already he hath shewed mercy, the rest which are not as yet enlightened, shall before they pass out of life be made partakers of the like grace Or if the Grace of him which saveth (for so we see it falleth out) overpass some, so that the Prayer of the Church for them be not received, this we may leave to the hidden judgments of God's Righteousness, and acknowledge that in this secret there is a gulf, which while we live we shall never found.

Of the Name, the Author, and the force of Sacraments, which Force consisteth in this, that God hath ordained them as means to make us Partakers of him in Christ, of life through Christ

50. Instruction and Prayer, whereof we have hitherto spoken, are duties which serve as elements, parts or principles to the rest that follow, in which number the Sacraments of the Church are chief. The Church is to us that very * Mother of our New Birth, in whose bowels we are all bred, at whose breasts we receive nourishment. As many therefore as are apparently to our judgment born of God, they have the seed of their Regeneration by the Ministry of the Church, which useth to that end and purpose not only the Word, but the Sacraments, both having generative force and virtue. As oft as we mention a Sacrament properly understood (for in the writings of the Ancient Fathers, all Articles which are peculiar to Christian Faith, all Duties of Religion containing that which Sense or natural Reason cannot of itself discern, are most commonly named Sacraments) our restraint of the Word to some few principal divine Ceremonies, importeth in every such Ceremony two things; the substance of the Ceremony itself which is visible,

* Gal. iv 26 Isai. liv. 3.

visible, and besides that somewhat else more secret, in reference whereunto we conceive that Ceremony to be a Sacrament. For we all admire and honour the holy Sacraments, not respecting so much the service which we do unto God in receiving them, as the dignity of that sacred and secret gift which we thereby receive from God. Seeing that Sacraments therefore consist altogether in relation to some such gift or grace supernatural, as only God can bestow, how should any but the Church administer those Ceremonies as Sacraments, which are not thought to be Sacraments by any but by the Church? There is in Sacraments to be observed their force and their form of Administration. Upon their force, their necessity dependeth. So that how they are necessary we cannot discern till we see how effectual they are. When Sacraments are said to be visible signs of invisible Grace, we thereby conceive how Grace is indeed the very end for which these heavenly Mysteries were instituted; and besides sundry other properties observed in them, the matter whereof they consist is such as signifieth, figureth, and representeth their end. But still their efficacy resteth obscure to our understanding, except we search somewhat more distinctly what Grace in particular that is whereunto they are referred, and what manner of operation they have towards it. The use of Sacraments is but only in this life, yet so, that here they concern a far better life than this, and are for that cause accompanied with Grace which worketh Salvation. Sacraments are the powerful instruments of God to eternal Life. For as our natural Life consisteth in the Union of the Body with the Soul, so our Life supernatural in the Union of the Soul with God. And for as much as there is no Union of God with Man,* without that mean between both, which is both; it seemeth requi- BOOK V.

* Oportebat Deum carnem fieri ut in semetipso concordiam confibularet terrenorum pariter atque cælestium, dum utriusque partis in se connectens pignora, et Deum pariter Homini et Hominem Deo copularet. Tertul. de Trinit.

 site,

 site, that we first consider how God is in Christ, then how Christ is in us, and how the Sacraments do serve to make us partakers of Christ. In other things we may be more brief, but the weight of these requireth largeness.

That God is in Christ by the personal Incarnation of the Son, who is very God.

51. The Lord our God is but one God. In which indivisible Unity notwithstanding we adore the Father, as being altogether of himself; we glorify that consubstantial Word which is the Son; we bless and magnify that co-essential Spirit eternally proceeding from both, which is the Holy Ghost. Seeing therefore the Father is of none, the Son is of the Father, and the Spirit is of both, they are by these their several properties really distinguishable each from other. For the Substance of God, with this property to be of none, doth make the Person of the Father; the very self-same Substance in number with this property to be of the Father, maketh the Person of the Son; the same Substance having added unto it the property of proceeding from the other two, maketh the Person of the Holy Ghost. So that in every Person there is implied both the Substance of God, which is one; and also that property which causeth the same Person really and truly to differ from the other two. Every Person hath his own subsistence which no other Person hath,* although there be others besides that are of the same Substance. As no man but Peter can be the person which Peter is, yet Paul hath the self-same Nature which Peter hath. Again, Angels have every of them the Nature of pure and invisible Spirits; but every Angel is not that Angel which appeared in a dream to Joseph. Now when God became Man, lest we should err in applying this to the Person of the

Isai. ix 6. Jer. xxiii 6. Rom. ix. 5. John xvi. 15, & v. 21. Col. ii. 9. 1 John v. 20.

* Πρόσωπον ἤγουν ὑπόστασίς ἐστι κατὰ τοὺς ἁγίους πατέρας τὸ ἴδιον παρὰ τὸ κοινόν· Κοινότης γὰρ ἐστὶν ἡ φύσις ἑκάστου πράγματος, ἴδιαι δὲ εἰσὶν αἱ ὑποστάσεις. Suid. Ἡ οὐσία καθ᾽ ἑαυτὴν οὐχ ὑφίσταται, ἀλλ᾽ ἐν ταῖς ὑποστάσεσι θεωρεῖται· τὸ δὲ κοινὸν μετὰ τοῦ ἰδιάζοντος ἔχει ἡ ὑπόστασις καὶ τὸ καθ᾽ ἑαυτὴν ὑπάρξαι. Damasc. de Orthod. Fide, lib. iii. cap. 6.

Father

Father or of the Spirit, St. Peter's confeſſion unto Christ was, *Thou art the Son of the Living God*; and St. John's Expoſition thereof was plain, that it is the * Word which was made Fleſh. † *The Father and the Holy Ghoſt* (ſaith Damaſcen) *have no communion with the Incarnation of the Word, otherwiſe than only by approbation and aſſent.* Notwithſtanding, for as much as the Word and Deity are one ſubject, we muſt beware we exclude not the Nature of God from Incarnation, and ſo make the Son of God incarnate not to be very God. For undoubtedly, ‡ even the Nature of God itſelf in the only Perſon of the Son is incarnate, and hath taken to itſelf Fleſh. Wherefore, Incarnation may neither be granted to any Perſon but only One, nor yet denied to that Nature which is common unto all Three. Concerning the cauſe of which incomprehenſible Myſtery, for as much as it ſeemeth a thing unconſonant that the World ſhould honour any other as the Saviour, but him whom it honoureth as the Creator of the World, and in the Wiſdom of God it hath not been thought convenient to admit any way of ſaving Man but by Man himſelf, though nothing ſhould be ſpoken of the Love and Mercy of God towards Man, which this way are become ſuch a ſpectacle as neither Men nor Angels can behold without a kind of heavenly aſtoniſhment, we may hereby perceive there is cauſe ſufficient why Divine Nature ſhould aſſume human, that ſo God might be in Chriſt reconciling to himſelf the World. And if ſome cauſe be likewiſe required why rather to this end and purpoſe the Son than either the Father or the Holy Ghoſt ſhould be made Man, could we which are born the

BOOK V.

Matt xvi. 16.

John i. 14.

2 Cor. v. 19.

* Ignat. Epiſt ad Magneſ. Ὅς ἐςιν αὐτȣ͂ Λόγος ὀ ῥητὸς ἀλλ' ὀσιώδης. Οὐ γάρ ἐςι λαλιᾶς ἐνάρθρȣ φώνημα, ἀλλ' ἐνεργείας θείης ȣ̓σία γεννητή.

† Κατ' ȣ̓δένα λογον κεκοινώνηκεν ὁ Πατὴρ καὶ τὸ Πνεῦμα τὸ ἅγιον τῇ σαρκώσει τȣ͂ Λόγȣ, εἰ μὴ κατ' εὐδοκίαν καὶ βȣ́λησιν. Damaſc.

‡ In illo Divinitas eſt Unigeniti facta particeps mortalitatis noſtræ, ut et nos participes ejus immortalitatis eſſemus. Aug. Epiſt. 57.

Children

BOOK V. Children of wrath, be adopted the Sons of God, through Grace, any other than the natural Son of God being Mediator between God and us? It became therefore him, by whom all things are, to be the way of Salvation to all, that the Institution and Restitution of the World might be both wrought by one hand. The World's Salvation was without the Incarnation of the Son of God a thing impossible; not simply impossible, but impossible, it being presupposed, that the Will of God was no otherwise to have it saved than by the Death of his own Son. Wherefore taking to himself our Flesh, and by his Incarnation, making it his own Flesh, he had now of his own, although from us, what to offer unto God for us. And as Christ took Manhood, that by it he might be capable of death, whereunto he humbled himself; so because Manhood is the proper subject of compassion and feeling pity, which maketh the Sceptre of Christ's Regency even in the Kingdom of Heaven be amiable, he which without our Nature could not on Earth suffer for the sins of the World, doth now also, by means thereof, both make intercession to God for Sinners, and exercise dominion over all Men with a true, a natural, and a sensible touch of mercy.

Heb. ii. 10.

Heb. iv. 15.

The misinterpretations which Heresy hath made of the manner how God and Man are united in one Christ.

52. It is not in Man's ability either to express perfectly, or conceive the manner how this was brought to pass. But the strength of our Faith is tried by those things wherein our wits and capacities are not strong. Howbeit, because this divine Mystery is more true than plain, divers, having framed the same to their own conceits and fancies, are found in their expositions thereof more plain than true: in so much, that by the space of five hundred years after Christ the Church was almost troubled with nothing else, saving only with care and travel to preserve this Article from the sinister construction of Hereticks; whose first mists when the light of the Nicene Council had dispelled, it was not long ere Macedonius transferred unto God's most holy Spirit the same blasphemy

An Dom. 325.

blaſphemy wherewith Arius had already diſhonoured BOOK V.
his co-eternal begotten Son; not long ere Apollinarius* began to pare away from Chriſt's Humanity. In refutation of which impieties, when the Fathers of the Church, Athanaſius, Baſil, and the two Gregories, had by their painful travels ſufficiently cleared the truth, no leſs for the Deity of the Holy Ghoſt than for the complete Humanity of Chriſt, there followed hereupon a final concluſion, whereby thoſe controverſies, as alſo the reſt which Paulus Samoſatenus, Sabellius, Photinus, Ætius, Eunomius, together with the whole ſwarm of peſtilent Demi-arians had from time to time ſtirred up ſince the Council of Nice, were both privately, firſt at Rome in a ſmaller Synod, and then at Conſtantinople in a general famous Aſ- An. Dom.
ſembly, brought to a peaceable and quiet end; ſeven- 381.
ſcore Biſhops and ten agreeing in that Confeſſion, which, by them ſet down, remaineth at this preſent hour a part of our Church-Liturgy, a memorial of their Fidelity and Zeal, a ſovereign preſervative of God's People from the venomous infection of Hereſy. Thus in Chriſt the verity of God, and the complete ſubſtance of Man, were with full agreement eſtabliſhed throughout the World, till ſuch time as the Hereſy of Neſtorius broached itſelf, † *dividing Chriſt into two Perſons, the Son of God, and the Son of Man; the one a Perſon begotten of God before all Worlds, the other alſo a Perſon born of the Virgin Mary, and in ſpecial favour choſen to be made entire to the Son of God above all Men, ſo that whoſoever will honour God, muſt together honour Chriſt, with whoſe Perſon God hath vouchſafed to join himſelf in ſo high a degree of gracious reſpect*

* Μηδὲ γὰρ δεηθῆναι φησὶ τὴν σάρκα ἐκείνην ἀνθρωπίνου νοὸς ἡγεμονευομένην ὑπὸ τοῦ αὐτὴν ἐνδεδυκότος θεοῦ. Suid.

† Οὐκ ἔτι τὴν ἕνωσιν ὁμολογεῖ μεθ' ἡμῶν. Cyril. Epiſt. ad Eulog. Οὐκ ἔλεγε γὰρ ἕνωσιν τοῦ Λόγου τοῦ Θεοῦ πρὸς Ἄνθρωπον, ἀλλὰ δύο ὑποστάσεις ἔλεγε καὶ διαίρεσιν. Εἰ δὲ καὶ Ἄνθρωπον καὶ Θεὸν ἀπεκάλει τὸν Χριστὸν, ἀλλ' οὐκ ἔτι ὡς ἡμεῖς, ἀλλὰ τῇ σχέσει καὶ τῇ οἰκειώσει κατὰ τὸ ταὐτὰ ἀλλήλοις ἀρέσκειν διὰ τὴν ὑπερβολὴν τῆς φιλίας. Leont. de Sect.

and

BOOK V. *and favour.* But that the self-same Person which verily is Man, should properly be God also, and that by reason not of two Persons linked in amity, but of two Natures human and divine, conjoined in one and the same Person, the God of Glory may be said as well to have suffered death as to have raised the dead from their graves; the Son of Man as well to have made, as to have redeemed the World, Nestorius in no case would admit. That which deceived him was want of heed to the first beginning of that admirable combination

John i. 14 of God with Man. *The Word* (saith St. John) *was made flesh, and dwelt in us.* The Evangelist useth the plural number, Men for Manhood, *us* for the Nature whereof we consist, even as the Apostle, denying the Assumption of Angelical Nature, saith likewise in the

Heb. ii. 16 plural number, he took not Angels, but the Seed of Abraham. It pleased not the Word or Wisdom of God, to take to itself some one Person amongst Men, for then should that one have been advanced which was assumed, and no more; but Wisdom, to the end she might save many, built her house of that Nature which is common unto all; she made not this or that Man her habitation, but dwelt *in us.* The seeds of herbs and plants at the first are not in act, but in possibility that which they afterwards grow to be. If the Son of God had taken to himself a Man now made and already perfected, it would of necessity follow that there are in Christ two Persons, the one assuming and the other assumed; whereas the Son of God did not assume a Man's Person into his own, but a Man's Nature to his own Person, and therefore took Semen, the Seed of Abraham, the very first original element of our Nature, before it was come to have any personal human subsistence. The Flesh and the conjunction of the Flesh with God began both at one instant;* his making and taking to himself our Flesh was

* Ἡ ἀνθρωπεία φύσις οὐ προϋπῆρχε τῆς λήψεως. Theod. Dial. Ἄτρεπτος.

but

but one act, so that in Christ there is no personal subsistence but one, and that from everlasting. By taking only the Nature of Man, he still continueth one Person, and changeth but the manner of his subsisting, which was before in the mere glory of the Son of God, and is now in the habit of our Flesh. For as much therefore as Christ hath no personal subsistence but one, whereby we acknowledge him to have been eternally the Son of God, we must of necessity apply to the Person of the Son of God, even that which is spoken of Christ according to his Human Nature. For example, according to the flesh, he was born of the Virgin Mary, baptized of John in the river Jordan, by Pilate adjudged to die, and executed by the Jews. We cannot say properly, that the Virgin bore, or John did baptize, or Pilate condemn, or the Jews crucify the Nature of Man, because these all are personal Attributes; his Person is the subject which receiveth them, his Nature that which maketh his Person capable or apt to receive. If we should say, that the Person of a Man in our Saviour Christ was the subject of these things, this were plainly to intrap ourselves in the very snare of the Nestorians Heresy, between whom and the Church of God there was no difference, saving only that Nestorius imagined in Christ as well a personal Human Substance, as a Divine; the Church acknowledging a Substance both Divine and Human, but no other personal Substance than Divine, because the Son of God took not to himself a Man's Person, but the Nature only of a Man. Christ is a Person both Divine and Human, howbeit not therefore two Persons in one; neither both these in one sense, but a Person Divine, because he is personally the Son of God, Human, because he hath really the Nature of the Children of Men. In Christ therefore God and Man, *There is* (saith Paschasius) *a twofold Substance, not a twofold Person, because one Person extinguisheth another, whereas one nature cannot in another become extinct.* For the personal Being which the Son of God already had, suffered

Pasch. lib. de Spir. Sanct.

ſuffered not the Subſtance to be perſonal which he took, although together with the Nature which he had, the Nature alſo which he took, continueth. Whereupon it followeth againſt Neſtorius, that no Perſon was born of the Virgin but the Son of God, no Perſon but the Son of God baptized, the Son of God condemned, the Son of God and no other Perſon crucified; which one only point of Chriſtian Belief, *The infinite worth of the Son of God*, is the very ground of all things believed concerning Life and Salvation, by that which Chriſt either did or ſuffered as Man in our behalf. But for as much as St. Cyril, the chiefeſt of thoſe two hundred Biſhops aſſembled in the Council of Epheſus, where the Hereſy of Neſtorius was condemned, had in his Writings againſt the Arians avouched, that the Word or Wiſdom of God hath but one Nature, which is eternal, and whereunto he aſſumed Fleſh (for the Arians were of opinion, that, beſides God's own eternal Wiſdom, there is a Wiſdom which God created before all things, to the end he might thereby create all things elſe; and that this created Wiſdom was the Word which took Fleſh): again, for as much as the ſame Cyril had given inſtance in the Body and the Soul of Man, no farther than only to enforce by example againſt Neſtorius, that a viſible and inviſible, a mortal and an immortal Subſtance, may united make one Perſon; the words of Cyril were in proceſs of time ſo taken, as though it had been his drift to teach, that even as in us the Body and the Soul, ſo in Chriſt God and Man, make but one Nature. Of which error, ſix hundred and thirty Fathers in the Council of Chalcedon condemned Eutyches. For as Neſtorius teaching rightly, that God and Man are diſtinct Natures, did thereupon miſ-infer, that in Chriſt thoſe Natures can by no conjunction make one Perſon; ſo Eutyches, of ſound belief as touching their true perſonal copulation, became unſound, by denying the difference which ſtill continueth between the one and the other Nature. We muſt

An. Dom. 431.

An. Dom. 451.

muſt therefore keep warily a middle courſe, ſhunning both that diſtraction of Perſons, wherein Neſtorius went awry; and alſo this later confuſion of Natures, which deceived Eutyches.* Theſe Natures from the moment of their firſt combination have been and are for ever inſeparable. For even when his Soul forſook the tabernacle of his Body, his Deity forſook neither Body nor Soul. If it had, then could we not truly hold, either that the Perſon of Chriſt was buried, or that the Perſon of Chriſt did raiſe up himſelf from the dead. For the Body ſeparated from the Word, can in no true ſenſe be termed the Perſon of Chriſt; nor is it true to ſay, that the Son of God, in raiſing up that Body, did raiſe up himſelf, if the Body were not both with him, and of him, even during the time it lay in the ſepulchre. The like is alſo to be ſaid of the Soul, otherwiſe we are plainly and inevitably Neſtorians. The very Perſon of Chriſt therefore, for ever one and the ſelf-ſame, was only, touching bodily Subſtance, concluded within the grave, his Soul only from thence ſevered; but by perſonal Union his Deity ſtill inſeparably joined with both.

That by the Union of the one with the other Nature in Chriſt, there groweth neither gain nor loſs of eſſential Properties to either.

53. The ſequel of which Conjunction of Natures in the Perſon of Chriſt is no aboliſhment of natural Properties appertaining to either Subſtance, no tranſition or tranſmigration thereof out of one ſubſtance into another: finally, no ſuch mutual infuſion, as really cauſeth the ſame natural Operations or Properties to be made common unto both Subſtances; but whatſoever is natural to Deity, the ſame remaineth in Chriſt uncommunicated unto his Manhood, and whatſoever natural to Manhood, his Deity thereof is uncapable. The true Properties and Operations of his Deity are, to know that which is not poſſible for created Natures to comprehend; to be ſimply the higheſt Cauſe of all things, the Well-ſpring of Immortality

* Ἀχώριστον προσήκει τῆς σαρκὸς εἶναι τὴν θείαν φύσιν ὁμολογεῖν, κἂν τῷ σταυρῷ κἂν τῷ τάφῳ. Theodor. Dial. Ἀπαθής.

and

BOOK V. and Life; to have neither end nor beginning of days; to be every where present, and inclosed no where; to be subject to no alteration nor passion; to produce of itself those effects which cannot proceed but from infinite Majesty and Power. The true Properties and Operations of his Manhood are such as Irenæus reckoneth up, * *If Christ* (saith he) *had not taken flesh from the very Earth, he would not have coveted those earthly nourishments, wherewith Bodies which be taken from thence are fed. This was the Nature which felt hunger after long fasting, was desirous of rest after travel, testified compassion and love by tears, groaned in heaviness, and with extremity of grief even melted away itself into bloody sweats.* To Christ we ascribe both working of wonders, and suffering of pains; we use concerning him speeches as well of humility, as of divine glory; but the one we apply unto that Nature which he took of the Virgin Mary, the other to that which was in the beginning. We may not therefore imagine, that the properties of the weaker Nature have vanished with the presence of the more glorious, and have been therein swallowed up as in a gulf. We dare not in this point give ear to them who over-boldly affirm, *That the Nature which Christ took weak and feeble from us, by being mingled with Deity, became the same which Deity is; that the Assumption of our Substance unto his, was like the blending of a drop of vinegar with the huge ocean, wherein although it continue still, yet not with those properties which severed it hath; because sithence the instant of their conjunction, all distinction and difference of the one from the other is extinct, and whatsoever we can now conceive of the Son of God is nothing else but mere Deity:* which words are so plain and direct for

Greg. Nyss. Epist. ad Theoph.l. Alexandr. Hilar. de Trin. lib. ix.

* Ταῦτα πάντα σύμβολα σαρκὸς τὴς ἀπὸ γῆς εἰλημμένης. Iren. l. iii. advers Hæres. Christ did all these ἀνθρωπίνε σώματ@ νόμῳ. Greg. Nazian. Orat. ii. de Filio. Τὲς μὲν ταπεινὲς λόγες τῷ ἐκ Μαριας ἀνθρώπῳ, τὲς δὲ ἀνηγμένες καὶ θεοπρεπεῖς τῷ ἐν ἀρχῇ ὄντι λόγῳ. Theod. Dial. Ἀσύγχυτ@.

Eutyches,

Eutyches, that I ſtand in doubt, they are not his whoſe name they carry. Sure I am they are far from truth, and muſt of neceſſity give place to the better adviſed ſentences of other Men. *He which in himſelf was appointed* (ſaith Hilary) *a Mediator to ſave his Church, and, for performance of that Myſtery of Mediation between God and Man, is become God and Man, doth now, being but one, conſiſt of both thoſe Natures united, neither hath he, through the Union of both, incurred the damage or loſs of either, leſt, by being born a Man, we ſhould think he hath given over to be God; or, that, becauſe he continued God, therefore he cannot be Man alſo; whereas the true belief which maketh a Man happy, proclaimeth jointly God and Man, confeſſeth the Word and Fleſh together.* Cyril more plainly, *His two Natures have knit themſelves the one to the other, and are in that nearneſs, as uncapable of confuſion, as of diſtraction. Their coherence hath not taken away the difference between them, Fleſh is not become God, but doth ſtill continue Fleſh, although it be now the Fleſh of God. Yea, of each Subſtance* (ſaith *Leo) *the Properties are all preſerved and kept ſafe.* Theſe two Natures are as cauſes and original grounds of all things which Chriſt hath done. Wherefore ſome things he doth as God, becauſe his Deity alone is the well-ſpring from which they flow; ſome things as Man, becauſe they iſſue from his mere human Nature; ſome things jointly as both God and Man, becauſe both Natures concur as principles thereunto. For albeit the Properties of each Nature do cleave only to that Nature whereof they are Properties; and therefore Chriſt cannot naturally be as God the ſame which he naturally is as Man; yet both Natures may very well concur unto one effect, and Chriſt in that reſpect be truly ſaid to work both as God and Man one and the ſelf-ſame thing. Let us therefore ſet it down for a rule or principle ſo neceſſary, as nothing more, to the plain

BOOK V.

Cyr. Epiſt. ad Neſt.

* Salva proprietate utriuſque naturæ, ſuſcepta eſt a Majeſtate humilitas, a virtute infirmitas, ab æternitate mortalitas. Leo. Epiſt. ad Flav.

BOOK V deciding of all doubts and queſtions about the Union of Natures in Chriſt, that of both Natures there is a Co-operation often, an Aſſociation always, but never any mutual Participation whereby the Properties of the one are infuſed into the other. Which rule muſt ſerve for the better underſtanding of that which *Damaſcene hath touching croſs and circulatory ſpeeches, wherein there are attributed to God ſuch things as belong to Manhood, and to Man ſuch as properly concern the Deity of Chriſt Jeſus, the cauſe whereof is the Aſſociation of Natures in one Subject. A kind of mutual commutation there is, whereby theſe concrete Names, God and Man, when we ſpeak of Chriſt, do take interchangeably one another's room, ſo that for truth of ſpeech, it ſkilleth not whether we ſay, that the Son of God hath created the World, and the Son of Man by his Death hath ſaved it; or elſe, that the Son of Man did create, and the Son of God die to ſave the World. Howbeit, as oft as we attribute to God what the Manhood of Chriſt claimeth, or to Man what his Deity hath right unto, we underſtand by the Name of God, and the Name of Man, neither the one nor the other Nature, but the whole Perſon of Chriſt, in whom both Natures are. When the Apoſtle ſaith of the Jews, that they crucified the Lord of Glory; and when the Son of Man, being on Earth, affirmeth, that the Son of Man was in Heaven at the ſame inſtant; there is in theſe two ſpeeches that mutual circulation before-mentioned. In the one, there is attributed to
1 Cor. ii. 8. God, or the Lord of Glory, Death, whereof Divine Nature is not capable; in the other Ubiquity unto

* Οὗτός ἐστιν ὁ τρόπος τῆς ἀντιδόσεως ἑκατέρας φύσεως τῇ ἑτέρᾳ τὰ ἴδια, διὰ τὴν τῆς ὑποστάσεως ταυτότητα, καὶ τὴν εἰς ἄλληλα αὐτῶν περιχώρησιν. Damaſc. de Orthod. Fid. l. iii. c. 4. Verum eſt duarum in Chriſto naturarum alteram ſuas alteri proprietates impertire, enunciando videlicet, idque non in abſtracto ſed in concreto ſolum, divinas homini non humanitati, humanas non deitati ſed Deo tribui. Cujus hæc eſt ratio, quia, cum ſuppoſitum prædicationis ſit ejuſmodi ut utramque naturam in ſe contineat, ſive ab una ſive ab altera denominetur, nihil refert.

Man,

Man, which Human Nature admitteth not. Therefore by the Lord of Glory, we muſt needs underſtand the whole Perſon of Chriſt, who being Lord of Glory, was indeed crucified, but not in that nature for which he is termed the Lord of Glory. In like manner, by the Son of Man, the whole Perſon of Chriſt muſt neceſſarily be meant, who being Man upon Earth, filled Heaven with his glorious preſence, but not according to that nature for which the title of Man is given him. Without this caution, the Fathers whoſe belief was ſincere, and their meaning moſt ſound, ſhall ſeem in their Writings, one to deny what another conſtantly doth affirm. Theodoret diſputeth, with great earneſtneſs, that God cannot be ſaid to ſuffer. But he thereby meaneth Chriſt's Divine Nature againſt * Apollinarius, which held even Deity itſelf paſſible. Cyril on the other ſide againſt Neſtorius as much contendeth, that whoſoever will deny very God to have ſuffered death, doth forſake the Faith. Which notwithſtanding to hold, were Hereſy, if the Name of God in this aſſertion did not import, as it doth, the Perſon of Chriſt, who being verily God, ſuffered death, but in the Fleſh, and not in that Subſtance for which the Name of God is given him.

BOOK V.

John iii. 13.

Apollinar. Epiſt. ad Flav.

54. If then both Natures do remain with their Properties in Chriſt thus diſtinct, as hath been ſhewed, we are, for our better underſtanding what either Nature receiveth from other, to note, that Chriſt is by three degrees a Receiver; firſt, in that he is the Son of God: ſecondly, in that his Human Nature hath had the honour of Union with Deity beſtowed upon it: thirdly, in that by means thereof ſundry eminent Graces have flowed as effects from Deity into that Nature which is coupled with it. On Chriſt therefore is beſtowed the Gift of eternal Generation, the Gift of Union, and the Gift of Unction. By

What Chriſt hath obtained according to the Fleſh, by the Union of his Fleſh with Deity.

* Θνητὸν τοῦ Υἱοῦ κατασκευάζουσι τὴν θεότητα. Greg. Nyſſ. de Sectator.

BOOK V. the Gift of eternal Generation, Christ hath received of the Father one, and in number the * self-same substance, which the Father hath of himself unreceived from any other. For every † beginning is a Father unto that which cometh of it, and every offspring is a Son unto that out of which it groweth. Seeing therefore the Father alone is ‡ originally that Deity which Christ § originally is not (for Christ is God ‖ by being of God; Light ¶ by issuing out of Light), it followeth hereupon, that whatsoever Christ hath ⟂ common unto him with his Heavenly Father, the same of necessity must be given him, but naturally and ** eternally given; not bestowed

* Nativitas Dei non potest non eam ex qua profecta est tenere naturam. Neque enim aliud quam Deus subsistit qui non aliunde quam ex Deo Deus subsistit. Hilar. de Trin. lib. v. Cum sit gloria, sempiternitate, virtute, regno, potestate, hoc quod Pater est, omnia tamen hæc non sine auctore sicut Pater, sed ex Patre tanquam Filius sine initio et æqualis habet Ruffin in Symb Apost. cap. 9. Filium aliunde non deduco, sed de substantia Patris omnem a Patre consecutum potestatem. Tertul contra Prax.

† Ephes. i. 15. πᾶσα πατρία, quicquid alteri quovis modo dat esse.

‡ Jac i. 17. Pater lumirum Ὑιȣ̃ τε καὶ Πνεύματος δηλονότι. Pachym. in Dionys. de Cœl. Hierar. cap. 1. Pater est principium totius divinitatis, quia ipse a nullo est. Non enim habet de quo procedat, sed ab eo et Filius est genitus et Spiritus sanctus procedit. Aug. de Trinit. lib. iv. cap. 40. Hinc Christus deitatis loco nomen ubique Patris usurpat, quia Pater nimirum est πηγαῖα θεότητος

§ Pater tota substantia est, Filius vero derivatio totius et propagatio Tertul contra Prax.

‖ Quod enim Deus est, ex Deo est. Hilar. de Trin. lib. v. Nihil nisi natum habet Filius. Hilar. lib. iv.

¶ Ἀπαύγασμα δόξης. Heb. i. 5. Ἐςὶν ἀπόῤῥεια τῆς τȣ̃ παντοκράτορος δόξης εἰλικρινὴς ἀπαύγασμα φωτὸς ἀιδίου. Sap. vii. 25, 26

⟂ Nihil in se diversum ac dissimile habent natus et generans. Hilar. de Synod. advers. Aria. In Trinitate alius atque alius, non aliud atque aliud. Vincent. Lyr. cap. 19.

** Ubi author æternus est, ibi et nativitatis æternitas est: quia sicut nativitas ab authore est, ita et ab æterno authore æterna nativitas est. Hilar. de Trin. lib. xii. Sicut naturam præstat Filio sine initio Generatio; ita Spiritus sancti præstat essentiam sine initio Processio. Aug. de Trin. lib. v. cap. 15.

by

by way of benevolence and favour, as the other gifts both are. And therefore * where the Fathers give it out for a rule, that whatsoever Christ is said in Scripture to have received, the same we ought to apply only to the Manhood of Christ; their assertion is true of all things which Christ hath received by Grace; but to that which he hath received of the Father, by eternal Nativity or Birth it reacheth not. Touching Union of Deity with Manhood, it is by Grace, because there can be no greater Grace shewed towards Men, than that God should vouchsafe to unite to Man's Nature the Person of his only begotten Son. Because *the Father loveth the Son* as Man, he hath, by uniting Deity with Manhood, *given all things into his hands*. (John iii. 35.) It hath pleased the Father, that in him *all Fulness should dwell*. (Col. i. 19.) The *Name* which he hath *above all Names* is given him. (Phil. ii. 9.) *As the Father hath life in himself, the Son in himself hath life also* by the gift of the Father. (John v 26.) The gift whereby God hath made Christ a Fountain of Life, is, that *Conjunction of the Nature of God with the Nature of Man*, in the Person of Christ, which gift (saith Christ to the Woman of Samaria) if thou didst know, and in that respect understand who it is which asketh water of thee, thou wouldest ask of him, that he might give thee living water. (Hic est verus Deus, et vita aterna. 1 John v 20. John iv. 10.) The Union therefore of the Flesh with Deity, is to that Flesh a gift of principal grace and favour. For by virtue of this grace, Man is really made God, a Creature is exalted above the dignity of all Creatures, and hath all Creatures else under it. This admirable Union of God with Man can enforce in that higher Nature no alteration, because unto God there is nothing more natural than not to be subject

* Ὅσα λέγει ἡ γραφὴ ὅτι ἔλαβεν ὁ Υἱὸς καὶ ἐδοξάσθη, διὰ τὴν ἀνθρωπότητα αὐτοῦ λέγει, οὐ τὴν θεότητα. Theod. fol. 42. et ex Greg. Nazian. Orat. ii. de Fol. ibid. 44.

BOOK V. to any * change. Neither is it a thing impoſſible, that the Word being made Fleſh, ſhould be that which it was not before as touching the manner of ſubſiſtence, and yet continue in all Qualities or Properties of Nature the ſame it was, becauſe the Incarnation of the Son of God conſiſteth merely in the Union of Natures, which Union doth add Perfection to the weaker, to the nobler no † alteration at all. If therefore it be demanded what the Perſon of the Son of God hath attained by aſſuming Manhood; ſurely, the whole ſum of all is this, to be as we are, truly, really, and naturally Man, by means whereof he is made capable of meaner offices than otherwiſe his Perſon could have admitted, the only gain he thereby purchaſed for himſelf was to be capable of loſs and detriment for the good of others. But may it rightly be ſaid concerning the Incarnation of Jeſus Chriſt, that as our Nature hath in no reſpect changed his, ſo from his to ours as little alteration hath enſued? The very cauſe of his taking upon him our Nature was to change it, to better the Quality, and to advance the condition thereof, although in no ſort to aboliſh the Subſtance which he took, nor to infuſe into it the natural Forces and Properties of his Deity. As therefore we have ſhewed how the Son of God by his Incarnation hath changed the manner of that perſonal Subſiſtence which before was ſolitary, and is now in the aſſociation of Fleſh, no alteration thereby accruing to the Nature of God; ſo neither are the Properties of Man's nature in the Perſon of Chriſt, by force and virtue of the ſame Conjunction,

* Ὥσπερ τῶν ἀνθρώπων κοινόν ἐςι τὸ θνητὸν, οὕτω τῆς ἁγίας Τριάδος κοινὸν τὸ ἄτρεπτόν τε καὶ ἀναλλοίωτον Theo. Dial. Ἄτρεπτος.

† Periculum ſtatus ſui Deo nullum eſt. Tertul. de Car. Chr. Majeſtati Filii Dei corporea Nativitas nihil contulit, nihil abſtulit. Leo de Nativit. Ser. viii. Μένει ὃ ἦν ἀπ' ἀρχῆς, Θέος μένει καὶ τὴν ἡμῶν ἐν ἑαυτῷ παρασκευάζων ὕπαρξιν. Theophil. In formam ſervi tranſiſſe non eſt naturam perdidiſſe Dei. Hilar. de Trin. lib. xii.

ſo

ſo much altered as not to ſtay within thoſe limits which our Subſtance is bordered withal; nor the ſtate and quality of our Subſtance ſo unaltered, but that there are in it many glorious effects proceeding from ſo near copulation with Deity. God from us can receive nothing; we by him have obtained much. For albeit the natural Properties of Deity be not communicable to Man's Nature, the ſupernatural Gifts, Graces, and Effects thereof are. The Honour which our Fleſh hath by being the Fleſh of the Son of God is in many reſpects great. If we reſpect but that which is common unto us with him, the Glory provided for him and his, in the Kingdom of Heaven, his right and title thereunto, even in that he is Man, differeth from other Men's, becauſe he is that Man of whom God is himſelf a part. We have right to the ſame Inheritance with Chriſt, but not the ſame right which he hath; his being ſuch as we cannot reach, and ours ſuch as he cannot ſtoop unto. Furthermore, to be the Way, the Truth, and the Life; to be the Wiſdom, Righteouſneſs, Sanctification, Reſurrection; to be the Peace of the whole World, the Hope of the Righteous, the Heir of all things; to be that Supreme Head whereunto all Power, both in Heaven and in Earth, is given — theſe are not Honours common unto Chriſt with other Men; they are Titles above the dignity and worth of any which were but a mere Man, yet true of Chriſt, even in that he is Man; but Man with whom Deity is perſonally joined, and unto whom it hath added thoſe excellencies which make him more than worthy thereof. Finally, ſith God hath deified our Nature, though not by turning it into himſelf, yet by making it his own inſeparable Habitation, we cannot now conceive how God ſhould, without Man, either * exerciſe divine Power, or receive the glory of

* Μετέχει ἡ ἀνθρωπίνη τῆς θείας ἐνεργείας. Theod.

BOOK V. of divine Praiſe. For Man is in * both an Aſſociate of Deity. But to come to the grace of Unction; did the parts of our Nature, the Soul and Body of Chriſt, receive, by the influence of Deity wherewith they were matched, no ability of operations, no virtue, or quality above Nature? Surely, as the ſword which is made fiery, doth not only cut by reaſon of the ſharpneſs which ſimply it hath, but alſo burn by means of that heat which it hath from fire; ſo, there is no doubt but the Deity of Chriſt hath enabled that Nature which it took of Man, to do more than Man in this World hath power to comprehend; foraſmuch as (the bare eſſential Properties of Deity excepted) he hath imparted unto it all things, he hath repleniſhed it with all ſuch Perfections as the ſame is any way apt to receive, at the leaſt, according to the exigence of that œconomy or ſervice for which
Luke ii. 47 it pleaſed him in love and mercy to be made Man. For, as the Parts, Degrees, and Offices of that Myſtical Adminiſtration did require which he voluntarily undertook, the beams of Deity did in operation always accordingly either reſtrain † or en-
Matt. xxvii. 46. large themſelves. From hence we may ſomewhat conjecture how the Powers of that Soul are illuminated, which being ſo inward unto God, cannot chooſe but be privy unto all things which God worketh, and muſt therefore of neceſſity be endued with
Col. ii. 3. knowledge ſo far forth univerſal, though not with infinite knowledge peculiar to Deity itſelf. The Soul of Chriſt, that ſaw in this life the face of God,

* Ἡ δεξιὰ τῦ Θεοῦ ἡ ποιητικὴ τῶν ὄντων τῶν πάντων, ἥτις ἐςὶν ὁ Κύριος, δι᾽ ὖ τὰ πάντα ἐγένετο, αὕτη τὸν ἑνωθέντα πρὸς αὐτὴν ἄνθρωπον εἰς τὸ ἴδιον ἀνήγαγεν ὕψος διὰ τῆς ἑνώσεως. Gregor. Nyſſ. apud Theod. Ἀπὸ τῆς φύσεως τῆς σῆς λαβὼν ἀπαρχὴν ἐκάθισεν ἐπάνω πάσης ἀρχῆς καὶ ἐξυσίας. Chryſ. in Pſal. xli.

† Ἡσυχάζοντος μὲν τῦ Λόγου ἐν τῷ πειράζεσθαι καὶ ςαυροῦσθαι καὶ ἀποθνήσκειν, συγγινομένου δὲ τῷ ἀνθρώπῳ ἐν τῷ νικᾶν καὶ ὑπομένειν καὶ χρηςεύεσθαι καὶ ἀνίςασθαι καὶ ἀναλαμβάνεσθαι. Theod. et Iren. lib. iii. adverſ. Hereſ.

was

was here, through ſo viſible preſence of Deity, filled BOOK V.
with all manner of Graces and Virtues in that un- Iſai. xi. 2.
matchable degree of perfection, for which, of him
we read it written, *That God with the oil of gladneſs* Iſai. lxi. 1.
anointed him above his fellows. And as God hath in Luke iv. 18. Acts iv. 27.
Chriſt unſpeakably glorified the nobler, ſo likewiſe Heb. i. 9.
the meaner part of our nature, the very bodily Sub- 2 Cor. i 21. 1 John ii.
ſtance of Man. Where alſo that muſt again be re- 20, 27.
membered which we noted before, concerning the degrees of the influence of Deity proportionable unto his own purpoſes, intents and counſels. For in this reſpect his Body, which by natural condition was corruptible, wanted the gift of everlaſting immunity from Death, Paſſion and Diſſolution, till God, which gave it to be ſlain for ſin, had for righteouſneſs ſake reſtored it to life, with certainty of endleſs continuance. Yea, in this reſpect, the very glorified Body
of Chriſt retained in it the ſcars and marks of former Joh. xx. 27.
mortality. But ſhall we ſay, that in Heaven his glorious Body, by virtue of the ſame cauſe, hath now power to preſent itſelf in all places, and to be every where at once preſent? We nothing doubt, but God hath, many ways above the reach of our capacities, exalted that Body which it hath pleaſed him to make his own, that Body wherewith he hath ſaved the World, that Body which hath been and is the Root of Eternal Life; the Inſtrument wherewith Deity worketh, the Sacrifice which taketh away Sin, the Price which hath ranſomed Souls from Death, the Leader of the whole Army of Bodies that ſhall riſe again. For though it had a beginning from us, yet God hath given it vital efficacy. Heaven hath endowed it with celeſtial power, that virtue it hath from above, in regard whereof all the Angels of Heaven adore it.* Notwithſtanding a Body ſtill it continueth, a Body conſubſtantial with our Bodies, a

* Μετὰ τὴν ἀνάστασιν ἀθάνατον μὲν ἐστὶ καὶ ἄφθαρτον καὶ θείας δόξης μεστὸν, σῶμα δὲ ὅμως τὴν οἰκείαν ἔχον περιγραφήν. Theod. fol. 80

Body

BOOK V. Body of the ſame both nature and meaſure which it had on Earth. To gather therefore into one ſum all that hitherto hath been ſpoken touching this point, there are but four things which concur to make complete the whole ſtate of our Lord Jeſus Chriſt; his Deity, his Manhood, the Conjunction of both, and the Diſtinction of the one from the other being joined in one. Four principal Hereſies there are which have in thoſe things withſtood the truth: Arians, by bending themſelves againſt the Deity of Chriſt; Apollinarians, by maiming and miſinterpreting that which belongeth to his Human Nature; Neſtorians, by renting Chriſt aſunder, and dividing him into two perſons; the followers of Eutyches, by confounding in his Perſon thoſe Natures which they ſhould diſtinguiſh. Againſt theſe there have been four moſt famous ancient General Councils: the Council of Nice, to define againſt Arians; againſt Apollinarians, the Council of Conſtantinople; the Council of Epheſus againſt Neſtorians; againſt Eutychians, the Chalcedon Council. In four words, ἀληθῶς, τελέως, ἀδιαιρέτως, ἀσυγχύτως, *truly, perfectly, indiviſibly, diſtinctly*; the firſt, applied to his being God; and the ſecond, to his being Man; the third, to his being of both One; and the fourth, to his ſtill continuing in that One both; we may fully, by way of abridgment, compriſe whatſoever Antiquity hath at large handled, either in declaration of Chriſtian belief, or in refutation of the aforeſaid Hereſies. Within the compaſs of which four heads, I may truly affirm, that all Hereſies which touch but the Perſon of Jeſus Chriſt (whether they have riſen in theſe latter days, or in any age heretofore), may be, with great facility, brought to confine themſelves. We conclude therefore, that to ſave the World it was of neceſſity the Son of God ſhould be thus incarnate, and that God ſhould ſo be in Chriſt, as hath been declared.

55. Having

Of the personal Presence of Christ every where, and in what sense it may be granted, he is every where present according to the Flesh.

55. Having thus far proceeded in speech concerning the Person of Jesus Christ, his two Natures, their Conjunction, that which he either is or doth in respect of both, and that which the one receiveth from the other; sith God in Christ is generally the medicine which doth cure the World, and Christ in us is that receipt of the same medicine whereby we are every one particularly cured: inasmuch as Christ's Incarnation and Passion can be available to no Man's good which is not made partaker of Christ, neither can we participate him without his presence; we are briefly to consider how Christ is present, to the end it may thereby better appear how we are made partakers of Christ, both otherwise, and in the Sacraments themselves. All things are in such sort divided into finite and infinite, that no one Substance, Nature or Quality, can be possibly capable of both. The World and all things in the World are stinted; all effects that proceed from them; all the powers and abilities whereby they work; whatsoever they do, whatsoever they may, and whatsoever they are, is limited. Which limitation of each Creature is both the perfection and also the preservation thereof. Measure is that which perfecteth all things, because every thing is for some end; neither can that thing be available to any end which is not proportionable thereunto; and to proportion as well excesses as defects are opposite. Again, forasmuch as nothing doth perish but only through excess or defect of that, the due proportioned measure whereof doth give perfection, it followeth, that measure is likewise the preservation of all things. Out of which premises we may conclude, not only, that nothing created can possibly be unlimited, or can receive any such accident, quality or property as may really make it infinite (for then should it cease to be a Creature), but also, that every Creature's limitation is according to his own kind; and therefore as oft as we note in them any thing above their kind, it argueth, that the same is not properly

BOOK V. properly theirs, but groweth in them from a cause more powerful than they are. Such as the Subſtance of each thing is, ſuch is alſo the Preſence thereof. Impoſſible it is, that God ſhould withdraw his Preſence from any thing, becauſe the very Subſtance of God is infinite. He filleth Heaven and Earth, although he take up no room in either, becauſe his Subſtance is immaterial, pure, and of us in this World ſo incomprehenſible, that albeit no part of us *be ever abſent from him who is preſent whole unto every particular thing, yet his Preſence with us we no way diſcern further than only that God is preſent; which partly by Reaſon, and more perfectly by Faith, we know to be firm and certain. Seeing therefore that Preſence every where is the ſequel of an infinite and incomprehenſible Subſtance (for what can be every where, but that which can no where be comprehended?) to enquire, whether Chriſt be every where, is to enquire of a natural Property, a Property that cleaveth to the Deity of Chriſt. Which Deity being common unto him with none but only the Father and the Holy Ghoſt, it followeth, that nothing of Chriſt which is limited, that nothing created, that neither the Soul nor the Body of Chriſt, and conſequently, not Chriſt as Man, or Chriſt according to his Human Nature, can poſſibly be every where preſent, becauſe thoſe phraſes of limitation and reſtraint do either point out the principal ſubject whereunto every ſuch attribute adhereth, or elſe they intimate the radical cauſe out of which it groweth. For example, when we ſay that Chriſt as Man, or according to his Human Nature, ſuffered Death; we ſhew what Nature was the proper ſubject of Mortality: when we ſay, that as God, or according to

Pſ. cxxxix. 7, 8. Jer. xxiii. 24.

* Ideo Deus ubique eſſe dicitur, quia nulli parti rerum abſens eſt; ideo totus, quia non parti rerum partem ſui præſentem præbet, et alteri parti alteram partem, ſed non ſolum univerſitati Creaturæ, verum etiam cuilibet parti ejus totus pariter adeſt. Aug. Epiſt. lvii.

his

his Deity, he conquered Death, we declare his Deity to have been the cause by force and virtue whereof he raised himself from the Grave. But neither is the Manhood of Christ that subject whereunto universal Presence agreeth, neither is it the cause original by force whereof his Person is enabled to be every where present. Wherefore Christ is essentially present with all things in that he is very God, but not present with all things as Man, because Manhood and the parts thereof can neither be the cause nor the true subject of such Presence. Notwithstanding, somewhat more plainly to shew a true immediate reason wherefore the Manhood of Christ can neither be every where present, nor cause the Person of Christ so to be; we acknowledge that of St. Augustin concerning Christ most true, * *In that he is personally the Word, he created all things; in that he is naturally Man, he himself is created of God*, and it doth not appear that any one Creature hath power to be present with all Creatures. Whereupon nevertheless it will not follow, that Christ cannot therefore be thus present because he is himself a Creature; forasmuch as only infinite Presence is that which cannot possibly stand with the Essence or Being of any Creature: as for Presence with all things that are, sith the whole Race, Mass and Body of them is finite, Christ by being a Creature is not in that respect excluded from possibility of Presence with them. That which excludeth him therefore, as Man, from so great largeness of Presence, is only his being Man, a Creature of this particular kind whereunto the God of Nature hath set those bounds of restraint and limitation beyond which to attribute unto it any thing more than

* Quod ad verbum attinet, Creator est; quod ad hominem, creatura est. Aug. Epist. lvii. Deus qui semper est, et semper erat, fit creatura. Leo. de Nativ. Multi timore trepidant ne Christum esse creaturam dicere compellantur; nos proclamamus non esse periculum dicere, Christum esse creaturam. Hier. in Epist. ad Eph. ii.

a Creature of that ſort can admit, were to give it another Nature, to make it a Creature of ſome other kind than in truth it is. Furthermore, if Chriſt, in that he is Man, be every where preſent, ſeeing this cometh not by the Nature of Manhood itſelf, there is no other way how it ſhould grow, but either by the grace of Union with Deity, or by the grace of Unction received from Deity. It hath been already ſufficiently proved, that by force of Union the Properties of both Natures are imparted to the Perſon only in whom they are, and not what belongeth to the one Nature, really conveyed or tranſlated into the other: it hath been likewiſe proved, that Natures united in Chriſt continue the very ſame which they are where they are not united. And concerning the Grace of Unction, wherein are contained the gifts and virtues which Chriſt as Man hath above Men, they make him really and habitually a Man more excellent than we are; they take not from him the Nature and Subſtance that we have; they cauſe not his Soul nor Body to be of another kind than ours is. Supernatural endowments are an advancement, they are no extinguiſhment of that Nature whereto they are given. The Subſtance of the Body of Chriſt hath no Preſence, neither can have, but only local. It was not therefore every where ſeen, nor did it every where ſuffer death, every where it could not be intombed, it is not every where now, being exalted into Heaven. There is no proof in the World ſtrong to enforce that Chriſt had a true Body, but by the true and natural Properties of his Body. Amongſt which Properties, definite or local Preſence is chief: *How is it true of Chriſt* (ſaith Tertullian) *that he died, was buried, and roſe again, if Chriſt had not that very fleſh, the nature whereof is capable of theſe things, fleſh mingled with blood, ſupported with bones, woven with ſinews, embroidered with veins?* If his majeſtical Body have now any ſuch new property, by force whereof it may every where really even in Subſtance preſent itſelf, or may at once be in many places;

Tertul de Car. Chr.

places; then hath the majeſty of his eſtate extinguiſhed the verity of his Nature. *Make thou no doubt or queſtion of it* (ſaith St. Auguſtin) *but that the Man Chriſt Jeſus is now in that very place from whence he ſhall come in the ſame Form and Subſtance of Fleſh which he carried thither, and from thence he hath not taken Nature, but given thereunto immortality. According to this Form he ſpreadeth not out himſelf into all places. For it behoveth us to take great heed, leſt, while we go about to maintain the glorious Deity of him which is Man, we leave him not the true bodily Subſtance of a Man.* According to St. Auguſtin's opinion therefore, that majeſtical Body which we make to be every where preſent, doth thereby ceaſe to have the Subſtance of a true Body. To conclude, we hold it in regard of the fore-alledged proofs, a moſt infallible truth, that Chriſt, as Man, is not every where preſent. There are which think it as infallibly true, that Chriſt is every where preſent as Man, which peradventure in ſome ſenſe may be well enough granted. His human Subſtance in itſelf is naturally abſent from the Earth; his Soul and Body not on Earth, but in Heaven only: yet becauſe this Subſtance is inſeparably joined to that perſonal Word, which by his very Divine Eſſence is preſent with all things; the Nature which cannot have in itſelf univerſal Preſence, hath it after a ſort, by being no where ſevered from that which every where is preſent. For in as much as that Infinite Word is not diviſible into parts, it could not in part, but muſt needs be wholly incarnate; and conſequently whereſoever the Word is it hath with it Manhood, elſe ſhould the Word be in part, or ſomewhere God only and not Man, which is impoſſible. For the Perſon of Chriſt is whole, perfect God and perfect Man, whereſoever; although the parts of his Manhood being finite, and his Deity infinite, we cannot ſay that the whole of Chriſt is ſimply every where, as we may ſay that his Deity is, and that his Perſon is by force of Deity. For, ſomewhat of the Perſon of Chriſt is not every where in that ſort; namely his Manhood,

Aug Epiſt. lvii.

BOOK V. Manhood, the only Conjunction whereof with Deity is extended as far as Deity, the actual position restrained and tied to a certain place; yet presence by way of Conjunction is in some sort presence. Again, as the Manhood of Christ may after a sort be every where said to be present, because that Person is every where present, from whose Divine Substance Manhood is no where severed; so the same Universality of Presence may likewise seem in another respect appliable thereunto, namely, by Co-operation with Deity, and that in all things. The Light created of God in the beginning did first by itself illuminate the World; but after that the Sun and Moon were created, the World sithence hath by them always enjoyed the same. And that Deity of Christ, which before our Lord's Incarnation wrought all things without Man, doth now work nothing wherein the Nature which it hath assumed is either absent from it or idle. Christ, as Man, hath all Power both in Heaven and Earth given him. He hath as Man, not as God only, supreme Dominion over quick and dead; for so much his Ascension into Heaven and his Session at the right hand of God do import. The Son of God, which did first humble himself by taking our flesh upon him, descended afterwards much lower, and became according to the flesh obedient so far as to suffer death, even the death of the Cross, for all Men, because such was his Father's will. The former was an Humiliation of Deity, the latter an Humiliation of Manhood; for which cause there followed upon the latter an Exaltation of that which was humbled: for with power he created the World, but restored it by obedience. In which obedience, as according to his Manhood he had glorified God on Earth; so God hath glorified in Heaven that Nature which yielded him obedience; and hath given unto Christ, even in that he is Man, such fulness of Power over the whole World, that he which before fulfilled in the state of humility and patience whatsoever God did require, doth now reign in glory till the time that all things be restored. He which came down

Matth. xxviii. Rom. xiv. 9.

Phil ii. 9. Heb. ii 9. Revel. v. 12.

Luke xxi. 27.

Acts iii. 21.

down from Heaven, and descended into the lowest BOOK V.
parts of the Earth, is ascended far above all Heavens; Ephes. iv.
that sitting at the right hand of God, he might from 9.
thence fill all things with the gracious and happy fruits of his saving Presence. Ascension into Heaven is a plain local translation of Christ, according to his Manhood, from the lower to the higher parts of the World. Session at the right hand of God is the actual exercise of that Regency and Dominion wherein the Manhood of Christ is joined, and matched with the Deity of the Son of God. Not that his Manhood was before without the possession of the same Power, but because the full use thereof was suspended till that humility which had been before as a veil to hide and conceal majesty were laid aside. After his rising again
from the dead, then did God set him at his right hand Ephes. i.
in heavenly places, far above all Principality and 20.
Power, and Might, and Domination, and every Name that is named, not in this World only, but also in that which is to come; and hath put all things under his feet, and hath appointed him over all, the Head to the Church, which is his Body, the fulness of him
that filleth all in all. The Sceptre of which spiritual Psal viii.
Regiment over us in this present World is at the 6
length to be yielded up into the hands of the Father Heb. ii 8. 1 Cor. xv.
which gave it; that is to say, the use and exercise thereof shall cease, there being no longer on Earth any Militant Church to govern. This Government therefore he exerciseth both as God and as Man; as God, by essential Presence with all things; as Man, by Co-operation with that which essentially is present. Touching the manner how he worketh as Man in all things; the principal powers of the Soul of Man are the Will and Understanding, the one of which two in Christ assenteth unto all things, and from the other nothing which Deity doth work is hid; so that by knowledge and assent the Soul of Christ is present with all things which the Deity of Christ worketh. And even the Body of Christ itself, although the de-

BOOK V. finite limitation thereof be most sensible, doth notwithstanding admit in some sort a kind of infinite and unlimited Presence likewise. For his Body being a part of that Nature, which whole Nature is presently joined unto Deity; wheresoever Deity is, it followeth, that his bodily Substance hath every where a Presence of true Conjunction with Deity. And for as much as it is, by virtue of that Conjunction, made the Body of the Son of God, by whom also it was made a Sacrifice for the Sins of the whole World, this giveth it a presence of force and efficacy throughout all Generations of Men. Albeit therefore nothing be actually infinite in substance but God only in that he is God; nevertheless, as every number is infinite by possibility of addition, and every line by possibility of extension infinite, so there is no stint which can be set to the value or merit of the sacrificed Body of Christ, it hath no measured certainty of limits, bounds of efficacy unto life it knoweth none, but is also itself infinite in possibility of application. Which things indifferently every way considered, that gracious Promise of our Lord and Saviour Jesus Christ concerning presence with his to the very end of the World, I see no cause but that we may well and safely interpret he doth perform, both as God, by essential presence of Deity, and as Man, in that order, sense and meaning, which hath been shewed.

The Union or mutual Participation which is between Christ and the Church of Christ, in this present World.

56. We have hitherto spoken of the Person and of the Presence of Christ. Participation is that mutual inward hold which Christ hath of us and we of him, in such sort that each possesseth other by way of special interest, property, and inherent copulation. For plainer explication whereof, we may from that which hath been before sufficiently proved, assume to our purpose these two Principles, *That every original cause imparteth itself unto those things which come of it*; *and whatsoever taketh being from any other, the same is after a sort in that which giveth it being.* It followeth hereupon, that the Son of God being Light of Light, must

muſt needs be alſo Light* in Light. The Perſons of the Godhead, by reaſon of the Unity of their Subſtance, do as neceſſarily remain one within another, as they are of neceſſity to be diſtinguiſhed one from another, becauſe two are the iſſue of one, and one the offſpring of the other two; only of three, one not growing out of any other. And ſith they all are but one God in number, one indiviſible Eſſence or Subſtance, their diſtinction cannot poſſibly admit ſeparation. For how ſhould that ſubſiſt ſolitarily by itſelf, which hath no Subſtance, but individually the very ſame whereby others ſubſiſt with it, ſeeing that the multiplication of Subſtances in particular is neceſſarily required to make thoſe things ſubſiſt apart which have the ſelfſame general Nature, and the Perſons of that Trinity are not three particular Subſtances to whom one general Nature is common, but three that ſubſiſt by one Subſtance which itſelf is particular; yet they all three have it, and their ſeveral ways of having it are that which maketh their perſonal diſtinction? The Father therefore is in the Son, and the Son in him; they both in the Spirit, and the Spirit in both them. So that the Father's firſt Offspring, which is the Son, remaineth eternally in the Father; the Father eternally alſo in the Son, no way ſevered or divided by reaſon of the ſole and ſingle Unity of their Subſtance. The Son in the Father, as Light in that Light out of which it floweth without ſeparation; the Father in the Son, as Light in that Light which it cauſeth and leaveth not. And becauſe in this reſpect his eternal Being is of the Father, which eternal Being is his Life, therefore he by the Father liveth. Again, ſith all things do accordingly love their Offspring as themſelves are more

* In the boſom of the Father, John i 18. Ecce dico alium eſſe Patrem, et alium Filium, non diviſione alium, ſed diſtinctione. Tertul. contra Prax. Nec in numerum pluralem defluit incorporea generatio, nec in diviſionem cadit, ubi qui naſcitur nequaquam a generante ſeparatur. Ruffin. in Symbol.

 or

BOOK V. or leſs contained in it, he which is thus the only begotten muſt needs be in this degree the only beloved of the Father. He therefore which is in the Father by eternal derivation of Being and Life from him, muſt needs be in him through an eternal affection of love. His Incarnation cauſeth him alſo as Man to be now in the Father, and the Father to be in him. For in that he is Man, he receiveth Life from the Father as from the Fountain of that Ever-living Deity, which in the Perſon of the Word hath combined itſelf with Manhood, and doth thereunto impart ſuch Life as to no other Creature beſides him is communicated. In which conſideration likewiſe, the Love of the Father towards him is more than it can be towards any other; neither can any attain unto that perfection of Love which he beareth towards his Heavenly Father. Wherefore God is not ſo in any, nor any ſo in God as Chriſt; whether we conſider him as the Perſonal Word of God, or as the natural Son of Man. All other things that are of God, have God in them, and he them in himſelf likewiſe. Yet becauſe their Subſtance and his wholly differeth, their coherence and communion either with him or amongſt themſelves, is in no ſort like unto that before-mentioned. God hath his influence into the very Eſſence of all things, without which influence of Deity ſupporting them, their utter annihilation could not chooſe but follow. Of him all things have both received their firſt being, and their continuance to be that which they are. All things are therefore partakers of God, they are his Offspring, his influence is in them, and the Perſonal Wiſdom of God is for that very cauſe ſaid to excel in nimbleneſs or agility, to pierce into all intellectual, pure and ſubtile Spirits, to go through all, and to reach unto every thing which is. Otherwiſe, how can the ſame Wiſdom be that which ſupporteth, beareth up, and ſuſtaineth all? Whatſoever God doth work, the hands of all three Perſons are jointly and equally in it, according to the order of that connexion whereby they each depend upon

Luke iii. 22. John iii 34, 35, & v 20. & x 17 & xiv 31. & xv 10.

Wiſd. vii. 23.

Heb. i 3.

upon other. And therefore albeit in that respect the Father be first, the Son next, the Spirit last, and consequently nearest unto every effect which groweth from all three; nevertheless, they all being of one Essence, are likewise all of one Efficacy. Dare any Man, unless he be ignorant altogether how inseparable the Persons of the Trinity are, persuade himself that every of them may have their sole and several possessions, or that we being not Partakers of all, can have fellowship with any one? The Father as Goodness, the Son as Wisdom, the Holy Ghost as Power, do all concur in every particular, outwardly issuing from that one only glorious Deity which they all are. For that which moveth God to work is Goodness; and that which ordereth his work is Wisdom; and that which perfecteth his work is Power. All things, which God in their times and seasons hath brought forth, were eternally and before all times in God, as a work unbegun is in the Artificer which afterward bringeth it unto effect. Therefore whatsoever we do behold now in this present World, it was inwrapped within the bowels of Divine Mercy, written in the Book of Eternal Wisdom, and held in the hands of Omnipotent Power, the first Foundations of the World being as yet unlaid. So that all things which God hath made are in that respect the Offspring of God, they are in him as effects in their highest cause; he likewise actually is in them, the assistance and influence of his Deity is their life. Let hereunto saving efficacy be added, and it bringeth forth a special Offspring amongst Men, containing them to whom God hath himself given the gracious and amiable name of Sons. We are by Nature the Sons of Adam. When God created Adam, he created us; and as many as are descended from Adam, have in themselves the root out of which they spring. The Sons of God we neither are all, nor any one of us, otherwise than only by grace and favour. The Sons of God have God's own natural Son as a second Adam from Heaven, whose

John xiv. 23.

Acts xvii. 28, 29

John i. 4. & 10

Isai. xl 26.

1 John iii. 1

1 Cor xv. 47.

 Race

BOOK V Race and Progeny they are by ſpiritual and heavenly Birth. God therefore loving eternally his Son, he muſt needs eternally in him have loved and preferred before all others, them which are ſpiritually ſithence deſcended and ſprung out of him. Theſe were in God as in their Saviour, and not as in their Creator only. It was the purpoſe of his ſaving Goodneſs, his ſaving Wiſdom, and his ſaving Power, which inclined itſelf towards them. They which thus were in God eternally by their intended admiſſion to life, have by vocation or adoption God actually now in them, as the Artificer is in the work which his hand doth preſently frame. Life as all other gifts and benefits groweth originally from the Father, and cometh not to us but by the Son; nor by the Son to any of us in particular, but through the Spirit. For this cauſe the Apoſtle wiſheth to the Church of Corinth, *the Grace of our Lord Jeſus Chriſt, and the Love of God, and the Fellowſhip of the Holy Ghoſt.* Which three St. Peter comprehendeth in one, *The participation of Divine Nature.* We are therefore in God through Chriſt eternally, according to that intent and purpoſe whereby we are choſen to be made his in this preſent World, before the World itſelf was made: we are in God, through the knowledge which is had of us, and the love which is borne towards us from everlaſting. But in God we actually are no longer than only from the time of our actual Adoption into the Body of his true Church, into the Fellowſhip of his Children. For his Church he knoweth and loveth, ſo that they which are in the Church, are thereby known to be in him. Our being in Chriſt by eternal fore-knowledge ſaveth us not without our actual and real Adoption into the Fellowſhip of his Saints in this preſent World. For in him we actually are by our actual incorporation into that Society which hath him for their Head; and doth make together with him one Body (he and they in that reſpect having one name); for which cauſe, by virtue of this myſtical Conjunction, we are of him, and in

Epheſ. i. 3, 4

1 John v. 11.

Rom. viii. 10.

2 Cor. xiii. 13.

2 Pet. i. 4.

Col. ii 10.

1 Cor. xii. 12.

in him, even as though our very flesh and bones should be made continuate with his. We are in Christ, because he knoweth and loveth us, even as parts of himself. No Man actually is in him, but they in whom he actually is. For *he which hath not the Son of God, hath not life: I am the Vine, and ye are the Branches: He which abideth in me, and I in him, the same bringeth forth much Fruit*, but the Branch severed from the Vine withereth. We are therefore adopted Sons of God to eternal Life by Participation of the only begotten Son of God, whose life is the well-spring and cause of ours. It is too cold an interpretation whereby some Men expound our being in Christ to import nothing else, but only, that the self-same Nature which maketh us to be Men is in him, and maketh him Man as we are. For what Man in the World is there, which hath not so far forth Communion with Jesus Christ? It is not this that can sustain the weight of such sentences as speak of the Mystery of our Coherence with Jesus Christ. The Church is in Christ, as Eve was in Adam. Yea, by Grace we are every of us in Christ and in his Church, as by Nature we were in those our first Parents. God made Eve of the rib of Adam, and his Church he frameth out of the very Flesh, the very wounded and bleeding side of the Son of Man. His Body crucified and his Blood shed for the Life of the World are the true Elements of that heavenly Being, which maketh us such as himself is of whom we come. For which cause the words of Adam may be fitly the words of Christ concerning his Church, *Flesh of my Flesh, and Bone of my Bones*, a true Nature extract out of my own Body. So that in him, even according to his Manhood, we, according to our heavenly Being, are as Branches in that Root out of which they grow. To all things he is Life, and to Men Light, as the Son of God, to the Church, both Life and Light eternal, by being made the Son of Man for us, and by being in us a Saviour, whether we respect him as God or as Man. Adam is in us as

Ephes. v. 30
John xv. 9.
1 John v. 12
John xv. 5, 6.
John xiv. 19.
Ephes. v. 23.
John xiv. 20. & xv. 4.
1 Cor xv. 48.
John i & vi 57.

BOOK V. an original cauſe of our Nature, and of that corruption of Nature which cauſeth death; Chriſt as the cauſe original of Reſtoration to Life. The Perſon of Adam is not in us, but his Nature, and the corruption of his Nature derived into all Men by propagation; Chriſt having Adam's Nature, as we have, but incorrupt, deriveth not Nature but incorruption, and that immediately from his own Perſon, into all that belong unto him. As therefore we are really Partakers of the Body of Sin and Death received from Adam, ſo except we be truly Partakers of Chriſt, and as really poſſeſſed of his Spirit, all we ſpeak of eternal Life is but a dream. That which quickeneth us is the Spirit of the Second Adam, and his Fleſh that wherewith he quickeneth. That which in him made our Nature uncorrupt was the Union of his Deity with our Nature. And in that reſpect the ſentence of Death and Condemnation, which only taketh hold upon ſinful fleſh, could no way poſſibly extend unto him. This cauſed his voluntary death for others to prevail with God, and to have the force of an expiatory Sacrifice. The Blood of Chriſt, as the Apoſtle witneſſeth, doth therefore take away ſin, becauſe, *through the Eternal Spirit, he offered himſelf unto God without ſpot.* That which ſanctified our Nature in Chriſt, that which made it a Sacrifice available to take away ſin, is the ſame which quickeneth it, raiſed it out of the grave after death, and exalted it unto Glory. Seeing therefore that Chriſt is in us a quickening Spirit, the firſt degree of Communion with Chriſt muſt needs conſiſt in the Participation of his Spirit, which Cyprian in that reſpect termeth *germaniſſimam Societatem*, the higheſt and trueſt Society that can be between Man and him, which is both God and Man in one. Theſe things St. Cyril duly conſidering, reproveth their ſpeeches which taught that only the Deity of Chriſt is the Vine whereupon we by Faith do depend as Branches, and that neither his Fleſh nor our Bodies are compriſed in this reſemblance. For doth any

Heb. v. 9.

1 Cor. xv. 45, 22.

Heb. ix. 14.

Cypr. de Cœna Dom. cap. vi.

Cyril. in Joan. lib. x cap. 13.

any Man doubt, but that even from the Fleſh of Chriſt our very Bodies do receive that Life which ſhall make them glorious at the latter day; and for which they are already accounted parts of his bleſſed Body? Our corruptible Bodies could never live the life they ſhall live, were it not that here they are joined with his Body which is incorruptible, and that his is in our's as a cauſe of Immortality, a cauſe by removing through the Death and Merit of his own Fleſh that which hindered the life of our's. Chriſt is therefore, both as God and as Man, that true Vine whereof we both ſpiritually and corporally are Branches. The mixture of his bodily Subſtance with our's is a thing which the ancient Fathers * diſclaim. Yet the mixture of his Fleſh with our's they † ſpeak of, to ſignify what our very bodies, through myſtical conjunction, receive from that vital efficacy which we know to be in his, and from bodily mixtures they borrow divers ſimilitudes, rather to declare the truth, than the manner of ‡ coherence between his ſacred, and the ſanctified Bodies of Saints. Thus much no Chriſtian Man will deny, that when Chriſt ſanctified his own Fleſh giving as God, and taking as Man the Holy Ghoſt, he did not this for himſelf only, but for our ſakes, that the Grace of Sanctification and Life, which was firſt received in him, might paſs from him to his whole Race, as Male-

* Noſtra quippe et ipſius conjunctio nec miſcet perſonas nec unit ſubſtantias, ſed affectus conſociat et confœderat voluntates. Cypr. de Cœn. Dom

† Quomodo dicunt carnem in corruptionem devenire, et non percipere vitam, quæ a corpore Domini et ſanguine alitur? Iren. lib. iv. adverſ. Hæreſ. cap. 34.

‡ Unde conſiderandum eſt non ſolum σχέσει ſeu conformitate affectionum, Chriſtum in nobis eſſe; verum etiam participatione naturali (id eſt reali et vera), quemadmodum ſi quis igne liquefactam ceram alii ceræ ſimiliter liquefactæ ita miſcuerit ut unum quid ex utriſque factum videatur; ſic communicatione Corporis et Sanguinis Chriſti ipſe in nobis eſt, et nos in ipſo. Cyril. in Joan. lib. x. cap. 13.

diction

BOOK V. diction came from Adam unto all Mankind. Howbeit, because the Work of his Spirit to those effects is in us prevented by Sin and Death, possessing us before; it is of necessity, that as well our present Sanctification unto newness of life, as the future restoration of our Bodies, should presuppose a participation of the Grace, Efficacy, Merit, or Virtue of his Body and Blood; without which foundation first laid, there is no place for those other operations of the Spirit of Christ to ensue. So that Christ imparteth plainly himself by degrees. It pleaseth him in mercy, to account himself incomplete and maimed * without us. But most assured we are, that we all receive of his Fulness, because he is in us as a moving and working Cause; from which many blessed effects are really found to ensue, and that in sundry both kinds and degrees, all tending to eternal Happiness. It must be confest, that of Christ working as a Creator and a Governor of the World by Providence all are partakers, not all partakers of that Grace whereby he inhabiteth whom he saveth. Again, as he dwelleth not by Grace in all, so neither doth he equally work in all them in whom he dwelleth. *Whence is it* (saith St. Augustin) *that some be holier than others are, but because God doth dwell in some more plentifully than in others?* And because the Divine Substance of Christ is equally in all, his Human Substance equally distant from all; it appeareth that the Participation of Christ, wherein there are many degrees and differences, must needs consist in such effects, as being derived from both Natures of Christ really into us, are made our own; and we, by having them in us, are truly said to have him from whom they come; Christ also more or less, to inhabit and impart himself, as the Graces are fewer or more, greater or smaller, which really

Aug. Epist. lvii.

* Ephes. i. 23. Ecclesia complementum ejus qui implet omnia in omnibus. Τὸ πλήρωμα τοῦ πάντα ἐν πᾶσι πληρουμένου.

flow

flow into us from Chriſt. Chriſt is whole with the whole Church, and whole with every part of the Church, as touching his Perſon, which can no way divide itſelf, or be poſſeſt by degrees and portions. But the Participation of Chriſt importeth, beſides the preſence of Chriſt's Perſon, and beſides the myſtical Copulation thereof with the Parts and Members of his whole Church, a true actual influence of Grace whereby the life which we live according to Godlineſs is his, and from him we receive thoſe perfections wherein our eternal Happineſs conſiſteth. Thus we participate Chriſt, partly by imputation; as when thoſe things which he did and ſuffered for us are imputed unto us for Righteouſneſs: partly by habitual and real infuſion, as when Grace is inwardly beſtowed while we are on Earth, and afterwards more fully both our Souls and Bodies made like unto his in Glory. The firſt thing of his ſo infuſed into our hearts in this life is the Spirit of Chriſt; whereupon, becauſe the reſt of what kind ſoever do all both neceſſarily depend and infallibly alſo enſue; therefore the Apoſtles term it, ſometime the ſeed of God, ſometime the pledge of our heavenly Inheritance, ſometime the hanſel or earneſt of that which is to come. From whence it is, that they which belong to the myſtical Body of our Saviour Chriſt, and be in number as the ſtars of heaven, divided ſucceſſively, by reaſon of their mortal condition, into many Generations, are notwithſtanding coupled every one to Chriſt their Head, and all unto every particular perſon amongſt themſelves, inaſmuch as the ſame Spirit which anointed the bleſſed Soul of our Saviour Chriſt, doth ſo formalize, unite, and actuate his whole Race, as if both he and they were ſo many Limbs compacted into one Body, by being quickened all with one and the ſame Soul. That wherein we are Partakers of Jeſus Chriſt by Imputation agreeth equally unto all that

Gal. ii. 20.
Iſai. liii. 5. Epheſ. i. 7.
Rom. viii. 9. Gal. iv. 6.
1 John iii 9. Epheſ. i. 14. Rom. viii. 23.
1 Cor. xii. 27. Epheſ. iv. 15
Rom xii. 5. Epheſ. iv. 25.

BOOK V. that have it. For it consisteth in such Acts and Deeds of his, as could not have longer continuance than while they were in doing, nor at that very time belong unto any other, but to him from whom they come; and therefore how Men, either then, or before, or sithence, should be made Partakers of them, there can be no way imagined, but only by Imputation. Again, a deed must either not be imputed to any, but rest altogether in him whose it is; or if at all it be imputed, they which have it by Imputation must have it such as it is, whole. So that degrees being neither in the personal Presence of Christ, nor in the Participation of those effects which are ours by Imputation only; it resteth that we wholly apply them to the Participation of Christ's infused Grace; although, even in this kind also, the first beginning of Life, the Seed of God, the first Fruits of Christ's Spirit, be without latitude. For we have hereby only the being of the Sons of God, in which number how far soever one may seem to excel another, yet touching this that all are Sons, they are all equals, some happily better Sons than the rest are, but none any more a Son than another. Thus therefore we see how the Father is in the Son, and the Son in the Father; how they both are in all things, and all things in them; what Communion Christ hath with his Church, how his Church and every Member thereof is in him by original derivation, and he personally in them, by way of mystical Association, wrought through the Gift of the Holy Ghost, which they that are his receive from him, and together with the same what benefit soever the vital force of his Body and Blood may yield; yea, by steps and degrees they receive the complete measure of all such divine Grace as doth sanctify and save throughout, till the day of their final Exaltation to a state of Fellowship in Glory with him, whose Partakers they are now in

those

thoſe things that tend to Glory. As for any mixture of the Subſtance of his Fleſh with our's, the Participation which we have of Chriſt includeth no ſuch kind of groſs ſurmiſe.

The neceſſity of Sacraments unto the Participation of Chriſt.

57. It greatly offendeth, that ſome, when they labour to ſhew the uſe of the holy Sacraments, aſſign unto them no end but only to teach the mind, by other ſenſes, that which the Word doth teach by hearing. Whereupon, how eaſily neglect and careleſs regard of ſo heavenly Myſteries may follow, we ſee in part by ſome experience had of thoſe Men with whom that opinion is moſt ſtrong. For where the Word of God may be heard which teacheth with much more expedition and more full explications any thing we have to learn, if all the benefit we reap by Sacraments be inſtruction, they which at all times have opportunity of uſing the better mean to that purpoſe will ſurely hold the worſe in leſs eſtimation. And unto Infants, which are not capable of inſtruction, who would not think it a mere ſuperfluity that any Sacrament is adminiſtered, if to adminiſter the Sacraments be but to teach Receivers what God doth for them? There is of Sacraments therefore, undoubtedly, ſome other more excellent and heavenly uſe. Sacraments, by reaſon of their mixed nature, are more diverſely interpreted and diſputed of than any other parts of Religion beſides; for that in ſo great ſtore of properties belonging to the ſelf-ſame thing, as every Man's wit hath taken hold of ſome eſpecial conſideration above the reſt, ſo they have accordingly ſeemed one to croſs another, as touching their ſeveral opinions about the neceſſity of Sacraments; whereas in truth their diſagreement is not great. For, let reſpect be had to the duty which every Communicant doth undertake, and we may well determine concerning the uſe of Sacraments, that they ſerve as Bonds of Obedience to God, ſtrict Obligations to the mutual exerciſe of Chriſtian Charity, Provocations to Godlineſs, Preſervations

BOOK V. servations from Sin, Memorials of the principal benefits of Christ; respect the time of their institution, and it thereby appeareth that God hath annexed them for ever unto the New Testament, as other Rites were before with the Old, regard the weakness which is in us, and they are warrants for the more security of our Belief; compare the Receivers of them with such as receive them not, and Sacraments are marks of distinction to separate God's own from Strangers; so that in all these respects, they are found to be most necessary. But their chiefest force and virtue consisteth not herein, so much as in that they are heavenly Ceremonies which God hath sanctified and ordained to be administered in his Church, first, as marks whereby to know when God doth impart the vital or saving Grace of Christ unto all that are capable thereof, and secondly, as means conditional, which God requireth in them unto whom he imparteth Grace. For, sith God in himself is invisible, and cannot by us be discerned working, therefore when it seemeth good in the eyes of his heavenly Wisdom that Men for some special intent and purpose should take notice of his glorious Presence, he giveth them some plain and sensible token whereby to know what they cannot see. For
Exod. iii 2. Moses to see God and live was impossible; yet Moses by fire knew where the glory of God extra-
John v. 4. ordinarily was present. The Angel by whom God endued the waters of the pool, called Bethesda, with supernatural virtue to heal, was not seen of any; yet the time of the Angel's presence known by the troubled motions of the Waters themselves.
Acts .i. 3. The Apostles by fiery tongues which they saw were admonished when the Spirit, which they could not behold, was upon them; in like manner it is with us. Christ and his holy Spirit with all their blessed effects, though entering into the Soul of Man, we are not able to apprehend or express how, do notwithstanding give notice of the times when they use

ufe to make their accefs, becaufe it pleafeth Almighty God to communicate by fenfible means thofe bleffings which are incomprehenfible. Seeing, therefore, that Grace is a confequent of Sacraments, a thing which accompanieth them as their end, a benefit which they have received from God himfelf, the Author of Sacraments, and not from any other natural or fupernatural quality in them; it may be hereby both underftood, that Sacraments are neceffary, and that the manner of their neceffity to Life fupernatural is not in all refpects as food unto natural life, becaufe they contain in themfelves no vital force or efficacy; they are not phyfical, but moral inftruments of Salvation, duties of fervice and worfhip; which unlefs we perform as the Author of Grace requireth, they are unprofitable: for, all receive not the Grace of God which receive the Sacraments of his Grace. Neither is it ordinarily his will to beftow the Grace of Sacraments on any but by the Sacraments; which Grace alfo, they that receive by Sacraments or with Sacraments, receive it from him, and not from them. For of Sacraments, the very fame is true which Solomon's wifdom obferveth in the brazen ferpent,* *He that turned towards it, was not healed by the thing he faw, but by thee, O Saviour of all.* This is therefore the neceffity of Sacraments. That faving Grace which Chrift originally is, or hath for the general good of his whole Church, by Sacraments he feverally deriveth into every member thereof. Sacraments ferve as the inftruments of God, to that end and purpofe: moral inftruments, the ufe whereof is in our own hands, the effect in his; for the ufe we have his exprefs Commandment, for the effect, his conditional Promife: fo that without our obedience to the one, there is of the other no apparent affurance; as contrariwife, where the Signs and Sacra-

BOOK V.

Wifd. xvi. 17.

* Spiritus Sancti munus eft gratiam implere myfterii. Ambr. in Luc. cap. iii. Sanctificans elementis effectum non propria ipfarum natura præbet, fed virtus divina potentius operatur. Cyp. de Chrifm.

ments

 ments of his Grace are not either through contempt unreceived, or received with contempt, we are not to doubt, but that they really give what they promise, and are what they signify. For we take not Baptism, nor the Eucharist, for bare resemblances or memorials of things absent, neither for naked signs and testimonies assuring us of Grace received before, but (as they are indeed and in verity) for means effectual, whereby God, when we take the Sacraments, delivereth into our hands that Grace available unto eternal Life, which Grace the Sacraments* represent or signify. There have grown in the Doctrine concerning Sacraments many difficulties for want of distinct explication, what kind or degree of Grace doth belong unto each Sacrament. For by this it hath come to pass, that the true immediate cause why Baptism and why the Supper of our Lord is necessary, few do rightly and distinctly consider. It cannot be denied but sundry the same effects and benefits which grow unto Men by the one Sacrament, may rightly be attributed unto the other. Yet then doth Baptism challenge to itself but the inchoation of those Graces, the consummation whereof dependeth on Mysteries ensuing. We receive Christ Jesus in Baptism once, as the first beginner; in the Eucharist often, as being by continual degrees the finisher of our life. By Baptism therefore, we receive Christ Jesus, and from him that saving Grace which is proper unto Baptism; by the other Sacrament we receive him also imparting therein himself and that Grace which the Eucharist properly bestoweth. So that each Sacrament having both that which is general or common, and that also which is peculiar unto itself, we may hereby gather, that the

* Dum homini bonum invisibile redditur, foris ei ejusdem significatio per species visibiles adhibetur, ut foris excitetur et intus reparetur. In ipsa vasis specie virtus exprimitur medicinæ. Hugo de Sacram. lib. 1. cap. 3. Si ergo vasa sunt spiritualis gratiæ sacramenta, non ex suo sanant, quia vasa ægrotum non curant, sed medicina. Idem. lib. i. cap. 4.

Participation

Participation of Chriſt, which properly belongeth to any one Sacrament, is not otherwiſe to be obtained but by the Sacrament whereunto it is proper.

BOOK V.

The Subſtance of Baptiſm; the Rites or Solemnities thereunto belonging, and that the Subſtance thereof being kept, other things in Baptiſm may give place to neceſſity.

58. Now even as the Soul doth organize the Body, and give unto every Member thereof that ſubſtance, quantity, and ſhape which Nature ſeeth moſt expedient; ſo the inward Grace of Sacraments may teach what ſerveth beſt for their outward form; a thing in no part of Chriſtian Religion, much leſs here to be neglected. Grace intended by Sacraments was a cauſe of the choice, and is a reaſon of the fitneſs of the elements themſelves. Furthermore, ſeeing that the Grace which here we receive, doth no way depend upon the natural force of that which we preſently behold, it was of neceſſity, that words of expreſs declaration, taken from the very mouth of our Lord himſelf, ſhould be added unto viſible Elements, that the one might infallibly teach what the other do moſt aſſuredly bring to paſs. In writing and ſpeaking of the bleſſed Sacrament we * uſe for the moſt part under the name of their Subſtance, not only to compriſe that whereof they outwardly and ſenſibly conſiſt, but alſo the ſecret Grace which they ſignify and exhibit. This is the reaſon wherefore commonly in † definitions, whether they be framed larger to augment, or ſtricter

* Euchariſtia duabus ex rebus conſtat, terrena et cœleſti. Iren. adverſ. Hæreſ. lib. iv. cap. 34. Arcanarum rerum ſymbola non nudis ſignis, ſed ſignis ſimul et rebus conſtant. Helvet. Confeſ. Prior. Art. 2.

† Sacramentum eſt, cum res geſta viſibilis longe aliud inviſibile intus operatur. Iſid Etym. lib. i. Sacramentum eſt per quod ſub tegumento rerum viſibilium divina virtus ſalutem ſecretius operatur. Greg. Mag. Sacramentum eſt ſignum ſignificans efficaciter effectum Dei gratuitum. Occa. Sent. lib. iv. d. 1 Sacramentum proprie non eſt ſignum cujuſlibet rei ſacræ, ſed tantum rei ſacræ ſanctificantis homines. Tho. xii. q. 101, 4. & q. 102, 5. Sacramentum eſt ſignum paſſionis Chriſti gratiæ et gloriæ. Ideo eſt commemoratio præteriti, demonſtratio præſentis, et prognoſticon futuri. Tho. iii. q. 60, 3. Sacramenta ſunt ſigna et ſymbola viſibilia rerum internarum et inviſibilium, per quæ, ſeu per media, Deus virtute Spiritus ſancti in nobis agit. Conf. Belg. Art. 33. Item Bohem. Conf. cap. 11.

BOOK V. to abridge the number of Sacraments, we find Grace exprefsly mentioned as their true effential form, Elements as the matter whereunto that form doth adjoin itfelf. But if that be feparated which is fecret, and that confidered alone which is feen, as of neceffity it muft in all thofe fpeeches that make diftinction of Sacraments from facramental Grace, the name of a Sacrament in fuch fpeeches can imply no more than what the outward fubftance thereof doth comprehend. And to make complete the outward fubftance of a Sacrament there is required an outward form, which form facramental Elements receive from facramental Words. Hereupon it groweth, that * many times there are three things faid to make up the Subftance of a Sacrament; namely, the Grace which is thereby offered, the Element which fhadoweth or fignifieth Grace, and the Word which expreffeth what is done by the Element. So that whether we confider the outward by itfelf, or both the outward and inward fubftance of any Sacraments, there are in the one refpect but two effential parts, and in the other but three that concur to give Sacraments their full being. Furthermore, becaufe definitions are to exprefs but the moft immediate and neareft parts of Nature, whereas other principles farther off, although not fpecified in defining, are notwithftanding in Nature implied and prefuppofed, we muft note, that in as much as Sacraments are actions religious and myftical, which Nature they have not unlefs they proceed from a ferious meaning; and what every Man's private mind is, as we cannot know, fo neither are we bound to examine; therefore always in thefe cafes the known intent of the Church generally doth fuffice; and where the contrary is not † manifeft, we may prefume that he which

* Sacramenta conftant verbo, fignis, et rebus fignificatis. Confef. Helvet. Poft. c. 19.

† Si aliquid Miniftri agere intendant, puta facris illudere myfteriis, vel aliud quod Ecclefiæ non confentiat, nihil agitur; fine fide enim fpiritualis poteftas exerceri quidem poteft, fine Ecclefiæ intentione non poteft. Lancel. Inft. Jur. Can. lib. ii. Tit. ii. 5. Hoc tamen.

outwardly

outwardly doth the work, hath inwardly the purpose of the Church of God. Concerning all other Orders, Rites, Prayers, Lessons, Sermons, Actions, and their circumstances whatsoever, they are to the outward Substance of Baptism but things accessory, which the wisdom of the Church of Christ is to order according to the exigence of that which is principal. Again, considering that such Ordinances have been made to adorn the Sacrament,* not the Sacrament to depend upon them; seeing also, that they are not of the Substance of Baptism, and that Baptism is far more necessary than any such incident Rite or Solemnity ordained for the better administration thereof;† if the case be such as permitteth not Baptism to have decent complements of Baptism, better it were to enjoy the body without his furniture, than to wait for this till the opportunity of that for which we desire it be lost. Which premises standing, it seemeth to have been no absurd collection, that in cases of necessity, which will not suffer delay till Baptism be administered with usual solemnities (to speak the least), it may be tolerably given without them, rather than any Man without it should be suffered to depart this life.

BOOK V.

The Grounds in Scripture whereupon a necessity of outward Baptism hath been built.

59. They which deny that any such case of necessity can fall, in regard whereof the Church should tolerate Baptism without the decent Rites and Solemnities thereunto belonging, pretend that such tolerations have risen from a false interpretation which certain Men have made of the Scripture, grounding a necessity of external Baptism upon the words of our Saviour Christ: *Unless a Man be born again of Water and of the Spirit, he cannot enter into the Kingdom of Heaven.*‡ For by Water and the Spirit, we are in that

* Accessorium non regulat principale, sed ab eo regulatur. 42. De Regul Jur in Sext. lib iii. ff. quod jussu

† Etsi nihil facile mutandum est ex solennibus, tamen ubi æquitas evidens poscit, subveniendum est Lib clxxxiii. de Reg. Jur.

‡ T. C. l. 1 p. 143. Private Baptism first rose upon a false interpretation of the place of St. John, ch. iii. 5. *Unless a Man be born again of Water, and of the Spirit,* &c where, certain do interpret the word Water, for [illegible]

BOOK V. place to underſtand (as they imagine) no more than if the Spirit alone had been mentioned, and Water not ſpoken of. Which they think is plain, becauſe elſewhere it is not improbable that *the Holy Ghoſt and Fire* do but ſignify the Holy Ghoſt in operation reſembling Fire. Whereupon they conclude, that ſeeing Fire in one place may be, therefore Water in another place is but a Metaphor; Spirit, the interpretation thereof; and ſo the Words do only mean, *That unleſs a Man be born again of the Spirit, he cannot enter into the Kingdom of Heaven.* I hold it for a moſt infallible rule in expoſitions of ſacred Scripture, that where a literal conſtruction will ſtand, the fartheſt from the Letter is commonly the worſt. There is nothing more dangerous than this licentious and deluding art, which changeth the meaning of words, as alchymy doth or would do the ſubſtance of metals, maketh of any thing what it liſteth, and bringeth in the end all Truth to nothing. Or howſoever ſuch voluntary exerciſe of wit might be borne with otherwiſe; yet in places which uſually ſerve, as this doth, concerning Regeneration by Water and the Holy Ghoſt, to be alledged for grounds and principles, leſs is permitted. To hide the general conſent of Antiquity, agreeing in the literal interpretation, they cunningly affirm, that certain have taken thoſe words as meant of material Water, when they know that of all the Ancients there is not one to be named that ever did otherwiſe either expound or alledge the place, than as implying external Baptiſm. Shall that which hath always * received

when as our Saviour Chriſt taketh Water there, by a borrowed ſpeech, for the Spirit of God, the effect whereof it ſhadoweth out. For even as in another place, Mat. iii 11. by *Fire and the Spirit*, he meaneth nothing but the Spirit of God, which purgeth and purifieth as the Fire doth; ſo in this place, by Water and the Spirit, he meaneth nothing elſe but the Spirit of God, which cleanſeth the filth of Sin, and cooleth the boiling heat of an unquiet Conſcience, as Water waſheth the thing which is foul, and quencheth the heat of the fire.

* Minime ſunt mutanda, quæ interpretationem certam ſemper habuerunt. D. lib. 1. tit. 2. lib. xviii.

this

this and no other construction be now disguised with the toy of novelty? Must we needs, at the only shew of a critical conceit, without any more deliberation, utterly condemn them of error, which will not admit that Fire in the words of John is quenched with the name of the Holy Ghost; or, with the Name of the Spirit, Water dried up in the words of Christ? When the letter of the Law hath two things plainly and expresly specified, Water and the Spirit; Water as a duty required on our parts, the Spirit as a gift which God bestoweth; there is danger in presuming so to interpret it, as if the clause which concerneth ourselves were more than needeth. We may by such rare expositions attain perhaps in the end to be thought witty, but with ill advice. Finally, if at * the time when that Baptism which was meant by John came to be really and truly performed by Christ himself, we find the Apostles that had been, as we are, before baptised, new baptised with the Holy Ghost; and in this their later Baptism as well a visible descent of Fire, as a secret miraculous infusion of the Spirit; if on us he accomplish likewise the heavenly work of our new birth, not with the Spirit alone, but with Water thereunto adjoined; sith the faithfullest Expounders of his words are his own deeds, let that which his hand hath manifestly wrought declare what his speech did doubtfully utter.

Acts ii. 3.

What kind of necessity in outward Baptism hath been gathered by the words of our Saviour Christ, and what the true necessity thereof indeed is.

60. To this they add, that as we err by following a wrong construction of the place before alledged; so our second oversight is, that we hereupon infer a necessity over rigorous and extreme.† The true necessity of Baptism, a few propositions considered will

* Acts i. 3. John baptized with Water, but you shall within few days be baptized with the Holy Ghost.

† T. C. lib. i. p. 143. Secondly, this error (of private Baptism) came by a false and unnecessary conclusion drawn from that place. For, although the Scripture should say, that none can be saved, but those which have the Spirit of God and are baptized with material and elemental Water; yet it ought to be understood of those which can conveniently and orderly be brought to Baptism;

BOOK V. ſoon decide. All things which either are known * cauſes or ſet means, whereby any great good is uſually procured, or Men delivered from grievous evil, the ſame we muſt needs confeſs neceſſary. And if Regeneration were not in this very ſenſe a thing neceſſary to eternal Life, would Chriſt himſelf have taught Nicodemus,
John iii 3. that to ſee the Kingdom of God is impoſſible, ſaving only for thoſe Men which are born from above? His words following in the next Sentence are a proof ſufficient, that to our Regeneration his Spirit is no leſs
Verſe 5. neceſſary, than Regeneration itſelf neceſſary unto Life. Thirdly, unleſs as the Spirit is a neceſſary inward cauſe, ſo Water were a neceſſary outward mean to our Regeneration, what conſtruction ſhould we give unto thoſe words wherein we are ſaid to be new born, and that ἐξ ὕδατος, even of Water?
Epheſ. v. 26. Why are we taught, that with Water God doth purify and cleanſe his Church? Wherefore do
Tit. iii. 5. the Apoſtles of Chriſt term Baptiſm a Bath of Regeneration? What purpoſe had they in giving Men advice to receive outward Baptiſm, and in perſuading
Acts ii. 38. them, it did avail to remiſſion of ſins? If outward Baptiſm were a cauſe in itſelf poſſeſſed of that power, either natural or ſupernatural, without the preſent operation whereof no ſuch effect could poſſibly grow; it muſt then follow, that ſeeing effects do never prevent the neceſſary cauſes out of which they ſpring, no

tiſm; as the Scripture, ſaying, that whoſo doth not believe the Goſpel, is condemned already, John iii 18 meaneth this ſentence of thoſe which can hear the Goſpel, and have diſcretion to underſtand it when they hear it; and cannot here ſhut under this condemnation, either thoſe that be born deaf and ſo remain, or little Infants, or natural Fools that have not wit to conceive what is preached.

* Ἀναγκαῖον λέγεται, οὗ ἄνευ οὐκ ἐνδέχεται ζῆν ὡς συναιτίου· καὶ ὧν ἄνευ τὸ ἀγαθὸν μὴ ἐνδέχεται ἢ εἶναι ἢ γένεσθαι, ἢ τὶ κακὸν ἀποβαλεῖν, ἢ στερηθῆναι. Neceſſarium id dicitur, ſine quo ut concauſa fieri non poteſt ut vivatur; et ea ſine quibus fieri nequit ut bonum aut ſit aut fiat; vel malum aliquod amoveatur, aut non adſit. Ariſt. Metaph. v. cap. v.

Man

Man could ever receive Grace before Baptiſm: which being apparently both known, and alſo confeſſed to be otherwiſe in many particulars, although in the reſt we make not Baptiſm a cauſe of Grace; yet the Grace which is given them with their * Baptiſm, doth ſo far forth depend on the very outward Sacrament, that God will have it embraced, not only as a ſign or token what we receive; but alſo as an inſtrument or mean whereby we receive Grace, becauſe Baptiſm is a Sacrament which God hath inſtituted in his Church, to the end that they which receive the ſame might thereby be † incorporated into Chriſt; and ſo through his moſt precious merit obtain, as well that ſaving Grace of Imputation which taketh away ‡ all former guiltineſs, as alſo that § infuſed divine Virtue of the Holy Ghoſt which giveth to the powers of the Soul their firſt diſpoſition towards future newneſs of life. There are that elevate too much the ordinary and im-

* Fideles ſalutem ex iſtis Elementis non quærunt, etiamſi in iſtis quærunt. Non enim iſta tribuunt quod per iſta tribuitur. Hugo de Sacram. lib. 1. cap. 3.

† Suſceptus a Chriſto, Chriſtumque ſuſcipiens, non idem fit poſt lavacrum qui ante Baptiſmum fuit; ſed corpus regenerati fit caro crucifixi. Leo. Serm. iv. de Paſ. Dom.

‡ Caro abluitur ut anima emaculetur. Tert. de Carn. Reſur. Homo per aquam Baptiſmi licet a foris idem eſſe videatur, intus tamen alter efficitur; cum peccato natus, ſine peccato renaſcitur; prioribus perit, ſuccedentibus proficit; deterioribus exuitur, in meliora innovatur; perſona tingitur, et natura mutatur. Euſeb. Emiſ. de Epiphan. Homil iii. Τριαχὴν γέννησιν ἡμῖν οἶδεν ὁ λόγος, τὴν ἐκ σώματος, τὴν ἐκ βαπτίσματος, τὴν ἐξ ἀναςάσεως Ἄυτη μὲν ἡ τῦ βαπτίσματος χάρις καὶ δύναμις οὐ κόσμυ κατακλυσμὸν ὡς πάλαι, τῆς δὲ τῦ καθ᾽ ἕκαςον ἁμαρτίας κάθαρσιν ἔχουσα. Greg. Homil. de Sanct. Bapt.

§ Unde genitalis auxilio ſuperioris ævi labe deterſa in expiatum pectus ac purum deſuper ſe lumen infundit. Cypr. Epiſt ad Donat. Ου μόνον τῶν παλαιῶν ἁμαρτημάτων δωρεῖται τὴν ἄφεσιν, ἀλλὰ καὶ τὴν ἐλπίδα τῶν ἐπηγγελμένων ἐντίθησιν ἀγαθῶν, καὶ τῦ δεσποτικῦ θανάτου καὶ τῆς ἀναςάσεως καθίςησι κοινωνὺς, καὶ τῆς τῦ πνεύματος δωρεᾶς τὴν μετουσίαν χαρίζεται. Theod. Epito. Divin. Dogmat. Baptizari, eſt purgari a ſordibus peccatorum, et donari varia Dei gratia ad vitam novam et innocentem. Confeſſ. Helvet. cap. xx.

BOOK V. mediate means of life, relying wholly upon the bare conceit of that eternal Election, which notwithstanding includeth a subordination of means, without which we are not actually brought to enjoy what God secretly did intend; and therefore to build upon God's Election, if we keep not ourselves to the ways which he hath appointed for Men to walk in, is but a self-deceiving vanity. When the Apostle saw Men called to the participation of Jesus Christ, after the Gospel of God embraced and the Sacrament of Life received,
Eph. i. 1. he feareth not then to put them in the number of
Eph. v. 8. elect Saints; he then accounteth them delivered from death, and clean purged from all sin. Till then, notwithstanding their preordination unto life, which none could know of saving God, what were they, in the
Eph. ii. 3, 12. Apostle's own account, but Children of Wrath, as well as others, plain Aliens, altogether without hope, Strangers, utterly without God in this present World? So that by Sacraments, and other sensible tokens of Grace, we may boldly gather, that he whose Mercy vouchsafeth now to bestow the means hath also long sithence intended us that whereunto they lead. But let us never think it safe to presume of our own last end by bare conjectural collections of his first intent and purpose, the means failing that should come between. Predestination bringeth not to life without
Ro. viii 30. the Grace of external Vocation, wherein our Baptism is implied. For as we are not naturally Men without birth, so neither are we Christian Men in the eye of the Church of God but by new birth; nor according to the manifest ordinary course of Divine Dispensation new-born, but by that Baptism which both declareth and maketh us Christians. In which respect, we justly hold it to be the door of our actual entrance into God's house, the first apparent * beginning of Life, a seal perhaps to the † Grace of Election before received;

* Ἀρχή μοι ζωῆς τὸ βάπτισμα. Basil. de Spir. Sanct. cap. x.

† T. C. lib. iii. p. 134. He which is not a Christian before he come to receive Baptism, cannot be made a Christian by Baptism; which is only the Seal of the Grace of God before received.

but

BOOK V.

but to our Sanctification here, a ſtep that hath not any before it. There were of the old Valentinian Hereticks ſome which had knowledge in ſuch admiration, that to it they aſcribed all, and ſo deſpiſed the Sacraments of Chriſt, pretending that as ignorance had made us ſubject to all miſery, ſo the full Redemption of the inward Man, and the work of our Reſtauration muſt needs belong unto knowledge only. They draw very near unto this error who fixing wholly their minds on the known neceſſity of Faith,* imagine that nothing but Faith is neceſſary for the attainment of all Grace. Yet is it a branch of Belief, that Sacraments are in their place no leſs required than Belief itſelf. For when our Lord and Saviour promiſeth eternal Life, is it any otherwiſe than as he promiſed reſtitution of health unto Naaman the Syrian, namely, with this condition, *Waſh and be clean?* or as to them which were ſtung of Serpents, health by beholding the brazen Serpent? If Chriſt himſelf which giveth Salvation do require Baptiſm; it is not for us that look for Salvation to ſound and examine him, whether unbaptized Men may be ſaved; but ſeriouſly to † do that which is required, and religiouſly to fear the danger which may grow by the want thereof. Had Chriſt only declared his will to have all Men baptized, and not acquainted us with any cauſe why Baptiſm is neceſſary, our ignorance in the reaſon of that he enjoineth, might perhaps have hindered ſomewhat the forwardneſs of our obedience thereunto; whereas now being taught that Baptiſm is neceſſary to take away ſin, how have we the fear of God in our hearts, if

Iren. contra Hæreſ. l. 1. c. 18.

2 Kings v. 14.
Numb. xxi. 8.
Mark xvi. 16.

* Hic ſceleſtiſſimi illi provocant quæſtiones. Adeo dicunt, Baptiſmus non eſt neceſſarius quibus fides ſatis eſt Tert. de Baptiſ. Huic nulla proderit fides, qui, cum poſſit, non percipit Sacramentum. Bern Epiſt lxx. ad Hugon

† Inſtitutio Sacramentorum quantum ad Deum Authorem, diſpenſationis eſt; quantum vero ad Hominem obedientem, neceſſitatis. Quoniam in poteſtate Dei eſt præter iſta Hominem ſalvare, ſed in poteſtate Hominis non eſt ſine iſtis ad ſalutem pervenire. Hugo de Sacra. lib. i. cap. 5.

BOOK V. care of delivering Men's Souls from ſin do not move us to uſe all means for their Baptiſm? * Pelagius, which denied utterly the guilt of original ſin, and in that reſpect the neceſſity of Baptiſm, did notwithſtanding both baptiſe Infants, and acknowledge their Baptiſm neceſſary for entrance into the Kingdom of God. Now the Law of Chriſt, which in theſe conſiderations maketh Baptiſm neceſſary, muſt be conſtrued and underſtood according to rules of † natural equity. Which rules if they themſelves did not follow in expounding the Law of God, would they ever be able to prove, that the Scripture, in ſaying, *Whoſo believeth not the Goſpel of Chriſt, is condemned already*, meaneth this ſentence of thoſe which can hear the Goſpel, and have diſcretion when they hear, to underſtand it, neither ought it to be applied unto Infants, deaf Men, and Fools? That which teacheth them thus to interpret the Law of Chriſt is Natural Equity. And (becauſe equity ſo teacheth) it is on all parts gladly confeſt, that there may be in divers caſes Life by virtue of inward Baptiſm, even where outward is not found. So that if any queſtion be made, it is but about the bounds and limits of this poſſibility. For example, to think that a Man whoſe Baptiſm the crown of Martyrdom preventeth, doth loſe in that caſe the happineſs which ſo many thouſands enjoy that only have had the grace to believe and not the honour to ſeal the teſtimony thereof with death, were almoſt barbarous. Again, when ſome certain opinionative Men in St. Bernard's time began privately to hold that, becauſe our Lord hath ſaid, *unleſs a Man be born again of Water*, therefore life, without either actual Baptiſm or Martyrdom inſtead of Baptiſm,

T. C. lib. i pag. 143.

Bern Epiſt. lxx. ad Hugonem.

* Pelagius aſſerere arrepta impietate præſumit non propter vitam, ſed propter regnum Cœlorum Baptiſmum parvulis conferendum. Euſeb. Emiſſ. Hom. v. de Paſch.

† Benignius leges interpretandæ ſunt, quo voluntas earum conſervetur. L. Benign. D. de Legib. et Sena. Tuſc.

cannot

cannot possibly be obtained at the hands of God; Bernard considering, that the same equity which had moved them to think the necessity of Baptism no bar against the happy estate of unbaptized Martyrs, is as forcible for the warrant of their Salvation, in whom, although there be not the sufferings of holy Martyrs, there are the virtues which sanctified those Sufferings, and made them precious in God's sight, professed himself an enemy to that severity and strictness which admitteth no exception but of Martyrs only. For, saith he, if a Man desirous of Baptism be suddenly cut off by death, in whom there wanted neither sound Faith, devout Hope, nor sincere Charity (God be merciful unto me, and pardon me if I err) but verily of such a one's Salvation, in whom there is no other defect besides his faultless lack of Baptism, despair I cannot, nor induce my mind to think his Faith void, his Hope confounded, and his Charity fallen to nothing, only because he hath not that which not contempt but impossibility withholdeth. *Tell me, I beseech you,* (saith Ambrose) *what there is in any of us more than to will, and to seek for our own good. Thy servant Valentinian, O Lord, did both.* (For Valentinian the Emperor died before his purpose to receive Baptism could take effect.) *And is it possible, that he which had purposely thy Spirit given him to desire Grace, should not receive thy Grace which that Spirit did desire? Doth it move you that the outward accustomed Solemnities were not done? As though Converts that suffer Martyrdom before Baptism, did thereby forfeit their right to the crown of eternal Glory in the Kingdom of Heaven. If the Blood of Martyrs in that case be their Baptism, surely his religious desire of Baptism standeth him in the same stead.* * It

BOOK V.

* Qui ad tolerandam omnem pro Dei gloria injuriam semel dicavit animum in Martyrium, mihi videtur implevisse. Summi ergo meriti est semel fixisse sententiam, atque ideo, ut dixi, ratio principatum obtinet passionis, et si sors perpetiendi deneget facultatem, pertulit tamen cuncta quæ voluit pati. Joseph. lib. de Imper. Ration.

hath

BOOK V. hath been therefore constantly held as well touching other Believers, as Martyrs, that Baptism, taken away by necessity, is supplied by desire of Baptism, because with equity this opinion doth best stand. Touching Infants which die unbaptized, sith they neither have this Sacrament itself, nor any sense or conceit thereof, the judgment of many hath gone hard against them. But yet seeing Grace is not absolutely tied unto Sacraments; and besides, such is the lenity of God, that unto things altogether impossible he bindeth no Man; but, where we cannot do what is enjoined us, accepteth our will to do instead of the deed itself; again, forasmuch as there is in their Christian Parents, and in the Church of God, a presumed desire, that the Sacrament of Baptism might be given them; yea, a purpose also that it shall be given, remorse of equity hath moved divers of the * School-Divines in these considerations, ingenuously to grant, that God, all-merciful to such as are not in themselves able to desire Baptism, imputeth the secret desire that others have in their behalf, and accepteth the same as theirs, rather than casteth away their Souls for that which no Man is able to help. And of the will of God to impart his Grace unto Infants without Baptism in that case, the very circumstance of their natural birth may serve as a just argument; whereupon it is not to be misliked, that Men in charitable presumption do gather a great likelihood of their Salvation, to whom the benefit of Christian Parentage being given, the rest that should follow is prevented by some such casualty, as Man hath himself no power to avoid. For, we are plainly taught of God, that the Seed of faithful Parentage is holy from the very birth. Which

1 Cor. vii. 12.

* Gers. Serm. in Nativit Beatæ Mar. Cajetan. in 3. Tho. ix. 68. Art. 1 et 2. Biel. in 4 Senten. d. 4 q. 2. Tilman. Segeberg. de Sacr. cap. 1. Elisius Neapol. in Clyp. advers. Hæres. cap. de Baptis.

albeit

albeit we may not ſo underſtand, as if the Children of believing Parents were without ſin; or grace from baptized Parents derived by propagation; or God, by Covenant and Promiſe, tied to ſave any in mere regard of their Parents' Belief: yet ſeeing, that to all profeſſors of the Name of Chriſt this pre-eminence above Infidels is freely given; the fruit of their Bodies bringeth into the World with it a preſent intereſt and right to thoſe means where-with the Ordinance of Chriſt is that his Church ſhall be ſanctified, it is not to be thought that he which, as it were, from Heaven, hath nominated and deſigned them unto Holineſs by ſpecial privilege of their very birth, will himſelf deprive them of Regeneration and inward Grace, only becauſe neceſſity depriveth them of outward Sacraments. In which caſe, it were the part of Charity to hope, and to make Men rather partial than cruel Judges, if we had not thoſe fair appearances which here we have. Wherefore a neceſſity there is of receiving, and a neceſſity of adminiſtering the Sacrament of Baptiſm; the one peradventure not ſo abſolute as ſome have thought, but out of all peradventure the other more ſtrait and narrow than that the Church, which is by office a Mother unto ſuch as crave at her hands the ſacred Myſtery of their new Birth, ſhould repel them; and ſee them die unſatisfied of theſe their ghoſtly deſires, rather than give them their Soul's rights with omiſſion of thoſe things which ſerve but only for the more convenient and orderly adminiſtration thereof. For as on the one ſide we grant, that thoſe ſentences of holy Scripture which make Sacraments moſt neceſſary to eternal life are no prejudice to their Salvation that want them by ſome inevitable neceſſity, and without any fault of their own,* ſo it ought, in reaſon, to be likewiſe acknow-

* T. C. l. iii. p. 218 It is in queſtion, whether there be any ſuch neceſſity of Baptiſm, as that for the miniſtering thereof, the common decent Orders ſhould be broken.

ledged,

BOOK V. ledged, that forasmuch as our Lord himself maketh Baptism necessary, necessary whether we respect the good received by Baptism, or the testimony thereby yielded unto God of that humility and meek obedience, which reposing wholly itself on the absolute authority of his Commandment, and on the Truth of his heavenly Promise, doubteth not but from Creatures despicable in their own condition and substance to obtain Grace of inestimable value; or rather not from them, but from him, yet by them, as by his appointed means. Howsoever he, by the secret ways of his own incomprehensible Mercy, may be thought to save without Baptism, this cleareth not the Church from guiltiness of blood, if, through her superfluous scrupulosity, letts and impediments of less regard should cause a Grace of so great moment to be withheld, wherein our merciless strictness may be our own harm, though not theirs towards whom we shew it; and we for the hardness of our hearts may perish, albeit they through God's unspeakable Mercy do live. God, which did not afflict that Innocent whose Circumcision Moses had over-long deferred, took revenge upon Moses himself for the injury which was done through so great neglect; giving us thereby to understand, that they whom God's own Mercy saveth without us, are on our parts notwithstanding, and as much as in us lieth, even destroyed, when under unsufficient pretences we defraud them of such ordinary outward helps as we should exhibit. We have for Baptism no day set, as the Jews had for Circumcision; neither have we by the Law of God, but only by the Churches discretion, a place thereunto appointed. Baptism therefore even in the meaning of the Law of Christ belongeth unto Infants capable thereof from the * very instant of their birth. Which if they have not howsoever, rather than lose it by

Exod. iv. 24.

* In omnibus obligationibus in quibus dies non ponitur, præsenti die debetur. Lib. xiv. D. de Reg. Jur.

being

being put off because the time, the place, or some such like circumstance doth not solemnly enough concur, the Church, as much as in her lieth, wilfully casteth away their Souls.

What things in Baptism have been dispensed with by the Fathers, respecting necessity.

61. The Ancients, it may be, were too severe, and made the necessity of Baptism more absolute than Reason would, as touching Infants. But will * any Man say, that they, notwithstanding their too much rigour herein, did not in that respect sustain and tolerate defects of local, or of personal Solemnities belonging to the Sacrament of Baptism? The Apostles themselves did neither use nor appoint for Baptism any certain time. The Church for general Baptism heretofore made choice of two chief days in the year; the Feast of Easter, and the Feast of Pentecost. Which Custom, when certain Churches in Sicily began to violate without cause, they were by Leo Bishop of Rome advised, rather to conform themselves to the rest of the World in things so reasonable, than to offend Men's minds through needless singularity; howbeit, always providing,

Leo Epist. iv ad Episc. Sicil.

* T. C. lib. i. pag. 146. The Authors themselves of that error, that they cannot be saved which are not baptized, did never seek a remedy of the mischief in Women's or private Baptism. T. C. lib. iii. p. 219. What plainer testimony can there be than that of Augustin? which noteth the use of the Church to have been, to come to the Church with their Children in danger of death, and that when some had opinion that their Children could not be saved if they were not baptized. Cont. Lit. Parm. lib. ii. cap. 13. I would also know of him what he will answer to that which is noted of a Christian Jew desperately sick of the palsy, that was with his Bed carried to the place of Baptism. Socr. lib. vii. cap. 4. What will he answer to this? that those which were baptized in their beds, were thereby made unapt to have any place amongst the Clergy (as they call them), doth it not leave a note of infamy in those which had procured that Baptism should be administered in private houses? Euseb. lib. vi. cap. 43. What unto the Emperor's Decree, which, upon authority of the ancient Laws, and of the Apostles, forbiddeth, that the holy things should be administered in any Man's house? Just. Novel. 57.

BOOK V. that nevertheleſs in apparent peril of death, danger of ſiege, ſtraits of perſecution, fear of ſhipwreck, and the like exigents, no reſpects of time ſhould cauſe this ſingular defence of true ſafety to be denied unto any. This of Leo did but confirm that ſentence which Victor had many years before given, extending the ſame exception as well unto places as times. That which St. Auguſtin ſpeaketh of Women haſting to bring their Children to the Church when they ſaw danger, is a weak proof, that when neceſſity did not leave them ſo much time, it was not then permitted them neither to make a Church of their own home. Which anſwer diſchargeth likewiſe their example of a ſick Jew carried in a bed to the place of Baptiſm, and not baptized at home in private. The cauſe why ſuch kind of Baptiſm barred Men afterwards from entering into holy Orders, the reaſon wherefore it was objected againſt Novatian, in what reſpect, and how far forth it did diſable, may be gathered by the twelfth Canon ſet down in the Council of Neocæſarea after this manner. *A Man which hath been baptized in ſickneſs, is not after to be ordained Prieſt.* For it may be thought, *That ſuch do rather at that time, becauſe they ſee no other remedy than of a voluntary mind, lay hold on the Chriſtian Faith, unleſs their true and ſincere meaning be made afterwards the more manifeſt, or elſe the ſcarcity of others enforce the Church to admit them.* They bring in Juſtinian's imperial Conſtitution, but to what purpoſe? Seeing it only forbiddeth Men to have the Myſteries of God adminiſtered in their Private Chapels, leſt under that pretence Hereticks ſhould do ſecretly thoſe things which were unlawful. In which conſideration he therefore commandeth, that if they would uſe thoſe private Oratories otherwiſe than only for their private Prayers, the Biſhop ſhould appoint them a Clerk whom they might entertain for that purpoſe. This is plain by later Conſtitutions made in the time of Leo: *It was thought good* (ſaith the Emperor) *in their judgment which have gone before, that in private Chapels*

Vict. Ep. ad Theoph. Alexand. in Pontif. Damaſc.

Leo. Conſt. iv.

Chapels none should celebrate the holy Communion but Priests belonging unto greater Churches. Which order they took as it seemeth for the Custody of Religion, lest Men should secretly receive from Hereticks, instead of the food, the bane of their Souls, pollution in the place of expiation. Again, *Whereas a sacred Canon of the sixth reverend Synod requireth Baptism, as others have likewise the holy Sacrifices and Mysteries, to be celebrated only in Temples hallowed for publick use, and not in private Oratories; which strict Decrees appear to have been made heretofore in regard of Hereticks which entered closely into such Men's Houses as favoured their opinions, whom, under colour of performing with them such religious Offices, they drew from the soundness of true Religion: now that perverse opinions, through the Grace of Almighty God, are extinct and gone, the cause of former restraints being taken away, we see no reason but that private Oratories may henceforward enjoy that Liberty, which to have granted them heretofore had not been safe.* In sum, all these things alledged are nothing, nor will it ever be proved while the World doth continue, but that the practice of the Church in cases of extreme necessity hath made for private Baptism always more than against it. Yea, *Baptism by any Man, in the case of necessity*, was the * voice of the whole World heretofore. Neither is Tertullian, Epiphanius, Augustin,† or any other of the Antients against it. The boldness of such, as, pretending Teclæ's example, took openly upon them both Baptism and all other publick Functions of Priesthood, Tertullian severely controuleth, saying, *To give Baptism is in truth the Bishop's right. After him*

BOOK V.

Leo Const. xv.

Tertul. de Virgin velland. & lib. de Baptis. Epipha. lib. i. & lib ii. cont. Hæref. Tertul de Bapt.

* T. C. lib. i. pag. 145. To allow of Women's baptising, is not only contrary to the learned Writers now, but also contrary to all learned Antiquity, and contrary to the practice of the Church whilst there was any tolerable estate

† St. Augustin, although he seem to allow of a Lay-man's Baptism in time of necessity, Cont. Epist. Parmen. lib. ii. cap. 13; yet there he mentioneth not Women's Baptism, and in the fourth council of Carthage, cap. c it is simply, without exception, decreed, that a Woman ought not to baptize.

BOOK V. *it belongeth unto Priests and Deacons; but not to them without authority from him received. For so the honour of the Church requireth, which, being kept, preserveth peace. Were it not in this respect, the Laity might do the same; all sorts might give, even as all sorts receive.* But because emulation is the mother of schisms, *Let it content thee,* (which art of the order of Lay-men) *to do it in necessity, when the state of time, or place, or Person thereunto compelleth. For then is their boldness privileged that help, when the circumstance of other Men's dangers craveth it.* What he granteth generally to Lay-persons of the house of God, the same we cannot suppose he denieth to any sort or sex contained under that name, unless himself did restrain the limits of his own speech; especially seeing that Tertullian's rule of interpretation is * elsewhere, *Specialties are signified under that which is general, because they are therein comprehended.* All which Tertullian doth † deny is, that Women may be called to bear, or publickly take upon them to execute Offices of Ecclesiastical Order, whereof none but Men are capable. As for Epiphanius, he striketh on the very self-same Anvil with Tertullian: and in necessity, if St. Augustin alloweth as much unto Lay-men as Tertullian doth, his not mentioning of Women is but a slender proof that his meaning was to exclude Women. Finally, the Council of Carthage likewise, although it make no express submission, may be very well presumed willing to stoop, as other positive Ordinances do, to the countermands of necessity. Judge therefore what the Ancients would have thought, if in their days it had

* Subjectum est generali speciale. In ipso significatur, quia in ipso continetur Tertul. de veland. Virg. Posito genere, supponitur species. Aug. in lib. ii. cap. de Transact.

† Non permittitur Mulieri in ecclesia loqui, sed nec docere, nec tingere, nec offerre, nec ullius virilis muneris nedum sacerdotalis officii sortem sibi vendicare. Tertul. de veland. Virg.

been

been heard, which is publiſhed in ours, * that becauſe *the Subſtance of the Sacrament doth chiefly depend on the Inſtitution of God, which is the form and as it were the life of the Sacrament*; therefore firſt, *if the whole Inſtitution be not kept, it is no Sacrament*; and ſecondly, if Baptiſm be private, his Inſtitution is broken, in as much as, *according to the orders which he hath ſet for Baptiſm, it ſhould be done in the Congregation*; from whoſe Ordinance in this point *we ought not to ſwerve, although we know that Infants ſhould be aſſuredly damned without Baptiſm.* O Sir, you that would ſpurn thus at ſuch, as in caſe of ſo dreadful extremity ſhould lie proſtrate before your feet; you that would turn away your face from them at the hour of their moſt need; you that would dam up your ears and harden your hearts as iron againſt the unreſiſtible cries of Supplicants, calling upon you for Mercy with terms of ſuch invocation as that moſt dreadful perplexity might miniſter, if God by miracle did open the mouths of Infants to expreſs their ſuppoſed neceſſity, ſhould firſt imagine yourſelf in their caſe, and them in your's. This done, let their Supplications proceed out of your mouth, and your anſwer out of theirs. Would you then contentedly hear, *My Son, the Rites and Solemnities of Baptiſm muſt be kept*; *we may not do ill, that good may come of it*; † *neither are Souls to be delivered from eternal death and condemnation, by breaking*

* T. C. lib. i. pag. 144. The Subſtance of the Sacrament dependeth chiefly of the Inſtitution and Word of God, which is the form, and, as it were, the life of the Sacrament T. C. lib. i. pag. 144. Although part of the Inſtitution be obſerved, yet if the whole Inſtitution be not, it is no Sacrament. T. C. lib. i. pag. 146. The Orders, which God hath ſet, are, that it ſhould be done in the Congregation, and by the Miniſter. T. C. lib. i. pag. 146. And I will further ſay, that although the Infants which die without Baptiſm, ſhould be aſſuredly damned (which is moſt falſe) yet ought not the Orders which God hath ſet in his Church, to be broken after this ſort.

† Noſtro peccato alterius ſaluti conſulere non debemus. Aug. lib. cont. Mend. cap. xvii.

BOOK V. *Orders which Chrift hath fet:* would you in their cafe yourfelf be fhaken off with thefe anfwers, and not rather embrace, enclofed with both your arms, a fentence, which now is no Gofpel unto you, *I will have Mercy and not Sacrifice?* To acknowledge Chrift's Inftitution the ground of both Sacraments, I fuppofe no Chriftian Man will refufe: for it giveth them their very nature, it appointeth the matter whereof they confift, the form of their adminiftration it teacheth; and it bleffeth them with that Grace whereby to us they are both pledges and inftruments of life. Neverthelefs, feeing Chrift's Inftitution containeth, befides that which maketh complete the effence or nature other things that only are parts, as it were, of the furniture of Sacraments; the difference between thefe two muft unfold that which the general terms of indefinite fpeech would confound. If the place appointed for Baptifm be a part of Chrift's Inftitution, it is but his Inftitution as Sacrifice, Baptifm his Inftitution as Mercy: in this cafe, he which requireth both Mercy and Sacrifice, rejecteth his own Inftitution of Sacrifice, where the offering of Sacrifice would hinder Mercy from being fhewed. External Circumftances, even in the holieft and higheft actions, are but the *leffer things of the Law*, whereunto thofe actions themfelves being compared, are the greater; and therefore as the greater are of fuch importance, that they muft be done; fo in that extremity before fuppofed, if our account of the leffer which are not to be omitted, fhould caufe omiffion of that which is more to be accounted of, were not this our ftrict obedience to Chrift's Inftitution touching Mint and Cummin, a difobedience to his Inftitution concerning Love? But fith no Inftitution of Chrift hath fo ftrictly tied Baptifm to public Affemblies, as it hath done all Men unto Baptifm; away with thefe mercilefs and bloody fentences, let them never be found ftanding in the Books and Writings of a Chriftian Man; they favour not of Chrift, nor of his moft gracious and meek Spirit,

Matth. ix 13

Matth. xxiii. 23.

Spirit, but under colour of exact obedience they nourish cruelty and hardness of heart.

Whether Baptism by Women, be true Baptism, good and effectual to them that receive it.

62. To leave private Baptism therefore, and to come unto Baptism by Women, which they say * is no more a Sacrament, than any other ordinary washing or bathing of a Man's body: the reason whereupon they ground their opinion herein is such, as making Baptism by Women void because Women are no Ministers in the Church of God, must needs generally annihilate the Baptism of all unto whom their conceit shall apply this exception, whether it be in regard of sex, of quality, of insufficiency, or whatsoever. For if want of calling do frustrate Baptism, they that baptize without calling do nothing, be they Women or Men. To make Women Teachers in the House of God, were a gross absurdity, seeing the Apostle hath said, *I permit not a Woman to teach.* And again, *Let your Women in Churches be silent.* Those extraordinary gifts of speaking with Tongues and Prophesying, which God at that time did not only bestow upon Men, but on Women also, made it the harder to hold them confined within private bounds; whereupon the Apostle's Ordinance was necessary against Women's publick admission to teach. And because, when Law hath begun some one thing or other well, it giveth good occasion either to draw by judicious exposition out of the very Law itself, or to annex to the Law by authority and jurisdiction things of like conveniency, therefore Clement extendeth this Apostolick Constitution to Baptism. *For* (saith he) *if we have denied them leave to teach, how should any Man dispense with Nature, and make them Ministers of holy things; seeing this unskilfulness is a part of the Grecians' impiety, which for the service of Women-Goddesses have*

1 Tim. ii. 12.
1 Tim. xiv. 34.
Clem. Const. Apostol. lib. iii. cap. 9.

* T. C. l. i. p. 144. On this point, whether he be a Minister, or no, dependeth not only the dignity, but also the being of the Sacrament. So that I take the Baptism of Women to be no more the holy Sacrament of Baptism, than any other daily or ordinary washing of the Child.

BOOK V. *Women-Priests?* I somewhat marvel, that Men which would not willingly be thought to speak or write but with good conscience, dare hereupon openly avouch Clement for a witness, *That as, when the Church began not only to decline, but to fall away from the sincerity of Religion, it borrowed a number of other profanations of the Heathens; so it borrowed this, and would needs have Women-Priests, as the Heathens had; and that this was one occasion of bringing Baptism by Women into the Church of God.* Is it not plain in their own eyes, that first, by an evidence which forbiddeth Women to be Ministers of Baptism, they endeavour to shew how Women were admitted unto that function in the wane and declination of Christian Piety? Secondly, that by an evidence rejecting the Heathens, and condemning them of impiety, they would prove such affection towards Heathens as ordereth the affairs of the Church by the pattern of their example: and, thirdly, that out of an evidence which nameth the Heathens as being in some part a reason why the Church had no Women-Priests, they gather the Heathens to have been one of the first occasions why it had? So that throughout every branch of this testimony their issue is yea; and their evidence directly no. But to Women's Baptism in private by occasion of urgent necessity, the reasons that only concern ordinary Baptism in publick are no just prejudice; neither can we by force thereof disprove the practice of those Churches which (necessity requiring) allow Baptism in private to be administered by Women. We may not, from Laws that prohibit any thing with restraint, conclude absolute and unlimitted prohibitions; although we deny not, but they which utterly forbid such Baptism may have perhaps wherewith to justify their Orders against it. For even things lawful * are well prohibited, when there

T. C. l. i. p. 144.

* Licita prohibentur, ne si permitterentur eorum occasione perveniatur ad illicita. Lib. neque tamen. Just. de Asuth. Tut. lib. Officium. D. de Rei Vind.

is

is fear left they make the way to unlawful more easy. And it may be the liberty of Baptism by Women at such times doth sometimes embolden the rasher sort to do it where no such necessity is. But whether of permission besides Law, or in presumption against Law, they do it, is it thereby altogether frustrate, void, and as though it were never given? They which have not at the first their right Baptism must of necessity be re-baptized, because the Law of Christ tieth all Men to receive Baptism. Iteration of Baptism once given hath been always thought a manifest contempt of that ancient Apostolick Aphorism, *One Lord, one Faith, one Baptism:* Baptism not only one, inasmuch as it hath every where the same Substance, and offereth unto all Men the same Grace; but one also, for that it ought not to be received by any one Man above once. We serve that Lord which is but one, because no other can be joined with him: we embrace that Faith which is but one, because it admitteth no innovation: that Baptism we receive which is but one, because it cannot be received often. For how should we practise iteration of Baptism; and yet teach, that we are by Baptism born anew; that by Baptism we are admitted unto the heavenly Society of Saints; that those things be really and effectually done by Baptism, which are no more possible to be often done * than a Man can naturally be often born, or civilly be often adopted into any one Stock and Family? This also is the cause, why they that present us unto Baptism are entituled forever after our Parents in God, and

Ephes. iv. 5.

* Una est Nativitas de terra, alia de cœlo; una de carne, alia de Spiritu; una de æternitate, alia de mortalitate; una de masculo et fœmina, alia de Deo et Ecclesia. Sed ipsæ duæ singulares sunt. Quo modo enim uterus non potest repeti, sic nec Baptismus iterari. Prosp. Senten. 331 Eja fratres lacteum genitalis fontis ad laticem convolate, ut semper vobis aqua sufficiat, hoc ante omnia scientes quia hanc nec effundere licet nec rursus haurire. Zenoph. Invit. ad Font.

BOOK V. the reaſon why there we receive new names, in token, that by Baptiſm we are made new Creatures. As Chriſt hath therefore died and riſen from the dead but once, ſo that Sacrament which both extinguiſheth in him our former ſin, and beginneth in us a new condition of life, is by one only actual adminiſtration forever available; according to that in the Nicene Creed, *I believe one Baptiſm for remiſſion of ſins*. And becauſe ſecond Baptiſm was ever abhorred in the Church of God as a kind of inceſtuous Birth, they that iterate Baptiſm are driven under ſome pretence or other to make the former Baptiſm void. Tertullian, the firſt that propoſed to the Church; Agrippinus, the firſt in the Church that accepted, and againſt the uſe of the Church; Novatianus, the firſt that publickly began to practiſe Rebaptization, did it therefore upon theſe two grounds; a true perſuaſion that Baptiſm is neceſſary; and a falſe, that the Baptiſm which others adminiſtered was no Baptiſm. Novatianus his conceit was, that none can adminiſter true Baptiſm but the true Church of Jeſus Chriſt; that he and his followers alone were the Church; and for the reſt, he accounted them wicked and prophane Perſons, ſuch as by Baptiſm could cleanſe no Man, unleſs they firſt did purify themſelves, and reform the faults wherewith he charged them. At which time St. Cyprian, with the greateſt part of African Biſhops, becauſe they likewiſe thought that none but only the true Church of God can baptize, and were of nothing more certainly perſuaded than that Hereticks are as rotten branches cut off from the life and body of the true Church, gathered hereby that the Church of God both may with good conſideration, and ought to reverſe that Baptiſm which is given by Hereticks. Theſe held and practiſed their own opinion, yet with great proteſtations often made, that they neither loved a whit the leſs, nor thought in any reſpect the worſe of them that were of a contrary mind. In requital

August. de Bapt. cont. Don. lib. ii cap. 14.

Tert. de Bapt. Cypr. Epiſt. 71.

Euſeb. lib. vii cap. 1, 2, 3. Cypr. Epiſt. 70, 71, 72, 73, 74, 75, 76 requital of which ingenuous moderation, the rest that withstood them, did it in a peaceable sort, with very good regard had of them, as of Men in error, but not in heresy. The Bishop of Rome against their novelties upheld, as beseemed him, the ancient and true Apostolick Customs, till they which unadvisedly before had erred became in a manner all * reconciled friends unto Truth, and saw that Heresy in the Ministers of Baptism could no way evacuate the force thereof; † such Heresy alone excepted, as by reason of unsoundness in the highest Articles of Christian Faith, presumed to change, and by changing to maim the Substance, the Form of Baptism. In which respect, the Church did neither simply disannul, nor absolutely ratify Baptism by Hereticks. For the Baptism which Novatianists gave stood firm, whereas they whom Samosatenians had baptized were re-baptized. It was likewise ordered in the Council of Arles, that if any Arian did reconcile himself to the Church, they should admit him without new Baptism, unless by examination they found him not baptized in the Name of the Trinity. Dionysius, Bishop of Alexandria, maketh report, how there lived under him a Man of good reputation and of very ancient continuance in that Church, who being present at the Rites of Baptism, and observing with better consideration than ever before, what was there done, came and with weeping submission craved of

BOOK V.

Synod. Nicæ. cap. 19.

Synod. i. Arelat. cap. 8.

Eufeb. Eccles. Hist. lib. vii. cap. 8.

* Illi ipsi Episcopi qui rebaptizandos Hæreticos cum Cypriano statuerant, ad antiquam consuetudinem revoluti novum emisere decretum. Hieron. cont. Lucifer Vide et August. contr. Crescon. lib. iii. cap. 2, 3. et Epist. 48.

† Dixisti fieri non posse ut in falso Baptismate inquinatus abluat, immundus emundet, supplantator erigat, perditus liberet, reus veniam tribuat, damnatus absolvat. Bene hæc omnia potuerunt ad solos Hæreticos pertinere, qui falsaverunt Symbolum, dum alter dixerit duos Deos cum Deus unus sit, alter Patrem vult in persona Filii cognosci, alter carnem subducens Filio Dei per quam Deo reconciliatus est mundus et cæteri hujusmodi, qui a Sacramentis Catholicis alieni noscuntur. Optat. lib. i.

his

BOOK V. his Biſhop not to deny him Baptiſm, the due of all which profeſs Chriſt, ſeeing it had been ſo long ſithence his evil hap to be deceived by the fraud of Hereticks, and at their hands (which till now he never throughly and duly weighed) to take a Baptiſm full fraught with blaſphemous impieties; a Baptiſm in nothing like unto which the true Church of Chriſt uſeth. The Biſhop was greatly moved thereat, yet durſt not adventure to re-baptize, but did the beſt he could to put him in good comfort, uſing much perſuaſion with him not to trouble himſelf with things that were paſt and gone, nor after ſo long continuance in the fellowſhip of God's People to call now in queſtion his firſt entrance. The poor Man that ſaw himſelf in this ſort anſwered, but not ſatisfied, ſpent afterwards his life in continual perplexity, whereof the Biſhop remained fearful to give releaſe; perhaps too fearful, if the Baptiſm were ſuch as his own declaration importeth. For that, the ſubſtance whereof was rotten at the very firſt, is never by tract of time able to recover ſoundneſs; and where true Baptiſm was not before given, the caſe of Re-baptization is clear. But by this it appeareth, that Baptiſm is not void in regard of Hereſy; and therefore much leſs through any other moral defect in the Miniſter thereof. Under which ſecond pretence, Donatiſts notwithſtanding took upon them to make fruſtrate the Church's Baptiſm, and themſelves to re-baptize their own fry. For whereas ſome forty years after the Martyrdom of
Circa An. 300. bleſſed Cyprian, the Emperor Diocleſian began to perſecute the Church of Chriſt; and for the ſpeedier aboliſhment of their Religion to burn up their ſacred Books; there were in the Church itſelf Traditors, content to deliver up the Books of God by compoſition, to the end their own lives might be ſpared. Which Men growing thereby odious to the reſt, whoſe conſtancy was greater; it fortuned that after, when one Cecilian was ordained Biſhop in the

Church

Church of Carthage, whom others endeavoured BOOK V.
in vain to defeat by excepting againſt him as a Traditor, they whoſe accuſations could not prevail, deſperately joined themſelves in one, and made a Biſhop of their own crew, accounting from that day forward, their faction the only true and ſincere Church. The firſt Biſhop on that part was Majorinus, whoſe Succeſſor Donatus being the firſt that wrote in defence of their Schiſm, the Birds that were hatched before by others have their names from him. Arians and Donatiſts began both about one time; which Hereſies, according to the different ſtrength of their own ſinews, wrought as hope of ſucceſs led them; the one with the choiceſt wits, the other with the multitude, ſo far that, after long and troubleſome experience, the perfecteſt view Men could take of both, was hardly able to induce any certain determinate reſolution whether error may do more by the curious ſubtilty of ſharp diſcourſe, or elſe by the mere appearance of zeal and devout affection; the latter of which two aids gave Donatiſts, beyond all Men's expectation, as great a ſway as ever any Schiſm or Hereſy had within that reach of the Chriſtian World, where it bred and grew; the rather perhaps, becauſe the Church, which neither greatly feared them, and beſides had neceſſary cauſe to bend itſelf againſt others that aimed directly at a far higher mark, the Deity of Chriſt, was contented to let Donatiſts have their courſe by the ſpace of threeſcore years and above, even from ten years before Conſtantine till the time that Optatus, Biſhop of Milevis, publiſhed his Books Circa An.
againſt Parmenian. During which term, and the 370.
ſpace of that Schiſm's continuance afterwards, they had, beſides many other ſecular and worldly means to help them forward, theſe ſpecial advantages; firſt, the very occaſion of their breach with the Church of God, a juſt hatred and diſlike of Traditors, ſeemed plauſible; they eaſily perſuaded their hearers that

ſuch

 ſuch Men could not be holy as held communion and fellowſhip with them that betrayed Religion: again, when to dazzle the eyes of the ſimple, and to prove that it can be no Church which is not holy, they had in ſhew and ſound of words, the glorious pretence of the Creed Apoſtolick, *I believe the holy Catholick Church*; we need not think it any ſtrange thing that with the multitude they gained credit: and avouching that ſuch as are not of the true Church can adminiſter no true Baptiſm, they had for this point whole Volumes of St. Cyprian's own writing, together with the judgments of divers African Synods, whoſe ſentence was the ſame with his. Whereupon, the Fathers were likewiſe in defence of their juſt cauſe very greatly prejudiced, both for that they could not enforce the duty of Men's communion with a Church, confeſt to be in many things blame-worthy, unleſs they ſhould oftentimes ſeem to ſpeak as half-defenders of the faults themſelves, or at the leaſt not ſo vehement accuſers thereof as their adverſaries; and to withſtand iteration of Baptiſm, the other branch of the Donatiſts' Hereſy, was impoſſible, without manifeſt and profeſt rejection of Cyprian, whom the World univerſally did in his life-time admire as the greateſt among Prelates, and now honour as not the loweſt in the Kingdom of Heaven. So true we find it by experience of all ages in the Church of God, that the Teacher's error is the People's trial, harder and heavier by ſo much to bear, as he is in worth and regard greater that miſperſuadeth them. Although there was odds between Cyprian's cauſe and theirs, he differing from others of ſounder underſtanding in that point, but not dividing himſelf from the Body of the Church by Schiſm, as did the Donatiſts. For which cauſe, ſaith Vincentius, *Of one and the ſame opinion we judge (which may ſeem ſtrange) the Authors Catholick and the Followers Heretical; we acquit the Maſters and condemn the Scholars; they are Heirs of Heaven which have*

Vincent. Lirin. adver. Hæreſ. cap. 11.

written

written those Books, the Defenders whereof are trodden down to the pit of Hell. The invectives of Catholick Writers therefore against them are sharp; the words of imperial Edicts by Honorius and Theodosius, made to bridle them, very bitter, the punishments severe in revenge of their folly. Howbeit, for fear (as we may conjecture) lest much should be derogated from the Baptism of the Church, and Baptism by Donatists be more esteemed of than was meet; if, on the one side, that which Hereticks had done ill should stand as good; on the other side, that be reversed which the Catholick Church had well and religiously done; divers better minded than advised Men, thought it fittest to meet with this inconvenience by re-baptizing Donatists as well as they re-baptized Catholicks. For stay whereof the same Emperors saw it meet to give their Law a double edge, whereby it might equally on both sides cut off not only Hereticks which re-baptized, whom they could pervert; but also Catholick and Christian Priests which did the like unto such as before had taken Baptism at the hands of Hereticks, and were afterwards reconciled to the Church of God. Donatists were therefore, in process of time, though with much ado, wearied, and at length worn out by the constancy of that Truth which teacheth that evil Ministers of good things are as torches, a light to others, a waste to none but themselves only; and that the foulness of their hands can neither any whit impair the virtue, nor stain the glory of the Mysteries of Christ. Now that which was done amiss by virtuous and good Men (as Cyprian, carried aside with hatred against Heresy, and was secondly followed by Donatists whom envy and rancour, covered with shew of godliness, made obstinate to cancel whatsoever the Church did in the Sacrament of Baptism) hath of later days, in another respect far different from both the former, been brought freshly again into practice: for the Anabaptist re-baptizeth, because,

BOOK V.

Vide C. Theod. lib. xvi. tit. 6. lib. Adversarios et lib. Nullus, circa An. 405.

Si quis C. Ne Sanct. Baptis. circa An. 413.

BOOK V. becaufe, in his eftimation, the Baptifm of the Church is fruftrate, for that we give it unto infants which have not Faith; whereas, according unto Chrift's inftitution, as they conceive it, true Baptifm fhould always prefuppofe actual Belief in Receivers, and is otherwife no Baptifm. Of thefe three errors there is not any but hath been able, at the leaft, to alledge in defence of itfelf many fair probabilities. Notwithftanding, fith the Church of God hath hitherto always conftantly maintained, that to re-baptize them which are known to have received true Baptifm is unlawful; that if Baptifm ferioufly be adminiftered in the fame element, and with the fame form of words which Chrift's inftitution teacheth, there is no other defect in the World that can make it fruftrate, or deprive it of the nature of a true Sacrament; and laftly, that Baptifm is only then to be re-adminiftered, when the firft delivery thereof is void, in regard of the fore-alledged imperfections, and no other; fhall we now in the cafe of Baptifm, which, having both for matter and form the fubftance of Chrift's inftitution, is by a fourth fort of Men voided, for the only defect of Ecclefiaftical Authority in the Minifter, think it enough that they blow away the force thereof with the bare ftrength of their very breath, by faying, *We take fuch Baptifm to be no more the Sacrament of Baptifm, than any other ordinary bathing to be a Sacrament?* It behoveth generally all fort of Men to keep themfelves within the limits of their own vocation; and feeing God, from whom Men's feveral degrees and pre-eminences do proceed, hath appointed them in his Church, at whofe hands his pleafure is that we fhould receive both Baptifm and all other publick medicinable helps of Soul, perhaps thereby the more to fettle our hearts in the love of our ghoftly fuperiors; they have fmall caufe to hope that with him their voluntary fervices will be accepted, who thruft themfelves into functions, either above their capacity, or befides their place, and

Numb. xvi. 10. Levit. x. 1. 1 Sam. xiii. 11. 2 Sam. vi. 6. 2 Chron. xxvi. 16. Heb. v. 4.

and over-boldly intermeddle with duties whereof no charge was ever given them. They that in any thing exceed the compaſs of their own order, do as much as in them lieth to diſſolve that order which is the harmony of God's Church. Suppoſe, therefore, that in theſe and the like conſiderations, the Law did utterly prohibit Baptiſm to be adminiſtered by any other than Perſons thereunto ſolemnly conſecrated what neceſſity ſoever happen; are not * many things firm being done, although in part done otherwiſe than poſitive rigour and ſtrictneſs did require? Nature, as much as is poſſible, inclineth unto validities and preſervations. Diſſolutions and nullities of things done are not only not favoured, but hated, when either urged without cauſe, or extended beyond their reach. If therefore at any time it come to paſs, that in teaching publickly or privately, in delivering this bleſſed Sacrament of Regeneration, ſome unſanctified hand, contrary to Chriſt's ſuppoſed Ordinance, do intrude itſelf to execute that whereunto the Laws of God and his Church have deputed others, which of theſe two opinions ſeemeth more agreeable with equity, our's that diſallow what is done amiſs, yet make not the force of the Word and Sacraments, much leſs their nature and very ſubſtance, to depend on the Miniſter's authority and calling, or elſe † their's which defeat, diſannul, and annihilate both, in reſpect of that one only perſonal defect; there being not any Law of God which ſaith, that if the Miniſter be incompetent, his Word ſhall

* 9. Q. ii. c. Lugdunenſis ex literis Decret. de Matrim. contract. Damaſc. Burch. Reg. 109. Prohibita fieri ſi fiant non tenent. In prohibitionibus autem circa res favorabiles, contrarium obtinet.

† T. C. lib i. pag. 144. As St. Paul ſaith, That a Man cannot preach which is not ſent, Rom. x. 15; no, not although he ſpeak the words of the Scripture, and interpret them; ſo I cannot ſee how a Man can baptize unleſs he be ſent to that end, although he pour water, and rehearſe the words which are to be rehearſed in the miniſtry of Baptiſm.

BOOK V. be no Word, his Baptiſm no Baptiſm? He which teacheth and is not ſent, loſeth the reward, but yet retaineth the name of a Teacher. His uſurped actions have in him the ſame nature which they have in others, although they yield not him the ſame comfort. And if theſe two caſes be Peers, the caſe of Doctrine and the caſe of Baptiſm both alike; ſith no defect in their vocation that teach the Truth is able to take away the benefit thereof from him which heareth, wherefore ſhould the want of a lawful calling in them that baptize make Baptiſm to be vain? *They grant, that the Matter and the Form in Sacraments are the only parts of Subſtance, and that if theſe two be retained, albeit other things beſides be uſed which are inconvenient, the Sacrament notwithſtanding is adminiſtered, but not ſincerely. Why perſiſt they not in this opinion? When by theſe fair ſpeeches they have put us in hope of agreement, wherefore ſup they up their words again, interlacing ſuch frivolous interpretations and gloſſes as diſgrace their ſentence? What ſhould move them, having named the Matter and the Form of the Sacrament, to give us preſently warning, that they mean by the Form of the Sacrament the Inſtitution? Which expoſition darkeneth whatſoever was before plain. For whereas, in common underſtanding, that Form which added to the Element doth make a Sacrament, and is of the outward ſubſtance thereof, containeth only the words of uſual application, they ſet it down (leſt common Dictionaries ſhould deceive us) that the Form doth ſignify in their language, the Inſtitution; which Inſtitution in truth comprehendeth both Form and Matter. Such are their fumbling ſhifts to en-

T. C. lib. i. pag. 117.

* T. C. lib. i. pag. 165. If either the Matter of the Sacrament, or the Form of it, which is the Inſtitution (which things are only ſubſtantial parts) were wanting, there ſhould then have been no Sacrament at all miniſtered. But they being retained, and yet other things uſed which are not convenient, the Sacrament is miniſtered, but not ſincerely.

close

close the Minister's vocation within the compass of some essential part of the Sacrament. A thing that can never stand with sound and sincere construction. For what if the Minister be *no circumstance, but a subordinate efficient cause in the work of Baptism?* What if the Minister's Vocation be a matter * *of perpetual necessity, and not a Ceremony variable as times and occasions require? What if his calling be a principal part of the Institution of Christ?* Doth it therefore follow, that the Minister's Authority is † *of the Substance of the Sacrament*, and as incident into the nature thereof as the Matter and the Form itself, yea, more incident? For whereas in case of necessity, the greatest amongst them professeth the change of the Element of Water lawful, and others, which like not so well this opinion, could be better content that voluntarily the Words of Christ's Institution were altered, and Men baptized in the Name of Christ without either mention made of the Father or of the Holy Ghost; nevertheless, in denying that Baptism administered by private Persons ought to be reckoned of as a Sacrament, they both agree. It may therefore please them both to consider, that Baptism is an action in part moral, in part ecclesiastical, and in part mystical: moral, as being a duty which Men perform towards God: ecclesiastical, in that it

BOOK V.

T. C. lib. iii. pag. 121.

* T. C. lib. iii. pag. 135. The Minister is of the Substance of the Sacrament, considering that it is a principal part of Christ's Institution. Beza. Epist. ii. Desit aqua, et tamen Baptismus alicujus differri cum ædificatione non possit, nec debeat; ego certe quovis alio liquore non minus rite quam aqua baptizarim.

† T. C. lib. iii. pag. 138. Shew me why the breach of the Institution in the Form should make the Sacrament unavailable, and not the breach of this part (which concerneth the Minister). T. C. ibid. Howsoever some learned and godly give some liberty in the change of the Elements of the holy Sacrament, yet I do not see how that can stand. Idem, pag. 137. I would rather judge him baptized, who is baptized into the name of Christ, without adding the Father and the Holy Ghost, when the Element of Water is added, than when the other words being duly kept, some other liquor is used.

BOOK V. belongeth unto God's Church as a publick duty: finally, myſtical, if we reſpect what God doth thereby intend to work. The greateſt moral perfection of Baptiſm conſiſteth in Men's devout obedience to the Law of God, which Law requireth both the outward act, or thing done, and alſo that religious affection which God doth ſo much regard, that without it whatſoever we do is hateful in his ſight; who therefore is ſaid to reſpect Adverbs more than Verbs, becauſe the end of his Law in appointing what we ſhall do is our own perfection; which perfection conſiſteth chiefly in the virtuous diſpoſition of the Mind, and approveth itſelf to him not by doing, but by doing well. Wherein appeareth alſo the difference between human and divine Laws, the one of which two are content with *Opus operatum*, the other require *Opus operantis*; the one do but claim the Deed, the other eſpecially the Mind. So that according to Laws, which principally reſpect the heart of Men, Works of Religion being not religiouſly performed cannot morally be perfect. Baptiſm as an eccleſiaſtical work is for the manner of performance ordered by divers eccleſiaſtical Laws, providing that as the Sacrament itſelf is a gift of no mean worth; ſo the miniſtry thereof might in all circumſtances appear to be a function of no ſmall regard. All that belongeth to the myſtical perfection of Baptiſm outwardly, is the Element, the Word, and the ſerious application of both unto him which receiveth both, whereunto, if we add that ſecret reference which this action hath to life and remiſſion of Sins, by virtue of Chriſt's own compact ſolemnly made with his Church, to accompliſh fully the Sacrament of Baptiſm, there is not any thing more required. Now put the queſtion, whether Baptiſm adminiſtered to infants, without any ſpiritual calling, be unto them both a true Sacrament, and an effectual inſtrument of Grace, or elſe an act of no more account than the ordinary waſhings are? The ſum of all that can be ſaid to defeat

defeat ſuch Baptiſm is, that thoſe things which have no being can work nothing; and that Baptiſm, without the power of ordination, is as a judgment without ſufficient juriſdiction, void, fruſtrate, and of no effect. But to this we anſwer, that the fruit of Baptiſm dependeth only upon the Covenant which God hath made: that God by Covenant requireth in the elder ſort, Faith and Baptiſm; in Children, the Sacrament of Baptiſm alone, whereunto he hath alſo given them right by ſpecial privilege of birth within the boſom of the holy Church: that Infants therefore which have received Baptiſm complete, as touching the myſtical perfection thereof, are by virtue of his own Covenant and Promiſe cleanſed from all Sin; foraſmuch as all other Laws, concerning that which in Baptiſm is either moral or eccleſiaſtical, do bind the Church which giveth Baptiſm, and not the Infant which receiveth it of the Church. So that if any thing be therein amiſs, the harm which groweth by violation of holy Ordinances, muſt altogether reſt where the bonds of ſuch Ordinances hold. For, that in actions of this nature it fareth not as in juriſdictions, may ſomewhat appear by the very opinion which Men have of them. The nullity of that which a Judge doth by way of authority without authority is known to all Men, and agreed upon with full conſent of the whole World; every Man receiveth it as a general Edict of Nature; whereas the nullity of Baptiſm, in regard of the like defect, is only a few Men's new, ungrounded, and as yet unapproved imagination. Which difference of generality in Men's perſuaſions on the one ſide, and their paucity whoſe conceit leadeth them the other way, hath riſen from a difference eaſy to obſerve in the things themſelves. The exerciſe of unauthoriſed juriſdiction is a grievance unto them that are under it, whereas they that without authority preſume to baptize, offer nothing but that which to all Men is good and acceptable. Sacraments are food, and the Mi-

BOOK V nifters thereof as Parents, or as Nurfes; at whofe hands, when there is neceffity, but no poffibility of receiving it, if that which they are not prefent to do in right of their Office, be of pity and compaffion done by others; fhall this be thought to turn celeftial bread into gravel, or the medicine of Souls into poifon? Jurifdiction is a yoke which Law hath impofed on the necks of Men in fuch fort, that they muft endure it for the good of others, how contrary foever it be to their own particular appetites and inclinations. Jurifdiction bridleth Men againft their wills; that which a Judge doth prevails by virtue of his very power, and therefore not without great reafon, except the Law hath given him Authority, whatfoever he doth vanifheth. Baptifm on the other fide, being a favour which it pleafeth God to beftow, a benefit of Soul to us that receive it, and a Grace which they that deliver are but as mere veffels, either appointed by others or offered of their own accord to this Service; of which two, if they be the one, it is but their own honour; their own offence to be the other. Can it poffibly ftand with *equity and right, that the faultinefs of their prefumption in giving Baptifm fhould be able to prejudice us, who by taking Baptifm have no way offended? I know there are many fentences found in the Books and Writings of the ancient Fathers, to prove both ecclefiaftical and alfo moral defects in the minifter of Baptifm a bar to the heavenly benefit thereof. Which fentences we always fo underftand, as Auguftin underftood in a cafe of like nature the words of St. Cyprian. When Infants baptized were, after their Parents revolt, carried by them in arms to the Stews of Idols, thofe wretched Creatures, as St. Cyprian thought, were not only their own ruin, but their Children's alfo: *Their Chil-*

August. Epist. 23.

* Factum alterius alii nocere non debet. Ulp. lib. de Pupillo, fect. Si plurimum. Item, Alphen. lib. Pater-familias. De Hære. Inftit. Maleficia tenent Authores fuos, non alios. Lib. Sançimus, 22. C. de Pœn.

dren,

dren, whom this their Apoſtacy prophaned, *did loſe what Chriſtian Baptiſm had given them being newly born. They loſt* (ſaith St. Auguſtin) *the Grace of Baptiſm, if we conſider to what their Parents impiety did tend*; although the Mercy of God preſerved them, and will alſo in that dreadful day of account give them favourable audience, pleading in their own behalf, *The harm of other Men's perfidiouſneſs it lay not in us to avoid.* After the ſame manner, whatſoever we read written, if it ſound to the prejudice of Baptiſm through any either moral or eccleſiaſtical defect therein, we conſtrue it as Equity and Reaſon teacheth, with reſtraint to the offender only; which doth, as far as concerneth himſelf and them which wittingly concur with him, make the Sacrament of God fruitleſs. St. Auguſtin's* doubtfulneſs, whether Baptiſm by a Lay-man may ſtand, or ought to be re-adminiſtered, ſhould not be mentioned by them which preſume to define peremptorily of that wherein he was content to profeſs himſelf unreſolved. Albeit, in very truth, his opinion is plain enough; but the manner of delivering his judgment being modeſt, they make of a virtue an imbecility, and impute his calmneſs of ſpeech to an irreſolution of mind. His diſputation in that place is againſt Parmenian, which held that a Biſhop or a Prieſt, if they fall into any Hereſy, do thereby loſe the power which they had before to baptize, and that therefore Baptiſm by Hereticks is merely void. For anſwer whereof, he firſt denieth that Hereſy can more deprive Men of power to baptize others, than it is of force to take from them their own Baptiſm; and in the ſecond place, he farther addeth, that if Hereticks did loſe the power which before was given

* T. C. lib. iii. pag. 136. Auguſtin ſtandeth in doubt, whether Baptiſm by a Lay-man be available or no. Cont Lit. Pyrm. lib. ii. cap 13. Where by all likelihood he was out of doubt, that that which was miniſtered by a Woman, whoſe unaptneſs herein is double to that of a Lay-man, was of no effect.

 them

BOOK V. them by Ordination, and did therefore unlawfully usurp as oft as they took upon them to give the Sacrament of Baptism, it followeth not, that Baptism by them administered without authority is no Baptism. For then what should we think of Baptism by Lay-men, to whom authority was never given? I doubt (saith St. Augustin) whether any Man which carrieth a virtuous and godly mind will affirm, that the Baptism which Lay-men do in case of necessity administer should be iterated; *For to do it unnecessarily, is to execute another Man's Office; necessity urging, to do it is then either no fault at all* (much less so grievous a crime that it should deserve to be termed by the name of Sacrilege*) *or, if any, a very pardonable fault. But suppose it even of very purpose usurped, and given unto any Man, by every Man that listeth; yet that which is given cannot possibly be denied to have been given, how truly soever we may say it hath not been given lawfully. Unlawful usurpation, a penitent affection must redress If not, the thing that was given shall remain to the hurt and detriment of him which unlawfully either administered or received the same; yet so, that in this respect it ought not to be reputed as if it had not at all been given.* Whereby we may plainly perceive, that St. Augustin was not himself uncertain what to think, but doubtful whether any well-minded Man in the whole World could think otherwise than he did. Their argument taken from a stolen Seal,† may return to the place out of which they had

* T. C. l. i. p 116. The Sacrilege of private Persons, Women especially, in administering the holy Sacrament of Baptism.

† T. C. lib. iii. p. 139. As by the Seal which the Prince hath set apart to seal his Grants with, when it is stolen and set to by him that hath no authority, there groweth no assurance to the party that hath it; so if it were possible to be the Seal of God which a Woman should set to, yet for that she hath stolen it, and put it to, not only without, but contrary to the Commandment of God; I see not how any can take any assurance by reason thereof.

it,

it, for it helpeth their cause nothing. That which Men give or grant to others, must appear to have proceeded of their own accord. This being manifest, their Gifts and Grants are thereby made effectual, both to bar themselves from revocation, and to assecure the right they have given. Wherein for further prevention of Mischiefs that otherwise might grow by the malice, treachery, and fraud of Men, it is both equal and meet that the strength of Men's Deeds and the Instruments which declare the same should strictly depend upon divers solemnities, whereof there cannot be the like reason in things that pass between God and us; because sith we need not doubt, lest the treasures of his heavenly Grace should without his consent be past by forged conveyances; nor lest he should deny at any time his own acts, and seek to revoke what hath been consented unto before; as there is no such fear of danger through deceit and falsehood in this case, so neither hath the circumstance of Men's persons that weight in Baptism, which for good and just considerations in the custody of Seals of Office it ought to have. The Grace of Baptism cometh by donation from God alone. That God hath committed the ministry of Baptism unto special Men, it is for order's sake in his Church, and not to the end that their Authority might give being or add force to the Sacrament itself. That Infants have right to the Sacrament in Baptism we all acknowledge. Charge them we cannot as guileful and wrongful possessors of that, whereunto they have right by the manifest will of the Donor, and are not parties unto any defect or disorder in the manner of receiving the same. And if any such disorder be, we have sufficiently before declared, that *delictum cum capite semper ambulat*, Men's own faults are their own harms. Wherefore, to countervail this and the like mischosen resemblances with that which more truly and plainly agreeth; the Ordinance of God, concerning

BOOK V. their Vocation that minister Baptism wherein the Mystery of our Regeneration is wrought, hath thereunto the same analogy which Laws of Wedlock have to our first Nativity and Birth: so that if Nature do effect procreation, notwithstanding the wicked violation and breach even of Nature's Law, made that the entrance of all Mankind into this present world might be without blemish; may we not justly presume that Grace doth accomplish the other, although there be faultiness in them that transgress the Order which our Lord Jesus Christ hath established in his Church? Some light may be borrowed from Circumcision, for explication of what is true in this question of Baptism. Seeing then, that even they which condemn Zipporah the Wife of Moses, *for taking upon her to circumcise her Son, a thing necessary at that time for her to do, and as I think very hard to reprove in her, considering how Moses, because himself had not done it sooner, was therefore stricken by the Hand of God, neither could in that extremity perform the Office; whereupon, for the stay of God's indignation there was no choice, but the action must needs fall into her hands; whose fact therein, whether we interpret as some have done, that being a Midianite and as yet not so

Exod. iv. 24.

* T. C. lib i. pag 144. I say, that the unlawfulness of that fact doth appear sufficiently, in that she did it before her husband Moses, which was a Prophet of the Lord, to whom that office of Circumcision did appertain. Besides, that she did cut off the fore-skin of the Infant, not of mind to obey the Commandment of God, or for the Salvation of the Child, but in a choler only, to the end that her Husband might be eased and have release; which mind appeareth in her, both by her words, and by casting away in anger, the fore-skin which she had cut off. And if it be said, that the event declared, that the act pleased God, because that Moses forthwith waxed better, and was recovered of his sickness; I have shewed before, that if we measure things by the event, we shall oftentimes justify the Wicked, and take the righteousness of the Righteous from them.

throughly

throughly acquainted with the Jewiſh Rites, it much diſcontented her to ſee herſelf, through her Huſband's overſight, in a matter of his own Religion, brought unto theſe perplexities and ſtreights; that either ſhe muſt now endure him periſhing before her eyes, or elſe wound the fleſh of her own Child; which ſhe could not do but with ſome indignation, ſhewed in that ſhe fumingly both threw down the fore-ſkin at his feet, and upbraided him with the cruelty of his Religion. Or, if we better like to follow their more judicious expoſition, which are not inclinable to think that Moſes was matched like Socrates, nor that Circumciſion could now in Eleazar be ſtrange unto her, having had Gerſom her elder Son before circumciſed; nor that any occaſion of choler could riſe from a ſpectacle of ſuch miſery, as doth * naturally move compaſſion and not wrath; nor that Zipporah was ſo impious, as in the viſible preſence of God's deſerved anger to ſtorm at the Ordinance and Law of God; nor that the words of the Hiſtory itſelf can enforce any ſuch affection: but do only declare how after the act performed ſhe touched the feet of Moſes, ſaying, † *Sponſus tu mihi es ſanguinum, Thou art unto me an Huſband of blood*; which might be very well, the one done and the other ſpoken, even out of the flowing abundance of commiſeration and love to ſignify, with hands laid under his feet, that her tender affection towards him

BOOK V.

* Mala paſſis non iraſcimur, ſed compatimur. Boet. de Conſol.

† Where the uſual Tranſlation hath, Exod iv. 25 She cut away the fore-ſkin of her ſon, and caſt it at his feet, and ſaid, Thou art indeed a bloody Huſband unto me. So he departed from him. Then ſhe ſaid, O bloody Huſband, becauſe of the Circumciſion. The words, as they lie in the original, are rather thus to be interpreted. and ſhe cut off the fore-ſkin of her Son. Which being done, ſhe touched his feet (the feet of Moſes), and ſaid, Thou art to me an Huſband of blood (in the plural number, thereby ſignifying effuſion of blood) And the Lord withdrew from him at the very time, when ſhe ſaid, A Huſband of blood, in regard of Circumciſion.

had

BOOK V. had caused her thus to forget Womanhood, to lay all motherly affection aside, and to redeem her Husband out of the hands of death with effusion of blood: the sequel thereof, take it which way you will, is a plain argument that God was satisfied with that she did, as may appear by his own testimony, declaring how there followed in the person of Moses present release of his grievous punishment, upon her speedy discharge of that duty which by him neglected had offended God; even, as after execution of justice by the hands of Phineas the Plague was immediately taken away, which former impunity of sin had caused. In which so manifest and plain cases, not to make that a reason of the event which God himself hath set down as a reason, were falsly to accuse whom he doth justify, and without any cause to traduce what we should allow; yet seeing they which will have it a breach of the Law of God for her to circumcise in that necessity, are not able to deny but Circumcision being in that very manner performed was to the innocent Child which received it true Circumcision; why should that defect, whereby Circumcision was so little weakened, be to Baptism a deadly wound? These premises therefore remaining, as hitherto they have been laid, because the Commandment of our Saviour Christ, * which

Psal. cvi. 30.

* T. C. lib iii. pag. 142. Seeing they only are bidden in the Scripture to administer the Sacraments which are bidden to preach the Word, and that the publick Ministers have only this charge of the Word; and seeing that the administration of both these are so linked together, that the denial of licence to do one, is a denial to do the other; as of the contrary part, licence to one, is licence to the other, considering also that to minister the Sacraments, is an honour in the Church which none can take unto him, but he which is called unto it, as was Aaron: and further, forasmuch as the baptizing by private Persons, and by Women especially, confirmeth the dangerous error of the Condemnation of young Children which die without Baptism; last of all, seeing we have the consent of the godly learned of all times against the Baptism by Women, and of the reformed Churches now, against the Baptism by private Men; we conclude, that the Administration

committeth jointly to publick Miniſters both Doctrine and Baptiſm, doth no more, by linking them together, import that the nature of the Sacrament dependeth on the Miniſter's authority and power to preach the Word, than the force and virtue of the Word doth on licence to give the Sacrament; and conſidering that the Work of external Miniſtry in Baptiſm is only a pre-eminence of honour, which they that take to themſelves, and are not thereunto called as Aaron was, do but themſelves in their own perſons, by means of ſuch uſurpation, incur the juſt blame of diſobedience to the Law of God, farther alſo, inaſmuch as it ſtandeth with no reaſon, that errors grounded on a wrong interpretation of other Men's deeds ſhould make fruſtrate whatſoever is miſconceived, and that Baptiſm by Women ſhould ceaſe to be Baptiſm as oft as any Man will thereby gather that Children which die unbaptized are damned; which opinion if the act of Baptiſm, adminiſtered in ſuch manner, did enforce, it might be ſufficient cauſe of diſliking the ſame, but none of defeating or making it altogether void: laſt of all, whereas general and full conſent of the godly learned in all ages doth make for validity of Baptiſm, yea, albeit adminiſtered in private, and even by Women; which kind of Baptiſm, in caſe of neceſſity, divers reformed Churches do both allow and defend, ſome others which do not defend, tolerate, few, in compariſon, and they without any juſt cauſe, do utterly diſannul and annihilate: ſurely, howſoever through defect on either ſide, the Sacrament may be without fruit, as well in ſome caſes to him which receiveth, as to him which giveth it; yet no diſability of either part can ſo far make it fruſtrate and without effect, as to deprive it of the very Nature of true Baptiſm, having all things elſe which the Or-

Adminiſtration of this Sacrament by private Perſons, and eſpecially by Women, is merely both unlawful and void.

dinance

BOOK V. dinance of Chrift requireth. Whereupon we may confequently infer, that the Adminiftration of this Sacrament by private Perfons, be it lawful or unlawful, appeareth not as yet to be merely void.

Interrogatories in Baptifm touching Faith, and the purpofe of a Chriftian life.

63. All that are of the Race of Chrift the Scripture nameth them, *Children of the Promife* which God hath made. The promife of eternal Life is the feed of the Church of God. And becaufe there is no attainment of life, but through the only begotten Son of God, nor by him otherwife than being fuch as the Creed Apoftolick defcribeth; it followeth that the Articles thereof are Principles neceffary for all Men to fubfcribe unto, whom by Baptifm the Church receiveth into Chrift's fchool. All points of Chriftian Doctrine are either demonftrable Conclufions, or demonftrative Principles. Conclufions have ftrong and invincible Proofs, as well in the School of Jefus Chrift, as elfewhere. And Principles be grounds which require no proof in any kind of Science, becaufe it fufficeth, if either their certainty be evident in itfelf, or evident by the light of fome higher knowledge; and in itfelf, fuch as no Man's knowledge is ever able to overthrow. Now the Principles whereupon we do build our Souls, have their evidence where they had their original; and as received from thence, we adore them, we hold them in reverend admiration, we neither argue nor difpute about them, we give unto them that affent which the Oracles of God require. We are not therefore afhamed of the Gofpel of our Lord Jefus Chrift, becaufe mifcreants in fcorn have upbraided us, that the higheft point of our Wifdom is, * *Believe*. That which is true, and neither can be difcerned by Senfe nor concluded by mere natural Principles, muft have Principles of revealed Truth whereupon to build itfelf, and an habit of Faith in us, wherewith

* Apoftatæ maledictum. Ουδὲν ὑπὲρ τὸ πίςευσον τῆς ὑμετέρας ἐςὶ σοφίας. Naz. Orat 1. contr. Julia

Principles

Principles of that kind are apprehended. *The Mysteries of our Religion are above the reach of our Understanding, above the discourse of Man's Reason above all that any Creature can comprehend. Therefore the first thing required of him which standeth for admission into Christ's Family, is Belief. Which Belief consisteth not so much in knowledge, as in acknowledgment of all things that Heavenly Wisdom revealeth; the Affection of Faith is above her reach, her Love to God-ward above the comprehension which she hath of God. And because only for Believers all things may be done, he which is Goodness itself loveth them above all. Deserve we then the Love of God, because we believe in the Son of God? What more opposite than Faith and Pride? When God had created all things, he looked upon them and loved them, because they were all as himself had made them. So the true reason wherefore Christ doth love Believers is, because their Belief is the gift of God, a gift than which flesh and blood in this World cannot possibly receive a greater. And as to love them, of whom we receive good things is duty, because they satisfy our desires in that which else we should want; so to love them on whom we bestow, is Nature, because in them we behold the effects of our own virtue. Seeing therefore no Religion enjoyeth Sacraments, the signs of God's love, unless it have also that Faith whereupon the Sacraments are built, could there be any thing more convenient than that our first admittance to the actual receipt of his grace in the Sacrament of Baptism should be consecrated with Profession of Belief?† which is to the Kingdom of God as a key, the want whereof excludeth Infidels both from that and from all other saving grace. We

Matt. xvi. 17. John i 12.

* Ὑπὲρ νοῦν, ὑπὲρ λόγον, ὑπὲρ κατάληψιν κτιστῆς φύσεως τὰ ἡμέτερα. Just. Mart. Expos. Fid.

† Spiritus Sanctus habitator ejus Templi non efficitur, quod Antistitem non habet veram fidem. Hieron adv Lucif. cap. iv.

find

BOOK V. find by experience, that, although Faith be an intellectual habit of the Mind, and have her seat in the Understanding; yet an evil moral disposition, obstinately wedded to the love of darkness, dampeth the very light of heavenly Illumination, and permitteth not the Mind to see what doth shine before it. Men are *lovers of pleasure, more than lovers of God.* Their assent to his saving Truth is many times withheld from it, not that the Truth is too weak to persuade, but because the stream of corrupt affection carrieth them a clean contrary way. That the Mind therefore may abide in the light of Faith, there must abide in the Will as constant a resolution to have no fellowship at all with the vanities and works of darkness. Two Covenants there

Isid de Offic. Eccles. lib. ii. cap. 24. are which Christian Men (saith Isidore) do make in Baptism, the one concerning relinquishment of Satan, the other touching obedience to the Faith of Christ.

Ambros Hexam. lib. i. cap. 4. In like sort St. Ambrose, *He which is baptized, forsaketh the intellectual Pharaoh, the Prince of this World, saying,* Abrenuncio; *Thee, O Satan, and thy Angels,*

Tertul de Spectac. *thy works and thy mandates I forsake utterly.* Tertullian having speech of wicked Spirits: *These* (saith he) *are the Angels which we in Baptism renounce.* The Declaration of *Justin the Martyr concerning Baptism sheweth how such as the Church in those days did baptize, made profession of Christian Belief, and undertook to live accordingly. Neither do I think it a matter easy for any Man to prove that ever Baptism did use to be administered without interrogatories of these two

1 Pet. iii. 21. kinds. Whereunto St. Peter (as it may be thought) alluding hath said, *That the Baptism which saveth us,* is not (as legal Purifications were) a cleansing of the flesh from outward impurity, but ἐπερώτημα, *an interrogative trial of a good conscience towards God.*

* Ὅσοι ἂν πεισθῶσι καὶ πιστεύωσιν ἀληθῆ ταῦτα τὰ ὑφ' ἡμῶν διδασκόμενα καὶ λεγόμενα εἶναι, καὶ βιοῦν οὕτως δύνασθαι ὑπισχνῶνται, εὔχεσθαί τε καὶ αἰτεῖν νηστεύοντες παρὰ τοῦ Θεοῦ τῶν προημαρτημένων ἄφεσιν διδάσκονται, ἔπειτα ἄγονται ὑφ' ἡμῶν, ἔνθα ὕδωρ ἐστὶ καὶ τρόπον ἀναγεννήσεως ὃν καὶ ἡμεῖς αὐτοὶ ἀνεγεννήθημεν ἀναγεννῶνται. Justin. Apol.

64. Now

Interrogatories propofed unto Infants in Baptifm, and anfwered as in their names by Godfathers.

64. Now the fault which they find with us concerning interrogatories is, our moving of thefe queftions unto Infants which cannot anfwer them, and the anfwering of them by others as in their names. The Anabaptift hath many pretences to fcorn at the Baptifm of Children: firft, becaufe the Scriptures, he faith, do no where give Commandment to baptize Infants: fecondly, for that, as there is no Commandment, fo neither any manifeft example fhewing it to have been done either by Chrift or his Apoftles: thirdly, in as much as the Word preached and the Sacraments muft go together, they which are not capable of the one, are not fit receivers of the other: laft of all, fith the Order of Baptifm continued from the firft beginning hath in it thofe things which are unfit to be applied to fucking Children, it followeth in their conceit, that the Baptifm of fuch is no Baptifm, but plain mockery. They with whom we contend are no enemies to the Baptifm of Infants; it is not their defire that the Church fhould hazard fo many Souls by letting them run on till they come to ripenefs of underftanding, that fo they may be converted and then baptized, as Infidels heretofore have been; they bear not towards God fo unthankful minds as not to acknowledge it even amongft the greateft of his endlefs Mercies, that by making us his own poffeffion fo foon, many advantages which Satan otherwife might take are prevented, and (which fhould be efteemed a part of no fmall happinefs) the firft thing whereof we have occafion to take notice is, how much hath been done already to our great good, though altogether without our knowledge. The Baptifm of Infants they efteem as an Ordinance which Chrift hath inftituted, even in fpecial love and favour to his own people: they deny not the practice thereof accordingly to have been kept, as derived from the hands, and continued from the days of the Apoftles themfelves unto this prefent; only it pleafeth them not, that to Infants there fhould be interrogatories pro-

BOOK V. posed in Baptism.* This they condemn as foolish, toyish and prophane mockery. But are they able to shew, that ever the Church of Christ had any publick Form of Baptism without interrogatories; or that the Church did ever use at the solemn Baptism of Infants to omit those Questions as needless in this case? Boniface, a Bishop in St Augustin's time, knowing that the Church did universally use this Custom of baptizing Infants with Interrogatories, was desirous to learn from St. Augustin the true cause and reason thereof. *If* (saith he) *I should set before thee a young Infant, and should ask of thee, whether that Infant when he cometh unto riper age will be honest and just, or no; thou wouldst answer (I know) that to tell in these things what shall come to pass, is not in the power of mortal Men. If I should ask, what good or evil such an Infant thinketh? Thine answer hereunto must needs be again with the like uncertainty. If thou neither canst promise for the time to come, nor for the present pronounce any thing in this case; how is it, that when such are brought unto Baptism, their Parents there undertake what the Child shall afterwards do? Yea, they are not doubtful to say, it doth that which is impossible to be done by Infants; at the least there is no Man precisely able to affirm it done. Vouchsafe me hereunto some short answer, such as not only may press me with the bare authority of Custom, but also instruct me in the cause thereof.* Touching which difficulty, whether it may truly be said for Infants at the time of their Baptism that they do believe, the effect of St. Augustin's answer is Yea; but with this distinction,† a present *actual habit*

Aug. Epist. XXIII.

* They prophane holy Baptism in toying foolishly; for that they ask Questions of an Infant which cannot answer, and speak unto them, as was wont to be spoken unto Men, and unto such as being converted, answered for themselves and were baptized. Which is but a mockery of God, and therefore against the holy Scriptures, Gal vi 7. Admonition to the Parliament. The same defended in T C. lib i. pag. 168

† Sicut credere respondetur, ita etiam fidelis vocatur; non rem ipsa mente annuendo, sed ipsius rei Sacramentum percipiendo. Aug.

of

of Faith there is not in them; there is delivered unto them that Sacrament a part of the due celebration whereof consisting in answering to the Articles of Faith, because the habit of Faith which afterwards doth come with years, is but a farther building up of the same edifice, *the first foundation whereof was laid by the Sacrament of Baptism.* For that which there we professed without any understanding, when we afterwards come to acknowledge, do we any thing else but only bring unto ripeness the very seed that was sown before? We are then Believers because then we begin to be that which process of time doth make perfect. And till we come to actual Belief, the very Sacrament of Faith is a shield as strong, as after this the Faith of the Sacrament against all contrary infernal Powers. Which whosoever doth think impossible, is undoubtedly farther off from Christian Belief, though he be baptized, than are these Innocents which at their Baptism, albeit they have no conceit or cogitation of Faith, are notwithstanding pure and free from all opposite cogitations; whereas the other is not free. If therefore without any fear or scruple we may account them and term them Believers, only for their outward profession's sake, which inwardly are farther from Faith than Infants, why not Infants much more at the time of their solemn initiation by Baptism, the Sacrament of Faith, whereunto they not only conceive nothing opposite, but have also that * Grace given them which is the first and most effectual cause out of which our Belief groweth? In sum, the whole Church is a multitude of Believers, all honoured with that

* Multum mirabilis res est, quemadmodum quorundam nondum cognoscentium Deum sit inhabitator Deus, et quorundam cognoscentium non sit Nec illi enim ad templum Dei pertinent, qui, cognoscentes Deum, non sicut Deum glorificaverunt. et ad templum Dei pertinent parvuli sanctificati Sacramento Christi, regenerati Spiritu Sancto qui per ætatem nondum possunt cognoscere Deum. Unde quem potuerunt illi nosse nec habere, isti potuerunt habere antequam nosse. Aug. Epist. lvii.

title

BOOK V. title, even Hypocrites for their Profession's sake, as well as Saints because of their inward sincere persuasion, and *Infants as being in the first degree of their ghostly motion towards the actual habit of Faith*; the first sort are faithful in the eye of the World, the second faithful in the sight of God; the last in the ready direct way to become both, if all things after be suitable to these their present beginnings. *This* (saith St. Augustin) *would not haply content such persons as are uncapable or unquiet; but to them which, having knowledge, are not troublesome, it may suffice. Wherein I have not for ease of myself objected against you that custom only, than which nothing is more firm, but of a custom most profitable, I have done that little which I could, to yield you a reasonable cause.* Were St. Augustin now living, there are which would tell him for his better instruction, that to say * of a Child, it is elect, and to say, it doth believe, are all one; for which cause, sith no Man is able precisely to affirm the one of any Infant in particular, it followeth, that precisely and absolutely we ought not to say the other. Which precise and absolute terms are needless in this case. We speak of Infants as the rule of piety alloweth both to speak and think. They that can take to themselves, in ordinary talk, a charitable kind of liberty to name Men of their own sort God's dear Children (notwithstanding the large reign of Hypocrisy) should not methinks be so strict and rigorous against the Church for presuming as it doth of a Christian Innocent. For when we know how Christ in general hath said that *of such is the Kingdom of Heaven*, which Kingdom is the Inheritance of God's Elect; and do withal behold, how his providence hath called them unto the first beginnings of

* T. C. lib. i. pag. 169. If Children could have Faith, yet, they that present the child cannot precisely tell whether that particular child hath Faith, or no, we are to think charitably, and to hope it is one of the Church, but it can be no more precisely said that it hath Faith, than it may be said precisely elected.

eternal

eternal Life, and presented them at the Well-spring of New-birth, wherein original sin is purged, besides which sin, there is no hindrance of their Salvation known to us, as themselves will grant; hard it were, that having so many fair inducements whereupon to ground, we should not be thought to utter, at the least, a truth as probable and allowable in terming any such particular Infant an elect Babe, as in presuming the like of others whose safety nevertheless we are not absolutely able to warrant. (2 John 2.) If any, troubled with these scruples, be only for instruction's sake desirous to know yet some farther reason why Interrogatories should be ministered to Infants in Baptism, and be answered unto by others as in their names; they may consider, that Baptism implieth a Covenant or League between God and Man, wherein as God doth bestow presently remission of sins and the Holy Ghost, binding also himself to add in process of time what Grace soever shall be farther necessary for the attainment of everlasting Life; so every baptized Soul, receiving the same Grace at the hands of God, tieth likewise itself forever to the observation of his Law, no less than the Jews by Circumcision bound themselves to the Law of Moses. (Gal. iii. 5.) The Law of Christ requiring therefore Faith and newness of Life in all Men, by virtue of the Covenant which they make in Baptism, is it toyish that the Church in Baptism exacteth at every Man's hands an express profession of Faith, and an irrevocable promise of Obedience by way of * solemn stipulation? That Infants may contract and covenant with God, the Law is plain. Neither is the (Gen. xvii. 14.) reason of the Law obscure: for sith it tendeth, we

* Stipulatio est verborum conceptio, quibus is qui interrogatur daturum facturumve se quod interrogatus est, respondet Lib. v. sect. 1. ff. de Oblig. et Act. In hac re olim talia verba tradita fuerunt Spondes? Spondeo. Promittis? Promitto. Fide promittis? Fide promitto. Fide jubes? Fide jubeo. Dabis? Dabo. Facies? Faciam. Instit. de Verb. oblig. lib. iii. tit. 15.

BOOK V. cannot sufficiently expreſs how much, to their own good, and doth no way hurt or endanger them to begin the race of their lives herewith; they are, as equity requireth, admitted hereunto, and, in favour of their tender years, such formal complements of Stipulation, as being requiſite are impoſſible by themſelves in their own perſons to be performed, leave is given that they may * ſufficiently diſcharge by others. Albeit therefore neither deaf, nor dumb Men, neither furious Perſons, nor Children, can receive any civil Stipulation; yet this kind of ghoſtly ſtipulation they may through his indulgence, who, reſpecting the ſingular benefit thereof, accepteth Children brought unto him for that end, entereth into Articles of Covenant with them, and in tender commiſeration granteth that other Men's profeſſions and promiſes in Baptiſm made for them ſhall avail no leſs than if they had been themſelves able to have made their own. None more fit to undertake this office in their behalf than ſuch as preſent them unto Baptiſm. A wrong conceit that none may receive the Sacrament of Baptiſm but they whoſe Parents, at the leaſt the one of them, are by the ſoundneſs of their Religion, and by their virtuous demeanor known T. C. l. i. p. 172. to be Men of God, hath cauſed ſome to repel Children, whoſoever bring them, if their Parents be miſperſuaded in Religion, or for other miſ-deſerts excommunicated; ſome likewiſe for that cauſe to withhold Baptiſm unleſs the Father, albeit no ſuch exception can juſtly be taken againſt him, do notwithſtanding make profeſſion of his Faith and avouch the Child to be his own. Thus whereas God hath appointed them Miniſters of holy things, they make themſelves inquiſitors of Men's perſons a great deal

* Accommodat illis mater Eccleſia aliorum pedes ut veniant, aliorum cor ut credant, aliorum linguam ut fateantur, ut quoniam quod ægri ſunt alio peccante prægravantur, ſic cum ſani fiant alio pio eis confitente ſalventur. Aug. Serm. x. de Verb. Apoſt.

farther

farther than need is. They should consider, that God hath ordained Baptism in favour of Mankind. To restrain favours is an odious thing; to enlarge them, acceptable both to God and Man. Whereas therefore the Civil Law gave divers Immunities to them that were Fathers of three Children, and had them living; those Immunities they held, although their Children were all dead, if War had consumed them, because it seemed in that case not against reason to repute them by a courteous construction of Law as live Men *, in that the honour of their Service done to the Commonwealth would remain always: can it hurt us, in exhibiting the Graces which God doth bestow on Men? or can it prejudice his glory, if the self-same equity guide and direct our hands? When God made his Covenant with such as had Abraham to their Father, was only Abraham's immediate issue, or only his lineal Posterity according to the flesh, included in that Covenant? Were not Proselytes as well as Jews always taken for the Sons of Abraham? Yea, because the very Heads of Families are Fathers in some sort, as touching providence and care for the meanest that belong unto them, the Servants which Abraham had bought with money were as capable of Circumcision, being newly born, as any natural Child that Abraham himself begat. Be it then that Baptism belongeth to none but such as either believe presently, or else being Infants are the Children of believing Parents, in case the Church do bring Children to the holy Font, whose natural Parents are either unknown, or known to be such as the Church accurseth, but yet forgetteth not in that severity to take compassion upon their Offspring, (for it is the Church † which

BOOK V.

* Hi enim qui pro Rep ceciderunt, in perpetuum per gloriam vivere intelliguntur. Instit. lib. ii. tit 25. sect. 1.

† Offeruntur quippe parvuli ad percipiendam spiritualem gratiam, non tam ab eis quorum gestantur manibus, quamvis et ab ipsis, si et ipsi boni et fideles sint, quam ab universa societate

sanctorum

BOOK V. doth offer them to Baptiſm by the Miniſtry of Preſenters) were it not againſt both equity and duty to refuſe the Mother of Believers herſelf, and not to take her in this caſe for a faithful Parent? It is not the virtue of our Fathers, nor the Faith of any other, that can give us the true Holineſs which we have by virtue of our New-birth. Yet even through the common Faith and Spirit of God's Church (a thing which no quality of Parents can prejudice) I ſay, through the Faith of the Church of God, undertaking the motherly care of our Souls, ſo far forth we may be and are in our Infancy ſanctified, as to be thereby made ſufficiently capable of Baptiſm, and to be intereſted in the Rites of our New-birth for their piety's ſake that offer us thereunto. *It cometh ſometime to paſs* (ſaith St. Auguſtin) *that the Children of Bond-ſlaves are brought to Baptiſm by their Lord; ſometime the Parents being dead, the Friends alive undertake that office; ſometime Strangers or Virgins conſecrated unto God, which neither have, nor can have Children of their own, take up Infants in the open ſtreets, and ſo offer them unto Baptiſm, whom the cruelty of unnatural Parents caſteth out and leaveth to the adventure of uncertain pity.* As therefore he which did the part of a Neighbour, was a Neighbour to that wounded Man whom the Parable of the Goſpel deſcribeth, ſo they are Fathers, although Strangers, that bring Infants to him which maketh them the Sons of God. In the phraſe of ſome kind of Men, they uſe to be termed Witneſſes, as if they came but to ſee and teſtify what is done. It ſavoureth more of piety to give them their old accuſtomed name of Fathers and Mothers in God, whereby they are well put in mind what affection they ought to bear towards thoſe Innocents for whoſe religious

ſanctorum atque fidelium. Aug. in Epiſt. xxiii. Ἀξιοῦνται δὲ τῶν διὰ τοῦ Βαπτίσματος ἀγαθῶν τὰ βρέφη τῇ πίστει τῶν προσφερόντων αὐτὰ τῷ Βαπτίσματι. Juſtin. Reſp. ad Orthod.

education

education the Church accepteth them as pledges. This therefore is their own duty: but because the answer which they make to the usual demands of stipulation proposed in Baptism is not their own; the Church doth best to receive it of them, in that form which best sheweth whose the act is. That which a Guardian doth in the name of his Guard or Pupil, standeth by natural equity forcible for his benefit, though it be done without his knowledge; and shall we judge it a thing unreasonable, or in any respect unfit, that Infants by words which others utter should, though unwittingly, yet truly and forcibly bind themselves to that whereby their estate is so assuredly bettered? Herewith Nestorius* the Heretick was charged, as having fallen from his first Profession, and broken the promise which he made to God in the arms of others. Of such as profaned themselves, being Christians, with irreligious delight in the ensigns of Idolatry, heathenish spectacles, shows and stage-plays, Tertullian, to strike them the more deep, claimeth the promise which they made in Baptism. Why were they dumb, being thus challenged? Wherefore stood they not up to answer it in their own defence, that such Professions and Promises made in their names were frivolous; that all which others undertook for them was but mockery and profanation?

Tertul. lib. de Spectac.

* Si Arrianæ aut Sabellianæ hereseos adsertor esses, et non tuo ipsius symbolo tecum uterer, convincerem te tamen testimoniorum sacrorum auctoritate. Quid tandem si sic apud te agerem? quid diceres? quid responderes? nonne obsecro illud, in eo te baptisatum, in eo te renatum esse? Et vere, in negotio quamvis improbo non importuna defensio, et quæ non absurde causam erroris diceres, si pertinaciam non sociares errori. Nunc autem cum in Catholica urbe natus, Catholica Fide institutus, Catholico Baptismate regeneratus sis, nunquid agere tecum quasi cum Arriano aut Sabelliano possim? Quod utinam fuisses. Minus dolerem in malis editum quam de bonis lapsum; minus Fidem non habitam quam amissam Non iniquum autem, Hæretice, non iniquum aut grave aliquid postulo. Hoc fac in Catholica Fide editus, quod fueras pro perversitate facturus. Cassia. de Incarn. lib. vi. cap. 5.

BOOK V. fanation? That which no Heretick, no wicked liver, no impious deſpiſer of God, no miſcreant or malefactor, which had himſelf been baptized, was ever ſo deſperate as to diſgorge in contempt of ſo fruitfully received Cuſtoms, is now their voice that reſtore, as they ſay, *the ancient Purity of Religion.*

Of the Croſs in Baptiſm.

65. In Baptiſm many things of very ancient continuance are now quite and clean aboliſhed, for that the virtue and Grace of this Sacrament had been therewith overſhadowed, as fruit with too great abundance of leaves. Notwithſtanding to them which think that always imperfect Reformation that doth but ſhear and not flay, our retaining certain of thoſe formal Rites, eſpecially the dangerous Sign of the Croſs, hath ſeemed almoſt an impardonable overſight. *The Croſs* (they ſay) *ſith it is but a mere invention of Man, ſhould not therefore at all have been added to the Sacrament of Baptiſm. To ſign Children's foreheads with a Croſs, in token that hereafter they ſhall not be aſhamed to make Profeſſion of the Faith of Chriſt, is to bring into the Church a new word, whereas there ought to be no Doctor heard in the Church but our Saviour Chriſt. That reaſon which moved the Fathers to uſe, ſhould move us not to uſe the Sign of the Croſs. They lived with Heathens that had the Croſs of Chriſt in contempt; we with ſuch as adore the Croſs; and therefore we ought to abandon it, even as, in like conſideration, Ezekias did of old the brazen ſerpent.* Theſe are the cauſes of diſpleaſure conceived againſt the Croſs; a Ceremony, the uſe whereof hath been profitable, although we obſerve it not as the Ordinance of God, but of Man. *For* (ſaith Tertullian) *if of this and the like Cuſtoms thou ſhouldſt require ſome Commandment to be ſhewed thee out of Scriptures, there is none found.* What reaſon there is to juſtify Tradition, Uſe or Cuſtom in this behalf, *either thou mayſt of thyſelf perceive, or elſe learn of ſome other that doth.* Leſt therefore the name of Tradition ſhould be offenſive to any, conſidering how far by ſome it hath been

Tertul. de Coron. Militis

and

and is abuſed, we mean by * Traditions, Ordinances made in the prime of Chriſtian Religion, eſtabliſhed with that Authority which Chriſt hath left to his Church for matters indifferent; and in that conſideration requiſite to be obſerved, till like Authority ſee juſt and reaſonable cauſe to alter them. So that Traditions Eccleſiaſtical are not rudely and in groſs to be ſhaken off, becauſe the Inventors of them were Men. Such as ſay, they allow no † invention of Men to be mingled with the outward Adminiſtration of Sacraments; and, under that pretence, condemn our uſing the Sign of the Croſs, have belike ſome ſpecial diſpenſation themſelves to violate their own Rules. For neither can they indeed decently, nor do they ever baptize any without manifeſt breach of this their profound Axiom, *That Men's Inventions ſhould not be mingled with Sacraments and Inſtitutions of God.* They ſeem to like very well in Baptiſm the Cuſtom of Godfathers, *becauſe ſo generally the Churches have received it.* Which Cuſtom being of God no more inſtituted than the other (howſoever they pretend the other hurtful and this profitable) it followeth, that even in their own opinion, if their words do ſhew their minds, there is no neceſſity of ſtripping Sacraments out of all ſuch attire of Ceremonies as Man's wiſdom hath at any time clothed them withal; and conſequently, that either they muſt reform their ſpeech as over-general, or elſe condemn their own practice as unlawful. Ceremonies have more in weight than in ſight; they work by commonneſs of uſe much, although in the ſeveral acts

BOOK V.

T. C. l. i. p. 170.

* Traditiones non ſcriptas, ſi doctrinam reſpiciant, cum doctrina ſcripta convenire debere dicimus. Quod ad rituales et eccleſiaſticas attinet, ordinis et ædificationis Eccleſiarum in his ſemper habenda ratio eſt; inutiles autem et noxias, nempe ineptas et ſuperſtitioſas Patronis ſuis relinquamus. Goulart. Geneven. Annot. in Epiſt. Cypr. lxxiv.

† T. C. lib. i. pag. 171. They ſhould not have been ſo bold as to have brought it into the holy Sacrament of Baptiſm; and ſo mingle the Ceremonies and Inventions of Men with the Sacraments and Inſtitutions of God.

of

BOOK V of their usage we scarcely discern any good they do. And because the use which they have for the most part is not perfectly understood, Superstition is apt to impute unto them greater virtue than indeed they have. For prevention whereof when we use this Ceremony, we always plainly express the end whereunto it serveth, namely, for a Sign of Remembrance to put us in mind of our duty. But by this mean, they say, *we make it a great deal worse. For why? Seeing God hath no where commanded to draw two lines in token of the duty which we owe to Christ, our practice with this exposition publisheth a new Gospel, and causeth another Word to have place in the Church of Christ, where no voice ought to be heard but his. By which good reason the Authors of those grave admonitions to the Parliament are well holpen up, which held, *That sitting at Communions betokeneth rest and full accomplishment of legal Ceremonies in our Saviour Christ.* For although it be the Word of God that such Ceremonies are expired; yet seeing it is not the Word of God, that Men to signify so much should sit at the Table of our Lord, these have their doom as well as others, *Guilty of a new devised Gospel in the Church of Christ.* Which strange imagination is begotten of a special dislike they have to hear, that Ceremonies now in use should be thought significant, whereas, in truth, such as are not significant must needs be vain. Ceremonies destitute of signification, are no better than the idle gestures of Men, whose broken wits are not masters of what they do. For if we look but into secular and civil complements, what other cause can

* T. C. l. i. p. 170. The profitable signification of the Cross maketh the thing a great deal worse, and bringeth in a new Word into the Church; whereas there ought to be no Doctor heard in the Church, but only our Saviour Christ. For although it be the Word of God, that we should not be ashamed of the Cross of Christ, yet is it not the Word of God, that we should be kept in remembrance of that, by two lines drawn across one over another in a Child's forehead.

there

there possibly be given why to omit them where of course they are looked for? for where they are not so due, to use them bringeth Men's secret intents oftentimes into great jealousy: I would know, I say, what reason we are able to yield, why things so light in their own nature should weigh in the opinions of Men so much, saving only in regard of that which they use to signify or betoken? Doth not our Lord Jesus Christ himself impute the omission of some courteous Ceremonies, even in domestical entertainment, to a colder degree of loving affection, and take the contrary in better part, not so much respecting what was less done, as what was signified less by the one than by the other? For, to that very end, he referreth in part those gracious expostulations. *Simon, seest thou this Woman? Since I entered into thine house, thou gavest me no water for my feet; but she hath washed my feet with tears, and wiped them with the hairs of her head: thou gavest me no kiss; but this Woman, since the time I came in, hath not ceased to kiss my feet: mine head with oil thou didst not anoint; but this Woman hath anointed my feet with ointment.* Wherefore as the usual dumb Ceremonies of common life are in request or dislike according to that they import; even so Religion having likewise her silent Rites, the chiefest rule, whereby to judge of their quality, is that which they mean or betoken. For if they signify good things (as somewhat they must of necessity signify, because it is of their very nature to be signs of intimation, presenting both themselves unto outward sense, and besides themselves some other thing to the understanding of beholders) unless they be either greatly mischosen to signify the same, or else applied where that which they signify agreeth not, there is no cause of exception against them, as against evil and unlawful Ceremonies; much less of excepting against them only in that they are not without sense. And if every religious Ceremony, which hath been invented of Men to signify any thing God himself alloweth, were the publication of another Gospel in the Church of Christ;

BOOK V.

Luke vii. 44.

BOOK V. Chrift; feeing that no Chriftian Church in the World is, or can be, without continual ufe of fome Ceremonies which Men have inftituted, and that to fignify good things (unlefs they be vain and frivolous Ceremonies); it would follow, that the World hath no Chriftian Church which doth not daily proclaim new Gofpels; a fequel, the manifeft abfurdity whereof argueth the rawnefs of that fuppofal out of which it groweth. Now the * caufe why Antiquity did the more, in actions of common life, honour the Ceremony of the Crofs, might be for that they lived with Infidels. But that which they did in the Sacrament of Baptifm was for the felf-fame good of Believers which is thereby intended ftill. The Crofs is for us an admonition no lefs neceffary than for them, to glory in the Service of Jefus Chrift, and not to hang down our heads

* T. C. lib i. pag 170. It is known to all that have read the Ecclefiaftical ftories, that the Heathens did object to Chriftians in times paft, in reproach, that the God which they believed on was hanged upon a Crofs. And they thought good to teftify, that they were not afhamed therefore of the Son of God, by the often ufing of the Sign of the Crofs. Which carefulnefs and good mind to keep amongft them an open Profeffion of Chrift crucified, although it be to be commended, yet is not this means fo. For they might otherwife have kept it, and with lefs danger than by this ufe of croffing. And as it was brought in upon no good ground, fo the Lord left a mark of his curfe of it, and whereby it might be perceived to come out of the forge of Men's brain, in that it began forthwith, while it was yet in the fwaddling clouts, to be fuperftitioufly abufed. The Chriftians had fuch a fuperftition in it, that they would do nothing without croffing. But if it were granted, that upon this confideration, which I have before mentioned, the ancient Chriftians did well; yet it followeth not, that we fhould fo do. For we live not among thofe Nations which do caft us in the teeth, or reproach us with the Crofs of Chrift. Now that we live amongft Papifts that do not contemn the Crofs of Chrift, but which efteem more of the wooden Crofs, than of the true Crofs which is his fufferings; we ought now to do clean contrariwife to the old Chriftians, and abolifh all ufe of thefe Croffes. For contrary difeafes muft have contrary remedies. If therefore the old Chriftians, to deliver the Crofs of Chrift from contempt, did often ufe the Crofs, the Chriftians now, to take away the fuperftitious eftimation of it, ought to take away the ufe of it.

heads as Men aſhamed thereof, although it procure us reproach and obloquy at the hands of this wretched World. Shame is a kind of fear to incur diſgrace and ignominy. Now whereas ſome things are worthy of reproach, ſome things ignominious only through a falſe opinion which Men have conceived of them; Nature, that generally feareth opprobrious reprehenſion, muſt by Reaſon and Religion be taught what it ſhould be aſhamed of, and what not. But be we never ſo well inſtructed what our duty is in this behalf, without ſome preſent admonition at the very inſtant of practice, what we know is many times not called to mind till that be done whereupon our juſt confuſion enſueth. To ſupply the abſence of ſuch as that way might do us good when they ſee us in danger of ſliding, there are judicious and wiſe Men which think we may greatly relieve ourſelves by a bare imagined preſence of ſome, whoſe authority we fear and would be loth to offend, if indeed they were preſent with us. Witneſſes at hand are a bridle unto many offences. Let the Mind have always ſome whom it feareth, ſome whoſe authority may keep even ſecret thoughts under awe. Take Cato, or, if he be too harſh and rugged, chooſe ſome other of a ſofter metal, whoſe gravity of life and ſpeech thou loveſt, his mind and countenance carry with thee, ſet him always before thine eyes, either as a watch or as a pattern. That which is crooked we cannot ſtraighten but by ſome ſuch level. If Men of ſo good experience and inſight in the maims of our weak fleſh, have thought theſe fancied remembrances available to awaken ſhamefacedneſs, that ſo the boldneſs of Sin may be ſtaid ere it look abroad; ſurely the wiſdom of the Church of Chriſt, which hath to that uſe converted the Ceremony of the Croſs in Baptiſm, it is no Chriſtian Man's part to deſpiſe; eſpecially ſeeing that by this mean, where Nature doth earneſtly import aid, Religion yieldeth her that ready aſſiſtance, than which there can be no help more

Ephef. v. 12. Rom vi. 21.

Sen. Epiſt. xi. lib. 1.

more forcible, serving only to relieve memory, and to bring to our cogitation that which should most make ashamed of Sin. The Mind, while we are in this present Life,* whether it contemplate, meditate, deliberate, or howsoever exercise itself, worketh nothing without continual recourse unto imagination, the only storehouse of wit, and peculiar chair of memory. On this anvil it ceaseth not day and night to strike, by means whereof, as the pulse declareth how the heart doth work, so the very † thoughts and cogitations of Man's mind, be they good or bad, do no where sooner bewray themselves than through the crevices of that wall, wherewith Nature hath compassed the cells and closets of Fancy. In the forehead nothing more plain to be seen than the fear of contumely and disgrace. For which cause the Scripture (as with great probability it may be thought) describeth them marked of God in the forehead, whom his Mercy hath undertaken to keep from final confusion and shame. Not that God doth set any corporal mark on his Chosen, but to note that he giveth his Elect security of preservation from reproach, the fear whereof doth use to shew itself in that part. Shall I say, that the Sign of the Cross (as we use it) is in some sort a mean to work our ‡ preservation from reproach? Surely, the Mind which as yet hath not hardened itself in sin, is seldom provoked thereunto in any gross and grievous manner, but Nature's secret suggestion objecteth against it ignominy as a bar. Which conceit

* Τὸ νοεῖν ἢ φαντασία τὶς ἢ οὐκ ἄνευ φαντασίας. Arist de Anim. lib. i. cap. 1. Ἡ μὲν αἰσθητικὴ φαντασία καὶ ἐν τοῖς ἀλόγοις ζώοις ὑπάρχει, ἡ δὲ βουλευτικὴ ἐν τοῖς λογιστικοῖς. Lib. iii. cap. 11. Τὰ μὲν οὖν εἴδη τὸ νοητικὸν ἐν τοῖς φαντάσμασι νοεῖ, καὶ ὡς ἐν ἐκείνοις ὥρισται αὐτῷ τὸ διωκτὸν, καὶ φευκτὸν, καὶ ἐκτὸς τῆς αἰσθήσεως ὂν, ὅταν ἐπὶ τῶν φαντασμάτων ᾖ, κινεῖται. Lib iii. cap 8.

† Frons hominis tristitiæ, hilaritatis, clementiæ, severitatis index est Plin lib. xi Ezek. ix. 4. Apoc. vii. 3. & ix. 4. Ἐρυθραίνονται γὰρ οἱ αἰσχυνόμενοι. Arist Eth iv. cap 9

‡ Caro signatur ut et anima muniatur. Tertul de Resur. Car.

being

being entered into that palace of Man's Fancy, the gates whereof have imprinted in them that holy Sign, which bringeth forthwith to mind whatsoever Christ hath wrought, and we vowed against sin, it cometh hereby to pass that Christian Men never want a most effectual, though a silent teacher, to avoid whatsoever may deservedly procure shame. So that in things which we should be ashamed of, we are by the Cross admonished faithfully of our duty, at the very moment when admonition doth most need. Other things there are which deserve honour, and yet do purchase many times our disgrace in this present World; as, of old, the very truth of Religion itself, till God by his own out-stretched arm made the glory thereof to shine over all the earth. Whereupon St. Cyprian exhorting to Martyrdom in times of heathenish persecution and cruelty, thought it not vain to alledge unto them, with other arguments, the very Ceremony of that Cross whereof we speak. Never let that hand offer sacrifice to Idols which hath already received the Body of our Saviour Christ, and shall hereafter the Crown of his Glory; *Arm your foreheads* unto all boldness, that the *Sign of God* may be kept safe. Again, when it pleased God, that, the fury of their Enemies being bridled, the Church had some little rest and quietness (if so small a liberty, but only to breathe between troubles, may be termed quietness and rest), to such as fell not away from Christ through former persecutions, he giveth due and deserved praise in the self-same manner: *You that were ready to endure imprisonment, and were resolute to suffer death; you that have courageously withstood the World, ye have made yourselves both a glorious spectacle for God to behold, and a worthy example for the rest of your Brethren to follow. Those mouths which had sanctified themselves with food coming down from Heaven, loathed, after Christ's own Body and Blood, to taste the poisoned and contagious scraps of Idols; those foreheads which the Sign of God had purified.*

Cypr Epist. lvi. ad Thibaritanos.

Cypr. de Lapi.

BOOK V *fied, kept themſelves to be crowned by him, the touch of the * garlands of Satan they abhorred.* Thus was the Memory of that Sign which they had in Baptiſm a kind of bar or prevention to keep them even from Apoſtaſy, whereunto the frailty of fleſh and blood, overmuch fearing to endure ſhame, might peradventure the more eaſily otherwiſe have drawn them. We have not now, through the gracious goodneſs of Almighty God, thoſe extreme conflicts which our Fathers had with blaſphemous contumelies every where offered to the Name of Chriſt, by ſuch as profeſſed themſelves Infidels and Unbelievers. Howbeit, unleſs we be ſtrangers to the age wherein we live, or elſe in ſome partial reſpect diſſemblers of that we hourly both hear and ſee, there is not the ſimpleſt of us but knoweth with what diſdain and ſcorn Chriſt is diſhonoured far and wide. Is there any burden in the World more heavy to bear than contempt? Is there any contempt that grieveth as theirs doth, whoſe quality no way making them leſs worthy than others are of reputation, only the Service which they do to Chriſt in the daily exerciſe of Religion treadeth them down? Doth any contumely which we ſuſtain for Religion's ſake pierce ſo deeply as that which would ſeem of mere conſcience religiouſly ſpiteful? When they that honour God are deſpiſed, when the chiefeſt ſervice of honour that Man can do unto him is the cauſe why they are deſpiſed, when they which pretend to honour him, and that with greateſt ſincerity, do, with more than heatheniſh petulancy, trample under foot almoſt whatſoever either we, or the whole Church of God by the ſpace of ſo many ages, have been accuſtomed unto, for the comelier and better exerciſe of our Religion according to the ſoundeſt Rules that Wiſdom directed by the Word

* Erant enim ſupplices coronarii. Tert. lib de Coro. Mil. In the ſervice of Idols, the doors of their temples, the ſacrifices, the altars, the Prieſts, and the Supplıants that were preſent, wore garlands.

of God, and by long experience confirmed, hath been able with common advice, with much deliberation and exceeding great diligence, to comprehend; when no Man fighting under Christ's banner can be always exempted from seeing or sustaining those indignities, the sting whereof not to feel, or feeling not to be moved thereat, is a thing impossible to flesh and blood: if this be any object for patience to work on, the strictest bond that thereunto tieth us, is our vowed obedience to Christ; the solemnest vow that we ever made to obey Christ, and to suffer willingly all reproaches for his sake was made in Baptism; and amongst other memorials to keep us mindful of that vow, we cannot think that the Sign which our new baptized foreheads did there receive, is either unfit or unforcible, the reasons hitherto alledged being weighed with indifferent balance. It is not (you will say) the Cross in our foreheads, but in our hearts the Faith of Christ that armeth us with patience, constancy, and courage. Which as we grant to be most true, so neither dare we despise, no not the meanest helps that serve, though it be but in the very lowest degree of furtherance, towards the highest services that God doth require at our hands. And if any Man deny that such Ceremonies are available, at the least, as memorials of duty; or do think that himself hath no need to be so put in mind what our duties are; it is but reasonable, that in the one the publick experience of the World over-weigh some few Men's persuasion; and in the other the rare perfection of a few condescend unto common imbecility. Seeing, therefore, that to fear shame, which doth worthily follow sin, and to bear undeserved reproach constantly, is the general duty of all Men professing Christianity; seeing also that our weakness, while we are in this present World, doth need towards spiritual duties the help even of corporal furtherance; and that by reason of natural intercourse between the highest and the lowest powers

BOOK V. of Man's mind in all actions, his fancy or imagination carrying in it that ſpecial note of remembrance, than which there is nothing more forcible, where either too weak or too ſtrong a conceit of infamy and diſgrace might do great harm, ſtandeth always ready to put forth a kind of neceſſary helping hand; we are in that reſpect to acknowledge the * good and profitable uſe of this Ceremony, and not to think it ſuperfluous that Chriſt hath his mark applied † unto that part where baſhfulneſs appeareth, in token that they which are Chriſtians ſhould be at no time aſhamed of his ignominy. But to prevent ſome inconveniencies which might enſue, if the over ordinary uſe thereof (as it fareth with ſuch Rites when they are too common) ſhould cauſe it to be of leſs obſervation or regard where it moſt availeth; we neither omit it in that place, nor altogether make it ſo vulgar, as the Cuſtom heretofore hath been. Although to condemn the whole Church of God when it moſt flouriſhed in zeal and piety, to mark that Age with the brand of error and ſuperſtition only becauſe they had this Ceremony more in uſe than we now think needful; boldly to affirm that this their practice grew ſo ſoon through a fearful malediction of God upon the Ceremony of the Croſs, as if we knew that his purpoſe was thereby to make it manifeſt in all Men's eyes how execrable thoſe things are in his ſight which have proceeded from human invention, is, as we take it, a cenſure of greater zeal than knowledge. Men whoſe judgments in theſe caſes are grown more moderate, although they retain not as we do the uſe of this Ceremony, perceive notwithſtanding very well, ſuch cenſures to

* Ἔστω δὴ ἀγαθὸν καὶ τὸ φυλακτικὸν τῶν τοιούτων καὶ ᾧ ἀκολουθεῖ τὰ τοιαῦτα καὶ τὰ κωλυτικὰ τῶν ἐναντίων καὶ τὰ φθαρτικά. Ariſt. Rhet. lib. 1. cap. 6.

† Ozias Rex lepræ varietate in fronte maculatus eſt, ea parte corporis notatus offenſo Domino ubi ſignantur qui Dominum promerentur. Cypr. de Unit. Eccleſ. cap. 16.

be

be out of ſquare; and do therefore not only * acquit the Fathers from Superſtition therein, but alſo think it ſufficient to anſwer in excuſe of themſelves, *This Ceremony which was but a thing indifferent even of old, we judge not at this day a matter neceſſary for all Chriſtian Men to obſerve.* As for their laſt upſhot of all towards this mark, they are of opinion that if the ancient Chriſtians to deliver the Croſs of Chriſt from contempt did well, and with good conſideration uſe often the Sign of the Croſs, in teſtimony of their Faith and Profeſſion, before Infidels which upbraided them with Chriſt's ſufferings; now that we live with ſuch as contrariwiſe adore the Sign of the Croſs (becauſe contrary diſeaſes ſhould always have contrary remedies), we ought to take away all uſe thereof. In which conceit they both ways greatly ſeduce themſelves; firſt, for that they imagine the Fathers to have had no uſe of the Croſs but with reference unto Infidels, which miſperſuaſion we have before diſcovered at large; and ſecondly, by reaſon that they think there is not any other way beſides univerſal extirpation to reform ſuperſtitious abuſes of the Croſs. Wherein, becauſe there are that ſtand very much upon the example of Ezechias, as if his breaking to pieces that Serpent of Braſs, whereunto the Children of Iſrael had burnt incenſe, did enforce the utter abolition of this Ceremony; the fact of that virtuous Prince, is by ſo much the more attentively to be conſidered. Our lives in this World are partly guided in Rules, and partly directed by Examples. To conclude out of general Rules and Axioms by diſcourſe of wit our duties in every particular action, is both troubleſome and many times ſo full of difficulty, that it maketh deliberations hard and tedious to the wiſeſt Men.

BOOK V.

Goulart. Annot. in Cypr. Epiſt. lvi. c 7

1 Kings, xviii 3

* Goulart. Annot. in Cypr. lib. ad Demetr. cap. 19. Quamvis veteres Chriſtiani externo ſigno Crucis uſi ſunt, id tamen fuit ſine ſuperſtitione, et doctrina de Chriſti merito ab errore qui poſtea irrepſit pios ſervavit immunes.

BOOK V. Whereupon we naturally all incline to obſerve Examples, to mark what others have done before us, and in favour of our own eaſe rather to follow them, than to enter into a new conſultation, if in regard of their virtue and wiſdom we may but probably think they have waded without error. So that the willingneſs of Men to be led by example of others both diſcovereth and helpeth the imbecility of our judgment. Becauſe it doth the one, therefore inſolent and proud Wits would always ſeem to be their own guides; and becauſe it doth the other, we ſee how hardly the vulgar ſort is drawn unto any thing for which there are not as well Examples as Reaſons alledged. Reaſons proving that which is more particular by things more general and farther from Senſe, are with the ſimpler ſort of Men leſs truſted, for that they doubt of their own judgment in thoſe things; but of Examples which prove unto them one doubtful particular by another, more familiarly and ſenſibly known, they eaſily perceive in themſelves ſome better ability to judge. The force of Examples therefore is great, when in matter of action, being doubtful what to do, we are informed what others have commendably done whoſe deliberations were like. But whoſoever doth perſuade by Example, muſt as well reſpect the fitneſs as the goodneſs of that he alledgeth. To Ezechias God himſelf in this fact giveth teſtimony of well-doing. So that nothing is here queſtionable, but only whether the Example alledged be pertinent, pregnant and ſtrong. The Serpent ſpoken of was firſt erected for the extraordinary and miraculous cure of the Iſraelites in the Deſart. This uſe having preſently an end, when the cauſe for which God ordained it was once removed, the thing itſelf they notwithſtanding kept for a monument of God's Mercy, as in like conſideration they did the Pot of Manna, the Rod of Aaron and the Sword which David took from Goliah. In proceſs of time they made of a monument of Divine Power a plain Idol, they burnt Incenſe before it contrary

trary to the Law of God, and did it the ſervices of honour due unto God only. Which groſs and grievous abuſe continued till Ezechias, reſtoring the purity of ſound Religion, deſtroyed utterly that which had been ſo long and ſo generally a ſnare unto them. It is not amiſs which the Canon Law hereupon concludeth, namely, *That if our Predeceſſors have done ſome things which at that time might be without fault, and afterwards be turned to error and ſuperſtition; we are taught by Ezechias breaking the Brazen Serpent, that Poſterity may deſtroy them without any delay, and with great authority.* But may it be ſimply and without exception hereby gathered, that Poſterity is bound to deſtroy whatſoever hath been either at the firſt invented, or but afterwards turned to like ſuperſtition and error? No, it cannot be. The Serpent therefore, and the Sign of the Croſs, although ſeeming equal in this point, that Superſtition hath abuſed both; yet being herein alſo unequal, that neither they have been both ſubject to the like degree of abuſe, nor were in hardneſs of redreſs alike, it may be, that even as the one for abuſe was religiouſly taken away, ſo now, when Religion hath taken away abuſe from the other, we ſhould by utter abolition thereof deſerve hardly his commendation, whoſe example there is offered us no ſuch neceſſary cauſe to follow. For by the words of Ezechias in terming the Serpent but *a lump of Braſs*, to ſhew that the beſt thing in it now was the metal or matter whereof it conſiſteth, we may probably conjecture, that the People whoſe error is therein controuled, had the ſelf-ſame opinion of it which the Heathens had of Idols. They thought that the power of Deity was with it; and when they ſaw it diſſolved, haply they might, to comfort themſelves, imagine as Olympius the Sophiſter did, beholding the diſſipation of Idols, *Shapes and Counterfeits they were, faſhioned of matter ſubject unto corruption, therefore to grind them to duſt was eaſy; but thoſe Celeſtial Powers which dwelt and reſided in them, are aſcended into Heaven.* Some difference

BOOK V.

Diſt. iii. Cyp. Quia.

Sozom. lib. vii. cap. 15.

BOOK V. ference there is between these opinions of palpable Idolatry, and that which the Schools in speculation have bolted out concerning the Cross. Notwithstanding, for as much as the Church of Rome hath hitherto practised, and doth profess the same Adoration to the Sign of the Cross, and neither less nor other than is due unto Christ himself, howsoever they varnish and qualify their sentence, pretending that the Cross which to outward Sense presenteth visibly itself alone is not by them apprehended alone, but hath in their secret surmise or conceit a reference to the Person of our Lord Jesus Christ; so that the honour which they jointly do to both respecteth principally his Person, and the Cross but only for his Person's sake; the People not accustomed to trouble their wits with so nice and subtile differences in the exercise of Religion, are apparently no less ensnared by adoring the Cross, than the Jews by burning Incense to the Brazen Serpent. It is by Thomas ingenuously granted, that because unto reasonable Creatures a kind of reverence is due for the Excellency which is in them, and whereby they resemble God, therefore if reasonable Creatures, Angels or Men, should receive at our hands holy and divine honour, as the Sign of the Cross doth at theirs, to pretend that we honour not them alone, but we honour God with them, would not serve the turn, neither would this be able to prevent the error of Men, or cause them always to respect God in their adorations, and not to finish their intents in the object next before them. But unto this he addeth, that no such error can grow by adoring in that sort a dead Image, which every Man knoweth to be void of excellency in itself, and therefore will easily conceive that the honour done unto it hath an higher reference. Howbeit, seeing that we have by over-true experience been taught how often, especially in these cases, the light even of common understanding faileth, surely their usual adoration of the Cross is not hereby freed. For in actions of this kind we are more to re-

Tho pag. 3 q 25 art 11. Resp. ad Tert.

spect

ſpect what the greateſt part of Men is commonly prone to conceive, than what ſome few Men's wits may deviſe in conſtruction of their own particular meanings. Plain it is, that a falſe opinion of ſome perſonal divine excellency to be in thoſe things which either Nature or Art hath framed, cauſes always religious Adoration. And as plain, that the like adoration applied unto things ſenſible, argueth to vulgar capacities, yea leaveth imprinted in them, the very ſame opinion of Deity from whence all idolatrous worſhip groweth. Yea, the meaner and baſer a thing worſhipped is in itſelf, the more they incline to think that every Man which doth adore it knoweth there is in it, or with it, a preſence of divine power. Be it therefore true, that Croſſes purpoſely framed or uſed for receipt of divine honour be even as ſcandalous as the Brazen Serpent itſelf, where they are in ſuch ſort adored; ſhould we hereupon think ourſelves in the ſight of God, and in conſcience charged to aboliſh utterly the very Ceremony of the Croſs, neither meant at the firſt nor now converted unto any ſuch offenſive purpoſe? Did the Jews, which could never be perſuaded to admit in the City of Jeruſalem that Image of Cæſar which the Romans were accuſtomed to * adore, make any ſcruple of Cæſar's Image in the Coin which they knew very well that Men were not wont to worſhip? Between the Croſs which ſuperſtition honoureth as Chriſt, and that Ceremony of the Croſs which ſerveth only for a ſign of remembrance, there is as plain and as great a difference as between thoſe brazen Images which Solomon made to bear up the Ciſtern of the Temple and (ſith both were of like ſhape, but of unlike uſe) that which the Iſraelites in the Wilderneſs did adore; or between the Altars which Joſias

BOOK V.

Joſeph. Antiquit. lib. xvi. cap. 8 & lib. xviii. cap. 3. & de Bel lib. ii. cap. Matth xxii. 20

2 Chron. iv 3.

Exod. xxxii. 4.

2 Chron. xxxiv. 7.

* Their Eagles, their Enſigns, and the Images of the Princes, they carried with them in all their Armies, and had always a kind of Chapel wherein they placed and adored them as their Gods. Dio. lib. xxx. Herodian. lib iv.

BOOK V. destroyed, because they were instruments of mere Idolatry, and that which the Tribe of Reuben with others erected near to the River Jordan; for which also they grew at the first into some dislike, and were by the rest of their Brethren suspected, yea hardly charged with open breach of the Law of God, accused of backwardness in Religion, upbraided bitterly with the fact of Peor and the odious example of Achan; as if the building of their Altar in that place had given manifest shew of no better than intended Apostasy, till by a true declaration made in their own defence it appeared that such as misliked, misunderstood their enterprize, in as much as they had no intent to build any Altar for Sacrifice, which God would have no where offered saving in Jerusalem only, but to a far other end and purpose, which being opened satisfied all parties, and so delivered them from causeless blame. In this particular, suppose the worst; imagine that the immaterial Ceremony of the Cross had been the subject of as gross pollution as any heathenish or prophane Idol. If we think the example of Ezechias a proof that things which error and superstition hath abused may in no consideration be tolerated, although we presently find them not subject to so vile abuse, the plain example of Ezechias proveth the contrary. The Temples and Idols, which under Solomon had been of very purpose framed for the honour of foreign Gods, Ezechias destroyed not, because they stood as forlorn things, and did now no harm, although formerly they had done harm. Josias for some inconvenience afterwards razed them up. Yet to both there is one commendation given even from God himself, that, touching matter of Religion, they walked in the steps of David, and did no way displease God. Perhaps it seemeth that by force and virtue of this example, although in bare detestation and hatred of Idolatry, all things which have been at any time worshipped are not necessarily to be taken out of the World, nevertheless for remedy and prevention of so great

Josh. xxii. 10.

1 Kings, xi. 7.

2 Kings, xxiii. 13.

2 Kings, xviii 3, 6. & xxii. 2.

great offences, Wiſdom ſhould judge it the ſafeſt courſe to remove altogether from the eyes of Men that which may put them in mind of evil. Some kinds of evil, no doubt, there are very quick in working on thoſe affections that moſt eaſily take fire, which evils ſhould in that reſpect no oftner than need requireth be brought in preſence of weak minds. But neither is the Croſs any ſuch evil, nor yet the Brazen Serpent itſelf ſo ſtrongly poiſoned, that our eyes, ears and thoughts ought to ſhun them both, for fear of ſome deadly harm to enſue the only repreſentation thereof, by geſture, ſhape, ſound, or ſuch like ſignificant means. And for mine own part, I moſt aſſuredly perſuade myſelf, that had Ezechias (till the days of whoſe moſt virtuous reign they ceaſed not continually to burn Incenſe to the Brazen Serpent)—had he found the Serpent, though ſometime adored, yet at that time recovered from the evil of ſo groſs abuſe and reduced to the ſame that was before in the time of David, at which time they eſteemed it only as a memorial, ſign or monument of God's miraculous goodneſs towards them, even as we in no other ſort eſteem the Ceremony of the Croſs; the due conſideration of an uſe ſo harmleſs, common to both, might no leſs have wrought their equal preſervation, than different occaſions have procured notwithſtanding the one's extinguiſhment, the other's lawful continuance. In all perſuaſions, which ground themſelves upon example, we are not ſo much to reſpect what is done, as the cauſes and ſecret inducements leading thereunto. The queſtion being therefore, whether the Ceremony, ſuppoſed to have been ſometimes ſcandalous and offenſive, ought for that cauſe to be now removed; there is no reaſon we ſhould forthwith yield ourſelves to be carried away with example, no not of them whoſe acts the higheſt judgment approveth for having reformed in that manner any publick evil; but before we either attempt any thing or reſolve, the ſtate and condition as well of our own affairs as theirs, whoſe example preſſeth us,

BOOK V is advisedly to be examined; because some things are of their own nature scandalous, and cannot choose but breed offence, as those sinks of execrable filth which Josias did overwhelm; some things, albeit not by nature, and of themselves, are notwithstanding so generally turned to evil by reason of an evil corrupt habit grown, and through long continuance incurably settled in the minds of the greatest part, that no redress can be well hoped for without removal of that wherein they have ruined themselves; which plainly was the state of the Jewish People, and the cause why Ezechias did with such sudden indignation destroy what he saw worshipped; finally, some things are as the Sign of the Cross, though subject either almost or altogether to as great abuse, yet curable with more facility and ease. And to speak as the truth is, our very nature doth hardly yield to destroy that which may be fruitfully kept, and without any great difficulty clean scoured from the rust of evil which by some accident hath grown into it. Wherefore to that which they build in this question upon the example of Ezechias let this suffice. When Heathens despised Christian Religion because of the sufferings of Jesus Christ, the Fathers, to testify how little such contumelies and contempts prevailed with them, chose rather the Sign of the Cross than any other outward mark, whereby the World might most easily discern always what they were. On the contrary side now, whereas they which do all profess the Christian Religion are divided amongst themselves, and the fault of the one part is, that in zeal to the sufferings of Christ they admire too much, and over-superstitiously adore the visible Sign of his Cross; if you ask what we that mislike them should do, we are here advised to cure one contrary by another. Which art or method is not yet so current as they imagine. For if, as their practice for the most part sheweth, it be their meaning that the scope and drift of Reformation, when things are faulty, should be to settle the Church in the contrary; it standeth

2 Kings, xxiii. 7.

ſtandeth them upon to beware of this rule, becauſe BOOK V. ſeeing Vices have not only Virtues, but other Vices alſo in nature oppoſite unto them, it may be dangerous in theſe caſes to ſeek but that which we find contrary to preſent evils. For in ſores and ſickneſſes of the Mind, we are not ſimply to meaſure good by diſtance from evil, becauſe one Vice may in ſome reſpect be more oppoſite to another, than either of them to that Virtue which holdeth the mean between them both. Liberality and Covetouſneſs, the one a Virtue and the other a Vice, are not ſo contrary as the Vices of Covetouſneſs and Prodigality. Religion and Superſtition have more affiance, though the one be Light and the other Darkneſs, than Superſtition and Prophaneneſs, which both are vicious extremities. By means whereof it cometh alſo to paſs, that the mean, which is Virtue, ſeemeth in the eyes of each extreme an extremity; the liberal hearted Man is by the opinion of the Prodigal miſerable, and by the judgment of the Miſerable laviſh: Impiety for the moſt part upbraideth Religion as ſuperſtitious, which Superſtition often accuſeth as impious; both ſo conceiving thereof, becauſe it doth ſeem more to participate each extreme than one extreme doth another, and is by conſequent leſs contrary to either of them, than they mutually between themſelves. Now, if he that ſeeketh to reform Covetouſneſs or Superſtition ſhould but labour to induce the contrary, it were but to draw Men out of lime into coal-duſt: ſo that their courſe, which will remedy the ſuperſtitious abuſe of things profitable in the Church, is not ſtill to aboliſh utterly the uſe thereof, becauſe not uſing at all is moſt oppoſite to ill uſing; but rather, if it may be, to bring them back to a right, perfect and religious uſage, which, albeit leſs contrary to the preſent ſore, is notwithſtanding the better and by many degrees the ſounder way of recovery: and unto this effect, that very precedent itſelf which they propoſe may be beſt followed. For as the Fathers, when the Croſs of Chriſt was in utter contempt,

BOOK V. ſcmpt, did not ſuperſtitiouſly adore the ſame, but rather declare that they ſo eſteemed it as was meet; in like manner where we find the Croſs to have that honour which is due to Chriſt, is it not as lawful for us to retain it in that eſtimation which it ought to have, and in that uſe which it had of old without offence, as by taking it clean away to ſeem followers of their example which cure wilfully by abſciſſion that which they might both preſerve and heal? Touching therefore the Sign and Ceremony of the Croſs, we no way find ourſelves bound to relinquiſh it; neither becauſe the firſt Inventors thereof were but mortal Men; nor leſt the ſenſe and ſignification we give unto it ſhould burden us as Authors of a new Goſpel in the Houſe of God; nor in reſpect of ſome cauſe which the Fathers had more than we have to uſe the ſame; nor, finally, for any ſuch offence or ſcandal as heretofore it hath been ſubject unto by error, now reformed in the minds of Men.

Of Confirmation after Baptiſm.

66. The ancient Cuſtom of the Church was, after they had baptized, to add thereunto Impoſition of Hands with effectual Prayer for the * Illumination of God's moſt Holy Spirit, to confirm and perfect that which the Grace of the ſame Spirit had already begun in Baptiſm. For our means to obtain the Graces which God doth beſtow are our Prayers. Our Prayers to that intent are available as well for others as for ourſelves. To pray for others, is to bleſs them for whom we pray; becauſe Prayer procureth the bleſſing of God upon them, eſpecially the Prayer of ſuch as God either moſt reſpecteth for their piety and zeal that way, or elſe regardeth for that their place and calling bindeth them above others unto this duty, as it doth both by natural and ſpiritual Fathers. With Prayers of ſpiritual and perſonal Benediction the manner hath been in all ages to uſe Impoſition of Hands, as a Ce-

* Caro manus Impoſitione adumbratur, ut et anima Spiritu illuminetur. Tertul. de Reſur. Car.

remony

remony betokening our reſtrained deſires to the party BOOK V.
whom we preſent unto God by Prayer. Thus when Iſrael bleſſed Ephraim and Manaſſes, Joſeph's Sons, Gen. xlviii. 14. he impoſed upon them his hands and prayed; *God, in whoſe ſight my Fathers Abraham and Iſaac did walk; God, which hath fed me all my life long unto this day, and the Angel which hath delivered me from all evil, bleſs theſe Children.* The Prophets which healed diſeaſes by Prayer uſed therein the ſelf-ſame Ceremony. And therefore when Eliſeus willed Naaman to waſh himſelf 2 Kings v. 11. ſeven times in Jordan for cure of his foul diſeaſe, it much offended him; *I thought* (ſaith he) *with myſelf, Surely the Man will come forth, and ſtand, and call upon the Name of the Lord his God, and put his hand on the place, to the end he may ſo heal the Leproſy.* In Con- Num. xxvii. 18. ſecrations and Ordinations of Men unto rooms of divine calling, the like was uſually done from the time of Moſes to Chriſt. Their ſuits that came unto Chriſt Matth. ix. 18. for help were alſo tendered oftentimes, and are ex- Mark v. 23. viii. 22. preſſed in ſuch forms or phraſes of ſpeech, as ſhew that he was himſelf an obſerver of the ſame cuſtom. He which with Impoſition of Hands and Prayer did ſo great Works of Mercy for reſtauration of bodily health, was worthily judged as able to effect the infuſion of Heavenly Grace into them, whoſe age was not yet depraved with that malice which might be ſuppoſed a bar to the goodneſs of God towards them. *They* Matth. xix. 13. *brought him* therefore *young Children to put his Hands* Mark x. 13. *upon them and pray.* After the Aſcenſion of our Lord Luke xviii. 15. and Saviour Jeſus Chriſt, that which he had begun continued in the daily practice of his Apoſtles, whoſe Prayer and Impoſition of Hands were a mean whereby thouſands became partakers of the wonderful gifts of God. The Church had received from Chriſt a promiſe, that ſuch as believed in him, theſe ſigns and tokens ſhould follow them; *To caſt out Devils, to ſpeak* Mark xvi. 17. *with tongues, to drive away ſerpents, to be free from the harm which any deadly poiſon could work, and to cure diſeaſes by Impoſition of Hands.* Which power, common

at

BOOK V. at the firſt in a manner unto all Believers, all Believers had not power to derive or communicate unto all other Men; but whoſoever was the inſtrument of Acts xix. 6. God to inſtruct, convert, and baptize them, the gift of miraculous Operations by the Power of the Holy Ghoſt they had not, but only at the Apoſtles own Acts viii. 17, 18. hands. For which cauſe Simon Magus perceiving that power to be in none but them, and preſuming that they which had it might ſell it, ſought to purchaſe it of them with money. And, as miraculous Graces of the Spirit continued after the Apoſtles' Iren. lib. ii. cap 57. times (*for*, ſaith Irenæus, *they which are truly his Diſciples do*, *in his Name*, *and through Grace received from him*, *ſuch works for the benefit of other Men*, *as every of them is by him enabled to work.—Some caſt out Devils*, *in ſo much*, *as they which are delivered from wicked Spirits have been thereby won unto Chriſt*, *and do conſtantly perſevere in the Church and ſociety of faithful Men*; *ſome excel in the knowledge of things to come*, *in the grace of Viſions from God*, *and the gift of prophetical prediction: ſome by laying on their Hands reſtore them to health*, *which are grievouſly afflicted with ſickneſs*; *yea*, *there are that of dead have been made alive*, *and have afterwards many years converſed with us. What ſhould I ſay? The Gifts are innumerable wherewith God hath enriched his Church throughout the World*, *and by virtue whereof*, *in the Name of Chriſt crucified under Pontius Pilate*, *the Church every day doth many Wonders for the good of Nations*, *neither fraudulently nor in any reſpect of lucre and gain to herſelf*, *but as freely beſtowing*, *as God on her hath beſtowed his divine Graces*): ſo it no where appeareth, that ever any did by Prayer and Impoſition of Hands, ſithence the Apoſtles' times, make others partakers of the like miraculous Gifts and Graces, as long as it pleaſed God to continue the ſame in his Church, but only Biſhops, the Apoſtles' Succeſſors, for a time, even in that power. St. Auguſtin acknowledgeth, that ſuch Gifts were not permitted to laſt always, leſt Men ſhould wax cold with the commonneſs nefs of that, the ftrangenefs whereof at the firft inflamed them. Which words of St. Auguftin, declaring how the vulgar ufe of thefe Miracles was then expired, are no prejudice to the like extraordinary Graces, more rarely obferved in fome, either then or of latter days. Now whereas the Succeffors of the Apoftles had but only for a time fuch power, as by Prayer and Impofition of Hands to beftow the Holy Ghoft; the reafon wherefore Confirmation, neverthelefs, by Prayer and Laying on of Hands hath hitherto always continued is for other very fpecial benefits which the Church thereby enjoyeth. The Fathers every where impute unto it that Gift or Grace of the Holy Ghoft, not which maketh us firft Chriftian Men, but when we are made fuch affifteth us in all virtue, armeth us againft temptation and fin. For, after Baptifm adminiftered, *there followeth* (faith Tertullian) *Impofition of Hands, with invocation and invitation of the Holy Ghoft, which willingly cometh down from the Father, to reft upon the purified and bleffed Bodies, as it were acknowledging the waters of Baptifm a fit feat.* St. Cyprian in more particular manner alluding to that effect of the Spirit, which here efpecially was refpected, *How great* (faith he) *is that power and force wherewith the mind is here* (he meaneth in Baptifm) *enabled, being not only withdrawn from that pernicious hold which the World before had of it, nor only fo purified and made clean, that no ftain or blemifh of the Enemies' invafion doth remain; but over and befides* (namely, through Prayer and Impofition of Hands) *becometh yet greater, yet mightier in ftrength, fo far as to reign with a kind of imperial dominion over the whole band of that roaming and fpoiling Adverfary.* As much is fignified by Eufebius Emiffenus, faying, *The Holy Ghoft which defcendeth with faving influence upon the waters of Baptifm doth there give that fulnefs which fufficeth for innocency, and afterwards exhibiteth in Confirmation an augmentation of further Grace.* The Fathers therefore being thus perfuaded held Confirmation as an

BOOK V.

Auguft de Veri Relig. cap. 25.

Tertul. de Baptil.

Cypr Epift. ii. ad Donat. c. 2

Eufeb Emif Ser. de Pente

Aug de Trin. lib. xv cap 26.
Heb. vi 2.

 an Ordinance Apostolick, always profitable in God's Church, although not always accompanied with equal largeness of those external effects which gave it countenance at the first. The cause of severing Confirmation from Baptism (for most commonly they went together) was sometimes in the Minister, which being of inferior degree, might baptize but not confirm, as in their case it came to pass whom Peter and John did confirm, whereas Philip had before baptized them; and in theirs of whom St. Jerom hath said, *I deny not but the Custom of the Churches is that the Bishop should go abroad, and, imposing his Hands, pray for the gift of the Holy Ghost on them whom Presbyters and Deacons far off, in lesser cities, have already baptized.* Which ancient Custom of the Church St. Cyprian groundeth upon the example of Peter and John in the eighth of the Acts before alledged. *The faithful in Samaria* (saith he) *had already obtained Baptism; only that which was wanting Peter and John supplied by Prayer and Imposition of Hands, to the end the Holy Ghost might be poured upon them. Which also is done amongst ourselves, when they which be already baptized, are brought to the Prelates of the Church to obtain by their Prayer and Imposition of Hands the Holy Ghost.* By this it appeareth, that when the Ministers of Baptism were persons of inferior degree, the Bishops did after confirm whom such had before baptized. Sometimes they which by force of their Ecclesiastical calling might do as well the one as the other, were notwithstanding Men whom Heresy had disjoined from the fellowship of true Believers. Whereupon, when any Man by them baptized and confirmed came afterwards to see and renounce their error, there grew in some Churches very hot contention about the manner of admitting such into the bosom of the true Church, as hath been declared already in the question of Rebaptization. But the generally received Custom was only to admit them with Imposition of Hands and Prayer. Of which Custom, while some imagined the reason to be, for that

Acts viii. 12, 15.

Jer. adverf Lucif. cap. 4.

Cypr. Epist. lxxiii ad Jubajanum.

that Hereticks might give Remiſſion of Sins by Baptiſm, but not the Spirit by Impoſition of Hands, becauſe themſelves had not God's Spirit, and that therefore their Baptiſm might ſtand; but Confirmation muſt be given again; the imbecility of this ground gave Cyprian occaſion to oppoſe himſelf againſt the practice of the Church herein, labouring many ways to prove, that Hereticks could do neither; and conſequently, that their Baptiſm in all reſpects was as fruſtrate as their Chriſm; for the manner of thoſe times was in confirming to uſe anointing. On the other ſide, againſt Luciferians which ratified only the Baptiſm of Hereticks, but diſannulled their Confirmations and Conſecrations, under pretence of the reaſon which hath been before ſpecified, *Hereticks cannot give the Holy Ghoſt*, St. Jerom proveth at large, that if Baptiſm by Hereticks be granted available to Remiſſion of Sins, which no Man receiveth without the Spirit, it muſt needs follow, that the reaſon taken from diſability of beſtowing the Holy Ghoſt was no reaſon wherefore the Church ſhould admit Converts with any new Impoſition of Hands. Notwithſtanding, becauſe it might be objected, that if the gift of the Holy Ghoſt do always join itſelf with true Baptiſm, the Church, which thinketh the Biſhop's Confirmation after other Men's Baptiſm needful for the obtaining of the Holy Ghoſt, ſhould hold an error; St. Jerom hereunto maketh anſwer, that the cauſe of this obſervation is not any abſolute impoſſibility of receiving the Holy Ghoſt by the Sacrament of Baptiſm, unleſs a Biſhop add after it the Impoſition of Hands, but rather a certain congruity and fitneſs to honour Prelacy with ſuch pre-eminences, becauſe the ſafety of the Church dependeth upon the dignity of her chief Superiors, to whom if ſome eminent offices of power above others ſhould not be given, there would be in the Church as many Schiſms as Prieſts. By which anſwer it appeareth his opinion was, that the Holy Ghoſt is received in Baptiſm;

 that

BOOK V that Confirmation is only a sacramental Complement; that the reason why Bishops alone did ordinarily confirm, was not because the benefit, grace and dignity thereof is greater than of Baptism; but rather, for that by the Sacrament of Baptism Men being admitted into God's Church, it was both reasonable and convenient that if he baptize them not unto whom the chiefest authority and charge of their Souls belongeth, yet for honour's sake, and in token of his spiritual superiority over them, because to bless is an act of authority, the performance of this annexed Ceremony should be sought for at his Hands. Now what effect their Imposition of Hands hath, either after Baptism administered by Hereticks or otherwise, St. Jerom in that place hath made no mention, because all Men understood that in Converts it tendeth to the fruits of Repentance, and craveth in behalf of the Penitent such grace as David after his fall desired at the hands of God; in others, the fruit and benefit thereof is that which hath been before shewed. Finally, sometime the cause of severing Confirmation from Baptism was in the Parties that received Baptism being Infants, at which age they might be very well admitted to live in the Family; but because to fight in the Army of God, to discharge the duties of a Christian Man, to bring forth the fruits, and to do the works of the Holy Ghost, their time of ability was not yet come (so that Baptism were not deferred), there could, by stay of their Confirmation, no harm ensue, but rather good. For by this means it came to pass, that Children in expectation thereof were seasoned with the principles of true Religion, before malice and corrupt examples depraved their minds, a good foundation was laid betimes for direction of the course of their whole lives, the seed of the Church of God was preserved sincere and sound, the Prelates and Fathers of God's Family, to whom the cure of their Souls belongeth, saw by trial and examination of them, a part of their own heavy burden discharged, reaped

Heb. vii. 7.

Psal li 10, 11, 12.

reaped comfort by beholding the firſt beginnings of true godlineſs in tender years, glorified him whoſe praiſe they found in the mouths of Infants, and neglected not ſo fit opportunity of giving every one fatherly encouragement and exhortation. Whereunto Impoſition of Hands and Prayer being added, our warrant for the great good effect thereof is the ſame which Patriarchs, Prophets, Prieſts, Apoſtles, Fathers, and Men of God have had for ſuch their particular Invocations and Benedictions, as no Man, I ſuppoſe, profeſſing truth of Religion, will eaſily think to have been without fruit. No, there is no cauſe we ſhould doubt of the benefit, but ſurely great cauſe to make complaint of the deep neglect of this Chriſtian Duty almoſt with all them, to whom, by right of their place and calling, the ſame belongeth. Let them not take it in evil part, the thing is true, their ſmall regard hereunto hath done harm in the Church of God. That which * error raſhly uttereth

* T. C. l. 1. p. 199. Tell me why there ſhould be any ſuch Confirmation in the Church, being brought in by the feigned Decretal Epiſtles of the Popes (this is retracted by the ſame T. C lib iii. pag. 232. That it is ancienter than the feigned Decretal Epiſtles, I yield unto) and no one tittle thereof being once found in the Scripture, and ſeeing that it hath been ſo horribly abuſed, and not neceſſary; why ought it not to be utterly aboliſhed? And thirdly, this Confirmation hath many dangerous points in it. The firſt ſtep of Popery in this Confirmation, is the Laying on of Hands upon the Head of the Child, whereby the opinion of it that it is a Sacrament, is confirmed; eſpecially when as the Prayer doth ſay, that it is done according to the example of the Apoſtles which is a manifeſt untruth, and taken indeed from the Popiſh Confirmation. The ſecond is, for that the Biſhop, as he is called, muſt be the only Miniſter of it; whereby the Popiſh opinion, which eſteemeth it above Baptiſm, is confirmed. For whilſt Baptiſm may be miniſtered of the Miniſter and not Confirmation, but only of the Biſhop, there is a great cauſe of ſuſpicion given to think that Baptiſm is not ſo precious a thing as Confirmation, ſeeing this was one of the principal reaſons whereby that wicked opinion was eſtabliſhed in Popery. I do not here ſpeak of the inconvenience that Men are conſtrained with charges to bring their Children oftentimes half a ſcore miles for that, which if it were needful might be as well

BOOK V. in disgrace of good things, may peradventure be spunged out, when the print of those evils which are grown through neglect will remain behind. Thus much therefore, generally spoken, may serve for answer unto their demands that require us to tell them, *why there should be any such Confirmation in the Church*, seeing we are not ignorant how earnestly they have protested against it; and how directly (although untruly, for so they are content to acknowledge) it hath by some of them been said, *to be first brought in by the feigned decretal Epistles of the Popes*; or, why it should not be *utterly abolished, seeing that no one tittle thereof can be once found in the whole Scrip-*
Heb. vi. 2 *ture*, except the Epistle to the Hebrews be Scripture. And again, seeing that how free soever it be now from abuse, if we look back to the times past which wise Men do always more respect than the present, it hath been abused, and is found at the length no such profitable Ceremony, as the whole silly Church of Christ for the space of these sixteen hundred years hath, through want of experience, imagined. Last of all, seeing also, besides the cruelty which is shewn towards poor country people, who are fain sometimes to let their ploughs stand still, and, with incredible wearisome toil of their feeble bodies, to wander over mountains and through woods, it may be now and then little less than a whole half-score of miles for a Bishop's blessing, *which, if it were needful, might as well be done at home in their own Parishes, rather than they to purchase it with so great loss and so intolerable pain.* There are, they say, in Confirmation, besides

done at home in their own Parishes. The third is, for that the Book saith, a cause of using Confirmation is, that by Imposition of Hands and Prayer, the Children may receive strength and defence against all temptations; whereas there is no promise, that, by the laying on of Hands upon Children, any such Gift shall be given; and it maintaineth the Popish distinction, that the Spirit of God is given at Baptism unto Remission of Sins; and in Confirmation, unto Strength.

this,

this, three terrible points. The firſt is, *Laying on of hands, with pretence that the ſame is done to the example of the Apoſtles*, which is not only, as they ſuppoſe, *a manifeſt untruth* (for all the World doth know that the Apoſtles did never after Baptiſm lay hands on any, and therefore St. Luke, which ſaith they did, was much deceived): but farther alſo, we thereby teach Men to think *Impoſition of Hands a Sacrament*, belike, becauſe it is a principle ingrafted by common light of Nature in the Minds of Men, that all things done by Apoſtolick example muſt needs be Sacraments. The ſecond high point of danger is, *that by tying Confirmation to the Biſhop alone, there is great cauſe of ſuſpicion given to think that Baptiſm is not ſo precious a thing as Confirmation:* for will any Man think that a velvet coat is of more price than a linen coif, knowing the one to be an ordinary garment, the other an ornament which only Serjeants at Law do wear? Finally, to draw to an end of perils, the laſt and the weightieſt hazard is, where the Book itſelf doth ſay, that Children by Impoſition of Hands and Prayer may receive ſtrength againſt all temptation; which ſpeech, as a two-edged ſword, doth both ways dangerouſly wound; partly becauſe it aſcribeth Grace to Impoſition of Hands, whereby we are able no more to aſſure ourſelves in the warrant of any promiſe from God, that his heavenly Grace ſhall be given, than the Apoſtle was that himſelf ſhould obtain Grace by the bowing of his knees to God; and partly, becauſe by uſing the very word *ſtrength* in this matter, a word ſo apt to ſpread infection, we maintain with Popiſh Evangeliſts an old forlorn diſtinction of the Holy Ghoſt beſtowed upon Chriſt's Apoſtles before his Aſcenſion into Heaven, and augmented upon them afterwards; a diſtinction of Grace infuſed into Chriſtian Men by degrees; planted in them at the firſt by Baptiſm, after cheriſhed, watered, and (be it ſpoken without offence) ſtrengthened as by other virtuous offices which

Acts viii. 15, 17.

Epheſ iii. 14.

John xx. 22.

Acts i. 8.

BOOK V which Piety and true Religion teacheth, even ſo by this very ſpecial Benediction whereof we ſpeak, the Rite or Ceremony of Confirmation.

Of the Sacrament of the Body and Blood of Chriſt.

67. The Grace which we have by the holy Euchariſt doth not begin but continue Life. No Man therefore receiveth this Sacrament before Baptiſm, becauſe no dead thing is capable of Nouriſhment. That which groweth muſt of neceſſity firſt live. If our Bodies did not daily waſte, food to reſtore them were a thing ſuperfluous. And it may be that the Grace of Baptiſm would ſerve to eternal life, were it not that the ſtate of our ſpiritual being is daily ſo much hindered and impaired after Baptiſm. In that Life therefore, where neither Body nor Soul can decay, our Souls ſhall as little require this Sacrament, as our Bodies corporal nouriſhment. But as long as the days of our warfare laſt, during the time that we are both ſubject to diminution and capable of augmentation in Grace, the Words of our Lord and Saviour Chriſt will remain forcible, *Except ye eat the Fleſh of the Son of Man, and drink his Blood, ye have no Life in you.* Life being therefore propoſed unto all Men as their end, they, which by Baptiſm have laid the foundation and attained the firſt beginning of a new Life, have here their nouriſhment and food preſcribed for continuance of Life in them. Such as will live the life of God, muſt eat the Fleſh and drink the Blood of the Son of Man, becauſe this is a part of that diet, which if we want we cannot live. Whereas therefore in our Infancy we are incorporated into Chriſt, and by Baptiſm receive the Grace of his Spirit without any ſenſe or feeling of the gift which God beſtoweth; in the Euchariſt we ſo receive the gift of God, that we know by Grace what the Grace is which God giveth us, the degrees of our own increaſe in holineſs and virtue we ſee, and can judge of them; we underſtand that the ſtrength of our Life, begun in Chriſt, is Chriſt; that his Fleſh is Meat, and his Blood Drink, not by ſurmiſed imagination,

John vi. 53

gination, but truly, even ſo truly, that through Faith we perceive in the Body and Blood ſacramentally preſented the very taſte of eternal Life; the Grace of the Sacrament is here as the food which we eat and drink. This was it that ſome did exceedingly fear, leſt Zuinglius and Oecolampadius would bring to paſs that Men ſhould account of this Sacrament but only as of a Shadow, deſtitute, empty, and void of Chriſt. But ſeeing, that, by opening the ſeveral opinions which have been held, they are grown, for ought I can ſee, on all ſides at the length to a general agreement concerning that which alone is material, namely, the real Participation of Chriſt, and of Life in his Body and Blood, by means of this Sacrament; wherefore ſhould the World continue ſtill diſtracted, and rent with ſo manifold contentions, when there remaineth now no controverſy, ſaving only about the ſubject where Chriſt is? Yea, even in this point no ſide denieth, but that the Soul of Man is the receptacle of Chriſt's Preſence. Whereby the Queſtion is yet driven to a narrower iſſue, nor doth any thing reſt doubtful but this; whether, when the Sacrament is adminiſtered, Chriſt be whole within Man only, or elſe his Body and Blood be alſo externally ſeated in the very conſecrated Elements themſelves. Which opinion they that defend, are driven either to conſubſtantiate and incorporate Chriſt with Elements ſacramental, or to tranſubſtantiate and change their ſubſtance into his; and ſo the one to hold him really, but inviſibly, moulded up with the ſubſtance of thoſe Elements; the other to hide him under the only viſible ſhew of Bread and Wine, the ſubſtance whereof, as they imagine, is aboliſhed, and his ſucceeded in the ſame room. All things conſidered, and compared with that ſucceſs which truth hath hitherto had by ſo bitter conflicts with errors in this point, ſhall I wiſh that Men would more give themſelves to meditate with ſilence what we have by the Sacrament, and leſs to diſpute of the manner how? If

BOOK V. any Man ſuppoſe that this were too great ſtupidity and dulneſs, let us ſee whether the Apoſtles of our Lord themſelves have not done the like. It appeareth by many examples, that they of their own diſpoſition were very ſcrupulous and inquiſitive, yea in other caſes of leſs importance, and leſs difficulty, always apt to move queſtions. How cometh it to paſs, that ſo few words of ſo high a Myſtery being uttered, they receive with gladneſs the gift of Chriſt, and make no ſhew of doubt or ſcruple? The reaſon hereof is not dark to them which have any thing at all obſerved how the powers of the Mind are wont to ſtir, when that which we infinitely long for preſenteth itſelf above and beſides expectation. Curious and intricate ſpeculations do hinder, they abate, they quench ſuch inflamed motions of delight and joy as divine Graces uſe to raiſe when extraordinarily they are preſent. The Mind therefore, feeling preſent joy, is always marvellous unwilling to admit any other cogitation, and in that caſe caſteth off thoſe diſputes whereunto the intellectual part at other times eaſily draweth. A manifeſt effect whereof may be noted, if we compare with our Lord's Diſciples, in the twentieth of John, the People that are ſaid in the ſixth of John to have gone after him to Capernaum. Theſe leaving him on the one ſide of the ſea of Tiberias, and finding him again as ſoon as themſelves by ſhip were arrived on the contrary ſide, whither they knew that by ſhip he came not, and by land the journey was longer than according to the time he could have to travel, as they wondered, ſo they aſked alſo, *Rabbi, when cameſt thou hither?* The Diſciples, when Chriſt appeared to them in far more ſtrange and miraculous manner, moved no queſtion, but rejoiced greatly in what they ſaw. For why? The one ſort beheld only that in Chriſt which they knew was more than natural, but yet their affection was not rapt therewith through any great extraordinary gladneſs; the other, when they looked on Chriſt, were

John vi. 26.

were not ignorant that they ſaw the well-ſpring of their own everlaſting felicity; the one, becauſe they enjoyed not, diſputed; the other diſputed not, becauſe they enjoyed. If then the preſence of Chriſt with them did ſo much move, judge what their thoughts and affections were at the time of this new preſentation of Chriſt, not before their eyes, but within their Souls. They had learned before that his Fleſh and Blood are the true cauſe of eternal Life; that this they are not by the bare force of their own ſubſtance, but through the dignity and worth of his Perſon, which offered them up by way of Sacrifice for the Life of the whole World, and doth make them ſtill effectual thereunto: finally, that to us they are Life in particular, by being particularly received. Thus much they knew, although as yet they underſtood not perfectly to what effect or iſſue the ſame would come, till at the length being aſſembled for no other cauſe which they could imagine but to have eaten the Paſſover only, that Moſes appointed, when they ſaw their Lord and Maſter, with hands and eyes lifted up to Heaven, firſt bleſs and conſecrate, for the endleſs good of all Generations till the World's end, the choſen Elements of Bread and Wine; which Elements, made for ever the inſtruments of Life by virtue of his divine Benediction, they being the firſt that were commanded to receive from him, the firſt which were warranted by his promiſe, that not only unto them at the preſent time, but to whomſoever they and their Succeſſors after them did duly adminiſter the ſame, thoſe Myſteries ſhould ſerve as conducts of Life, and conveyances of his Body and Blood unto them; was it poſſible they ſhould hear that voice, *Take, eat, this is my Body; drink ye all of this, this is my blood*; poſſible, that doing what was required, and believing what was promiſed, the ſame ſhould have preſent effect in them, and not fill them with a kind of fearful admiration at the Heaven which they ſaw in themſelves? They had at that time a ſea of comfort and joy to wade in,

and

BOOK V. and we by that which they did are taught that this Heavenly Food is given for the satisfying of our empty Souls, and not for the exercising of our curious and subtile wits. If we doubt what those admirable Words may import, let him be our Teacher for the meaning of Christ, to whom Christ was himself a School-master; let our Lord's Apostle be his Interpreter, content we ourselves with his explication; My Body, *the Communion of my Body:* my Blood, *the Communion of my Blood.* Is there any thing more expedite, clear and easy, than that as Christ is termed our Life, because through him we obtain Life; so the parts of this Sacrament are his Body and Blood, for that they are so to us; who receiving them, receive that by them which they are termed? The Bread and Cup are his Body and Blood, because they are causes instrumental, upon the receipt whereof the Participation of his Body and Blood ensueth. For that which produceth any certain effect, is not vainly nor improperly said to be that very effect whereunto it tendeth. Every cause is in the effect which groweth from it. Our Souls and Bodies quickened to eternal Life are effects, the cause whereof is the Person of Christ: his Body and Blood are the true well-spring out of which this Life floweth. So that his Body and Blood are in that very subject whereunto they minister Life; not only by effect or operation, even as the influence of the Heavens is in Plants, Beasts, Men, and in every thing which they quicken; but also by a far more divine and mystical kind of Union, which maketh us one with him, even as he and the Father are one. The real Presence of Christ's most Blessed Body and Blood is not therefore to be sought for in the Sacrament, but in the worthy Receiver of the Sacrament. And with this the very order of our Saviour's Words agreeth, first, *Take and eat;* then, *This is my Body which was broken for you:* First, *Drink ye all of this;* then followeth, *This is my Blood of the New Testament, which is shed for many for the Remission of*

Mark xiv. 22.

of Sins. I ſee not which way it ſhould be gathered by the Words of Chriſt when and where the Bread is his Body, or the Cup, his Blood; but only in the very Heart and Soul of him which receiveth them. As for the Sacraments, they really exhibit, but for aught we can gather out of that which is written of them they are not really, nor do really contain in themſelves that Grace which with them, or by them, it pleaſeth God to beſtow. If on all ſides it be confeſſed that the Grace of Baptiſm is poured into the Soul of Man; that by Water we receive it, although it be neither ſeated in the Water, nor the Water changed into it; what ſhould induce Men to think, that the Grace of the Euchariſt muſt needs be in the Euchariſt before it can be in us that receive it? The fruit of the Euchariſt is the Participation of the Body and Blood of Chriſt. There is no ſentence of holy Scripture which ſaith, that we cannot by this Sacrament be made Partakers of his Body and Blood, except they be firſt contained in the Sacrament, or the Sacrament converted into them. *This is my Body*, and *This is my Blood*, being words of promiſe, ſith we all agree, that by the Sacrament Chriſt doth really and truly in us perform his promiſe, why do we vainly trouble ourſelves with ſo fierce contentions, whether by Conſubſtantiation, or elſe by Tranſubſtantiation the Sacrament itſelf be firſt poſſeſſed with Chriſt, or no? A thing which no way can either further or hinder us, howſoever it ſtand, becauſe our Participation of Chriſt in this Sacrament dependeth on the co-operation of his omnipotent power which maketh it his Body and Blood to us, whether with change or without alteration of the Element, ſuch as they imagine, we need not greatly to care or enquire. Take therefore that wherein all agree, and then conſider by itſelf what cauſe why the reſt in queſtion ſhould not rather be left as ſuperfluous than urged as neceſſary. It is on all ſides plainly confeſſed, firſt, that this Sacrament is a true and a real Participation of Chriſt, who thereby

thereby imparteth himſelf, even his whole intire Perſon, *as a myſtical Head* unto every Soul that receiveth him, and that every ſuch Receiver doth thereby incorporate or unite himſelf unto Chriſt *as a myſtical Member* of him, yea of them alſo whom he acknowledgeth to be his own. Secondly, that to whom *the Perſon of Chriſt* is thus communicated, to them he giveth by the ſame Sacrament his holy Spirit to ſanctify them, as it ſanctifieth him which is their Head. Thirdly, that what *merit, force, or virtue ſoever there is in his Sacred Body and Blood*, we freely, fully and wholly have it by this Sacrament. Fourthly, that *the effect thereof in us, is a real tranſmutation of our Souls and Bodies* from ſin to Righteouſneſs, from death and corruption to Immortality and Life. Fifthly, that becauſe the Sacrament being of itſelf but a corruptible and earthly creature, muſt needs be thought an unlikely inſtrument to work ſo admirable effects in Man, we are therefore to reſt ourſelves altogether upon *the ſtrength of his glorious Power*, who is able and will bring to paſs, that the Bread and Cup which he giveth us ſhall be truly the thing he promiſeth. It ſeemeth therefore much amiſs, that againſt them whom they term Sacramentaries ſo many invective diſcourſes are made, all running upon two points, that the Euchariſt is not a bare ſign or figure only, and that the efficacy of his Body and Blood is not all we receive in this Sacrament. For no Man, having read their Books and Writings which are thus traduced, can be ignorant that both theſe aſſertions they plainly confeſs to be moſt true. They do not ſo interpret the Words of Chriſt, as if the name of his Body did import but the figure of his Body; and to be, were only to ſignify his Blood. They grant that theſe holy Myſteries, received in due manner, do inſtrumentally both make us partakers of the Grace of that Body and Blood which were given for the Life of the World, and beſides alſo impart unto us, even in true and real, though myſtical manner, the very Perſon of

our

our Lord himſelf, whole, perfect and entire, as hath been ſhewed. Now whereas all three opinions do thus far accord in one, that ſtrong conceit which two of the three have embraced, as touching a literal, corporal and oral manducation of the very Subſtance of his Fleſh and Blood, is ſurely an opinion no where delivered in holy Scripture, whereby they ſhould think themſelves bound to believe it; and (to ſpeak with the ſofteſt terms we can uſe) greatly prejudiced in that, when ſome others did ſo conceive of eating his Fleſh, our Saviour, to abate that error in them, gave them directly to underſtand how his Fleſh ſo eaten could profit them nothing, becauſe the words which he ſpake were Spirit; that is to ſay, they had a reference to a myſtical Participation; which myſtical Participation giveth Life. Wherein there is ſmall appearance of likelihood that his meaning ſhould be only to make them Marcionites by inverſion, and to teach them, that as Marcion did think Chriſt ſeemed to be Man, but was not; ſo they contrariwiſe ſhould believe that Chriſt in truth would ſo give them, as they thought, his Fleſh to eat; but yet, leſt the horror thereof ſhould offend them, he would not ſeem to do that he did. When they which have this opinion of Chriſt in that bleſſed Sacrament go about to explain themſelves, and to open after what manner things are brought to paſs, the one ſort lay the union of Chriſt's Deity with his Manhood, as their firſt foundation and ground: from thence they infer a power which the Body of Chriſt hath, thereby to preſent itſelf in all places; out of which Ubiquity of his Body they gather the preſence thereof with that ſanctified Bread and Wine of our Lord's table; the Conjunction of his Body and Blood with thoſe Elements they uſe as an argument to ſhew how the Bread may as well in that reſpect be termed his Body, becauſe his Body is therewith joined, as the Son of God may be named Man, by reaſon that God and Man in the Perſon of Chriſt are united; to this they add, how the Words of of Chriſt commanding us to eat muſt needs import, that as he hath coupled the Subſtance of his Fleſh and the Subſtance of Bread together, ſo we together ſhould receive both; which labyrinth as the other ſort doth juſtly ſhun, ſo the way which they take to the ſame inn is ſomewhat more ſhort, but no whit more certain. For through God's omnipotent power they imagine that Tranſubſtantiation followeth upon the Words of Conſecration; and, upon Tranſubſtantiation, the Participation of Chriſt's both Body and Blood, in the only ſhape of ſacramental Elements. So that they all three do plead God's Omnipotency; Sacramentaries, to that alteration which the reſt confeſs he accompliſheth; the Patrons of Tranſubſtantiation, over and beſides that, to the change of one Subſtance into another; the Followers of Conſubſtantiation, to the kneading of both Subſtances, as it were, into one lump. Touching the ſentence of Antiquity in this cauſe; firſt, for as much as they knew that the force of this Sacrament doth neceſſarily preſuppoſe the verity of Chriſt's both Body and Blood, they uſed oftentimes the ſame as an argument to prove, that Chriſt hath as truly the Subſtance of Man as of God, becauſe here we receive Chiſt, and thoſe Graces which flow from him, in that he is Man. So that if he have no ſuch being, neither can the Sacrament have any ſuch meaning as we all confeſs it hath. Thus * Tertullian, thus † Irenæus, thus

* Acceptum panem et diſtributum diſcipulis Corpus ſuum illum fecit, hoc eſt Corpus meum dicendo, id eſt figura corporis mei. Figura autem non fuiſſet niſi veritatis eſſet Corpus, cum vacua res quod eſt phantaſma figuram capere non poſſit. Tertul. contra Marc lib. iv. cap 40.

† Secundum hæc (that is to ſay, if it ſhould be true which Hereticks have taught, denying that Chriſt took upon him the very nature of Man) nec Dominus ſanguine ſuo redemit nos, neque calix Euchariſtiæ communicatio ſanguinis ejus erit, nec panis quem frangimus communicatio corporis ejus eſt. Sanguis enim non eſt, niſi a venis et carnibus et a reliqua quæ eſt ſecundum hominem ſubſtantia. Iren. lib. v. cap. 1.

Theodoret

* Theodoret disputeth. Again, as evident it is how they teach that Christ is personally there present, yea present whole, albeit a part of Christ be corporally absent from thence, that † Christ, assisting this heavenly Banquet with his personal and true Presence, ‡ doth by his own divine power add to the natural substance thereof supernatural efficacy, which § addition to the nature of those consecrated elements changeth them, and maketh them that unto us which otherwise they could not be, that to us they are thereby made such instruments, as ** mystically yet

* Ἐι τοίνυν τȣ̃ ὄντος σώματος ἀντίτυπά ἐςὶ τὰ θεῖα μυςήρια, σῶμα ἄρα ἐςὶ καὶ νῦν τȣ̃ δεσπότου τὸ σῶμα, ȣ̓κ εἰς θεότητος φύσιν μεταβληθὲν ἀλλὰ θείας δόξης ἀναπλησθέν. Theod. Dial. Ἀσύγχυτος.

† Sacramenta quidem quantum in se est sine propria virtute esse non possunt, nec ullo modo se absentat majestas mysteriis. Cypr. de Cœn. cap. vii.

‡ Sacramento visibili ineffabiliter divina se infundit essentia ut esset Religioni circa Sacramenta devotio. Idem cap. vi. Invisibilis Sacerdos visibiles creaturas in substantiam corporis et sanguinis sui verbo suo secreta potestate convertit. In spiritualibus Sacramentis, verbi præcipit virtus et servit effectus. Euseb. Emissen. Hom. v. de Pasch.

§ Τὰ σύμβολα τȣ̃ δεσποτικȣ̃ σώματός τε καὶ αἵματος ἄλλα μὲν εἰσὶ πρὸ τῆς ἱερατικῆς ἐπικλήσεως, μετὰ δὲ γε τὴν ἐπίκλησιν μεταβάλλεται καὶ ἕτερα γίνεται. Ἀλλ' ȣ̓κ οἰκείας ἐξίςαται φύσεως. Μένει γὰρ ἐπι τῆς προτέρας ȣ̓σίας καὶ τȣ̃ σχήματος καὶ τȣ̃ εἴδους, κ̀ ὁρατὰ ἐςι καὶ ἁπτὰ οἷα καὶ πρότερον ἦν, νοεῖται δὲ ἅπερ ἐγένετο καὶ πιςεύεται καὶ προσκυνεῖται ὡς ἐκεῖνα ὄντα ἅπερ πιςεύεται. Theodor.. Ex quo a Domino dictum est, hoc facite in meam commemorationem, Hæc est caro mea, et hic est sanguis meus, quotiescunque his verbis et hac fide actum est, panis iste supersubstantialis, et calix benedictione solenni sacratus, ad totius hominis vitam salutemque proficit. Cypr. de Cœn. cap. iii. Immortalitatis alimonia datur, a communibus cibis differens, corporalis substantiæ retinens speciem, sed virtutis divinæ invisibili efficientia probans adesse præsentiam. Ibid cap. ii.

** Sensibilibus Sacramentis inest vitæ æternæ effectus, et non tam corporali quam spirituali transitione Christo unimur. Ipse enim et panis et caro, et sanguis, idem cibus, et substantia et vita factus est Ecclesiæ suæ quam corpus suum appellat, dans ei participationem spiritus. Ibid cap. v. Nostra et ipsius conjunctio nec miscet personas, nec unit substantias, sed effectus consociat et confœderat voluntates. Ibid cap. vi. Mansio nostra in ipso est manducatio, et potus quasi quædam incorporatio. Ibid cap. ix. Ille

BOOK V. truly, invisibly yet really work our Communion or Fellowship with the Person of Jesus Christ, as well in that he is Man as God, our Participation also in the fruit, grace and efficacy of his Body and Blood; whereupon there ensueth a kind of Transubstantiation in us, a true * change both of Soul and Body, an alteration from Death to Life. In a Word, it appeareth not, that of all the ancient Fathers of the Church any one did ever conceive or imagine other than only a mystical Participation of Christ's both Body and Blood in the Sacrament; neither are their speeches concerning the change of the Elements themselves into the Body and Blood of Christ such, that a Man can thereby in conscience assure himself it was their meaning to persuade the World, either of a corporal Consubstantiation of Christ with those sanctified and blessed Elements before we receive them, or of the like Transubstantiation of them into the Body and Blood of Christ. Which both to our mystical Communion with Christ are so unnecessary, that the Fathers who plainly hold but this mystical Communion, cannot easily be thought to have meant any other change of sacramental Elements,

est in Patre per naturam Divinitatis, nos in eo per corporalem ejus Nativitatem, ille rursus in nobis per Sacramentorum mysterium. Hilar. de Trin lib viii.

* Panis hic azymus cibus verus et sincerus per speciem et Sacramentum nos tactu sanctificat, fide illuminat, veritate Christo conformat Cypr. de Cœn cap. vi. Non aliud agit participatio corporis et sanguinis Christi, quam ut in id quod sumimus transeamus, et in quo mortui et sepulti et corresuscitati sumus, ipsum per omnia et spiritu et carne gestemus. Leo de Pasch Serm. xiv. Quemadmodum qui est a terra panis percipiens Dei vocationem (id est facta invocatione divini numinis) jam non communis panis est, sed Eucharistia ex duabus rebus constans, terrena et cœlesti, sic et corpora nostra percipientia Eucharistiam, jam non sunt corruptibilia, spem resurrectionis habentia. Iren. lib. iv. cap. 34. Quoniam salutaris caro verbo Dei quod naturaliter vita est conjuncta, vivifica effecta est; quando eam comedimus, tunc vitam habemus in nobis; illi carni conjuncti, quæ vita effecta est. Cyril. in Johan. lib. iv. cap. 14.

than

than that which the same spiritual Communion did BOOK V. require them to hold. These things considered, how should that Mind which, loving Truth and seeking comfort out of holy Mysteries, hath not perhaps the leisure, perhaps not the wit nor capacity to tread out so endless mazes as the intricate disputes of this cause have led Men into, how should a virtuously disposed Mind better resolve with itself than thus? *Variety of judgments and opinions argueth obscurity in those things whereabout they differ. But that which all parts receive for Truth, that which every one having sifted, is by no one denied or doubted of, must needs be matter of infallible certainty. Whereas therefore there are but three expositions made of*, This is my Body; *the first, this is in itself before Participation really and truly the natural Substance of my Body, by reason of the co-existence which my omnipotent Body hath with the sanctified Element of Bread, which is the Lutherans' interpretation; the second, this is in itself and before Participation the very true and natural Substance of my Body, by force of that Deity, which with the words of Consecration abolisheth the Substance of Bread, and substituteth in the place thereof my Body, which is the Popish construction; the last, this hallowed Food, through concurrence of Divine Power, is in verity and truth, unto faithful Receivers, instrumentally a cause of that mystical Participation, whereby as I make myself wholly theirs, so I give them in hand an actual possession of all such saving Grace as my sacrificed Body can yield, and as their Souls do presently need, this is to them, and in them, my Body; of these three rehearsed interpretations, the last hath in it nothing but what the rest do all approve and acknowledge to be most true; nothing but that which the Words of Christ are on all sides confessed to enforce; nothing but that which the Church of God hath always thought necessary; nothing but that which alone is sufficient for every Christian Man to believe concerning the use and force of this Sacrament; finally, nothing but that wherewith the Writings of all Antiquity are consonant, and all Christian Confessions agreeable. And as Truth*

BOOK V. *Truth, in what kind ſoever, is by no kind of Truth gainſaid, ſo the Mind, which reſteth itſelf on this, is never troubled with thoſe perplexities which the other do find, by means of ſo great contradiction between their opinions and true principles of Reaſon grounded upon Experience, Nature, and Senſe. Which albeit, with boiſterous courage and breath, they ſeem oftentimes to blow away; yet whoſo obſerveth how again they labour and ſweat by ſubtilty of wit to make ſome ſhew of agreement between their peculiar conceits and the general edicts of Nature, muſt needs perceive they ſtruggle with that which they cannot fully maſter. Beſides, ſith of that which is proper to themſelves, their diſcourſes are hungry and unpleaſant, full of tedious and irkſome labour, heartleſs, and hitherto without fruit; on the other ſide, read we them or hear we others, be they of our own or of antienter times, to what part ſoever they be thought to incline, touching that whereof there is controverſy; yet in this, where they all ſpeak but one thing, their diſcourſes are heavenly, their words ſweet as the honey-comb, their tongues melodiouſly tuned inſtruments, their ſentences mere conſolation and joy, are we not hereby, almoſt even with voice from heaven, admoniſhed which we may ſafelieſt cleave unto? He which hath ſaid of the one Sacrament,* Waſh and be clean, *hath ſaid concerning the other likewiſe,* Eat and live. *If therefore, without any ſuch particular and ſolemn warrant as this is, that poor diſtreſſed Woman, coming unto Chriſt for health, could ſo conſtantly reſolve herſelf,* May I but touch the ſkirt of his Garment, I ſhall be whole, *what moveth us to argue of the manner how Life ſhould come by Bread, our duty being here but to take what is offered, and moſt aſſuredly to reſt perſuaded of this, that can we but eat, we are ſafe? When I behold with mine eyes ſome ſmall and ſcarce diſcernible grain or ſeed, whereof Nature maketh a promiſe that a tree ſhall come; and when afterwards of that tree any ſkilful Artificer undertaketh to frame ſome exquiſite and curious work, I look for the event, I move no queſtion about performance either of the one, or of the other. Shall*

I ſimply

I simply credit Nature in things natural? Shall I in things artificial rely myself on art, never offering to make doubt? and in that which is above both Art and Nature refuse to believe the Author of both, except he acquaint me with his ways, and lay the secret of his skill before me? Where God himself doth speak those things which, either for height and sublimity of the matter, or else for secresy of performance, we are not able to reach unto, as we may be ignorant without danger, so it can be no disgrace to confess we are ignorant. Such as love piety will, as much as in them lieth, know all things that God commandeth, but especially the duties of service which they owe to God. As for his dark and hidden Works, they prefer, as becometh them in such cases, simplicity of Faith before that Knowledge, which, curiously sifting what it should adore, and disputing too boldly of that which the wit of Man cannot search, chilleth for the most part all warmth of zeal, and bringeth soundness of belief many times into great hazard Let it therefore be sufficient for me, presenting myself at the Lord's Table, to know what there I receive from him, without searching or enquiring of the manner how Christ performeth his promise; let disputes and questions, enemies to piety, abatements of true devotion, and hitherto in this cause but over-patiently heard, let them take their rest; let curious and sharp-witted Men beat their heads about what questions themselves will; the very letter of the Word of Christ giveth plain security, that these Mysteries do, as nails, fasten us to his very Cross, that by them we draw out, as touching efficacy, force, and virtue, even the blood of his gored side; in the wounds of our Redeemer we there dip our tongues, we are dyed red both within and without; our hunger is satisfied, and our thirst for ever quenched; they are things wonderful which he feeleth, great which he seeth, and unheard of which he uttereth, whose Soul is possessed of this Paschal Lamb, and made joyful in the strength of this new Wine; this Bread hath in it more than the Substance which our eyes behold, this Cup hallowed with solemn Benediction availeth to the

BOOK V.

 endless life and welfare both of Soul and Body; in that it serveth as well for a medicine to heal our Infirmities and purge our Sins, as for a Sacrifice of Thanksgiving; with touching it sanctifieth, it enlighteneth with belief, it truly conformeth us unto the image of Jesus Christ. What these Elements are in themselves, it skilleth not; it is enough, that to me which take them they are the Body and Blood of Christ, his promise in witness hereof sufficeth; his word he knoweth which way to accomplish; why should any cogitation possess the mind of a faithful Communicant but this, O my God, thou are true; O my Soul, thou art happy! Thus therefore we see, that howsoever Men's opinions do otherwise vary; nevertheless, touching Baptism and the Supper of our Lord, we may with one consent of the whole Christian World conclude they are necessary, the one to initiate or begin, the other to consummate or make perfect our Life in Christ.

Of Faults noted in the Form of administering the holy Communion.

68. In administering the Sacrament of the Body and Blood of Christ, the supposed faults of the Church of England are not greatly material, and therefore it shall suffice to touch them in few words. *The first is, that we do not use in a generality once for all to say to Communicants,* Take, eat, and drink; *but unto every particular Person,* Eat thou, drink thou, *which is according to the Popish manner, and not the Form that our Saviour did use. Our second oversight is, by gesture. For in kneeling there hath been superstition, sitting agreeth better to the action of a Supper; and our Saviour, using that which was most fit, did himself not kneel. A third accusation is, for not examining all Communicants, whose knowledge in the Mystery of the Gospel should that way be made manifest; a thing every where, they say, used in the Apostles' times, because all things necessary were used; and this in their opinion is necessary, yea it is commanded, inasmuch as the Levites are commanded to prepare the People for the Passover;* (2 Chron. xxxv. 6.) *and Examination is a part of their preparation, our Lord's Supper in place of the Passover. The fourth thing misliked*

misliked is, that against the Apostle's prohibition, to have any familiarity at all with notorious Offenders, Papists being not of the Church are admitted to our very Communion, before they have by their religious and gospel-like behaviour purged themselves of that suspicion of Popery which their former life hath caused. They are dogs, swine, unclean beasts, Foreigners and Strangers from the Church of God; and therefore ought not to be admitted, though they offer themselves. We are, fifthly, condemned, inasmuch as when there have been store of People to hear Sermons and Service in the Church, we suffer the Communion to be ministered to a few. It is not enough, that our Book of Common-Prayer hath godly exhortations to move all thereunto which are present. For it should not suffer a few to communicate, it should by Ecclesiastical Discipline and civil punishment provide that such as would withdraw themselves might be brought to communicate, according both to the Law of God and the ancient Church Canons. In the sixth and last place, cometh the enormity of imparting this Sacrament privately unto the Sick. Thus far accused, we answer briefly to the first, * that seeing God by Sacraments doth apply in particular unto every Man's Person the Grace which himself hath provided for the benefit of all Mankind, there is no cause why administering the Sacraments we should forbear to express that in our forms of speech, which he by his Word and Gospel teacheth all to believe. In the one Sacrament, *I baptize thee*, displeaseth them not. If, *Eat thou*, in the other offend them, their fancies are no

BOOK V.

1 Cor. v. 11.

Num. ix. 13. Can ix. Apost Concil 11 Brac. cap. 83.

* T. C. lib iii. pag. 166. Besides that it is good to leave the Popish form in those things, which we may so conveniently do, it is best to come as near the manner of celebration of the Supper which our Saviour Christ did use, as may be And if it be a good argument to prove that therefore we must rather say, *Take thou*, than *Take ye*, because the Sacrament is an application of the Benefits of Christ, it behoveth that the Preacher should direct his admonitions particularly, one after another, unto all those which hear his Sermon, which is a thing absurd.

BOOK V. rules for Churches to follow. Whether Chriſt at his laſt Supper did ſpeak generally once to all, or to every one in particular, is a thing uncertain. His Words are recorded in that form which ſerveth beſt for the ſetting down with hiſtorical brevity what was ſpoken; they are no manifeſt proof that he ſpake but once unto all which did then communicate, much leſs that we in ſpeaking unto every Communicant ſeverally do amiſs, although it were clear that we herein do otherwiſe than Chriſt did. Our imitation of him conſiſteth not in tying ſcrupulouſly ourſelves unto his ſyllables, but rather in ſpeaking by the heavenly direction of that inſpired Divine Wiſdom, which teaches divers ways to one end; and doth therein controul their boldneſs, by whom any profitable way is cenſured as reprovable, only under colour of ſome ſmall difference from great examples going before. To do throughout every the like circumſtance the ſame which Chriſt did in this action, were, by following his footſteps in that ſort, to err more from the purpoſe he aimed at, than we now do by not following them with ſo nice and ſevere ſtrictneſs. They little weigh with themſelves how dull, how heavy, and almoſt how without ſenſe, the greateſt part of the common Multitude every where is, who think it either unmeet or unneceſſary to put them, even Man by Man, eſpecially at that time, in mind whereabout they are. It is true, that in Sermons we do not uſe to repeat our ſentences ſeverally to every particular Hearer; a ſtrange madneſs it were if we ſhould. The ſoftneſs of wax may induce a wiſe Man to ſet his ſtamp or image therein; it perſuadeth no Man, that becauſe wool hath the like quality, it may therefore receive the like impreſſion. So the reaſon taken from the uſe of Sacraments, in that they are inſtruments of Grace unto every particular Man, may with good congruity lead the Church to frame accordingly her words in Adminiſtration of Sacraments, becauſe they eaſily admit

this

this form; which being in Sermons a thing impossible, without apparent ridiculous absurdity, agreement of Sacraments with Sermons, in that which is alledged as a reasonable proof of conveniency for the one, proveth not the same allegation impertinent, because it doth not enforce the other to be administered in like sort. For equal principles do then avail unto equal conclusions, when the matter whereunto we apply them is equal, and not else. * Our kneeling at Communions is the gesture of Piety. If we did there present ourselves but to make some shew or dumb resemblance of a spiritual Feast, it may be that sitting were the fitter ceremony; but coming as Receivers of inestimable Grace at the Hands of God, what doth better beseem our Bodies at that hour, than to be sensible witnesses of Minds unfeignedly humbled? Our Lord himself did that which custom and long usage had made fit; we, that which fitness and great decency hath made usual. The trial of ourselves, before we eat of this Bread, and drink of this Cup, is, by express commandment, every Man's precise duty. As for necessity of calling others unto account besides ourselves, albeit we be not thereunto drawn by any great strength which is in their arguments, who first press us with it as a thing necessary, by affirming that the Apostles did use it, and then prove the † Apostles to have used it, by affirming it to be necessary; again, albeit we greatly muse how they can avouch that God did command the Levites

* T C lib 1. pag. 165. Kneeling carrieth a shew of worship; sitting agreeth better with the action of the Supper. Christ and his Apostles kneeled not.

† T. C. lib. 1. pag. 164. All things necessary were used in the Churches of God in the Apostles' times; but Examination was a necessary thing, therefore used. In the Book of Chronicles, 2 Chron. xxxv. 6. the Levites were commanded to prepare the People to the receiving of the Passover, in place whereof we have the Lord's Supper. Now Examination being a part of preparation, it followeth that here is commandment of the Examination.

BOOK V. to prepare their Brethren against the Feast of the Passover, and that the Examination of them was a part of their Preparation. when the place alledged to this purpose doth but charge the Levite, saying, *Make ready* Laahhechem *for your Brethren*, to the end they may do according to the Word of the Lord by Moses: wherefore in the self-same place it followeth, how lambs, and kids, and sheep, and bullocks were delivered unto the Levites, and that thus the service was made ready, it followeth likewise, how the Levites having in such sort provided for the People, they made provision for themselves, *and for the Priests, the Sons of Aaron:* so that confidently from hence to conclude the necessity of Examination, argueth their wonderful great forwardness in framing all things to serve their turn; nevertheless, the Examination of Communicants when need requireth, for the profitable use it may have in such cases, we reject not. Our fault in admitting Popish Communicants, is it in that we are forbidden to eat, and therefore much more to communicate with notorious Malefactors? The name of a Papist is not given unto any Man for being a notorious Malefactor: and the Crime wherewith we are charged, is suffering Papists to communicate; so that, be their life and conversation whatsoever in the sight of Man, their Popish opinions are in this case laid as bars and exceptions against them; yea, those opinions which they have held in former times, * although they now both profess by word, and offer to shew by fact the contrary. All this doth not justify us, which ought not (they say) to admit them in any wise, till their gospel-like behaviour have removed all suspicion of Popery from them, because Papists are *dogs*,

1 Cor. v. 11. T. C. lib. 1 pag. 167.

* Although they would receive the Communion, yet they ought to be kept back, until such time as, by their religious and gospel-like behaviour, they have purged themselves of that suspicion of Popery which their former life and conversation hath caused to be conceived. T. C. lib. i. pag. 167.

swine,

ſwine, beaſts, Foreigners and Strangers from the Houſe of God; in a word, *they are not of the Church.* What the Terms of goſpel-like behaviour may include, is obſcure and doubtful, but of the viſible Church of Chriſt in this preſent World, from which they ſeparate all Papiſts, we are thus perſuaded. Church is a word which art hath deviſed, thereby to ſever and diſtinguiſh that Society of Men, which profeſſeth the true Religion, from the reſt which profeſs it not. There have been in the World, from the very firſt foundation thereof, but three Religions, Paganiſm, which lived in the blindneſs of corrupt and depraved Nature; Judaiſm, embracing the Law which reformed heatheniſh impieties, and taught Salvation to be looked for through One, whom God in the laſt days would ſend, and exalt to be Lord of all. Finally, Chriſtian Belief, which yieldeth obedience to the Goſpel of Jeſus Chriſt, and acknowledgeth him the Saviour whom God did promiſe. Seeing then that the Church is a name, which art hath given to Profeſſors of true Religion, as they which will define a Man, are to paſs by thoſe qualities wherein one Man doth excel another, and to take only thoſe eſſential Properties whereby a Man doth differ from Creatures of other kinds, ſo he that will teach what the Church is, ſhall never rightly perform the work whereabout he goeth, till in matter of Religion he touch that difference which ſevereth the Church's Religion from theirs who are not the Church. Religion being therefore a matter partly of contemplation, partly of action; we muſt define the Church, which is a religious Society, by ſuch differences as do properly explain the eſſence of ſuch things, that is to ſay, by the object or matter whereabout the Contemplations and Actions of the Church are properly converſant. For ſo all Knowledges and all Virtues are defined. Whereupon, becauſe the only object which ſeparateth ours from other Religions, is Jeſus Chriſt, in whom none but the Church doth believe;

and

BOOK V. and whom none but the Church doth worſhip; we find that accordingly the Apoſtles do every where diſtinguiſh hereby the Church from Infidels and from Jews, *accounting them which call upon the Name of our Lord Jeſus Chriſt to be his Church.* If we go lower, we ſhall but add unto this certain caſual and variable accidents which are not properly of the being, but make only for the happier and better being of the Church of God, either in deed, or in Men's opinions and conceits. This is the error of all Popiſh definitions that hitherto have been brought. They define not the Church by that which the Church eſſentially is, but by that wherein they imagine their own more perfect than the reſt are. Touching parts of eminency and perfection, parts likewiſe of imperfection and defect in the Church of God, they are infinite, their degrees and differences no way poſſible to be drawn unto any certain account. There is not the leaſt contention and variance, but it blemiſheth

Rom xv. 5. 1 Cor. i. 10.

ſomewhat the Unity that ought to be in the Church of Chriſt, which notwithſtanding may have not only without offence or breach of concord her manifold varieties in Rites and Ceremonies of Religion, but alſo her ſtrifes and contentions many times, and that about matters of no ſmall importance, yea, her Schiſms, Factions, and ſuch other evils whereunto the Body of the Church is ſubject, ſound and ſick remaining both of the ſame Body, as long as both parts retain by outward profeſſion that vital ſubſtance of Truth, which maketh Chriſtian Religion to differ from theirs which acknowledge not our Lord Jeſus Chriſt, the Bleſſed Saviour of Mankind, give no credit to his glorious Goſpel, and have his Sacraments, the ſeals of eternal Life, in deriſion. Now the privilege of the viſible Church of God (for of that we ſpeak) is to be herein like the Ark of Noah, that, for any thing we know to the contrary, all without it are loſt Sheep; yet in this was the Ark of Noah privileged above the Church, that whereas none

none of them which were in the one could perish, BOOK V.
numbers in the other are cast away, because to eternal Life our Profession is not enough. Many things exclude from the Kingdom of God, although from the Church they separate not. In the Church there arise sundry grievous storms, by means whereof whole Kingdoms and Nations professing Christ, both have been heretofore, and are at this present day divided about Christ. During which divisions and contentions amongst Men, albeit each part do justify itself, yet the one of necessity must needs err, if there be any contradiction between them, be it great or little; and what side soever it be that hath the truth, the 1 John ii. 19.
same we must also acknowledge alone to hold with the true Church in that point, and consequently the other as an Enemy, in that case fallen away from the true Church. Wherefore of Hypocrites and Dissemblers, whose profession at the first was but only from the teeth outward, when they afterwards took occasion to oppugn certain principal Articles of Faith, the Apostles which defended the Truth against them, pronounce them gone out from the Fellowship of sound and sincere Believers, when as yet the Christian Religion they had not utterly cast off. In like sense and meaning throughout all ages, Hereticks have justly been hated as branches cut off from the body of the true Vine; yet only so far forth cut off as their Heresies have extended. Both Heresy, and many other crimes which wholly sever from God, do sever from the Church of God in part only. The Mystery of Piety, saith the Apostle, is without peradventure great, *God hath been manifested in the* 1 Tim. iii. 16.
Flesh, hath been justified in the Spirit, hath been seen of Angels, hath been preached to Nations, hath been believed on in the World, hath been taken up into Glory. The Church a pillar and foundation of this Truth, which no where is known or professed but only within the Church, and they all of the Church that profess it. In the mean while, it cannot be denied, that

many

BOOK V many profeſs this who are not therefore cleared ſimply from all, either faults or errors, which make ſeparation between us and the well-ſpring of our happineſs. Idolatry ſevered of old the Iſraelites, iniquity, thoſe Scribes and Phariſees from God, who notwithſtanding were a part of the Seed of Abraham, a part of that very Seed which God did himſelf acknowledge to be his Church. The Church of God may therefore contain both them which indeed are not his, yet muſt be reputed his by us that know not their inward thoughts, and them, whoſe apparent wickedneſs teſtifieth even in the ſight of the whole World that God abhorreth them. For to this

Matt xiii. 24, 47.

and no other purpoſe are meant thoſe Parables, which our Saviour in the Goſpel hath concerning mixture of Vice with Virtue, Light with Darkneſs, Truth with Error, as well and openly known and ſeen, as a cunningly cloaked mixture. That which ſeparateth therefore utterly, that which cutteth off clean from the viſible Church of Chriſt, is plain Apoſtaſy, direct denial, utter rejection of the whole Chriſtian Faith, as far as the ſame is profeſſedly different from Infidelity. Hereticks, as touching thoſe points of Doctrine wherein they fail; Schiſmaticks, as touching the quarrels for which, or the duties wherein they divide themſelves from their Brethren; looſe, licentious, and wicked Perſons, as touching their ſeveral offences or crimes, have all forſaken the true Church of God; the Church which is ſound and ſincere in the Doctrine that they corrupt; the Church that keepeth the Bond of Unity, which they violate; the Church that walketh in the Laws of Righteouſneſs, which they tranſgreſs; this very true Church of Chriſt they have left, howbeit not altogether left, nor forſaken ſimply the Church; upon the main foundations whereof they continue built, notwithſtanding theſe breaches whereby they are rent at the top aſunder. Now becauſe for redreſs of profeſſed Errors and open Schiſms it is, and muſt be the Church's care that all may in outward

outward Conformity be one, as the laudable Polity of former Ages, even ſo our own to that end and purpoſe hath eſtabliſhed divers Laws, the moderate ſeverity whereof is a mean both to ſtay the reſt, and to reclaim ſuch as heretofore have been led awry. But ſeeing that the offices which Laws require are always definite, and when that they require is done they go no farther, whereupon ſundry ill-affected Perſons, to ſave themſelves from danger of Laws, pretend obedience, albeit inwardly they carry ſtill the ſame hearts which they did before; by means whereof it falleth out, that receiving unworthily the bleſſed Sacrament at our hands, they eat and drink their own Damnation; it is for remedy of this miſchief * here determined, that whom the Law of the

* T. C. lib. i. pag. 167. If the place of the fifth to the Corinthians do forbid that we ſhould have any familiarity with notorious Offenders, it doth more forbid that they ſhould be received to the Communion: and therefore Papiſts being ſuch, as which are notoriouſly known to hold heretical opinions, ought not to be admitted, much leſs compelled to the Supper. For ſeeing that our Saviour Chriſt did inſtitute his Supper amongſt his Diſciples, and thoſe only which were, as St. Paul ſpeaketh, within; it is evident, that the Papiſts being without, and Foreigners and Strangers from the Church of God, ought not to be received if they would offer themſelves, and that Miniſter that ſhall give the Supper of the Lord to him which is known to be a Papiſt, and which hath never made any clear renouncing of Popery with which he hath been defiled, doth profane the Table of the Lord, and doth give the meat that is prepared for the Children, unto Dogs; and he bringeth into the paſture, which is provided for the Sheep, ſwine, and unclean beaſts, contrary to the Faith and Truſt that ought to be in a Steward of the Lord's Houſe, as he is. For albeit, that I doubt not, but many of thoſe which are now Papiſts, pertain to the Election of God, which God alſo in his good time will call to the knowledge of his Truth; yet, notwithſtanding, they ought to be unto the Miniſter, and unto the Church, touching the miniſtering of Sacraments, as Strangers, and as unclean Beaſts. The miniſtering of the holy Sacraments unto them is a declaration and ſeal of God's favour and reconciliation with them, and a plain preaching, partly, that they be waſhed already from their ſin, partly that they are of the Houſhold of God, and ſuch as the Lord will feed to eternal Life; which

BOOK V. Realm doth punish unless they communicate, such, if they offer to obey Law, the Church notwithstanding should not admit without probation before had of their gospel-like behaviour. Wherein they first set no time, how long this supposed probation must continue; again, they nominate no certain judgment, the verdict whereof shall approve Men's behaviour to be gospel-like; and, that which is most material, whereas they seek to make it more hard for dissemblers to be received into the Church than Law and Polity as yet hath done, they make it in truth more easy for such kind of Persons to wind themselves out of the Law, and to continue the same they were. The Law requireth at their hands that duty which in conscience doth touch them nearest, because the greatest difference between us and them is the Sacrament of the Body and Blood of Christ, whose Name in the Service of our Communion we celebrate with due honour, which they in the error of their Mass prophane. As therefore on our part to hear Mass, were an open departure from that sincere Profession wherein we stand; so if they on the other side receive our Communion, they give us the strongest pledge of fidelity that Man can demand. What their hearts are, God doth know. But if they which mind treachery to God and Man, should once apprehend this advantage given them, whereby they may satisfy Law in pretending themselves conformable (for what can Law with reason or justice require more?) and yet be sure the Church will accept no such offer till their gospel-like behaviour be allowed,

which is not lawful to be done unto those which are not of the Houshold of Faith. And therefore I conclude, that the compelling of Papists unto the Communion, and the dismissing and letting of them go, when as they be to be punished for their stubbornness in Popery (with this condition, if they will receive the Communion) is very unlawful; when as, although they would receive it, yet they ought to be kept back till such time as by their religious and gospel-like behaviour, &c.

after

after that our own ſimplicity hath once thus fairly eaſed them from the ſting of the Law; it is to be thought they will learn the myſtery of goſpel-like behaviour when leiſure ſerveth them. And ſo while without any cauſe we fear to prophane Sacraments, we ſhall not only defeat the purpoſe of moſt wholeſome Laws, but loſe or wilfully hazard thoſe Souls, from whom the likelieſt means of full and perfect recovery are by our indiſcretion with-held. For neither doth God thus bind us to dive into Men's conſciences, nor can their fraud and deceit hurt any Man but themſelves. To him they ſeem ſuch as they are; but of us they muſt be taken for ſuch as they ſeem. In the eye of God they are againſt Chriſt, that are not truly and ſincerely with him; in our eyes, they muſt be received as with Chriſt, that are not to outward ſhew againſt him. The caſe of impenitent and notorious Sinners is not like unto theirs, whoſe only imperfection is error ſevered from pertinacy, error in appearance content to ſubmit itſelf to better inſtruction; error ſo far already cured, as to crave at our hands that Sacrament, the hatred and utter refuſal whereof, was the weightieſt point wherein heretofore they ſwerved and went aſtray. In this caſe therefore they cannot reaſonably charge us with remiſs dealing, or with careleſſneſs to whom we impart the Myſteries of Chriſt; but they have given us manifeſt occaſion to think it requiſite that we earneſtly adviſe rather, and exhort them to conſider as they ought their ſundry overſights; firſt, in equalling undiſtinctly crimes with errors, as touching force to make uncapable of this Sacrament; ſecondly, in ſuffering indignation at the faults of the Church of Rome to blind and with-hold their judgments from ſeeing that which withal they ſhould acknowledge, concerning ſo-much, nevertheleſs, ſtill due to the ſame Church, as to be held and reputed a part of the Houſe of God, a limb of the viſible Church of Chriſt; thirdly, in impoſing upon the Church

BOOK V. Church a burthen, to enter farther into Men's hearts, and to make a deeper ſearch of their conſciences, than any Law of God, or Reaſon of Man enforceth; fourthly and laſtly, in repelling under colour of longer trial ſuch from the Myſteries of heavenly Grace, as are both capable thereof by the Laws of God, for any thing we hear to the contrary; and ſhould in divers conſiderations be cheriſhed according to the merciful examples and precepts whereby the Goſpel of Chriſt hath taught us towards ſuch to ſhew compaſſion, to receive them with lenity and all meekneſs; if any thing be ſhaken in them, to ſtrengthen it; not to quench with delays and jealouſies that feeble ſmoak of Conformity which ſeemeth to breathe from them; but to build whereſoever there is any foundation; to add perfection unto ſlender beginnings; and that as by other offices of piety, even ſo by this very Food of Life which Chriſt hath left in his Church, not only for preſervation of ſtrength, but alſo for relief of weakneſs.

T. C. l. i. p. 147. But to return to our own ſelves, in whom the next thing ſeverely reproved is the paucity of Communicants. If they require at Communions frequency, we wiſh the ſame, knowing how acceptable unto God ſuch ſervice is, when multitudes cheerfully concur unto it, if they encourage Men thereunto, we alſo (themſelves acknowledge it) are not utterly forgetful to do the like; if they require ſome publick coaction for remedy of that, wherein by milder and ſofter means, little good is done, they know our Laws and Statutes provided in that behalf, whereunto whatſoever convenient help may be added more by the wiſdom of Man, what cauſe have we given the World to think that we are not ready to hearken to it, and to uſe any good means of ſweet compulſion to have this high and heavenly Banquet largely furniſhed? Only we cannot ſo far yield as to judge it convenient, that the holy deſire of a competent number ſhould be unſatisfied becauſe the greater part

2 Chron. xxx. 13. Pſal. cxxii. 1.

Luke xiv. 23.

is

is carelefs and undifpofed to join with them. Men fhould not (they fay) be permitted a few by themfelves to communicate when fo many are gone away, becaufe this Sacrament is a token of our Conjunction with our Brethren; and therefore by communicating apart from them, we make an apparent fhew of diftraction. I afk then, on which fide Unity is broken, whether on theirs that depart, or on theirs who, being left behind, do communicate? Firft, in the one it is not denied but that they may have reafonable caufes of departure, and that then even they are delivered from juft blame. Of fuch kind of caufes two are allowed, namely, danger of impairing health, and neceffary bufinefs requiring our prefence otherwhere. And may not a third caufe, which is unfitnefs at the prefent time, detain us as lawfully back as either of thefe two? True it is, that we cannot hereby altogether excufe ourfelves, for that we ought to prevent this and do not. But if we have committed a fault in not preparing our minds before, fhall we therefore aggravate the fame with a worfe; the crime of unworthy participation? He that abftaineth doth want for the time that grace and comfort which religious Communicants have; but he that eateth and drinketh unworthily, receiveth death; that which is life to others, turneth in him to poifon. Notwithftanding, whatfoever be the caufe for which Men abftain, were it reafon that the fault of one part fhould any way abridge their benefit that are not faulty? There is in all the Scripture of God no one fyllable which doth condemn communicating amongft a few, when the reft are departed from them. As for the laft thing, which is our imparting this Sacrament privately to the Sick, whereas there have been of old (they grant) two kinds of neceffity wherein this Sacrament might be privately adminiftered; of which two, the one being erroneoufly imagined, and the other (they fay) continuing no longer in ufe, there remaineth unto us no neceffity at

T. C. l. i. p. 146.

BOOK V. at all, for which that Cuſtom ſhould be retained. The falſely ſurmiſed neceſſity is that whereby ſome have thought all ſuch excluded from poſſibility of Salvation, as did depart this Life, and never were made partakers of the holy Euchariſt. The other caſe of neceſſity was, when Men which had fallen in time of perſecution, and had afterwards repented them, but were not as yet received again unto the Fellowſhip of this Communion, did at the hour of death requeſt it, that ſo they might reſt with greater quietneſs and comfort of mind, being thereby aſſured of departure in unity of Chriſt's Church; which virtuous deſire, the Fathers did think it great impiety not to ſatisfy. This was Serapion's caſe of neceſſity. Serapion, a faithful aged Perſon, and always of very upright life, till fear of perſecution in the end cauſed him to ſhrink back, after long ſorrow for his ſcandalous offence, and ſuit oftentimes made to be pardoned of the Church, fell at length into grievous ſickneſs, and being ready to yield up the ghoſt, was then more inſtant than ever before to receive the Sacrament. Which Sacrament was neceſſary in this caſe, not that Serapion had been deprived of everlaſting life without it, but that his end was thereby to him made the more comfortable. And do we think, that all caſes of ſuch neceſſity are clean vaniſhed? Suppoſe that ſome have by miſperſuaſion lived in Schiſm, withdrawn themſelves from holy and publick Aſſemblies, hated the Prayers, and loathed the Sacraments of the Church, falſely preſuming them to be fraught with impious and antichriſtian corruptions; which error the God of Mercy and Truth opening at the length their eyes to ſee, they do not only repent them of the evil which they have done, but alſo in token thereof deſire to receive comfort by that whereunto they have offered diſgrace (which may be the caſe of many poor ſeduced Souls, even at this day); God forbid we ſhould think that the Church doth ſin, in permitting

permitting the wounds of ſuch to be ſupplied with that oil which this gracious Sacrament doth yield, and their bruiſed Minds not only need but beg. There is nothing which the Soul of Man doth deſire in that laſt hour ſo much as comfort againſt the natural terrors of death, and other ſcruples of conſcience which commonly do then moſt trouble and perplex the weak; towards whom the very Law of God doth exact at our hands all the helps that Chriſtian lenity and indulgence can afford. Our general conſolation departing this life is, the hope of that glorious and bleſſed Reſurrection which the Apoſtle St. Paul nameth Ἐξανάστασιν,* to note that as all Men ſhould have their Ἀνάστασιν, and be raiſed again from the dead, ſo the Juſt ſhall be taken up and exalted above the reſt, whom the power of God doth but raiſe, and not exalt. This Life, and this Reſurrection of our Lord Jeſus Chriſt, is for all Men, as touching the ſufficiency of that he hath done; but that which maketh us partakers thereof, is our particular Communion with Chriſt; and this Sacrament a principal mean, as well to ſtrengthen the bond, as to multiply in us the fruits of the ſame Communion. For which cauſe St. Cyprian † termeth it a joyful ſolemnity of expedite and ſpeedy Reſurrection; Ignatius, ‡ a medicine which procureth Immortality and preventeth Death; Irenæus, § the nouriſhment of our Bodies to eternal Life, and their preſervative from corruption. Now becauſe that Sacrament, which at all times we may

1 Cor. xv. 21

Phil. iii. 11.

* Δια την εκ τ γης επαρσιν Theophyl. Πάντες οἱ ἄνθρωποι ἀνίστανται, μόνοι δὲ πιστοὶ ἀξιοῦνται τῶν ἀγαθῶν. Ammon Vide 1 Th ff. iv. 17.

† Maturatæ Reſurrectionis lætabunda ſolemnia. Cypr. de Cœn Dom. cap. x.

‡ Φάρμακον ἀθανασίας, ἀντίδοτον μὴ θανεῖν. Ignat. Epiſt. ad Epheſ Iren. lib. iv. cap. 34.

§ Etſi nihil facile mutandum eſt ex ſolemnibus, tamen ubi æquitas evidens poſcit, ſubveniendum eſt Lib. cxxxviii. ff. de Reg. Jur.

BOOK V. receive unto this effect, is then most acceptable and most fruitful when any special extraordinary occasion, nearly and presently urging, kindleth our desires towards it, their severity, who cleave unto that alone which is generally fit to be done, and so make all Men's conditions alike, may add much affliction to divers troubled and grieved Minds, of whose particular estate particular respect being had, according to the charitable Order of the Church wherein we live, there ensueth unto God that glory which his righteous Saints comforted in their greatest distresses do yield; and unto them which have their reasonable petitions satisfied the same contentment, tranquillity and joy, that others before them, by means of like satisfaction, have reaped, and wherein we all are or should be desirous finally to take our leave of the World, whensoever our own uncertain time of most assured departure shall come. Concerning therefore both Prayers and Sacraments, together with our usual and received Form of administering the same in the Church of England, let thus much suffice.

Of Festival-Days, and the natural causes of their convenient Institution.

69. As the Substance of God alone is infinite and hath no kind of limitation, so likewise his Continuance is from everlasting to everlasting, and knoweth neither beginning nor end. Which demonstrable conclusion being presupposed, it followeth necessarily, that besides him, all things are finite both in Substance and in Continuance. If in Substance all things be finite, it cannot be but that there are bounds without the compass whereof their Substance doth not extend, if in Continuance also limited, they all have, it cannot be denied, their set and their certain terms, before which they had no being at all. This is the reason why, first, we do most admire those things which are greatest, and, secondly, those things which are ancientest; because the one are least distant from the infinite Substance, the other from the infinite Continuance of God. Out of this we gather that only God hath true Immortality or Eternity, that is

to

to ſay, Continuance wherein there groweth no difference by addition of hereafter unto now, whereas the nobleſt and perfecteſt of all things beſides have continually, through continuance, the time of former continuance lengthened, ſo that they could not heretofore be ſaid to have continued ſo long as now, neither ſo long as hereafter. God's own eternity is the hand which leadeth Angels in the courſe of their perpetuity; their perpetuity the hand that draweth out celeſtial Motion; the line of which Motion, and the thread of Time, are ſpun together. Now as Nature bringeth forth Time with Motion, ſo we by Motion have learned how to divide Time, and by the ſmaller parts of Time both to meaſure the greater, and to know how long all things elſe endure. For Time, conſidered in itſelf, is but the flux of that very inſtant wherein the Motion of the Heaven began; being coupled with other things, it is the quantity of their continuance meaſured by the diſtance of two inſtants: as the Time of a Man, is a Man's continuance from the inſtant of his firſt breath till the inſtant of his laſt gaſp. Hereupon ſome have defined Time to be the meaſure of the Motion of Heaven; becauſe the firſt thing which Time doth meaſure, is that Motion wherewith it began, and by the help whereof it meaſureth other things; as when the Prophet David ſaith, that a Man's continuance doth not commonly exceed threeſcore and ten years, he uſeth the help both of Motion and Number to meaſure Time. They which make Time an effect of Motion, and Motion to be in nature before Time, ought to have conſidered with themſelves, that albeit we ſhould deny, as Meliſſus did, all Motion, we might notwithſtanding acknowledge Time, becauſe Time doth but ſignify the quantity of Continuance, which Continuance may be in things that reſt and are never moved. Beſides, we may alſo conſider in reſt both that which is paſt, and that which is preſent, and that which is future; yea, farther, even length and ſhortneſs in every of theſe, although we

BOOK V. never had conceit of Motion. But to define, without Motion, how long, or how ſhort ſuch Continuance is, were impoſſible. So that herein we muſt of neceſſity uſe the benefit of Years, Days, Hours, Minutes, which all grow from celeſtial Motion. Again, for as much as that Motion is circular, whereby we make our diviſions of Time, and the compaſs of that Circuit ſuch, that the Heavens, which are therein continually moved and keep in their Motions uniform celerity, muſt needs touch often the ſame points, they cannot chooſe but bring unto us by equal diſtances frequent returns of the ſame Times. Furthermore, whereas Time is nothing but a mere quantity of that Continuance which all things have, that are not, as God is, without beginning, that which is proper unto all quantities agreeth alſo to this kind, ſo that Time doth but meaſure other things, and neither worketh in them any real effect, nor is itſelf ever capable of any. And therefore when commonly we uſe to ſay, that Time doth eat or fret out all things; that Time is the wiſeſt thing in the World, becauſe it bringeth forth all knowledge; and that nothing is more fooliſh than Time, which never holdeth any thing long, but whatſoever one day learneth, the ſame another day forgetteth again, that ſome Men ſee proſperous and happy days, and that ſome Men's days are miſerable; in all theſe, and the like ſpeeches, that which is uttered of the Time, is not verified of Time itſelf, but agreeth unto thoſe things which are in Time, and do by means of ſo near conjunction either lay their burden upon the back, or ſet their crown upon the head of Time. Yea, the very opportunities which we aſcribe to Time,* do in truth cleave to the things themſelves wherewith the Time is joined. As for Time, it neither cauſeth things, nor opportunities of things, although it compriſe and contain both. All things

* Χρόνος ἐστὶν ἐν ᾧ καιρὸς, καὶ καιρὸς ἐν ᾧ χρόνος οὐ πολύς. Hippoc. Lib. qui præceptiones inſcribitur.

whatſoever

whatſoever having their Time, the Works of God have always that Time which is ſeaſonableſt and fitteſt for them. His Works are ſome ordinary, ſome more rare; all worthy of obſervation, but not all of like neceſſity to be often remembered; they all have their Times, but they all do not add the ſame eſtimation and glory to the Times wherein they are. For as God by being every where, yet doth not give unto all places one and the ſame degree of holineſs; ſo neither one and the ſame dignity to all Times by working in all. For if all either places or Times were in reſpect of God alike; wherefore was it ſaid unto Moſes by particular deſignation, *That very place wherein thou ſtandeſt is holy ground?* Why doth the Prophet David chooſe out of all the days of the year but one, whereof he ſpeaketh by way of principal admiration, *This is the day the Lord hath made?* No doubt, as God's extraordinary Preſence hath hallowed and ſanctified certain places, ſo they are his extraordinary Works that have truly and worthily advanced certain times; for which cauſe they ought to be with all Men that honour God more holy than other days. The Wiſe Man therefore compareth herein not unfitly the Times of God with the Perſons of Men. If any ſhould aſk how it comes to paſs that one day doth excel another, ſeeing the light of all the days in the year proceedeth from one ſun; to this he anſwereth, *That the Knowledge of the Lord hath parted them aſunder, he hath by them diſpoſed the Times and ſolemn Feaſts; ſome he hath choſen out and ſanctified, ſome he hath put among the days to number:* even as Adam and all other Men are of one ſubſtance, all created of the Earth: *But the Lord hath divided them by great knowledge; and made their ways divers, ſome he hath bleſſed and exalted, ſome he hath ſanctified and appropriated unto himſelf, ſome he hath curſed, humbled and put them out of their dignity.* So that the cauſe being natural and neceſſary for which there ſhould be a difference in days, the ſolemn obſervation whereof declareth religious

BOOK V.

Exod. iii. 5.

Pſal. cxviii. 24.

Ecclus xxxiii. 7.

BOOK V. thankfulneſs towards Him, whoſe Works of principal reckoning we thereby admire and honour, it cometh next to be conſidered, what kinds of Duties and Services they are, wherewith ſuch Times ſhould be kept holy.

The manner of celebrating of Feſtival-Days.

70. The Sanctification of Days and Times is a token of that thankfulneſs, and a part of that publick honour which we owe to God for admirable Benefits, whereof it doth not ſuffice that we keep a ſecret kalender, taking thereby our private occaſions as we liſt ourſelves to think how much God hath done for all Men; but the Days which are choſen out to ſerve as publick memorials of ſuch his Mercies ought to be clothed with thoſe outward robes of Holineſs, whereby their difference from other Days may be made ſenſible. But becauſe Time in itſelf, as hath been already proved, can receive no alteration, the hallowing of Feſtival-Days muſt conſiſt in the ſhape or countenance which we put upon the affairs that are incident into thoſe Days. *This is the Day which the Lord hath made*, ſaith the Prophet David, *let us rejoice and be glad in it.* So that generally Offices and Duties of * religious joy are that wherein the hallowing of Feſtival-Times conſiſteth. The moſt natural teſtimonies of our rejoicing in God, are, firſt, his Praiſes ſet forth with cheerful alacrity of mind, ſecondly, our Comfort and Delight expreſſed by a charitable largeneſs of ſomewhat more than common Bounty; thirdly, Sequeſtration from ordinary Labours, the

* Grande videlicet officium, focos et choros in publicum educere, vicatim epulari, civitatem tabernæ halitu obolefacere, vino lutum cogere, catervatim curſitare ad injurias, ad impudicitias, ad libidinis illecebras. Siccine exprimitur publicum gaudium per publicum dedecus? Tert. Apol. cap 35. Dies feſtos Majeſtati altiſſimæ dedicatos nullis volumus voluptatibus occupari. Cl. xii. tit. 12. lib. 1. Ἀντὶ τῆς πάλαι πομπείας κὶ αἰσχρουργίας κὶ αἰχρορῥημοσύνης σώφρονες ἑορτάζονται πανηγύρεις, οὐ μέθην ἔχουσαι καὶ κῶμον καὶ γέλωτα, ἀλλ᾽ ὕμνους θείους κὶ ἱερῶν λογίων ἀκρόασιν, κὶ προσευχὴν ἀξιεπαίνοις κοσμουμένην δακρύοις. Theod. ad Græc. Infidel. ſer. ix. Τῆς γὰρ αὐτῆς φύσεώς ἐστιν εὐσεβῆ τε εἶναι κὶ φιλάνθρωπον. Philo. lib. de Abraha.

toils

toils and cares whereof are not meet to be companions of ſuch gladneſs. Feſtival Solemnity, therefore, is nothing but the due mixture, as it were, of theſe three elements, Praiſe, Bounty and Reſt. Touching Praiſe, for as much as the Jews, who alone knew the way how to magnify God aright, did commonly (as appeared by their wicked lives) more of cuſtom and for faſhion-ſake execute the ſervice of their Religion, than with hearty and true devotion (which God eſpecially requireth) he therefore proteſteth againſt their Sabbaths and ſolemn Days, as Iſa. i. 13. being therewith much offended. Plentiful and liberal expence is required in them that abound, partly as a ſign of their own joy in the goodneſs of God towards them, and partly as a mean whereby to refreſh thoſe poor and needy, who being eſpecially at theſe times Deut lxi. 14 made partakers of relaxation and joy with others, do Nehemiah the more religiouſly bleſs God, whoſe great Mercies viii. 9. were a cauſe thereof, and the more contentedly endure the burthen of that hard eſtate wherein they continue. Reſt is the end of all Motion, and the laſt perfection of all things that labour. Labours in us are journeys, and even in them which feel no wearineſs by any work, yet they are but ways whereby to come unto that, which bringeth not Happineſs till it do bring Reſt. For as long as any thing which we deſire is unattained, we reſt not. Let us not here take Reſt for Idleneſs. They are idle, whom the painfulneſs of action cauſeth to avoid thoſe labours whereunto both God and Nature bindeth them; they reſt, which either ceaſe from their work when they have brought it unto perfection, or elſe give over a meaner labour becauſe a worthier and better is to be undertaken. God hath created nothing to be idle or ill employed. As therefore Man doth conſiſt of different and diſtinct parts, every part endued with manifold abilities, which all have their ſeveral ends and actions thereunto referred, ſo there is in this great variety of duties which belong to Men that dependency and order,

BOOK V. der, by means whereof, the lower ſuſtaining always the more excellent, and the higher perfecting the more baſe, they are in their times and ſeaſons continued with moſt exquiſite correſpondence. Labours of bodily and daily toil purchaſe freedom for actions of religious Joy, which benefit theſe actions requite with the gift of deſired Reſt; a thing moſt natural and fit to accompany the ſolemn Feſtival duties of honour which are done to God. For if thoſe principal Works of God, the memory whereof we uſe to celebrate at ſuch times, be but certain taſtes and ſays, as it were, of that final benefit wherein our perfect Felicity and Bliſs lieth folded up, ſeeing that the preſence of the one doth direct our cogitations, thoughts and deſires towards the other, it giveth ſurely a kind of life, and addeth inwardly no ſmall delight to thoſe ſo comfortable expectations, when the very outward countenance of that we preſently do, repreſenteth after a ſort that alſo whereunto we tend; as Feſtival Reſt doth that Celeſtial Eſtate whereof the very Heathens themſelves,* which had not the means whereby to apprehend much, did notwithſtanding imagine that it needs muſt conſiſt in Reſt, and have therefore taught that above the higheſt moveable Sphere there is nothing which feeleth alteration, motion or change, but all things immutable, unſubject to paſſion, bleſt with eternal continuance in a Life of the higheſt Perfection, and of that complete abundant ſufficiency within itſelf, which no poſſibility of want, maim, or defect can touch. Beſides, whereas ordinary Labours are both in themſelves painful and baſe in compariſon of Feſtival Services done to God, doth not the natural difference between them ſhew that the one, as it were by way of ſubmiſſion and homage, ſhould ſurrender them-

* Οὐδ᾽ ἐστιν οὐδενὸς οὐδεμία μεταβολὴ τῶν ὑπὲρ ἐξωτάτω φερομένην φορὰν, ἀλλ᾽ ἀναλλοίωτα καὶ ἀπαθῆ τὴν ἀρίστην ἔχοντα ζωὴν καὶ τὴν αὐταρκεστάτην διατελεῖ τὸν ἅπαντα αἰῶνα. Ariſt.

ſelves

ſelves to the other, wherewith they can neither eaſily concur, becauſe painfulneſs and joy are oppoſite, nor decently, becauſe while the Mind hath juſt occaſion to make her abode in the houſe of gladneſs, the weed of ordinary toil and travel becometh her not? Wherefore even Nature hath taught the Heathens, and God the Jews, and Chriſt us, firſt that Feſtival Solemnities are a part of the publick exercife of Religion; ſecondly, that Praiſe, Liberality and Reſt, are as natural elements whereof Solemnities conſiſt. But theſe things the Heathens converted to the honour of their falſe Gods; and, as they failed in the end itſelf, ſo neither could they diſcern rightly what form and meaſure Religion therein ſhould obſerve. Whereupon when the Iſraelites impiouſly followed ſo corrupt example, they are in every degree noted to have done amiſs; their Hymns or Songs of Praiſe were Idolatry; their Bounty, Exceſs; and their Reſt, Wantonneſs. Therefore the Law of God, which appointed them Days of Solemnity, taught them likewiſe in what manner the ſame ſhould be celebrated. According to the pattern of which inſtitution, David eſtabliſhing the ſtate of Religion ordained Praiſe to be given unto God in the Sabbaths, Months, and appointed Times, as their Cuſtom had been always before the Lord. Now, beſides the times which God himſelf in the Law of Moſes particularly ſpecified, there were through the wiſdom of the Church certain other deviſed by occaſion of like occurrents to thoſe whereupon the former had riſen; as namely, that which Mordecai and Eſther did firſt celebrate in memory of the Lord's moſt wonderful Protection, when Haman had laid his inevitable plot, to Man's thinking, for the utter extirpation of the Jews even in one day. This they call the Feaſt of Lots, becauſe Haman had caſt their life and their death, as it were, upon the hazard of a lot. To this may be added that other alſo of Dedication, mentioned in the tenth of St. John's Goſpel, the inſtitution whereof is declared in

BOOK V.

1 Chron. xxiii. 30.

Eſther ix. 27.

John x. 22.

BOOK V. in the Hiſtory of the Maccabees. But for as much as their Law by the coming of Chriſt is changed, and we thereunto no way bound, St. Paul, although it were not his purpoſe to favour invectives againſt the ſpecial Sanctification of Days and Times to the ſervice of God, and to the honour of Jeſus Chriſt, doth notwithſtanding bend his forces againſt that opinion which impoſed on the Gentiles the yoke of Jewiſh Legal obſervations, as if the whole World ought for ever, and that upon pain of condemnation, to keep and obſerve the ſame. Such as in this perſuaſion hallowed thoſe Jewiſh Sabbaths the Apoſtle ſharply reproveth, ſaying, *Ye obſerve Days, and Months, and Times, and Years; I am in fear of you, leſt I have beſtowed upon you labour in vain.* Howbeit, ſo far off was Tertullian from imagining how any Man could poſſibly hereupon call in queſtion ſuch Days as the Church of Chriſt doth obſerve,* that the obſervation of theſe Days he uſeth for an argument whereby to prove, it could not be the Apoſtle's intent and meaning to condemn ſimply all obſerving of ſuch Times. Generally therefore touching Feaſts in the Church of Chriſt, they have that profitable uſe whereof St. Auguſtin ſpeaketh, *By Feſtival Solemnities and ſet Days, we dedicate and ſanctifie to God the memory of his Benefits, leſt unthankful forgetfulneſs thereof ſhould creep upon us in courſe of time.* And concerning particulars, their Sabbath the Church hath changed into our Lord's Day; that as the one did continually bring to mind the former World finiſhed by Creation, ſo the other might keep us in perpetual remembrance of a far better World, begun by him which came to reſtore all things, to make both Heaven and Earth new. For which cauſe they honoured the laſt Day, we the

1 Mac. iv. 54.

Gal. iv. 10.

Aug. de Civit Dei, lib. x. cap. 4.

* Si omnem in totum devotionem temporum et dierum et menſium et annorum eraſit Apoſtolus, cur Paſcha celebramus annuo circulo in menſe primo? Cur quinquaginta exinde diebus in omni exultatione decurrimus? Lib. adverſ. Pſych.

firſt

first in every seven throughout the Year. The rest of the Days and Times which we celebrate have relation all to one Head. We begin therefore our Ecclesiastical Year with the glorious Annunciation of his Birth by Angelical Embassage. There being hereunto added his blessed Nativity itself, the Mystery of his Legal Circumcision; the testification of his true Incarnation by the Purification of her which brought him into the World, his Resurrection, his Ascension into Heaven, the admirable sending down of his Spirit upon his Chosen, and (which consequently ensued) the notice of that incomprehensible Trinity thereby given to the Church of God. Again, for as much as we know that Christ hath not only been manifested great in himself, but great in other his Saints also, the days of whose departure out of the World are to the Church of Christ as the birth and coronation-days of Kings or Emperors; therefore especial choice being made of the very flower of all occasions in this kind, there are annual selected Times to meditate of Christ glorified in them, which had the honour to suffer for his sake, before they had age and ability to know him; glorified in them, which knowing him as Stephen, had the sight of that before death, whereinto so acceptable death did lead; glorified in those Sages of the East, that came from far to adore him, and were conducted by strange light; glorified in the second Elias of the World, sent before him to prepare his way; glorified in those Apostles, whom it pleased him to use as Founders of his Kingdom here; glorified in the Angels, as in Michael; glorified in all those happy Souls, that are already possessed of Heaven. Over and besides which number not great, the rest be but four other Days heretofore annexed to the Feast of Easter and Pentecost, by reason of general Baptism usual at those two Feasts; which also is the cause why they had not, as other Days, any proper name given them. Their first institution was therefore through necessity, and

Luke i. 26.

Luke ii. 21.

their

BOOK V. their present continuance is now for the greater honour of the principals whereupon they still attend. If it be then demanded, whether we observe these Times as being thereunto bound by force of divine Law, or else by the only positive Ordinances of the Church? I answer to this, that the very Law of Nature itself, which all Men confess to be God's Law, requireth in general no less the Sanctification of Times, than of Places, Persons, and Things, unto God's Honour. For which cause it hath pleased him heretofore, as of the rest, so of Times likewise, to exact some parts by way of perpetual homage, never to be dispensed withal, nor remitted; again, to require some other parts of Time with as strict exaction, but for less continuance; and of the rest which were left arbitrary, to accept what the Church shall in due consideration consecrate voluntarily unto like religious uses. Of the first kind, amongst the Jews, was the Sabbath-day; of the second, those Feasts which are appointed by the Law of Moses, the Feast of Dedication, invented by the Church, standeth in the number of the last kind. The Moral Law requiring therefore a seventh part throughout the age of the whole World to be that way employed, although with us the Day be changed, in regard of a new revolution begun by our Saviour Christ; yet the same proportion of Time continueth which was before, because in reference to the benefit of Creation, and now much more of Renovation thereunto added by him which was Prince of the World to come, we are bound to account the sanctification of one Day in seven a duty which God's immutable Law doth exact for ever. The rest, they say, we ought to abolish, because the continuance of them doth nourish wicked Superstition in the minds of men; besides, they are all abused by Papists, the Enemies of God, yea, certain of them, as Easter and Pentecost, even by the Jews.

71. Touching

Exceptions against our keeping of other Festival-Days, besides the Sabbath.

71. Touching Jews, their Eafter and Pentecoft have with ours as much affinity as Philip the Apoftle with Philip the Macedonian King. As for imitation of Papifts and the breeding of Superftition, they are now become fuch common guefts, that no Man can think it difcourteous to let them go as they came. The next is a rare obfervation and ftrange;* you fhall find, if you mark it (as it doth deferve to be noted well) that many thoufands there are, who if they have virtuoufly during thofe times behaved themfelves, if their devotion and zeal in prayer have been fervent, their attention to the Word of God fuch as all Chriftian Men fhould yield, imagine that herein they have performed a good duty; which notwithftanding to think is a very dangerous error, in as much as the Apoftle Saint Paul hath taught that we ought not to keep our Eafter as the Jews did for certain days; but in the unleavened bread of Sincerity and of Truth to feaft continually: whereas

* T.C. lib. vi pag. 151. If they had been never abufed neither by the Papifts, nor by the Jews, as they have been, and are daily; yet fuch making of Holidays is never without fome great danger of bringing in fome evil and corrupt opinions into the minds of Men. I will ufe an example in one, and that the chief of Holidays, and moft generally and of longeft time obferved in the Church, which is the Feaft of Eafter, which was kept of fome more days, of fome fewer. How many thoufands are there, I will not fay of the ignorant Papifts, but of thofe alfo which profefs the Gofpel, which when they have celebrated thofe days with diligent heed taken unto their life, and with fome earneft devotion in praying, and hearing the Word of God, do not by and by think that they have well celebrated the Feaft of Eafter: and yet have they thus notably deceived themfelves: for Saint Paul teacheth, 1 Cor. v. 8. that the celebrating of the feaft of the Chriftians Eafter is not, as the Jews was, for certain days; but fheweth that we muft keep this Feaft all the days of our life in the unleavened bread of Sincerity and of Truth. By which we fee, that the obferving of the Feaft of Eafter for certain days in the year doth pull out of our minds, ere ever we be aware, the Doctrine of the Gofpel, and caufeth us to reft in that near confideration of our duties, for the fpace of a few days, which fhould be extended to all our life.

 the reſtraint of Eaſter to a certain number of days, cauſeth us to reſt for a ſhort ſpace in that near conſideration of our duties, which ſhould be extended throughout the courſe of our whole lives, and ſo pulleth out of our Minds the Doctrine of Chriſt's Goſpel ere we be aware. The Doctrine of the Goſpel, which here they mean, or ſhould mean, is, that, Chriſt having finiſhed the Law, there is no Jewiſh Paſchal Solemnity, nor abſtinence from ſour bread now required at our hands; there is no leaven which we are bound to caſt out, but malice, ſin and wickedneſs; no bread but the food of ſincere Truth wherewith we are tied to celebrate our Paſſover. And ſeeing no time of ſin is granted us, neither any intermiſſion of ſound belief, it followeth, that this kind of feaſting ought to endure always. But how are ſtanding Feſtival Solemnities againſt this? That which the Goſpel of Chriſt requireth is the perpetuity of virtuous duties; not perpetuity of exerciſe or action; but diſpoſition perpetual, and practice as oft as times and opportunities require. Juſt, valiant, liberal, temperate and holy Men are they, which can whenſoever they will, and will whenſoever they ought, execute what their ſeveral perfections import. If virtues did always ceaſe to be when they ceaſe to work, there ſhould be nothing more pernicious to virtue than ſleep; neither were it poſſible that Men, as Zachary and Elizabeth, ſhould in all the Commandments of God walk unreprovable; or that the chain of our converſation ſhould contain ſo many links of divine virtues, as the Apoſtles in divers places have reckoned up, if in the exerciſe of each virtue perpetual continuance were exacted at our hands. Seeing therefore all things are done in time, and many offices are not poſſible at one and the ſame time to be diſcharged, duties of all ſorts muſt have neceſſarily their ſeveral ſucceſſions and ſeaſons, in which reſpect the School-men have well and ſoundly determined, that God's affirmative Laws and Precepts, the Laws that enjoin

any

any actual duty, as Prayer, Alms, and the like, do bind us *ad semper velle* but not *ad semper agere*; we are tied to iterate and resume them when need is, howbeit not to continue them without any intermission. Feasts, whether God himself hath ordained them, or the Church by that authority which God hath given, they are of Religion such publick services as neither can nor ought to be continued otherwise than only by iteration. Which iteration is a most effectual mean to bring unto full maturity and growth those seeds of Godliness, that these very Men themselves do grant to be sown in the hearts of many thousands, during the while that such Feasts are present. The constant habit of well doing is not gotten without the custom of doing well, neither can virtue be made perfect but by the manifold works of virtue often practised. Before the powers of our Minds be brought unto some perfection, our first essays and offers towards virtue must needs be raw; yet commendable, because they tend unto ripeness. For which cause, the Wisdom of God hath commanded, especially this circumstance amongst others in solemn Feasts, that to Children and Novices in Religion they minister the first occasion to ask and enquire of God. Whereupon, if there follow but so much piety as hath been mentioned, let the Church learn to further imbecility with prayer; *Preserve, Lord, these good and gracious beginnings, that they suddenly dry not up like the morning dew, but may prosper and grow as the trees, which rivers of waters keep always flourishing*. Let all Men's acclamations be, *Grace, Grace unto it*, as to that first laid corner-stone in *Zerubbabel*'s buildings. For who hath despised the day of those things which are small? Or, how dare we take upon us to condemn that very thing which voluntarily we grant maketh us of nothing somewhat; seeing all we pretend against it, is only, that as yet this somewhat is not much? The Days of Solemnity which are but few, cannot choose but soon finish that

BOOK V. outward exercise of Godliness which properly appertaineth to such times; howbeit, Men's inward disposition to Virtue they both augment for the present, and, by their often returns, bring also the same at the length unto that perfection which we most desire. So that although by their necessary short continuance they abridge the present exercise of piety in some kind, yet because by repetition they enlarge, strengthen and confirm the habits of all Virtue, it remaineth, that we honour, observe and keep them as Ordinances many ways singularly profitable in God's Church. This exception being taken against Holidays, for that they restrain the Praises of God unto certain times, another followeth condemning restraint of Men from their ordinary trades and labours at those times. * It is not (they say) in the power of the

* T C. lib i. pag. 152. I confess, that it is in the power of the Church to appoint so many days in the week, or in the year (in the which, the Congregation shall assemble to hear the Word of God, and receive the Sacraments, and offer up Prayers unto God) as it shall think good, according to those Rules which are before alledged. But that it hath power to make so many Holidays as we have, wherein Men are commanded to cease from their daily vocations of plowing and exercising their handicrafts, that I deny to be in the power of the Church. For proof whereof I will take the fourth Commandment, and no other interpretation of it than Mr. Doctor alloweth of, which is, that God licenseth and leaveth it at the liberty of every Man to work six days in the week, so that he rest the seventh day. Seeing, therefore, that the Lord hath left it to all Men at liberty, that they might labour, if they think good, six days; I say, the Church, nor no Man can take this liberty away from them, and drive them to a necessary rest of the body. And if it be lawful to abridge the liberty of the Church in this point; and instead, that the Lord saith, six days thou mayest labour, if thou wilt, to say, thou shalt not labour six days, I do not see, why the Church may not as well, whereas the Lord saith, *Thou shalt rest the seventh Day*, command that thou shalt not rest the seventh Day. For if the Church may restrain the liberty which God hath given them, it may take away the yoke also which God hath put upon them. And whereas you say, that notwithstanding this fourth Commandment, the Jews had certain other Feasts which they observed; indeed the Lord, which gave this general Law, might make as many exceptions as

Church to command rest, because God hath left it to all Men at liberty, that if they think good to bestow six whole days in labour, they may; neither is it more lawful for the Church to abridge any Man of that liberty which God hath granted, than to take away the yoke which God hath laid upon them, and to countermand what he doth expresly enjoin. They deny not, but in times of publick calamity, that Men may the better assemble themselves to fast and pray, the Church, because it hath received Commandment from God to proclaim a prohibition from ordinary works, standeth bound to do it, as the Jews afflicted did in Babylon But without some express Commandment from God there is no power, they say, under Heaven, which may presume by any degree to restrain the liberty that God hath given. Which opinion, albeit applied here no farther than to this present cause, shaketh universally the fabrick of Government, tendeth to anarchy and mere confusion, dissolveth Families, dissipateth Colleges, Corporations, Armies, overthroweth Kingdoms, Churches,

as he thought good, and so long as he thought good. But it followeth not, because the Lord did it, that therefore the Church may do it, unless it hath Commandment and Authority from God so to do As when there is any general plague or judgment of God either upon the Church, or coming towards it, the Lord commandeth in such a case, Joel ii 15, that they should sanctify a general Fast, and proclaim *Ghnatsaroh*, which signifieth a prohibition, or forbidding of ordinary works, and is the same Hebrew word wherewith those Fast-days are noted in the Law, wherein they should rest. The reason of which Commandment of the Lord was, that as they abstained that day as much as might be conveniently from meats, so they might abstain from their daily works, to the end they might bestow the whole day in hearing the Word of God, and humbling themselves in the Congregation, confessing their faults, and desiring the Lord to turn away from his fierce wrath. In this case the Church having Commandment to make a Holiday, may, and ought to do it, as the Church which was in Babylon did during the time of their Captivity; but where it is destitute of a Commandment, it may not presume by any Decree to restrain that liberty which the Lord hath given.

BOOK V. and whatſoever is now through the providence of God by authority and power upheld. For whereas God hath foreprized things of the greateſt weight, and hath therein preciſely defined, as well that which every Man muſt perform, as that which no Man may attempt, leaving all ſorts of Men in the reſt, either to be guided by their own good diſcretion if they be free from ſubjection to others, or elſe to be ordered by ſuch Commandments and Laws as proceed from thoſe Superiors under whom they live, the Patrons of Liberty have here made ſolemn proclamation that all ſuch Laws and Commandments are void, inaſmuch as every Man is left to the freedom of his own mind in ſuch things as are not either exacted or prohibited by the Law of God. And becauſe, only in theſe things, the poſitive Precepts of Men have place, which Precepts cannot poſſibly be given without ſome abridgment of their Liberty to whom they are given; therefore if the Father command the Son, or the Huſband the Wife, or the Lord the Servant, or the Leader the Soldier, or the Prince the Subject, to go or ſtand, ſleep or wake, at ſuch times as God himſelf in particular commandeth neither; they are to ſtand in defence of the freedom which God hath granted, and to do as themſelves liſt, knowing that Men may as lawfully command them things utterly forbidden by the Law of God, as tie them to any thing which the Law of God leaveth free. The plain contradictory whereunto is infallibly certain. Thoſe things which the Law of God leaveth arbitrary and at liberty, are all ſubject to the poſitive Laws of Men, which Laws, for the common benefit, abridge particular Men's liberty in ſuch things as far as the rules of Equity will ſuffer. This we muſt either maintain, or elſe over-turn the World, and make every Man his own Commander. Seeing then that Labour and Reſt upon any one day of the ſix throughout the year, are granted free by the Law of God, how exempt we them

them from the force and power of Ecclefiaftical Law, BOOK V. except we deprive the World of power to make any Ordinance or Law at all? Befides, is it probable that God fhould not only allow, but command concurrency of Reft with extraordinary occafions of doleful events befalling (peradventure) fome one certain Church, or not extending unto many, and not as much as permit or licence the like, when Piety, triumphant with Joy and Gladnefs, maketh folemn commemoration of God's moft rare and unwonted Mercies, fuch efpecially as the whole race of Mankind doth or might participate? Of vacation from labour in times of forrow the only caufe is, for that the general publick Prayers of the whole Church, and our own private bufinefs, cannot both be followed at once; whereas of Reft in the famous folemnities of publick Joy, there is both this confideration the fame, and alfo farther a kind of natural repugnancy, which maketh labours (as hath been proved) much more unfit to accompany Feftival Praifes of God, than offices of Humiliation and Grief. Again, if we fift what they bring for proof and approbation of Reft with Fafting, doth it not in all refpects as fully warrant, and as ftrictly command Reft, whenfoever the Church hath equal reafon by Feafts and gladfome Solemnities to teftify publick thankfulnefs towards God? I would know fome caufe why thofe words of the Prophet Joel, *Sanctify a Faft, call a folemn Affembly*, Joel ii 15. which words were uttered to the Jews in mifery and great diftrefs, fhould more bind the Church to do at all times after the like in their like perplexities, than the words of Mofes to the fame People in a time of Exod. xiii. 3. joyful deliverance from mifery, *Remember this day*, may warrant any annual celebration of benefits no lefs importing the good of Men, and alfo juftify, as touching the manner and form thereof, what circumftance foever we imitate only in refpect of natural fitnefs or decency, without any Jewifh regard to

 Ceremonies,

BOOK V. Ceremonies, such as were properly theirs, and are not by us expedient to be continued. According to the Rule of which general directions taken from the Law of God, no less in the one than the other, the practice of the Church commended unto us in holy Scripture, doth not only make for the justification of black and dismal days (as one of the Fathers termeth them), but plainly offereth itself to be followed by such Ordinances (if occasion require) as that which Mordecai did sometimes devise, Esther what lay in her power help forward, and the rest of the Jews establish for perpetuity; namely, that the fourteenth and fifteenth days of the Month Adar should be every year kept throughout all Generations, as days of Feasting and Joy, wherein they would rest from bodily labour, and what by Gifts of Charity bestowed upon the poor, what by other liberal signs of amity and love, all testify their thankful minds towards God, which almost beyond possibility had delivered them all, when they all were as Men dead. But this Decree, they say, was Divine not Ecclesiastical,* as

Esth. ix.

* T. C. l. iii. p. 193. The example out of Esther is no sufficient warrant for these Feasts in question. For first, as in other cases, so in this case of days, the estate of Christians under the Gospel ought not to be so ceremonious as was theirs under the Law. Secondly, that which was done there, was done by a special direction of the Spirit of God, either through the ministry of the Prophets which they had, or by some other extraordinary means, which is not to be followed by us. This may appear by another place, Zach. viii. where the Jews changed their Fasts into Feasts, only by the mouth of the Lord, through the ministry of the Prophet. For further proof whereof, first, I take the 28th verse, where it appeareth, that this was an order to endure always, even as long as the other Feast-days which were instituted by the Lord himself. So that what abuses soever were of that Feast, yet as a perpetual Decree of God it ought to have remained; whereas our Churches can make no such Decree, which may not upon change of times, and other circumstances, be altered. For the other proof hereof I take the last verse: for the Prophet contenteth not himself with that, that he had rehearsed the Decree, as he doth sometimes the Decree of prophane Kings, but addeth precisely, that as soon as ever the Decree was made, it

may appear in that there is another Decree in another Book of Scripture, which Decree is plain not to have proceeded from the Church's authority, but from the Mouth of the Prophet only; and as a poor simple Man sometime was fully persuaded that if Pontius Pilate had not been a Saint, the Apostles would never have suffered his name to stand in the Creed; so these Men have a strong opinion, that because the Book of Esther is Canonical, the Decree of Esther cannot be possibly Ecclesiastical. If it were, they ask how the Jews could bind themselves always to keep it, seeing Ecclesiastical Laws are mutable? As though the purposes of Men might never intend constancy in that, the nature whereof is subject to alteration. Doth the Scripture itself make mention of any divine Commandment? Is the Scripture witness of more, than only that Mordecai was the Author of this Custom, that by Letters written to his Brethren the Jews throughout all Provinces under Darius the King of Persia, he gave them charge to celebrate yearly those two Days, for perpetual remembrance of God's miraculous Deliverance and Mercy; that the Jews hereupon undertook to do it, and made it with general consent an order for perpetuity; that Esther, secondly, by her Letters confirmed the same which Mordecai had before decreed; and that, finally, the Ordinance was written to remain forever upon record? Did not the Jews in Provinces abroad observe at the first the fourteenth Day, the Jews in Susis the fifteenth? Were they not all reduced to an uniform Order by means of those two Decrees, and so every where three Days

it was registered in this Book of Esther, which is one of the Books of Canonical Scripture, declaring thereby in what esteem they had it. If it had been of no further authority than our Decrees, or than a Canon of one of the Councils, it had been presumption to have brought it into the Library of the Holy Ghost. The sum of my Answer is, that this Decree was Divine, and not Ecclesiastical only.

BOOK V. kept; the firſt with Faſting, in memory of danger; the reſt, in token of Deliverance, as Feſtival and joyful Days? Was not the firſt of theſe three afterwards, the Day of Sorrow and Heavineſs, abrogated, when the ſame Church ſaw it meet that a better Day, a Day in memory of like Deliverance out of the bloody hands of Nicanor, ſhould ſucceed in the room thereof? But foraſmuch as there is no end of anſwering fruitleſs oppoſitions, let it ſuffice Men of ſober minds to know, that the Law both of God and Nature alloweth generally Days of Reſt and Feſtival Solemnity to be obſerved by way of thankful and joyful Remembrance, if ſuch miraculous Favours be ſhewed towards Mankind as require the ſame; that ſuch Graces God hath beſtowed upon his Church, as well in latter as in former times; that in ſome particulars, when they have fallen out, himſelf hath demanded his own honour, and in the reſt hath left it to the wiſdom of the Church, directed by thoſe precedents, and enlightened by other means, always to judge when the like is requiſite. About Queſtions therefore, concerning Days and Times, our manner is not to ſtand at bay with the Church of God, demanding wherefore the memory of * Paul ſhould be rather kept than the memory of † Daniel, we are content to imagine, it may be perhaps true, that the leaſt in the Kingdom of Chriſt is greater than the greateſt of all the Prophets of God that have gone before; we never yet ſaw cauſe to deſpair, but that the ‡ ſimpleſt of the People might be taught the

2 Mac. xv. 36.

1 Mac. iv. 55.

* Commemoratio Apoſtolica Paſſionis, totius Chriſtianitatis magiſtra, a cunctis jure celebratur. Cod. lib. iii. tit. 12. l. 7.

† T. C. lib. i. pag 153. For ſo much as the old People did never keep any Feaſt or Holiday for remembrance, either of Moſes, &c.

‡ T. C. lib. i. pag. 153. The People, when it is called St. Paul's Day, or the Bleſſed Virgin Mary's Day, can underſtand nothing thereby, but that they are inſtituted to the honour of St. Paul, or the Virgin Mary, unleſs they be otherwiſe taught. And if you ſay, let them ſo be taught, I have anſwered, that the teaching

right conſtruction of as great Myſteries as the * name of a Saint's Day doth comprehend, although the times of the year go on in their wonted courſe; we had rather glorify and bleſs God for the fruit we daily behold reaped by ſuch Ordinances, as his gracious Spirit maketh the ripe wiſdom of this National Church to bring forth, than vainly boaſt of our own peculiar and private inventions, as if the ſkill of † profitable Regiment had left her publick habitation to dwell in retired manner with ſome few Men of one livery; we make not our childiſh appeals, ſometimes from our own to foreign Churches, ſometimes from both unto Churches ancienter than both are, in effect always from all others to our own ſelves; but, as becometh them that follow with all humility the ways of Peace, we honour, reverence and obey, in the very next degree unto God, the voice of the Church of God wherein we live. They, whoſe wits are too glorious to fall to ſo low an ebb, they which have riſen and ſwoln ſo high that the walls of ordinary rivers are unable to keep them in, they whoſe wanton contentions in the cauſe whereof we have ſpoken, do make all where they go a ſea, even they, at their higheſt float, are conſtrained both to ſee and ‡ grant, that what their fancy will not yield to like, their judgment cannot with reaſon condemn.

BOOK V.

T. C. l. i. p. 154.

teaching in this Land cannot, by any Order which is yet taken, come to the moſt part of thoſe which have drunk this Poiſon, &c.

* Scilicet ignorant nos nec Chriſtum unquam relinquere, qui pro totius ſervandorum mundi ſalute paſſus eſt, nec alium quempiam colere poſſe. Nam hunc quidem tanquam Filium Dei adoramus, Martyres verò tanquam Diſcipulos et Imitatores Domini digne propter inſuperabilem in Regem ipſorum ac Præceptorem benevolentiam diligimus, quorum et nos conſortes et diſcipulos fieri optamus. Euſeb. Hiſt. Eccleſ. lib. iv cap. 15.

† T. C. lib. i. pag. 153. As for all the commodities, &c.

‡ T. C. lib. i. pag 154. We condemn not the Church of England, neither in this, nor in other things, which are meet to be reformed. For it is one thing to miſlike, another thing to condemn; and it is one thing to condemn ſomething in the Church, and another thing to condemn the Church for it.

Such

BOOK V Such is evermore the final victory of all Truth, that they which had not the hearts to love her, acknowledge that to hate her they have no cause. Touching those Festival Days therefore which we now observe, their number being no way felt * discommodious to the Commonwealth, and their grounds such as hitherto hath been shewed, what remaineth, but to keep them throughout all Generations holy, severed by manifest notes of difference from other times, adorned with that which most may betoken true, virtuous, and celestial Joy? To which intent, because surcease from labour is necessary, yet not so necessary, no not on the Sabbath or seventh day itself, but that rarer occasions in Men's particular affairs, subject to manifest detriment unless they be presently followed, may with very good conscience draw them sometimes aside from the ordinary rule, considering the favourable dispensation which our

Mark ii. 27 Numb. xv. 32. Lord and Saviour groundeth on this axiom, *Man was not made for the Sabbath, but the Sabbath ordained for Man*, so far forth as concerneth Ceremonies annexed to the principal Sanctification thereof, howsoever the rigour of the Law of Moses may be thought to import the contrary; if we regard with what severity the violation of Sabbaths hath been sometime punished, a thing perhaps the more requisite at that instant, both because the Jews, by reason of their long abode in a place of continual servile toil, could not suddenly be weaned and drawn unto contrary offices without some strong impression of terror; and also for that there is nothing more needful, than to punish with extremity the first transgressions of those Laws that require a more exact observation for many ages to come; therefore as the Jews, superstitiously addicted to their Sabbaths' rest for a long time, not

* Πολλὰς μὲν θυσίας, πολλὰς δὲ καὶ ἱερομηνίας ἔπαυσε· τό τε γὰρ πλεῖστον τοῦ ἔτους εἰς αὐτὰς ἀνηλίσκετο καὶ τῷ δημοσίῳ ζημία οὐκ ἐλαχίστη ἐγίγνετο. De Claudio dictum apud Dionys. lib. lx.

without

without danger to themſelves and * obloquy to their very Law, did afterwards perceive and amend wiſely their former error, not doubting that bodily labours are made by neceſſity venial, though otherwiſe, eſpecially on that day, reſt be more convenient; ſo at all times, the voluntary ſcandalous contempt of that reſt from labour, wherewith publickly God is ſerved, we cannot too ſeverely correct and bridle. The Emperor Conſtantine having with over-great facility licenſed Sunday's labour in country villages, under that pretence, whereof there may juſtly no doubt ſometime conſideration be had, namely, leſt any thing which God by his providence hath beſtowed ſhould miſcarry not being taken in due time; Leo, which afterwards ſaw that this ground would not bear ſo general and large indulgence as had been granted, doth by a contrary Edict both reverſe and ſeverely cenſure his Predeceſſor's remiſſneſs, ſaying, *We ordain, according to the true meaning of the Holy Ghoſt and of the Apoſtles thereby directed, that on the ſacred day, wherein our own integrity was reſtored, all do reſt and ſurceaſe labour, that neither Huſbandman, nor other, on that Day put their hands to forbidden works. For if the Jews did ſo much reverence their Sabbath, which was but a ſhadow of ours, are not we, which inhabit the Light and Truth of Grace, bound to honour that Day which the Lord himſelf hath honoured, and hath therein delivered us both from diſhonour and from death? Are we not bound to keep it ſingular and inviolable, well contenting ourſelves with ſo liberal a grant of the reſt, and not incroaching upon that one Day which God hath*

BOOK V.

1 Mac 1. 40.

Neh. xiii. 15.

Cod lib iii. tit. 12. l. 3.

Leo Conſtit. liv.

* Hi vacare conſueti ſunt ſeptima die, et neque arma portare in prædictis diebus, neque terræ culturam contingere, neque alterius cujuſpiam curam habere patiuntur, ſed in templis extendentes manus adorare uſque ad veſperam ſoliti ſunt. Ingrediente vero in civitatem Ptolomæo Lago cum exercitu et multis hominibus, cum cuſtodire debuerint civitatem, ipſis ſtultitiam obſervantibus, provincia quidem dominum ſuſcepit amariſſimum, Lex vero manifeſtata eſt malam habere ſolennitatem. Agatharchid. apud Joſeph. lib. i. contra Appion. Vide & Dionyſ. lib. xxxvii.

choſen

BOOK V *chosen to his own honour? Were it not reckless neglect of Religion to make that very Day common, and to think we may do with it as with the rest?* Imperial Laws which had such care of hallowing, especially our Lord's Day, did not omit to provide that other Festival times might be kept with vacation from labour, whether they were days appointed on the sudden, as extraordinary occasions fell out, or days which were celebrated yearly for politick and civil considerations; or, finally, such days as Christian Religion hath ordained in God's Church. The joy that setteth aside labour, disperseth those things which labour gathereth. For gladness doth always rise from a kind of fruition and happiness, which happiness banisheth the cogitation of all want, it needeth nothing but only the bestowing of that it hath, in as much as the greatest felicity that felicity hath, is to spread and enlarge itself. It cometh hereby to pass, that the first effect of joyfulness is to rest, because it seeketh no more; the next, because it aboundeth, to give. The root of both, is the glorious presence of that Joy of Mind, which ariseth from the manifold considerations of God's unspeakable Mercy, into which considerations we are led by occasion of sacred times. For, how could the Jewish Congregations of old be put in mind by their weekly Sabbaths what the World reaped through his goodness, which did of nothing create the World; by their yearly Passover, what farewell they took of the Land of Egypt; by their Pentecost, what Ordinances, Laws and Statutes their Fathers received at the hands of God; by their Feast of Tabernacles, with what protection they journeyed from place to place, through so many fears and hazards, during the tedious time of forty years travel in the Wilderness; by their annual solemnity of Lots, how near the whole Seed of Israel was unto utter extirpation, when it pleaseth that Great God which guideth all things in Heaven and Earth, so to change the counsels and purposes of Men, that the same hand which had signed a Decree, in the opinion both

T. C. lib. iii. tit 12. Dies festus

both of them that granted and of them that procured BOOK V.
it irrevocable, for the general massacre of Man, Woman and Child, became the buckler of their preservation, that no one hair of their heads might be touched; the same days which had been set for the pouring out of so much innocent blood were made the days of their execution whose malice had contrived the plot thereof; and the self-same Persons that should have endured whatsoever violence and rage could offer, were employed in the just revenge of cruelty, to give unto blood-thirsty Men the taste of their own cup; or how can the Church of Christ now endure to be so much called on, and preached unto,
by that which every Dominical day throughout the Matth.
year, that which year by year so many Festival times, xxviii 1. Mark xvi.
* if not commanded by the Apostles themselves, whose 1.
care at that time was of greater things, yet instituted Luke xxiv. 1.
either by such † universal Authority as no Man, or at John xx.
the least such as we with no reason may despise, doth 1. 1 Cor. xvi.
as sometime the holy Angels did from Heaven, sing, 2.
Glory be unto God on high, Peace on Earth, towards Men Apoc. i. 10
good will (for this in effect is the very Song that all Luke ii. 14.
Christian Feasts do apply as their several occasions require), how should the days and times continually thus inculcate what God hath done, and we refuse to agnize the benefit of such remembrances; that very benefit which caused Moses to acknowledge those guides of day and night, the Sun and Moon, which enlighten the World, not more profitable to Nature by giving all things life, than they are to the Church of God by occasion of the use they have in regard of

* Apostolis propositum fuit, non ut leges de festis diebus celebrandis sancirent, sed ut recte vivendi rationis et pietatis nobis authores essent. Socra. Hist. lib. v. cap. 21.

† Quæ toto terrarum orbe servantur, vel ab ipsis Apostolis vel conciliis generalibus quorum est saluberrima in Ecclesia authoritas, statuta esse intelligere licet; sicuti quod Domini Passio et Resurrectio, et in Cœlum Ascensus, et Adventus Spiritus Sancti, anniversaria solemnitate celebrarentur. August. Epist. cxviii.

the

BOOK V. the appointed Feſtival times? That which the head of all Philoſophers hath ſaid of Women, *If they be good, the half of the Commonwealth is happy wherein they are*; the ſame we may fitly apply to times; well to celebrate theſe religious and ſacred Days, is to ſpend the flower of our time happily. They are the ſplendor and outward dignity of our Religion, forcible witneſſes of ancient Truth, provocations to the exerciſes of all Piety, ſhadows of our endleſs Felicity in Heaven, on Earth everlaſting records and memorials; wherein they which cannot be drawn to hearken unto that we teach, may only, by looking upon that we do, in a manner read whatſoever we believe.

Of Days appointed as well for ordinary, as for extraordinary Faſts in the Church of God.

72. The matching of contrary things together is a kind of illuſtration to both. Having therefore ſpoken thus much of Feſtival Days, the next that offer themſelves to hand are Days of penſive Humiliation and Sorrow. Faſtings are either of Men's own free and voluntary accord, as their particular devotion doth move them thereunto; or elſe they are publickly enjoined in the Church, and required at the hands of all Men. * There are which altogether diſallow not

* T. C. lib. i. pag. 30. I will not enter now to diſcuſs, whether it were well done to faſt in all places according to the cuſtom of the place. You oppoſe Ambroſe and Auguſtin; I could oppoſe Ignatius and Tertullian; whereof the one ſaith, It is *nefas*, a deteſtable thing to faſt upon the Lord's Day; the other, that it is to kill the Lord. Tertul. de Coron. Mil. Ignatius, Epiſt. ad Philippen. And although Ambroſe and Auguſtin, being private Men at Rome, would have ſo done, yet it followeth not, that if they had been Citizens and Miniſters there, they would have done it. And if they had done ſo, yet it followeth not, but that they would have ſpoken againſt that appointment of days, and νομοθεσίαν of Faſting, whereof Euſebius ſaith, that Montanus was the firſt Author. I ſpeak of that which they ought to have done. For otherwiſe I know, they both thought corruptly of Faſting; when as the one ſaith, it was a remedy or reward to faſt other days, but in Lent not to faſt was ſin; and the other aſketh, what Salvation we can obtain, if we blot not out our ſins by Faſting, ſeeing that the Scripture ſaith, That Faſting and Alms doth deliver from ſin; and therefore calleth them new Teachers, that ſhut out the merit of Faſting. Auguſt. de Temp. lxii. Serm. Ambr. lib. x. Epiſt.

the

the former kind; and the latter they greatly commend, so that it be upon extraordinary occasions only, and after one certain manner exercised. But yearly or weekly Fasts, such as ours in the Church of England, they allow no farther than as the temporal state of the Land doth require the same, for the maintenance of sea-faring Men and preservation of Cattle; because the decay of the one, and the waste of the other, could not well be prevented but by a politick Order appointing some such usual change of diet as ours is. We are therefore the rather to make it manifest in all Men's eyes, that set-times of Fasting, appointed in spiritual considerations to be kept by all sorts of Men, took not their beginning either from Montanus, or any other, whose Heresies may prejudice the credit and due estimation thereof, but have their ground in the Law of Nature, are allowable in God's sight, were in all ages heretofore, and may till the World's end be observed not without singular use and benefit. Much hurt hath grown to the Church of God through a false imagination that Fasting standeth Men in no stead for any spiritual respect, but only to take down the frankness of Nature, and to tame the wildness of flesh. Whereupon the World being bold to surfeit, doth now blush to fast, supposing that Men, when they fast, do rather bewray a disease than exercise a virtue. I much wonder what they who are thus persuaded do think, what conceit they have concerning the Fasts of the Patriarchs, the Prophets, the Apostles, our Lord Jesus Christ himself. The affections of joy and grief are so knit unto all the actions of Man's life, that whatsoever we can do, or may be done unto us, the sequel thereof is continually the one or the other affection. Wherefore considering that they which grieve and joy as they ought, cannot possibly otherwise live than as they should, the Church of Christ, the most absolute and perfect School of all Virtue, hath, by the special direction of God's good Spirit, hitherto always inured Men from their infancy, partly with days of Festival

BOOK V. Feſtival exerciſe for the framing of the one affection, and partly with times of a contrary ſort for the perfecting of the other. Howbeit, over and beſides this, we muſt note, that as reſting, ſo Faſting likewiſe attendeth ſometimes no leſs upon the actions of the higher, than upon the affections of the lower part of the Mind. Faſting, ſaith Tertullian, is a work of reverence towards God. The end thereof, ſometimes elevation of Mind; ſometime the purpoſe thereof clean contrary. The cauſe why Moſes in the Mount did ſo long faſt was mere divine Speculation; the cauſe why David, * Humiliation. Our life is † a mixture of good with evil. When we are partakers of good things, we joy; neither can we but grieve at the contrary. If that befal us which maketh glad, our Feſtival Solemnities declare our rejoicing to be in Him, whoſe mere undeſerved mercy is the author of all happineſs; if any thing be either imminent or preſent which we ſhun, our Watchings, Faſtings, Cries and Tears, are unfeigned teſtimonies that ourſelves we condemn as the only cauſes of our own miſery, and do all acknowledge him no leſs inclinable than able to ſave. And becauſe as the memory of the one, though paſt, reneweth gladneſs; ſo the other, called again to mind, doth make the wound of our juſt remorſe to bleed anew; which wound needeth often touching the more, for that we are generally more apt to kalendar Saints than ſinners days; therefore there is in the Church a care not to iterate the one alone, but to have frequent repetition of the other. Never to ſeek after God ſaving only when either the crib or the whip doth conſtrain, were brutiſh ſervility, and a great

* Tertul. de jejun. Neque enim cibi tempus in periculo: ſemper inedia mœroris ſequela eſt.

† Μηδεὶς δ' ὑπολαβέτω τὴν ἄκρατον καὶ ἀμιγῆ λύπης χαρὰν ἀπ' οὐρανοῦ καταβαίνειν ἐπὶ τὴν γῆν, ἀλλ' ἐγκέκραται ἐξ ἀμφοῖν· οὐ γὰρ εἴασεν ὁ πατὴρ τὸ ἀνθρώπων γένος λύπαις καὶ ὀδύναις καὶ ἄχθεσιν ἀνιάτοις ἐμφέρεσθαι, παρέμιξε δὲ καὶ τῆς ἀμείνονος φύσεως, ἐνδιάσας ποτὲ καὶ γαληνιάσαι τὴν ψυχὴν δικαιώσας. Philo. l. de Abrah.

derogation

derogation to the worth of that which is moſt predominant in Man, if ſometime it had not a kind of voluntary acceſs to God, and of conference, as it were, with God, all theſe inferior conſiderations laid aſide. In which ſequeſtration, for as much as higher cogitations do naturally drown and bury all inferior cares, John iv 34. the Mind may as well forget natural both food and ſleep, by being carried above itſelf with ſerious and heavenly meditation, as by being caſt down with heavineſs, drowned and ſwallowed up of ſorrow. Albeit therefore, concerning Jewiſh Abſtinence from certain kinds of meats as being unclean, the Apoſtle doth teach, that *the Kingdom of Heaven is not meat nor drink*, Rom. xiv. 17. that *food commendeth us not unto God*, whether we take it, or abſtain from it; that if we eat, we are not thereby the more acceptable in his ſight; nor the leſs, if we eat not; his purpoſe notwithſtanding was far from any intent to derogate from that Faſting, which is no ſuch ſcrupulous Abſtinence as only refuſeth ſome kinds of meats and drinks, leſt they make them unclean that taſte them; but an Abſtinence whereby we either interrupt, or otherwiſe abridge the care of our bodily ſuſtenance, to ſhew by this kind of outward exerciſe the ſerious intention of our Minds fixed on heavenlier and better deſires, the earneſt hunger and thirſt whereof depriveth the Body of thoſe uſual contentments, which otherwiſe are not denied unto it. Theſe being in Nature the firſt cauſes that induce Faſting, the next thing which followeth to be conſidered, is the ancient practice thereof amongſt the Jews. Touching whoſe private voluntary Faſts the Precept which our Saviour gave them was, *When* Matth vi. 16. *ye faſt, look not ſour, as Hypocrites: For they disfigure their faces, that they might ſeem to Men to faſt. Verily, I ſay unto you, they have their reward. When thou faſteſt, anoint thy head, and waſh thy face, that thou ſeem not unto Men to faſt, but unto thy Father which is in ſecret; and thy Father which ſeeth in ſecret, will reward thee openly.* Our Lord and Saviour would not teach the

BOOK V. manner of doing, much leſs propoſe a reward for doing that which were not both holy and acceptable in God's ſight. The Phariſees weekly bound themſelves unto double Faſts, neither are they for this reproved. Often faſting, which was a virtue in John's Diſciples, could not in them of itſelf be a vice; and therefore not the oftenneſs of their Faſting, but their Hypocriſy

2 Chron. xx. Jerem. xxxvi. Ezra viii. therein was blamed. Of publick enjoined Faſts, upon cauſes extraordinary, the examples in Scripture are ſo far frequent, that they need no particular rehearſal.

1 Sam. vii. Judg. xx. 26. 2 Mac. xiii. 12. 1 Sam. xxxi. 13. 1 Chron. x. 12. Publick extraordinary Faſtings were ſometimes for one only day, ſometimes for three, ſometimes for ſeven. Touching Faſts not appointed for any ſuch extraordinary cauſes, but either yearly, or monthly, or weekly obſerved and kept; firſt, upon the * ninth day of that month, the tenth whereof was the Feaſt of

Levit. xxiii. Levit. xvi. Expiation, they were commanded of God that every Soul, year by year, ſhould afflict itſelf. Their yearly Faſts every fourth month, in regard of the City of Jeruſalem entered by the Enemy, every fifth, for the memory of the overthrow of their temple; every ſeventh, for the treacherous deſtruction and death of Gedaliah, the very laſt ſtay which they had to lean unto in their greateſt miſery; every tenth, in remembrance of the time when ſiege began firſt to be laid againſt them; all theſe not commanded by God himſelf, but ordained by a publick Conſtitution of their

Zach. viii. 16. Exod. xxxii. Numb. xiv. own, the Prophet Zachary expreſly toucheth. That St. Jerom, following the Tradition of the Hebrews, doth make the firſt a memorial of the breaking of thoſe two Tables, when Moſes deſcended from Mount Sinai; the ſecond, a memorial as well of God's indignation, condemning them to forty years travel in the

* Philo de hujus feſti jejunio ita loquitur Οὐ σιτίον οὐ ποτὸν ἔξεστι προσενέγκασθαι, καθαραῖς ὅπως διανοίαις μηδενὸς ἐνοχλοῦντος μηδὲ ἐμποδίζοντος σωματικοῦ πάθους ὁποῖα φιλεῖ συμβαίνειν ἐκ πλησμονῆς ἑορτάζωσιν ἱλασκόμενοι τὸν Πατέρα τοῦ παντὸς ὁσίαις εὐχαῖς, δι' ὧν ἀμνηστείαν μὲν παλαιῶν ἁμαρτημάτων, κτῆσιν δὲ καὶ ἀπόλαυσιν νέων ἀγαθῶν εἰώθασιν αἰτεῖσθαι. Pag. 447.

Deſart,

Deſart, as of his wrath, in permitting Chaldeans to waſte, burn and deſtroy their City; the laſt a memorial of heavy tidings, brought out of Jewry to Ezekiel and the reſt, which lived as Captives in foreign parts; the difference is not of any moment, conſidering that each time of ſorrow is naturally evermore a regiſter of all ſuch grievous events as have happened either in, or near about the ſame time. To theſe I might add ſundry other Faſts, above twenty in number, ordained amongſt them by like occaſions, and obſerved in like manner, beſides their weekly Abſtinence, Mondays and Thurſdays, throughout the whole year. When Men faſted, it was not always after one and the ſame ſort; but either by depriving themſelves wholly of all food, during the time that their Faſts continued; or by abating both the quantity and kind of diet. We have of the one a plain example in the Ninevites Faſting; and as plain a precedent for the other in the Prophet Daniel; *I was* (ſaith he) *in heavineſs for three weeks of days; I ate no pleaſant bread, neither taſted fleſh nor wine.* Their Tables, when they gave themſelves to faſting, had not that uſual furniture of ſuch diſhes as do cheriſh blood with blood; but * for food, they had bread; for ſuppage, ſalt; and for ſauce, herbs. Whereunto the Apoſtle may be thought to allude, ſaying, *One believeth he may eat all things, another which is weak* (and maketh a conſcience of keeping thoſe Cuſtoms which the Jews obſerve) *eateth herbs.* This auſtere repaſt they took in the evening after abſtinence the whole day: for to forfeit a noon's meal, and then to recompence themſelves at night, was not their uſe; nor did they ever accuſtom themſelves on Sabbaths, or Feſtival days, to faſt. And yet it may be a queſtion, whether in ſome ſort they did not always faſt the Sabbath. Their

Vide Riber. lib. v. cap. 21.

Dan. x. 2, 3.

Rom xiv. 2.

Hieron lib. ii contr Jovinian.

Judith viii. 6.

R Mcſ in Miſne. Tora lib in Qui eſt de tempor. cap. de Sab & cap de Jejun.

* Puram et ſine animalibus cœnam. Apul. in Aſclep. in fine. Paſtum et potum pura noſſe, non ventris ſcilicet ſed animæ cauſa. Tertul. de Pœnit. Vide Phil. lib. de Vita contempl.

BOOK V. Faſtings were partly in token of penitency, humiliation, grief and ſorrow, partly in ſign of devotion and reverence towards God. Which ſecond conſideration (I dare not peremptorily and boldly affirm any thing) might induce to abſtain till noon, as their manner was on Faſting days to do till night. May it not very well be thought, that hereunto the ſacred Scripture doth give ſome ſecret kind of teſtimony? Joſephus is plain, * that the ſixth hour (the day they divided into twelve) was wont on the Sabbath always to call them home unto meat. Neither is it improbable, but that the † Heathens did therefore ſo often upbraid them with faſting on that day. Beſides, they which found ſo great fault with our Lord's Diſciples, for rubbing a few ears of corn in their hands on the Sabbath-day, are not unlikely to have aimed alſo at the ſame mark. For neither was the bodily pain ſo great, that it ſhould offend them in that reſpect, and the very manner of defence which our Saviour there uſeth, is more direct and literal to juſtify the breach of the Jewiſh cuſtom in faſting, than in working at that time. Finally, the Apoſtles afterwards themſelves, when God firſt gave them the gift of tongues, whereas ſome in diſdain and ſpite, termed grace, drunkenneſs, it being then the day of Pentecoſt, and but only a fourth part of the day ſpent, they uſe this as an argument againſt the other cavil, *Theſe Men*, ſaith Peter, *are not drunk as you ſuppoſe, ſince as yet the third hour of the day is not over-paſt.* Howbeit, leaving this in ſuſpenſe as a thing not altogether certainly known, and to come from Jews to Chriſtians, we find that of private voluntary Faſtings the Apoſtle St. Paul ſpeaketh more than once. And (ſaith Tertullian) they are ſometime

Nehem. viii. 3, 12.

Acts ii. 15.

1 Cor. vii. 5. 2 Cor. vi. 5, & xi 27. Col. iv. 4.

* Hora ſexta quæ Sabbatis noſtris ad prandium vocare ſolet, ſupervenit Joſeph. lib de Vita ſua.

† Sabbata Judæorum a Moſe in omne ævum jejunio dicata. Juſtin. lib. xxxvi. Ne Judæus quidem, mi Tiberi, tam libenter Sabbati jejunium ſervat, quam ego hodie ſervavi. Sueton. in Octav. c. lxxvi.

commanded

commanded throughout the Church, *Ex aliqua ſollicitudinis Eccleſiaſticæ cauſa*, the care and fear of the Church ſo requiring. It doth not appear, that the Apoſtles ordained any ſet and certain days to be generally kept of all. Notwithſtanding, for as much as Chriſt hath fore-ſignified, that when himſelf ſhould be taken from them, his abſence would ſoon make them apt to faſt, it ſeemeth, that even as the firſt feſtival-day appointed to be kept of the Church was the day of our Lord's return from the dead, ſo the firſt ſorrowful and mournful day was that which we now obſerve in memory of his departure out of this World. And becauſe there could be no abatement of grief till they ſaw him raiſed, whoſe death was the occaſion of their heavineſs; therefore the day he lay in the Sepulchre hath been alſo kept and obſerved as a weeping day. The Cuſtom of Faſting theſe two days before Eaſter is undoubtedly moſt ancient; in ſo much, that Ignatius not thinking him a Catholick Chriſtian Man which did not abhor, and (as the ſtate of the Church was then) avoid faſting on the Jews' Sabbath, doth notwithſtanding except for ever that one Sabbath or Saturday which falleth out to be the Eaſter-Eve, as with us it always doth, and did ſometimes alſo with them, which kept at that time their Eaſter the fourteenth day of March, as the cuſtom of the Jews was. It came afterwards to be an order, that even as the day of Chriſt's Reſurrection, ſo the other two, in memory of his Death and Burial, were weekly. But this, when St. Ambroſe lived, had not as yet taken place throughout all Churches, no not in Milan, where himſelf was Biſhop. And for that cauſe, he ſaith, that although at Rome he obſerved the Saturday's Faſt, becauſe ſuch was then the cuſtom in Rome, nevertheleſs in his own Church at home he did otherwiſe. The Churches which did not obſerve that day had another inſtead thereof, which was the Wedneſday, for that when they judged it meet to have weekly a day of humiliation, beſides that whereon our

Ignat. Epiſt. ad Philip.

BOOK V. Saviour ſuffered death, it ſeemed beſt to make their choice of that day eſpecially whereon the Jews are thought to have firſt contrived their treaſon together with Judas againſt Chriſt. So that the inſtituting and ordaining both of theſe, and of all other times of like exerciſe, is as the Church ſhall judge expedient for Men's good. And concerning every Chriſtian Man's duty herein, ſurely that which Auguſtin and Ambroſe are before alledged to have done, is ſuch, as all Men favouring equity muſt needs allow and follow, if they affect peace. As for their ſpecified errors, I will not in this place diſpute, whether voluntarily faſting with a virtuous purpoſe of mind, be any medicinable remedy of evil, or a duty acceptable unto God, and in the World to come even rewardable as other offices are which proceed from Chriſtian Piety; whether wilfully to break and deſpiſe the wholeſome Laws of the Church herein be a thing which offendeth God; whether truly it may not be ſaid, that penitent both weeping and Faſting are means to blot out ſin, means whereby through God's unſpeakable and undeſerved mercy we obtain or procure to ourſelves pardon; which attainment unto any gracious benefit by him beſtowed, the phraſe of Antiquity uſeth to expreſs by the name of Merit; but if either St. Auguſtin or St. Ambroſe have taught any wrong opinion, ſeeing they which reprove them are not altogether free from error, I hope they will think it no error in us ſo to cenſure Men's ſmaller faults, that their virtues be not thereby generally prejudiced. And if in Churches abroad, where we are not ſubject to power or juriſdiction, diſcretion ſhould teach us for peace and quietneſs ſake to frame ourſelves to other Men's example, is it meet that at home, where our freedom is leſs, our boldneſs ſhould be more? Is it our duty to oppugn, in the Churches whereof we are Miniſters, the Rites and Cuſtoms which in foreign Churches piety and modeſty did teach us as Strangers not to oppugn, but to keep without ſhew of contradiction or diſlike? Why oppoſe they

they the name of a Minister in this case unto the state of a private Man? Doth their order exempt them from obedience to Laws? That which their office and place requireth, is to shew themselves patterns of reverend subjection, not Authors and Masters of contempt towards Ordinances; the strength whereof when they seek to weaken, they do but in truth discover to the World their own imbecilities, which a great deal wiselier they might conceal. But the practice of the Church of Christ we shall by so much the better both understand and love, if to that which hitherto hath been spoken, there be somewhat added for more particular declaration, how Hereticks have partly abused Fasts, and partly bent themselves against the lawful use thereof in the Church of God. Whereas therefore Ignatius hath said, * if any keep Sundays or Saturdays Fasts (one only Saturday in the year excepted) that Man is no better than a murtherer of Christ; the cause of such his earnestness at that time, was the impiety of certain Hereticks, which thought that this World being corruptible could not be made but by a very evil Author. And therefore as the Jews did, by the Festival Solemnity of their Sabbath, rejoice in the God that created the World as in the Author of all Goodness; so those Hereticks, in hatred of the Maker of the World, sorrowed, wept and fasted on that day as being the birth-day of all evil. And as Christian Men of sound belief did solemnize the Sunday in joyful memory of Christ's Resurrection, so likewise at the self-same time such Hereticks as denied his Resurrection did the contrary to them which held it; when the one sort rejoiced, the other fasted. Against those Hereticks which have urged perpetual Abstinence from certain meats, as being in their very nature unclean, the Church hath still bent herself as an enemy; St. Paul giving charge to take heed of them, which

Vide Irenæ. lib. i cap. 20, 21, 22, 23, 24, 25. Epiph. Hæres. 20, 21, 22, 23, 24, 27, 28, & 41, 42. Vide Canon. Apost. 55.

* Εἴ τις κυριακὴν ἢ σάββατον νηστεύει πλὴν ἑνὸς σαββάτου, οὗτος χριστοκτόνος ἐστί. Epist. ad Philip.

BOOK V. under any ſuch opinion, ſhould utterly forbid the uſe of meats or drinks. The Apoſtles themſelves forbad ſome, as the order taken at Jeruſalem declareth; but the cauſe of their ſo doing we all know. Again, when Tertullian, together with ſuch as were his followers, began to Montanize, and, pretending to perfect the ſeverity of Chriſtian Diſcipline, brought in ſundry unaccuſtomed Days of Faſting, continued their Faſts a great deal longer, and made them more rigorous than the uſe of the Church had been; the minds of Men being ſomewhat moved at ſo great and ſo ſudden novelty, the cauſe was preſently inquired into. After notice taken how the Montaniſts held theſe additions to be ſupplements of the Goſpel, whereunto the Spirit of Prophecy did now mean to put, as it were, the laſt hand, and was therefore newly deſcended upon Montanus, whoſe orders all Chriſtian Men were no leſs to obey than the Laws of the Apoſtles themſelves; this Abſtinence the Church abhorred likewiſe, and that juſtly. Whereupon Tertullian proclaiming even open War to the Church, maintained Montaniſm, wrote a Book in defence of the new Faſt, and intituled the ſame, *A Treatiſe of Faſting againſt the opinion of the carnal ſort.* In which Treatiſe nevertheleſs, becauſe ſo much is ſound and good, as doth either generally concern the uſe, or in particular declare the Cuſtom of the Churches Faſting in thoſe times, Men are not to reject whatſoever is alledged out of that Book for confirmation of the Truth. His error diſcloſeth itſelf in thoſe places where he defendeth his Faſts to be duties neceſſary for the whole Church of Chriſt to obſerve, as commanded by the Holy Ghoſt, and that with the ſame authority from whence all other Apoſtolical Ordinances came, both being the Laws of God himſelf, without any other diſtinction or difference, ſaving only, that he which before had declared his will by Paul and Peter, did now farther reveal the ſame by Montanus alſo. *Againſt us ye pretend*, ſaith Tertullian, *that the publick Orders which Chriſtianity is bound*

bound to keep, were delivered at the first, and that no new thing is to be added thereunto. Stand if you can upon this point; for behold, I challenge you for fasting more than at Easter, yourselves. But in fine ye answer, that these things are to be done as established by the voluntary appointment of Men, and not by virtue or force of any divine commandment. Well then (he addeth) *ye have removed your first footing, and gone beyond that which was delivered, by doing more than was at the first imposed upon you. You say, you must do that which your own judgments have allowed: we require your obedience to that which God himself doth institute. Is it not strange, that Men to their own will should yield that, which to God's commandment they will not grant? Shall the pleasure of Men prevail more with you, than the power of God himself?* These places of Tertullian for Fasting have worthily been put to silence; and as worthily Aërius condemned for opposition against Fasting. The one endeavoured to bring in such Fasts as the Church ought not to receive; the other, to overthrow such as already it had received and did observe: the one was plausible unto many, by seeming to hate carnal looseness and riotous excess, much more than the rest of the World did; the other drew hearers, by pretending the maintainance of Christian liberty: the one thought his cause very strongly upheld by making invective declamations with a pale and withered countenance against the Church, by filling the ears of his starved hearers with speech suitable to such Men's humours, and by telling them, no doubt, to their marvellous contentment and liking, *Our new Prophecies are refused, they are despised. Is it because Montanus doth preach some other God, or dissolve the Gospel of Jesus Christ, or overthrow any Canon of Faith and Hope? No, our crime is, we teach that Men ought to fast more often than marry; the best Feast-maker is with them the perfectest Saint, they are assuredly mere Spirit; and therefore these our corporal devotions please them not:* thus the one for Montanus and his Superstition. The other in a clean

BOOK V.

BOOK V. clean contrary tune againſt the Religion of the Church; *theſe ſet faſts away with them, for they are Jewiſh, and bring Men under the yoke of ſervitude; if I will faſt, let me chooſe my time, that Chriſtian liberty be not abridged.* Hereupon their glory was to faſt eſpecially upon the Sunday, becauſe the order of the Church was on that day not to faſt. *On Church Faſting-days, and eſpecially the week before Eaſter, when with us* (ſaith Epiphanius) *Cuſtom admitteth nothing but lying down upon the earth, abſtinence from fleſhly delights and pleaſures, ſorrowfulneſs, dry and unſavoury diet, Prayer, Watching, Faſting, all the medicines which holy affections can miniſter, they are up betimes to take in of the ſtrongeſt for the belly, and when their veins are well ſwoln, they make themſelves mirth with laughter at this our ſervice, wherein we are perſuaded we pleaſe God.* By this of Epiphanius it doth appear, not only what Faſtings the Church of Chriſt in thoſe times uſed, but alſo what other parts of Diſcipline were together therewith in force, according to the ancient uſe and cuſtom of bringing all Men at certain times to a due conſideration and an open humiliation of themſelves.

Epiph. Hæreſ. lxxv.

Two kinds there were of publick Penitency; the one belonging to notorious Offenders, whoſe open wickedneſs had been ſcandalous; the other appertaining to the whole Church, and unto every ſeveral Perſon whom the ſame containeth. It will be anſwered, that touching this latter kind, it may be exerciſed well enough by Men in private. No doubt, but Penitency is as Prayer, a thing acceptable unto God, be it in publick or in ſecret. Howbeit, as in the one, if Men were only left to their own voluntary meditations in their cloſets, and not drawn by Laws and Orders unto the open Aſſemblies of the Church that there they may join with others in Prayer, it may be ſoon conjectured what Chriſtian devotion that way would come unto in a ſhort time; even ſo in the other, we are by ſufficient experience taught, how little it booteth to tell Men of waſhing away their Sins

Sins with tears of Repentance, and ſo to leave them altogether unto themſelves. O Lord, what heaps of grievous tranſgreſſions have we committed, the beſt, the perfecteſt, the moſt righteous amongſt us all; and yet clean paſs them over unſorrowed for, and unrepented of, only becauſe the Church hath forgotten utterly how to beſtow her wonted times of Diſcipline, wherein the publick example of all was unto every particular Perſon a moſt effectual mean to put them often in mind, and even in a manner to draw them to that which now we all quite and clean forget, as if Penitency were no part of a Chriſtian Man's duty. Again, beſides our private offences which ought not thus looſely to be overſlipt; ſuppoſe we the body and corporation of the Church ſo juſt, that at no time it needeth to ſhew itſelf openly caſt down, in regard of thoſe faults and tranſgreſſions, which though they do not properly belong unto any one, had notwithſtanding a ſpecial Sacrifice appointed for them in the Law of Moſes; and being common to the whole Society which containeth all, muſt needs ſo far concern every Man in particular, as at ſome time in ſolemn manner to require acknowledgment with more than daily and ordinary teſtifications of grief. There could not hereunto a fitter preamble be deviſed, than that memorable Commination ſet down in the Book of Common Prayer, if our practice in the reſt were ſuitable. The head already ſo well drawn doth but wiſh a proportionable body. And by the Preface to that very part of the Engliſh Liturgy it may appear, how at the firſt ſetting down thereof no leſs was intended. For ſo we are to interpret the meaning of thoſe words wherein *reſtitution of the primitive Church Diſcipline is greatly wiſhed for*, touching the manner of publick Penance in time of Lent. Wherewith ſome being not much acquainted, but having framed in their minds the conceit of a new Diſcipline far unlike to that of old, they make themſelves believe, it is undoubtedly this their Diſcipline which at the firſt was ſo much deſired.

BOOK V. desired. They have long pretended, that the whole Scripture is plain for them. If now the Communion-Book make for them too (I well think the one doth as much as the other), it may be hoped, that being found such a well-wisher unto their cause, they will more favour it than they have done. Having therefore hitherto spoken both of Festival-days, and so much of solemn Fasts, as may reasonably serve to shew the ground thereof in the Law of Nature; the practice partly appointed, and partly allowed of God in the Jewish Church; the like continued in the Church of Christ; together with the sinister oppositions, either of Hereticks erroneously abusing the same, or of others thereat quarrelling without cause, we will only collect the chiefest points as well of resemblance as of difference between them, and so end. First, in this they agree, that because Nature is the general root of both, therefore both have been always common to the Church with Infidels and Heathen Men. Secondly, they also herein accord, that as oft as joy is the cause of the one, and grief the well-spring of the other, * they are incompatible. A third degree of affinity between them is, that neither being acceptable to God of itself, but both tokens of that which is acceptable, their approbation with him must necessarily depend on that which they ought to import and signify; so that if herein the mind dispose not itself aright, whether we rest or fast, we offend. A fourth thing common unto them, is, that the greatest part of the World hath always grossly and palpably offended in both; Infidels, because they did all in relation to false gods; godless, sensual and careless Minds, for that there is in them no constant, true and sincere affection towards those things which are pretended by such exercise; yea, certain flattering oversights there are, wherewith sundry, and they not of the worst sort,

Isai i. 13. Isai. lviii. 3.

* Con Laod. c. li. 52. Vetat Natalitia Martyrum in Quadragesima celebrari.

may

may be eaſily in theſe caſes led awry, even through abundance of love and liking to that which muſt be embraced by all means, but with caution, in as much as the very admiration of Saints, whether we celebrate their glory, or follow them in humility; whether we laugh or weep, mourn or rejoice with them, is (as in all things the affection of love) apt to deceive; and doth therefore need the more to be directed by a watchful guide, ſeeing there is manifeſtly both ways, even in them whom we honour, that which we are to obſerve and ſhun. The beſt have not ſtill been ſufficiently mindful, that God's very Angels in Heaven are but Angels; and that bodily exerciſe, conſidered in itſelf, is no great matter. Finally, ſeeing that both are Ordinances well deviſed for the good of Man, and yet not Man created purpoſely for them as for other offices of Virtue, whereunto God's immutable Law for ever tieth; it is but equity to wiſh or admoniſh that where, by uniform order, they are not as yet received, the example of Victor's extremity in the one, and of John's Diſciples' curioſity in the other, be not followed; yea, where they are appointed by Law, that notwithſtanding we avoid Judaiſm: and, as in Feſtival-days, Men's neceſſities for matter of labour, ſo in times of Faſting, regard be had to their imbecilities, leſt they ſhould ſuffer harm, doing good. Thus therefore we ſee how theſe two Cuſtoms are in divers reſpects equal. But of Faſting the uſe and exerciſe, though leſs pleaſant, is by ſo much more requiſite than the other, as grief of neceſſity is a more familiar gueſt than the contrary paſſion of mind, albeit gladneſs to all Men be naturally more welcome. For firſt, we ourſelves do many more things amiſs than well, and the fruit of our own ill-doing is remorſe, becauſe nature is conſcious to itſelf that it ſhould do the contrary. Again, foraſmuch as the World overaboundeth with malice, and few are delighted in doing good to other Men, there is no Man ſo ſeldom croſſed as pleaſured at the hands of others; whereupon it cannot

1 Tim. iv. 8.
Eccleſ. xii. 13.
Iſai. lviii. 6, 7.
Rom. xiv. 17.
Jam. i. 27.
Heb. xii. 14.
Epheſ. ii 4.
Euſeb. Eccleſ Hiſt. lib v. c. 23.
Matth. ix. 14.
Col. ii. 16.

BOOK V. cannot be chosen but every Man's woes must double in that respect the number and measure of his delights. Besides, concerning the very choice which oftentimes we are to make, our corrupt inclination well considered, there is cause why our Saviour should account them the happiest that do most mourn, and why Solomon might judge it better to frequent mourning than feasting houses; not better simply and in itself (for then would Nature that way incline), but in regard of us and our common weakness better. Job was not ignorant that his Children's banquets, though tending to amity, needed Sacrifice. Neither doth any of us all need to be taught that in things which delight we easily swerve from mediocrity, * and are not easily led by a right direct line. On the other side, the sores and diseases of mind which inordinate Pleasure breedeth are by Dolour and Grief cured. For which cause as all offences use to seduce by pleasing, so all punishments endeavour by vexing to reform transgressions. We are of our own accord apt enough to give entertainment to things delectable, but patiently to lack what flesh and blood doth desire, and by virtue to forbear what by Nature we covet, this no Man attaineth unto but with labour and long practice. From hence it ariseth that in former ages, Abstinence and Fasting more than ordinary was always a special branch of their praise in whom it could be observed and known, were they such as continually gave themselves to austere life; or Men that took often occasions in private virtuous respects to lay Solomon's counsel aside, *Eat thy bread with joy*, and to be followers of David's example, which saith, *I humbled my soul with fasting*, or but they who, otherwise worthy of no great commendation, have made of hunger, some their gain, some their physick, some their art, that by mastering sensual appetites without constraint,

Matth vi. 4
Eccles. vii. 4.
Job i. 5.
Eccles. ix. 7.
Psal. xxxv. 13.

* Ἐν παντὶ δὲ μάλιστα φυλακτέον τὸ ἡδὺ καὶ τὴν ἡδονήν, οὐ γὰρ ἀδέκαστοι κρίνομεν αὐτήν. Arist. Eth. ii. cap. 13.

they

they might grow able to endure hardneſs whenſoever need ſhould require: for the body accuſtomed to emptineſs pineth not away ſo ſoon as having ſtill uſed to fill itſelf. Many ſingular effects there are which ſhould make Faſting even in publick conſiderations the rather to be accepted. For I preſume we are not altogether without experience how great their advantage is in martial enterpriſes, that lead armies of Men trained in a ſchool of Abſtinence. It is therefore noted at this day in ſome, that patience of hunger and thirſt hath given them many victories; in others, that becauſe if they want, there is no Man able to rule them, nor they in plenty to moderate themſelves, he which can either bring them to hunger or overcharge them, is ſure to make them their own overthrow. What Nation ſoever doth feel theſe dangerous inconveniencies, may know that ſloth and fulneſs in peaceable times at home is the cauſe thereof, and the remedy a ſtrict obſervation of that part of Chriſtian Diſcipline, which teacheth Men in practice of ghoſtly warfare againſt themſelves, thoſe things, that afterwards may help them, juſtly aſſaulting or ſtanding in lawful defence of themſelves againſt others. The very purpoſe of the Church of God both in the number and in the order of her Faſts, hath been not only to preſerve thereby throughout all ages the remembrance of miſeries heretofore ſuſtained, and of the cauſes in ourſelves out of which they have riſen, that Men conſidering the one might fear the other the more, but farther alſo to temper the mind, leſt contrary affections coming in place ſhould make it too profuſe and diſſolute, in which reſpect it ſeemeth that Faſts have been ſet as uſhers of Feſtival-days, for preventing of thoſe diſorders as much as might be; wherein, notwithſtanding, the World always will deſerve, * as it hath done, blame; becauſe ſuch evils being not poſ-

* Valde abſurdum eſt nimia fatuitate velle honorare Martyrem quem ſcias Deo placuiſſe jejuniis. Hier. Epiſt. ad Euſt.

ſible

BOOK V. ſible to be rooted out, the moſt we can do, is in keeping them low, and (which is chiefly the fruit we look for) to create in the minds of Men a love towards a frugal and ſevere life, to undermine the palaces of wantonneſs; to plant parſimony as nature, where riotouſneſs hath been ſtudied; to harden whom pleaſure would melt; and to help the tumours which always fulneſs breedeth; that Children, as it were in the wool of their infancy dyed with hardneſs, may never afterwards change colour; that the Poor, whoſe perpetual Faſts are of neceſſity, may with better contentment endure the hunger which Virtue cauſeth others ſo often to chooſe; and by advice of Religion itſelf ſo far to eſteem above the contrary, that they which for the moſt part do lead ſenſual and eaſy lives, they which, as the Prophet David deſcribeth them, *are not plagued like other Men*, may by the publick ſpectacle of all be ſtill put in mind what themſelves are; finally, that every Man may be every Man's daily guide and example, as well by faſting to declare humility, as by praiſe to expreſs joy in the ſight of God, although it have herein befallen the Church, as ſometimes David, ſo that the ſpeech of the one may be truly the voice of the other, *My ſoul faſted, and even that was alſo turned to my reproof.*

Pſal. lxxiii. 5.

Pſal. lxix. 10.

The Celebration of Matrimony. T. C. l. 1. p. 199.

73. In this World there can be no Society durable otherwiſe than only by propagation. Albeit therefore ſingle Life be a thing more angelical and divine, yet ſith the repleniſhing firſt of Earth with bleſſed Inhabitants, and then of Heaven with Saints everlaſtingly praiſing God, did depend upon conjunction of Man and Woman, he which made all things complete and perfect, ſaw it could not be good to leave Men without any helper unto the fore-alledged end. In things which ſome farther end doth cauſe to be deſired, choice ſeeketh rather proportion than abſolute perfection of goodneſs. So that Woman being created for Man's ſake to be his helper, in regard of the end before mentioned, namely, the having, and bringing up of Children,

Children, whereunto it was not poſſible they could concur, unleſs there were ſubalternation between them, which ſubalternation is naturally grounded upon inequality, becauſe things equal in every reſpect are never willingly directed one by another: Woman therefore was even in her firſt eſtate framed by Nature, not only after in time, but inferior in excellency alſo unto Man, howbeit in ſo due and ſweet proportion, as being preſented before our eyes, might be ſooner perceived than defined. And even herein doth lie the Reaſon why that kind of Love which is the perfecteſt ground of Wedlock, is ſeldom able to yield any reaſon of itſelf. Now, that which is born of Man muſt be nouriſhed with far more travel, as being of greater price in Nature, and of ſlower pace to perfection, than the offſpring of any other creature beſides. Man and Woman being therefore to join themſelves for ſuch a purpoſe, they were of neceſſity to be linked with ſome ſtrait and inſoluble knot. The bond of Wedlock hath been always, more or leſs, eſteemed of as a thing religious and ſacred. The title which the very Heathens themſelves do thereunto oftentimes give * is, *holy*. Thoſe Rites and Orders which were inſtituted in the Solemnization of Marriage the Hebrews term by the name of conjugal † *Sanctification.* Amongſt ourſelves, becauſe ſundry things appertaining unto the publick Order of Matrimony, are called in queſtion by ſuch as know not from whence thoſe Cuſtoms did firſt grow, to ſhew briefly ſome true and ſufficient reaſon of them ſhall not be ſuperfluous; although we do not hereby intend to yield ſo far unto Enemies of all Church Orders ſaving their own, as though every thing were unlawful, the true cauſe and reaſon whereof at the firſt might hardly perhaps be now rendered. Wherefore, to begin with the times wherein the liberty of Marriage is reſtrained; *There is*, ſaith Solo-

BOOK V.

Eccleſ. iii. 1. Joel ii 16. 1 Cor vii. 5

* Τὰς ἱερὰς γάμους. Dionyſ. ant. lib. ii.

† Kidduſchin in Rituali Heb de benedictione nuptiarum.

BOOK V. mon, *a time for all things, a time to laugh, and a time to mourn.* That duties belonging unto Marriage, and offices appertaining to Penance, are things unſuitable and unfit to be matched together, the Prophets and Apoſtles themſelves do witneſs. Upon which ground, as we might right well think it marvellous abſurd to ſee in a Church a Wedding on the day of a publick Faſt, ſo likewiſe in the ſelf-ſame conſideration our Predeceſſors thought it not amiſs to take away the common liberty of Marriages during the time which was appointed for preparation unto, and for exerciſe of general Humiliation by Faſting and Praying, weeping for ſins. As for the delivering up of the Woman either by her Father or by ſome other, we muſt note that in ancient times * all Women which had not Huſbands nor Fathers to govern them, had their Tutors, † without whoſe authority there was no act which they did warrantable; and for this cauſe, they were in Marriage delivered unto their Huſbands by others. Which Cuſtom retained hath ſtill this uſe, that it putteth Women in mind of a duty whereunto the very imbecility of their nature and ſex doth bind them, namely, to be always directed, guided and ordered by others, although our poſitive Laws do not tie them now as Pupils. The cuſtom of laying down money ſeemeth to have been derived from the Saxons, whoſe manner was to buy their Wives. But, ſeeing there is not any great cauſe wherefore the memory of that cuſtom ſhould remain, it ſkilleth not much, although we ſuffer it to lie dead, even as we ſee it in a manner already worn out. The Ring hath been always uſed as a ſpecial pledge of faith and fide-

* Mulieres antiquo jure tutela perpetua continebat. Recedebant vero a Tutoris poteſtate quæ in manum conveniſſent. Boet. in Topic. Cic.

† Nullam ne privatam quidem rem Fœminas ſine auctore agere majores noſtri voluerunt. Liv l. 4 The reaſon yielded by Tully is this, propter infirmitatem conſilii. Cic. pro Mur. Vide Leg. Saxon. tit. vi. & xvii.

lity;

lity; nothing more fit to ſerve as a token of our purpoſed endleſs continuance in that which we never ought to revoke. This is the cauſe wherefore the Heathens themſelves did in ſuch caſes uſe the Ring, whereunto Tertullian alluding, ſaith, that in ancient times, * *No Woman was permitted to wear gold, ſaving only upon one finger, which her Huſband had faſtened unto himſelf, with that Ring which was uſually given for aſſurance of future Marriage.* The cauſe why the Chriſtians uſe it, as ſome of the Fathers think, is either to teſtify mutual love, or rather to ſerve for a pledge of conjunction in heart and mind agreed upon between them. But what rite and cuſtom is there ſo harmleſs, wherein the wit of Man bending itſelf to deriſion may not eaſily find out ſomewhat to ſcorn and jeſt at? He that ſhould have beheld the Jews when they ſtood with a four-cornered garment, ſpread over the heads of eſpouſed Couples, while their Eſpouſals were in making; he that ſhould have beheld their praying over a cup, and their delivering the ſame at the Marriage-feaſt, with ſet forms of Benediction, as the order amongſt them was, might, being lewdly affected, take thereat as juſt occaſion of ſcornful cavil, as at the uſe of the Ring in Wedlock amongſt Chriſtians. But of all things the moſt hardly taken is the uttering of theſe words, *With my body I thee worſhip*; in which words, when once they are underſtood, there will appear as little cauſe as in the reſt for any wiſe Man to be offended. Firſt, therefore, inaſmuch as unlawful copulation doth pollute and diſhonour both Parties, this proteſtation that we do worſhip and honour another with our bodies, may import a denial of all ſuch lets and impediments to our knowledge as might cauſe any ſtain, blemiſh, or diſgrace that way; which kind of conſtruction being probable, would eaſily approve that ſpeech to a peaceable and quiet mind. Secondly, in

BOOK V.

Iſidor. de Eccleſ. Offic. l. ii. c. 19

Elias Theſb. in dict. Hupha In Ritual. de benedict. nuptiarum.

Rom. i. 24. 1 Cor. vii. 4.

* Aurum nulla norat præter unico digito quem ſponſus oppignoraſſet pronubo annulo. Tertul. Apol. cap. vi.

BOOK V. that the Apoſtle doth ſo expreſsly affirm that Parties married have not any longer entire power over themſelves, but each hath intereſt in other's Perſon, it cannot be thought an abſurd conſtruction to ſay, that worſhipping with the body is the imparting of that intereſt in the body unto another which none before had, ſave only ourſelves. But if this were the natural meaning, the words ſhould perhaps be as requiſite to be uſed on the one ſide as on the other; and therefore a third ſenſe there is, which I rather rely upon. Apparent it is that the ancient difference between a lawful Wife and a Concubine, was only in the different purpoſe of Man betaking himſelf to the one or the other. If his purpoſe were only fellowſhip, there grew to the Woman by this means no worſhip at all, but the contrary. In profeſſing that his intent was to add by his perſon honour and worſhip unto hers, he took her plainly and clearly to Wife. This is it which the Civil Law doth mean, when it maketh a Wife to differ from a Concubine in dignity; a Wife to be taken where conjugal honour and affection do go before. The worſhip that grew unto her being taken with declaration of this intent was, that her children became by this means legitimate and free; herſelf was made a Mother over his Family; laſt of all, ſhe received ſuch advancement of ſtate, as things annexed unto his perſon might augment her with; yea, a right of participation was thereby given her both in him, and even in all things which were his. This doth ſomewhat the more plainly appear, by adding alſo that other clauſe, *With all my worldly goods I thee endow*. The former branch having granted the principal, the latter granteth that which is annexed thereunto. To end the publick Solemnity of Marriage with receiving the bleſſed Sacrament is a Cuſtom ſo religious and ſo holy, that if the Church of England be blameable in this reſpect, it is not for ſuffering it to be ſo much, but rather for not providing that it may be more put

L. penul. D. de concub.

L. item legato ſect. penult. D. de leg 3. L. Donationes D de donationibus.

in

in ure. The Laws of Romulus concerning Marriage* are therefore extolled above the reſt amongſt the Heathens which were before, in that they eſtabliſhed the uſe of certain ſpecial Solemnities, whereby the minds of Men were drawn to make the greater conſcience of Wedlock, and to eſteem the bond thereof a thing which could not be without impiety diſſolved. If there be any thing in Chriſtian Religion ſtrong and effectual to like purpoſe, it is the Sacrament of the holy Euchariſt; in regard of the force whereof Tertullian breaketh out into theſe words, concerning Matrimony therewith ſealed; *Unde ſufficiam ad enarrandam fælicitatem ejus Matrimonii, quod Eccleſia conciliat, et confirmat Oblatio? I know not which way I ſhould be able to ſhew the happineſs of that Wedlock, the knot whereof the Church doth faſten, and the Sacrament of the Church confirm.* Touching Marriage therefore let thus much be ſufficient.

Tertul. lib. ii. ad uxorem.

Churching of Women.

74. The fruit of Marriage is Birth; and the companion of Birth, Travail; the grief whereof being ſo extreme, and the danger always ſo great, dare we open our mouths againſt the things that are holy, and preſume to cenſure it as a fault in the Church of Chriſt, that Women after their Deliverance do publickly ſhew their thankful minds unto God? But behold what reaſon there is againſt it! *Forſooth, if there ſhould be ſolemn and expreſs giving of Thanks in the Church for every benefit, either equal or greater than this, which any ſingular Perſon in the Church doth receive, we ſhould not only have no preaching of the Word, nor miniſtering of the Sacraments, but we ſhould not have ſo much leiſure as to do any corporal or bodily work, but ſhould be like thoſe Maſſilian Hereticks which do nothing elſe but pray.* Surely, better a great deal to be like unto thoſe Hereticks which do nothing elſe but pray,

T. C. l. i. p. 150.

* Οὗτος ὁ νόμος τάς τε γυναῖκας ἠνάγκασε τὰς γαμετὰς, οἷα μηδεμίαν ἐχούσας ἑτέραν ἀποστροφὴν πρὸς ἕνα τὸν τοῦ γεγαμηκότος ζῆν τρόπον, καὶ τοὺς ἄνδρας ὡς ἀναγκαίου τε καὶ ἀναφαιρέτου χρήματος τῆς γυναικὸς κρατεῖν. Dionyſ. Hal. Antiq lib. ii.

BOOK V. than thoſe which do nothing elſe but quarrel. Their heads it might haply trouble ſomewhat more than as yet they are aware of, to find out ſo many benefits greater than this, or equivalent thereunto, for which if ſo be our Laws did require ſolemn and expreſs Thankſgivings in the Church, the ſame were like to prove a thing ſo greatly cumberſome as is pretended. But if there be ſuch ſtore of Mercies, even ineſtimable, poured every day upon thouſands (as indeed the Earth is full of the Bleſſings of the Lord, which are day by day renewed without number and above meaſure), ſhall it not be lawful to cauſe ſolemn Thanks to be given unto God for any Benefit, than which greater, or whereunto equal are received, no Law binding Men in regard thereof to perform the like duty? Suppoſe that ſome bond there be, that tieth us at certain times to mention publickly the names of ſundry our Benefactors. Some of them, it may be, are ſuch, that a day would ſcarcely ſerve to reckon up together with them the Catalogue of ſo many Men beſides, as we are either more or equally beholden unto. Becauſe no Law requireth this impoſſible labour at our hands, ſhall we therefore condemn that Law, whereby the other, being poſſible and alſo dutiful, is enjoined us? So much we owe to the Lord of Heaven, that we can never ſufficiently praiſe him, nor give him thanks for half thoſe benefits, for which this ſacrifice were moſt due. Howbeit, God forbid we ſhould ceaſe performing this duty when publick Order doth draw us unto it, when it may be ſo eaſily done, when it hath been ſo long executed by devout and virtuous People, God forbid that, being ſo many ways provoked in this caſe unto ſo good a duty, we ſhould omit it, only becauſe there are other caſes of like nature, wherein we cannot ſo conveniently, or at leaſt wiſe do not perform the ſame moſt virtuous office of piety. Wherein we truſt that as the action itſelf pleaſeth God, ſo the order and manner thereof is not ſuch as

may

may juſtly offend any. It is but an overflowing of gall, which cauſeth the Woman's abſence from the Church during the time of her lying-in to be traduced and interpreted, as though ſhe were ſo long judged unholy, and were thereby ſhut out or ſequeſtered from the Houſe of God, according to the ancient Levitical Law. Whereas the very Canon Law itſelf doth not ſo hold, but directly profeſſeth the contrary;* ſhe is not barred from thence in ſuch ſort as they interpret it, nor in reſpect of any unholineſs forbidden entrance into the Church, although her abſtaining from publick Aſſemblies and her abode in ſeparation for the time be moſt convenient.† To ſcoff at the manner of attire, than which there could be nothing deviſed for ſuch a time more grave and decent, to make it a token of ſome folly committed, for which they are loth to ſhew their faces, argueth that ſome Divines are ſometimes more merry than wiſe. As for the Women themſelves, God accepting the ſervice which they faithfully offer unto him, it is no great diſgrace, though they ſuffer pleaſant-witted Men a little to intermingle with zeal, ſcorn. The

* Dict. v. cap. Hæc quæ. In lege præcipiebatur, ut mulier ſi maſculum pareret 40. ſi fœminam 80 diebus a templi ceſſaret ingreſſu. Nunc autem ſtatim poſt partum Eccleſiam ingredi non prohibetur.

† Leo Conſt 17. Quod profecto non tam propter muliebrem immunditiem, quam ob alias cauſas in intima legis ratione reconditas, et veteri prohibitum eſſe lege, et gratiæ tempus traditionis loco ſuſcepiſſe puto. Exiſtimo ſiquidem ſacram legem id præſcripſiſſe, quo protervam eorum qui intemperanter viverent concupiſcentiam caſtigaret; quemadmodum et alia multa per alia præcepta ordinantur et præſcribuntur, quo indomitus quorundam in mulieres ſtimulus retundatur. Quin et hæc providentiæ quæ legem conſtituit voluntas eſt, ut partus a depravatione liberi ſint. Quia enim quicquid natura ſupervacaneum eſt, idem corruptivum eſt et inutile, quod hic ſanguis ſuperfluus ſit, quæ illi obnoxiæ eſſent in immunditie, ad id temporis vivere illa lex jubet, quo ipſo etiam nominis ſono laſcivi concupiſcentia ad temperantiam redigatur, ne ex inutili et corrupta materia ipſum animans coagmentetur.

BOOK V. name of Oblations, applied not only here to thoſe ſmall and petit payments which yet are a part of the Miniſter's right, but alſo generally given unto all ſuch allowances as ſerve for their needful maintenance, is both ancient and convenient. For as the life of the Clergy is ſpent in the ſervice of God, ſo it is ſuſtained with his revenue. Nothing therefore more proper than to give the name of Oblations to ſuch payments, in token that we offer unto him whatſoever his Miniſters receive.

Of the Rites of Burial. T. C. lib iii. p. 236.

75. But to leave this, there is a duty which the Church doth owe to the Faithful departed, wherein foraſmuch as the Church of England is ſaid to do thoſe things which are, though not unlawful, yet inconvenient, becauſe it appointeth a preſcript Form of Service at Burials, ſuffereth mourning Apparel to be worn, and permitteth Funeral-Sermons; a word or two concerning this point will be neceſſary, although it be needleſs to dwell long upon it. The end of Funeral duties is, firſt, to ſhew that love towards the Party deceaſed, which Nature requireth; then to do him that honour, which is fit both generally for Man, and particularly for the quality of his perſon, laſt of all, to teſtify the care, which the Church hath to comfort the living, and the hope, which we all have concerning the Reſurrection of the Dead. For ſignification of love towards them that are departed, Mourning is not denied to be a thing convenient, as in truth the Scripture every where doth approve lamentation made unto this end. John xi. 36. The Jews by our Saviour's tears therefore gathered in this caſe that his love towards Lazarus was great. And that as Mourning at ſuch times is fit, ſo likewiſe that there may be a kind of Attire ſuitable to a ſorrowful affection, and convenient for Mourners to wear, how plainly doth David's example ſhew, who, being in heavineſs, went up the mount with his head covered, and all the People that were with him in like ſort? White Garments being fit to uſe at Marriage

2 Sam. xv. 30.

riage Feafts, and fuch other times of joy, whereunto Solomon alluding, when he requireth continual cheerfulnefs of mind, fpeaketh in this fort, *Let thy Garments be always white*; what doth hinder the contrary from being now as convenient in grief, as this heretofore in gladnefs hath been? *If there be no forrow*, they fay, *it is hypocritical to pretend it*; *and if there be, to provoke it by wearing fuch attire, is dangerous*. Nay, if there be, to fhew it, is natural; and if there be not, yet the figns are meet to fhew what fhould be, efpecially, fith it doth not come oftentimes to pafs, that Men are fain to have their mourning gowns pulled off their backs for fear of killing themfelves with forrow that way nourifhed. The honour generally due unto all Men maketh a decent interring of them to be convenient, even for very humanity's fake. And therefore, fo much as is mentioned in the Burial of the Widow's Son, the *carrying of him forth upon a Bier*, and the accompanying of him to the Earth, hath been ufed even amongft Infidels; all Men accounting it a very extreme deftitution not to have at the leaft this honour done them. Some Man's eftate may require a great deal more, according as the fafhion of the Country where he dieth doth afford. And unto this appertained the ancient ufe of the Jews, to embalm the Corpfe with fweet Odours, and to adorn the Sepulchres of certain. In regard of the quality of Men, it hath been judged fit to commend them unto the World at their death, amongft the Heathen in funeral Orations, amongft the Jews in facred Poems; and why not in funeral Sermons alfo amongft Chriftians? Us it fufficeth, that the known benefit hereof doth countervail millions of fuch inconveniencies as are therein furmifed, although they were not furmifed only, but found therein. The life and the death of Saints is precious in God's fight. Let it not feem odious in our eyes, if both the one and the other be fpoken of then efpecially, when the prefent occafion doth make Men's minds the more capable

Ecclef. ix. 8.

Luke vii. 12.

Pfal. lxxix. 3
John xix. 40.
Matt. xxiii. 27.

2 Sam. i. 19.

BOOK V. capable of ſuch ſpeech. The care, no doubt, of the living, both to live and to die well, muſt needs be ſomewhat increaſed, when they know that their departure ſhall not be folded up in ſilence, but the ears of many be made acquainted with it. Moreover, when they hear how mercifully God hath dealt with their Brethren in their laſt need, beſides the praiſe which they give to God, and the joy which they have or ſhould have by reaſon of their fellowſhip and communion with Saints, is not their hope alſo much confirmed againſt the day of their own diſſolution? Again, the ſound of theſe things doth not ſo paſs the ears of them that are moſt looſe and diſſolute in life, but it cauſeth them one time or other to wiſh, *O that I might die the death of the righteous, and that my end might be like his!* Thus much peculiar good there doth grow at thoſe times by ſpeech concerning the dead, beſides the benefit of publick inſtruction common unto funeral with other Sermons. For the comfort of them whoſe Minds are through natural affection penſive in ſuch caſes, no Man can juſtly miſlike the cuſtom which the Jews had to end their Burials with funeral Banquets, in reference whereunto the Prophet Jeremy ſpake concerning the People, whom God had appointed unto a grievous Manner of deſtruction, Jer. xvi. 7 ſaying, *That Men ſhould not give them the cup of conſolation to drink for their Father, or for their Mother,* becauſe it ſhould not be now with them as in peaceable times with others, who bringing their Anceſtors unto the grave with weeping eyes, have notwithſtanding means wherewith to be re-comforted. *Give wine,* Prov. xxxi. 6 ſaith Solomon, *unto them that have grief of heart.* 1 Chro. xix. 2 Surely he, that miniſtereth unto them comfortable Job ii. 11 ſpeech, doth much more than give them wine. But the greateſt thing of all other about this duty of Chriſtian Burial is an outward teſtification of the hope which we have touching the Reſurrection of the Dead. For which purpoſe, let any Man of reaſonable judgment examine, whether it be more convenient for a Company

pany

pany of Men, as it were, in a dumb ſhow, to bring a Corſe to the place of Burial, there to leave it covered with Earth, and ſo end, or elſe have the Exequies devoutly performed with ſolemn recital of ſuch Lectures, Pſalms and Prayers, as are purpoſely framed for the ſtirring up of Men's minds unto a careful conſideration of their eſtate both here and hereafter. Whereas therefore it is objected, that neither the People of God under the Law, nor the Church in the Apoſtles' times, did uſe any form of Service in Burial of the Dead; and therefore, that this order is taken up without any good example or precedent followed therein; firſt, while the World doth ſtand they ſhall never be able to prove, that all things which either the one or the other did uſe at Burials are ſet down in holy Scripture, which doth not any where of purpoſe deliver the whole manner and form thereof, but toucheth only ſometime one thing, and ſometime another, which was in uſe, as ſpecial occaſions require any of them to be either mentioned or inſinuated. Again, if it might be proved that no ſuch thing was uſual amongſt them, hath Chriſt ſo deprived his Church of judgment, that what Rites and Orders ſoever the latter ages thereof have deviſed, the ſame muſt needs be inconvenient? Furthermore, that the Jews before our Saviour's coming had any ſuch form of Service, although in Scripture it be not affirmed, yet neither is it there denied (for the forbidding of Prieſts to be preſent at Burials letteth not but that others might diſcharge that duty, ſeeing all were not Prieſts which had rooms of publick function in their Synagogues), and if any Man be of opinion that they had no ſuch form of Service; thus much there is to make the contrary more probable. The Jews at this day have, as appeareth in their form of funeral Prayers, and in certain of their funeral Sermons publiſhed; neither are they ſo affected towards Chriſtians, as to borrow that order from us; beſides that, the Form thereof is ſuch as hath in it ſundry things which the

the very words of the Scripture itſelf doth ſeem to allude unto, as namely, after departure from the Sepulchre unto the houſe whence the Dead was brought, it ſheweth the manner of their Burial-feaſt, and a conſolatory Form of Prayer, appointed for the Maſter of the Synagogue thereat to utter; albeit I may not deny, but it hath alſo ſome things which are not perhaps ſo ancient as the Law and the Prophets. But whatſoever the Jews cuſtom was before the days of our Saviour Chriſt, hath it once at any time been heard of that either Church or Chriſtian Man of ſound belief did ever judge this a thing unmeet, indecent, unfit for Chriſtianity, till theſe miſerable days, wherein, under the colour of removing ſuperſtitious abuſes, the moſt effectual means both to teſtify and to ſtrengthen true Religion are plucked at, and in ſome places even pulled up by the very roots? Take away this which was ordained to ſhew at Burials the peculiar hope of the Church of God concerning the Dead; and in the manner of thoſe dumb Funerals what one thing is there whereby the World may perceive we are Chriſtian Men?

Of the nature of that Miniſtry, which ſerveth for performance of divine duties in the Church of God; and how happineſs, not eternal only, but alſo temporal, doth depend upon it.

76. I come now unto that Function which undertaketh the publick Miniſtry of holy things according to the Laws of Chriſtian Religion. And becauſe the nature of things, conſiſting as this doth in action, is known by the object whereabout they are converſant, and by the end or ſcope whereunto they are referred, we muſt know that the object of this Function is both God and Men; God, in that he is publickly worſhipped of his Church, and Men, in that they are capable of happineſs by means which Chriſtian Diſcipline appointeth. So that the ſum of our whole labour in this kind is to honour God and to ſave Men. For whether we ſeverally take, and conſider Men one by one, or elſe gather them into one ſociety and body, as it hath been before declared, that every Man's Religion is in him the well-ſpring of all other ſound and ſincere virtues, from whence both here in ſome ſort,

ſort, and hereafter more abundantly, their full joy and felicity ariſeth; becauſe while they live they are bleſſed of God, and when they die their works follow them: ſo at this preſent we muſt again call to mind how the very worldly peace and proſperity, the ſecular happineſs, the temporal and natural good eſtate both of all Men, and of all Dominions, hangeth chiefly upon Religion, and doth evermore give plain teſtimony, that, as well in this as in other conſiderations, the Prieſt is a pillar of that Commonwealth wherein he faithfully ſerveth God. For if theſe aſſertions be true, firſt, that nothing can be enjoyed in this preſent World againſt his will which hath made all things; ſecondly, that albeit God doth ſometime permit the impious to have, yet impiety permitteth them not to enjoy, no not temporal bleſſings on Earth; thirdly, that God hath appointed thoſe bleſſings to attend as handmaids upon Religion; and fourthly, that without the work of the Miniſtry, Religion by no means can poſſibly continue, the uſe and benefit of that ſacred Function even towards all Men's worldly happineſs muſt needs be granted. Now the * firſt being a Theorem both underſtood and confeſſed by all, to labour in proof thereof were ſuperfluous. The ſecond perhaps may be called in queſtion, except it be perfectly underſtood. By good things temporal therefore we mean length of days, health of body, ſtore of friends and well-willers, quietneſs, proſperous ſucceſs of thoſe things we take in hand, riches with fit opportunities to uſe them during

* Si creaturæ Dei, merito et diſpenſatio Dei ſumus; quis enim magis diligit, quam ille qui fecit? Quis autem ordinatius regit, quam is qui et fecit et diligit? Quis vero ſapientius et fortius ordinare et regere facta poteſt, quam qui et facienda providit et proviſa perfecit? Quapropter omnem poteſtatem a Deo eſſe omnemque ordinationem, et qui non legerunt ſentiunt, et qui legerunt cognoſcunt. Paul Oroſ Hiſt. adverſ. Pagan. lib. ii. Οὔτοι τὰ χρήματ' ἴδια κέκτηνται βροτοὶ τὰ τῶν θεῶν δ' ἔχοντες ἐπιμελούμεθα. Eurip. Phœniſ.

life,

BOOK V. life, reputation following us both alive and dead, Children, or ſuch as inſtead of Children we wiſh to leave ſucceſſors and partakers of our happineſs. Theſe things are naturally every Man's deſire, becauſe they are good, and on whom God beſtoweth the ſame, them we confeſs he graciouſly bleſſeth. Of earthly bleſſings the meaneſt is wealth, reputation the chiefeſt. For which cauſe we eſteem the gain of honour an ample recompence for the loſs of all other worldly benefits. But for as much as in all this there is no certain perpetuity of goodneſs, Nature hath taught to affect theſe things, not for their own ſake, but with reference and relation to ſomewhat independently good, as is the exerciſe of virtue and ſpeculation of Truth. None, whoſe deſires are rightly ordered, would wiſh to live, to breath, and move, without performance of thoſe actions which are beſeeming Man's excellency. Wherefore having not how to employ it, we wax weary even of life itſelf. Health is precious, becauſe ſickneſs doth breed that pain which diſableth action. Again, why do Men delight ſo much in the multitude of friends, but for that the actions of life, being many, do need many helping hands to further them? Between troubleſome and quiet days we ſhould make no difference, if the one did not hinder and interrupt, the other uphold our liberty of action. Furthermore, if thoſe things we do, ſucceed, it rejoiceth us not ſo much for the benefit we thereby reap, * as in that it probably argueth our actions to have been orderly and well-guided. As for riches, to him which hath and doth nothing with them, they are a contumely. Honour is commonly preſumed a ſign of more than ordinary virtue and merit, by means whereof when ambitious Minds thirſt after it, their endeavours are teſtimonies how much it is in the eye of Nature to poſſeſs that body, the very

* Ὀιόμεθα γὰρ τὸν εὐτυχοῦντα πάντ' ἐπίςασθαι καλῶς. Eurip. Heracl.

ſhadow

ſhadow whereof is ſet at ſo high a rate. Finally, ſuch is the pleaſure and comfort which we take in doing, that when life forſaketh us, ſtill our deſires to continue action and to work, though not by ourſelves, yet by them whom we leave behind us, causeth us providently to reſign into other Men's hands the helps we have gathered for that purpoſe, deviſing alſo the beſt we can to make them perpetual. It appeareth, therefore, how all the parts of temporal felicity are only good in relation to that which uſeth them as inſtruments, and that they are no ſuch good as wherein a right deſire doth ever ſtay or reſt itſelf. Now temporal bleſſings are enjoyed of thoſe which have them, know them, *eſteem them according to that they are in their own nature.* Wherefore of the Wicked whom God doth hate, his uſual and ordinary ſpeeches are, that *blood-thirſty and deceitful Men ſhall not live out half their days*; that God ſhall cauſe a peſtilence to cleave unto the Wicked, and ſhall ſtrike them with conſuming grief, with fevers, burning diſeaſes, and ſores which are paſt cure; that when the impious are fallen, all Men ſhould tread them down, and none ſhew countenance of love towards them, as much as by pitying them in their miſery; that the ſins of the ungodly ſhall bereave them of peace; that all counſels, complots and practices againſt God ſhall come to nothing; that the lot and inheritance of the unjuſt is beggary; that the name of unrighteous Perſons ſhall putrefy, and the poſterity of Robbers ſtarve. If any think that Iniquity and Peace, Sin and Proſperity can dwell together, they err, becauſe they diſtinguiſh not aright between the matter, and that which giveth it the form of happineſs, between poſſeſſion and fruition, between the having and enjoying of good things. The impious cannot enjoy that they have, partly becauſe they receive it not as at God's hands, which only conſideration maketh temporal bleſſings comfortable; and partly becauſe through error, placing it above things of far more price and worth, they turn that to poiſon which

BOOK V.

Pſal. lv. 23.

Deut xxviii. 22.

Prov. x.

BOOK V. which might be food, they make their proſperity their own ſnare; in the neſt of their higheſt growth they lay fooliſhly thoſe eggs out of which their woful overthrow is afterwards hatched. Hereby it cometh to paſs, that wiſe and judicious Men, obſerving the vain behaviour of ſuch as are riſen to unwonted greatneſs, have thereby been able to prognoſticate their ruin. So that in very truth no impious or wicked Man doth proſper on Earth, but either ſooner or later the World may perceive eaſily, how at ſuch time as others thought them moſt fortunate, they had but only the good eſtate which fat oxen have above lean; when they appeared to grow, their climbing was towards ruin.* The groſs and beſtial conceit of them which want underſtanding is, only that the fulleſt bellies are happieſt. Therefore the greateſt felicity, they wiſh to the Commonwealth wherein they live, is that it may but abound and ſtand, that they which are riotous may have to pour out without ſtint; that the poor may ſleep, and the rich feed them; that nothing unpleaſant may be commanded, nothing forbidden Men which themſelves have a luſt to follow; that Kings may provide for the eaſe of their Subjects, and not be too curious about their manners; that wantonneſs, exceſs and lewdneſs of life may be left free; and that no fault may be capital, beſides diſlike of things ſettled in ſo good terms. But be it far from the Juſt to dwell either in, or near to the tents of theſe ſo miſerable felicities. Now whereas we thirdly affirm, that Religion and the Fear of God as well induceth ſecular Proſperity as everlaſting Bliſs in the World to come, this alſo is true. For otherwiſe Godlineſs could not be ſaid to have the promiſes of both lives; to be that ample revenue wherein there is always ſufficiency; and to carry with it a general diſ-

* Prov xvi. 18. Ante ruinam elatio. Φιλέει ὁ Θεὸς πάντα τὰ ὑπερέχοντα κωλύειν· οὐ γὰρ ἐᾷ φρονέειν ἄλλον μέγα ἢ ἑαυτὸν. Herodot. lib. vii.

charge

charge of want, even ſo general, that David himſelf ſhould proteſt, *he never ſaw the Juſt forſaken.* Howbeit, to this we muſt add certain ſpecial limitations; as firſt, that we do not forget how crazed and diſeaſed Minds (whereof our heavenly Phyſician muſt judge) receive oftentimes moſt benefit by being deprived of thoſe things which are to others beneficially given, as appeareth in that which the Wiſe Man hath noted concerning them, whoſe lives God mercifully doth abridge, leſt wickedneſs ſhould alter their underſtanding; again, that the meaſure of our outward proſperity be taken by proportion with that which every Man's eſtate in this preſent life requireth. External abilities are inſtruments of action. It contenteth wiſe Artificers to have their inſtruments proportionable to their work, rather fit for uſe, than huge and goodly to pleaſe the eye. Seeing then the actions of a Servant do not need that which may be neceſſary for Men of calling and place in the World, neither Men of inferior condition many things which greater Perſonages can hardly want, ſurely they are bleſſed in worldly reſpects that have wherewith to perform * ſufficiently what their ſtation and place aſketh, though they have no more. For, by reaſon of Man's imbecility and proneneſs to elation of mind, † too high a flow of proſperity is dangerous, too low an ebb again as dangerous, for that the virtue of patience is rare, and the hand of neceſſity ſtronger than ordinary virtue is able to withſtand. Solomon's diſcreet and moderate deſire we all know; *Give me, O Lord, neither riches nor penury.* Men over-high exalted either in honour or in power, or in nobility, or in wealth; they likewiſe that are as much on the contrary hand

BOOK V.

* Ἐπεὶ τά γ' ἀρκοῦνθ' ἱκανὰ τοῖς γε σώφροσιν. Eurip Phœniſ

† Ταπεινοτέρων ὁ λογισμὸς ἴσως, ἀλλ' οὖν ἀσφαλεστέρων, ἴσον ἀπέχειν καὶ ὕψους καὶ πτώματος. Greg. Nazian. Apol. iii. They may haply be the moſt deject, but they are the wiſeſt for their own ſafety, which fear climbing no leſs than falling. Ariſt. Polit lib. iv. cap 11.

BOOK V. ſunk either with beggary, or through dejection, or by baſeneſs, do not eaſily give ear to reaſon; but the one exceeding apt unto outrages, and the other unto petty miſchiefs. For greatneſs delighteth to ſhew itſelf by effects of power, and baſeneſs to help itſelf with ſhifts of malice. For which cauſe, a moderate, indifferent temper, between fulneſs of bread and emptineſs, hath been evermore thought and found (all circumſtances duly conſidered) the ſafeſt and happieſt for all Eſtates, even for Kings and Princes themſelves. Again, we are not to look that theſe things ſhould always concur, no not in them which are accounted happy, neither that the courſe of Men's lives, or of publick affairs ſhould continually be drawn out as an even thread (for that the nature of things will not ſuffer), but a juſt ſurvey being made, as thoſe particular Men are worthily reputed good whoſe virtues be great and their faults tolerable; ſo him we may regiſter for a Man fortunate, and that for a proſperous and happy State, which having flouriſhed doth not afterwards feel any tragical alteration, ſuch as might cauſe them to be a ſpectacle of miſery to others. Beſides, whereas true felicity conſiſteth in the higheſt operations of that nobler part of Man, which ſheweth ſometime greateſt perfection, not in uſing the benefits which delight nature, but in ſuffering what nature can hardlieſt endure, there is no cauſe why either the loſs of good, if it tend to the purchaſe of better, or why any miſery, the iſſue whereof is their greater praiſe and honour that have ſuſtained it, ſhould be thought to impeach that temporal happineſs wherewith Religion, we ſay, is accompanied; but yet in ſuch meaſure as the ſeveral degrees of Men may require by a competent eſtimation, and unleſs the contrary do more advance, as it hath done, thoſe moſt heroical Saints whom afflictions have made glorious. In a word, not to whom no calamity falleth, but whom neither miſery nor proſperity is able to move from a right mind, them we may truly pronounce fortunate, and whatſoever doth outwardly happen

without

without that precedent improbity, for which it appeareth in the eyes of ſound and unpartial Judges to have proceeded from divine revenge, it paſſeth in the number of human caſualties, whereunto we are all alike ſubject. No miſery is reckoned more than common or human, if God ſo diſpoſe that we paſs thorough it, and come ſafe to ſhore; even as contrariwiſe, Men do not uſe to think thoſe flouriſhing days happy, which do end with tears. It ſtandeth therefore with theſe cautions firm and true, yea, ratified by all Men's unfeigned confeſſions, drawn from the very heart of experience, that whether we compare Men of Note in the World with others of like degree and ſtate, or elſe the ſame Men with themſelves, whether we confer one Dominion with another, or elſe the different times of one and the ſame Dominion, the manifeſt odds between their very outward condition, as long as they ſtedfaſtly were obſerved to honour God, and their ſucceſs, being fallen from him, are remonſtrances more than ſufficient, how all our welfare, even on earth, dependeth wholly upon our Religion. Heathens were ignorant of true Religion. Yet ſuch as that little was which they knew, it much impaired or bettered always their worldly affairs, as their love and zeal towards it did wane or grow. Of the Jews, did not even their moſt malicious and mortal Adverſaries all acknowledge, that to ſtrive againſt them it was in vain as long as their amity with God continued, that nothing could weaken them but Apoſtaſy? In the whole courſe of their own proceedings did they ever find it otherwiſe, but that, during their faith and fidelity towards God, every Man of them was in war as a thouſand ſtrong, and as much as a grand Senate for counſel in peaceable deliberations? contrariwiſe, that if they ſwerved, as they often did, their wonted courage and magnanimity forſook them utterly, their Soldiers and military Men trembled at the ſight of the naked ſword; when they entered into mutual conference and ſate in counſel for their own good, that which Children might have ſeen their graveſt Senators could not diſcern; their Prophets ſaw darkneſs inſtead of viſions; the wiſe and prudent were as Men bewitched, even that which they knew (being ſuch as might ſtand them in ſtead) they had not the grace to utter; or if any thing were well propoſed, it took no place, it entered not into the minds of the reſt to approve and follow it, but, as Men confounded with ſtrange and unuſual amazements of ſpirit, they attempted tumultuouſly they ſaw not what; and by the iſſues of all attempts they found no certain concluſion but this, *God and Heaven are ſtrong againſt us in all we do.* The cauſe whereof was ſecret fear which took heart and courage from them; and the cauſe of their fear, an inward guiltineſs that they all had offered God ſuch apparent wrongs as were not pardonable. But it may be the cauſe is now altogether changed, and that in Chriſtian Religion there is not the like force towards temporal felicity. Search the ancient records of time, look what hath happened by the ſpace of theſe ſixteen hundred years, ſee if all things to this effect be not luculent and clear, yea all things ſo manifeſt, that for evidence and proof herein, we need not by uncertain dark conjectures ſurmiſe any to have been plagued of God for contempt, or bleſt in the courſe of faithful obedience towards true Religion more than only them, whom we find in that reſpect, on the one ſide, guilty by their own confeſſions, and happy on the other ſide by all Men's acknowledgment; who beholding the proſperous eſtate of ſuch as are good and virtuous, impute boldly the ſame to God's moſt eſpecial favour, but cannot in like manner pronounce that whom he afflicteth above others, with them he hath cauſe to be more offended. For Virtue is always plain to be ſeen, rareneſs cauſeth it to be obſerved, and goodneſs to be honoured with admiration. As for Iniquity and Sin, it lieth many times hid; and becauſe we be all Offenders, it becometh us not to incline towards hard and ſevere ſentences touching others, unleſs their notorious wicked-

neſs

neſs did ſenſibly before proclaim that which afterwards came to paſs. Wherefore the ſum of every Chriſtian Man's duty is, to labour by all means toward that which other Men ſeeing in us may juſtify; and what we ourſelves muſt accuſe if we fall into it, that, by all means we can, to avoid; conſidering eſpecially, that as hitherto upon the Church there never yet fell tempeſtuous ſtorm, the vapours whereof were not firſt noted to riſe from coldneſs in affection and from backwardneſs in duties of ſervice towards God, ſo if that which the tears of antiquity have uttered concerning this point ſhould be here ſet down, it were aſſuredly enough to ſoften and to mollify an heart of ſteel. On the contrary part, although we confeſs with St. Auguſtin moſt willingly, that the chiefeſt happineſs for which we have ſome Chriſtian Kings in ſo great admiration above the reſt, is not becauſe of their long reign; their calm and quiet departure out of this preſent life; the ſettled eſtabliſhment of their own fleſh and blood ſucceeding them in Royalty and Power; the glorious overthrow of foreign Enemies, or the wiſe prevention of inward danger, and of ſecret attempts at home; all which ſolaces and comforts of this our unquiet life it pleaſeth God oftentimes to beſtow on them which have no ſociety or part in the joys of Heaven, giving thereby to underſtand that theſe in compariſon are toys and trifles, far under the value and price of that which is to be looked for at his hands; but in truth the reaſon wherefore we moſt extol their felicity is, if ſo be they have virtuouſly reigned, if honour hath not filled their hearts with pride, if the exerciſe of their power hath been ſervice and attendance upon the Majeſty of the Moſt High, if they have feared him as their own Inferiors and Subjects have feared them, if they have loved neither pomp nor pleaſure more than Heaven, if revenge hath ſlowly proceeded from them, and mercy willingly offered itſelf, if ſo they have tempered rigour with lenity, that neither extreme ſeverity might utterly

 cut

 cut them off, in whom there was manifeſt hope of amendment, nor yet the eaſineſs of pardoning offences embolden offenders; if, knowing that whatſoever they do, their potency may bear it out, they have been ſo much the more careful not to do any thing but that which is commendable in the beſt, rather than uſual with greateſt Perſonages; if the true knowledge of themſelves hath humbled them in God's ſight, no leſs than God in the eyes of Men hath raiſed them up; I ſay, albeit we reckon ſuch to be the happieſt of them that are mightieſt in the World, and albeit thoſe things alone are happineſs, nevertheleſs, conſidering what force there is even in outward bleſſings to comfort the minds of the beſt diſpoſed, and to give them the greater joy when Religion and Peace, heavenly and earthly Happineſs are wreathed in one crown, as to the worthieſt of Chriſtian Princes it hath by the providence of the Almighty hitherto befallen; let it not ſeem to any Man a needleſs and ſuperfluous waſte of labour, that there hath been thus much ſpoken, to declare how in them eſpecially it hath been ſo obſerved, and withal univerſally noted, even from the higheſt to the very meaneſt, how this particular benefit, this ſingular grace and pre-eminence Religion hath, that either it guardeth as an heavenly ſhield from all calamities, or elſe conducteth us ſafe through them, and permitteth them not to be miſeries; it either giveth honours, promotions and wealth, or elſe more benefit by wanting them than if we had them at will; it either filleth our houſes with plenty of all good things, or maketh a ſallad of green herbs more ſweet than all the ſacrifices of the ungodly. Our fourth Propoſition before ſet down was, that Religion without the help of ſpiritual Miniſtry is unable to plant itſelf, the fruits thereof not poſſible to grow of their own accord. Which laſt Aſſertion is herein as the firſt, that it needeth no farther confirmation: if it did, I could eaſily declare how all things which are of God, he hath by wonderful art and wiſdom ſodered as it

were

were together with the glue of mutual affiftance, appointing the loweft to receive from the neareft to themfelves what the influence of the higheft yieldeth. And therefore the Church, being the moft abfolute of all his works, was in reafon to be alfo ordered with like harmony, that what he worketh might, no lefs in grace than in nature, be effected by hands and inftruments duly fubordinated unto the Power of his own Spirit. A thing both needful for the humility of Man, which would not willingly be debtor to any but to himfelf; and of no fmall effect to nourifh that divine love, which now maketh each embrace other, not as Men, but as Angels of God. Minifterial actions tending immediately unto God's honour, and Man's happinefs, are either as Contemplation, which helpeth forward the principal work of the Miniftry, or elfe they are parts of that principal work of Adminiftration itfelf, which work confifteth in doing the fervice of God's Houfe, and in applying unto Men the fovereign medicines of Grace, already fpoken of the more largely to the end it might thereby appear, that we * owe to the Guides of our Souls even as much as our Souls are worth, although the debt of our temporal bleffings fhould be ftricken off.

Luke xii. 42. 1 Cor. iv. 1 Tit. i. 7. 1 Pet. iv. 10. Ephef. iii. 2.

77. The Miniftry of things divine is a Function, which as God did himfelf inftitute, fo neither may Men undertake the fame but by authority and power given them in lawful manner. That God which is no way deficient or wanting unto Man in neceffaries, and hath therefore given us the light of his heavenly Truth, becaufe without that ineftimable benefit we muft needs have wandered in darknefs to our endlefs perdition and woe, hath, in the like abundance of mercies, ordained certain to attend upon the due execution of requifite Parts and Offices therein prefcribed for the good of the whole World, which Men thereunto affigned do hold their Authority from him,

Of power given unto Men to execute that heavenly Office, of the gift of the Holy Ghoft in Ordination; and whether conveniently the power of Order may be fought or fued for.

* Καὶ σεαυτόν μοι προσοφείλεις. Epift. ad Philem.

BOOK V. whether they be ſuch as himſelf immediately, or as the Church in his name inveſteth; it being neither poſſible for all, nor for every Man without diſtinction convenient to take upon him a charge of ſo great importance. They are therefore Miniſters of God, not only by way of ſubordination as Princes and civil Magiſtrates, whoſe execution of Judgment and Juſtice the ſupreme hand of Divine Providence doth uphold; but Miniſters of God, as from whom their authority is derived, and not from Men. For in that they are Chriſt's Ambaſſadors and his Labourers, who ſhould give them their commiſſion but he whoſe moſt inward affairs they manage? Is not God alone the Father of Spirits? Are not Souls the purchaſe of Jeſus Chriſt? What Angel in Heaven could have ſaid to Man, as our Lord did unto Peter, *Feed my Sheep? preach? baptize? do this in remembrance of me? whoſe Sins ye retain, they are retained; and their offences in Heaven pardoned, whoſe faults you ſhall on earth forgive?* What think we? Are theſe terreſtrial ſounds, or elſe are they voices uttered out of the clouds above? The power of the Miniſtry of God tranſlateth out of darkneſs into glory; it raiſeth Men from the Earth, and bringeth God himſelf from Heaven; by bleſſing viſible Elements it maketh them inviſible Grace; it giveth daily the Holy Ghoſt, it hath to diſpoſe of that Fleſh which was given for the life of the World, and that Blood which was poured out to redeem Souls; when it poureth Malediction upon the heads of the wicked, they periſh, when it revoketh the ſame, they revive. O wretched blindneſs, if we admire not ſo great power; more wretched if we conſider it aright, and notwithſtanding imagine that any but God can beſtow it! To whom Chriſt hath imparted power, both over that myſtical Body which is the Society of Souls, and over that natural which is himſelf, for the knitting of both in one (a work which Antiquity doth call the making of Chriſt's Body), the ſame power is in ſuch not amiſs both termed

termed a kind of mark or character, and acknowledged to be indelible. Ministerial power is a mark of separation, because it severeth them that have it from other Men, and maketh them a special Order consecrated unto the service of the Most High in things wherewith others may not meddle. Their difference therefore from other Men is in that they are a distinct Order. So Tertullian calleth them. And St. Paul himself dividing the Body of the Church of Christ into two moieties, nameth the one part ἰδιώτας, which is as much as to say the Order of the Laity, the opposite part whereunto we in like sort term the Order of God's Clergy, and the spiritual power which he hath given them, the power of their Order, so far forth as the same consisteth in the bare execution of holy things, called properly the affairs of God. For of the power of their Jurisdiction over Men's persons we are to speak in the Books following. They which have once received this power may not think to put it off and on like a cloke, as the weather serveth, to take it, reject and resume it as oft as themselves list; of which prophane and impious contempt these latter times have yielded, as of all other kinds of iniquity and apostasy, strange examples. But let them know, which put their hands unto this plough, that once consecrated unto God, they are made his peculiar inheritance for ever. Suspensions may stop, and Degradations utterly cut off the use or exercise of power before given; but voluntarily it is not in the power of Man to separate and pull asunder what God by his authority coupleth. So that although there may be through misdesert Degradation, as there may be cause of just separation after Matrimony; yet if (as sometimes it doth) restitution to former dignity, or reconciliation after breach doth happen, neither doth the one nor the other ever iterate the first knot. Much less is it necessary, which some have urged, concerning the Re-ordination of such, as others in times more corrupt did consecrate heretofore.

Tertul. de Adhort. Castit.

Heb. ii. 17.

Matth. xix.

Which

BOOK V Which error, already quelled by Saint Jerom, doth not now require any other refutation. Examples I grant there are which make for restraint of those Men from admittance again into rooms of spiritual function, whose fall by Heresy, or want of constancy in professing the Christian Faith, hath been once a disgrace to their calling. Neverthelesss, as there is no Law which bindeth, so there is no cause that should always lead to shew one and the same severity towards Persons culpable. Goodness of nature itself more inclineth to clemency than rigour. And we in other Men's offences do behold the plain image of our own imbecility. Besides also them that wander out of the way * it cannot be unexpedient to win with all hopes of favour, lest strictness used towards such as reclaim themselves should make others more obstinate in error. Wherefore after that the Church of Alexandria had somewhat recovered itself from the tempests and storms of Arianism, being in consultation about the re-establishment of that which by long disturbance had been greatly decayed and hindered, the ferventer sort gave quick sentence, that touching them which were of the Clergy, and had stained themselves with Heresy, there should be none so received into the Church again as to continue in the order of the Clergy. The rest, which considered how many Men's cases it did concern, thought it much more safe and consonant to bend somewhat down towards them which were fallen; to shew severity upon a few of the chiefest Leaders, and to offer to the rest a friendly reconciliation, without any other demand, saving only the abjuration of their error; as in the Gospel that wasteful young Man which returned home to his Father's house was with joy both admitted and honoured, his elder Brother

Ruffin. Hist Eccles lib. cap. 28.

* In 12 tabulis cautum est, ut idem juris esset sanantibus quod fortibus, id est bonis et qui nunquam defecerunt a populo Romano. Fest. in ver. Samnites.

hardly

hardly thought of for repining thereat; neither commended so much for his own fidelity and virtue, as blamed for not embracing him freely, whose unexpected recovery ought to have blotted out all remembrance of misdemeanors and faults past. But of this sufficient. A thing much stumbled at in the manner of giving Orders is our using those memorable words of our Lord and Saviour Christ, *Receive the Holy Ghost.* The Holy Ghost, they say, we cannot give, and therefore we * foolishly bid Men receive it. Wise Men, for their authority's sake, must have leave to befool them whom they are able to make wise by better instruction. Notwithstanding, if it may please their wisdom, as well to hear what Fools can say, as to controul that which they do, thus we have heard some wise Men teach, namely, that the Holy Ghost may be used to signify not the Person alone, but the Gift of the Holy Ghost; and we know that spiritual gifts are not only abilities to do things miraculous, as to speak with tongues which were never taught us, to cure diseases without art, and such like; but also that the very Authority and Power which is given Men in the Church to be Ministers of holy things, this is contained within the number of those gifts whereof the Holy Ghost is Author; and therefore he which giveth this Power may say without absurdity or folly, *Receive the Holy Ghost*, such Power as the Spirit of Christ hath endued his Church withal, such Power as neither Prince nor Potentate, King nor Cæsar on earth can give. So that if Men alone had devised this form of speech, thereby to express the heavenly well-spring of that Power which Ecclesiastical Ordinations do bestow, it is not so foolish but that wise Men might bear with

BOOK V.

Eccles Discip fol. 52. p. 2 l. 1.

* Papisticus quidam ritus, stulte quidem ab illis et sine ullo Scripturæ fundamento institutus, et a disciplinæ nostræ autoribus (pace illorum dixerim) non magno primum judicio acceptus, minore adhuc in Ecclesia nostra retinetur. Ecclesiast. Discip. pag. 53.

BOOK V. it. If then our Lord and Saviour himself have used the self-same form of words, and that in the self-same kind of action, although there be but the least shew of probability, yea or any possibility that his meaning might be the same which ours is, it should teach sober and grave Men not to be too venturous in condemning that of folly, which is not impossible to have in it more profoundness of wisdom, than flesh and blood should presume to controul. Our Saviour, after his Resurrection from the dead, gave

Matth. xxviii. 18.

his Apostles their Commission, saying, *All power is given me in Heaven and in Earth: Go therefore and teach all Nations, baptizing them in the Name of the Father, and the Son, and the Holy Ghost, teaching them to observe all things whatsoever I have commanded you.* In sum, *As my Father sent me, so send I you.* Where-

John xx. 22.

unto St. John doth add farther, that *having thus spoken, he breathed on them, and said, Receive the Holy Ghost.* By which words he must of likelihood understand some gift of the Spirit which was presently at that time bestowed upon them, as both the speech of actual delivery in saying *Receive*, and the visible sign thereof, his breathing, did shew. Absurd it were to imagine our Saviour did both to the ear, and also to the very eye, express a real donation, and they at that time receive nothing. It resteth then that we search what special Grace they did at that time receive. Touching miraculous power of the Spirit most apparent it is, that as then they received it not, but the promise thereof was to be shortly after performed. The words of St. Luke concerning that power are therefore set down with signifi-

Luke xxiv. 49.

cation of the time to come, *Behold I will send the promise of my Father upon you, but tarry you in the city of* Jerusalem *until ye be endued with power from on high.* Wherefore, undoubtedly, it was some other effect of the Spirit, the Holy Ghost in some other kind, which our Saviour did then bestow. What other likelier than that which himself doth mention, as it should

ſhould ſeem of purpoſe to take away all ambiguous conſtructions, and to declare that the Holy Ghoſt which he then gave was an holy and a ghoſtly authority, authority over the Souls of Men, authority, a part whereof conſiſteth in power to remit and retain ſins? *Receive the Holy Ghoſt: whoſe ſins ſoever ye remit, they are remitted; whoſe ſins ye retain, they are retained.* John xx. 23. Whereas therefore the other Evangeliſts had ſet down, that Chriſt did before his ſuffering promiſe to give his Apoſtles the keys of the Kingdom of Heaven, and being riſen from the dead promiſed moreover at that time a miraculous power of the Holy Ghoſt, St. John addeth, that he alſo inveſted them even then with the power of the Holy Ghoſt for caſtigation and relaxation of ſin, wherein was fully accompliſhed that which the Promiſe of the Keys did import. Seeing therefore that the ſame power is now given, why ſhould the ſame form of words expreſſing it be thought fooliſh? The cauſe why we breathe not, as Chriſt did on them unto whom he imparted power, is, for that neither Spirit nor ſpiritual authority may be thought to proceed from us, who are but Delegates or Aſſigns to give Men poſſeſſion of his Graces. Now beſides that the power and authority delivered with thoſe words is itſelf χάρισμα, a gracious donation which the Spirit of God doth beſtow, we may moſt aſſuredly perſuade ourſelves, that the hand which impoſeth upon us the function of our Miniſtry, doth under the ſame form of words ſo tie itſelf hereunto, that he which receiveth the burden is thereby for ever warranted to have the Spirit with him, and in him, for his aſſiſtance,* aid, countenance and ſupport in

* Et ſi neceſſarium eſt trepidare de merito, religioſum eſt tamen gaudere de dono: quoniam qui mihi oneris eſt autor, ipſe fiet adminiſtrationis adjutor; et ne magnitudine gratiæ ſuccumbat infirmus, dabit virtutem qui contulit dignitatem. Leo. ſer. 1. in anniver. die A. Τὸ πνεῦμα τὸ ἅγιον ἔθετο ἡμᾶς εἰς τὴν διακονίαν ταύτην. Greg. Nazian.

whatſoever

BOOK V. whatsoever he faithfully doth to discharge duty. Knowing therefore that when we take Ordination we also receive the presence of the Holy Ghost, partly to guide, direct and strengthen us in all our ways, and partly to assume unto itself for the more authority those actions that appertain to our place and calling, can our ears admit such a speech uttered in the reverend performance of that solemnity; or can we at any time renew the memory and enter into serious cogitation thereof, but with much admiration and joy? Remove what these foolish words do imply, and what hath the Ministry of God besides wherein to glory? Whereas now, forasmuch as the Holy Ghost, which our Saviour in his first Ordinations gave, doth no less concur with spiritual vocations throughout all ages, than the Spirit, which God derived from Moses to them that assisted him in his Government, did descend from them to their Successors in like authority and place, we have for the least and meanest duties, performed by virtue of ministerial power, that to dignify, grace and authorize them, which no other offices on earth can challenge. Whether we preach, pray, baptize, communicate, condemn, give absolution, or whatsoever; as Disposers of God's Mysteries, our words, judgments, acts and deeds are not ours, but the Holy Ghost's. Enough, if unfeignedly and in heart we did believe it, enough to banish whatsoever may justly be thought corrupt either in bestowing, or in using, or in esteeming the same otherwise than is meet. For profanely to bestow, or loosely to use, or vilely to esteem of the Holy Ghost, we all in shew and profession abhor. Now because the Ministry is an office of dignity and honour, some are doubtful whether any Man may seek for it without offence; or, to speak more properly, doubtful they are not, but rather bold to accuse our Discipline in this respect, as not only permitting, but requiring also ambitious suits, or other oblique ways or means whereby to

Numb. xi. 17.

Author. Lib Discip. Ecclesiast.

to obtain it. Againſt this they plead, that our Saviour did ſtay till his Father ſent him, and the Apoſtles till he them, that the ancient Biſhops in the Church of Chriſt were examples and patterns of the ſame modeſty. Whereupon in the end they infer, *Let us therefore at the length amend that cuſtom of repairing from all parts unto the Biſhop at the day of Ordination, and of ſeeking to obtain Orders; let the cuſtom of bringing commendatory letters be removed; let Men keep themſelves at home, expecting there the voice of God, and the authority of ſuch as may call them to undertake charge.* Thus ſeverely they cenſure and controul ambition, if it be ambition which they take upon them to reprehend. For of that there is cauſe to doubt. Ambition, as we underſtand it, hath been accounted a vice which ſeeketh after honours inordinately. Ambitious minds, eſteeming it their greateſt happineſs to be admired, reverenced, and adored above others, uſe all means lawful and unlawful which may bring them to high rooms. But as for the power of Order conſidered by itſelf, and as in this caſe it muſt be conſidered, ſuch reputation it hath in the eye of this preſent World, that they, which affect it, rather need encouragement to bear contempt, than deſerve blame as Men that carry aſpiring minds. The work whereunto this power ſerveth is commended, and the deſire thereof allowed by the Apoſtle for good. Nevertheleſs, becauſe the burden thereof is heavy, and the charge great, it cometh many times to paſs, that the minds even of virtuous Men are drawn into clean contrary affections, ſome in humility declining that by reaſon of hardneſs, which others in regard of goodneſs only do with fervent alacrity covet. So that there is not the leaſt degree in this ſervice, but it may be both in * reve- 1 Tim. iii. 1.

* Τῶν παλαιῶν τοὺς εὐδοκιμωτάτους ἀναγνοπῶν εὑρίσκω ὅσους πώποτε εἰς ἐπιστασίαν ἢ προφητείαν ἡ χάρις προυβάλετο, τοὺς μὲν εἴξαντας προθύμως τῇ κλήσει, τοὺς δὲ ἀναβαλλομένους τὸ χάρισμα, καὶ οὐδετέρων μεμπτὴν οὔτε τῶν [illegible]

BOOK V. rence ſhunned, and of very devotion longed for. If then the deſire thereof may be holy, religious and good, may not the profeſſion of that deſire be ſo likewiſe? We are not to think it ſo long good as it is diſſembled, and evil if once we begin to open it. And allowing that it may be opened without ambition, what offence, I beſeech you, is there in opening it there, where it may be furthered and ſatisfied, in caſe they to whom it appertaineth think meet? In vain are thoſe deſires allowed, the accompliſhment whereof it is not lawful for Men to ſeek. Power therefore of Eccleſiaſtical Order may be deſired, the deſire thereof may be profeſſed, they which profeſs themſelves that way inclined may endeavour to bring their deſires to effect, and in all this no neceſſity of evil. Is it the bringing of teſtimonial Letters wherein ſo great obliquity conſiſteth? What more ſimple, more plain, more harmleſs, more agreeable with the law of common humanity, than that Men, where they are not known, uſe for their eaſier acceſs the credit of ſuch as can beſt give teſtimony of them? Letters of any other conſtruction our Church Diſcipline alloweth not; and theſe to allow, is neither to require ambitious ſuings, nor to approve any indirect or unlawful act. The Prophet Eſay receiving his meſſage at the hands of God, and his charge by heavenly viſion, heard the voice of

Eſay vi. 8. the Lord, ſaying, *Whom ſhall I ſend? Who ſhall go for us?* Whereunto he recordeth his own anſwer, *Then I ſaid, Here, Lord, I am, ſend me.* Which in effect is the Rule and Canon whereby touching this point the very Order of the Church is framed. The appointment of times for ſolemn Ordination is but the publick demand of the Church in the name of the Lord himſelf, *Whom ſhall I ſend? Who ſhall go for us?*

ὑποχωρησάντων τὴν δειλίαν, οὔτε τῶν ὁρμησάντων τὴν προθυμίαν, οἱ μετὰ γὰρ τῆς διακονίας τὸ μέγεθος εὐλαβήθησαν, οἱ δὲ τῷ καλοῦντι πιστεύσαντες ἠκολούθησαν. Greg. Nazian. Apologet.

The

The confluence of Men, whose inclinations are bent that way, is but the answer thereunto, whereby the labours of sundry being offered, the Church hath freedom to take whom her Agents in such case think meet and requisite. As for the example of our Saviour Christ, who took not to himself this honour to be made our High Priest, but received the same from him which said, *Thou art a Priest for ever after* Heb v 5.
the order of Melchisedeck, his waiting and not attempting to execute the office till God saw convenient time, may serve in reproof of usurped honours, forasmuch as we ought not of our own accord to assume dignities, whereunto we are not called as Christ was. But yet it should be withal considered, that a proud usurpation without any orderly calling is one thing, and another the bare declaration of willingness to obtain admittance; which willingness of mind, I suppose, did not want in him whose answer was to the voice of his heavenly calling, *Behold I am come* Heb. vi. 9.
to do thy Will. And had it been for him, as it is for us, expedient to receive his commission signed with the hands of Men, to seek it might better have beseemed his humility, than it doth our boldness to reprehend them of pride and ambition, that make no worse kind of suits than by letters of information. Himself in calling his Apostles prevented all cogitations of theirs that way, to the end it might truly be said of them, *Ye chose not me, but I of my own voluntary motion made choice of you.* Which kind of undesired nomination to Ecclesiastical Places befel divers of the most famous amongst the ancient Fathers of the Church in a clean contrary consideration. For our Saviour's election respected not any merit or worth, but took them which were farthest off from likelihood of fitness; that afterwards their supernatural ability and performance, beyond hope, might cause the greater admiration; whereas in the other, mere admiration of their singular and rare virtues was the reason why honours were enforced upon

 them,

BOOK V. them, which they of meeknefs and modefty did what they could to avoid. But did they ever judge it a thing unlawful to wifh or defire the office, the only charge and bare function of their Miniftry? Towards which labour, what doth the bleffed Apoftle elfe but encourage, faying, *He, which defireth it, is defirous of a good work?* What doth he elfe by fuch fentences but ftir, kindle and inflame ambition; if I may term that defire ambition, which coveteth more to teftify love by painfulnefs in God's fervice, than to reap any other benefit? Although of the very honour itfelf, and of other emoluments annexed to fuch labours for more encouragement of Man's induftry, we are not fo to conceive neither, as if no affection could be caft towards them without offence. Ecclus. vii. 6. Only as the Wife Man giveth counfel, *Seek not to be made a Judge, left thou be not able to take away iniquity, and left thou, fearing the perfon of the mighty, fhouldeft commit an offence againft thine uprightnefs*; fo it always behoveth Men to take good heed, left affection to that, which hath in it as well difficulty as goodnefs, fophifticate the true and fincere judgment which before-hand they ought to have of their own ability, for want whereof many forward minds have found, inftead of contentment, repentance. But forafmuch as hardnefs of things in themfelves moft excellent cooleth the fervency of Men's defires, unlefs there be fomewhat naturally acceptable to incite labour (for both the method of fpeculative knowledge doth, by things which we fenfibly perceive, conduct to that which is in nature more certain, though lefs fenfible, and the method of virtuous actions is alfo to train beginners at the firft by things acceptable unto the tafte of natural appetite, till our minds at the length be fettled to embrace things precious in the eye of reafon, merely and wholly for their own fakes), howfoever inordinate defires do hereby take occafion to abufe the polity of God and Nature, either affecting without worth, or procuring by unfeemly means that which

which was inſtituted, and ſhould be reſerved for better minds to obtain by more approved courſes, in which conſideration the Emperors Anthemius and Leo did worthily oppoſe againſt ſuch ambitious practices that ancient and famous Conſtitution, wherein they have theſe ſentences: *Let not a Prelate be ordained for reward or upon requeſt, who ſhould be ſo far ſequeſtered from all ambition, that they which advance him might be fain to ſearch where he hideth himſelf, to entreat him drawing back, and to follow him till importunity have made him yield. Let nothing promote him but his excuſes to avoid the burden. They are unworthy of that vocation which are not thereunto brought unwillingly*; notwithſtanding, we ought not therefore with the odious name of ambition to traduce and draw into hatred every poor requeſt or ſuit, wherein Men may ſeem to affect honour; ſeeing that ambition and modeſty do not always ſo much differ in the mark they ſhoot at, as in the manner of their proſecutions. Yea, even in this may be error alſo, if we ſtill imagine them leaſt ambitious, which moſt forbear to ſtir either hand or foot towards their own preferments. For there are that make an idol of their great ſufficiency, and becauſe they ſurmiſe the place ſhould be happy that might enjoy them, they walk every where like grave pageants, obſerving whether Men do not wonder why ſo ſmall account is made of ſo rare worthineſs; and in caſe any other Man's advancement be mentioned, they either ſmile or bluſh at the marvellous folly of the World, which ſeeth not where dignities ſhould offer themſelves. Seeing therefore that ſuits after ſpiritual Functions may be as ambitiouſly forborne as proſecuted, it remaineth that the * eveneſt line of moderation between both

* Μέσος εἰμί τις τῶν τε ἄγαν τολμηρῶν καὶ τῶν λίαν δειλῶν, τῶν μὲν πάσαις ἐπιπηδώντων προστασίαις δειλότερος, τῶν δὲ φευγόντων πάσας θαρσαλεώτερος. Greg. Nazian. Apologet.

BOOK V. is, neither to follow them without conſcience; nor of pride to withdraw ourſelves utterly from them.

Of Degrees, whereby the power of Order is diſtinguiſhed, and concerning the Attire of Miniſters

78. It pleaſed Almighty God to chooſe to himſelf, for diſcharge of the * legal Miniſtry, one only Tribe out of twelve others, the Tribe of Levi; not all unto every divine ſervice, but Aaron and his Sons to one charge, the reſt of that ſanctified Tribe to another. With what Solemnities they were admitted into their Functions, in what manner Aaron and his ſucceſſors the High-Prieſts aſcended every Sabbath and Feſtival-day, offered and miniſtered in the Temple; with what Sin-offering once every year they reconciled firſt themſelves and their own houſe, afterwards the People unto God; how they confeſſed all the iniquities of the Children of Iſrael, laid all their treſpaſſes upon the head of a ſacred goat, and ſo carried them out of the city; how they purged the Holy Place from all uncleanneſs; with what reverence they entered within the Veil, preſented themſelves before the Mercy-ſeat, and conſulted with the Oracle of God, what ſervice the other Prieſts did continually in the Holy Place, how they miniſtered about the Lamps, morning and evening; how every Sabbath they placed on the Table of the Lord thoſe twelve Loaves with pure incenſe, in perpetual remembrance of that mercy which the Fathers, the twelve Tribes, had found by the providence of God for their food, when hunger cauſed them to leave their natural ſoil, and to ſeek for ſuſtenance in Egypt; how they employed themſelves in ſacrifice day by day, finally, what Offices the Levites diſcharged, and what Duties the reſt did execute, it were a labour too long to enter into it, if I ſhould collect that which Scriptures and other ancient Records do mention. Beſides theſe, there were indifferently out of all Tribes from time to

* Πρὸς διατήρησιν ϗ φυλακὴν ὁσιότητος ϗ εὐσεβείας ϗ λειτουργιῶν αἳ πρὸς τὴν τοῦ Θεοῦ τιμὴν ἀναφέρονται. Philo, p 297.

time

time ſome called of God as Prophets, foreſhewing them things to come, and giving them counſel in ſuch particulars as they could not be directed in by the Law; ſome choſen Men to read, ſtudy and interpret the Law of God, as the Sons or Scholars of the old Prophets, in whoſe room afterwards Scribes and Expounders of the Law ſucceeded. And, becauſe where ſo great variety is, if there ſhould be equality, confuſion would follow, the Levites were in all their ſervice at the appointment and direction of the Sons of Aaron, or Prieſts; they ſubject to the principal Guides and Leaders of their own Order; and they all in obedience under the High-Prieſt. Which difference doth alſo manifeſt itſelf in the very titles that Men for honour's ſake gave unto them, terming Aaron and his Succeſſors, High or Great; the Ancients over the companies of Prieſts, Arch-Prieſts; Prophets, Fathers; Scribes and Interpreters of the Law, Maſters. Touching the Miniſtry of the Goſpel of Jeſus Chriſt, the whole body of the Church being divided into Laity and Clergy, the Clergy are either Preſbyters or Deacons. I rather term the one ſort Preſbyters than * Prieſts, becauſe in a matter of ſo ſmall moment I would not willingly offend their ears to whom the name of Prieſthood is odious, though without cauſe. For as things are diſtinguiſhed BOOK V.

* T. C. lib. i. pag. 198. For ſo much as the common and uſual ſpeech of England is to note by the word Prieſt, not a Miniſter of the Goſpel, but a Sacrificer, which the Miniſter of the Goſpel is not, therefore we ought not to call the Miniſters of the Goſpel Prieſts. And that this is the Engliſh ſpeech, it appeareth by all the Engliſh Tranſlations, which tranſlate always ἱερεῖς, which were Sacrificers, Prieſts, and do not on the other ſide, for any that ever I read, tranſlate πρεσβύτερον a Prieſt. Seeing therefore a Prieſt with us, and in our tongue, doth ſignify both by the Papiſts' judgment, in reſpect of their abominable Maſs, and alſo by the judgment of the Proteſtants, in reſpect of the beaſts which were offered in the Law, a ſacrificing office, which the Miniſter of the Goſpel neither doth nor can execute; it is manifeſt, that it cannot be without great offence ſo uſed.

BOOK V. one from another by thoſe true eſſential forms, which being really and actually in them do not only give them the very laſt and higheſt degree of their natural perfection, but are alſo the knot, foundation and root whereupon all other inferior perfections depend; ſo if they that firſt do impoſe names did always underſtand exactly the nature of that which they nominate, it may be that then by hearing the terms of vulgar ſpeech we ſhould ſtill be taught what the things themſelves moſt properly are. But becauſe words have ſo many artificers by whom they are made, and the things whereunto we apply them are fraught with ſo many varieties, it is not always apparent what the firſt Inventors reſpected, much leſs what every Man's inward conceit is which uſeth theſe words. For any thing myſelf can diſcern herein, I ſuppoſe that they which have bent their ſtudy to ſearch more diligently ſuch matters, do, for the moſt part, find that Names adviſedly given had either regard unto that which is naturally moſt proper; or if perhaps to ſome other ſpeciality, to that which is ſenſibly moſt eminent in the thing ſignified; and concerning popular uſe of words, that which the wiſdom of their Inventors did intend thereby is not commonly thought of, but by the name the thing altogether conceived in groſs; as may appear in that if you aſk of the common ſort what any certain word, for example, what a Prieſt doth ſignify; their manner is not to anſwer, a Prieſt is a Clergyman which offereth ſacrifice to God; but they ſhew ſome particular Perſon whom they uſe to call by that name. And if we liſt to deſcend to Grammar, we are told by maſters in thoſe Schools, that the word Prieſt

Etymol. [illegible] hath his right place ἐπὶ τȣ̃ ψιλῶς προεςῶτος τῆς θεραπείας τȣ̃ Θεȣ̃, in him whoſe mere function or charge is the ſervice of God. Howbeit, becauſe the eminenteſt part both of Heatheniſh and Jewiſh ſervice did conſiſt in Sacrifice, when learned Men declare what the word Prieſt doth properly ſignify, according to the mind of the firſt impoſer of that name, their ordinary

Schools

* Schools do well expound it to imply Sacrifice. Seeing then that Sacrifice is now no part of the Church-Miniſtry, how ſhould the name of Prieſthood be thereunto rightly applied? Surely even as St. *Paul* applieth the name of † *Fleſh* unto that very ſubſtance of fiſhes, which hath a proportionable correſpondence to fleſh, although it be in nature another thing. Whereupon, when Philoſophers will ſpeak warily, they ‡ make a difference between fleſh in one ſort of living Creatures, and that other ſubſtance in the reſt which hath but a kind of analogy to fleſh: the Apoſtle contrariwiſe having matter of greater importance whereof to ſpeak, nameth indifferently both fleſh. 1 Cor. xv. 39. The Fathers of the Church of Chriſt with like ſecurity of ſpeech call uſually the Miniſtry of the Goſpel *Prieſthood*, in regard of that which the Goſpel hath proportionable to ancient Sacrifices; namely, the communion of the bleſſed Body and Blood of Chriſt, although it hath properly now no Sacrifice. As for the People, when they hear the name, it draweth no more their minds to any cogitation of Sacrifice, than the name of a Senator or of an Alderman cauſeth them to think upon old age, or to imagine that every one ſo termed muſt needs be ancient, becauſe years were reſpected in the firſt nomination of both. Wherefore, to paſs by the name, let them uſe what dialect they will, whether we call it a Prieſthood, a Preſbyterſhip, or a Miniſtry, it ſkilleth not: although in truth the word *Preſbyter* doth ſeem more fit, and in propriety of ſpeech more agreeable than *Prieſt* with the drift of the whole Goſpel of Jeſus Chriſt. For what are they that embrace the Goſpel but Sons of God? What are Churches but his Families? Seeing

* Ἱερεῦσαι, θυσιάσαι.

† Heſy. Chriſtus Homo dicitur, quia natus eſt; Propheta, quia futura revelavit, Sacerdos, quia pro nobis hoſtiam ſe obtulit. Iſid. Orig. lib. vii. cap. 2.

‡ Ἔχει δ᾽ ἀπορίαν τὶ τὸ αἰσθητήριον τὸ τοῦ ἁπτοῦ ἁπλῶς, πότερον ἡ σάρξ καὶ ἐν τοῖς ἄλλοις τὸ ἀνάλογον ἢ οὔ. Ariſt. de Anim. lib. ii. c. 11.

BOOK V therefore we receive the Adoption and ſtate of Sons by their Miniſtry whom God hath choſen out for that purpoſe; ſeeing alſo that when we are the Sons of God, our continuance is ſtill under their care which were our Progenitors, what better title could there be given them than the reverend name of *Preſbyters*, or fatherly Guides? The Holy Ghoſt throughout the body of the New Teſtament, making ſo much mention of them, doth not any where call them Prieſts.
Eſay lxvi. 21. The Prophet Eſay, I grant, doth, but in ſuch ſort as the ancient Fathers, by way of analogy. A Preſbyter, according to the proper meaning of the New Teſtament, is he unto whom our Saviour Chriſt hath communicated the power of ſpiritual procreation. Out of twelve Patriarchs iſſued the whole multitude of Iſrael according to the fleſh. And, according to the myſtery of heavenly birth, our Lord's Apoſtles we all acknowledge to be the Patriarchs of his whole Church.
Rev. iv. 4. Rev. xxi. 14. Matt. xix. 28. 1 Pet. v. 1. St. John therefore beheld ſitting about the Throne of God in Heaven four and twenty Preſbyters, the one half Fathers of the old, the other of the new Jeruſalem. In which reſpect the Apoſtles likewiſe gave themſelves the ſame title, albeit that name were not proper, but common unto them with others. For of Preſbyters, ſome were greater, ſome leſs in power, and that by our Saviour's own appointment, the greater, they which received fulneſs of ſpiritual power; the leſs, they to whom leſs was granted. The Apoſtles' peculiar charge was to publiſh the Goſpel of Chriſt unto all Nations, and to deliver them his Ordinances received by * immediate relation from himſelf. Which pre-eminence excepted,
Acts ii 41, 47. to all other offices and duties incident unto their Order, it was in them to ordain and conſecrate whomſoever they thought meet, even as our Saviour did himſelf aſſign ſeventy other of his own Diſciples inferior Preſbyters, whoſe commiſſion to preach and baptize was the ſame which the Apoſtles had. Whereas there-

* Οἱ τῶν ἱερῶν θεοπαραδότως νομοθέται. Dionyſ. Areop. p. 110.

fore

ſore we find that the very firſt Sermon which the Apoſtles did publickly make, was the converſion of above three thouſand Souls, unto whom there were every day more and more added, they having no open place permitted them for the exerciſe of Chriſtian Religion, think we that twelve were ſufficient to teach and adminiſter Sacraments in ſo many private places, as ſo great a multitude of People did require? This harveſt our Saviour (no doubt) foreſeeing, provided accordingly Labourers for it before-hand. By which means it came to paſs that the growth of that Church, being ſo great and ſo ſudden, they had notwithſtanding in a readineſs Preſbyters enough to furniſh it. And therefore the Hiſtory doth make no mention by what occaſion Preſbyters were inſtituted in Jeruſalem, only we read of things which they did, and how the like were made afterwards elſewhere. To theſe two degrees appointed of our Lord and Saviour Chriſt, his Apoſtles ſoon after annexed Deacons. Deacons therefore muſt know, ſaith Cyprian, that our Lord himſelf did elect Apoſtles; but Deacons, after his aſcenſion into Heaven, the Apoſtles ordained. Deacons were Stewards of the Church, unto whom at the firſt was committed the diſtribution of Church-goods, the care of providing therewith for the Poor, and the charge to ſee that all things of expence might be religiouſly and faithfully dealt in. A part alſo of their office was attendance upon their Preſbyters at the time of divine Service. For which cauſe Ignatius, to ſet forth the dignity of their calling, ſaith, that they are in ſuch caſe to the Biſhop, as if Angelical Powers did ſerve him. Theſe only being the uſes for which Deacons were firſt made, if the Church have ſithence extended their Miniſtry further than the circuit of their labour at the firſt was drawn, we are not herein to think the Ordinance of Scripture violated, except there appear ſome prohibition which hath abridged the Church of that liberty. Which I note chiefly in regard of them to whom it ſeemeth a thing

Cypr. Ep. ix. l. 3. ad Rogatianum.

Ignat. Epiſt. ad Tral.

ſo

 ſo monſtrous that Deacons ſhould ſometime be licenced to preach, whoſe inſtitution was at the firſt to another end. To charge them for this as Men not contented with their own vocations, and as breakers into that which appertaineth unto others, is very hard. For when they are thereunto once admitted, it is part of their own vocation, it appertaineth now unto them as well as others, neither is it intruſion for them to do it, being in ſuch ſort called, but rather in us it were temerity to blame them for doing it. Suppoſe we the office of teaching to be ſo repugnant unto the office of Deaconſhip that they cannot concur in one and the ſame Perſon? What was there done in the Church by Deacons, which the Apoſtles did not firſt diſcharge being Teachers? Yea, but the Apoſtles found the burden of teaching ſo heavy, that they judged it meet to cut off that other charge, and to have Deacons which might undertake it. Be it ſo. The multitude of Chriſtians increaſing in Jeruſalem, and waxing great, it was too much for the Apoſtles to teach, and to miniſter unto tables alſo. The former was not to be ſlacked, that this latter might be followed. Therefore unto this they appointed others. Whereupon we may rightly ground this axiom, that when the ſubject wherein one Man's labours of ſundry kinds are employed doth wax ſo great, that the ſame Men are no longer able to manage it ſufficiently as before, the moſt natural way to help this is, by dividing their charge into ſlips, and ordaining of Under-Officers; as our Saviour under twelve Apoſtles, ſeventy Preſbyters; and the Apoſtles by his example ſeven Deacons to be under both. Neither ought it to ſeem leſs reaſonable, that when the ſame Men are ſufficient both to continue in that which they do and alſo to undertake ſomewhat more, a combination be admitted in this caſe, as well as diviſion in the former. We may not therefore diſallow it in the Church of Geneva, that Calvin and Beza were made both Paſtors and Readers in Divinity, being Men ſo able to diſcharge both. To

ſay

ſay they did not content themſelves with their paſtoral vocations, but brake into that which belongeth to others; to alledge againſt them, *He that exhorteth on exhortation*, as againſt us, *He that diſtributeth in ſimplicity*, is alledged in great diſlike of granting licence for Deacons to preach, were very hard. The ancient cuſtom of the Church was to yield the Poor much relief, eſpecially Widows. But as poor People are always querulous, and apt to think themſelves leſs reſpected than they ſhould be, we ſee that when the Apoſtles did what they could without hindrance to their weightier buſineſs, yet there were which grudged that others had too much and they too little, the Grecian Widows ſhorter commons than the Hebrews. By means whereof the Apoſtles ſaw it meet to ordain Deacons. Now tract of time having clean worn out thoſe firſt occaſions, for which the Deaconſhip was then moſt neceſſary, it might the better be afterwards extended to other ſervices, and ſo remain, as at this preſent day, a Degree in the Clergy of God which the Apoſtles of Chriſt did inſtitute. That the firſt ſeven Deacons were choſen out of the ſeventy Diſciples, is an error in Epiphanius. For to draw Men from places of weightier, unto rooms of meaner labour, had not been fit. The Apoſtles, to the end they might follow teaching with more freedom, committed the miniſtry of tables unto Deacons. And ſhall we think they judged it expedient to chooſe ſo many out of thoſe ſeventy to be miniſters unto tables, when Chriſt himſelf had before made them Teachers? It appeareth therefore how long theſe three degrees of Eccleſiaſtical Order have continued in the Church of Chriſt; the higheſt and largeſt, that which the Apoſtles, the next that which Preſbyters, and the loweſt that which Deacons had. Touching Prophets, they were ſuch Men as having otherwiſe learned the Goſpel, had from above beſtowed upon them a ſpecial gift of expounding Scriptures, and of foreſhewing things to come. Of this ſort Agabus was, and beſides him in

Rom. xii. 8.

Epiph. l. i. c. 21.

Acts xxi. 10.

Jeruſalem

Jerusalem sundry others, who notwithstanding are not therefore to be reckoned with the Clergy, because no Man's gifts or qualities can make him a Minister of holy things, unless Ordination do give him power. And we no where find Prophets to have been made by Ordination; but all whom the Church did ordain were either to serve as Presbyters or as Deacons. Evangelists were Presbyters of principal sufficiency, whom the Apostles sent abroad, and used as Agents in Ecclesiastical affairs wheresoever they saw need. They whom we find to have been named in Scripture Evangelists, Ananias, Apollos, Timothy and others were thus employed. And concerning Evangelists, afterwards in Trajan's days, the History Ecclesiastical noteth that many of the Apostles' Disciples and Scholars which were then alive, and did with singular love of wisdom affect the heavenly Word of God, to shew their willing minds in executing that which Christ first of all requireth at the hands of Men, they sold their possessions, gave them to the Poor, and betaking themselves to travel, undertook the labour of Evangelists, that is, they painfully preached Christ, and delivered the Gospel to them who as yet had never heard the doctrine of Faith. Finally, whom the Apostle nameth Pastors and Teachers, what other were they than Presbyters also, howbeit settled in some charge, and thereby differing from Evangelists? I beseech them therefore which have hitherto troubled the Church with questions about Degrees and Offices of Ecclesiastical calling, because they principally ground themselves upon two places, that, all partiality laid aside, they would sincerely weigh and examine whether they have not misinterpreted both places, and all by surmising incompatible offices, where nothing is meant but sundry graces, gifts and abilities which Christ bestowed. To them of Corinth, his words are these: *God placed in the Church, first of all, some Apostles; secondly, Prophets; thirdly, Teachers; after them Powers, then gifts of Cures, Aids, Governments, kinds*

Acts xi. 27.

Acts ix. 18
Acts xviii. 24.
2 Tim iv. 5, 9
1 Tim. iii. 15 v. 14.
ii 8.
Euseb Ecclef Hist. l iii. c. 34.

1 Cor. xii. 28.

kinds of Languages. Are all Apoſtles? Are all Prophets? Are all Teachers? Is there power in all? Have all grace to cure? Do all ſpeak with tongues? Can all interpret? But be you deſirous of the better graces. They which plainly diſcern firſt, that ſome one general thing there is which the Apoſtle doth here divide into all theſe branches, and do ſecondly conceive that general to be Church-Offices, beſides a number of other difficulties, can by no means poſſibly deny but that many of theſe might concur in one Man, and peradventure in ſome one all; which mixture, notwithſtanding, their form of Diſcipline doth moſt ſhun. On the other ſide, admit that Communicants of ſpecial infuſed grace, for the benefit of Members knit into one body, the Church of Chriſt, are here ſpoken of, which was in truth the plain drift of that whole Diſcourſe; and ſee if every thing do not anſwer in due place with that fitneſs which ſheweth eaſily what is likelieſt to have been meant. For why are Apoſtles the firſt, but becauſe unto them was granted the revelation of all Truth from Chriſt immediately? Why Prophets the ſecond, but becauſe they had of ſome things knowledge in the ſame manner? Teachers the next, becauſe whatſoever was known to them it came by hearing, yet God withal made them able to inſtruct, which every one could not do that was taught? After gifts of edification there follow general abilities to work things above Nature, Grace to cure Men of bodily diſeaſes, ſupplies againſt occurrent defects and impediments, dexterities to govern and direct by counſel, finally, aptneſs to ſpeak or interpret foreign tongues. Which Graces, not poured out equally, but diverſely ſorted and given, were a cauſe why not only they all did furniſh up the whole body, but each benefit and help other. Again, the ſame Apoſtle, otherwhere in like ſort, *To every one of us is given Grace, according to the meaſure of the gift of Chriſt. Wherefore he ſaith, when he aſcended up on high, he led captivity captive, and gave gifts unto Men. He therefore gave* *ſome*

BOOK V.

Epheſ iv. 7.
Pſal. lxviii. 18.

BOOK V. *ſome Apoſtles, and ſome Prophets, and ſome Evangeliſts, and ſome Paſtors and Teachers, for the gathering together of Saints, for the work of the Miniſtry, for the edification of the Body of Chriſt.* In this place none but gifts of inſtruction are expreſſed. And becauſe of Teachers ſome were Evangeliſts, which neither had any part of their knowledge by revelation as the Prophets, and yet in ability to teach were far beyond other Paſtors, they are, as having received one way leſs than Prophets, and another way more than Teachers, ſet accordingly between both. For the Apoſtle doth in neither place reſpect what any of them were by office or power given them through Ordination, but what by grace they all had obtained through miraculous infuſion of the Holy Ghoſt. For in Chriſtian Religion, this being the ground of our whole Belief, that the promiſes, which God of old had made his Prophets concerning the wonderful gifts and graces of the Holy Ghoſt, wherewith the Reign of the true Meſſias ſhould be made glorious, were immediately after our Lord's Aſcenſion performed, there is no one thing whereof the Apoſtles did take more often occaſion to ſpeak. Out of Men thus endued with gifts of the Spirit upon their converſion to Chriſtian Faith, the Church had her Miniſters choſen, unto whom was given Eccleſiaſtical power by Ordination. Now, becauſe the Apoſtle, in reckoning degrees and varieties of Grace, doth mention Paſtors and Teachers, although he mention them not in reſpect of their Ordination to exerciſe the Miniſtry, but as examples of Men eſpecially enriched with the gifts of the Holy Ghoſt, divers learned and ſkilful Men have ſo taken it, as if thoſe places did intend to teach what Orders of Eccleſiaſtical Perſons there ought to be in the Church of Chriſt; which thing we are not to learn from thence, but out of other parts of holy Scripture, whereby it clearly appeareth that Churches Apoſtolick did know but three degrees in the power of Eccleſiaſtical Order; at the firſt Apoſtles, Preſbyters and Deacons; afterwards,

afterwards, inftead of Apoftles, Bifhops, concerning whofe Order we are to fpeak in the feventh Book. There is an error which beguileth many who do much entangle both themfelves and others by not diftinguifhing Services, Offices and Orders Ecclefiaftical. The firft of which three, and in part the fecond may be executed by the Laity; whereas none have, or can have the third but the Clergy. Catechifts, Exorcifts, Readers, Singers and the reft of like fort, if the nature only of their labour and pains be confidered, may in that refpect feem Clergymen, even as the Fathers for that caufe term them ufually Clerks; as alfo in regard of the end whereunto they were trained up, which was to be ordered when years and experience fhould make them able. Notwithftanding, in as much as they no way differed from others of the Laity longer than during that work of fervice, which at any time they might give over, being thereunto but admitted, not tied by irrevocable Ordination, we find them always exactly fevered from that body, whereof thofe three before rehearfed Orders alone are natural parts. Touching Widows, of whom fome Men are perfuaded, that if fuch as St. Paul defcribeth may be gotten, we ought to retain them in the Church for ever, certain mean fervices there were of Attendance; as about Women at the time of their Baptifm, about the bodies of the Sick and Dead, about the neceffities of Travellers, way-faring Men, and fuch like, wherein the Church did commonly ufe them when need required, becaufe they lived of the Alms of the Church, and were fitteft for fuch purpofes; St. Paul doth therefore, to avoid fcandal, require that none but Women well experienced and virtuoufly given, neither any under threefcore years of age fhould be admitted of that number. Widows were never in the Church fo highly efteemed as Virgins. But feeing neither of them did or could receive Ordination, to make them Ecclefiaftical Perfons were abfurd. The ancienteft therefore of the Fathers mention thofe three degrees of Ecclefiaftical

BOOK V.

T. C. l. i. p. 191.
1 Tim. v. 9.

BOOK V. siastical Order specified, and no more. *When your Captains* (saith Tertullian), *that is to say, the Deacons, Presbyters and Bishops fly, who shall teach the Laity that they must be constant?* Again, *What should I mention Lay-men* (saith Optatus), *yea, or divers of the Ministry itself? To what purpose Deacons, which are in the third, or Presbyters in the second degree of Priesthood, when the very Heads and Princes of all, even certain of the Bishops themselves were content to redeem life with the loss of Heaven?* Heaps of allegation in a case so evident and plain are needless. I may securely therefore conclude, that there are at this day in the Church of England no other than the same Degrees of Ecclesiastical Orders, namely, Bishops, Presbyters and Deacons, which had their beginning from Christ and his blessed Apostles themselves. As for Deans, Prebendaries, Parsons, Vicars, Curates, Archdeacons, Chancellors, Officials, Commissaries and such other like names, which being not found in holy Scripture, we have been thereby through some Men's error thought to allow of Ecclesiastical Degrees not known, nor ever heard of in the better ages of former times; all these are in truth but titles of office, whereunto partly Ecclesiastical Persons, and partly others are in sundry forms and conditions admitted, as the state of the Church doth need, degrees of Order still continuing the same they were from the first beginning. Now what habit or attire doth beseem each Order to use in the course of common life, both for the gravity of his place and for example sake to other Men, is a matter frivolous to be disputed of. A small measure of wisdom may serve to teach them how they should cut their coats. But seeing all well-ordered Polities have ever judged it meet and fit by certain special distinct ornaments to sever each sort of Men from other when they are in publick, to the end that all may receive such compliments of civil honour as are due to their rooms and callings, even when their Persons are not known,

Tertul de Persecut.

Optat. l. 1.

known, it argueth a diſproportioned mind in them whom ſo decent Orders diſpleaſe.

Of Oblations, Foundations, Endowments, Tithes, all intended for perpetuity of Religion, which purpoſe being chiefly fulfilled by the Clergy's certain and ſufficient maintenance, muſt needs by alienation of Church-livings be made fruſtrate.

79. We might ſomewhat marvel what the Apoſtle St. Paul ſhould mean to ſay that *Covetouſneſs is Idolatry*, if the daily practice of Men did not ſhew, that whereas Nature requireth God to be honoured with wealth, we honour for the moſt part wealth as God. Fain we would teach ourſelves to believe, that for worldly goods it ſufficeth frugally and honeſtly to uſe them to our own benefit, without detriment and hurt to others, or if we go a degree farther, and perhaps convert ſome ſmall contemptible portion thereof to charitable uſes, the whole duty which we owe unto God herein is fully ſatisfied. But for as much as we cannot highly honour God, unleſs both our Souls and Bodies be ſometime employed merely in his ſervice; again, ſith we know that Religion requireth at our hands the taking away of ſo great a part of the time of our lives quite and clean from our own buſineſs, and the beſtowing of the ſame in his; ſuppoſe we that nothing of our wealth and ſubſtance is immediately due to God, but all our own to beſtow and ſpend as ourſelves think meet? Are not our riches as well his, as the days of our life are his? Wherefore, unleſs with part we acknowledge his ſupreme dominion by whoſe benevolence we have the whole, how give we honour to whom honour belongeth, or how hath God the things that are God's? I would know what Nation in the World did ever honour God, and not think it a point of their duty to do him honour with their very goods. So that this we may boldly ſet down as a Principle clear in Nature, an Axiom that ought not to be called in queſtion, a Truth manifeſt and infallible, that Men are eternally bound to honour God with their ſubſtance, in token of thankful acknowledgment that all they have is from him. To honour him with our worldly goods, not only by ſpending them in lawful manner, and by uſing them without offence, but alſo by alienating from ourſelves ſome

BOOK V. reasonable part or portion thereof, and by offering up the same to him as a sign that we gladly confess his sole and sovereign dominion over all, is a duty which all Men are bound unto, and a part of that very worship of God, which, as the Law of God and Nature itself requireth, so we are the rather to think all Men no less strictly bound thereunto, than to any other natural duty, inasmuch as the hearts of Men do so cleave to these earthly things, so much admire them for the sway they have in the World, impute them so generally either to Nature or to Chance and Fortune, so little think upon the Grace and Providence from which they come, that unless by a kind of continual tribute we did acknowledge God's dominion, it may be doubted that in short time Men would learn to forget whose tenants they are, and imagine that the World is their own absolute, free and independent inheritance. Now, concerning the kind or quality of gifts which God receiveth in that sort, we are to consider them, partly as first they proceed from us, and partly as afterwards they are to serve for divine uses. In that they are testimonies of our affection towards God, there is no doubt but such they should be as beseemeth most his glory to whom we offer them. In this respect the fatness of Abel's sacrifice is commended; the flower of all Men's increase assigned to God by Solomon; the gifts and donations of the People rejected as oft as their cold affection to God-ward made their presents to be little worth. Somewhat the Heathens saw touching that which was herein fit, and therefore they unto their gods did not think they might consecrate any thing which was * impure or unsound, or already given, or else not truly their own to give. Again, in regard of use, for as much as we know that God hath himself no need of worldly commodities, but taketh them because it is our good to be so exercised, and with no

* Purum, probum, profanum, suum. Fest. lib. xiv.

other

other intent accepteth them, but to have them ufed for the endlefs continuance of Religion; there is no place left of doubt or controverfy, but that we in the choice of our gifts are to level at the fame mark, and to frame ourfelves to his own intents and purpofes. Whether we give unto God therefore that which himfelf by commandment requireth, or that which the publick confent of the Church thinketh good to allot, or that which every Man's private devotion doth beft like, in as much as the gift which we offer proceedeth not only as a teftimony of our affection towards God, but alfo as a means to uphold Religion, the exercife whereof cannot ftand without the help of temporal commodities; if all Men be taught of Nature to wifh, and as much as in them lieth to procure the perpetuity of good things; if for that very caufe we honour and admire their wifdom, who, having been Founders of Common-weals, could devife how to make the benefit they left behind them durable; if, efpecially in this refpect, we prefer Lycurgus before Solon, and the Spartan before the Athenian Polity, it muft needs follow, that as we do unto God very acceptable fervice in honouring him with our fubftance, fo our fervice that way is then moft acceptable when it tendeth to perpetuity. The firft permanent donations of honour in this kind are Temples. Which works do fo much fet forward the exercife of Religion, that while the World was in love with Religion, it gave to no fort greater reverence than to whom it could point and fay, *Thefe are the Men that have built us Synagogues.* But of Churches we have fpoken fufficiently heretofore. The next things to Churches are the Ornaments of Churches, memorials which Men's devotion hath added to remain in the treafure of God's Houfe, not only for ufes wherein the exercife of Religion prefently needeth them, but alfo partly for fupply of future cafual neceffities, whereunto the Church is on earth fubject, and partly to the end that while they are kept they may continually

BOOK V. ſerve as teſtimonies, giving all Men to underſtand that God hath in every Age and Nation ſuch as think it no burden to honour him with their ſubſtance. The riches firſt of the Tabernacle of God, and then of the Temple of Jeruſalem, ariſing out of voluntary gifts and donations, were, as we commonly ſpeak, a *Nemo ſcit*, the value of them above that which any Man would imagine. After that the Tabernacle was made, furniſhed with all neceſſaries, and ſet up, although in the wilderneſs their ability could not poſſibly be great, the very metal of thoſe veſſels, which the Princes of the Twelve Tribes gave to God for their firſt preſents, amounted even then to two thouſand and four hundred ſhekels of ſilver, an hundred and twenty ſhekels of gold, every ſhekel weighing half an ounce. What was given to the Temple which Solomon erected we may partly conjecture, when over and beſides wood, marble, iron, braſs, veſtments, precious ſtones and money, the ſum which David delivered into Solomon's hands for that purpoſe, was of gold in maſs eight thouſand, and of ſilver ſeventeen thouſand cichars, every cichar containing a thouſand and eight hundred ſhekels, which riſeth to nine hundred ounces in every one cichar, whereas the whole charge of the Tabernacle did not amount unto thirty cichars. After their return out of Babylon, they were not preſently in caſe to make their ſecond Temple of equal magnificence and glory, with that which the Enemy had deſtroyed. Notwithſtanding what they could they did. Inſomuch that the buildings finiſhed, there remained in the coffers of the Church, to uphold the fabrick thereof, ſix hundred and fifty cichars of ſilver, one hundred of gold. Whereunto was added by Nehemias of his own gift a thouſand drams of gold, fifty veſſels of ſilver, five hundred and thirty Prieſts veſtments; by other the Princes of the Fathers twenty thouſand drams of gold, two thouſand and two hundred pieces of ſilver; by the reſt of the People twenty thouſand of gold, two thouſand of ſilver, threeſcore

Numb. vii 85, 86.

1 Chron. xxix. Exod. xxv. 28 & xxxvii. 24. Ezra ii. 68, 69 Hag ii 4. Ezra viii. 24.

Nehem. vii. 70.

BOOK V.

threefcore and feven attires of Priefts. And they furthermore bound themfelves towards other charges to give by the poll, in what part of the World foever they fhould dwell, the third of a fhekel, that is to fay, the fixth part of an ounce yearly. * This out of foreign Provinces they always fent in gold. Whereof Mithridates is faid to have taken up by the way before it could pafs to Jerufalem from Afia, in one adventure, eight hundred talents†; Craffus after that to have borrowed of the Temple itfelf eight thoufand; at which time Eleazar having both many other rich ornaments, and all the tapeftry of the Temple under his cuftody, thought it the fafeft way to grow unto fome compofition; and fo to redeem the refidue by parting with a certain beam of gold about feven hundred and an half weight, a prey fufficient for one Man, as he thought who had never bargained with Craffus till then, and therefore upon the confidence of a folemn oath that no more fhould be looked for, he fimply delivered up a large morfel, whereby the value of that which remained was betrayed, and the whole loft. Such being the cafualties whereunto moveable treafures are fubject, the Law of Mofes did both require eight and forty Cities, together with their fields and whole territories in the Land of Jury, to be referved for God himfelf, and not only provide for the liberty of farther additions, if Men of their own accord fhould think good, but alfo for the fafe prefervation thereof unto all Pofterities, that no Man's avarice or fraud, by defeating fo virtuous intents, might difcourage from like purpofes. God's third endowment did therefore of old confift in Lands. Furthermore, fome caufe no doubt there is why be-

Nehe. x. 32

Jofeph. Anti. l. xiv. c. 7

Num. xxxv. Levit. xxv 34. & xxvii. 28.

* Cic. orat pro L. Flac. Cum aurum Judæorum nomine quotannis ex Italia et ex omnibus veftris provinciis Hierofolymam exportari foleret, Flaccus fanxit edicto, ne ex Afia exportari liceret

† Every talent in value fix hundred crowns.

BOOK V. ſides ſundry other more rare donations of uncertain rate, the Tenth ſhould be thought a revenue ſo natural to be allotted out unto God. For of the ſpoils which Abraham had taken in war, he delivered unto Melchiſedeck the Tithes. The vow of Jacob, at ſuch time as he took his journey towards Haran, was, *If God will be with me, and will keep me in this voyage which I am to go, and will give me bread to eat, and clothes to put on, ſo that I may return to my Father's houſe in ſafety, then ſhall the Lord be my God; and this ſtone which I have ſet up as a pillar, the ſame ſhall be God's-houſe, and of all thou ſhalt give me I will give unto thee the Tithe.* And as Abraham gave voluntarily, as Jacob vowed to give God Tithes, ſo the Law of Moſes did require at the hands of all Men the ſelf-ſame kind of tribute, the Tenth of their Corn, Wine, Oil, Fruit, Cattle and whatſoever increaſe his heavenly Providence ſhould ſend. Inſomuch, that Painims being herein followers of their ſteps, paid Tithes likewiſe. Imagine we that this was for no cauſe done, or that there was not ſome ſpecial inducement to judge the Tenth of our worldly profits the moſt convenient for God's portion? Are not all things by him created in ſuch ſort, that the forms which give them their diſtinction are number, their operations meaſure, and their matter weight? Three being the myſtical number of God's unſearchable perfection within himſelf; Seven the number whereby our own perfections, through grace, are moſt ordered; and * Ten the number of Nature's perfections (for the beauty of Nature is Order; and the foundation of Order, Number; and of Number, Ten the higheſt we can riſe unto without iteration of numbers under it) could Nature better acknowledge the power of the God of Nature, than by aſſigning unto him that quantity which is the continent of all ſhe poſſeſſeth?

Gen. xiv. 20.

Gen. xxviii. 20.

Deut. xiv. 22.

Plin. Hiſt. Nat. l. xii. § 14.

* Δεκὰς ἀριθμῶν τῶν ἀπὸ μονάδος ἐςὶ πέρας τελειότατον. Philo. περὶ ἀποικ.

There

There are in Philo the Jew, many arguments to ſhew the great congruity and fitneſs of this number in things conſecrated unto God. But becauſe over-nice and curious ſpeculations become not the earneſtneſs of holy things, I omit what might be farther obſerved, as well out of others, as out of him, touching the quantity of this general ſacred tribute; whereby it cometh to paſs that the meaneſt and the very pooreſt amongſt Men yielding unto God as much in proportion as the greateſt, and many times in affection more, have this as a ſenſible token always aſſuring their minds, that in his ſight, from whom all good is expected, they are concerning acceptation, protection, divine privileges and pre-eminences whatſoever, equals and peers with them unto whom they are otherwiſe in earthly reſpects inferiors; being furthermore well aſſured that the top as it were thus preſented to God is neither loſt, nor unfruitfully beſtowed, but doth ſanctify to them again the whole maſs, and that he by receiving a little undertaketh to bleſs all. In which conſideration the Jews were accuſtomed to name their Tithes, the ***hedge* of their riches. Albeit a hedge do only fence and preſerve that which is contained, whereas their Tithes and Offerings did more, becauſe they procured increaſe of the heap out of which they were taken. God demanded no ſuch debt for his own need, but for their only benefit that owe it. Wherefore detaining the ſame, they hurt not him whom they wrong, and themſelves, whom they think they relieve, they wound; except Men will haply affirm, that God did, by fair ſpeeches and large promiſes, delude the World in ſaying, *Bring ye all the Tithes into the ſtore-houſe, that there may be meat in mine houſe* (deal truly, defraud not God of his due, but bring all), *and prove if I will not open unto you the windows of Heaven, and pour down upon you an immea-*

BOOK V.

Mal. iii.

* Maſſoreth ſepes eſt legis, divitiarum ſepes decimæ. R. Aquiba in Pirk Aboth.

BOOK V. *ſurable bleſſing.* That which St. James hath concerning the effect of our Prayers unto God, is for the moſt part of like moment in our Gifts; we pray and obtain not, becauſe he which knoweth our hearts, doth know our deſires are evil. In like manner we give, and we are not the more accepted, * becauſe he beholdeth how unwiſely we ſpill our gifts in the bringing. It is to him, which needeth nothing, all one whether any thing or nothing be given him. But for our own good, it always behoveth that whatſoever we offer up into his hands, we bring it ſeaſoned with this cogitation, *Thou, Lord, art worthy of all honour.* With the Church of Chriſt, touching theſe matters, it ſtandeth as it did with the whole World before Moſes. Whereupon for many years Men being deſirous to honour God, in the ſame manner as other virtuous and holy Perſonages before had done, both during the time of their life, and, if farther ability did ſerve, by ſuch device as might cauſe their works of piety to remain always, it came by theſe means to paſs that the Church from time to time had treaſure, proportionable unto the poorer or wealthier eſtate of Chriſtian Men. And as ſoon as the ſtate of the Church could admit thereof, they eaſily condeſcended to think it moſt natural and moſt fit that God ſhould receive, as before, of all Men his ancient accuſtomed revenues of Tithes. Thus therefore both God and Nature have taught to convert things temporal to eternal uſes, and to provide for the perpetuity of Religion, even by that which is moſt tranſitory. For to the end that in worth and value there might be no abatement of any thing once aſſigned to ſuch purpoſes, the Law requireth preciſely the beſt of what we poſſeſs; and to prevent all damages by way of commutation, where, inſtead of natural commodities or other rights, the price of them might be taken, the

* Nemo libenter dedit quod non accepit ſed expreſſit. Sen de Benef. l. i. c. 1.

Law of Mofes determined their rates, and the payments to be always made by the Shekel of the Sanctuary, wherein there was great advantage of weight above the ordinary current Shekel. The trueft and fureft way for God to have always his own, is by making him payment in kind, out of the very felffame riches which through his gracious benediction the earth doth continually yield. This, where it may be without inconvenience, is for every Man's confcience fake. That which cometh from God to us, by the natural courfe of his providence, which we know to be innocent and pure, is perhaps beft accepted, becaufe leaft fpotted with the ftain of unlawful or indirect procurement. Befides, whereas prices daily change, Nature, which commonly is one, muft needs be the moft indifferent and permanent ftandard between God and Man. But the main foundation of all, whereupon the fecurity of thefe things dependeth as far as any thing may be afcertained amongft Men, is that the title and right which Man had in every of them before donation doth by the act, and from the time of any fuch donation, dedication, or grant, remain the proper poffeffion of God till the World's end, unlefs himfelf renounce or relinquifh it. For if equity have taught us, that one ought to enjoy his own; that what is ours no other can alienate from us, but with our own * deliberate confent; finally, that no Man having paffed his confent or deed, may † change it to the prejudice of any other, fhould we prefume to deal with God worfe than God hath allowed any Man to deal with us? Albeit therefore we be now free from the Law of Mofes, and confequently not thereby bound to the payment of Tithes; yet becaufe Nature hath taught Men to honour God

Levit xxvii. 25.

Lib xi. de Reg. Jur.

* Cujus per errorem dati repetitio eft, ejus confulto dati donatio eft. L. i D. de cond. indeb. This is the ground of confideration in alienations from Man to Man

† Nemo poteft mutare confilium fuum in alterius præjudicium. L. lxxv. de Reg. Jur.

with

BOOK V. with their ſubſtance, and Scripture hath left us an example of that particular proportion, which for moral conſiderations hath been thought fitteſt by him whoſe wiſdom could beſt judge; furthermore, ſeeing that the Church of Chriſt hath long ſithence entered into like obligation, it ſeemeth in theſe days a queſtion altogether vain and ſuperfluous, whether Tithes be a matter of divine right: becauſe howſoever at the firſt, it might have been thought doubtful, our caſe is clearly the ſame now with theirs unto whom St. Peter
Acts v. 4. ſometime ſpake, ſaying, *While it was whole, it was whole thine.* When our Tithes might have probably ſeemed our own, we had colour of liberty to uſe them as we ourſelves ſaw good. But having made them his whoſe they are, let us be warned by other Men's example what it is νοσφίσασθαι, to waſh or clip that coin which hath on it the mark of God. For that all theſe are his poſſeſſions, and that he doth himſelf ſo reckon them, appeareth by the form of his own
Exod. xxii. 29, 30. ſpeeches. Touching Gifts and Oblations, *Thou ſhalt give them me*; touching Oratories and Churches, *My*
Mat. xxi. 13. *Houſe ſhall be called the Houſe of Prayer*; touching
Mal. iii. 8. Tithes, *Will a Man ſpoil God?* Yet behold, even me your God ye have * ſpoiled, notwithſtanding ye aſk wherein, as though ye were ignorant, what injury there hath been offered in Tithes: ye are heavily accurſed, becauſe with a kind of publick conſent ye have joined yourſelves in one to rob me, imagining the commonneſs of your offence to be every Man's particular
Ezech. xlv. 3, 4. juſtification; touching Lands, *Ye ſhall offer to the Lord a ſacred portion of ground, and that ſacred portion ſhall belong to the Prieſts.* Neither did God only thus ordain amongſt the Jews; but the very purpoſe, intent, and meaning of all that have honoured him with their ſubſtance, was to inveſt him with the property of thoſe benefits, the uſe whereof muſt needs be

* Non videntur rem amittere quibus propria non fuit. L. lxxxiii. de Reg. Jur.

committed

committed to the hands of Men. In which reſpect the ſtyle of ancient Grants and Charters, is, *We have given unto God both for us, and our Heirs for ever.* Yea, *We know*, ſaith Charles the Great, that *the goods of the Church are the ſacred endowments of God, to the Lord our God we offer and dedicate whatſoever we deliver unto his Church.* Whereupon the Laws Imperial do likewiſe divide all things in ſuch ſort, that they make ſome to belong by right of Nature indifferently unto every Man, ſome to be the certain goods and poſſeſſions of Common-weals, ſome to appertain unto ſeveral Corporations and Companies of Men, ſome to be privately Men's own in particular, and ſome to be ſeparated quite * from all Men; which laſt branch compriſeth things ſacred and holy, becauſe thereof God alone is Owner. The ſequel of which received opinion, as well without as within the walls of the Houſe of God touching ſuch poſſeſſions, is, as hath been ever, that there is not an act more honourable than by all means to amplify and to defend the patrimony of Religion, not any more † impious and hateful than to impair thoſe poſſeſſions which Men in former times, when they gave unto holy uſes, were wont at the Altar of God, and in the preſence of their ghoſtly ſuperiors, to make as they thought inviolable by words of fearful execration, ſaying, *Theſe things we offer to God, from whom if any take them away (which we hope no Man will attempt to do), but if any ſhall, let his account be without favour in the laſt day, when he cometh to receive the doom which is due for Sacrilege againſt that Lord and God unto whom we dedicate the ſame.* The beſt and moſt renowned Prelates of the Church of Chriſt have in this conſideration rather ſuſtained the wrath, than yielded to ſatisfy the hard deſire of their greateſt

Mag. Char. c. i.

Capit. Carol. l. vi. c. 284.

* Nullius autem ſunt res ſacræ et religioſæ et ſanctæ. Quod enim divini juris eſt, id nullius in bonis eſt. Inſt. l. ii. tit. i.

† Soli cum Diis ſacrilegi pugnant. Curt. l. vii. Sacrum ſacrove commendatum qui demſerit rapſeritve, parricida eſto. Leg. xii. tab. Capit. Carol. l. vi. c. 285.

Commanders

BOOK V. Commanders on Earth, coveting with ill advice and counsel that which they willingly should have suffered God to enjoy. There are of Martyrs, whom posterity doth much honour, for that having under their hands the custody of such * treasures, they could by virtuous delusion invent how to save them from prey, even when the safety of their own lives they gladly neglected; as one, sometime an Archdeacon under Xistus the Bishop of Rome, did, whom when his Judge understood to be one of the Church-stewards, thirst of blood began to slake, and another humour to work, which first by a favourable countenance, and then by quiet speech did thus calmly disclose itself: *You that profess the Christian Religion make great complaint of the wonderful cruelty we shew towards you. Neither peradventure altogether without cause. But for myself, I am far from any such bloody purpose. Ye are not so willing to live, as I unwilling that out of these lips should proceed any capital sentence against you. Your Bishops are said to have rich vessels of gold and silver, which they use in the exercise of their Religion; besides the fame is, that numbers sell away their lands and livings, the huge prices whereof are brought to your Church-coffers; by which means the devotion, that maketh them and their whole Posterity poor, must needs mightily enrich you, whose God we know was no coiner of money, but left behind him many wholesome and good Precepts, as namely, that Cæsar should have of you the things that are fit for, and due to Cæsar. His wars are costly and chargeable unto him. That which you suffer to rust in corners, the affairs of the Commonwealth do need. Your profession is not to make account of things transitory. And yet if ye can be contented but to forego that which ye care not for, I dare undertake to warrant you both safety of life, and freedom of using your conscience, a thing more acceptable to you than wealth.* Which fair parly the happy Martyr quietly hearing, and perceiving it necessary to make

* Deposita pietatis. Tertul Apologet Prudent. Peristeph.

some

ſome ſhift for the ſafe concealment of that, which being now deſired, was not unlikely to be more narrowly afterwards ſought, he craved reſpite for three days to gather the riches of the Church together, in which ſpace againſt the time the Governor ſhould come to the doors of the Temple, big with hope to receive his prey, a miſerable rank of poor, lame and impotent Perſons was provided, their names delivered him up in writing as a true inventory of the Church's goods, and ſome few words uſed to ſignify how proud the Church was of theſe treaſures. If Men did not naturally abhor Sacrilege, to reſiſt and defeat ſo impious attempts would deſerve ſmall praiſe. But ſuch is the general deteſtation of rapine in this kind, that whereas nothing doth either in peace or war more uphold Men's reputation than proſperous ſucceſs, becauſe in common conſtruction, unleſs notorious improbity be joined with proſperity, it ſeemeth to argue favour with God; they which once have ſtained their hands with theſe odious ſpoils do thereby faſten unto all their actions an eternal prejudice, in reſpect whereof, for that it paſſeth through the World as an undoubted rule and principle that Sacrilege is open defiance to God, whatſoever afterwards they undertake, if they proſper in it, Men reckon it but Dionyſius his navigation, and if any thing befall them otherwiſe, it is not, as commonly, ſo in them aſcribed to the great uncertainty of caſual events, wherein the providence of God doth controul the purpoſes of Men oftentimes much more for their good, than if all things did anſwer fully their hearts deſire, but the cenſure of the World is ever directly againſt them both * bitter and peremptory. To make ſuch actions

* Novimus multa regna, et reges eorum, propterea cecidiſſe; quia Eccleſias ſpoliaverunt, reſque earum vaſtaverunt, alienaverunt vel diripuerunt, Epiſcopiſque et Sacerdotibus, atque, quod magis eſt, Eccleſiis eorum abſtulerunt, et pugnantibus dederunt. Quapropter nec fortes in bello nec in fide ſtabiles fuerunt, nec victores extiterunt; ſed terga multi vulnerati, et plures interfecti verterunt, regnaque

BOOK V. therefore leſs odious, and to mitigate the envy of them, many colourable ſhifts and inventions have been uſed, as if the World did hate only wolves, and think the fox a goodly creature. The * time it may be will come, when they that either violently have ſpoiled, or thus ſmoothly defrauded God, ſhall find they did but deceive themſelves. In the mean while there will be always ſome ſkilful Perſons, which can teach a way how to grind treatably the Church with jaws that ſhall ſcarce move, and yet devour in the end more than they that come ravening with open mouth, as if they would worry the whole in an inſtant; others alſo, who having waſtefully eaten out their own patrimony would be glad to repair, if they might, their decayed eſtates with the ruin they care not of what nor of whom, ſo the ſpoil was theirs; whereof in ſome part if they happen to ſpeed, yet commonly they are Men born under that conſtellation which maketh them, I know not how, as unapt to enrich themſelves as they are ready to impoveriſh others; it is their lot to ſuſtain during life both the miſery of Beggars and the infamy of Robbers. But though no other plague and revenge ſhould follow ſacrilegious violations of holy things, the natural ſecret diſgrace and ignominy, the very turpitude of ſuch actions in the eye of a wiſe underſtanding heart,† is itſelf a heavy puniſhment. Men of virtuous quality are by this ſufficiently moved to beware how they anſwer and requite the mercies of

regnaque et regiones, et, quod pejus eſt, regna cœleſtia perdiderunt, atque propriis hæreditatibus caruerunt, et hactenus carent. Verba Carol. Ma in Capitu. Carol. l. vii cap. 104.

* Turno tempus erit magno cum optaverit emptum
Intactum Pallanta, et cum ſpolia iſta diemque
Oderit. Virg. Æn. lib. x

† Ἡ τῶν πραγμάτων αἰσχύνη οὐδεμίας ἐλάττων ζημία τοῖς γε σώφροσι. Demoſth Pœnam non dico legum quas ſæpe perrumpunt, ſed ipſius turpitudinis quæ acerbiſſima eſt non vident. Cic. Offic l. iii. Impunita tu credes eſſe quæ inviſa ſunt? aut illum ſupplicium gravius exiſtimas publico odio? Sen. de Benef. l. iii. c. 17.

God

God with injuries, whether openly or indirectly offered. I will not absolutely say concerning the goods of the Church, that they may in no case be seized on by Men, or that no obligation, commerce and bargain made between Man and Man, can ever be of force to alienate the property which God hath in them. Certain cases I grant there are, wherein it is not so dark what God himself doth warrant, but that we may safely presume him as willing to forego for our benefit, as always to use and convert to our benefit whatsoever our Religion hath honoured him withal. But surely under the name of that which may be, many things that should not be are often done. By means whereof the Church most commonly for gold hath flannel; and whereas the usual saw of old was *Glaucus his change*, the Proverb is now, *A Church Bargain.* And for fear lest covetousness alone should linger out the time too much, and not be able to make havock of the House of God, with that expedition which the mortal Enemy thereof did vehemently wish, he hath by certain strong enchantments so deeply bewitched Religion itself, as to make it in the end an earnest Solicitor, and an eloquent Persuader of Sacrilege, urging confidently that the very best service which Men of power can do to Christ, is without any more ceremony to sweep all, and to leave the Church as bare as in the day it was first born; that fulness of bread having made the Children of the Houshold wanton, it is without any scruple to be taken away from them and thrown to dogs; that they which laid the prices of their lands as offerings at the Apostles' feet, did but sow the seeds of Superstition; that they which endowed Churches with lands, poisoned Religion; that Tythes and Oblations are now in the sight of God as the sacrificed blood of goats; that if we give him our hearts and affections, our goods are better bestowed otherwise; that Irenæus, Polycarp's Disciple, should not have said, *We offer unto God our goods as tokens*

BOOK V.

Iren. l. iv. c. 34.

BOOK V. *tokens of thankfulneſs for that we receive*; neither Origen, *He which worſhippeth God, muſt by Gifts and Oblations acknowledge him the Lord of all*; in a word, that to give unto God is error; reformation of error, to take from the Church that which the blindneſs of former ages did unwiſely give: by theſe or the like ſuggeſtions, received with all joy, and with like ſedulity practiſed in certain parts of the Chriſtian World, they have brought to paſs that as David doth ſay of Man, ſo it is in hazard to be verified concerning the whole Religion and Service of God; *The time thereof may peradventure fall out to be threeſcore and ten years, or if ſtrength do ſerve unto fourſcore, what followeth is likely to be ſmall joy for them whoſoever they be that behold it.* Thus have the beſt things been overthrown, not ſo much by puiſſance and might of Adverſaries, as through defect of counſel in them that ſhould have upheld and defended the ſame.

Orig in 18 Num hom xi.

Pſalm xc. 10.

Of Ordinations lawful without title, and without any popular election precedent, but in no caſe without regard of due information what their quality is, that enter into holy Orders.

80. There are in a Miniſter of God theſe four things to be conſidered, his Ordination which giveth him power to meddle with things ſacred; the charge or portion of the Church allotted unto him for exerciſe of his office; the performance of his Duty, according to the exigence of his charge; and, laſtly, the Maintenance which in that reſpect he receiveth. All Eccleſiaſtical Laws and Canons which either concern the beſtowing or the uſing of the power of miniſterial Order have relation to theſe four. Of the firſt we have ſpoken before at large. Concerning the next, for more convenient diſcharge of Eccleſiaſtical Duties, as the body of the People muſt needs be ſevered by divers precincts, ſo the Clergy likewiſe accordingly diſtributed. Whereas therefore Religion did firſt take place in Cities, and in that reſpect was a cauſe why the name of Pagans, which properly ſignifieth a country People, came to be uſed in common ſpeech for the ſame that Infidels and unbelievers were; it followed thereupon that

all

all ſuch Cities had their Eccleſiaſtical Colleges, conſiſting of Deacons and of Preſbyters, whom firſt the Apoſtles or their Delegates the Evangeliſts did both ordain and govern. Such were the Colleges of Jeruſalem, Antioch, Epheſus, Rome, Corinth, and the reſt where the Apoſtles are known to have planted our Faith and Religion. Now becauſe Religion and the cure of Souls was their general charge in common over all that were near about them, neither had any one Preſbyter his ſeveral cure apart, till Evariſtus, Biſhop in the See of Rome, about the year 112, began to aſſign precincts unto every Church or Title which the Chriſtians held, and to appoint unto each Preſbyter a certain compaſs whereof himſelf ſhould take charge alone, the commodiouſneſs of this invention cauſed all parts of Chriſtendom to follow it, and at the length among the reſt our own Churches about the year 636, became divided in like manner. But other diſtinction of Churches there doth not appear any in the Apoſtles' Writings, ſave only, according to thoſe Cities wherein they planted the Goſpel of Chriſt, and erected Eccleſiaſtical Colleges. Wherefore to ordain κατὰ πόλιν throughout every City, and κατὰ ἐκκλησίαν throughout every Church, do in them ſignify the ſame thing. Churches then neither were, nor could be in ſo convenient ſort limited as now they are; firſt, by the bounds of each ſtate, and then within each ſtate by more particular precincts, till at the length we deſcend unto ſeveral Congregations, termed Pariſhes, with far narrower reſtraint than this name at the firſt was uſed. And from hence hath grown their error, who, as oft as they read of the duty which Eccleſiaſtical Perſons are now to perform towards the Church, their manner is always to underſtand by that Church, ſome particular Congregation or Pariſh Church. They ſuppoſe that there ſhould now be no Man of Eccleſiaſtical Order which is not tied to ſome certain Pariſh. Becauſe the names of all Church-

Acts xv. 36.
Apoc i. 20.
Tit i 5.
Acts xiv. 23.

Officers are words of relation, becaufe a Shepherd muft have his Flock, a Teacher his Scholars, a Minifter his company which he minifttereth unto, therefore it feemeth a thing in their eyes abfurd and unreafonable that any Man fhould be ordained a Minifter, otherwife than only for fome particular Congregation. Perceive they not how by this means they make it unlawful for the Church to employ Men at all in converting Nations? For if fo be the Church may not lawfully admit to an Ecclefiaftical Function, unlefs it tie the party admitted unto fome particular Parifh, then furely a thanklefs labour it is whereby Men feek the converfion of Infidels which know not Chrift, and therefore cannot be as yet divided into their fpecial Congregations and Flocks. But, to the end it may appear how much this one thing among many more hath been miftaken, there is no precept requiring that Prefbyters and Deacons be made in fuch fort and not otherwife. Albeit therefore the Apoftles did make them in that order, yet is not their example fuch a Law, as without all exception bindeth to make them in no other order but that. Again, if we will confider that which the Apoftles themfelves did, furely no Man can juftly fay, that herein we practife any thing repugnant to their example. For by them there was ordained only in each Chriftian City a College of Prefbyters and Deacons to adminifter holy things. Evariftus did a hundred years after the birth of our Saviour Chrift begin the diftinction of the Church into Parifhes. Prefbyters and Deacons having been ordained before to exercife Ecclefiaftical Functions in the Church of Rome promifcuoufly, he was the firft that tied them each one to his own ftation. So that of the two, indefinite Ordination of Prefbyters and Deacons doth come more near the Apoftles' example, and the tying of them to be made only for particular Congregations may more juftly ground itfelf upon the example of Evariftus than of any Apoftle of Chrift.

Chriſt. It hath been the opinion of wiſe and good Men heretofore, that nothing was ever deviſed more ſingularly beneficial unto God's Church than this which our honourable Predeceſſors have to their endleſs praiſe found out by the erecting ſuch houſes of ſtudy, as thoſe two moſt famous Univerſities do contain, and by providing that choice Wits, after reaſonable time ſpent in contemplation, may at the length either enter into that holy vocation for which they have been ſo long nouriſhed and brought up, or elſe give place and ſuffer others to ſucceed in their rooms, that ſo the Church may be always furniſhed with a number of Men whoſe ability being firſt known by publick trial in Church-labours there where Men can beſt judge of them, their calling afterwards unto particular charge abroad may be accordingly. All this is fruſtrate, thoſe worthy foundations we muſt diſſolve, their whole device and religious purpoſe which did erect them is made void, their Orders and Statutes are to be cancelled and diſannulled, in caſe the Church be forbidden to grant any power of order unleſs it be with reſtraint to the Party ordained unto ſome particular Pariſh or Congregation. Nay, might we not rather affirm of Preſbyters and of Deacons, that the very nature of their Ordination is unto neceſſary local reſtraint a thing oppoſite and repugnant? The Emperor Juſtinian doth ſay of Tutors, *Certæ rei vel cauſæ tutor dari non poteſt, quia perſonæ, non cauſæ vel rei, tutor datur.* He that ſhould grant a tutorſhip, reſtraining his grant to ſome one certain thing or cauſe, ſhould do but idly, becauſe Tutors are given for perſonal defence generally, and not for managing of a few particular things or cauſes. So he that ordaining a Preſbyter or a Deacon ſhould, in the form of Ordination, reſtrain the one or the other to a certain place, might with much more reaſon be thought to uſe a vain and a frivolous addition, than they reaſonably to require ſuch local reſtraint as a thing which

Juſt. lib. i. tit 14 ſect. 4.

BOOK V. muſt of neceſſity concur evermore with all lawful Ordination. Preſbyters and Deacons are not by Ordination conſecrated unto places, but unto functions. In which reſpect, and in no other, it is that ſith they are by virtue thereof bequeathed unto God, ſevered and ſanctified to be employed in his ſervice, which is the higheſt advancement that mortal creatures on earth can be raiſed unto, the Church of Chriſt hath not been acquainted in former ages with any ſuch prophane and unnatural cuſtom, as doth hallow Men with Eccleſiaſtical Functions of Order only for a time, and then diſmiſs them again to the common affairs of the world. Whereas, contrariwiſe from the place or charge where that power hath been exerciſed, we may be by ſundry good and lawful occaſions tranſlated, retaining nevertheleſs the ſelf-ſame power which was firſt given. It is ſome grief to ſpend thus much labour in refuting a thing that hath ſo little ground to uphold it, eſpecially ſith they themſelves that teach it do not ſeem to give thereunto any great credit, if we may judge their minds by their actions. There are amongſt them that have done the work of Eccleſiaſtical Perſons, ſometime in the families of Noblemen, ſometime in much more publick and frequent Congregations; there are that have ſucceſſively gone through perhaps ſeven or eight particular Churches after this ſort; yea, ſome that at one and the ſame time have been, ſome which at this preſent hour are, in real obligation of Eccleſiaſtical Duty, and poſſeſſion of commodity thereto belonging, even in ſundry particular Churches within the land; ſome there are amongſt them which will not ſo much abridge their liberty, as to be faſtened or tied unto any place; ſome which have bound themſelves to one place, only for a time, and that time being once expired, have afterwards voluntarily given unto other places the like experience and trial of them. All this I preſume they would not do, if their perſuaſion

were

were as ſtrict as their words pretend. But for the avoiding of theſe and ſuch other the like confuſions as are incident unto the cauſe and queſtion whereof we preſently treat, there is not any thing more material, than firſt to ſeparate exactly the nature of the Miniſtry from the uſe and exerciſe thereof; ſecondly, to know that the only true and proper act of Ordination is to inveſt Men with that power which doth make them Miniſters, by conſecrating their perſons to God and his ſervice in holy things during term of life, whether they exerciſe that power or no; thirdly, that to give them a title or charge where to uſe their Miniſtry, concerneth not the making, but the placing of God's Miniſters; and therefore the laws which concern only their election or admiſſion unto place of charge, are not appliable to infringe any way their Ordination; fourthly, that as oft as any ancient Conſtitution, Law, or Canon, is alledged concerning either Ordinations or Elections, we forget not to examine whether the preſent caſe be the ſame which the ancient was, or elſe do contain ſome juſt reaſon for which it cannot admit altogether the ſame rules which former affairs of the Church, now altered, did then require. In the queſtion of making Miniſters without a title, which to do, they ſay is a thing unlawful, they ſhould at the very firſt have conſidered what the name of Title doth imply, and what affinity or coherence Ordinations have with Titles, which thing obſerved would plainly have ſhewed them their own error. They are not ignorant, that when they ſpeak of a Title, they handle that which belongeth to the placing of a Miniſter in ſome charge, that the place of charge wherein a Miniſter doth execute his office requireth ſome Houſe of God for the People to reſort unto, ſome definite number of Souls unto whom he there adminiſtereth holy things, and ſome certain allowance whereby to ſuſtain life; that the Fathers at the firſt named Oratories, and Houſes of Prayer Titles; thereby ſignifying how

BOOK V. God was interested in them, and held them as his own possessions. But because they know that the Church had Ministers before Christian Temples and Oratories were, therefore some of them understand by a Title, a definite Congregation of People only, and so deny that any Ordination is lawful which maketh Ministers that have no certain Flock to attend: forgetting how the seventy whom Christ himself did ordain Ministers, had their calling in that manner, whereas yet no certain charge could be given them. Others referring the name of a Title, especially to the maintenance of the Minister, infringe all Ordination made,* except they which receive Orders be first entituled to a competent Ecclesiastical Benefice, and (which is most ridiculously strange) except besides their present Title to some such Benefice they have likewise some other Title of annual rent or pension whereby they may be relieved, in case, through infirmity, sickness, or other lawful impediment, they grow unable to execute their Ecclesiastical Function. So that every Man lawfully ordained must bring a bow which hath two strings, a Title of present right, and another to provide for future possibility or chance. Into these absurdities and follies they slide by mis-conceiving the true purpose of certain Canons, which indeed have forbidden to ordain a Minister without a Title; not that simply it is unlawful so to ordain, but because it might grow to an inconveniency if the Church did not somewhat restrain that liberty. For, seeing they which have once received Ordination cannot again return into the World, it behoveth them which or-

* Unlawful to ordain a Minister without a Title. Abstra. p. 243. et p. 246. The Law requireth, that every one admitted unto Orders having for his present relief some Ecclesiastical Benefice, should also have some other Title unto some annual rent or pension whereby he might be relieved in case he were not able through infirmity, sickness, or other lawful impediment to execute his Ecclesiastical Office and Function.

dain

dain to foresee how such shall be afterwards able to live, lest their poverty and destitution should redound to the disgrace and discredit of their calling. Which evil prevented, those very Laws, which in that respect forbid, do expressly admit Ordinations to be made at large and without Title; namely, if the Party so ordained have of his own for the sustenance of this life; or if the Bishop which giveth him Orders will find him competent allowance, till some place of administration from whence his maintenance may arise be provided for him; or if any other fit and sufficient means be had against the danger before-mentioned. Absolutely therefore it is not true, that any ancient Canon of the Church, which is or ought to be with us in force, doth make Ordinations at large unlawful; and as the state of the Church doth stand, they are most necessary. If there be any conscience in Men, touching that which they write or speak, let them consider as well what the present condition of all things doth now suffer, as what the Ordinances of former ages did appoint; as well the weight of those causes for which our affairs have altered, as the reasons in regard whereof our Fathers and Predecessors did some time strictly and severely keep that, which for us to observe now is neither meet nor always possible. In this our present cause and controversy, whether any not having Title of right to a Benefice may be lawfully ordained a Minister, is it not manifest in the eyes of all Men, that whereas the name of a Benefice doth signify some standing Ecclesiastical Revenue taken out of the treasure of God and allotted to a Spiritual Person, to the end he may use the same and enjoy it as his own for term of life, unless his default cause deprivation, the Clergy for many years after Christ had no other Benefices, but only their canonical portions, or monthly dividends allowed them according to their several degrees and qualities, out of the common stock of such Gifts, Oblations and Tithes, as the fervour of Chriſtian Piety did then yield? Yea, that even when Miniſters had their Churches and Flocks aſſigned unto them in ſeveral, yet for maintenance of life, their former kind of allowance continued, till ſuch time as Biſhops and Churches Cathedral being ſufficiently endowed with lands, other Preſbyters enjoyed, inſtead of their firſt Benefices, the Tithes and Profits of their own Congregations whole to themſelves? Is it not manifeſt, that in this Realm, and ſo in other the like Dominions, where the tenure of Lands is altogether grounded on military Laws, and held as in fee under Princes which are not made Heads of the People by force of voluntary election, but born the ſovereign Lords of thoſe whole and entire Territories, which Territories their famous Progenitors, obtaining by way of conqueſt, retained what they would in their own hands, and divided the reſt to others with reſervation of ſovereignty and capital intereſt, the building of Churches, and conſequently the aſſigning of either Pariſhes or Benefices was a thing impoſſible without conſent of ſuch as were principal Owners of Land; in which conſideration, for their more encouragement hereunto, they which did ſo far benefit the Church had by common conſent granted (as great equity and reaſon was) a right for them and their Heirs till the World's end, to nominate in thoſe Benefices Men whoſe quality the Biſhop allowing might admit them thereunto? Is it not manifeſt, that from hence inevitably ſuch inequality of Pariſhes hath grown, as cauſeth ſome through the multitude of people which have reſort unto one Church to be more than any one Man can wield, and ſome to be of that nature by reaſon of Chapels annexed that they which are Incumbents ſhould wrong the Church if ſo be they had not certain Stipendiaries under them, becauſe where the corps of the Profit or Benefice is but one, the Title can be but one Man's, and yet the charge may require more? Not to mention therefore

therefore any other reaſon whereby it may clearly appear how expedient it is, and profitable for this Church to admit Ordinations without Title, this little may ſuffice to declare how impertinent their allegations againſt it are out of ancient Canons; how untrue their confident aſſeverations, that only through negligence of popiſh Prelates the cuſtom of making ſuch kind of Miniſters hath prevailed in the Church of Rome againſt their Canons, and that with us it is expreſsly againſt the Laws of our own Government when a Miniſter doth ſerve as a ſtipendiary Curate, which kind of ſervice nevertheleſs the greateſt Rabbins of that part do altogether follow. For howſoever they are loth peradventure to be named Curates, Stipendiaries they are, and the labour they beſtow is in other Men's Cures; a thing not unlawful for them to do, yet unſeemly for them to condemn which practiſe it. I might here diſcover the like overſight throughout all their Diſcourſes, made in behalf of the People's pretended right to elect their Miniſters before the Biſhop may lawfully ordain. But becauſe we have otherwhere at large diſputed of popular Elections, and of the right of patronage, wherein is drowned whatſoever the People under any pretence of colour may ſeem to challenge about admiſſion and choice of the Paſtors that ſhall feed their Souls, I cannot ſee what one duty there is which always ought to go before Ordination, but only care of the Party's worthineſs as well for integrity and virtue as knowledge; yea, for virtue more: inaſmuch as defect of knowledge may ſundry ways be ſupplied, but the ſcandal of vicious and wicked life is a deadly evil.

Of the Learning that ſhould be in Miniſters, their reſidence and the number of their Livings.

81. The truth is, that of all things hitherto mentioned, the greateſt is that threefold blot or blemiſh of notable ignorance, unconſcionable abſence from the Cures whereof Men have taken charge, and unſatiable hunting after ſpiritual preferments without either care or conſcience of the publick good. Whereof,

BOOK V. Whereof, to the end that we may conſider as in God's own ſight and preſence with all uprightneſs, ſincerity and truth, let us particularly weigh and examine in every of them, firſt, how far forth they are reprovable by reaſons and maxims of common right; ſecondly, whether that which our Laws do permit be repugnant to thoſe maxims, and with what equity we ought to judge of things practiſed in this caſe, neither on the one hand defending that which muſt be acknowledged out of ſquare, nor on the other ſide condemning raſhly whom we liſt for whatſoever we diſallow. Touching arguments therefore taken from the principles of common right to prove that Miniſters ſhould be learned, that they ought to be reſident upon their Livings, and that more than one only Benefice or ſpiritual Living may not be granted unto one Man; the firſt, becauſe St. Paul requireth in a Miniſter ability to teach, to convince, to diſtribute the Word rightly; becauſe alſo the Lord himſelf hath proteſted they ſhall be no Prieſts to him which have rejected knowledge, and becauſe if the blind lead the blind, they muſt both needs fall into the pit; the ſecond, becauſe Teachers are Shepherds whoſe Flocks can be no time ſecure from danger; they are Watchmen whom the Enemy doth always beſiege; their labours in the Word and Sacrament admit no intermiſſion; their duty requireth inſtruction and conference with Men in private; they are the living Oracles of God, to whom the People muſt reſort for counſel; they are commanded to be Patterns of Holineſs, Leaders, Feeders, Superviſors amongſt their own; it ſhould be their grief, as it was the Apoſtles', to be abſent, though neceſſarily, from them over whom they have taken charge; finally, the laſt, becauſe Plurality and Reſidence are oppoſite; becauſe the placing of one Clerk in two Churches is a point of merchandize and filthy gain; becauſe no Man can ſerve two Maſters; becauſe every one ſhould remain in that vocation whereto he is called;

T. C. lib. i. p. 70. 66. 69. 1 Tim. iii. 2. Titus i. 9. 2 Tim. ii. 15. Hoſ. iv. 6. Matth. xv. 14. Luke ii. 8. Acts xx. 2. 1 Sam. i. 19. 1 Tim. iv. 12. John x. 4. 1 Pet. v. 2. Acts xx. 38. 1 Theſſ. ii. 17. Coun. Nic. cap. 15. Matth. vi. 24. 1 Cor. vii. 24.

called; what conclude they of all this? Againſt Ignorance, againſt Non-reſidence, and againſt Plurality of Livings, is there any Man ſo raw and dull, but that the volumes which have been written both of old and of late may make him in ſo plentiful a cauſe eloquent? For by that which is generally juſt and requiſite, we meaſure what knowledge there ſhould be in a Miniſter of the Goſpel of Chriſt; the Arguments which Light of Nature offereth; the Laws and Statutes which Scripture hath; the Canons that are taken out of ancient Synods; the Decrees and Conſtitutions of ſincereſt Times; the Sentences of all Antiquity; and in a word, even every Man's full conſent and conſcience is againſt Ignorance in them that have Charge and Cure of Souls. Again, what availeth it if we be learned and not faithful? or what benefit hath the Church of Chriſt, if there be in us ſufficiency without endeavour or care to do that good which our place exacteth? Touching the pains and induſtry therefore, wherewith Men are in conſcience bound to attend the work of their Heavenly Calling, even as much as in them lieth bending thereunto their whole endeavour, without either fraud, ſophiſtication, or guile; I ſee not what more effectual obligation or bond of duty there ſhould be urged, than their own only vow and promiſe made unto God himſelf at the time of their Ordination. The work which they have undertaken requireth both care and fear. Their ſloth, that negligently perform it, maketh them ſubject to malediction. Beſides, we alſo know that the fruit of our pains in this Function is life both to ourſelves and others. And do we yet need incitements to labour? Shall we ſtop our ears both againſt thoſe conjuring exhortations which Apoſtles, and againſt the fearful comminations which Prophets have uttered out of the mouth of God, the one for prevention, the other for reformation of our ſluggiſhneſs in this behalf? Saint Paul, *Attend to yourſelves, and to all the Flock, whereof the Holy Ghoſt hath* Acts xx. 27.

BOOK V. *hath made you Overseers, to feed the Church of God which he hath purchased with his own Blood.* Again, *I charge thee before God, and the Lord Jesus Christ, which shall judge the quick and the dead at his coming, preach the Word, be instant.* Jeremiah, *Woe unto the Pastors that destroy and scatter the Sheep of my Pasture; I will visit you for the wickedness of your works, saith the Lord, the remnant of my Sheep, I will gather together out of all countries, and will bring them again to their folds; they shall grow and increase, and I will set up Shepherds over them which shall feed them.* Ezekiel, *Should not the Shepherds, should they not feed the Flocks? Ye eat the fat, and ye clothe yourselves with the wool, but the weak ye have not strengthened, the sick ye have not cured, neither have ye bound up the broken, nor brought home again that which was driven away: ye have not enquired after that which was lost, but with cruelty and rigour have ruled.* And ver. 8. *Wherefore, as I live, I will require my Sheep at their hands, nor shall the Shepherds feed themselves any more; for I will deliver my Sheep from their mouths, they shall no more devour them.* Nor let us think to excuse ourselves if haply we labour, though it be at random, and sit not altogether idle abroad. For we are bound to attend that part of the Flock of Christ, whereof the Holy Ghost hath made us Overseers. The residence of Ministers upon their own peculiar Charge is by so much the rather necessary, for that absenting themselves from the place where they ought to labour, they neither can do the good which is looked for at their hands, nor reap the comfort which sweeteneth life to them that spend it in these travels upon their own. For it is in this, as in all things else which are through private interest dearer than what concerneth either others wholly, or us but in part, and according to the rate of a general regard. As for Plurality, it hath not only the same inconveniencies which are observed to grow by absence; but over and besides, at the least in common construction, a shew of that worldly humour which Men do

Jer. xxiii. 2.

Ezek. xxxiv. 2.

do think ſhould not reign ſo high. Now from hence their collections are, as followeth; firſt, a repugnancy or contradiction between the principles of common right, and that which our Laws in ſpecial conſiderations have allowed; ſecondly, a nullity or fruſtration of all ſuch acts as are by them ſuppoſed oppoſite to thoſe principles, and invalidity in all Ordinations of Men unable to preach, and in all Diſpenſations which mitigate the Law of common right for the other two. And why ſo? Forſooth, becauſe whatever we do in theſe three caſes, and not by virtue of common right, we muſt yield it of neceſſity done by warrant of peculiar right or Privilege. Now a Privilege is ſaid to be that, that for favour of certain Perſons cometh forth againſt common right; things prohibited are diſpenſed with, becauſe things permitted are diſpatched by common right, but things forbidden require Diſpenſations. By which deſcriptions of a Privilege and Diſpenſation it is (they ſay) apparent, that a Privilege muſt licenſe and authorize the ſame which the Law againſt ignorance, non-reſidence, and plurality doth infringe; and ſo be a Law contrariant or repugnant to the Law of Nature and the Law of God, becauſe all the reaſons whereupon the poſitive Law of Man againſt theſe three was firſt eſtabliſhed are taken and drawn from the Law of Nature and the Law of God. For anſwer whereunto we will but lead them to anſwer themſelves. Firſt therefore if they will grant (as they muſt) that all direct oppoſitions of ſpeech require one and the ſelf-ſame ſubject to be meant on both parts where oppoſition is pretended, it will follow that either the maxims of common right do inforce the very ſame things not to be good which we ſay are good, grounding ourſelves on the reaſons by virtue whereof our Privileges are eſtabliſhed, or if the one do not reach unto that particular ſubject for which the other have provided, then is there no contradiction between them. In all contradictions, if the one part be true, the other eternally muſt be

BOOK V.

Abſtract p. 117.

f'':

BOOK V. falſe. And therefore if the principles of common right do at any time truly enforce that particular not to be good which Privileges make good, it argueth invincibly that ſuch Privileges have been grounded upon ſome error. But to ſay, that every Privilege is oppoſite unto the principles of common right, becauſe it diſpenſeth with that which common right doth prohibit, hath groſs abſurdity. For the voice of Equity and Juſtice is, that a general Law doth never derogate from a ſpecial Privilege; whereas if the one were contrariant to the other, a general Law being in force ſhould always diſſolve a Privilege. The reaſon why many are deceived by imagining that ſo it ſhould do, and why Men of better inſight conclude directly it ſhould not, doth reſt in the ſubject or matter itſelf; which matter indefinitely conſidered in Laws of common right, is in Privileges conſidered as beſet and limited, with ſpecial circumſtances; by means whereof to them which reſpect it but by way of generality, it ſeemeth one and the ſame in both, although it be not the ſame, if once we deſcend to particular conſideration thereof. Precepts do always propoſe perfection, not ſuch as none can attain unto, for then in vain ſhould we aſk or require it at the hands of Men, but ſuch perfection as all Men muſt aim at; to the end that as largely as human providence and care can extend it, it may take place. Moral Laws are the rules of politick; thoſe politick, which are made to order the whole Church of God, rules unto all particular Churches; and the Laws of every particular Church, rules unto every particular Man within the body of the ſame Church: now, becauſe the higher we aſcend in theſe rules, the further ſtill we remove from thoſe ſpecialties, which being proper to the ſubject, whereupon our actions muſt work, and therefore chiefly conſidered by us, by them leaſt thought upon that wade altogether in the two firſt kinds of general directions, their judgment cannot be exact and ſound concerning either Laws of Churches, or actions of Men in particular,

becauſe

because they determine of effects by a part of the causes only out of which they grow; they judge conclusions by demi-premises and half-principles; they lay them in the balance stript from those necessary material circumstances which should give them weight; and by shew of falling uneven with the scale of most universal and abstracted rules, they pronounce that too light which is not, if they had the skill to weigh it. This is the reason why Men altogether conversant in study do know how to teach, but not how to govern; Men experienced contrariwise govern well, yet know not which way to set down orderly the precepts and reasons of that they do. He that will therefore judge rightly of things done, must join with his forms and conceits of general speculation the matter wherein our actions are conversant. For by this shall appear what equity there is in those Privileges and peculiar grants or favours which otherwise will seem repugnant to Justice, and because in themselves considered they have a shew of repugnancy, this deceiveth those great Clerks, which hearing a Privilege defined to be * *an especial right brought in by their power and authority that make it for some publick benefit against the general course of reason*, are not able to comprehend how the word *against* doth import exception without any opposition at all. For inasmuch as the hand of Justice must distribute to every particular what is due, and judge what is due with respect had no less of particular circumstances than of general rules and axioms; it cannot fit all sorts with one measure, the wills, counsels, qualities and states of Men being divers. For example, the Law of common right bindeth all Men to keep their Promises, perform their Compacts, and answer the Faith they have given either

* Jus singulare est, quod contra tenorem rationis propter aliquam utilitatem authoritate constituentium introductum est. Paulus ff. de Legib.

for

BOOK V. for themſelves or others. Notwithſtanding he which bargaineth with one under years can have no benefit by this allegation, becauſe he bringeth it againſt a Perſon which is exempt from the common rule. Shall we then conclude, that thus to exempt certain Men from the Law of common right is againſt God, againſt Nature, againſt whatſoever may avail to ſtrengthen and juſtify that Law before alledged; or elſe acknowledge (as the truth is) that ſpecial cauſes are to be ordered by ſpecial rules; that if Men grown unto ripe age diſadvantage themſelves by bargaining, yet what they have wittingly done is ſtrong and in force againſt them, becauſe they are able to diſpoſe and manage their own affairs; whereas youth for lack of experience and judgment, being eaſily ſubject to circumvention, is therefore juſtly exempt from the Law of common right whereunto the reſt are juſtly ſubject? This plain inequality between Men of years and under years is a cauſe why Equity and Juſtice cannot apply equally the ſame general rule to both, but ordereth the one by common right, and granteth to the other a ſpecial Privilege. Privileges are either tranſitory or permanent: tranſitory, ſuch as ſerve only ſome one turn, or at the moſt extend no farther than to this or that Man,* with the end of whoſe natural life they expire; permanent, ſuch as the uſe whereof doth continue ſtill, for that they belong unto certain kinds of Men and cauſes which never die. Of this nature are all immunities and pre-eminences, which for juſt conſiderations one ſort of Men enjoyeth above another both in the Church and Common-wealth, no Man ſuſpecting them of contrariety to any branch of thoſe Laws or Reaſons whereupon the general right is grounded. Now there being general Laws and Rules whereby it can-

* Privilegium perſonale cum perſona extinguitur, et privilegium datum actioni tranſit cum actione. Op. de Regulis, p. 1. 227.

not be denied but the Church of God ſtandeth bound to provide that the Miniſtry may be learned, that they which have charge may reſide upon it, and that it may not be free for them in ſcandalous manner to multiply Eccleſiaſtical Livings; it remaineth in the next place to be examined, what the Laws of the Church of England do admit, which may be thought repugnant to any thing hitherto alledged, and in what ſpecial conſideration they ſeem to admit the ſame. Conſidering, therefore, that to furniſh all places of Cure of this Realm, it is not an army of twelve thouſand learned Men that would ſuffice, nor two Univerſities that can always furniſh as many as decay in ſo great a number, nor a fourth part of the Livings with Cure, that when they fall are able to yield ſufficient maintenance for learned Men, is it not plain that unleſs the greateſt part of the People ſhould be left utterly without the publick uſe and exerciſe of Religion, there is no remedy but to take into the Eccleſiaſtical Order a number of Men meanly qualified in reſpect of Learning? For whatſoever we may imagine in our private cloſets, or talk for communication ſake at our boards, yea, or write in our books through a notional conceit of things needful for performance of each Man's duty, if once we come from the theory of Learning, to take out ſo many learned Men, let them be diligently viewed out of whom the choice ſhall be made, and thereby an eſtimate made what degree of ſkill we muſt either admit or elſe leave numbers utterly deſtitute of Guides, and I doubt not but that Men endued with ſenſe of common equity will ſoon diſcern, that, beſides eminent and competent knowledge, we are to deſcend to a lower ſtep, receiving knowledge in that degree which is but tolerable. When we commend any Man for Learning, our ſpeech importeth him to be more than meanly qualified that way; but when Laws do require Learning as a quality, which maketh capable of any function,

BOOK V. our meaſure to judge a learned Man by muſt be ſome certain degree of Learning, beneath which we can hold no Man ſo qualified. And if every Man that liſteth may ſet that degree himſelf, how ſhall we ever know when Laws are broken, when kept, ſeeing one Man may think a lower degree ſufficient, another may judge them unſufficient that are not qualified in ſome higher degree? Wherefore of neceſſity either we muſt have ſome Judge, in whoſe conſcience they that are thought and pronounced ſufficient are to be ſo accepted and taken, or elſe the Law itſelf is to ſet down the very loweſt degree of fitneſs that ſhall be allowable in this kind. So that the queſtion doth grow to this iſſue. St. Paul requireth Learning in Preſbyters, yea ſuch Learning as doth enable them to exhort in Doctrine which is ſound, and to diſprove them that gainſay it. What meaſure of ability in ſuch things ſhall ſerve to make Men capable of that kind of office he doth not himſelf preciſely determine, but referreth it to the conſcience of Titus, and others which had to deal in ordaining Preſbyters. We muſt therefore of neceſſity make this demand, whether the Church, lacking ſuch as the Apoſtle would have choſen, may with good conſcience take out of ſuch as it hath in a meaner degree of fitneſs, them that may ſerve to perform the ſervice of publick Prayer, to miniſter the Sacraments unto the People, to ſolemnize Marriage, to viſit the Sick, and bury the Dead, to inſtruct by reading, although by preaching they be not as yet ſo able to benefit and feed Chriſt's Flock. We conſtantly hold, that in this caſe the Apoſtle's Law is not broken. He requireth more in Preſbyters than there is found in many whom the Church of England alloweth. But no Man being tied unto impoſſibilities, to do that we cannot we are not bound. It is but a ſtratagem of theirs therefore, and a very indirect practice, when they publiſh large declamations to prove that Learning is required in the Miniſtry,

Tit. i. 9.

niſtry, and to make the ſilly People believe that the contrary is maintained by the Biſhops, and upheld by the Laws of the Land; whereas the queſtion in truth is not whether Learning be required, but whether a Church, wherein there is not ſufficient ſtore of learned Men to furniſh all Congregations, ſhould do better to let thouſands of Souls grow ſavage, to let them live without any publick ſervice of God, to let their Children die unbaptized, to with-hold the benefit of the other Sacrament from them, to let them depart this World like Pagans, without any thing ſo much as read unto them concerning the way of life, than, as it doth in this neceſſity, to make ſuch Preſbyters as are ſo far forth ſufficient, although they want that ability of preaching which ſome others have. In this point therefore we obey neceſſity, and of two evils we take the leſs; in the reſt a publick utility is ſought, and in regard thereof ſome certain inconveniencies tolerated becauſe they are recompenſed with greater good. The Law giveth liberty of Non-reſidence for a time to ſuch as will live in Univerſities, if they faithfully there labour to grow in knowledge, that ſo they may afterwards the more edify and the better inſtruct their Congregations. The Church in their abſence is not deſtitute, the People's ſalvation not neglected for the preſent time, the time of their abſence is in the intendment of Law beſtowed to the Church's great advantage and benefit; thoſe neceſſary helps are procured by it, which turn by many degrees more to the People's comfort in time to come, than if their Paſtors had continually abidden with them. So that the Law doth hereby provide in ſome part to remedy and help that evil which the former neceſſity hath impoſed upon the Church. For compare two Men of equal meanneſs, the one perpetually reſident, the other abſent for a ſpace in ſuch ſort as the Law permitteth. Allot unto both ſome nine years continuance with Cure of Souls. And muſt not three years abſence

BOOK V. in all probability and likelihood make the one more profitable than the other unto God's Church, by so much as the increase of his knowledge, gotten in those three years, may add unto six years travail following? For the greater ability there is added to the instrument, wherewith it pleaseth God to save Souls, the more facility and expedition it hath to work that which is otherwise hardlier effected. As much may be said touching absence granted to them that attend in the families of Bishops; which Schools of gravity, discretion and wisdom, preparing Men against the time that they come to reside abroad, are, in my poor opinion, even the fittest places that any ingenious mind can wish to enter into, between departure from private study and access to a more publick charge of Souls; yea no less expedient for Men of the best sufficiency and most maturity in knowledge, than the very Universities themselves are, for the ripening of such as be raw. Employments in the families of Noblemen, or in Princes' courts, hath another end for which the self-same leave is given, not without great respect to the good of the whole Church. For assuredly, whosoever doth well observe how much all inferior things depend upon the orderly courses and motions of those greater Orbs, will hardly judge it either meet or good, that the Angels assisting them should be driven to betake themselves to other stations, although by Nature they were not tied where they now are, but had charge also elsewhere, as long as their absence from beneath might but tolerably be supplied, and by descending their rooms above should become vacant. For we are not to dream in this case of any platform which bringeth equally high and low unto Parish Churches, nor of any constraint to maintain at their own charge Men sufficient for that purpose; the one so repugnant to the majesty and greatness of English Nobility, the other so improbable and unlikely to take effect, that they which mention either of

both,

both, ſeem not indeed to have conceived what either is. But the eye of the Law is the eye of God, it looketh into the hearts and ſecret diſpoſitions of Men, it beholdeth how far one ſtar differeth from another in glory, and as Men's ſeveral degrees require, accordingly it guideth them; granting unto principal Perſonages Privileges correſpondent to their high eſtates, and that not only in civil, but even in ſpiritual affairs, to the end they may love that Religion the more, which no way ſeeketh to make them vulgar, no way diminiſhes their dignity and greatneſs, but to do them good doth them honour alſo, and by ſuch extraordinary favours teacheth them to be in the Church of God, the ſame which the Church of God eſteemeth them, more worth than thouſands. It appeareth therefore in what reſpect the Laws of this Realm have given liberty of Non-reſidence to ſome, that their knowledge may be increaſed, and their labours by that mean be made afterwards the more profitable to others, leſt the houſes of great Men ſhould want that daily exerciſe of Religion, wherein their example availeth as much, yea many times peradventure more than the Laws themſelves with the common ſort. A third thing reſpected both in permitting abſence, and alſo in granting to ſome that liberty of addition or Plurality, which neceſſarily enforceth their abſence, is a mere both juſt and conſcionable regard that as Men are in quality, and as their ſervices are in weight for the publick good, ſo likewiſe their rewards and encouragements by ſpecial Privilege of Law might ſomewhat declare how the State itſelf doth accept their pains, much abhorring from their beſtial and ſavage rudeneſs, which think that oxen ſhould only labour, and aſſes feed. Thus to Readers in Univerſities, whoſe very paper and book-expences their ancient allowances and ſtipends at this day do either not, or hardly ſuſtain; to Governors of Colleges, leſt the great overplus of charges neceſſarily enforced upon

 them,

BOOK V. them, by reason of their place, and very slenderly supplied, by means of that charge in the present condition of things which their Founders could not foresee; to Men called away from their Cures, and employed in weightier business either of the Church or Commonwealth, because to impose upon them a burden which requireth their absence, and not to release them from the duty of Residence, were a kind of cruel and barbarous injustice; to Residents in Cathedral Churches, or upon Dignities Ecclesiastical, forasmuch as these being rooms of greater hospitality, places of more respect and consequence than the rest, they are the rather to be furnished with Men of best quality, and the Men for their quality's sake to be favoured above others—I say unto all these, in regard of their worth and merit, the Law hath therefore given leave while themselves bear weightier burdens, to supply inferior by reputation, and in like consideration partly, partly also by way of honour to Learning, Nobility, and Authority, permitteth, that Men which have taken Theological Degrees in Schools, the Suffragans of Bishops, the Houshold Chaplains of Men of Honour or in great Offices, the Brethren and Sons of Lords Temporal, or of Knights, if God shall move the hearts of such to enter at any time into holy Orders, may obtain to themselves a faculty or licence to hold two Ecclesiastical Livings though having Cure, any spiritual Persons of the Queen's Council, three such Livings; her Chaplains, what number of promotions herself in her own princely wisdom thinketh good to bestow upon them. But, as it fareth in such cases, the gap which for just considerations we open unto some, letteth in others through corrupt practices, to whom such favours were neither meant nor should be communicated. The greatness of the Harvest, and the scarcity of able Workmen hath made it necessary that Law should yield to admit numbers of Men but slenderly and meanly qualified. Hereupon, because

whom

whom all other worldly hopes have forſaken, they commonly reſerve miniſterial vocation as their laſt and ſureſt refuge ever open to forlorn Men; the Church, that ſhould nouriſh them whoſe ſervice ſhe needeth, hath obtruded upon her their ſervice that know not otherwiſe how to live and ſuſtain themſelves. Theſe finding nothing more eaſy than means to procure the writing of a few lines to ſome one or other which hath authority, and nothing more uſual than too much facility in condeſcending unto ſuch requeſts, are often received into that vocation whereunto their unworthineſs is no ſmall diſgrace. Did any thing more aggravate the crime of Jeroboam's prophane apoſtacy, than that he choſe to have his Clergy the ſcum and refuſe of his whole land? Let no Man ſpare to tell it them, that they are not faithful towards God that burden wilfully his Church with ſuch ſwarms of unworthy creatures. I will not ſay of all degrees in the Miniſtry, that which St. Chryſoſtom doth of the higheſt, *He that will undertake ſo weighty a charge, had need to be a Man of great underſtanding, rarely aſſiſted with divine grace, for integrity of manners, purity of life, and for all other virtues, to have in him more than a Man:* but ſurely this I will ſay with Chryſoſtom, *We need not doubt whether God be highly diſpleaſed with us, or what the cauſe of his anger is, if things of ſo great fear and holineſs as are the leaſt and loweſt duties of his ſervice, be thrown wilfully on them whoſe not only mean, but bad and ſcandalous quality doth defile whatſoever they handle.* Theſe eye-ſores and blemiſhes in continual Attendants about the ſervice of God's Sanctuary, do make them every day fewer that willingly reſort unto it, till at length all affection and zeal towards God be extinct in them through a weariſome contempt of their perſons, which for a time only live by Religion, and are for recompence, in fine, the death of the nurſe that feedeth them. It is not obſcure, how incommodious the Church hath found both this abuſe of the liberty

Chryſoſt. de Sacerd lib. III. c. 15.

BOOK V. which Law is enforced to grant; and not only this, but the like abuſe of that favour alſo which Law in other conſiderations already mentioned afforded touching Reſidence and Plurality of ſpiritual Livings. Now that which is practiſed corruptly to the detriment and hurt of the Church againſt the purpoſe of thoſe very Laws which notwithſtanding are pretended in defence and juſtification thereof, we muſt needs acknowledge no leſs repugnant to the grounds and principles of common right, than the fraudulent proceedings of Tyrants to the principles of juſt Sovereignty. Howbeit not ſo thoſe ſpecial Privileges which are but inſtruments wreſted and forced to ſerve malice. There is in the Patriarch of heathen Philoſophers this Precept, * *Let no Huſbandman nor no Handicraftſman be a Prieſt.* The reaſon whereupon he groundeth is a maxim in the Law of Nature; *it importeth greatly the good of all Men that God be reverenced*, with whoſe honour it ſtandeth not that they which are publickly employed in his ſervice ſhould live of baſe and manuary trades. Now
Acts xx. 34. compare herewith the Apoſtle's words, *Ye know that*
1 Cor. iv. 12. *theſe hands have miniſtered to my neceſſities, and them*
1 Theſſ. ii. 9. *that are with me.* What think we? Did the Apoſtle any thing oppoſite herein, or repugnant to the rules
2 Theſſ. iii. 8. and maxims of the Law of Nature? The ſelf-ſame reaſons, that accord his actions with the Law of Nature, ſhall declare our Privileges and his Laws no leſs conſonant. Thus therefore we ſee, that although they urge very colourably the Apoſtle's own ſentences, requiring that a Miniſter ſhould be able to divide rightly the Word of God, that they who are placed in charge ſhould attend unto it themſelves, which in abſence they cannot do, and that they which have divers Cures muſt of neceſſity be abſent from ſome, whereby the Law apoſtolick ſeem-

* Οὔτε γεωργὸν οὔτε βάναυσον ἱερέα καταστατέον· ὑπὸ γὰρ τῶν πολιτῶν πρέπει τιμᾶσθαι τοὺς θεούς. Ariſt. Po. vii c. 9.

eth

eth apparently broken, which Law requiring attendance cannot otherwise be underſtood than ſo as to charge them with perpetual Reſidence: again, though in every of theſe cauſes they indefinitely heap up the Sentences of Fathers, the Decrees of Popes, the ancient edicts of imperial authority, our own national Laws and Ordinances prohibiting the ſame, and grounding evermore their prohibitions partly on the Laws of God, and partly on reaſons drawn from the Light of Nature, yet hereby to gather and infer contradiction between thoſe Laws which forbid indefinitely, and ours which in certain caſes have allowed the ordaining of ſundry Miniſters whoſe ſufficiency for Learning is but mean; again, the licenſing of ſome to be abſent from their Flocks, and of others to hold more than one only Living which hath Cure of Souls, I ſay, to conclude repugnancy between theſe eſpecial permiſſions and the former general prohibitions which ſet not down their own limits, is erroneous, and the manifeſt cauſe thereof ignorance in difference of matter which both ſorts of Law concern. If then the conſiderations be reaſonable, juſt and good, whereupon we ground whatſoever our Laws have by ſpecial right permitted, if only the effects of abuſed Privileges be repugnant to the maxims of common right, this main foundation of repugnancy being broken, whatſoever they have built thereupon falleth neceſſarily to the ground. Whereas therefore, upon ſurmiſe, or vain ſuppoſal of oppoſition between our ſpecial and the principles of common right, they gather that ſuch as are with us ordained Miniſters, before they can preach be neither lawful, becauſe the Laws already mentioned forbid generally to create ſuch, neither are they indeed Miniſters, although we commonly ſo name them, but whatſoever they execute by virtue of ſuch their pretended vocation is void; that all our grants and toleraations, as well of this as the reſt, are fruſtrate and of no effect; the Perſons that enjoy them poſſeſs them

BOOK V. them wrongfully, and are deprivable at all hours; finally, that other juſt and ſufficient remedy of evils there can be none, beſides the utter abrogation of theſe our mitigations, and the ſtrict eſtabliſhment of former Ordinances to be abſolutely executed whatſoever follow: albeit the anſwer already made in diſcovery of the weak and unſound foundation whereupon they have built theſe erroneous collections may be thought ſufficient; yet becauſe our deſire is rather to ſatisfy, if it be poſſible, than to ſhake them off, we are with very good will contented to declare the cauſes of all particulars more formally and largely than the equity of our own defence doth require.

There is crept into the minds of Men, at this day, a ſecret pernicious and peſtilent conceit, that the greateſt perfection of a Chriſtian Man doth conſiſt in diſcovery of other Men's faults, and in wit to diſcourſe of our own profeſſion. When the World moſt abounded with juſt, righteous and perfect Men, their chiefeſt ſtudy was the exerciſe of piety, wherein for their ſafeſt direction they reverently hearkened to the readings of the Law of God, they kept in mind the Oracles and Aphoriſms of Wiſdom which tended unto virtuous life; if any ſcruple of conſcience did trouble them for matter of actions which they took in hand, nothing was attempted before counſel and advice were had for fear leſt raſhly they might offend. We are now more confident, not that our knowledge and judgment is riper, but becauſe our deſires are another way. Their ſcope was obedience, ours is ſkill; their endeavour was reformation of life, * our virtue nothing but to hear gladly the reproof of vice; they in the practice of

* Ἀλλ᾽ οἱ πολλοὶ ταῦτα μὲν οὐ πράττουσιν, ἐπὶ δὲ τὸν λόγον καταφεύγοντες οἴονται φιλοσοφεῖν, καὶ οὕτως ἔσεσθαι σπουδαῖοι· ὅμοιόν τι ποιοῦντες τοῖς κάμνουσιν, οἳ τῶν ἰατρῶν ἀκούουσι μὲν ἐπιμελῶς, ποιοῦσι δὲ οὐδὲν τῶν προσταττομένων· ὥσπερ οὖν οὐδὲ ἐκεῖνοι εὖ ἕξουσι τὸ σῶμα οὕτω θεραπευόμενοι, οὐδὲ οὗτοι τὴν ψύχην οὕτω φιλοσοφοῦντες. Ariſt. Eth. lib. ii. c. 5.

their

their Religion wearied chiefly their knees and hands, BOOK V. we ſpecially our ears and tongues. We are grown as in many things elſe, ſo in this, to a kind of intemperancy, which (only Sermons excepted) hath almoſt brought all other duties of Religion out of taſte. At the leaſt they are not in that account and reputation which they ſhould be. Now, becauſe Men bring all Religion in a manner to the only office of hearing Sermons, if it chance that they who are thus conceited do embrace any ſpecial opinion different from other Men, the Sermons that reliſh not that opinion can in no wiſe pleaſe their appetite. Such therefore as preach unto them, but hit not the ſtring they look for, are reſpected as unprofitable, the reſt as unlawful; and indeed no Miniſters, if the faculty of Sermons want. For why? A Miniſter of the Word ſhould, they ſay, be able rightly to *divide* the Word. Which Apoſtolick Canon many think they do well obſerve, when in opening the ſentences of holy Scripture they draw all things favourably ſpoken unto one ſide; but whatſoever is reprehenſive, ſevere and ſharp, they have others on the contrary part whom that muſt always concern, by which their over-partial and un-indifferent proceeding, while they thus labour amongſt the People to divide the Word, they make the Word a mean to divide and diſtract the People. Ὀρθοτομεῖν *to divide aright*, doth note in the Apoſtles' Writings ſoundneſs of Doctrine only; and in meaning ſtandeth oppoſite to καινοτομεῖν *the broaching of new opinions againſt that which is received.* For queſtionleſs the firſt things delivered to the Church of Chriſt were pure and ſincere Truth; which whoſoever did afterwards oppugn could not chooſe but divide the Church into two moieties; in which diviſion, ſuch as taught what was firſt believed, held the truer part; the contrary ſide, in that they were Teachers of novelty, erred. For prevention of which evil there are in this Church many ſingular and deviſed remedies; as namely, the

uſe

BOOK V. uſe of ſubſcribing to the Articles of Religion before admiſſion to Degrees of Learning or to any Eccleſiaſtical Living; the cuſtom of reading the ſame Articles, and of approving them in publick Aſſemblies whereſoever Men have Benefices with Cure of Souls; the order of teſtifying under their hands allowance of the Book of Common-Prayer, and the Book of ordaining Miniſters; finally, the diſcipline and moderate ſeverity which is uſed either in otherwiſe correcting or ſilencing them that trouble and diſturb the Church with Doctrines which tend unto innovation; it being better that the Church ſhould want altogether the benefit of ſuch Men's labours, than endure the miſchief of their inconformity to good Laws; in which caſe, if any repine at the courſe and proceedings of Juſtice, they muſt learn to content themſelves with the anſwer of M. Curius, which had ſometime occaſion to cut off one from the body of the Commonwealth; in whoſe behalf becauſe it might have been pleaded that the Party was a Man ſerviceable, he therefore began his judicial ſentence with this preamble, *Non eſſe opus Reip. eo cive qui parere neſciret; The Commonwealth needeth Men of quality, yet never thoſe Men which have not learned how to obey.* But the ways which the Church of England hath taken to provide that they who are Teachers of others may do it ſoundly, that the purity and unity as well of ancient Diſcipline as Doctrine may be upheld, that avoiding ſingularities we may all glorify God with one heart and one tongue, they of all do leaſt approve that do moſt urge the Apoſtles' Rule and Canon. For which cauſe they alledge it not ſo much to that purpoſe, as to prove that unpreaching Miniſters (for ſo they term them) can have no true nor lawful calling in the Church of God. St. Auguſtin hath ſaid of the will of Man, that *ſimply to will proceedeth from Nature, but our well-willing is from Grace.* We ſay as much of the Miniſters of God, *publickly to teach and inſtruct the Church, is neceſſary in every*

Valer lib. vi. c. 5.

every Ecclesiastical Minister; but ability to teach by Sermons is a grace which God doth bestow on them whom he maketh sufficient for the commendable discharge of their duty. That therefore wherein a Minister differeth from other Christian Men is not, as some have childishly imagined, the *sound preaching of the Word of God*; but as they are lawfully and truly Governors to whom authority of Regiment is given in the Commonwealth according to the order which Polity hath set, so Canonical Ordination in the Church of Christ is that which maketh a lawful Minister *as touching the validity of any act which appertaineth to that Vocation.* The cause why St. Paul willed Timothy not to be over-hasty in ordaining Ministers, was (as we very well may conjecture) because imposition of hands doth consecrate and make them Ministers whether they have gifts and qualities fit for the laudable discharge of their duties or no. If want of learning and skill to preach did frustrate their vocation, Ministers ordained before they be grown unto that maturity should receive new Ordination whensoever it chanceth that study and industry doth make them afterwards more able to perform the office, than which what conceit can be more absurd? Was not St. Augustin himself contented to admit an Assistant in his own Church, a Man of small erudition, considering that what he wanted in knowledge was supplied by those virtues which made his life a better orator than more learning could make others whose conversation was less holy? Were the Priests sithence Moses all able and sufficient Men, learnedly to interpret the Law of God? Or was it ever imagined that this defect should frustrate what they executed, and deprive them of right unto any thing they claimed by virtue of their Priesthood? Surely, as in Magistrates the want of those gifts which their office needeth is cause of just imputation of blame in them that wittingly choose unsufficient and unfit Men when they might do otherwise, and yet therefore is not their choice

BOOK V.

Ox. man. p. 27.

BOOK V. choice void, nor every action of Magistracy frustrate in that respect; so whether it were of necessity, or even of very carelessness that Men unable to preach should be taken in Pastors' rooms, nevertheless it seemeth to be an error in them which think the lack of any such perfection defeateth utterly their calling. To wish that all Men were qualified as their place and dignities require, to hate all sinister and corrupt dealings which hereunto are any lett, to covet speedy redress of those things whatsoever whereby the Church sustaineth detriment, these good and virtuous desires cannot offend any but ungodly minds. Notwithstanding, some in the true vehemency, and others under the fair pretence of these desires, have adventured that which is strange, that which is violent and unjust. There are which in confidence of their general allegation concerning the knowledge, the Residence and the single Livings of Ministers, presume not only to annihilate the solemn Ordinations of such as the Church must of force admit, but also to urge a kind of universal proscription against them to set down Articles, to draw Commissions, and almost to name themselves of the Quorum, for inquiry into Men's estates and dealings, whom at their pleasure they would deprive and make obnoxious to what punishment themselves list, and that not for any violation of Laws either spiritual or civil, but because Men have trusted the Laws too far, because they have held and enjoyed the liberty which Law granteth, because they had not the wit to conceive as these Men do, that Laws were made to entrap the simple, by permitting those things in shew and appearance which indeed should never take effect, forasmuch as they were but granted with a secret condition to be put in practice if they should be profitable and agreeable with the Word of God; which condition failing in all Ministers that cannot preach, in all that are absent from their Livings, and in all that have divers Livings (for so it must be presumed, though never as yet proved) therefore

The Author of the Abstract.

as

as Men which have broken the Law of God and Nature they are deprivable at all hours. Is this the juſtice of that Diſcipline whereunto all Chriſtian Churches muſt ſtoop and ſubmit themſelves? Is this the equity wherewith they labour to reform the World? I will no way diminiſh the force of thoſe Arguments whereupon they ground: but if it pleaſe them to behold the viſage of theſe collections in another glaſs, there are Civil as well as Eccleſiaſtical Unſufficiencies, Non-reſidences, and Pluralities; yea the reaſons which Light of Nature hath miniſtered againſt both are of ſuch affinity, that much leſs they cannot enforce in the one than in the other. When they that bear great offices be Perſons of mean worth, the contempt whereinto their authority groweth * weakeneth the ſinews of the whole State. Notwithſtanding, where many Governors are needful, and they not many whom their quality can commend, † the penury of worthier muſt needs make the meaner ſort of Men capable. Cities, in the abſence of their Governors, are as ſhips wanting pilots at ſea: but were it therefore ‡ juſtice to puniſh whom ſuperior authority pleaſeth to call from home, or alloweth to be employed elſewhere? In committing § many offices to one Man there are apparently theſe inconveniencies; the Commonwealth doth loſe the benefit of ſerviceable Men which might be trained up in thoſe rooms; it is not eaſy for one Man to diſcharge many Men's duties well; in ſervice of

* Μεγάλων κύριοι καθεϛῶτες ἂν εὐτελεῖς ὦσι μεγάλα βλάπτουσι. Ariſt. Polit ii. c. 11.

† Nec ignoro maximos honores ad parum dignos penuria meliorum ſolere deferri. Mamertin. Paneg. ad Julian

‡ Neque enim æquum viſum eſt abſentem Reipub. cauſa inter reos referri dum Reipub. operatur. Ulpian. l. xv. Si maritus ad legem Julian de Adulter.

§ Ariſt. Polit. l. i. c. 11. See the like Preamble framed by the Author of the Abſtract, where he fancieth a Biſhop depoſing one unapt to preach, whom himſelf had before ordained.

warfare

BOOK V. warfare and navigation, were it not the overthrow of whatsoever is undertaken if one or two should ingross such offices, as being now divided into many hands, are discharged with admirable both perfection and expedition? Nevertheless, be it far from the mind of any reasonable Man to imagine, that in these considerations Princes either ought of duty to revoke all such kind of grants, though made with very special respect to the extraordinary merit of certain Men, or might in honour demand of them the resignation of their offices with speech to this or the like effect: *Forasmuch as you A. B. by the space of many years have done us that faithful service in most important affairs, for which we always judging you worthy of much honour, have therefore committed unto you from time to time very great and weighty offices, which hitherto you quietly enjoy; we are now given to understand, that certain grave and learned Men have found in the books of ancient Philosophers divers Arguments drawn from the common light of Nature, and declaring the wonderful discommodities which use to grow by dignities thus heaped together in one; for which cause, at this present, moved in conscience and tender care for the publick good, we have summoned you hither to dispossess you of those places, and to depose you from those rooms whereof indeed by virtue of our own grant, yet against Reason, you are possessed. Neither ought you, or any other to think us rash, light, or inconstant, in so doing: for we tell you plain, that herein we will both say and do that thing which the noble and wise Emperor sometime both said and did in a matter of far less weight than this;* Quod inconsulto fecimus, consulto revocamus, *That which we unadvisedly have done, we advisedly will revoke and undo.* Now for mine own part the greatest harm I would wish them who think that this were consonant with equity and right is, that they might but live where all things are with such kind of justice ordered till experience have taught them to see their error. As for the last thing which is is incident into the caufe whereof we fpeak, namely, what courfe were the beft and fafeft whereby to remedy fuch evils as the Church of God may fuftain, where the prefent liberty of Law is turned to great abufe, fome light we may receive from abroad, not unprofitable for direction of God's own facred Houfe and Family. The Romans being a People full of generofity, and by nature courteous, did no way more fhew their gentle difpofition than by eafy condefcending to fet their Bond-men at liberty. Which benefit in the happier and better times of the Commonwealth, was beftowed for the moft part as an ordinary reward of virtue, fome few now and then alfo purchafing freedom with that which their juft labours could gain, and their honeft frugality fave. But as the Empire daily grew up, fo the manners and conditions of Men decayed, wealth was honoured, and virtue not cared for; neither did any thing feem opprobrious out of which there might arife commodity and profit, fo that it could be no marvel in a State thus far degenerated, if when the more ingenuous fort were become bafe, the bafer laying afide all fhame and face of honefty, did fome by robberies, burglaries and proftitution of their bodies, gather wherewith to redeem liberty; others obtain the fame at the hands of their Lords, by ferving them as vile inftruments in thofe attempts, which had been worthy to be revenged with ten thoufand deaths. A learned, judicious and polite Hiftorian, having mentioned fo foul diforders, giveth his judgment and cenfure of them in this fort: *Such eye-fores in the Commonwealth have occafioned many virtuous minds to condemn altogether the cuftom of granting liberty to any Bond flave, forafmuch as it feemed a thing abfurd that a People which commands all the World fhould confift of fo vile refufe. But neither is this the only cuftom wherein the profitable inventions of former are depraved by latter ages; and for myfelf I am not of their opinion that wifh the abrogation of fo grofly ufed cuftoms, which abrogation might*

BOOK V.

Dionyf. Halicar. Rom Ant. lib. iv.

BOOK V. *might peradventure be cause of greater inconveniencies ensuing: but as much as may be, I would rather advise that redress were sought through the careful providence of chief Rulers and Overseers of the Commonwealth, by whom a yearly survey being made of all that are manumised, they which seem worthy might be taken and divided into Tribes with other Citizens, the rest dispersed into Colonies abroad, or otherwise disposed of, that the Commonwealth might sustain neither harm nor disgrace by them.* The ways to meet with disorders growing by abuse of Laws are not so intricate and secret, especially in our case, that Men should need either much advertisement or long time for the search thereof. And if counsel to that purpose may seem needful, this Church (God be thanked) is not destitute of Men endued with ripe judgment, whensoever any such thing shall be thought necessary. For which end, at this present, to propose any special inventions of my own, might argue in a Man of my place and calling more presumption perhaps than wit. I will therefore leave it entire unto graver consideration, ending now with request only and most earnest suit, first, that they which give Ordination would, as they tender the very honour of Jesus Christ, the safety of Men, and the endless good of their own Souls, take heed lest unnecessarily, and through their default the Church be found worse or less furnished than it might be: secondly, that they which by right of Patronage have power to present unto Spiritual Livings, and may in that respect much damnify the Church of God, would, for the ease of their own account in that dreadful day, somewhat consider what it is to betray for gain the Souls which Christ hath redeemed with blood, what to violate the sacred bond of fidelity and solemn promise given at the first to God and his Church by them, from whose original interest together with the self-same title of right, the same obligation of duty likewise is descended: thirdly, that they unto whom the granting

granting of Diſpenſations is committed, or which otherwiſe have any ſtroke in the diſpoſition of ſuch Preferments as appertain unto learned Men, would bethink themſelves what it is to reſpect any thing either above or beſide merit; conſidering how hardly the World taketh it when to Men of commendable note and quality there is ſo little reſpect had, or ſo great unto them whoſe deſerts are very mean, that nothing doth ſeem more ſtrange than the one ſort becauſe they are not accounted of, and the other becauſe they are; it being every Man's hope and expectation in the Church of God eſpecially, that the only purchaſe of greater rewards ſhould be always greater deſerts, and that nothing ſhould ever be able to plant a thorn where a vine ought to grow: fourthly, that honourable Perſonages, and they who by virtue of any principal office in the Commonwealth are enabled to qualify a certain number, and make them capable of favours or faculties above others, ſuffer not their names to be abuſed, contrary to the true intent and meaning of wholeſome Laws, by Men in whom there is nothing notable beſides covetouſneſs and ambition: fifthly, that the graver and wiſer ſort in both Univerſities, or whoſoever they be, with whoſe approbation the marks and recognizances of all learning are beſtowed, would think the Apoſtles' caution againſt unadviſed Ordinations not impertinent or unneceſſary to be borne in mind, even when they grant thoſe Degrees of Schools, which Degrees are not *gratiæ gratis datæ*, kindneſſes beſtowed by way of humanity, but they are *gratiæ gratum facientes*, favours which always imply a teſtimony given to the Church and Commonwealth concerning Men's ſufficiency for manners and knowledge; a teſtimony upon the credit whereof ſundry Statutes of the Realm are built; a teſtimony ſo far available, that nothing is more reſpected for the warrant of divers Men's abilities to ſerve in the affairs of the Realm, a teſtimony wherein if they violate

BOOK V.

 that

that religion wherewith it ought to be always given, and do thereby induce into error ſuch as deem it a thing uncivil to call the credit thereof in queſtion, let them look that God ſhall return back upon their heads, and cauſe them in the ſtate of their own Corporations to feel either one way or other the puniſhment of thoſe harms which the Church through their negligence doth ſuſtain in that behalf: finally, and to conclude, that they who enjoy the benefit of any ſpecial indulgence or favour which the Laws permit, would as well remember what in duty towards the Church and in conſcience towards God they ought to do, as what they may do by uſing to their own advantage whatſoever they ſee tolerated; no Man being ignorant that the cauſe why abſence in ſome caſes hath been yielded unto and in equity thought ſufferable, is the hope of greater fruit through induſtry elſewhere; the reaſon likewiſe wherefore Pluralities are allowed unto Men of note, a very ſovereign and ſpecial care, that as Fathers in the ancient World did declare the pre-eminence of priority in birth by doubling the worldly portions of their firſt-born; ſo the Church by a courſe not unlike in aſſigning Men's rewards might teſtify an eſtimation had proportionably of their virtues, according to the ancient rule Apoſtolick, *They which excel in labour, ought to excel in honour*; and therefore unleſs they anſwer faithfully the expectation of the Church herein, unleſs ſincerely they bend their wits day and night both to ſow becauſe they reap, and to ſow ſo much more abundantly as they reap more abundantly than other Men, whereunto by their very acceptance of ſuch benignities they formally bind themſelves, let them be well aſſured that the honey which they eat with fraud ſhall turn in the end into true gall, foraſmuch as Laws are the ſacred image of his Wiſdom who moſt ſeverely puniſheth thoſe colourable and ſubtle crimes that ſeldom are taken within the walk of human

Juſtice.

Juſtice.* I therefore conclude, that the grounds and maxims of common right whereupon Ordinations of Miniſters unable to preach, tolerations of abſence from their Cures, and the multiplications of their Spiritual Livings are diſproved, do but indefinitely enforce them unlawful, not unlawful univerſally and without exception; that the Laws which indefinitely are againſt all theſe things, and the Privileges which make for them in certain caſes are not the one repugnant to the other; that the Laws of God and Nature are violated through the effects of abuſed Privileges; that neither our Ordinations of Men unable to make ſermons, nor our Diſpenſations for the reſt, can be juſtly proved fruſtrate by virtue of any ſuch ſurmiſed oppoſition between the ſpecial Laws of this Church which have permitted, and thoſe general which are alledged to diſprove the ſame; that when Privileges by abuſe are grown incommodious, there muſt be redreſs; that for remedy of ſuch evils, there is no neceſſity the Church ſhould abrogate either in whole or in part the ſpecialties before mentioned; and that the moſt to be deſired were a voluntary reformation thereof on all hands which may give paſſage unto any abuſe. BOOK V.

* For the main hypotheſis or foundation of theſe concluſions, let that before ſet down in the 9th, be read together with this laſt the 81ſt Paragraph.

End of the Second Volume.

LaVergne, TN USA
03 February 2011
215109LV00003B/46/P

9 781178 232066